D1126097

MACARTNEY'S ILLUSTRATIONS

MACARTNEY'S ILLUSTRATIONS

Illustrations from the Sermons

of

Clarence Edward Macartney

Minister, First Presbyterian Church

Pittsburgh, Pennsylvania

ABINGDON-COKESBURY PRESS

New York · Nashville

Wartime Books

*Wartime shortage of pulp, manpower, and transportation has
produced a severe shortage of paper. In compliance with orders
of the War Production Board, wartime books are printed on
lighter-weight paper. This reduces thickness and weight. New
books have more words to the page and smaller margins. This reduces the number of pages without reducing reading content.*

*Thinner books save paper, critical copper, and other metals.
They help also to avoid wartime increases in book prices.
Wartime books appear to be smaller, but their content has not
been cut. They are complete. The only change is in appearance.*

K
PRINTED IN THE UNITED STATES OF AMERICA

To Three Congregations:

FIRST PRESBYTERIAN CHURCH, *Paterson, New Jersey*

ARCH STREET PRESBYTERIAN CHURCH, *Philadelphia, Pennsylvania*

FIRST PRESBYTERIAN CHURCH, *Pittsburgh, Pennsylvania*

FOREWORD

As THE TITLE INDICATES, THIS BOOK IS NOT A GENERAL COMPILATION OF sermon illustrations but a carefully selected collection of illustrations which have been used by Dr. Macartney in his sermons. They are drawn from his wide reading, his extensive travels, his pastoral experience, and from his own imagination.

The best recommendation for these illustrations is the fact that they are taken from sermons which commanded a wide and popular hearing when preached in the three pulpits which Dr. Macartney has served in the heart of three American cities.

THE PUBLISHERS

A

ABRAHAM

Under the roof of the mosque at Hebron are the cenotaphs of the three patriarchs Abraham, Isaac, and Jacob—not the tombs, but their monuments, or cenotaphs. Each one is covered with gorgeous green brocade, and each is shielded by a silver grille. In the middle of the floor is a circular opening covered with a grating. From this grating a lamp is suspended. Looking down through the opening, you can see the lamp burning in the darkness far below.

You are looking into the cave of Machpelah, and there rests the dust of Abraham, Isaac, and Jacob. The wind of the ages seems to be blowing there, and you seem to hear the voice of the remotest past. You are standing where Abraham bought the Cave of Machpelah to bury his dead out of his sight. There he buried Sarah, there he himself was laid to rest, and there Isaac and Jacob were gathered to their fathers. On all the earth is there an authentic sepulcher which evokes such memories as this one beneath the mosque at Hebron?

ABSTINENCE—*see* TOTAL ABSTINENCE

ACTION

When the Pennsylvania west-bound train on which I was traveling stopped recently at Altoona before beginning the ascent of the mountains, I saw in the yards there many powerful engines, their bunkers filled with coal, steam up, smoke issuing from the stacks, fires glowing under the boilers, and engineer and firemen at their posts. The engines were ready to go into action. They had been fueled and fired and manned for action

—and they *did* go into action, pulling the long trains over the mountains.

Too often in human life enthusiasm is aroused, emotion is stirred, noble goals are glimpsed, high purposes are entertained; but no action follows. Nothing is done about it. The splendid enthusiasms are wasted, and the emotions are dissipated. The soul has not capitalized on what it desired, but did not will.

ADVERSITY—*see also* AFFLICTION, COURAGE, PROVIDENCE AND ADVERSITY, SORROW, SUFFERING, TRIAL

"Detour!" This highway sign is greeted with smothered groans or ejaculations of impatience. The motorist glares at the sign and the barrier across the road as if he were half determined to go on regardless of sign or barrier. But if so, he runs the risk of danger, and ultimately meets with failure and is compelled to turn back. The detour is rough, dusty, and at right angles to the direction in which he has been traveling. Yet it is a necessary change of route, and if followed patiently it brings the traveler back to the main highway.

Life has many detours. After many miles of smooth going in fine spirits and rapid progress, suddenly we come upon this sign, "Detour!" and are arrested by the barrier. Then we leave a fine road for the rough way, and life is heavy and labored and difficult.

———

—**Blessings of**—At the time of his serious sickness and operation in August, 1893, Grover Cleveland wrote: "I have learned how weak the strongest man is under God's decrees; and I see in a new light the necessity of doing my allotted

9

work in the full apprehension of the coming night." Thus to be laid aside for a season from our task not only teaches us humility but makes us more earnest and industrious when strength returns to us. This was the verdict of David after his trouble: "It is good for me that I have been afflicted" (Ps. 119:71). This was the verdict of Hezekiah after his near approach to the gates of death: "By these things men live" (Isa. 38:16).

Jeremy Taylor, author of so many wonderful sayings, strikes the note that I am trying to strike when he says, in his inimitable way, "We are safe at sea, safer in the storm God sends us, than when we are befriended by the world." God's storms blow us to the port of repentance and faith.

I remember an officer in a Presbyterian church who had been very successful in his operations but who at length failed in some great business enterprise. He said to his pastor, "I am glad that I failed, for I was getting away from God."

In Jerusalem today there is an institution known as the American Colony, founded to help little children in the city where our Saviour died. And this is how it came to be. A well-to-do, beautiful, and talented young woman, resident in Chicago, was crossing the Atlantic on her way to visit her aged parents in Paris. On the journey the steamer was struck amidships by a large sailing vessel, and immediately began to sink. The four daughters who were with this woman were drowned, but she herself was rescued.

When she reached land she sent a cable back to her husband in Chicago, "Saved alone!" Then she began to think about that word "alone"; and, accepting her great sorrow in the death of her

children, and her own deliverance from death, as a divine message, she resolved to give her life to the welfare of her fellow passengers on life's long voyage, and so established in Jerusalem the Colony, which has brought the knowledge and the spirit of Christ to so many of the children and youth of the Holy Land.

Richard Cobden, the Manchester manufacturer, and John Bright, the Rochdale spinner, were men who were not content merely to make money and to succeed in life in the business sense. They looked upon the masses of Great Britain and were moved with compassion. They began to think and to write and to speak of a better day. They met first in the chapel of a Baptist church at Rochdale, where Bright had asked Cobden to come and speak in the interests of education for the children of laborers. But it is doubtful if Bright would ever have become the colaborer and codisciple of Cobden in the work of reform had it not been for the sorrow that crushed his early hopes, and the ministry of his friend Cobden in the critical hour.

Bright, who was a Quaker, had written to Cobden informing him of the death of his young wife: "It has pleased the Almighty to take from me my beloved and cherished companion. She sank peacefully to her rest about one o'clock this day. She had almost no suffering, and death to her had long lost his terrors. Until she became mine, I did not know that mortality ever was the abode of so much that was pure and lovely. Her sainted spirit, I cannot doubt, is now an inhabitant of that city 'where none can say he is sick,' and in this deep affliction my heart rejoices in the full assurance that to my precious wife the change is inconceivably glorious. I know thou wilt sympathize with me in this very deep trial and it is therefore I

10

write to inform thee of it. I hope this may reach thee before thou leaves tomorrow."

In his speech at the unveiling of the Cobden statue at Bradford in 1877, Bright told the story of Cobden's response to his letter. "At that time I was at Leamington, and on the day when Mr. Cobden called upon me—for he happened to be there at the time on a visit to some relatives—I was in the depths of grief, I might almost say of despair, for the light and sunshine of my house had been extinguished. All that was left on earth of my young wife, except the memory of a sainted life and a too-brief happiness, was lying still and cold in the chamber above us. Mr. Cobden called upon me as his friend, and addressed me, as you might suppose, with words of condolence. After a time he looked up and said: 'There are thousands of houses in England at this moment where wives, mothers, and children are dying of hunger. Now,' he said, 'when the first paroxysm of your grief is past, I would advise you to come with me, and we will never rest till the Corn Law is repealed.'

"I accepted his invitation. And since then, though there has been suffering, and much suffering, in many homes in England, yet no wife and no mother and no little child has been starved to death as the result of a famine made by law."

—**Meeting**—In writing of the final and heroic period of Walter Scott's life, when troubles came in on him like a flood, R. H. Hutton applies to him the words with which Cicero described a contemporary: "a man who had borne adversity wisely, who had not been broken by fortune, and who, amidst the buffets of fate, had maintained his dignity." In that description of character there is something which makes the heart leap

in quick and generous response. The greatest, highest task that can ever fall to man is that of maintaining the awful dignity of the soul amid the buffetings of fate.

When the Confederate army retreated after Gettysburg, General Lee wrote to Jefferson Davis a remarkable letter in which he said: "We must expect reverses, even defeats. They are sent to teach us wisdom and prudence, to call forth greater energies, and to prevent our falling into greater disasters." True of a nation's life, this is also profoundly true of the life of the individual. And what shall we say of sickness, sorrow, and affliction? Shall these things overwhelm us, or shall we be able to say, with that great spirit who kept both his soul and his body under the dominion of a great and holy purpose, "Nay, in all these things we are more than conquerors through him that loved us" (Rom. 8:37)?

Happy is that man who, as when Jacob by the fords wrestled with the angel and refused to let him go unless he blessed him, is resolved that life, however much it may baffle him or wound him, will not be permitted to come to a close without having blessed him, without having taught him that fear of God which endureth forever!

—**Physical handicaps**—Our own American history affords a shining example of fortitude under misfortune and sickness. The preface to General Grant's *Memoirs* opens with the quotation, "Man proposes, and God disposes." Then follows an account of how he came to write the *Memoirs*. First, a fall from his horse, which kept him indoors; then the rascality of business partners, which plunged him into debt and made him dependent upon the kindness of friends. To pay his debts he commenced the laborious task of writing his story of the war. He had not gone far with the work when his mortal sickness fastened itself upon him. From then on it was a race with death. There he sat on the porch at Mount McGregor, propped up in his chair with pillows, the awful disease clutching his throat, toiling at the manuscript, until, just four days before his death, he wrote these final and prophetic sentences: "I feel that we are on the eve of a new era, when there is to be a great harmony between Confederate and Federal. I cannot stay to be a living witness to the correctness of this prophecy; but I feel it within me that it is to be so." That was Grant's greatest victory. Donelson, Shiloh, Vicksburg, Chattanooga, Appomattox, are nothing alongside of that last heroic battle against poverty and cancer.

———•◆•———

Heroic witness to the strength that is latent in human nature has been borne by men who were sick or frail in body, but who fused the salient energies of the soul and called upon their souls and all within them to do the work at hand. Most people in the physical condition of the Apostle Paul would spend their days in a home for the incurable, yet Paul, animated by a mighty love for Christ, traversed the Mediterranean world and survived incredible hardships.

John Calvin, the intellectual genius and the real organizer of Protestantism, was a man who hardly knew a well day; but his indomitable spirit carried him through almost unbelievable labors. "And so he continued," in the words of Bancroft, "solitary and feeble, toiling for humanity, till after a life of glory he bequeathed to the world a fortune in books and furniture, in stocks and bonds, not exceeding $200, and to the world a purer Reformation, Republican liberty,

and the kindred spirit of Republican institutions."

———•◆•———

I have two books in my library that I like to take up, for both their interesting narration and their style. One is Parkman's *Pioneers of France in the New World*. In the preface the distinguished author relates how it has taken him eighteen years to write the brief volume, and how through those years he has secured access to all records of value that bore upon his subject. "The extreme slowness," he says, writing of himself, "was unavoidable." During the past eighteen years, he says, the state of his health has exacted throughout an extreme caution in regard to mental application, reducing it at best within narrow and precarious limits, and often precluding it. Indeed, for two periods, each of several years, any attempt at bookish occupation would have been merely suicidal. A condition of sight arising from kindred sources has also retarded the work, since it has never permitted reading or writing continuously for more than five minutes.

The other books are the writings of Prescott. In his preface to one of his volumes he craves the indulgence of the readers as to possible errors in the text, for, he says, "Owing to the state of my eyes, I have been obliged to use a writing case made for the blind, which does not permit the writer to see his own manuscript." There they are on the shelves, brightly burnished monuments to the power of the energized spirit to overcome obstacles, to make blind men write better than men who see.

———•◆•———

Let those who think they are handicapped by some affliction in body or in spirit for a noble work in life remember Paul. And let them also remember:

*Milton the blind, who looked on
    Paradise!
Beethoven, deaf, who heard vast har-
    monies!
Byron, the lame, who climbed to-
    ward Alpine skies!
Who pleads a handicap, remember-
    ing these?* [1]

—**Uses of**—Steel is made in the furnace, and there is no wine until the grapes are crushed. In a day when his struggles and hardships were behind him, Charles Lamb wrote of those struggles and contrary winds against which he and his sister Mary had fought together: "That we had much to contend with as we grew up together, we have reason to be most thankful. It strengthened and knit our compact closer together. We never would have been what we have been to each other if we had always had the sufficiency which you now complain of."

The strongest characters are those who have faced the contrary winds. "They that go down to the sea in ships, that do business in great waters; these see the works of the Lord, and his wonders in the deep."

I know of no writer who has dealt so tenderly and in so helpful a manner with the misfortunes of men as Saint-Pierre, the author of the immortal *Paul and Virginia*. He chose for his motto the line from Vergil, "Taught by calamity, I pity the unhappy." In *Indian Cottage* he not only comments on the spiritual gain from his own misfortunes but throws out this exquisite suggestion for all who may need it: "Misfortune resembles the Black Mountain of Bember, situated at the extremity of the burning kingdom of Lahore; while you are climbing it, you see before you only barren rocks; but when you have reached its summit, you see heaven above your head, and at your feet the kingdom of Cashmere."

By the discipline of adversity we learn sympathy, and sympathy leads to usefulness.

At the end of his great book *The Republic* Plato tells of the dream of the Greek soldier Erus, who had fallen in battle, and, according to his story, was transported into the future world, where he saw the wicked condemned and the righteous rewarded. He tells how after a period of years those who had been sent to the lower regions and punished, and those who came down from heaven to commence life over again, were given an opportunity by Lachesis, the Daughter of Necessity, to choose their own lot in a new life. Some very strange choices were made out of those which Lachesis cast down on the plain before this multitude of souls. Some of the worst choices, Socrates says—or rather Plato, who put the words in his mouth—were made by those who had come down from heaven and had never had the discipline and experience of trouble. Those who came up from the earth and the lower regions were much more careful in their choices. So trouble is one of life's great teachers.

Out of adversity and trial come the virtues of a Christian life, such as patience, courage, kindness, sympathy. Power and influence are won out of the struggles of life. In his *Heredity and Environment* Professor Conklin writes: "What is needed in education more than anything else is some means or system which will train the powers of self-discovery and self-control. Easy lives and so-called 'good environment' will not arouse the dormant powers. It usually takes the stress and strain of hard necessity to make us acquainted with our hidden selves, to rouse the sleeping giant

[1] Violet Alleyn Storey, in *Tea in an Old House*.

within us. How often it is said that the worthless sons of worthy parents are mysteries; with the best of heredity and environment they amount to nothing, whereas the sons of poor and ignorant farmers, blacksmiths, tanners and backwoodsmen, with few opportunities and with many hardships and disadvantages, become world figures. Probably the inheritance in these last named cases was no better than in the former, but the environment was better."[1]

———•—•—•———

A traveler in Africa saw one of the large butterflies of the tropics struggling to free itself from the cocoon. He took pity on its struggles and with his knife cut the cords at which it was straining, and it came safely and easily out. But all the brilliant coloring was gone! The anguish of the struggle was necessary for that. The beautiful colors of the soul are won in the struggle with, and the victory over, trial and adversity.

———•—•—•———

On the shores of the Baltic Sea, after a great storm has passed, the fishermen go down into the water and rake the beach for the precious ambergris which has been cast up on the shores by the tumult of the waves. Life's storms have their treasures that they bring with them, and we are wise fishermen if we go out after the great billows have been raging and gather up the heavenly ambergris with which they have strewn the shores of our life. Who knows but this is the real treasure that we are intended to glean in life, instead of those lesser things whose destruction we so lament but the possession of which brings us no abiding joy.

———•—•—•———

[1] Edwin Grant Conklin, *Heredity and Environment* (Princeton: Princeton University Press, 1922), p. 335.

Like many another good man, David Livingstone was sorely tried in his son. This son, Robert, a restless, uneasy spirit, went out to Africa to join his father but, unable to reach him, found his way to Boston. The Civil War was then raging, and he enlisted in the Federal army. In his nineteenth year he fell on the field of Gettysburg. Before his father knew of his death, he wrote to a friend: "I hope your oldest boy will do well in the distant land to which he has gone. My son is in the Federal army in America, and no comfort. The secret ballast is often applied by a kind hand above, when to outsiders we appear to be sailing gloriously with the wind."

AFFLICTION—*see also* ADVERSITY, BURDENS, SORROW, SUFFERING

Recently I heard of an affliction which has befallen an old friend in the ministry. He has had sorrow upon sorrow. First of all, his sight failed him; then his child was crippled; then came the death of his wife—and now this last sorrow, the death at college of a promising son, upon whose sympathy and help the father leaned. What could one say to such a man? All I could say to him was that the Lord must love him more than most of us, because it is written, "Whom the Lord loveth he chasteneth" (Heb. 12:6).

———•—•—•———

When Aaron Burr's beautiful daughter, Thedosia Burr Alston, lost her boy of twelve at Charleston, South Carolina, her heart was crushed with sorrow. In a letter to her father she wrote as follows: "There is no more joy for me. The world is a blank. I have lost my boy. My own child is gone forever. Alas! my dear father, I live, but how does it happen? Of what am I formed that I live, and why? Of what service can I be in this world, either to you or anyone else, with a body reduced to premature old age and a mind enfeebled and wretched and bewildered? Yet, since it is my lot to live, I will endeavor to fulfill my part and exert myself to the utmost, though this life must henceforth be to me a bed of thorns!"

The letter was the expression of the first paroxysms of grief, the exposing of the desolation of a broken heart. But making allowance for that, there is still the evidence of a state of mind and heart when one feels, and has good reason to feel, that the song has gone out of life, and that whatever part is played thereafter must be by sheer determination and a sense of obligation.

—Blessings of—Late on a May day I climbed Walnut Hills, leaving the smoke and grime and warehouses and noise and din of Cincinnati far below me. On the heights all was fair and quiet and lovely, with the flowers blossoming in the springtime, and my own heart soft and tender with the memories of my father and mother and their early associations with this same Cincinnati. I strolled through the grounds of the Lane Theological Seminary, thinking of Lyman Beecher and his greater son, Henry Ward, and Harriet Beecher Stowe, all associated with that seminary.

It was while her husband was a professor there that Mrs. Stowe got the material and the inspiration for *Uncle Tom's Cabin.* In her letters she tells how that Cabin was built out of the sorrows of her own life: "I have been the mother of seven children, the most beautiful and most loved of whom lies buried near my Cincinnati residence. It was at his dying bed and at his grave that I learned what a poor slave mother may feel when her child is torn away from her. In these depths of sorrow which seemed to me immeasurable, it was my own prayer to God that such anguish might not be suffered in vain. There were circumstances about his death of such peculiar bitterness, of what seemed almost cruel suffering, that I felt that I could never be consoled for it unless this crushing of my own heart might enable me to work out some great good to others. I allude to this here, for I have often felt that much that is in that book, *Uncle Tom's Cabin,* had its root in the awful scene and bitter sorrows of that summer. It has left now, I trust, no trace on my mind except a deep compassion for the sorrowful, especially for mothers who are separated from their children."

This land of ours is linked together with a chain of homes for the refuge of those for whom men care but little—unfortunate and fallen girls and women. When the giver of those Crittenton homes died in the Far West and his body was brought across the continent to New York, at nearly every large city where the train that transported his dust stopped there were groups of girls and women with flowers in their hands and tears in their eyes.

As a boy in a California school, I heard him speak one day and marveled at his power. Now I understand. He had a daughter. She was the desire of his eyes. Life for him was the music of the brook. But the brook dried up: the child died. But in the grave of that child the heartbroken father gave his heart to Christ and consecrated his all—his vast wealth, his time, his strength, mind, soul, and body—to the ministry of compassion for homeless and unfortunate women more sinned against than sinning. Have you had losses, disappointments, total eclipses of the sun of joy? Let them lead you to Christ and, through him, to the healing of others.

—Courage in—On the third of October, just as Sherman was starting eastward to support the Union army in Chattanooga, defeated at Chickamauga, his oldest child, a boy of nine, died at Memphis. War does not stop for private sorrow, and while his wife turned northward to bury the child in the valley of the Hocking in Ohio, Sherman, mastering his anguish, but confessing to his wife that "the chief stay to his faltering heart was now gone," headed his divisions for the relief of Chattanooga.

This sentence in a letter written to a brother officer the day after the boy died tells the whole story of his sorrow and heroism: "The child who bore my name, and in whose future I reposed with more confidence than I did in my own plan of life, now floats a mere corpse, seeking a grave in a distant land, with a weeping mother, brothers, and sisters clustered about him. For myself I ask no sympathy. On, on, I must go, to meet a soldier's fate, or to live to see our country rise superior to all factions, till its flag is adored and respected by ourselves and by all the powers of the earth."

—————

—And will of God—I stood recently by the coffin of a young man who had been cut off untimely—untimely, that is, as to man's view and measurement. After the young widow had poured out her soul in grief, and asked questions which no man could answer, I said to her, "God will give you strength and faith, and out of this will come good."

"No," she answered, "good will *not* come out of it!"

And, no matter how much God wills it, good will not come out of it unless she also wills it. That was what the apostle meant when he said that "no chastening for the present seemeth to be joyous, but grievous: *nevertheless* afterward it yieldeth the peaceable fruit of righteousness unto them which are exercised thereby." (Heb. 12:11.)

ALTAR, FAMILY—*see* FAMILY ALTAR

AMBITION—*see also* IDEALS, OPPORTUNITY, PROVIDENCE, PURPOSE, YOUTH

The former president of Czechoslovakia, Dr. Masaryk, who died recently, in his autobiography writes of the high purpose of his life for the establishment of Czechoslovakia as a nation. Speaking of some of the hardships which he endured, he says, "I had a sincere and high purpose, and you can endure a great many difficulties and hardships when you follow a great aim."

—————

Gibbon's *The Decline and Fall of the Roman Empire* will probably endure till many another empire has risen and fallen. In his autobiography the author tells us how the great purpose was born within him: "It was at Rome, on the eleventh of October, 1764, as I sat musing amid the ruins of the Capitol, while the barefooted friars were singing vespers in the Temple of Jupiter, that the idea of writing the decline and fall of the city first started to my mind."

In June, 1787, twenty-three years later, we find these lines entered at Lausanne: "I have presumed to mark the moment of conception; I shall now commemorate the moment of my final deliverance. It was in the day, or rather the night, of the twenty-seventh of June, 1787, that I wrote the last line of the last page in a summer house in my garden. After laying down my pen, I took several turns in a covered walk of acacias, which commands a prospect of the country, the lakes, and the mountains. The air was temperate, the sky was serene, the silver orb of the moon was reflected from the waters, and all nature was silent. I will not dissemble the emotions of joy I felt in the recovery of my freedom, and perhaps the establishment of my fame.

"But my pride was soon humbled, and a sober melancholy was spread over my mind by the idea that I had taken everlasting leave of an old and agreeable companion, and whatsoever may be the future fate of my history, the life of the historian must be short and precarious."

The price had been great: he had given up much of his freedom; old age was coming on—but the great work had been done. His fame was secure, and one can open his pages and see the walls of Rome go down, and, in the words of Milman, "behold the gorgeous coloring in which Gibbon has invested the dying form of paganism."

───────

The minister who can speak of a sermon of the past as his "great" sermon simply confesses that he has ceased to aspire, for the only great sermon must be the one that has never been preached. The physician who says he has achieved complete mastery of disease and bodily conditions advertises his incompetency. The artist who feels that he has produced his masterpiece tells the world that he is not a master at all. The Christian who can say—what Paul could not say—that he has already attained, has already been made perfect, simply shows his complete ignorance of the fundamental law of Christianity. That law is growth, development. Joshua at the age of a hundred and ten, with his fingers releasing their firm grip upon the sword, went down to death saying, "There remaineth yet very much land to be possessed." (Josh. 13:1.) That showed him to be a great general and soldier. Frederick Watts at eighty felt that he could yet paint better pictures than he had done in the past; and that showed him to be a great painter. Paul the "aged" counted not himself to have apprehended, but reached forth to the

things that are before—and that showed him to be a great Christian.

───────

—Perils of—The Shakespearean scholar Furness wrote to Webster in those critical days of the great debate on slavery that if he "would only throw his great nature into the cause of human freedom, his fellow men would behold such a demonstration of personal power as it is seldom given to the world to witness." Webster's answer was his famous seventeenth of March speech, in which he denounced the Abolition party, said that California and Mexico could come in without any provision regarding slavery, because the nature of the country was such that no man would ever think of taking slaves and settling there. It is difficult to avoid the impression that in making that speech Daniel Webster was seeking to hold the votes of the South while getting the votes of the North for the presidential nomination. If so, he must have been bitterly disappointed. What Horace Mann said, whether true or not, expressed the opinion of many who hitherto had followed him: "Webster is a fallen star, Lucifer descending from heaven."

───────

When Macbeth had his ambition stirred by the three witches and saw his opportunity to become king by assassinating his faithful lord, yet drew back from the dreadful crime, his more hardened wife read his letter hinting at his emotions and mused of him:

> *Thou wouldst be great;*
> *Art not without ambition, but*
> *without*
> *The illness should attend it.*

What is the illness which should attend worldly ambition? It is a willingness and readiness to lower one's principle, silence one's conscience, and so bow down to Satan for the sake of securing some worldly aim.

AMERICA

As our nation grew, the people opened their doors to all the sons of men. In the words of Emma Lazarus, written as an inscription for the Statue of Liberty, the nation said:

> Give me your tired, your poor,
> Your huddled masses yearning to breathe free,
> The wretched refuse of your teeming shore,
> Send these, the homeless, tempesttossed, to me:
> I lift my lamp beside the golden door.

Once over the entrance to a cemetery in the Southern mountains where are buried the dead who fell for their country, I read these words: "Erected by the Government of the United States." The government of the United States! Ah, thought I, there is something here more than crops, and mines, and fleets, and armies, and stocks, and bonds, and country clubs, and highways; something far beyond that—something that has to do with the soul!

—**Its danger**—In 1857 Macaulay, the British historian, wrote these words to an American friend: "Your Republic will be as fearfully plundered and laid waste by barbarians in the twentieth century as the Roman Empire was in the fifth, with this difference, that the Huns and Vandals who ravaged the Roman Empire came from without, and that your Huns and Vandals will have been engendered within your own country by your own institutions."

—**Its opportunities**—On a ship on the Adriatic, sailing from Greece to Italy, I met a young businessman from New York, of Syrian parentage, who had been on a visit to his father on the island of Cyprus. He was contrasting conditions as he found them there and elsewhere in that part of the world with the advantages and opportunities he had in New York. He said to me: "If I had to live now in this part of the world, it would be a slow death."

—**Its true greatness**—A man walked down through the narrow canyon of New York's financial district. As he contemplated the great buildings and saw the names of famous financial houses, he said to himself, "Here is the power and greatness of America." A short time afterward he was in Washington and visited the Capitol. As he walked under the great dome and viewed the statues of celebrated statesmen and presidents, he said to himself, "Here is the greatness of America."

But sometime later he was a guest at an old-fashioned farm in southern Ohio. When the time came for the noonday meal, the bell on the post back of the house was rung, and presently the hired men who had been working in the fields appeared for their dinner. They washed their faces in a tin basin on a bench near the pump and then filed into the dining room, taking their places at the table. The farmer and his wife were seated at either end of the table, which groaned with plenty. The farmer took up a Bible and read in solemn and reverent accent the noble sentences of the Ninetieth Psalm. Then, with every head bowed, he led in prayer and thanked God for his goodness. When he left this home with that scene fresh in his mind, the visitor concluded that he had discovered the *real* greatness of America. "Except the Lord build the house, they labor in vain that build it: except the Lord keep the city, the watchman waketh but in vain."

At the end of the Civil War, when the news of Appomattox came, the secretary of war, Edwin M. Stanton, caused to be displayed from the dome of the Capitol a transparency on which were inscribed these words from Psalm 118: "This is the Lord's doing; it is marvelous in our eyes" (v. 23).

In his message to the Congress, December 1, 1862, Abraham Lincoln, after sketching the great possible destiny and future for a united nation on this continent if the one issue which divided it could be settled, said: "Fellow Citizens, we cannot escape history. We of this Congress and this Administration will be remembered in spite of ourselves. No personal significance or insignificance can spare one or another of us. The fiery trial through which we pass will light us down in honor or dishonor to the latest generation. . . . We shall nobly save or meanly lose the last best hope of earth."

—Lincoln's faith in—When the fall of the Confederacy was at hand, General Grant invited Lincoln to come down to visit him at his headquarters at City Point on the James River. As they sat that night about the campfire, Lincoln related some of his characteristic anecdotes, and then sat in silence, looking into the fire. Grant looked up and said to him, "Mr. President, did you at any time doubt the final success of the cause?"

Straightening himself up in his camp chair, and leaning forward and lifting his hand by way of emphasis, Lincoln answered with the greatest solemnity, "Never, for a moment!"

ANCHORS FOR LIFE

Even in appearance a ship's anchor remains much the same today as it always has been. Compare Paul's grain ship with the *Queen Mary* or the *Queen Elizabeth;* there is hardly anything about one ship that is like the other. The oars are gone, the sails are gone, the masts are mostly gone. The ship of today is completely changed; and yet in one respect, except for size, there is not so much difference: the anchor on Paul's ship and the anchor on the *Queen Elizabeth* are much the same in form. Human life changes outwardly, but not inwardly. We have automobiles, radios, airships, and all the devices of our modern civilization; but *inwardly* life is much the same—the same perils, the same sorrows, the same temptations, the same joy and hope. The soul of man still needs the anchor on its voyage across life's sea.

Paul and his companions who sailed on that ship that was wrecked on the coast of Malta were saved from destruction by the four anchors which they cast out of the stern. On this dangerous voyage of life there are anchors that every man ought to carry on his ship—anchors which will not drag in time of storm.

ANGELS, GUARDIAN—*see also* MOTHER

A GUARDIAN ANGEL

When Theodosia Burr, the beautiful and gifted daughter of Aaron Burr, who afterward perished at sea, thought that the end of her life was at hand, she wrote to her husband, the governor of South Carolina: "If it is permitted, I will hover around you and guard you and intercede for you."

As a mere lad in the Confederate army, Henry M. Stanley was taken prisoner at the Battle of Shiloh and confined at Fort Douglas, Chicago. In his autobiography he relates how, as he was one day playing cards, he felt a slight blow in the back of his neck and in a moment was by the bedside of his aunt in the farmhouse in Wales where he had lived for a year or more. His aunt lay dying and was asking his forgiveness for having turned him out into the world. He was about to take her hand when he "came to" and asked his fellows what had happened. They wondered what he meant, for the vision had been too rapid for calculation. In due time he received word telling him that on the corresponding day and hour his aunt had died and that she left such a message for him.

Stanley goes on to say that he believes the intelligence of the swift vision was brought to him by a guardian spirit and that every man has such a spirit, striving in every way to warn, help, and encourage its mortal charge. It is not strange that such an office—the guardian angel's ministry—should be assigned to our loved ones who have gone before us.

ANGER—*see also* REMORSE, SELF-CONTROL, TEMPER

—**Dangers of**—Alexander the Great was one of the few men of history who deserved the adjective "great." His biographer describes him as by nature fervently passionate and impulsive. He was strong in his loves and his loyalties; and, although hatred was foreign to his magnanimous nature, he was often swept by storms of anger. Yet by a magnificent display of will power he held the reins upon his passions. In the midst of the sensuous temptations of the Asiatic courts, where his army passed in conquest, he seems to have held himself in complete mastery and kept himself unspotted from the world.

But to this long chapter of noble self-control there is one sad and tragic exception. At a banquet given for Dionysius a song was sung comparing Alexander with Castor and Pollux, to his advantage. Then someone disparaged the old Macedonian officers who had fought under Alexander's father, Philip. This aroused one of Alexander's generals, Clitus, who commanded the famous Hetairoi. Clitus reminded Alexander how he had saved his life in one of the recent battles, and said Alexander had bought his fame with the blood of the Macedonian officers. He told Alexander to associate with his lickspittle Persians, who bowed the knee to him and told him only what he wanted to hear. Alexander, stung by this remark of Clitus, reached for his sword, which a discreet officer had hidden away. Then in his anger, falling—as men always do at such a time—into his native idiom, the Macedonian, he ordered the trumpeter to sound the call, and when he delayed, smote him with his fist.

Before he could inflict hurt upon Clitus, the friends of that half-intoxicated officer hurried him out of the banqueting hall. But he soon entered by another door, where he stood under the curtains quoting lines from a Greek poet to the disparagement of Alexander's conquests. "Quick as a flash, Alexander snatched a spear from the hand of the guard and hurled it at the figure by a raised curtain. The deed was done. The friend of his childhood, his life companion and rescuer, lay gasping out his life."

The passion of remorse followed quickly upon the fury of his anger. Alexander himself drew out the fatal spear, and but for his officers he would have fallen upon it himself. All through the night, and for several days, he lay writhing in his remorse, piteously calling Clitus by name and chiding himself as the murderer of his friend. Alexander the Great conquered the world, but he could not conquer himself. In his conquests he stormed and took almost every great city of the ancient world. Yet he was not able to subdue that more important city, to conquer which is the greatest of all achievements—the city and citadel of his own spirit.

Jonah is an example of how the character of a good and a great man can be marred by anger, and his usefulness impaired. His story suggests the folly, the danger, and the injury of anger. Unfortunately, when a man feels anger and gives unrestrained expression to it, as Jonah did, his fellowman is not as patient and long suffering as God was and does not always return the soft answer which God returned to the angry and petulant Jonah. Anger is one of the most common sins, yet one of the most dangerous and injurious to the peace and well-being of man. More than any other sin, it blasts the flower of friendship, turns men out of Eden, destroys peace and concord in the home, incites to crime and violence, and turns love and affection into hatred.

Another great man injured by anger was Moses. When the people murmured and asked for water, Moses was commanded to strike the rock at Horeb. Out of all patience with the people and their waywardness, Moses struck the rock twice, as if the rock had been the head of the people, crying out as he did so, "Hear, ye rebels!" This burst of rage cost Moses the Promised Land, because it was for this transgression that Moses —in spite of his grand service and his pathetic pleading at the end of Israel's long wandering—was not permitted to go into the land of Canaan. That was not the first nor the last time that a land of promise and of happiness was lost through anger. Moses was not as patient as God.

Anger weakens a man. It puts him at a disadvantage in every undertaking in life. When Sinbad and his sailors landed on one of their tropical islands, they saw high up in the trees coconuts which could quench their thirst and satisfy their hunger. The coconuts were far above the reach of Sinbad and the sailors, but in the branches of the trees were the chattering apes. Sinbad and his men began to throw stones and sticks up at the apes. This enraged the monkeys and they began to seize the coconuts and hurl them down at the men on the ground. That was just what Sinbad and his men wanted. They got the apes angry so that the apes would gather their food for them. That is a good illustration of how by indulgence in anger we play into the hands of our foes.

—Restraining—When Lee's army escaped across the Potomac into Virginia after the defeat at Gettysburg, Lincoln was greatly distressed; and in his disappointment and anger he wrote a sharp letter to the commander of the Union army, General Meade. But after the letter had been written he decided not to send it. That letter contains many true sentiments, and to us at this distance it does seem that Meade should never have permitted Lee to get safely over the river into Virginia. But lest in the intensity of his feeling, and in his mortification, he should wound or do an injustice to a faithful general, Lincoln did not send the letter. Some of the best letters ever written are those which were never sent.

—Righteous—What would one not give to have seen Elijah confronting Ahab after the murder of Naboth, and telling him that "in the place where dogs licked the blood of Naboth shall dogs lick thy blood" (I Kings 21:19)? What would one not give to have seen John the Baptist stand before Herod and Herodias and denounce them for their adulterous union? What would one not give to have seen Paul in the Sanhedrin, when the high priest commanded one to smite Paul, and Paul turned on the high priest like a flame, exclaiming, "God shall smite thee, thou whited wall: and sittest thou to judge me according to the law, and commandest me to be smitten contrary to the law?" (Acts 23:3). What would one not give to have seen Ambrose forbidding the bloodstained Emperor Theodosius from entering his church at Milan? Or John Knox, almost too ill to stand, when the news came of the massacre of St. Bartholemew's Day in Paris, mounting the pulpit in St. Giles in Edinburgh to express the righteous indignation and horror of the Protestant world, commanding the French ambassador to "tell his master, that murderer, the King of France, that God's vengeance shall not depart from him nor from his house"?

These are magnificent exhibitions of righteous anger and indignation.

—And a soft answer—"A soft answer turneth away wrath: but grievous words stir up anger." (Prov. 15:1.) It is said that when an elephant is enraged nothing calms him so well as a little lamb, and it is a well-known fact that Andrew Jackson in the battle of New Orleans stopped the cannon balls of the British artillery with bales of cotton.

APPRECIATION

A minister, once walking through one of the new-made American cemeteries in France after the first World War, saw a mother weeping over a grave.

Going up to her, he said, "Madam, you have my sympathy."

The woman looked up and answered, "I don't want your sympathy."

Somewhat taken aback, the minister answered, "Well, you have it whether you want it or not."

The woman then said, "No, I do not want your sympathy; I do not ask for your prayers. What I want is your appreciation."

ARMAGEDDON

From the summit of Mount Tabor one commands a grand view of the Holy Land. To the north and east, on a clear day, the waters of Galilee can be seen; to the north, the hills of Nazareth, where He was brought up; to the northwest, Carmel and the Mediterranean; to the south, the mountains of Gilboa and the mountains of Samaria. Immediately at the foot of the mountain is the great plain of Esdraelon, which belts its way clear across the Holy Land. On the slopes of the mountain which mark the southern end of the plain, one can make out Endor, where Saul consulted the witch the night before he fell at Gilboa; Nain, where Christ stopped the funeral procession and raised the widow's son; and, farther to the west in the direction of Carmel, the ruins of Jezreel and Megiddo.

But it is more than a great stretch of the Holy Land that one surveys from the summit of Tabor. It is a cyclorama of the history of Israel. One is looking down on the battleground of the nations. From the dawn of history that plain of Esdraelon has resounded with the tread of marching hosts, and the banners of invading and clashing armies have been wet with the dews of Tabor and of Hermon. The plain is exceedingly fertile, for it has been irrigated with blood and fertilized with men's bones as has no other part of the earth's surface.

ATONEMENT—*see also* BLOOD OF CHRIST, THE CROSS, FORGIVENESS OF SIN, LAMB OF GOD, RECONCILIATION

The Atonement is God's own mystery. The best that we can do is to stretch forth humble hands of faith and touch the outermost fringe of its crimson garment. The cherubim and the seraphim cover the rest with their wings.

The Jews have a legend about David which shows how deeply in the most ancient days men were moved by David's immortal lament over Absalom and felt that in some way God must honor such immeasurable grief. According to the tradition, at each cry of David—every time he uttered the words "My son! My son!"—one of the sevenfold gates of hell opened, until at length the soul of Absalom was admitted to paradise. What the Jews unwittingly were grasping after in that legend was the truth of the Atonement. At every cry of Christ on the cross as he hangs and suffers for sinners, one of the gates of condemnation swings open and the soul of the redeemed sinner is admitted unto paradise.

In the Boston library is the great mural painting "Christianity and Judaism," by Sargent. At one end are depicted the law and the prophets in majestic splendor and noble array; at the other is a representation of the Redemption. Surmounting all are the three colossal figures of the Trinity. On the cross hangs the Son of God, with Adam and Eve, emblematic of humanity, kneeling on either side and bound, by what seems to be cloud or purple banner, close to the body of Christ. Thus the artist has related to mankind the death of Christ. His death on the cross for sin has its direct and peculiar effect upon mankind. Humanity, identified with Christ in the Incarna-tion, suffers in Christ and is redeemed in Christ.

There is an old story of how the celebrated Greek poet Aeschylus was about to be sentenced and banished by the citizens of Athens. But his brother, who had lost an arm at the battle of Salamis, appeared at the tribunal and displayed his wounds as a reason why the citizens should show mercy to Aeschylus. Upon that ground, and with that appeal, the poet was set free.

This is but a poor illustration of how the wounds of Christ, his death upon the cross, are forever with God the ground of our forgiveness and his mercy. That is what we mean every time we conclude our prayers, in church or in private, by saying, "For Christ's sake. Amen." We ask God to answer our prayers and forgive our sins, for Christ's sake—that is, not merely for the sake of who Christ was, but of *what* Christ *did* upon the cross.

For several generations the *Edinburgh Review* has carried on its cover the Latin epigram, "The Judge is condemned when the guilty is acquitted." The guilty is sometimes acquitted in human courts, but this never happens in the Divine Court. There, if man is justified, or, to put it in plain present-day English, acquitted or found not guilty, it is in strict harmony with the law of right, of justice. How, then, shall mortal man be just with God? Man is a sinner. The penalty upon sin as announced by God is death, eternal death, spiritual death; and God will by no means clear the guilty.

The fact that Christ has bought us makes us desire to belong to him. See the account of the beautiful mulatto girl put upon the auction block at New Orleans. "$500, $700"—"knocked down" at $2,500! The next day the successful bidder called at the home where the girl was a slave; and when she saw him who was now her owner she said sadly, "I am ready to go with you."

But the man replied, "I do not want you to go with me. I bought you in order to set you free."

When the amazed girl was able to take in the meaning of his words, she said, "Then I will be your servant forever!"

So the purchase of Christ binds us to him with the bonds of love.

—And gospel—As Dr. Dale finely puts it in his work on the Atonement, "The real truth is that while He came to preach the gospel, his chief object in coming was that there might be a gospel to preach."

—For the nation—Great evils and great wrongs can be met and conquered only by great suffering. Perhaps there lies the key to the mystery of life.

On a November day in 1859 at Charles Town, Virginia, an old man was led out to be hanged by the neck until dead. The sentence of death was quickly executed. Stonewall Jackson, who had come up with a company of cadets from the Virginia Military Institute to suppress any attempt at rescue—who says he prayed earnestly for the man's soul—watching the hanging, said that soon the wind blew his lifeless body to and fro. North and south, nearly everyone said he died as the fool dieth. But just before he died the old man handed his executioners a bit of paper on which he had written these words: "I now believe that the sins of this guilty nation will never be purged away except with blood." That was in November, 1859.

Three short years passed, and on the seventeenth of September, 1862, the very ground on which the old man was hanged shook with the thunder and concussion of the guns firing on the banks of the Antietam. In the morning of that day the little river flowed quietly under stone bridges on its way to the Potomac, and the sentient fields of corn stood waiting for the reaper's hand. But when the moon came up that night over the distant mountains, it looked down upon one of those scenes which must ever humble man's vaunted wisdom and pride. The fields of corn which at sunrise had been waving their tassels in the morning wind now lay prostrate and trampled, swept by the sleet of lead. The trim hedges and fences were broken down, the orchards mangled and splintered. In the great barns or at the field hospitals the army surgeons, with bare and bloody arms, cut and hacked and sawed in the flickering light of the lanterns. Down by the river banks and in the river, under the stone bridges and along the roads and lanes, in the trampled corn fields, in the woods and in the orchards, the wounded and the dead, most of them under twenty—23,481 of them—lay in rows and heaps, their white faces pleading a mute protest to the autumnal moon. Yet that scene of sorrow and suffering played its part in righting a great wrong and in cementing anew the foundations and walls of the nation.

—Substitution—There has never been found a better illustration of sacrificial love than that in Charles Dickens' *Tale of Two Cities,* where Sidney Carton dies for Charles Darnay. The young Frenchman has been condemned to die by the guillotine. Sidney Carton is a dissipated English lawyer who has wasted great gifts and quenched high possibilities in riotous living. When he learns the plight of his friend, he determines to save him by laying down his own life—not for the love he has for the man, but for the sake of the man's wife and child.

To that end Carton gains admission to the dungeon the night before the execution, changes garments with the condemned man, and the next day is led out and put to death as Charles Darnay. Before he went to the dungeon he had entered the courtyard and remained there for a few minutes alone, looking up at the light in the window of the daughter's room. He was led by the light of love, but it led straight to a dungeon and thence to the guillotine.

As we see him ascending the steps to the place of death, his hands bound behind his back, taking his last look at the world, we feel that a noble ending has sanctified an ignoble life; and these words of our Saviour come to mind: "Greater love hath no man than this, that a man lay down his life for his friends" (John 15:13).

———

Only the precious blood of Christ can cover our transgressions. In Stroudsburg, Pennsylvania, there is the grave of a Civil War soldier. The stone bears the date of his birth and death, and then these words: "Abraham Lincoln's substitute." In the woe and anguish of the war, realizing that thousands upon thousands were falling in his place on the field of battle, Lincoln chose to honor one particular soldier as his substitute and make him a symbol, as it were, of the fact that the soldiers who perished in battle were dying that others might live. When you and I come to the Cross of Christ, each one of us, supplying his own name, can say, "My substitute!"

———

At the crisis of the Civil War, a New York State farmer was drafted for the army. His wife had died and left him the sole support of a family of little children. He was wondering what he could do, when a young man of the neighborhood who had none depending upon him came to his house and offered to go in his place. For the sake of his children the farmer accepted the offer. The generous friend marched off to war. In the first engagement he was shot and killed. The news filtered back to the New York farm. The man took his horses from the field and drove to the scene of battle. There he sought until he found the body of his friend. He carried him back to his home and laid him tenderly in a grave in the village churchyard. From the hills he hewed a stone and cut upon it these words, "He died for me."

———

—**Trust in Christ's salvation**—His chaplain said to Bishop Butler on his deathbed, "My lord, you have forgotten that Jesus Christ is the Saviour."

"True," said Butler, "but how shall I know that he is a Saviour for me?"

"My lord," answered the chaplain, "it is written, 'Him that cometh to me I will in no wise cast out'" (John 6:37).

At this, Butler said: "True. I am surprised that, although I have read that scripture a thousand times over, I never felt its virtue until this moment; and now I die happy."

AUTHORITY

In answer to a centurion's earnest request to heal his slave who was desperately sick, Jesus was on his way to the house of the Roman centurion who was in command of the garrison at Capernaum. When the centurion heard that Jesus was coming in person he was amazed, and at once sent messengers to intercept him, protesting that he was not worthy that Christ should go to such trouble. Surely all he had to do was to speak the word, without coming in person, and the sick slave would be healed; for, he said, "I am a man under authority, having soldiers under me: and I say to this man, Go, and he goeth; and to another, Come, and he cometh; and to my servant, Do this, and he doeth it" (Matt. 8:9). What he meant was that if he, a junior noncommissioned officer in the Roman army, could have things done by word of command, without going in person, surely Jesus, the great prophet of Israel, could do likewise.

"A man under authority." At first that seems an odd way of putting it. Why did he not say a man *with* authority, or a man *invested with* authority? But this is what he said: "a man *under* authority." When you stop to think of it, there was sound sense in the way he put it. Above the centurion was the senior centurion, and above the senior centurion, the sixty centurions of the Roman legion. Above the sixty centurions were the six tribunes, and above the six tribunes the two consuls, and—in the imperial system—above the two consuls, the emperor himself. It was because he stood—although the last and the lowest—in this long line of delegated authority that the Romnaan centurion was able to give orders and have them obeyed. He could give orders because he received orders. He *had* authority because he was *under authority himself*.

AVARICE—*see also* COVETOUSNESS, ENVY, MONEY

Once in medieval Rome there stood in one of the squares an image with an outstretched hand. On the forefinger of the image was a golden ring inscribed with the device "Strike Here." Men often stopped to look at the image and read the device on the finger, but they did not know what it meant. However, a learned clerk often passing the image was careful to observe the place on the street where the shadow of the finger fell.

Coming one night at midnight, he began to dig in that spot—and soon came upon a secret stairway, leading underground until it brought him into a spacious hall which was lighted by a flaming jewel on the wall. Opposite the flaming jewel there was a statue, a man holding a bow and shaft ready to shoot, and upon the forehead of this image were the words, "That which I am I am. My fatal aim none can escape." Midway in the hall there was a table upon which the cloth, the cups, the plates and knives, and all the meats and bread, were gold or studded with precious stones. Around the table, silent, motionless, and sad, were seated knights and ladies and men from every rank of life. But they were turned to stone.

The clerk looked at the scene in amazement and then, stirred by greed, began to gather up the silver and the gold. Whereupon the figures seated about the table suddenly leaped to their feet, the archer shot his arrow, and the clerk lay dead on the floor in the midst of darkness.

The image is the adversary, the tempter whose finger points to the realms of gold. The downward stair is our lusts and passions, the archer is death, the flaming jewel, life. The table heaped with gold and silver is the things of this world, the knights and ladies those whose flesh and bone have been hardened into stone by avarice.

———•———

Tolstoi has a powerful tale of a young Russian who fell heir to his father's small farm. He was no sooner in possession of this land than he began to dream eagerly of how he could add to it. One morning a stranger, evidently a person of power and authority, came to him and told him, as they were standing near the old homestead, that he could have, for nothing, all the land he could walk over in one day—but at sundown he must be back at the very place from which he started. Pointing to the grave of the young man's father, the stranger said, "This is the point to which you must return."

The youth looked eagerly over the rich fields in the distance and, throwing off his coat and without waiting to say a word to his wife and children, started off across the fields. His first plan was to cover a tract of ground six miles square; but when he had walked the six he decided to make it nine, then twelve, and then fifteen—which would give him sixty miles to walk before sundown!

By noon he had covered two sides of this square, or thirty miles. But eager to get on and compass the whole distance, he did not stop for food. An hour later he saw an old man drinking at a spring, but in his hunger for land he brushed aside the cup which the old man offered him and rushed on in his eager quest for possession of land. When he was a few miles from the goal he was worn down with fatigue.

A few hundred yards from the line, he saw the sun approaching the horizon and knew that he had but a few minutes left. Hurrying on and ready to faint, he summoned all his energies for one last effort—and managed to stagger across the line just as the sun was sinking. But as he crossed the line he saw a cruel, cynical smile on the face of the stranger who had promised him the land, and who was waiting for him there at his father's grave. Just as he crossed the line —the master and possessor, as he thought, of fifteen square miles of rich land—the

youth fell dead upon the ground which he had coveted.

The stranger then said to the servants, "I offered him all the land he could cover. Now you see what that is: six feet long by two feet wide; and I thought he would like to have the land close to his father's grave, rather than to have it anywhere else." With that the stranger, who was Death, vanished, saying as he did so, "I have kept my pledge."

"Whose shall those things be?" (Luke 12:20.)

———•••———

One of the old saints, according to the legend, in his journey overtook two travelers. One was a greedy, avaricious, covetous man; the other was of a jealous and envious nature. When they came to the parting of the ways, the saint said he would give them a parting gift. Whichever made a wish first would have his wish fulfilled, and the other man would get a double portion of what the first had asked for. The greedy man knew what he wanted; but he was afraid to make his wish, because he wanted a double portion and could not bear the thought of his companion getting twice as much as he had. But the envious man was also unwilling to wish first, because he could not stand the idea of his companion getting twice as much as he would get. So each waited for the other to wish first. At length the greedy man took his fellow by the throat and said he would choke him to death unless he made his wish. At that the envious man said, "Very well; I will make my wish. I wish to be made blind in one eye." Immediately he lost the sight of his eye —and his companion went blind in both eyes.

So avarice and its companion, envy, blind and curse the soul of man.

27

B

BALAAM

A battlefield is not a pleasant place for a walk, at least, not for half a century or so after the battle has been fought. But let us walk over this battlefield in Moab, across the Jordan, where the children of Israel took vengeance on the Midianites who had tempted them into licentiousness and sin. Here the slain lie in heaps, rows, piles, and avenues, hecatombs of the dead. Already the vultures and the jackals have come to the feast, for where the carcass is, there also will the eagles be gathered together.

But who is this lying dead here in this pyramid of fallen tribesmen and Bedouins, this man with the robes of divination all rent and torn, his gray hair clotted with blood, and his wild and sightless eyes staring heavenward? Balaam, is it thou? Art thou also among the slain? How camest *thou* here, Balaam? Art thou not he who once uttered those great and eloquent words concerning the children of Israel and their destiny? Art thou not the man who said, "God is not a man, that he should lie; neither the son of man, that he should repent" (Num. 23:19)? Art thou not he who said, "There shall come a star out of Jacob, and a Sceptre shall rise out of Israel"? Art thou not he who made the prayer, "Let me die the death of the righteous, and let my last end be like his!" And yet, here thou liest—dead, slain among the enemies of Israel! "Balaam, also the son of Beor they slew with the sword."

BARNABAS

Paul lived to write a great and beautiful description of a Christian man. He described that man, in the immortal accents of the thirteenth chapter of First Corinthians, as having the love that "suffereth long, and is kind," that "envieth not," that "vaunteth not itself," that "seeketh not its own," that "rejoiceth not in unrighteousness, but rejoiceth with the truth," that "beareth all things, believeth all things, hopeth all things."

When I read that beautiful chapter, that masterpiece of Paul's inspired brush, I feel sure that the model, the man that Paul had in mind, was his old friend Barnabas, the "son of consolation."

BEAUTY

After a minister had preached a searching sermon on pride, a woman who had heard the sermon waited upon him and told him that she was in much distress of mind, and that she would like to confess to a great sin. The minister asked her what the sin was.

She answered, "The sin of pride, for I sat for an hour before my mirror some days ago admiring my beauty."

"Oh," responded the minister, "that was not a sin of pride—that was a sin of imagination!"

———

—And money—Betsey Patterson of Baltimore was regarded as the most beautiful woman in America, and the charm of her beauty was acknowledged in the highest circles of Europe. In 1804 Napoleon's youngest brother, on a visit to America, became infatuated with Elizabeth and married her; but the marriage was afterward annulled through the influence of Napoleon.

Toward the end of her remarkable career, Betsey Patterson said, "Once I had everything but money. Now I have nothing but money." Writing in middle life to a friend, she confessed, "I am dying with ennui. I am tired of reading, and of all my ways of killing time. I doze away my existence. I am too old to coquet, and without this stimulus I die of ennui. The Princess Gallitizin tries to keep me up to the toil of dressing by telling me I am a beauty. I am tired of life, and tired of having lived." Such was the melancholy confession of a woman who had great beauty of body and delighted to adorn that body, but had no inner beauty of the soul—what Peter calls the "hidden man of the heart" (I Pet. 3:4).

BELIEF

The houses built by the two men in the parable were exactly alike. They had the same walls, the same kind of roof, the same doors, and the same windows; but when the storm was over, one was a heap of rubbish, and the other stood just as it was before the storm. The difference was due to the fact that one was built on sand and the other on the rock. Such, Christ said, is the difference between the man who hears and obeys and believes his words, and the one who does not.

BENEDICTION—*see* PREACHING AFTER THE BENEDICTION

BIBLE—*see also* MOTHER'S BIBLE

The Bible is the last voice. It is the voice that speaks to us from the other world, or God has never spoken. The truth about the Bible is told in those words in "The Monastery" which Scott puts into the mouth of the apparition which speaks to the young Glendinning:

Within that awful volume lies
The mystery of mysteries!
Happiest they of human race,
To whom God has granted grace

To read, to fear, to hope, to pray,
To lift the latch, and force the way;
And better had they ne'er been born,
Who read to doubt, or read to scorn.

Among the interesting relics of Thomas Jefferson is his copy of the New Testament. He has gone through the Gospels, scoring out with his pen all passages which present Jesus as a supernatural person. The records of his miraculous birth and all the miracles are deleted, together with all statements which declare Jesus to be the Son of God. In this deleted New Testament the Gospel of Matthew ends with these words: "And he rolled a great stone to the door of the sepulchre, and departed" (Matt. 27:60).

"But the word of God is not bound." That is the inscription on a pillar in the crypt of a church in Rome where Paul is said to have been imprisoned. The heroic apostle, bound with a chain and awaiting death, is not disheartened, discouraged, nor despairing. He has full confidence in the spread of the gospel, and in the conquest of Christ, telling Timothy at Ephesus to be true to Christ and the gospel, for which, he says, "I suffer . . . unto bonds; but the word of God is not bound" (II Tim. 2:9). How true that statement of the apostle was—and is—is demonstrated by the simple, yet tremendous, fact that nineteen hundred years after Paul wrote from his prison at Rome, "The word of God is not bound," the words are taken as the text for a sermon on the invincible power of the Bible.

—Belief in the—A friend once said to President Grant that Sumner did not believe in the Bible. "Of course Sumner doesn't believe in the Bible," answered Grant. "He didn't write it." That attitude of mind toward Christian truth, however justly or unjustly imputed to the brilliant senator from New England, is typical of many of those who vent their doubts loudly and boast that they do not accept anything the way other people do but must have infallible proofs. There are some people who would never believe in any Bible that they themselves did not write.

————◆◆◆————

During one of the most critical periods of the Civil War, Lincoln wrote to his friend Joshua Speed, "I am profitably engaged in reading the Bible. Take all of this book upon reason that you can and the balance upon faith, and you will live and die a better man."

The intimation might be that most of the Bible you can take on reason, and only a small portion will require the exercise of faith. But if you are to receive the Bible as a revelation from God, you must take it all upon faith.

————◆◆◆————

—Church and the—On a summer trip to the Pacific Coast I broke the journey on a Saturday night at Fargo, North Dakota. I worshiped the next morning in a Baptist church, the Presbyterian and the Congregational churches being closed. After the service, as I walked through the town—and let me say I have great sympathy for the man who comes to a strange city to spend Sunday—I saw a beautiful structure which bore the name of the Norwegian Lutheran Church. I slipped into a seat at the rear of the long nave and heard just the concluding part of the sermon. The closing hymn was sung to the music of Luther's great hymn, "A Mighty Fortress Is Our God." But the words of the hymn were these:

God's Word is our great heritage,
And shall be ours forever;
To spread its light from age to age
Shall be our chief endeavor.

Through life it guides our way,
In death it is our stay.
Lord, grant while worlds endure,
We keep its teachings pure
Throughout all generations.

As these words went up on the wings of Luther's grand music, I said to myself, "That is all that the Church has, God's Word; that is our great heritage; that is all that man has to guide him in life and stay him in death; and to spread that Word throughout the world unto all generations is all that Christ has given his Church to do in this world."

————◆◆◆————

—Civilization and the—When Thomas Paine showed Benjamin Franklin the manuscript of *The Age of Reason,* Franklin advised him not to publish it, saying, "The world is bad enough *with* the Bible; what would it be without it?"

————◆◆◆————

In recent years the thrilling story of Pitcairn Island and the mutiny of the *Bounty* has been retold and popularized in newspaper articles and books. There is one incident in that story which, indeed, is worth retelling. The mutineers sank their ship and landed with their native women on the lonely island named Pitcairn. There were nine white sailors, six natives, ten women, and a girl of fifteen. One of the sailors discovered a method of distilling alcohol, and the island colony was debauched with drunkenness and vice.

After a time only one of the white sailors who had landed survived, surrounded by native women and half-breed children. This sailor, Alexander Smith, found in one of the chests that had been taken from the *Bounty* a copy of the Bible. He began to teach his fellow exiles its principles, with the result that his own life was changed, and finally the life of that island colony.

In 1808 the United States ship *Topaz* visited the island and found a thriving and prosperous community, without whiskey, without a jail, without crime, and without an insane asylum. The Bible had changed the life of that island community.

So it has been from age to age: "The entrance of thy words giveth light" (Ps. 119:130).

—Devil and the—I saw the chamber of Luther, with the bed in which he slept, his wash basin, and his desk—a notable desk, too, for on that desk Luther translated the New Testament into German. On one of the walls of the room there is a place bare of plaster. It is the spot where Luther hurled his inkstand at the devil, whose fearful apparition he had seen. This may be but legend. But there is no doubting the fact that by his translation of the New Testament into the language of the people Luther did hurl an inkstand of considerable weight at the devil and all his works.

—Lincoln and the—In an Indiana wilderness near Gentryville I went once to visit the old Pigeon Creek Baptist Church. The original church is gone, but the present structure is just about the same as the church of a hundred years ago. Backless benches are the only pews. In front of the pulpit platform is an old-fashioned marble-topped table. On the plain wooden pulpit lies a Bible from which the preacher preaches—a Bible whose declarations he believes and upon which he does not try to improve. A water bucket stands in one corner at the back of the church, and a stove in the middle. On the two sides are two windows with little squares of glass in them. Outside, the wind sighs in the oaks and hickory-nut trees.

The Sabbath morning has come and the congregation is assembling. Here they come from every direction, on foot and on horseback—hardy, God-fearing pioneers. Among the worshipers comes Sally Bush, with two stepchildren by her side. One of these children is Sarah, the other a tall, gangling boy with sallow complexion and a shock of coarse, tawny hair. The mother sits on a backless bench with Sarah on one side and Abraham on the other. The preacher prays long and preaches longer, and on his lips are the accents of predestination, preterition, regeneration, sanctification, and adoption.

Years afterward, that tall, sallow boy with his shock of coarse hair stirred the nation with his speeches on the Union and slavery. The most striking thing about these speeches was the use Abraham Lincoln made of the Bible. As Lowell said of him, "He spoke in the grand simplicites of the Old and New Testament." Where did he get that familiarity with the saving truths and the noble music of the Bible? He got it sitting Sunday after Sunday by the side of Sally Bush on a backless bench, listening to a Hard-Shell Baptist preacher who knew little else besides the Bible—but who *knew* his Bible, and preached its truths and spoke its language.

—Preaching and the—A preacher without faith in the Bible, or one who does not make it the ground of his preaching and teaching, is as useless in the warfare with sin as a soldier who uses a blank cartridge. And, aside from the doctrinal significance of the Bible, what a territory it is for the intellect, for the imagination, for the conscience! "Sight, riches, healing of the mind"—all are there in the Bible. Joseph Parker, whose *The People's Bible* is a great window into the Bible, used to be credited with sitting for hours in his study, tapping an open Bible with his fingertips and murmuring: "This is history—exhausts all history! This is poetry—exhausts all poetry! This is truth—exhausts all truth!" Thomas à Kempis said that the Bible is the one book whose wealth rebukes us more the older we grow, because we knew and loved it so late. It is sad, but true, that many preachers are well along in their ministerial race before they awake to the power and beauty of the Bible.

—**Prophecy and the**—No man can unlock the door of the future. Even the wisest man cannot penetrate the secrets of futurity. Anyone, however, can make a shrewd guess. When Croesus consulted the Delphic oracle as to his contemplated war against the Persians, he was told he would destroy a great empire. That was a safe prediction; for whether Croesus or the Persians were victorious in the war, a great empire would be destroyed.

Seneca predicted that one day the Shetland Islands would no longer mark the limits of the inhabited world. That, also, was a sensible conclusion, but not prophecy. A trained scientist can predict heavenly movements a long time in advance. The astronomers who observed the transit of Venus in South Carolina left the stone on which their meridian circle rested for the use of those who in June, 2004, will have need of it to watch another transit. These astronomers knew to a certainty that at that period far in the future Venus would cross the disc of the sun. That is calculation, not prophecy.

Neither is it prophecy to venture generalities about the future. In that famous passage in his "Review of Ranke's *History of the Popes*," Macaulay predicted the lasting prosperity of the Catholic Church, even when a traveler from New Zealand, in the midst of a vast solitude, should stand on a broken arch of London Bridge and sketch the ruins of St. Paul's.

In view of what has happened to great cities and kingdoms in the past, anyone could have made a similar prediction. But that is not prophecy. If Macaulay had named the century when London would be destroyed, and the kingdom or conqueror who would destroy it, that would have been prophecy, the sort of thing we meet with in the Old Testament. But Macaulay was wise enough not to attempt a prediction of that nature. As Justin Martyr, who was converted from paganism by the evidence of prophecy, has well put it: "To declare a thing should come to pass long before it is in being, and to bring it to pass, this or nothing is the work of God."

—**Purpose of the**—As the Stagirite philosopher, Aristotle, said of his work, "This book is given for action and not for discussion," so the Scriptures of the New Testament are given to us for action and not for discussion. Arguments about the Bible reverberate through the centuries; vast libraries house the literature on the study of the sacred writings. But it was not for this purpose that God gave the Scriptures and that holy men of old spake through the Holy Ghost. The Bible was given to man in order that he might have eternal life through Jesus Christ. What John said at the close of his Gospel is true of every book in the Bible: "But these are written, that ye might believe that Jesus is the Christ, the Son of God; and that believing ye might have life through his name" (John 20:31).

—**A refuge**—Her world was the upstairs room, and her journeys were from the bed to the chair and from the chair back to the bed. How will it fare with you and me when our goings out and comings in are thus circumscribed, when the only world in which we live and move is that upstairs world on the second story?

When I went in to greet her, I saw the Bible lying near her chair and said something about how I saw she had the best literature near at hand. "Yes," she answered, "that is my best friend."

The gifted Oscar Wilde fell into deep and shameful sin. He was sentenced to gloomy Reading Gaol, where, as he says in his powerful *Ballad of Reading Gaol,* the inmates could rarely look

Upon that little tent of blue
Which prisoners call the sky.[1]

In writing of his experiences in the jail, he tells us how in his deep distress and woe the only literature which meant anything to him was the New Testament.

The real values of life come out in the days of loneliness and deprivation. Souls taken captive have found that God's Word is the only pillar upon which they can lean. In the African wilds Stanley had the Bible and old newspapers. He whiled away the feverish hours in bed by reading, and he recorded his impression of the Bible and the press: "The one reminded me that apart from God my life was but a bubble of air, and it bade me remember my creator; the other fostered arrogance and worldliness. The Bible, however, with its noble and simple language, I continued to read with a higher and truer understanding than I had ever before conceived. Its powerful verses had a different meaning, a more penetrative influence, in the silence of the wilds. I came to feel a stronger glow while absorbed in its pages, and a charm peculiarly appropriate to the deep melancholy of African scenery."

—Treasures of the—In Derbyshire, England, there is a rock which on the out-

side looks just like a dull lump of clay, a clod. But when it is broken with a hammer it is found to have within a hollow space which is lined with beautiful crystalline spar. So is it with some of the most unpromising passages of the Bible, such as genealogical tables. It always pays to read them, for in the midst of them you may come upon some beautiful treasure of the Scriptures—for example, in the First Book of the Chronicles, the prayer of Jabez in the monotonous list of those who were begotten and died.

—Truth of the—A zealous believer in the Bible once asked a rich relative to contribute toward a fund for an archaeological exploration in Palestine. His cautious uncle wanted to know the real purpose of the expedition. "To prove that the Bible is true," was the answer.

"But," said his uncle, "suppose you prove the Bible is *not* true?"

The reply of the man is not given. But if the interview had taken place within the last few years the man might have answered that in view of the vast and ever-increasing evidence from the remains of ancient cities, kingdoms, and civilizations, there is no cause to fear that the spade of the archaeologist will prove the Bible to be false.

Alexander of Macedon was painted with his hand resting on his face, as if in reverie. But the real purpose was to hide an ugly scar on his cheek. The German emperor was photographed and painted standing in such a position that his withered arm would not appear. But in the Bible, men are painted just as they are. No scar, however hideous, no ugly deformity, is omitted.

—Understanding the—In the second part of *Pilgrim's Progress* Prudence questions Matthew about the Bible:

[1] From *The Poems of Oscar Wilde,* John W. Luce & Company, publishers.

PRUD. What do you think of the Bible?

MATT. It is the holy word of God.

PRUD. Is there nothing written therein but what you understand?

MATT. Yes, a great deal.

PRUD. What do you do when you meet with places therein that you do not understand?

MATT. I think God is wiser than I. I pray also that he will please to let me know all therein that he knows will be for my good.

The above dialogue is to be read on a tablet on the walls of Canterbury Cathedral. It contains a world of sense, and Bunyan was not unmindful in his own preaching of the principles expressed therein.

BLINDNESS AND DEAFNESS

Would you rather be blind or deaf? One might say, "I would rather be deaf than blind, for if I were deaf I could still see." But if you were deaf you would never hear the sigh of the wind in the treetops on a summer evening, like the sigh of infinite pity and sadness. You would never hear the breaking of the waves on the seashore, like the voice of eternity. You would never hear the matins of the birds, or the voice of the orator, or the voice of the mother, or the cry of a little child, or the whisper of love, or the voice of a great congregation uplifted in praise of the triune God. Another might say, "I would rather be blind than deaf, for if I were blind I could still hear the human voice and communicate with my fellow man." But think of what you would never see—the waving blossoms on the trees in the springtime, the blue sky, the sun rejoicing as a strong man to run a race, the stars and the moon at night. You would never see the light in a woman's eyes, you would never look on the ocean as it rolls in splendor such as creation's dawn beheld.

BLOOD—*see also* ATONEMENT, FORGIVENESS OF SIN, RECONCILIATION BY THE BLOOD

In the moment of great victory in the Battle of Chancellorsville, Stonewall Jackson was wounded. As he was being taken to a field hospital in an ambulance, Dr. Hunter McGuire held the artery in the shoulder with his finger so that if the tourniquet should slip there would be no fatal bleeding. Life is in the blood.

———•———

—Of Christ—The blood of Christ delivers us from the stain of sin because it assures us of the love of God. Somewhere in England there is a cathedral with two graves, and over them are the effigies of a crusader knight and his lady. The exquisite effigy of the lady, however, is without a right hand. The tradition is that in the wars of the crusades this knight was captured by the Moslem conqueror, Saladin. When the knight besought Saladin to spare his life for the sake of the love which his lady in England bore him, Saladin scoffed at him and said that she would soon forget him and marry another. Assured that she would never do that, Saladin asked for a proof. He said that if the lady sent him her right hand he would release the knight from the sentence of death. A letter to this effect reached the lady in England, who promptly had her right hand cut off and sent to the Moslem conqueror. When Saladin saw it, he set the knight free and sent him back to England. The severed hand was the proof of great love. So the blood of Christ, which was shed for our redemption, is the proof that God loves us; and that knowledge gives us hope.

———•———

34

A Presbyterian minister in Ireland told of an incident which took place at an after meeting in his church at Belfast. It was during the days of the strife between Catholics and Protestants, when murder and outrage were everyday and commonplace facts. A young man came into the inquiry room, where faithful Christians talked with him and prayed with him. But no one was able to do anything or say anything which helped him or relieved him of the distress under which he was laboring.

Then this minister was called in to see him. He told him to put his trust in Christ for forgiveness. "But how can I," he said—"one who has shot down nine persons in cold blood?" Then there came to the mind of the minister that great verse of John's: "The blood of Jesus Christ his Son cleanseth us from all sin" (I John 1:7). This was the word that the young man's troubled soul was waiting to hear, and, casting himself on the mercy of Christ, he found peace.

Martin Luther once had a dream in which he stood, in the Day of Judgment, before God. Satan was there to accuse him; and when the books were opened, he pointed to transgression after transgression of which Luther was guilty. Luther's heart sank in despair.

Then he remembered the Cross and, turning upon the devil, he said, "There is one entry which thou hast not made, Satan."

"What is that?" asked the devil.

"It is this," answered Luther: "The blood of Jesus Christ his Son cleanseth us from all sin" (I John 1:7).

Hedley Vicars, a well-known officer of the British army, was sitting one day at his quarters waiting for another officer to come to see him. While he was waiting, he began to turn over the leaves of a Bible which was lying on the table. The words that caught his eye were these: "The blood of Jesus Christ his Son cleanseth us from all sin" (I John 1:7). He closed the Bible and said, "If this be true for me, henceforth I will live by the grace of God as a man should live who has been washed in the blood of Christ."

In Lee's official report of the Battle of Fredericksburg only one person below the rank of major general is mentioned— a young officer of the artillery whom Lee speaks of as the "gallant Pelham." He fell in the Battle of Brandy Station, March 17, 1863. His West Point and army comrades always remembered his fine figure, his bright face, and his beautiful spirit. After the battle his body was taken home to his widowed mother in Alabama. As they bore him up the lane to his mother's home, the moon was full: "Her still light lay white upon the way by the cotton fields he knew so well, and white on the roof, and in the dooryard of his home. His mother stood waiting for him on the doorstep; and as they bore him up to her, she whispered through falling tears, 'Washed in the blood of the Lamb that was slain.'"

In our home we sang only the Psalms. But whenever my father was in a particularly good humor—when his work in the study was over or things had gone well at the college—he used to whistle the tune of a hymn. It was always the same tune, "There Is a Fountain Filled with Blood." Yes, the Cross alone can make a man truly happy. It is the sense of sin forgiven that tunes our hearts to sing His praise.

I have heard it intimated here and there that this is one of the hymns which must be omitted from the books, that its metaphors offend sensitive souls. So far as the matter of good literary taste is concerned, it will do for me to remember that the hymn was written by him who wrote the exquisite sonnet commencing, "Mary! I want a lyre with other strings"; and for the religious propriety of the hymn it is sufficient to recall that it was written by one who had knelt as a penitent sinner at the foot of the Cross. No one who has done that will find anything in the hymn to offend him—but much to thrill him.

The ancient legend of the Holy Grail tells how Joseph of Arimathea, who got permission from Pilate to take the body of Jesus down from the cross and bury it, caught in a golden cup which Christ had held at the Last Supper the blood which flowed from a wound in his side. This cup he carried to Glastonbury, on an island in Somerset in England. There he formed an order of knights whose work it was to protect the precious blood. The chief of these knights was made their king. At certain times the king unveiled the golden cup that held the precious blood, at which times a glorious and radiant light fell on the faces of all who stood about, filling them with rapture and enduing them with strength from on high. Only the pure in heart could look upon the cup and behold the wondrous light which streamed from the precious blood.

This is a beautiful story, which has played a great part in the history of our race. But there is one respect in which it is in sharp contrast with the conception of the blood of Christ presented to us in the Gospels. Only the pure in heart, according to the legend of the Holy Grail, could look upon the precious blood. But in the New Testament the thing which is emphasized is that the blood of Christ—and only the blood of Christ—cleanses the stained and sinful heart.

Pursued once by the English with bloodhounds, Bruce and his followers were in desperate straits. His companions had given up all hope of escape. But the courageous Bruce took them down into a small stream and, walking with them for some distance in the waters up the bed of the river, threw the dogs off their scent, and so escaped. Even so, that retribution, penalty, and punishment which is man's due is turned back in the crimson tide that flowed from Calvary's tree.

On the night of Daniel Webster's death at Marshfield, October 24, 1852, his physician, Dr. Jeffries, knowing Mr. Webster's religious faith, suggested that he should read to him one of his favorite hymns. Mr. Webster having intimated his consent, Dr. Jeffries read Cowper's hymn, beginning

There is a fountain filled with blood
Drawn from Immanuel's veins.

He read on till he had finished the last stanza:

Then in a nobler, sweeter song,
I'll sing thy power to save,
When this poor lisping, stammering
*   tongue*
Lies silent in the grave.

Then, although his tongue was one of the least feeble and stammering of human tongues, Webster in a clear, strong voice replied, "Amen! Amen! Amen!"

BODY

That master soul, the Apostle Paul, was in Ephesus when he wrote to the Christians in distant Corinth, "Know ye not that ye are the temple of God?" (I Cor. 3:16). Ephesus was a city famed throughout the world for its temple to

Diana. As he wrote, Paul may have been looking out upon that most glorious temple, with its 120 pillars of Parian marble, its doors of carved cypress wood, its cedar roof, supported by columns of jasper, its masterpieces of Praxiteles and Phidias, its great altar, and the monstrous image of Diana, ever shrouded in thick darkness. That was the pagan world's idea of a temple. Of its kind, it has never been surpassed.

But the apostle of Jesus Christ had another idea of a temple. As he looked out from the school of Tyrannus, where he wrote and taught, and saw the flashing splendors of the marvelous shrine to Diana, he thought of another and a more glorious temple; and to the believers at Corinth he wrote of the temple of the body, God's incomparable temple, compared with which the Fourth Wonder of the World was but a poor and mean thing. Man could make the temple of Diana, but only God could make the temple of man.

Belshazzar perished just at the time he was desecrating and profaning the sacred vessels taken from the temple at Jerusalem. In a figurative sense, all of us possess sacred vessels. Every person is in a certain sense a king, and has within him that which is holy—which ought not to be desecrated, profaned, or given to the dogs. That is the sad thing about every form of desecration: it profanes a sacred vessel. The body, Paul said, is the temple of the Holy Ghost, and whoever defiles that temple God will destroy, just as he destroyed Belshazzar when he defiled the vessels of Jehovah's temple.

Esau is termed a "profane person" who sold his birthright. The root meaning of the word used and translated "profane" is "unfenced," "common." There was no temple area in Esau's life, no sacred enclosure. You have a heavenly birthright; when you are tempted to sell it for the savory morsel of passing appetite, remember Esau the profane. His body was just a sty where a beast was fed, not a temple in which a god was worshiped.

A student in a medical college allowed the fence of awe and reverence about his life to be broken down. "For Sale" was written over the temple where his birthright was stored. Bidders and buyers were not wanting. The markets of the world may be ever so dull, but the business of buying and exchanging birthrights is always brisk. Things went from bad to worse, from one disillusionment to another, till the wretched student ended his scholastic career in the police station. Then his father, an honored physician in a Western State, came and took that wreck, that ruined temple, home with him. Perhaps now the son looks after his father's garage or runs his car for him, a grief to his father, a heaviness to his mother, ashamed to lift his head in the village—if indeed, he has not by this time been submerged in the stream of crime. Complete shipwreck! The temple defiled, and the man who defiled it destroyed!

BOOK OF LIFE

Under the trees of life in a corner of the Protestant cemetery in Rome is the grave of the English poet John Keats, with the inscription, "Here lies one whose name was writ in water." That is not true, for Keats's name will live as long as that of most poets. Nevertheless, it is a true description of all earthly things, efforts, honors, renown, achievements. Your name is writ in water. The wind blows, the ripples flow—and your name is gone. All efforts at length come to nothing. Seek first, therefore, the Kingdom of God. Seek to have your name written in the Lamb's book of life.

BOOKS

Take the advice which Saint-Pierre makes the old man utter in the story that has touched so many thousands of hearts —*Paul and Virginia,* a great book and a good book: "Literature, my son, is the gift of heaven. Like the rays of the sun, it enlightens, it rejoices, it warms, it is a divine fire. It is this that reminds us of the rules of human life. It calms the passions, it represses the vices, it excites to virtue by the august examples of the good and great men which it records, and of whom it presents to us the ever-honored images. It is a daughter of heaven which has descended to earth to charm away the evils of the human race. Read, then, my son. The wise men who have written before our time are travelers who have preceded us in the paths of misfortune, and who reach out to us their hands to invite us to join their society when all else have abandoned us. A good book is a good friend."

BOYS—*see also* SOUL WINNING

In England a returned missionary to Russia was a guest in the Congregational minister's home. Visiting there at the time was the minister's grandson. One night after evening worship the missionary, who had been "taken" with the lad, asked him to point out the chamber where he slept. Early in the morning he called him, and as they sat together in the garden he told him of the love of Christ. A few days later, as they were concluding family worship, the missionary took the boy on his knee and said to those assembled, "I am convinced that this boy will preach the gospel. I am convinced that he will be a great preacher of the gospel, and that he will stand one day in the pulpit of Rowland Hill." Then he said to the boy, as he gave him a shilling, "I want you to promise that when that day comes and you stand in Rowland Hill's pulpit, you will give out the hymn, 'God Works in a Mysterious Way His Wonders to Perform.'"

Several years passed by; and the minister's grandson, now a lad of fifteen, was on his way to church in Colchester. A storm came up, and he turned into the first church he came to—the Primitive Methodist Chapel in Artillery Street. The regular minister did not appear, and a layman arose in the pulpit and gave out the text, Isaiah 45:22: "Look unto me, and be ye saved, all the ends of the earth: for I am God, and there is none else." The boy sitting in the rear of the dark and almost empty church answered the text and was saved.

That boy was Charles H. Spurgeon, who preached in the great Metropolitan Tabernacle for thirty years!

———

One day an old minister in England walked into his churchyard and, sitting down on a tombstone, began to weep. He wept because his church officers had just notified him that he was getting old and that he ought to resign and let a younger man take his place. As he sat there disconsolate, he saw a boy, with sunshine in his face and joy in his heart, coming down the street beyond the cemetery fence. The old preacher was fond of boys, and he called this boy to him and had him sit down beside him on the tombstone. There he forgot his sorrow as he talked with the boy about the meaning of life and told him about Christ and his salvation. Presently the boy left him and went on his happy way down the street. The old preacher went back to his manse and to his sorrow. Not long afterward he was called to his eternal home.

If it is permitted the redeemed in the life to come to behold what transpires on earth, then this is what that old preacher has seen: He has seen that boy with whom he talked become a lay preacher, a teacher, and a cobbler. In his schoolroom and cobbler shop he has fashioned a large leather globe; and scholars in his class and customers who come in for their shoes have seen the face of the teacher-cobbler suffused with emotion as he pointed to land after land on that globe and said, "And these are pagans!" After a few years he saw that boy to whom he had talked in the cemetery become the pioneer missionary to India, who translated the Scriptures into the dialects of the East.

That boy was William G. Carey!

Early in the last century the Presbyterian minister at Darlington, Pennsylvania, out on his pastoral round, was riding his horse down a country lane. As he drew up before a humble cottage he heard the sound of a woman's voice lifted in earnest prayer. As he listened he heard this widowed mother, with her boys kneeling at her side, earnestly entreating God that he would open a door for the education of these boys, so that they might become good and useful men. The pastor dismounted and went in to speak with the widow who had prayed so earnestly, and yet with a note of sorrow in her voice. Struck with the alertness of one of these boys and touched by the woman's petitions, he took the boy with him to the old Stone Academy at Darlington, and there gave him the instruction for which his mother had prayed.

That boy, so handicapped in his birth, and for whom there seemed to be no opportunity, influenced more young minds in America in the last century than any other man; for he was William McGuffey, the author of the famous Eclectic Readers, which reached the extraordinary circulation of a hundred million copies.

BRAVERY—*see* COURAGE

BUNYAN

Leaving the noisy and ill-smelling street in a now rather shabby part of the city, one enters by an ancient iron gateway into Bunhill Fields, one of London's most famous burial grounds. Venerable trees with outstretched arms cast shadows across the closely crowded tombs of the dead. On the benches along the paths poor and decayed old men, more welcome among the dead than the living, sit and chat amiably together, undisturbed by their gloomy surroundings. Passing down the narrow lanes between the graves, the visitor surveys a dismal harvest of the trophies and tokens of mortality. But here and there the eye lights upon a name which can never die.

Here on this stone he reads the name "Susanna Wesley"—the great mother of the Wesleys. Here on another tomb the name "Isaac Watts"—and as he looks he seems to hear the melody of Watts's grand hymn, "When I Survey the Wondrous Cross." Over here is the grave of Daniel Defoe, author of *Robinson Crusoe,* one of the two most popular books in the English tongue.

Not far off is another famous grave. Before the visitor can make out the name carved upon it, the sculptured relief of a pilgrim kneeling at the foot of the cross, while his bundle rolls from his back, tells him that he is standing by the grave of the author of the other best-known English book, *Pilgrim's Progress.*

BURDENS

Writing on a saying of Socrates—that if all the misfortunes of mankind were cast into a public stock and equally distributed among the whole species, those who now think themselves the most unhappy would prefer the share they already possess before that which would fall to them by such a division—Addison relates a dream he once had.

In his dream he heard a proclamation by Jupiter that every mortal should bring his griefs and calamities and throw them together in a heap. Into the central plain marched the whole army of mankind, led by an airy figure named Fancy. Each one laid down his burden of real or imagined woe. Slowly the heap of discarded burdens grew until it reached the heavens.

Then Jove issued a second proclamation, to the effect that each was now at liberty to exchange his affliction and return to his habitat with any other burden he might choose. Fancy stood about and recommended to each one his particular packet. Eagerly the deluded mortals rushed into the most foolish and absurd bargains. But when all had selected their new burdens the whole plain was filled with lamentation and murmuring, for their last state was worse than their first.

Taking pity on them, Jove ordered them to lay down their burdens a second time so that each might resume his own. With that, the phantom Fancy was commanded to disappear; and a new figure, the goddess Patience, stood by the mountain of misery, which straightway sank to such a degree that it did not seem a third the size it was before. Each man then resumed his old burden, well pleased that the burden to fall to his lot had not been left to his own choice. Men have their own burdens, and their own burdens are the ones best suited to them.

What a procession it is, if we could only have eyes to see it, this long parade of those who bear burdens! There are burdens visible, and some—ofttimes the heavier—invisible. There are burdens physical—the burden of failing strength, or chronic illness, or other "thorns in the flesh." There are burdens, too, of lost happiness, of baffled ambition, of disappointment; burdens of anxiety and care;

burdens of temptation; and the heavy burden of sin. Tramp! Tramp! Tramp! The army of the burden bearers marches by! During the day the streets of our city are thronged with people, but late at night the crowds have departed. The army of the marchers has passed by, and the sound of their feet is no longer heard. The streets of the city are left to the policemen and the watchmen, the night reveler and the homeless. But on the highway of life the night is no different from the day; and at midnight, as well as at noon, we can hear the tramp, tramp, tramp of the army of the burden bearers.

When Lincoln was talking with a friend during the Civil War, he told him how often he was driven to his knees—because there was nowhere else to go. The time comes when we have none but God to whom we can go. We are driven to our knees because we have nowhere else to go. But always he is there, inviting us to cast our burden upon him.

BURNING BUSH

The burning bush was a striking, unforgettable sign and experience. To a certain extent, there is a bush that burns for each of us; some little radiance, at least, each of us has caught from that bush, and life's most sacred memories gather about that flame. You know best when it was and what it was in your life. Perhaps it was a deep conviction, a strong urge to do good, to serve God in your generation. Perhaps it was a light that kindled in the still countenance of a loved one who had passed through the gates of death. Perhaps it was a light and a voice that came to you in the midst of some great trial or sorrow. But whatever and wherever it was, you recognize it now as something different and apart from the common territory of life, the ordinary experiences of life. Moses was faithful to that desert experience. Even at the very end, in his farewell to the people of Israel, he spoke of "the good will of him that dwelt in the bush."

Have you been faithful to your voice, to your experience? If you have not, then now is the time to find your way back to the burning bush and renew your vows, ere the holy light goes out.

C

CALVIN

"To the man not utterly corrupt," one has written, "the thoughts which come by the grave of the dead fall like dew from heaven." This is true not only of the thoughts which come by the grave of one whom we have loved and lost awhile but also of those by the graves of the mighty men of God.

After much searching in the old cemetery of Plain Palais, at Geneva, I found the grave of John Calvin. Not far from the wall, it was covered with grass, and the shadows of the cypress tree above it were playing to and fro over the grave as if to remind one of the shadow brevity of human life. On the stone, hardly a foot high, are the letters "J. C."

Across the lake rises the costly and magnificent cenotaph of one of the dukes of Brunswick. But who today is the Duke of Brunswick? Who was he then? But the man whose initials are graven on that humble grave, in keeping with his theology which exalted God and humbled man, lives forever.

CARE—*see also* BURDENS, TRUST, WORRY

The burden of care is not to be dismissed or dealt with lightly. There is no abiding satisfaction in the reflection that the thing that is a burden of care will one day pass away. An Eastern king who was tormented with indecision and vacillation once called upon the wise men of his court to give him some word that would steady him. They tried, but in vain. But where the wise men failed the king's daughter succeeded. She gave him on his birthday a ring inscribed with two Arabic words meaning, "This, too, shall pass away." But the Christian remedy for care is not that. It is to cast our care upon God. Do not try to support the load of your care all by yourself.

———————

In that great tale we liked to read as children, and which we can read again as men with great profit, *Gulliver's Travels,* the shipwrecked Gulliver was set upon in his slumber by the tiny Lilliputians, who bound him with hundreds of ropes. These ropes were only the smallest threads, and yet by the very multitude of them he was bound. He could have broken each of them or several of them in his hand, but not the hundreds with which they bound him.

Sometimes man in our complex society of today seems bound as Gulliver was— bound by a multiplicity of things which are regarded as essential to existence, but which in reality are not.

CEDARS OF LEBANON

Far beyond the highest villages—at an altitude of nine thousand feet, where all other vegetation had ceased—nestling in a crevice of the highest ridge of Lebanon, I came upon a sacred grove of four hundred of the cedars of Lebanon. I went often to visit them and to worship in this forest shrine—at twilight, when the great shadows were falling over the face of the yellow mountains; at night, when the stars were looking down upon the trees; and at sunrise, when bars of golden light lay across the evergreen branches of the trees. Our ancestors are said to have worshiped in the forests of England and Europe. After visiting the cedars of Lebanon one will not think it strange that such a mode of worship arose.

Sometimes the cedars, moving in the evening wind like colossal harps touched by the fingers of the wind, give forth a sad, but beautiful, music. But most impressive are the cedars when not a breath of air is stirring. In that awesome and overwhelming silence those great trees reign like monarchs of another world. The silence is vocal with the history of the kingdoms and empires which have waxed and waned during the life of a single one of those trees. At night when the stars come out and pitch their shining tents in the canopy of heaven, looking down upon the mighty mass of the mountains and the cedars of Lebanon, all silent, sad, and majestic, it seems as if the world has come to worship at this throne and altar of nature's trinity of grandeur, silence, and peace—the stars, the mountains, and the cedars of Lebanon.

CEMETERIES—*see also* SOULS (CEMETERY OF)

I have no dread of a cemetery. Sometimes it is better to be there and have fellowship with the dead who are buried than to walk down the streets of our cities and meet the unburied dead, that is, those in whom faith and hope and love and purity have long been dead, leaving only the animal alive.

In the cemetery the bible of life is open and a passionless voice reads to us its great lessons and tells us to apply our hearts unto wisdom. Sometimes we can learn more from the silence of the dead than from the speech of the living. Whether it be a little churchyard, where under ancient elms the dead lie close to holy walls, or the dark spaces of some hoary cathedral, where the dead sleep under sculptured sarcophagus and lettered marble, or some wilderness battlefield where the nation has gathered the bodies of the soldiers who there gave their last full measure of devotion, or some rural hillside where the wind blows free like the viewless and intangible spirit which has returned to God who gave it, or some quiet acre by the banks of a river that flows silently and swiftly away like man's life—wherever it may be, the resting place of the dead has always something worth while to say to the living.

CHANCE—*see also* THE PAST (CONQUERING), PROVIDENCE

Speaking of the part played by chance, Oliver Goldsmith writes, in *The Vicar of Wakefield*: "Nor can I go on without a reflection on those accidental meetings, which though they happen every day, seldom excite our surprise but upon some extraordinary occasion. To what a fortuitous concurrence do we owe every pleasure and convenience of our lives!"

Upon reflection you see the truth of that. Look back! One day it was your hap to go into the field of Boaz, and your life since then has been a series of events growing out of that chance incident. You happened to visit a friend in a certain city, and there you have been ever since. One day you happened to open a book, and that book opened the world for you

—spread before you the great page of life and its pulsing opportunities. You took a temporary position, and that has been your lifework.

You went one day into a church and heard a sermon, a prayer, a hymn, which altered the course of your life just as clearly as stones divide the waters and alter the course of a river. You happened one day to go into a drawing room or a public assembly, and you saw there a face. That moment, consciously or unconsciously, life was changed for you, enriched or impoverished, expanded or contracted; from that moment life was never the same, for it was the face of your wife, the face of your husband, the face of posterity, the face of your friend, the face of one who was to bring joy and peace or woe and shame into your life.

Oh, these chances! How they spin out the garment of our destiny, and we never know it! How these chance happenings have worked out our careers in life! Compared with them, how insignificant appear all our night dreaming and planning and all our day toiling. The best verdict on the past would seem to be this: "It was my hap!"

—**And determination**—The lots were cast in the lap, and the seamen gathered round for the drawing of the lot. The dim light of the swinging ship's lantern revealed the anxiety stamped on every face. Each man's past, each man's sin, was making him say, "Lord, is it I?" Each searched his past. One thought of the merchant he had drowned in the harbor at Sidon. Another said, "That woman I robbed at the Piraeus." Another, "That girl I seduced in Egypt." Each one said to himself, "Is it I?" But when the lot came out, it had Jonah's number on it. The lot fell on Jonah. This was just chance, you say. Yes, it was chance; but chance overruled by the de-

termination of God. "The lot is cast into the lap; but the whole disposing thereof is of the Lord." (Prov. 16:33.)

—**Second**—I have preached a good many sermons on a good many texts, but I can still feel the thrill of a text like this: "The word of the Lord came unto Jonah the second time" (Jonah 3:1). The first time it came there was failure, disobedience, flight, disgrace, judgment, and disaster. But when he had been delivered out of the peril of the sea, "the word of the Lord came unto Jonah the second time." God, who spake once, spake to him again.

In his account of the Battle of Shiloh, General Grant tells of seeing hundreds of Union soldiers cowering under the banks of the river during the critical first days' fighting. Their regiments had been driven from the field, and these men were panic-stricken refugees. Grant tells how General Buell berated them and cursed them and vainly tried to get them back to join their commands on the firing line. Then he goes on to say, "Most of these men afterward proved themselves as gallant as any of those who saved the battle from which they had deserted." It takes more than one battle to make a campaign. Because a man has failed in one engagement does not mean that he will not be a hero in the next.

CHANGES IN THE SOUL

Now and then we see strange changes come over the once godly man—sometimes slowly, hardly to be discerned at the time, and sometimes with a strange rapidity. The man's character has changed, his personality has deteriorated. This may not be noted in any one particular thing, but the tone and atmosphere of his life is different. Speaking of an old student of his, occupying a position of importance in a distant city, a venerable college president once said to me after his last visit to this man, "There's something wrong." He could not *see* anything wrong. Just what it was he could not state; yet he was sure that there was something different, something wrong. Such a difference can be accounted for only by an internal change.

CHARACTER—*see also* YOUTH AND CHARACTER MAKING

In the old cemetery at Princeton there is a row of graves called the "Presidents' Row." The long line of flat stones marks the resting places of the presidents of Princeton College and University. A little to one side is a small, upright stone which bears the inscription, "Aaron Burr, A Colonel in the Continental Army, Vice President of the United States."

The man whose dust lies there had all that heredity and training could bestow. Just at hand is the grave of his pious father, Aaron Burr, the second president of Princeton, and the grave of his renowned grandfather, Jonathan Edwards. Burr's career in the college was one of attainment and brilliancy such as perhaps has never been equaled. Ability of mind and fascination of manner were his, but one thing was lacking.

After the duel with Hamilton, finding that men mistrusted him and would not give him their votes or their confidence, he turned his face toward the Western frontiers. He crossed the mountains to Pittsburgh and floated down the Ohio. Everything that he touched withered. He went into the home on Blennerhasset Island as the serpent into Eden, and that island home became a desolation. After the trial in Richmond he wandered abroad. Ordered out of England, he went to France and was scorned by Napoleon. At length he came back to New York in disguise, landing in the night so that his old friends might not see him, and resumed the practice of law. Had we been alive then, we might have seen the brown-faced little old man sitting by his green desk in his office on Nassau Street, his head resting on his hand, thinking of the days that had been, of what might have been—with no clients coming to disturb his reverie.

After his last wife left him, he took rooms in the basement of a boarding house. While he was still able to walk, he would every day go down toward the Narrows—watching for the return of the *Patriot,* the ship on which his daughter Theodosia had sailed from Georgia, the ship that never came to port. When no longer able to walk, he hung her portrait where he might gaze upon it, sitting or reclining, the first thing in the morning and the last thing at night. Thus he lived, "severed from humanity," until death relieved his loneliness. He was carried to Princeton and buried near the feet of his father and grandfather. The spot was unmarked; and no man to this day would know his sepulcher were it not that some nameless woman came in the night, put the stone over his grave, and departed.

That is the story of the brightest man who ever took a degree at Princeton. His life was long, but neither happy nor useful. It was a life which learned much and acquired much, but which ignored the common and familiar laws of manhood and character, without which there can be no true happiness—and with which there can be no failure.

———•◆•———

The enemies of Daniel were determined to bring him down. But how to do it, that was the question. Daniel administered the exchequer of the great empire. Possibly they might find some irregularity or peculation in the discharge of his stewardship. But when they looked into the matter they were unable to discover anything which even malice or hate could distort into dishonesty. "He was," it is written, "faithful; neither was there any error or fault found in him." That is the way a man ought to live, so that when his enemies would bring him down they can find no occasion against him. Spurgeon, threatened with blackmail by evil men who said that if he did not meet their demands they would publish things which would ruin his reputation, answered, saying, "Write all you know about me across the heavens."

CHILD—*see also* LOVE (REVIVING POWER OF), SOUL OF A CHILD

When you stand on the brink of a volcano's crater, you tremble to think of the dreadful and explosive powers which are hidden there, sleeping now, but one day to burst forth with devastating terror and spread ruin and death o'er the smiling land. But what are the explosive forces lodged in that volcano compared with the explosive forces for evil that are lodged in an infant's heart? Hitler was once an infant!

On the top of some high mountain you pause to rest by a spring, whence flows forth with musical voice a little stream of water. In your imagination you can follow it as it goes down the mountainside, gaining new volume and breadth and depth with every mile, until it has become a mighty river which carries on its bosom the commerce of a nation, or, suddenly swollen by the rains, overflows its banks and smites the earth with a curse. But what is the power lodged in that mountain spring which becomes a great river compared with the power to bless or to hurt, to add to the sum and total of human happiness or human woe, which is lodged in the soul of a single child?

A number of years ago a young man was coming from California to visit the East. In the Pullman car with him were three or four race-track gamblers. They were rough, hardened, godless, but somewhat interesting men, and this young man, who himself had been wandering from the training of his youth, became familiar with them. At a town on the way east a little boy was put on the car and given into the custody of the Pullman conductor. When night came the porter made up the berth for the boy. The gamblers and the young man were sitting across the aisle from the boy's berth. Presently the boy came out in his nightdress and, first looking timidly up and down the aisle, knelt to say his prayers. At once the gamblers ceased from their loud conversation and removed their hats in reverential pose. The young man felt a lump in his throat as he looked at the praying child. What had happened? The prayer of a child had carried them all back to their Bethel. The young man afterward entered the ministry and became a well-known preacher of the gospel. Thus was fulfilled the saying of the Bible, "And a little child shall lead them" (Isa. 11:6).

CHILDHOOD—*see also* MEMORY (CHILDHOOD)

The deepest loss of youth is the loss of the innocency and trust which belong to childhood. In his glorious and yet terrible *Confessions* Rousseau struck the note which vibrates with the sense of that loss. After the death of his mother at Geneva he was sent with a comrade to live with a Protestant minister, M. Lambercier, at Bossey. There he underwent the first budding of evil on the tree of his own nascent experience, and also his first encounter with injustice, and that from the hands of those whom he had loved and trusted.

45

Though he was only a boy, he later wrote, from that hour the gates of Eden were closed against him: "Here was the term of the serenity of my childish days. From this moment I ceased to enjoy a pure happiness and I feel even this day that the reminiscence of the delights of my infancy came to an end. Even the country lost in my eyes that charm of sweetness and simplicity which goes to the heart; it seemed somber and deserted, and was as if covered by a veil, hiding its beauties from our sight. We no longer tended our little gardens, our plants, our flowers; we went no more lightly to scratch the earth, shouting for joy as we discovered the germ of the seed we had sown."

If you ever visit the Episcopal hospital in Philadelphia, you will see on the wall of the main hall the inscription, or dedication, which tells of the donors and how they came to give that property. It was the home where sisters had lived, and the dedication makes touching reference to the memories of their childhood, telling how in that home and in those grounds, before they knew pain and sickness and sorrow, they had spent the happiest days of their life.

I wonder if that is not always so. I wonder if even men who have had what seems to us cheerless and dismal surroundings in their youth do not from the heights of success and renown in life look back to childhood as the happiest and most blessed time. I believe it is usually true.

Henry M. Stanley is the only man I know of who speaks of his childhood as a lonely and starless night, without love and without hope. Hearing the chaplain in the almshouse read the words of the divine John (15:12), "Love one another," he wondered in his boyish heart why it was that with a heart so ready for love,

so responsive to its tiniest ray, he never felt its sunshine in his life. But we must remember that it is the man who writes the autobiography, that it is the man with a sense of what life might have been, who takes pity on the boy who once was himself.

David was intensely human in his desire to turn back to the things of yesterday. Few who have traveled any distance on the path of life are strangers to this emotion, this longing of David's heart. There are those, indeed, who, like Charles Dickens or Henry M. Stanley, had a bleak, cheerless, and loveless youth —no love, no play, only want and fear. But most of us have happy recollections of our childhood days. When life hurts, when the way grows weary, when we are vexed and baffled by unattainable but deep desires, or saddened by losses, or burdened with a sense of our mistakes and blunders, our failures and our sins, then does not David's longing for the water out of the well of yesterday become our longing? How true this is, is demonstrated by the hold on the heart of such songs as "The Barefoot Boy," "My Old Kentucky Home," "The Old Oaken Bucket," "Carry Me Back to Ole Virginny," and "Backward, Turn Backward, O Time, in Your Flight." These songs appeal to all ages, all classes, all conditions of life, because their major note touches one of the deep and elemental things in human nature.

CHILDREN—*see also* HOME TRAINING, PARENTS SACRIFICING FOR CHILDREN

—Training of—Coleridge was once talking with a man who told him that he did not believe in giving little children any religious instruction whatsoever. His theory was that the child's mind should not be prejudiced in any direction, but when he came to years of discretion he should be permitted to choose his religious opinions for himself. Coleridge said nothing; but after a while he asked his visitor if he would like to see his garden. The man said he would, and Coleridge took him out into the garden, where only weeds were growing. The man looked at Coleridge in surprise, and said, "Why this is not a garden! There is nothing but weeds here!"

"Well, you see," answered Coleridge, "I did not wish to infringe upon the liberty of the garden in any way. I was just giving the garden a chance to express itself and to choose its own production."

A very timely parable! We go astray from the womb; if we are not trained to go in the right way, we go naturally in the wrong way.

CHOICE—*see also* PREDESTINATION

In the "Marble Faun" Hawthorne describes the beautiful statue in Sculpture Gallery on Capitoline Hill representing the soul and its choice between good and evil—a child clasping a dove to its breast and assailed by a serpent. The symbolism of this allegory fits everybody. A tale of human life which centers about the temptation of a human spirit is never out of date, whether it be the story of Joseph in Egypt or that of the last popular novel.

———————

One of the most distinguished and useful men in the religious world today has written that he regards a certain night in New York as a parting of the way, a turning point, in his life. With his college friends he had gone down from Princeton to New York. Some of these men asked him to accompany them to a place where soul and body would have been defiled. He had the courage and independence to say No, and that refusal he now looks back to as a turning point in his life.

One can almost hear the clock of his heart tick when he stops to remember that there are thousands of young men and women confronted by a similar choice tonight. If it were possible to do so, one would choose for them, so that their recollection of the parting of the way shall be as happy as that of the man to whom I have just referred. Alas, for those with whom it will be otherwise! Yet every man must choose for himself. The choice he makes now, tonight, may determine the future course of his life and the destiny of his soul.

———————

At Noyon there were born in a family two brothers, John and Charles. John from his earliest days was studious, thoughtful, and reverent. At the early age of twenty-seven he wrote one of the world's greatest books, *The Institutes of the Christian Religion.* When he died at Geneva in 1564 he bequeathed to the world the great principles of democracy and religious freedom. The other brother, Charles, pursued a course of profligacy and dissipation and lived a life as worthless and infamous as his brother's life was noble and glorious. How do you explain the difference between those two men? Not in heredity, not in environment, not in education, for they had the same heredity, the same environment, the same home, the same early influences. The difference is to be explained in choice.

———————

As a boy, hearing the story of the great and good Hezekiah and his wicked father and son, Ahaz and Manasseh, read at morning worship, I used to wonder just what it was that made one king do that which was evil in the sight of the Lord and another do that which was right. I cannot answer that question now;

and if I should live for a thousand years, I would not be able to answer it. Only God knows the secrets of the human heart. We cannot tell why one turns in the right direction and another in the wrong direction. But there is no doubt that they do, or that they are responsible for the direction they take. Strange mystery! From the same home, from the same mother's knee, from the same training, one goes out and does that which is right in the sight of the Lord, and another through a long life does that which is evil.

CHRIST—*see also* LOVE OF CHRIST, LOYALTY TO CHRIST, MARKS OF CHRIST, TRIUMPH OF CHRIST, WOMAN AND CHRIST

—Changing the world—It was a cruel world into which Christ was born. Grim Herod, waiting to destroy the newborn King, is a true picture of the attitude of the early world toward childhood. How different Christ has made the world by his coming could not be better expressed than in this fragment of a letter written June 17, 1 B.C., by Hilarion to his wife, Alis, concerning his own child, and concerning a babe about to be born to his daughter:

"Hilarion to Alis, his sister:

Many greetings. . . . Be not distressed if at the general coming in I remain at Alexandria. I pray thee and beseech thee take care of the little child, and as soon as we receive wages, I will send them to thee. If —— is delivered, if it be a male baby, let it live. If it be a female, expose it."

That awful Greek word *ekbale*—"cast out," "expose"—is sufficient to measure the difference between the world with and without Christ.

—Character of—There is one tiny book that, I believe, is the most famous book on religion ever written. *Pilgrim's Progress* is famous and beautiful, but it is read only by Protestants. The circulation of this other book, however, is not limited by creedal or ecclesiastical barriers: "It has diffused itself like incense through the aisles and alcoves of the universal church." It takes its title from these opening words, "He that followeth Me, walketh not in darkness, saith the Lord." These are the words of Christ by which we are admonished to imitate his life and manner. Only one person has appeared on this earth who was worthy of having a book written about him with such a title—*The Imitation of Christ.* The perfection and beauty in the character and person of Christ is at once the treasure and the proof of Christianity. Before Christ appeared men had never seen the perfect, nor could they altogether agree as to what it ought to be. But the character of Christ, which Thomas à Kempis urges men to imitate, is the final pattern of perfection.

—Deity of—The first church building dedicated to the worship of God in all of western Pennsylvania was the church the Moravians built in 1771 on the Beaver River for the Delaware Indians. The Moravians were founded by Count Zinzendorf, who was converted in an art gallery in Düsseldorf by contemplating a painting of Christ on the cross, which had the inscription, "I did this for thee. What hast thou done for me?"

This painting was done by an artist three hundred years before. When he had finished his first sketch of the face of the Redeemer, this artist called in his landlady's little daughter and asked her who she thought it was. The girl looked at it and said, "It is a good man." The painter knew that he had failed. He destroyed the first sketch, and after praying for greater skill he finished a second.

Again he called the little girl in and asked her to tell him whom she thought the face represented. This time the girl said she thought it looked like a great sufferer. Again the painter knew that he had failed, and again he destroyed the sketch he had made. After meditation and prayer, a third sketch was made. When it was finished, he called the girl in a third time and asked her who it was. Looking at the portrait, the girl knelt down and exclaimed, "It is the Lord!"

That alone makes the coming of Christ meaningful to the world—not that a good man came, not that a wise teacher came, not that a great sufferer came, but that *God* came—Immanuel, God with us.

One hears quoted very often, and very thoughtlessly, Richard Watson Gilder's lines:

If Jesus Christ is a man,—
    And only man,—I say
That of all mankind I cleave to him,
    And to him will I cleave alway.

If Jesus Christ is a god,—
    And the only God,—I swear
I will follow Him through heaven
    and hell
    The earth, the sea, and the air! [1]

The last part is sense and reason; the first part is nonsense. If Jesus Christ be man, and only a man, there is nothing in him worth following and worth cleaving to. The poet sings as if it made little difference which way the vote fell—man, or Son of God. But it *does* make a difference—an immeasurable difference.

In "Death in the Desert," where Browning imagines the death and the

[1] Used by permission of the publishers, Houghton Mifflin Company.

last words of John, he makes the evangelist speak thus:

I say, the acknowledgment of God
    in Christ
Accepted by thy reason, solves for
    thee
All questions in the earth and out
    of it.

Yes, if God was in Christ, and if he loved me and gave himself for me, then all problems are solved and all wants are satisfied.

Thou, O Christ, art all I want;
More than all in thee I find.

But if Christ was not the Son of God, who died for us, then chaos is come again. In the words of Milton in *Comus,*

The pillared firmament is rotten-
    ness,
And earth's base built on stubble.

—Denying—Father St. Philip used to make a protest to God with the Blessed Sacrament in his hand, saying, "Lord, beware of me today, lest I should betray thee, and do thee all the mischief in the world. . . . The wound in Christ's side is large, but if God did not guard me, I should make it larger."

—At the door—The conclusion to John's severe and condemnatory letter to the church at Laodicea is the most beautiful of all his conclusions and promises. Here we have love's beautiful climax, "Behold, I stand at the door, and knock" (Rev. 3:20). The mighty actor and conqueror of the Apocalypse, before whom all things in heaven and earth and under the earth bow down in worship and adoration, appears here as a suppliant at man's heart: "Behold, I stand at the door, and knock."

There he is, like a weary traveler, just as you have seen him in Holman Hunt's famous painting—the dews of night distilling upon his brow, a lantern in one hand, and knocking with the other, the head bent forward eagerly to hear if there is an answer to his knock.

This, I think, is the most moving thing in the Apocalypse—not the great white throne, not the sound of many waters, not the sea of glass mingled with fire, not the fourfold hallelujah that rings out over a reconciled and conquered universe, not the New Jerusalem, but *Christ, knocking at the door of the sinner's heart!*

— — —

—**The eternal**—On a visit to the Covenanter church, Northwood, Ohio, where I was baptized, and where my father preached, I thought of the changes in the world—in methods of transportation and communication, in geography and politics—since he first began to preach there. Yet, standing in that pulpit, I realized that I had no Christ to preach but the Christ whom my father preached. His judgment, his power, and his mercy are the same from age to age.

— — —

High up on the cliffs overlooking a noble river, like the Orontes or the Rhine or the Hudson, you will see some great outjutting rock. From century to century the rock has remained the same, while the river beneath it has changed with every moment of its flow. So the stream of time and of history, ever changing, flows past the changeless Christ, the Rock of Ages.

— — —

Last summer I stood in a little room in a house on Tenth Street in Washington, a room in which there was barely space for the great bed that filled it. At twenty minutes past seven on the morning of the fifteenth of April, 1865, the secretary of war, Edwin Stanton, rose from the bedside where he had been kneeling, pulled down the blind at the window to shut out the bright April sunlight, and then, turning to look at the still form on the bed, said, "Now he belongs to the ages." That is the briefest—and perhaps the best—biography of Abraham Lincoln. Yet it is only relatively true that Lincoln and the other great figures of history belong to the ages.

The only one who belongs to the ages is He who is Alpha and Omega, and to whom, by divine appointment and decree, the ages belong. "Who shall declare his generation?" (Acts 8:33.) Christ has no age, no epoch. His personality bridges the ages. He is the same yesterday, today, and forever.

— — —

In his vision St. John saw on the right hand of him that sat on the throne a book sealed with seven seals. When the angel proclaimed with the great voice, "Who is worthy to open the book, and to loose the seals thereof?" (Rev. 5:2). no one in heaven, or on the earth, or under the earth, was able to loose the seals or open the book. Then John saw one standing in the midst of the throne, a Lamb, as though it had been slain. The Lamb came and took the book out of the right hand of him that sat on the throne, and to the full-chorused ascription and adoration of the host of heaven, "Worthy art thou to take the book," the Lamb—that is, Christ—proceeded to loose the seven seals. Here we have presented the truth that Christ alone holds the key to the future destiny of mankind, and that in him all things consist. He is the Alpha and Omega of human history.

— — —

—**Glory of**—No one ever saw more of the glory of Christ than Isaiah—not

50

even Abraham, who saw his day and rejoiced; nor Moses, who wrote of him; nor David, who sang of him; nor Peter, nor Paul, nor John, who saw him standing in the midst of the seven golden candlesticks on the Isle of Patmos. More than any one of them, more than all of them together, Isaiah saw his glory and spake of him.

In the Apocryphal Old Testament book, the Ascension of Isaiah, it is related how when the prophet was talking with King Hezekiah he was suddenly carried away by an angel. He traversed the firmament and between the earth and the moon witnessed the battle of the angels and the demons. He entered and passed through the six heavens and saw all their glory. Then he ascended to the seventh heaven itself, where he looked upon the Holy Trinity and beheld all the events of futurity pass in review before him.

The legend of the Apocryphal book is only a legend; but it expresses a great truth—that all the glory of the heavenly places, the glory of the prophets and the apostles, the angels and the martyrs, the glory of the Father, Son, and Holy Ghost, and the future glory of the Kingdom of God, is reflected in the pages of Isaiah's book.

Once when reading through Isaiah I took a red pencil and thought to mark, as I passed from chapter to chapter, those verses or passages which were of striking beauty, marvelous sublimity, or tender and appealing pathos. But as I drew near to the end of the book I came to the conclusion that the best plan would be to take my red pencil and draw a circle around the entire book, for on every page there is glory.

—In the heart—When I was in Russia in 1912, every house—the great winter palace of the czar, the house of the nobleman, the hotel for lodgers for the night, and the thatched hut of the peasant— had in one of the rooms, in the corner looking toward the East, an icon, a little painting or mosaic of Christ or the Virgin Mother. At that time no Russian home was a home until it was consecrated by the icon. Before that image the devout offered their prayers and made their devotions.

In your House of the Soul have you a place for worship—an altar before which you bow? Among the many guests who come and go, swift as the play of thought—guests on pleasures or on business bent—do you entertain the Heavenly Guest. Has Jesus Christ a place in your life? If you have never admitted him, will you not do it now?

I remember a toiling, afflicted woman who once came to see me. While relating her sorrows and her tribulations, met with such wonderful fortitude and faith, she exclaimed in the midst of her recital, more to herself than to me, "Oh, if I had not known Him . . ." She did not finish her sentence. That was left to me, as I leave it now to your imagination. "If I had not known Him . . ." What does he mean to *you?* Is he your friend, your counselor, your comforter, your inspirer, your eternal hope? Can you, too, say, with all the calm and beautiful conviction of that troubled woman, "Oh, if I had not known Him?"

How many, I wonder, in some moment of spiritual uplift—a moment of quiet meditation or high communion— have had a quickening sense of the nearness and reality of Christ, a feeling that there is no doubt that he is near to your life? Such an experience is too sacred to talk of; but it brings strength and comfort, and you walk in the light of it. Such an experience, one of those special moments when the soul seems to be in close fellowship with Christ, lets us know that he is always there, close to us. On a dark night a sudden flash of lightning, illuminating the sky and the earth, reveals to the traveler houses, hillsides, fields, trees. But the flash of lightning does not create these. It only reveals what is always there. In like manner, these special soul-refreshing views of Christ do but reveal to us the truth that he is ever with us and ever near us.

Once a little band of Christians were forced to meet in secret to worship their Lord and Saviour. A spy betrayed them to the secret police, and an officer with several men surprised them one night at their place of prayer. Looking about him in anger and contempt, the officer ordered one of his men to count all who were present and to record their names. When he had done so he reported to the officer that there were thirty men and women there.

At that an old man stepped forward and said, "Officer, there is one whom you have missed. There is one more here."

The officer looked at him in scorn and said, "What do you mean? We have counted them carefully. There are just thirty here."

"No," the old man insisted, "there is another here whom you have missed."

"Very well," said the officer, "we will count them again."

Again he counted them and again the count was thirty. "There," he said, "it is just as I told you. There are only thirty. Thirty of you miserable Christians. Thirty and no more."

"Yes," said the old man, "but there is one more here, one whom you missed— and that is our Lord Jesus Christ!"

"The form of the fourth is like the Son of God." (Dan. 3:25.) Wherever men are faithful and true to Christ, there in their midst, to comfort and cheer them, is "the form of the fourth"—one who is like, and one who *is,* "the Son of God."

Thousands upon thousands who have followed Christ through all the pilgrimage of life are on record as saying what John Bunyan said in those beautiful and incomparable words: "I have loved to hear my Lord spoken of; and wherever I have seen the print of his shoe in the earth, there I have coveted to set my foot too. His name has been to me as a civet-box; yea, sweeter than all perfumes. . . . And his countenance I have more desired than they that have most desired the light of the sun."

—In the life—W. C. Stead was a great figure in the journalistic world a generation ago. He was one of the notable persons who perished at sea when the *Titanic* went down on that April night in 1912. One of the survivors saw him as he stood alone at the edge of the deck, silent, and in what seemed to be a prayerful attitude, or one of profound meditation.

Stead was a courageous reformer, and in one of his campaigns in London to protect young girls and to raise the age of consent, he was arrested on some technical charge, convicted, and sentenced to prison. On Christmas Day he was writing a letter to a reclaimed girl, encouraging her to stand fast and be a Christian. He was in the organ loft of the chapel prison, looking down on the six hundred prisoners, when he heard a voice say, "Why are you telling that girl to be a Christian? Never again tell anyone to be a *Christian.* Always tell him to be a *Christ."*

A few years ago a group of distinguished historians amused themselves by writing a book called *If, or History Re-*

written. Among these historians were Van Loon, Maurois, Belloc, Chesterton, and Ludwig. Some of the "ifs" which they discussed were these: If Lee had not lost the Battle of Gettysburg; If the Moors in Spain had won; If the Dutch had kept New Amsterdam; If Louis XVI had had an atom of firmness; If Booth had missed Lincoln; If Napoleon had escaped to America. The attempt to reconstruct the past on the ground of these hypotheses and to imagine what might have been was indeed an interesting intellectual enterprise. But there are no "ifs" in history.

The greatest fact of history is the incarnation of God in Jesus Christ; and therefore the greatest "if"—the greatest possible imagination—would be "If Christ had not come." Such an "if" is almost too staggering for our minds. It is like imagining the world without a sunrise, or the heavens without a sky. Yet one of the best ways to get at the value and importance of the incarnation and to rescue Christmas from mere commercialism and festivity and sentimentalism, is to try to think of the world without Christ. Try to think of your own life without Christ. "If I had not come . . ." (John 15:22.)

—**Suffering for martyrs**—Paul's fellowship with Christ was so close that he could make bold to say that Christ suffered in him. . . . Scotland has given many martyrs to the Church and to civil liberty, but there is no tale of martyrdom which so touches a Scottish heart as that of the two Wigtown martyrs, Mary Wilson and Agnes McLaughlin, who perished in the Solway tide. For refusing to retract their Christian declarations the friends were condemned to drown. The elder woman was fastened to a stake much farther out than the younger, with the thought that when the younger saw the suffering and death struggle of her friend she would recant. Quickly the inexorable tide of the Solway came in—first to the older girl's ankles, then to her knees, then to her waist, then to her neck, then to her lips.

The executioners called to the younger girl, "Look! What seest thou?"

Turning her head a little, she saw the struggles of her drowning friend, and then made her calm answer, "What do I see? I see the Lord Jesus suffering in one of his members."

—**Triumph of**—It was a great day for Washington and a great day for the nation when, at the close of the Civil War, the victorious armies—the army of the Potomac and the army of Sherman—marched down Pennsylvania Avenue and past the reviewing platform where stood the President of the United States and General Grant. The multitudes cheered the famous generals as they rode by on their war horses, the sun flashed from thousands of gleaming bayonets, and over all waved the starry banner of a reunited and redeemed nation.

But history shows us a greater and a grander triumph. Mounted on a white horse, his vesture and his thigh bearing a name—King of Kings and Lord of Lords—Christ, the conqueror of Calvary, passes by in triumph. In the chains of captivity and defeat we behold his great enemies, spoiled now of their dread weapons and power—sin, and death, and hell, and Satan himself. And following the King come the great host, the armies of those whom Christ has released from captivity, emancipated from death, and led to victory: Moses and his host who marched through the Red Sea, Joshua and his army of conquest, Gideon and his three hundred men, Elijah and his seven thousand, Peter and the thousands he brought into the Kingdom, Paul and the great host whom he led to Christ— men of every nation and kindred and tribe of the then-known world. Legion after legion, regiment after regiment, army after army, they wheel by and salute their captain and king, who is the King of kings and the Lord of lords.

——— • • • • • ———

That same amazing Wiertz who painted Napoleon in hell gave us two other great canvases. One is entitled, "One of Earth's Great Ones." It is a terrific indictment of man's worship of the warrior, showing a monstrous and colossal giant crushing the bones of men and trampling them under his feet as he cruelly leers upon them.

The other is "The Triumph of Christ." On the cross hangs the Saviour. It is one of the most beautiful bodies of Christ to be seen in any gallery of the world. From the points of the crown of thorns streams ineffable light. Great angels sound their trumpets; and dark, sinister, evil figures flee away into the darkness. So at length will it be! Christ is the Last Conqueror! The Light of the World shall banish the darkness of the world! Divine love shall conquer sin, and the whole earth shall be filled with the knowledge of the glory of the Lord, as the waters cover the sea!

——— • • • • • ———

When Julian the Apostate, who sought to light again the fires on the altars of the pagan gods, and thus destroy Christianity, was on the march with his army in the campaign against Persia, in the year 363, one of the soldiers of his army said to a Christian who was being abused by the soldiery, "Where is your carpenter now?"

"He is making a coffin for your emperor," was the reply of the Christian.

A few months afterward Julian received a mortal wound in battle. The rumor spread through the army that the wound was inflicted by a Christian soldier in the ranks of the Roman army. According to the story of Theoderet, Julian, realizing that his death was near, dipped his hand in the blood of his wound and threw the blood toward heaven, exclaiming as he did so, "Thou hast conquered, O Galilean!"

Yes, the carpenter of Nazareth, exalted to the right hand of God, is making a coffin for all the kings and kingdoms of this world. One by one they flourish and are gone. But Christ's is an everlasting kingdom. All that is not obedient to him, and subject to him, shall perish. That alone endures which belongs to him.

——— • • • • • ———

A convict who had been for twenty-six years a prisoner on Devil's Island, the notorious French penal colony off the coast of South America, of his own volition returned to the colony where he spent a quarter of a century. Asked to give his impressions of the world and of civilization when he went back to it, he said the thing that most impressed him was "the extraordinary spiritual collapse in the world and the decline in conscience and in intelligence." Periods of darkness, such as the one we are now experiencing, come over the earth from time to time; and the cause of truth and righteousness seems to have suffered irrevocable defeat. But even in the darkest age there are silent tokens of the coming triumph.

——— • • • • • ———

—Victory in—When Lord Nelson reported to the British admiralty his great victory over the French fleet in the Battle of the Nile, he said that "victory" was not a large enough word to describe what had taken place. When Paul spoke of the victory which through Jesus Christ he had won over all the ills and adversaries and temptations and woes of life, that greatest of all words, "conqueror," was not sufficient to describe it; and therefore he said *"more* than conquerors." "Nay, in all these things we are more than conquerors, through him that loved us."

On one occasion, after he had been delivered out of great peril at Ephesus, where he had the sentence of death passed on him, and after he had been delivered out of deep and painful anxiety concerning the church at Corinth by the return of his messenger, Titus, Paul cried out in the joy of his soul, "Thanks be unto God, which always causeth us to have a triumph in Christ!" There he made use of the greatest of all Roman scenes and pageants—a Roman triumph. The triumphal arch was the last word in Roman art and splendor. With their sculptured reliefs depicting battles and sieges in all parts of the world, these great arches, such as those of Titus and Constantine, look grandly down today upon the heap of rubbish and the sea of ruins that once was Rome. Bitten and defaced by the winds and rains of ages, scarred and battered by catapult and cannon, these arches have survived the vicissitudes of centuries.

Before the triumphal arch came the triumphal procession. Sometimes, as in the case of Julius Caesar, these great spectacles of victory came after a long lapse of years, when peace had been established. Arrayed in silken garments and crowned with garlands, the conqueror rode in his chariot at the head of his victorious legions. At the wheel of his chariot walked the princes and potentates who had been taken captive, and who, after having helped to make a Roman holiday, would be strangled or decapitated. As the procession moved toward the walls of the city along the Ap-

pian Way, or the *Via Sacra,* successive pageants and pantomimes recalled the incidents of the conqueror's battles and campaigns, while clouds of incense went up to heaven from the altars which had been reared along the line of march. It was this greatest of Roman scenes and exhibitions which Paul had in mind when he employed it as a metaphor to describe the triumph he had won through faith in Christ. Always he is the triumphant man, the "more than conqueror."

Those who overcame through the blood of the Lamb loved not their own lives unto the death. They gladly surrendered their lives in testimony to Christ. Call the long roll of those who in all ages loved not their own lives unto the death, and ask them where they got the power to live such noble lives and die such vicarious deaths, and the answer is always the same, "We overcame through the blood of the Lamb. The Cross was our motive, the Cross inspired us, the Cross strengthened us, the Cross constrained us." I call them from their graves—the apostolic martyrs, Peter, Paul; the martyrs of the Neronian persecution; the martyrs of Domitian; the martyrs of the Colosseum; the martyrs of the Reformation; the missionaries whose blood blends with the soil of China, India, Japan, Africa, and the islands of the sea; and all those who have lived beautiful, Christlike, sacrificial lives amid darkness and sin, woe and hate. I bid them arise from their graves. Yes, I invoke the whole blood-besprinkled throng, those who have been redeemed out of every kindred and tribe and nation; and when I ask them to tell us the secret of their life and death and victory, always it is the same: The Cross! The Lamb of God! Worthy is the Lamb that was slain!

*I ask them whence their victory
   come:*
  They, with united breath,
  Ascribe their conquest to the Lamb,
  Their triumph to his death.
           —Isaac Watts

—**The water of life**—On the last day of the Feast of Tabernacles there was a great procession from the Temple through the streets of Jerusalem to the pool of Siloam. It was led by the temple band, with the white-robed priests marching in front. It passed through Jerusalem, out at the Water Gate, and down the hill of Zion to the pool of Siloam, where each of the priests filled his golden vessel with water. When the procession returned to the Temple, the priests gathered around the altar of sacrifice, where each one emptied his vessel of water on the side of the altar. As they did so, the Levitic choir chanted the words of Isaiah 12:3: "With joy shall ye draw water out of the wells of salvation."

Seven and a half centuries after Isaiah wrote those words, Jesus stood near the Temple watching the procession and listening to the music of the trumpets and the chanting of the Levites on the last great day of the Feast of Tabernacles. Lifting up his voice, he cried out, "If any man thirst, let him come unto me, and drink." (John 7:37.)

So today Christ, watching us as we seek worldly satisfaction, as we attempt to fill our vessels and quench our thirst at the broken cisterns of this world, cries out, as he did on that last day of the Feast at Jerusalem, "If any man thirst, let him come unto me, and drink."

CHRISTIAN LIVING

"Except these chains." (Acts 26:29.) In wishing that Agrippa were as he was, the only thing that Paul had to except was his chains. But how is it with you and me? If we ask someone to be a Christian as we are, what would we have to except? One would have to say, "Except my bad temper"; and another, "Except my speaking evil of others"; another, "Except my tainted imagination"; and another, "Except my little denial of myself for Christ"; and another, "Except my little effort to serve Christ." Christ said that every Christian is to be a witness unto him. Oh, let everyone think of that, and now with shame and confusion confess and seek pardon for those things in his life he would have to name as exceptions when he asked another to be the kind of Christian he is!

CHRISTIAN TRUTH

We must not confuse acceptance of secondary Christianity with acceptance of primary Christianity. In the words of Vinet in his *Outlines of Theology*: "The time may not be far distant when in a certain sense the whole world will be Christian. But even then, it will not be the fundamental principles, but the secondary ideas, the applications of Christianity, that the world will have adopted. The truths which are at the base of the faith of the Church will be nonetheless contrary and odious to the natural man; and while that natural man, of whom even the Christian so long finds some remnant within himself, shall form the majority in this world, so long it is evident the Church must fight and struggle for its very life and suffer therefore even as its Head suffered. . . . It is our strength as well as our duty to hope. God wills that we believe all things possible, yea, even in this our world grown old, the possibility of the glory and force of earlier days."

CHRISTIANITY

In one of the parks of Dublin there is a monument to a young Irish poet who fell fighting by the side of the British in the first World War. Under his bust are cut these words: "He died fighting, not for king or country, or flag or emperor, but for a dream born in a herdsman's hut."

—And education—On the chapel of Williams College is the following beautiful and significant inscription:

"Brethren, Alumni, Fellow Students, Fellow Citizens: We are here gathered to lay the cornerstone of an edifice that is to be sacred to the worship of Almighty God, to the teachings of Christian truth, and to the joyful meeting of man with man as sons of the common Father of us all. It is to be reared, and it is to stand, as a majestic and enduring symbol of the democratic, catholic faith of Williams College.

"In accepting this gift, we declare anew our belief that an education in which the religious nature is ignored cannot produce the noblest type of man. We thus reassert that the citizen whom the republic needs, and the leader whom the republic must have, is the man who fears and loves God and keeps his commandments.

"We here record in imperishable stone our unalterable conviction—that the highest education must always be carried on in the light and warmth of those great truths which make our holy religion immortal."

—Survival of—As Disraeli said so eloquently at Oxford concerning the French Revolution, so it might be said today concerning the vast upheaval that our eyes have witnessed and our ears have heard: "When the turbulence was over, when the waters had subsided, the sacred heights of Sinai and of Calvary were again revealed; and amidst the wreck of thrones, extinct nations, and abolished laws, mankind, tried by so many sorrows, purified by so much suffering, and wise with such unprecedented experience, bowed again before the divine truths that Omnipotence had entrusted to the custody and promulgation of a chosen people."

CHRISTIANS AND CHAMELEONS

The chameleon takes the color of his background and environment—tree, bush, or sod. Many Christians are chameleonlike in the facility with which they can take on the color of the world about them; and, just as it is difficult to distinguish the chameleon from the background, the color of which he has taken, so it is very difficult to distinguish many Christians from the background of the world in which they live.

CHRISTIANS, SLEEPING

Luther had a parable or dream of how on one occasion the devil sat upon his throne listening to the reports of his agents and ambassadors on the progress they had made in opposing the truth of Christ and destroying the souls of men.

One spirit said: "There was a company of Christians crossing the desert. I loosed the lions upon them, and soon the sands of the desert were strewn with their mangled corpses."

"What of that?" answered Satan. "The lions destroyed their bodies, but their souls were saved. It is their souls that I am after."

Then another made his report. He said: "There was a company of Christian pilgrims sailing through the sea on a vessel. I sent a great wind against the ship, which drove the ship on the rocks, and every Christian aboard the ship was drowned."

"What of that?" said Satan. "Their bodies were drowned in the sea, but their souls were saved. It is their souls that I am after."

Then a third came forward to give his report, and he said: "For ten years I have been trying to cast a Christian into a deep sleep, and at last I have succeeded."

And with that the corridors of hell rang with shouts of malignant triumph.

CHURCH—*see also* KINGDOM OF GOD, SECOND COMING AND THE CHURCH

—Blessings of the—A ship was once wrecked on an island in the South Pacific. The sailors who had survived the buffeting of the waves were now seized with a dread lest the island should prove to be inhabited by cannibals. They sent one of their companions before them into the interior of the island to explore. He made his way to the top of a hill, took a look at the valley in front of him, and then, turning, waved to his companions and said, "Come on, boys; here's a church!" That is so all over the world and all through the ages. Where there is a church there are no cannibals.

———·◆·———

—Enemies of the—Gideon had reduced his army to three hundred, as the Lord instructed him; but, when he gazed from the slopes of Gilead upon the hosts of the Midianites encamped in the valley below, he still felt some misgivings about the forthcoming battle. So God said to him, Go down into the camp of the enemy, and "thou shalt hear what they say." (Judges 7:11.) With his ear close to the tent of the Midianites, Gideon heard one tell to his fellow his dream of the barley loaf which tumbled down the hill and knocked over the tent, and his interpretation of it: "This is nothing else save the sword of Gideon . . . for into his hand hath God delivered Midian, and all the host." When Gideon heard that, he worshiped and returned to his

army, to whom he said, "Arise; for the Lord hath delivered into your hand the host of Midian!"

"Thou shalt hear what they say!" We hear what they say to us—what they say in criticism of the Church, in hostility or derision or bitterness, but not what they say among themselves, in their own camp. Would that we might lie quietly by the tents of this world and hear what they think and say! Could we but hear what they think and say of some noble and guileless Christian character; could we but hear their anxious misgivings for the tomorrow of a life without God; could we but see their blank despair as they stand by the grave of one they have loved; could we but hear the restless tossing of their remorse; could we but hear their secret verdict about the ultimate victory of the Kingdom of God— like Gideon, we should worship and return to our posts full of joy and confidence; for we should then know how true it is that the sword of the Lord is also the sword of the Church.

———·◆·———

—Glory of the—As Timothy went to and fro at Ephesus on his pastoral rounds, looking after his church, in which there were not many noble and not many great, he saw the sun reflected from the glorious temple of Diana. The sight reminded him that he was the minister of a grander temple, the temple of Christian truth; for the Church of the Living God is the pillar and the ground of the truth.

———·◆·———

When the seventh angel sounded, there were great voices heard in heaven. The temple of God was opened to the accompaniment of voices, lightning, thundering, great hail, and earthquake. Then appeared a great wonder—a woman clothed with the sun, the moon under her feet and upon her head a crown of twelve stars. This woman clothed in incomparable glory—the sun, the moon, and the stars—has generally been taken to represent the Church of Christ. Wherever the Church appears in the Scriptures, she appears in majesty and glory. The magnificent description of the Church in Revelation is in keeping with that in the Song of Solomon (6:10): "fair as the moon, clear as the sun, and terrible as an army with banners." But greater than the glory of the sun and the moon and the stars is the glory with which the Apostle Paul clothes the Church when he calls it "the body of Christ" (Rom. 7:4).

—Going to—Writing for the *Ladies' Home Journal* an article called "Shall We Do Away with the Church?" Theodore Roosevelt said certain things of permanent import to the nation:

"In the pioneer days of the West, we found it an unfailing rule that after a community had existed for a certain length of time, either a church was built or else the community began to go downhill.

"I doubt whether the frank protest of nothing but amusement has really brought as much happiness as if it had been alloyed with and supplemented by some minimum meeting of obligation toward others. Therefore, on Sunday go to church. Yes—I know all the excuses; I know that one can worship the Creator and dedicate oneself to good living in a grove of trees or by a running brook or in one's own house just as well as in a church, but I also know that as a matter of cold fact, the average man *does not* worship or thus dedicate himself. If he stays away from church he does not spend his time in good works or in lofty meditation. . . . He may not hear a

good sermon at church, but unless he is very unfortunate he will hear a sermon by a good man.

"Besides, even if he does not hear a good sermon, the probabilities are that he will listen to and take part in reading some beautiful passages from the Bible, and if he is not familiar with the Bible, he has suffered a loss which he had better make all possible haste to correct. He will meet and nod to or speak to good, quiet neighbors. If he doesn't think about himself too much, he will benefit himself very much, especially as he begins to think chiefly of others." [1]

—And the Holy Spirit—In a vision John Bunyan saw a man throwing water on a flame, and yet the flame continued to burn. He wondered how it could burn on—until he saw that there was one behind the door pouring oil on the flame!

—Influence of the—Going through the countries of the old world and standing silently and retrospectively beneath the roofs of the venerable fanes, one feels that the Church is an old, old institution. Yet what a world still lives and sins and dies without the walls of the cathedral! Passing out of the glorious cathedral of Toledo, I saw the throngs hurrying to secure their yellow tickets for the unspeakable brutalities of the bull ring. Still only a step from the cathedral to the bull ring, from the Christian to the barbarian! And in our own lands and cities, how closely the world presses upon the Church! But sursum corda! The important thing is not the present or past effect and influence of the Church, but the fact that in it are lodged the eternal principles. These principles must conquer. Christ must reign from the river unto the ends of the earth.

[1] Copyright 1917 The Curtis Publishing Co.

—A pillar—When he called the Church of the Living God a pillar, Paul was thinking not of a building but rather of the institution—the family of God, the company of Christain believers. Yet he drew his metaphor about the pillar and ground of the truth from a building, one of the greatest and most beautiful buildings the world has ever seen, the temple of Diana. Paul and Timothy had seen it often. This temple was four times as large as the Parthenon at Athens and constructed on the same general plan. It was adorned with paintings and sculptures of Praxiteles, Apelles, and Phidias. The roof was covered with white marble tiles, and to sailors on approaching ships the temple gleamed in the distance with the brilliancy of a star. But the chief glory of the temple was the 120 jasper columns which upheld the roof. How magnificent those columns were, one who has visited the Mosque of St. Sofia will be able to judge, for eight of them now help to hold up that great dome, having been transported thither by the Emperor Justinian after the destruction of Ephesus by the Goths in A.D. 260.

As these great pillars upheld the marble roof of Diana's temple, so the Church, declares Paul, is a mighty pillar which holds up in this world the truth, and by the truth he means the truth that is above all other truth, which takes in and embraces all truth—the truth of redemption through Christ, the everlasting gospel.

—Survival of the—In the Apocalypse of St. John we have a magnificent prediction and prefiguration of an age-long conflict. A woman, clothed with the sun and with a crown of twelve stars on her head, is about to give birth to a child. Before the woman stands a dragon, waiting to devour the child as soon as it is born. But the woman flees into the wilderness where she has a place prepared of God. The very powers of nature helped the woman in her escape from the dragon: the wings of a great eagle carry her into the wilderness, and the earth swallows up the flood which the dragon casts out of his mouth.

A strange picture, you say; and yet it is natural history of good and evil. It is a conflict which appears and reappears in the age-long drama of man's history. Always waits the dragon—and yet the child is always miraculously preserved.

Shortly before the great prophet of Florence—Savonarola—was burned at the stake, he said, "If you ask me in general as to the issue of this trouble, I reply, Victory. If you ask me in a particular sense, I reply, Death; for the Master who wields the hammer, when he has used it, throws it away. So he did with Jeremiah, whom he caused to be stoned at the end of his ministry. But Rome will not put out this fire; and if this be put out, God will light another."

On his way to Greece in his campaign against Pompey, Caesar tried to calm the fears of the sailors in the storm by the impious words, "Remember you carry Caesar and his fortunes." But in the case of Christ that is true. The Church carries Christ and his redeeming fortunes; therefore no storm can overwhelm it. The whole Church of Christ was present one night in a little ship tossed by the sea—present in the person of Peter and James and John and Matthew, Bartholmew, and the rest of the disciples. If they had gone down, the Church would have been lost, for these were the men chosen by Christ to found it; but the Church did not go down, it did not sink, for *Christ was with it.*

The old Reformed churches of Europe, and some of their successors in this country, with scriptural and historical appropriateness chose for their motto a phrase referring to the burning bush— "Nevertheless, it was not consumed" (Exod. 3:2). That is the sentence with which you must conclude every chapter of the history of the church. After every fire of false teaching, of schism, of persecution, of corruption and apostasy, that is the record: *"Nevertheless, it was not consumed."*

- - • - -

"The gates of hell shall not prevail." (Matt. 16:18.) "Watchman, what of the night?" (Isa. 21:11.) When in the fifth century Rome was sacked by the Goths under their king, Alaric, and eleven centuries of progress and civilization seemed to be going down into darkness, the heathen—and some faithless Christians—attributed these disasters to Christianity and supposed that they were the prelude to the destruction of the whole world. The great Augustine, however, sat down to write his famous work, *The City of God,* picturing the sublime city of the Christian Church which rises out of the ruins of the civilizations of this world, survives all disasters and catastrophes, and one day will bring the Kingdom of Everlasting Justice and Righteousness and Peace. It is our privilege, it is our high heritage, to have the faith to see that Kingdom—to see it even in this darkest hour of the world's history, for it was the eternal Son of God, the King of all kingdoms, the blessed and only Potentate, Lord of lords, and King of kings, who said, "Upon this rock I will build my church; and the gates of hell shall not prevail against it."

- - • - -

In his dream a man once found himself in a city where there were many splendid and notable buildings—great granite temples of finance, towering structures where great business was transacted; marble halls where a university was housed; spacious palaces of pleasure; and costly and ornate homes. In the midst of these splendid buildings there stood a plain structure, humble and modest in comparison with the mighty buildings which looked down upon it. Men and women were going into and coming out of that humble structure.

A hundred years passed in the dream, and the man found himself again in the same city, but he could hardly recognize it, for all the great buildings upon which he had looked a hundred years before had disappeared and other and more imposing structures had taken their places. But still in the midst of these great buildings stood the modest frame building, with men and women going in and out, just as he had seen them do a century before.

A thousand years passed, and the man returned to that same city, and again he noted a complete transformation. All buildings that he had seen before had vanished and new buildings with new architecture and new grandeur had taken their places—all except the little frame building, and out of it he saw men and women coming with the light of joy and satisfaction upon their faces. At length he asked some of the citizens what this building might be, and what was the explanation of its remaining unchanged and still frequented after all other buildings had vanished and disappeared? Then he learned the secret of the endurance of that one building: it was the house of God, where men found the way of life eternal.

- - • - -

Through all the storms and convulsions of time the gospel survives, the Church lives on. It is because there is something in the Church that is imperishable and indestructible, something built to the music of faith, "and therefore never built at all, and therefore built forever." Chateaubriand somewhere speaks of Christanity as the most glorious rainbow that ever smiled upon our troubled world. So after the storm of war Christian faith will again build its iridescent ladder of hope upon the bloodstained earth.

———

—Triumph of the—It was a beautiful church, built of pine logs, and all within was white and fragrant. The windows, as befitted the grandeur of the scenery in which the church was set, were of plain glass. On the altar between the pulpit and the lectern was a cross. Looking through the great window back of the altar, one saw the pine trees, the cloudless sky, and the towering mountains. The service was a dedication of the little church which was to minister to the people of that mountain community almost two miles above the level of the sea. In other parts of the world churches were being bombed and blasted and torn down. But here was a church which, in the midst of world turmoil and confusion and anguish, had been built by the gifts of followers of Jesus Christ. It was a symbol of the timelessness and perpetuity of Christ's Kingdom, the Kingdom of Heaven. Leaving the church, one seemed to hear the music of the old hymn:

> *O where are kings and empires*
>   *now,*
> *Of old that went and came?*
> *But, Lord, thy Church is praying*
>   *yet,*
> *A thousand years the same.*

———

Not far from Lake Geneva, out of which it flows, the river Rhone disappears from view; but farther to the south

it emerges again in full sweep and power. From age to age the river of God's truth has flowed through the world, sometimes through quiet valleys, sometimes over rocks and rapids—and sometimes, like the Rhone, disappearing altogether, as far as man can judge, but finally emerging again with undiminished sweep and power. An exploration of the river of the gospel fills us with invincible confidence that its course and history are directed of God and that one day the river shall become a flood of righteousness which will cover the earth as the waters cover the sea.

———

In a day of indifference and apostasy in England, Samuel Wesley, the father of John Wesley and Charles, looked forward to a period of restoration and resurrection of spiritual life and power when he said to his son Charles, "Charles, be steady. The Christian faith will surely revive in these kingdoms. You shall see it, though I shall not." Years afterward, forbidden to preach from his father's pulpit, John Wesley, standing on the flat stone of his father's grave, remembered that remark as he preached the gospel to a great multitude.

Yes, out of every eclipse the cause of Christ arises more glorious and resplendent than ever. If the present age seems spiritually dark, if the glory of the Church seems obscured, have faith in God. His gospel shall again shine forth in glory and in power.

———

From age to age the enemies of the gospel have proclaimed that the Church is dying, that it has lost its hold upon mankind, that ere long its temples will be forsaken. Some years ago two noted unbelievers were passing the beautiful Corinthian-columned Madeleine Church in Paris. It was a Sabbath morning and many worshipers were coming out of the church.

One of these men remarked to the other, "God has a good many callers this morning."

"Yes," replied his companion, "but they are making their last call."

Yet that last call has never been made, and never shall be made; and until all the redeemed shall gather about the throne of the Lamb in heaven, the followers of Christ will "enter into his gates with thanksgiving, and into his courts with praise: be thankful unto him, and bless his name" (Ps. 100:4).

———————

Christians among the soldiers of the Allied armies of World War II who marched into Cologne and saw that majestic cathedral, with its heaven-aspiring towers, standing unhurt and unscarred in the midst of that great desolation, must have thought of the perdurance of the Christian faith and the indestructibility of the Kingdom of God. Theaters, mills, factories, banks, shops, warehouses, schools, universities—all had disappeared. But still the spires of the cathedral pointed heavenward. Things which can be shaken, and ought to be shaken, are shaken down; but the things which cannot be shaken always remain.

The majestic spires of Cologne Cathedral call Germany back to God; and they call America back to God, too.

———————

—Unity of the—The Roman soldiers on guard at the crucifixion of Jesus were, according to custom, appropriating to themselves the prisoner's raiment. When they came to his coat they discovered that it was a seamless garment. To rend it into four parts, one for each soldier, would ruin it. For this reason they decided to keep it intact and cast lots for the ownership of it. By so doing, John comments, the soldiers fulfilled the prophecy of the great messianic psalm:

> *They part my garments among them,*
> *And upon my vesture do they cast lots.*

I have no idea who first employed the seamless robe of Christ as a metaphor for the unity of his Church. The first time I ever came upon it was in a prayer of Henry Ward Beecher, where he prayed that the Church might be one again, like the seamless robe of her Lord. All agree that the metaphor is one of the great beauty and appropriateness. The strife of the sects and the wrangling of the parties within the Church of Christ have been angry efforts to tear in pieces the sacred garment of the truth, while the Crucified One looks sadly down upon the miserable conflict between those he died to redeem; and his look of love and sorrow seems to repeat the prayer of the sacramental table, "That they may be one . . . that the world may know that thou didst send me" (Jno. 17:21).

CHURCH MEMBERS

—Dead—"Thou livest, and art dead." (Rev. 3:1.) Every church has on its roll members of whom this is a true description. The greatest of all names is "Christian." By virtue of their connection with the Church, believers bear that great name—and that name implies life, and life eternal. But as a matter of fact the *name* is all they have. They are dead.

A minister was asked to conduct the service of a godless man who was a member of his congregation, and the family insisted that a public funeral be held in the church. This was the brief and powerful sermon preached by the minister. Pointing to the coffin in front of him, he said, "This corpse has been a member of my church for twenty-five years."

CITY—*see also* LONELINESS OF THE CITY

—The lost of the—At the close of a sermon which I preached in Toronto, a young woman of a good family and superior personality asked to see me in the vestry. Her story was brief, but sad. A year before, her brother had left home and had gone to the States. The last they heard of him he was employed in Pittsburgh under an assumed name. During his absence his mother had died. All their efforts to get in touch with him had failed; the investigations of detectives and police had accomplished nothing. When I went back to Pittsburgh, would I try to find her brother? Of course, I said I would; and when I went back I did try to find that lost brother, but in vain. He belongs to the number of those who must be listed as "lost" in the city. Not a few like that vanish completely, the very name and place that once knew them knowing them no more forever. But in addition to such persons, a much vaster army, made up of those, who, although their places of work and residence may be well known, must nevertheless—if we take into the reckoning the high and holy purposes of life—be listed among the lost. O City, O Pittsburgh, O Philadelphia, O Chicago, O New York, if thou couldst open thy graves and give up thy dead, restore thy lost, how they would stand tonight by Wisdom's side and cry in our streets!

—Sins of the—O City, City, City! Thy sins, thy shame, thy woes, thy devils, and thy death! In all this is there none to plead thy cause, that thou mayest be bound up? Hast thou no healing medicines? Is thy wound incurable? Have all thy lovers forsaken thee? No, there is One who has not forsaken thee. He who wept over the city that crucified him still comes to visit thee. I walked round thy walls as the prophet of old walked at midnight round the walls of Jerusalem; and amid all the scenes of revelry and shame and sin and woe and misery his friends—the friends of Jesus Christ—were the only ones who cared for thy misery, who sought to heal thy wound or wipe away thy tears. O hear his voice as he speaks unto thee and to thy children saying, "Come unto me, all ye that labor and are heavy laden, and I will give you rest" (Matt. 11:28).

—Voice of the—Whenever I think of London I recall my first visit to the metropolis and how, in a hotel not far from Euston Station, I lay on my bed and all through the night listened to the thunder and roar and rumble of the city's streets, as the never-ending procession of omnibuses rolled up and down the avenues. It was the voice of London. Every great city utters a great voice.

An organist once visited Niagara Falls and spent much time standing on the brink of the falls listening to the thunder of the cataract. His conclusion was that the falls were striking one of the chords of the scale. It was more than just a thunder of noise he heard.

In the streets of our great cities, where the cataract of humanity, with its business, its pleasure, its joy, and its sorrow, is forever pouring, it is more than just noise that we hear. Music is there, weird, melancholy, grand, sad, awful—for in that tremendous chord, love, greed, lust, hate, fear, and despair endeavor to make themselves heard.

COLLEGE

—Robert E. Lee and—Late on a summer's afternoon, after a long ride through the beautiful valley of the Shenandoah, that starlit abbey of the Confederacy, well-watered like the garden of the Lord, and with mountains on either side to guard it, I alighted at the little town of

Lexington, Virginia. It is a town dear to all the Southland, for it holds the dust of her two great military heroes, Lee and Jackson. There is the university, with its sloping lawns and gracious trees and white-pillared buildings. Fifty years ago it was a small, broken-down, bankrupt college, with neither students nor funds.

Had I been there on another summer's evening I might have seen a chunky gray horse come steadily up the hill and pass down the main street of the village. Astride his back sat a tall, grave man, clad in Confederate gray. The horse was Traveler, and the rider Robert E. Lee. When the war was over an English nobleman offered him an estate in England and an insurance company of New York offered him fifty thousand dollars for the use of his name. The trustees of this little Presbyterian college borrowed a suit of broadcloth from a local judge and sent one of their members down to Richmond to proffer Lee the presidency of Washington College—at the munificent salary of fifteen hundred dollars a year! This was the offer Lee accepted, and there in that little mountain college he wrote the noblest chapter of his life, and took "captivity captive."

COLLEGE IDEALS—*see* IDEALS, WILL OF GOD, YOUTH (IDEALS OF; OPPORTUNITIES OF)

COLLEGE TRAGEDY—*see* DREAMS (LOST)

COLOSSEUM

This huge structure was commenced by the Emperor Vespasian and finished by his son Titus, conqueror of the Jews. It was built to satisfy the Roman lust for the spectacular and the exciting, for bloodshed and for cruelty. Covering five acres of ground, the colossal bowl could accommodate eighty-five thousand of the populace of Rome. Built in the shape of an ellipse, and founded on eighty acres, it rises to the dizzy height of 160 feet.

The outside consists of four rows of columns, representing successive orders of architecture—Doric, Ionic, and Corinthian—and was encrusted with marble and decorated with statues. Inside, tiers of stone benches rose one above the other. Sixty-four exits, or vomitories, in a short time admitted or poured forth the blood-loving throngs; and to this day you can see the Roman numerals on fragments of the arches showing the number of the entrance corresponding to the ticket held by the patron. Huge canopies could be spread over the seats to protect from rain and sun.

Gushing fountains cooled and refreshed the air and aromatics diffused a pleasant odor to offset that of the wild beasts. The open space in the center was called the arena, from the Latin word for the sand with which it was carefully overlaid. Under the lowest tier of benches were the dens of the wild beasts, for which the whole earth had been ransacked, and side by side with them the gloomy caverns where the prisoners and martyrs spent their last hours before they were thrust forth into the blazing arena to fight with beasts.

Dark and somber, the colosseum is like the vast shadow of a departed world falling across the face of our generation. It stands as a crowning indictment of the pagan civilization which reached its awful climax in these bloody spectacles. When the enormous show house was dedicated by the Emperor Titus in the year A.D. 80, ten years after the fall of Jerusalem, more than five thousand wild beasts were slain in the games. Here, on the very ground where I was standing, thousands had fallen in combat with one another or with wild animals. That was the Roman estimate of the barbarian. All he was good for was to make a Roman holiday.

COMMUNION—*see* LORD'S SUPPER

COMMUNION OF THE SAINTS

Faith unites us, and yet we are conscious of the division of time and death. This thought is beautifully expressed by Charles Wesley:

One family we dwell in him,
  One Church above, beneath,
Though now divided by the stream,
  The narrow stream of death;

One army of the living God,
  To his command we bow:
Part of his host have crossed the
  flood,
And part are crossing now.

COMPASSION, LINCOLN'S

An old man whose son had been convicted of gross crimes in the army and sentenced to be shot came to plead with Lincoln. As the boy was an only son, the case appealed to Lincoln; but he had just received a telegram from Butler which read: "Mr. President, I beg you not to interfere with the court-martials of this army. You will destroy all discipline in the army." Lincoln handed the old man the telegram, and he watched the shadow of disappointment and sorrow come over the man's face as he read the message. He suddenly seized his hand and exclaimed, "By jingo! Butler or no Butler, here goes!" He wrote out an order and handed it to the father. The man read the order, which was as follows: "Job Smith is not to be shot until further orders from me. Abraham Lincoln."

"Why," said the father, "I thought it

was going to be a pardon. You may order him to be shot next week."

"My old friend," said Lincoln, "evidently you do not understand my character. If your son is never shot until an order comes from me, he will live to be as old as Methuselah."

CONSCIENCE—*see also* REMORSE

A certain king had a magic ring. The ring sat on his finger as any other ring, yet it had mystic qualities. Whenever an evil thought came into the mind of the prince, or he was tempted to do an evil deed, or had done a wrong thing, the ring pressed painfully upon his finger. Such a ring, by virtue of his creation, belongs to every man, prince or peasant; and the name of it is Conscience.

———•◦•———

Here is John Ruskin's interpretation of Holman Hunt's "Light of the World": The light from the lantern in Christ's hand is the light of conscience; its red light falls only on the closed door. But the light from the head is that of hope and salvation. Conscience condemns. Christ delivers and forgives.

———•◦•———

Jesus said to the woman at the well, "Go call thy husband." To another he may say, "Go call thy wife, whom thou hast wronged." To another, "Go call thy child, whom thou hast neglected." To another, "Go call thy father and mother." To another he says, "Go bring thy bankbook." To another, "Go call the record of that business transaction." To another, "Go call that slander which you uttered against another's name." To another, "Go call that hatred or enmity which you treasure up in your heart." To another, "Go call that secret habit which stains and defiles thy soul." Can you meet these tests?

—A battlefield—I like to visit old battle-fields. I have wandered over Marathon and walked through the pass of Thermopylae; I have stood on the plains of Philippi and driven over the field of Issus, where Alexander crushed the Persians under Darius. But more thrilling than all these battlefields is the battle-field of the soul, the battlefield of conscience.

—Condemnation of—The raven that came in the darkness into the chamber of Poe and perched upon a bust of Pallas just above his chamber door, whose only word was "Nevermore," seems to be a metaphor, a symbol of remorse. Poe beseeches the raven to take his beak from out his heart, and his form from off his door, but all the raven answers is, "Nevermore."

And the lamp-light o'er him streaming throws his shadow on the floor;
And my soul from out that shadow that lies floating on the floor
Shall be lifted—nevermore!

Yes, the shadow that conscience casts upon the soul—because of evil done, because of sin—is a shadow which man is not able to lift. Only God in Christ can lift that shadow.

During a session of the legislature of Illinois at Springfield, a Chicago businessman had prepared for passage in the legislature a measure which would bring profit to him and others, but which was not just, honest, or right. All things having been arranged for the successful introduction and passage of the bill, and having a few hours to spend before his train left for Chicago, he went out to Oak Hill Cemetery to visit the tomb of Lincoln. As he walked in the soft twi-light about the monument and looked upon the statue of Lincoln, a feeling of great discomfort came over him with regard to the bill which was to be passed in the legislature. The image of Lincoln and the thought of his noble character made the man uneasy and unhappy. He canceled his reservation on the night train to Chicago; and, after spending a sleepless night tossing on his bed at the hotel, he sent for his attorneys and had the bill withdrawn.

What caused this action? It was conscience, awakened by the memory of Abraham Lincoln, warning the man to restrain his hand from doing evil.

—Dulled by sin—How was it possible for guilty David to have missed the point of the parable and not to have known who was meant by the rich man and the poor man and the ewe lamb? His conscience had been dulled by sin. Not until the sword was a hairbreadth from the heart did he know that it was meant for him.

—A good—When Mr. Honest received his summons to present himself at his Father's house, and addressed himself to go over the river, the river at that time overflowed its banks. "But Mr. Honest, in his lifetime, had spoken to one Good-conscience to meet him there, the which he also did, and lent him his hand, and so helped him over."

In Victor Hugo's great *Les Misérables* Jean Valjean, the ex-convict, under a new name, had buried his past and become the prosperous mayor of a provincial town. But one day he learned that in a neighboring village an old man arrested for stealing apples had been identified as the notorious and long-sought ex-convict, Jean Valjean. That news precipitated a crisis in the soul of the real Jean Valjean. Should he keep silent, or should he reveal his identity and be sent back to the gallows? Should he remain in paradise and become a demon, or go to hell and become an angel?

His first impulse was to say nothing and do nothing. Out of a secret closet in the wall he drew a blue linen blouse, an old pair of trousers, an old knapsack, and a huge cudgel shod with iron at both ends. These were the last ties which attached him to the old Jean Valjean. He threw them into the fire, and then seized the candlesticks which the Bishop had given him and flung them into the flame. But a voice said, "Jean Valjean, there will be many voices around you which will bless you, and only one which will curse you in the dark. All those benedictions will fall back before they ascend to God." This made him take the candlesticks out of the fire and replace them on the mantel. All through the night he fought his awful battle, until, in the morning, his servant told him that the carriage he had ordered to take him to the town where the old man was on trial waited at the door.

The next day as the president of the court was about to pronounce sentence, the true convict stood up before the court and said, "I am Jean Valjean." Some thought that he was mad, and others pitied him for the sacrifice he had made. As he left the courtroom, he said: "All of you consider me worthy of pity, do you not? When I think what I was on the point of doing, I consider that I am to be envied. God, who is on high, looks down on what I am doing at this moment, and that suffices."

—**A guiding beam**—The airship has a radio beam in the shape of a V, which guides the plane like a path of light. At its widest portion, five miles, the sounds can still be heard. When the ship veers off the course to the right the pilot gets the signal *N,* or dash and dot. When he veers to the left he gets the signal *A,* or dot and dash. When he is directly on the beam he hears a constant hum. Thus the ship is guided unerringly to its destination, and when it is immediately over the field there is a zone of silence.

A wonderful triumph of man's inventive genius, a marvelous conquest of the laws of nature! But there is something within man which is more wonderful and more mysterious than that radio beam. It is that divine beam of truth and light—man's conscience—showing him the path of safety. To obey that voice means safety and happiness; to disobey it means disaster and sorrow.

———

—**A guilty**—One of the old manuscripts of John's Gospel has an interesting and striking addendum to the text of John 8:6 as most of us know it. Our Bible reads, "Jesus stooped down, and with his finger wrote on the ground." The old manuscript adds these words: ". . . the sin of each one of them." Those added words help us to see the scribes and Pharisees looking over the shoulder of Jesus as he wrote, each man blanching at one of the words written there, at one of the sins—profane swearing, dishonor of parents, extortion, bribe taking, wife beating, theft, lying, adultery. No wonder, then, that each man, convicted in his own conscience, turned and with lowered countenance walked silently away.

However true to the original text may be that sentence ". . . and with his finger wrote on the ground the sin of each one of them," it is at least true to the spirit of this interview; for nothing is plainer than that each man felt his own sin. Christ wrote out each man's guilt, and then let each man condemn himself.

———

Here is a man on the deck of a palatial Atlantic liner. He has planned and carried out a long-cherished trip to the sites and nurseries of ancient and modern civilization. He has stood before the colossal monuments of Egypt and has marveled at the broken grace of the Parthenon. He has wandered at moonlight amid the solitudes of the Colosseum, and from the towers of the Alhambra has seen the sun set on the Sierras. He has breathed the light air of Paris and heard the central roar of London. Yet enjoyment and satisfaction of mind have escaped him. He did not have it at home, and he could not find its dwelling place abroad. Wherever he went, he was confronted by his own shadow. Wherever he went, he found himself there in advance. However eloquently spoke the voice of ancient castle or venerated field of battle, or priceless sculpture or painting, his own self-accusing voice spoke with a louder and more penetrating accent. Something was not right within, and that something trailed him with unsleeping persistence and unbribable determination. Almost anything in the world he could have. He could get passports to other lands, but not a passport to the land of happiness and peace of mind; he could buy tickets and food, drink and raiment, and what the world calls pleasures; but he could not buy a good conscience. A good conscience cannot be purchased—even though a man offers all he possesses for it.

When, in that play within the play, the assassin poured the poison into the sleeper's ear, the guilty king rose up in terror; for he saw just what Hamlet intended he should see—he saw his own crime.

—Inescapable—There is no grave deep enough permanently to bury evil. It must have its resurrection. The man who has done wrong has a serpent hibernating in his heart. For months, for years, it will show no sign of life; but one day it will lift its head and strike. The evil deed has been hidden, the sin buried, for years; but suddenly it will have a fearful resurrection. "Angels hear the throb of the heart and God counts the thoughts of the mind." The smallest trifle will suffice to call the sin out of its grave—the stirring of a leaf, the murmur of water, the sound of a voice, the sight of a face, the pronunciation of a name or a number—and lo! the graves are opened, and the ghosts of our former transgressions come forth to accuse us to our faces! In that great tale of conscience, *Toilers of the Sea,* Victor Hugo says: "You can no more keep thought from returning to past transgression than keep the sea from returning to the shore after it has gone out. In the sea we call it the tide; but the guilty man calls it conscience. Conscience heaves the soul as the tide does the ocean."

It is impossible for an evildoer to get safely by the judgment seat of conscience. Some of you may have seen grim Alcazar Island, now the federal prison in San Francisco Bay. One day a group of prisoners was being taken into the prison enclosure. They had all been searched at the receiving station. Then, one by one, and with considerable distance between them, they were marched past the little guardhouse and through the gates into the prison. Several had passed; but as one prisoner was walking in, an order rang out—"Halt!" The guards took the man into the guardhouse, and after careful search they drew out of his ear a minute saw. In the guardhouse was a powerful magnet which by its vibrations disclosed the presence of any bit of metal on a prisoner who passed through the gates. The prisoner could not escape the magnet. So it is impossible for the evildoer to pass successfully by the deep scrutiny of conscience.

In his extraordinary *Confessions* Rousseau tells us how, in order to protect himself, he falsely charged a lady in waiting at a castle in Italy with the theft of a ribbon, and how to the end of his days he was haunted by the pained expression upon the face of that innocent maid.

In Dickens' powerful tale *Barnaby Rudge,* you have the confession of the evildoer that for eight and twenty years the man whom he had slain has never changed. He is always there before him —in the dark night and in the sunshine, in the twilight and the moonlight, in the light of the fire and the lamp and the candle, in the gloom of winter, in company and in solitude, on sea and on land, on the quays and in the market places, in the center of the busy crowd. Always he has been conscious of that terrible form, towering above him with uplifted and avenging hand.

One of the most powerful verses in English poetry is Thomas Hood's "The Dream of Eugene Aram"—a poem based on historic fact. It is the tale of an usher at a boy's school in England who has committed a terrible crime. In charge of the boys on the playing field, he sees one of them reading a book under a tree and asks him what he is reading. He answers, "It is 'The Death of Abel.'" The usher sits down by his side and tells the boy of a dream that he has had—how he murdered an innocent old man and robbed him of his gold, how he flung the body into the river, how some strange urge in the night made him go back and look on the body lying in the bed of the stream, and how he took it out of the river bed and quickly buried it under the leaves in the forest, only to see the wind uncover it by sweeping the leaves away. The frightened boy listens to the usher in amazement. And that very night Eugene Aram is carried off to prison.

Before he talked to the boy he had sat reading a book as he watched the boys at play. As he shut the ponderous tome, strained the dusky covers close, and fixed the brazen clasp, he exclaimed:

"Oh, God! could I so close my mind,
And clasp it with a clasp!"

But that is impossible. You cannot close the mind and "clasp it with a clasp," as you can close and clasp a book. You can no more keep thought from returning to transgression than you can keep the sea when it is gone out from returning to the shore. In the sea we call that the tide; in that deeper and mysterious sea, the soul of man, we call it conscience.

Oh, strange, mysterious, indefinable, inescapable conscience! If, even in the busy arena of this life, conscience has been able to bring you into a corner, if in spite of all the pleasure and business and occupations which divert or amuse you here, conscience has been able to give you a most unpleasant moment, then how will it be in that great day when you stand before the judgment seat of Christ—and every word comes back, every deed is reproduced, and every secret thought is called forth? What will you do then, when there is no business, and no occupation, and no pleasure, to divert you, or to anesthetize the thorn of conscience? Oh, in that hour you will need—and thank God you can have— the protection and refuge of your Redeemer and Advocate, who takes your place, and in whom you have put your trust, and concerning whom you can say, "I . . . am persuaded that he is able to keep that which I have committed unto him against that day" (II Tim. 1:12).

—Loyalty to—"A man must live," the world said to Daniel when he read the proclamation of the king, Darius, that for thirty days no prayer should be offered save to Darius himself. "You need not pray at the open window where your enemies will see you; you can say your prayers, Daniel, in your secret chamber. Thus you will escape the lion's den." Such was the worldly counsel.

But Daniel said, "The man of faith and prayer must live within me"; and three times, as his wont was, Daniel opened his window toward Jerusalem and knelt down and prayed to the God of Abraham, Isaac, and Jacob.

"A man must live," the world might have said to John the Baptist when he was confronted with the enormous transgression of Herod and Herodias. "Limit your strictures on immoral conduct to vague general principles," the world might have advised John. But John invaded the king's palace and, standing before Herod and Herodias, said to him, "It is not lawful for thee to have her!" (Matt. 14:4.)

"A man must live," said the world to John the Baptist.

But John answered, "No, a man must *not* live. A man may have to *die* in order that the true, the high, the spiritual, in him—the man of God—shall live."

And here on a silver charger is John's head—to please the whim of a half-naked dancing girl, to satisfy the vengeance of a bad woman! John died; yet in the highest sense John lived—and lives—and the mention of his name today is like an army with banners.

"A man must live," the world said to John Bunyan when he was arrested un-

der Charles II. If John Bunyan had signed a paper saying he would not preach in public he could have escaped prison; and if at any time during his twelve years' imprisonment he had been willing to say that, he would have been released.

"A man must live," the world said to Bunyan, "especially a man with a dependent wife and little children, and especially when one of those children is blind, like your poor girl, Mary." In the dungeon, Bunyan thought of that. He said that his heart was like to break when he thought of his poor family, and especially when he thought of his poor blind girl. "Oh, my poor blind one," he would say to himself, "what sorrows thou art likely to have in this life! How thou must go naked and hungry, and beg on the streets, and be beaten and starved; and now I cannot so much as endure the thought that the winds should blow upon thee!" Yes, a man must live, and a man's family must live; but John Bunyan remained in the dungeon, and gave over his concerns, blind Mary and all, to the keeping of God. Toward the end of his imprisonment he wrote that glorious passage in which he said, "Unless I am willing to make of my conscience a continual slaughter shop and butchery; unless I am willing to pluck out my eyes and let the blind lead me, then God Almighty being my witness and my defense —if it shall please him to let frail life last that long—the moss shall grow upon these eyebrows before I surrender my principles or violate my conscience."

—Warning of—What would you think of a ship's captain who, sailing off a dangerous coast, saw suddenly through the clouds and the mist the flash of a lighthouse but, instead of at once altering his course, decided to go on a little farther and wait for a second or a third flash? He would be guilty, you say, of criminal folly and carelessness. Yet as the captain and master of your own soul, do you not often act as foolishly as the captain of that ship? Do not tamper with your conscience. Do not lightly dismiss, as only an inherited prejudice, the distinction which it makes between good and evil. Muffle not that warning bell. If it kept you awake last night, thank God that even if you did sin, at least your conscience condemned you for your transgression—and the Spirit has not departed from you!

———•◆•———

Robert Southey has a poem about the Inchcape Bell. This was a bell buoy off a dangerous shore of Scotland. In a drunken spree a wild sea captain, to injure the folk in the harbor, cut the bell from its mooring; and it sank into the depths of the sea. Months afterward that same captain's ship was driven before the storm. His men listened in vain for the sound of the bell buoy which would guide them to port. Missing the channel, the ship drove on the rocks—and all perished.

This is a parable of piercing truth. He who muffles conscience may live to see that day when conscience will not speak. In the words of the prophet, "Ye have set at nought all my counsel, and would none of my reproof: I also will laugh at your calamity; I will mock when your fear cometh." (Prov. 1:25-26.)

CONSECRATION

At a meeting in a hay mow in Dublin, which Moody attended in the year 1872, Henry Varley said in a quiet way, "The world has yet to see what God can do with and for and through and in a man who is fully and wholly consecrated to him." The next Sabbath, sitting high up in Spurgeon's Tabernacle in the same seat he had occupied in 1867, Moody, as he thrilled to the preaching of Spurgeon, heard those words of Varley over and over. He said to himself, "The world has yet to see! 'With and for and through and in a man'! Varley meant *any* man! Varley didn't say he had to be educated, or brilliant, or anything else—just a man! Well, by the Holy Spirit in me, I'll *be* one of those men." In his joy he began to weep. Sympathetic Christians who went to talk with him, thinking that he was under great conviction, learned that it was not a case of sin or penitence, but great joy, the joy of dedication to a high purpose.

Still the world has yet to see what God can do with a man who is wholly consecrated to his will. It saw it once in the divine man, Christ Jesus—only imperfectly in any other man. But among those who have demonstrated what a man who is consecrated to the will of God can do with the limitations of human nature, Moody stands high in the list.

CONTROVERSY AND "HARD NAMES"

There is a place for righteous indignation, but there is also a place for reasoning together; and it may be that we can accomplish as much by a conference as by a long-range bombardment of invisible foes. In this connection I like to read those fine words of John Wesley, written in the preface to his sermons: "Point me out a better way than I have yet known. Show me it is so, by plain proof of Scripture. . . . May I not request of you, farther, not to give me hard names in order to bring me into the right way. . . . Nay, perhaps, if you are angry, so shall I be too; and then there will be small hopes of finding the truth. If once anger arise, . . . this smoke will so dim the eyes of my soul, that I shall be able to see nothing clearly."

To these sentiments I heartily subscribe. It may be, too, that conservative and evangelical men, in deep distress over what they deem false teaching in the name of the gospel, have denounced too much and conferred too little. "Hard names," too, may have been sometimes relied upon instead of "plain proof of Scripture." Yet permit me to say, after several years' personal experience with the liturgy of execration, that all the "hard names" have not come from one camp.

CONVERSION—*see also* DECISION FOR CHRIST, PREACHING AND CONVERSION, PROVIDENCE AND CONVERSION

The night when he wrestled with the angel marked the turning point, the change, in the life of Jacob. There were other events, no doubt, that prepared for it, but this was the decisive night, the turning point, in the history of his soul.

On some journey you have felt as you went along that you had turned into the wrong road. Yet you were not quite sure, and you continued driving or walking along. At length you came to a dead end, or some other certain intimation that you were off the road; and you turned about and went back. That was the turning point. Although the incidents that had gone before had prepared you for it, there was a definite moment when you turned about.

So is it with repentance, with conversion, with the new birth. The change came for Jacob when, weak and halt and lame, he made the prayer, "I will not let thee go, except thou bless me" (Gen. 32:26).

—**Of Augustine**—A remarkable example of how Christ can touch man into greatness is found in the life of Augustine, perhaps after Paul and the apostles the most influential of Christians. In his *Con-fessions* he tells of his long and desperate struggle with sensuality—how he gave up one mistress only to take another. He desired to become a Christian, and yet feared that the break with his old life would occasion more suffering than he could endure. As Michael and the devil disputed over the body of Moses, so did faith and lust, Christ and the world, dispute over the soul of Augustine. One day, in gloom and sorrow, he heard amid his tears and groanings in the garden at Milan a voice which seemed to say to him, "Take and read." He picked up his New Testament, and this is what he read: "Not in rioting and drunkenness. . . . But put ye on the Lord Jesus Christ, and make not provision for the flesh, to fulfill the lusts thereof" (Rom. 13:13-14). There and then the chains fell from him. He had put on Christ, henceforth the strength of his life, and from that day he was a new man in Christ Jesus.

—**Of George Fox**—In the year 1643 a young shoemaker's apprentice in Leicestershire, England, on business at a fair, was invited by a cousin and another friend to have a jug of beer with them. Being thirsty, he joined them. When they had drunk a glass apiece, his friends began to drink healths, agreeing that he who would not drink should pay all. This shocked the serious youth; and, rising from the table, he took out a groat and laid it before them, saying, "If it be so, I will leave you." That night he walked up and down and prayed and cried to the Lord. The Lord spoke to him, saying, "Thou seest how young people go together into vanity, and old people into the earth. Thou must forsake all—young and old—keep out of all, and be as a stranger unto all."

In obedience to this command, the young man left his relations and his home and became a wanderer in England. His name was George Fox, and he became the founder of the Quakers.

————◆◆◆————

—Of Colonel Gardiner—In a park near Prestonpans, not far from Edinburgh, there is a grave which bears the name of a Colonel James Gardiner, who fell fighting gallantly when the royal army was defeated in the Battle of Prestonpans by the Highlanders under Prince Charles Edward in 1745. His death is related in the pages of Scott's *Waverley,* and the remarkable story of his conversion and visitation is told by Philip Doddridge, the author of many of our hymns, who was his friend and preached his funeral sermon.

The son of an officer, Gardiner had followed his father in the profession of arms, and through gallantry in action and personal attractiveness he soon rose to be a colonel. On the field of battle he had many narrow escapes from death, but none of these encounters with death sobered his mind or won him from the licentious living to which he had abandoned himself. The prayers of his widowed and devout mother were apparently to go unanswered.

On a July Sabbath evening in 1719 he had been dining with a company of dissolute companions. The company broke up at eleven o'clock. At midnight he had an assignation with a married woman. As he sat in his chambers, impatiently waiting for the clock to strike the hour, he took out of his portmanteau a book which his mother had put in it when he left home. It was *The Christian Soldier, or Heaven Taken by Storm*—a strange prophecy of what was shortly to happen. As he was glancing through its pages, not heeding what he read, a sudden blaze of light seemed to fall on the book. He glanced up, supposing that some accident had befallen the candle. As he lifted his eyes he saw a visible representation of Christ on the cross, surrounded with glory. Then there came a voice which said, "Oh, sinner, did I suffer this for thee, and are these the returns?"

It is possible, as Doddridge intimates, that it was a dream. But dream or not, it makes no difference as to the moral and spiritual result. At once Gardiner knew himself to be the vilest sinner, who all his lifetime had been crucifying Christ anew by his sins. He was sure that the justice of God required that such an enormous sinner should be made an example of everlasting vengeance. Yet his keenest pangs were not from any dread of hell, but from the sense of having been so ungrateful a monster to him whom he now saw pierced for his transgressions.

Convinced of his doom, Gardiner nevertheless determined that the remainder of his life should be God-fearing and decent, and he cast himself upon the mercy of God. For months no relief came to him; but at once the corrupt fires of his nature sank and went out, leaving him with an abhorrence for the licentious sensualities to which he had been a slave all his life, and to which he had been so devoted that he had said that Omnipotence itself could not reform him without destroying his body and giving him another. But now the chains of his disgusting bondage fell from him. In the course of time the terrors of the law were supplanted by the assurance of peace and forgiveness, and the remaining years of his life were a noble and courageous witness to the Christ who had sought him and found him. As he lay dying on the fatal field of Prestonpans, he said to a Highland officer whom he saw lying near him, also fatally wounded, "You are fighting for an earthly crown; I am about to receive an heavenly."

————◆◆◆————

—Of Admiral Mahan—Admiral Mahan was the great authority on sea power and author of *The Influence of Sea Power on History*. One day during Lent he chanced to wander into a church in Boston. The preacher, whose name he never knew, in the midst of his sermon lifted up his hands and quoted from Matthew's Gospel, "Thou shalt call his name Jesus: for he shall save his people from their sins" (Matt. 1:21). "Almost the first words of the first Gospel," said Admiral Mahan. "I had seen them for years, but at last perceived them. Scales seemed to fall from my eyes, and I began to see Jesus Christ and life as I had never seen them before."

—**Of Moody**—This is a story which commenced on a bright May day in a shoe store on Court Street in Boston, not far from Boston Common, in the year 1856. Had you and I been standing outside Samuel Holton's shoe store on that morning, we would have seen a young man, Edward Kimball, teacher of a Sunday school class in the Mount Vernon Congregational Church, walking up and down before the store as if hesitating to enter. In the back of the store was a young lad nineteen years old, a country boy from Northfield, Massachusetts, who had been given employment in his uncle's shoe store on condition that he do what he was told—never go anywhere his mother would not like to find him, and attend the services and the Sunday school of Mount Vernon Church every Sunday. At length we would have seen the hesitating young man outside pluck up his courage and enter the store. If we had followed him in we would have seen him go up to Dwight L. Moody, in the rear of the building wrapping up shoes, put his hand on his shoulder, and tell him of Christ's love and the love Christ wanted in return.

It was the word spoken in season, and there in the back of the shoe store Moody gave himself to Christ.

—**In old age**—In an address delivered at the centennial celebration of the First Presbyterian Church of Pittsburgh, in 1884, Dr. William Speer told of a man, Luke Short, who died in New England at the age of 116. When over a century old, this man was converted by remembering a sermon which he had heard a century before in England on the text, "If any man love not the Lord Jesus Christ, let him be anathema" (I Cor. 16:22). As we hear today the voices of a century ago echoing within the walls of this church, let us pray that the message they bring to us shall not be without profit and inspiration.

—**Of Charles Spurgeon**—On a stormy January day in 1850 an English lad fifteen years of age started down the street to go to his regular place of worship. A storm came up, and he turned into the Primitive Methodist Chapel in Artillery Street. The regular preacher did not appear, and a man, to this day unknown, stepped into the pulpit and took his place. What happened is best told by the lad himself: "Six years ago today, as near as possible at this very hour of the day, I was in the gall of bitterness and in the bonds of iniquity, but had yet by divine grace been led to feel the bitterness of that bondage and to cry out by reason of the soreness of its slavery. Seeking rest and finding none, I stepped within the house of God and sat there afraid to look upward lest I should be utterly cut off and lest his fierce wrath should consume me. The minister rose in his pulpit, and, as I have done this morning, read this text, 'Look unto me, and be ye saved, all the ends of the earth: for I am God, and there is none else' [Isa. 45:22]. I looked that moment.

The grace of faith was vouchsafed to me in the self-same instant, and now I think I can say with truth,

> *'E'er since, by faith, I saw the stream*
> *Thy flowing wounds supply,*
> *Redeeming love has been my theme,*
> *And shall be till I die.'"*
> —WILLIAM COWPER

The lad was Charles H. Spurgeon.

—Sudden—The conversion of the jailor was sudden and dramatic. It was accompanied by an earthquake. The converted man was full of excitement, emotion, and alarm. Some great men have been converted that way.

One was Paul. Another was Luther, who, terrified by a thunderstorm as he was going through the wood to his home at Erfurt, fell on his knees and determined to give his life to God, which resolution at that time meant entering a monastery. John Newton started toward God while the ship on which he was a passenger was being tossed in a storm on the wild Atlantic. Peter Waldo, generally thought to be the first of the Waldensians, was changed from a gay man of the world to a servant of Christ when a friend seated near him at a banquet in Lyons fell dead, and Waldo asked himself, "Where would I now be if it had been I who had fallen dead?"

One of the most eloquent of Presbyterian divines of the last century left college and entered the Civil War a skeptic, proud of his unbelief. But when in battle a cannon ball annihilated his companion, who was lying face down on the earth during an artillery bombardment, his unbelief and skepticism were blown up—and he entered the ministry. Some come into the Kingdom of God by the earthquake gate.

COUNTRY—*see* FLOWERS, NATURE

COURAGE—*see also* MARKS OF CHRIST, PREACHING (COURAGEOUS)

Between St. Giles and the Parliament House you can see today a stone with "J. K." on it, marking the spot where John Knox's dust reposes. Knox was full worthy of the verdict of the Regent Morton, who, as he saw him laid in the grave, exclaimed, "There lies he who never feared the face of man!"

—Through Christ—In the first World War an officer was leading back to the front a company of British soldiers who had been on furlough. The country was war-scarred and desolate. The cold rain had fallen; the road was trampled and muddy. The men knew what they were going back to—mud and blood, and possibly death. Their shoulders sagged. None spoke or sang. Glancing through the door of a ruined church on the line of march, the officer happened to see the figure of Christ on a cross above the high altar. It came to him like a breath of courage, like a voice of assurance. Turning to his company, he gave the command, "Eyes, right! March!" The depressed and discouraged soldiers saw what he had seen, and in the suffering but triumphant Christ they found their strength. Their heads lifted, their shoulders squared, and they marched on like conquerors.

—Moral—Tertullian relates how when the Emperor Severus was distributing bounty to the troops after his victory over the Parthians a great review of the army was held, and the soldiers were asked to march by the imperial stand crowned with laurel. The Christians of that day believed it was disloyal to God to wear such a crown. There was one Christian soldier in the army more steadfast than the others, who could imagine that they could serve two masters. His head alone was uncovered as he approached the stand, and he held the useless crown in his hand. His fellow soldiers began to jeer at him and to revile him. When he was brought before the tribune, he was asked, "Why are you so different in your attire? Why do you not wear the crown like the others?" The soldier answered that he had no liberty to wear the crown like the rest. When a reason for this was demanded, he answered, "I am a Christian!"

Wellington used to speak of what he called "three o'clock in the morning" courage. What a man thinks, does, determines, when things are at their worst, makes or mars his future. Bitter disappointment, broken trust, the fading of cherished hopes, precipitate a crisis for every soul thus tried; for the soul must choose hate, bitterness, and despair—or have the courage to choose the way of forgiveness and heroic endurance.

Great scenes have been staged by those who in the hour of trial stood boldly for Christ, ever since Stephen lighted a flame that has never gone out. By the side of Stephen stands Luther in the great moment of his life. Anyone who has seen the Luther monument at Worms, representing the reformer just at the moment when he made his grand defiance of this world—"Here I stand, I cannot do otherwise"—must have been deeply impressed with the look on the uplifted face of Luther. You could say of him, as his murderers said of Stephen, that his face looks like that of an angel. In this day, when the popular tide runs away from morality and religion, there is all the greater need on the part of the followers of Christ for that courage which is born of fellowship with him, the courage which can make a man say to all the rest of the world, "Stand thou on that side, for on this am I."

—To face a beast—We have a stirring example of the courage of a man facing a beast in the great story of Rome and the early Christian Church, *Quo Vadis,* where Ursus grapples with the wild bull across whose horns is strapped the naked body of a Christian.

When I was at Princeton there was current the story of a well-known missionary in India who was bowing one night in prayer at the side of his bed when a great python lowered itself from the rafters of his bungalow and encircled his body with its cold and powerful coils. It made no attempt to constrict, and yet the missionary knew that if he struggled the great serpent would tighten the coils and crush him. With marvelous self-control, and courage born of faith, he went on quietly praying, until at length the animal unwound itself and went back into the roof.

—To face death—The annals of men of letters reveal many a tale of heroic fortitude, but none more honorable than that of Sidney Lanier. With his flute in his pocket he fought in the ranks of the Confederate army—and returned to blackened Georgia with the seeds of disease in his body. Soon after, he had his first hemorrhage; and from that day until his death in 1881 it was one long battle with sickness, but he never forgot his vision of distinction in poetry. Supported by the implicit faith of one heart that believed in his genius, he was driven by disease from state to state—Texas, Florida, Pennsylvania, Virginia, Maryland, North Carolina—between the periods of sickness stirring up and exercising the gift that was in him. It was in December, 1880, at Baltimore, when "too feeble to raise his food to his mouth, with a fever of 104 degrees, that he penciled his last and greatest poem, "Sunrise." The "thing to be done" for him was death, but even so he sang:

> But I fear not, nay, I fear not the
>   thing to be done;
> I am strong with the 'strength of
>   my lord the Sun:
> How dark, how dark soever the race
>   that must needs be run,
>   I am lit with the Sun.

—To face the mob—An example of that rare courage, the courage to face a mob undaunted, is related by Dickens in one of his greatest stories, the somber tale *Barnaby Rudge*. The locksmith, Gabriel Varden, stood before the doors of Newgate Prison during the Gordon riots of 1799. A basket of tools was put on the ground before him, and it was demanded that he pick the lock of the prison. "He had never loved his life so well as then, but nothing could move him. The savage faces that glared upon him, look where he would; the cries of those who thirsted like wild animals for his blood; the sight of men pressing forward and trampling down their fellows as they strove to reach him and struck at him above the heads of other men with axes and with iron bars—all failed to daunt him. He looked from man to man, and face to face, and still with quickened breath and lessening color, cried firmly, 'I will not!' "

—To persevere—When Christian in the battle with Apollyon was hard pressed by the black fiend—fallen to the ground, his sword had slipped from his hand; and Apollyon was lifting his weapon to dispatch him—Bunyan's hero grasped his sword again, and springing to his feet, cried out, "Rejoice not against me, O mine enemy: when I fall, I shall arise";

and with that he drove his cruel foe from the field. Human nature assumes its grandest proportion when, in the battle with sin, it reaches again for the lost sword and puts the foes to rout.

In 1825, at the height of his fame, surrounded by his family and friends, Scott was living at Abbotsford, his "romance in stone." In that year his printing house failed and left him in debt more than a hundred thousand pounds. In his diary of that period we find such entries as this: "Naked we entered the world and naked we leave it; blessed be the name of the Lord"; "I have walked my last in the domains I have planted—sat the last time in the halls I have built. But death would have taken them from me if misfortune had spared them." With splendid courage he took arms against a sea of troubles and began to write the new romances which were to clear his house of debt. Year after year he toiled on, until his health gave way under the strain, and still he continued to write until death stilled the wand of his imagination.

—In war—One of the bravest things in the Civil War was an incident that took place at the explosion of the Petersburg mine. The engineers of the army of the Potomac under General Grant had dug a gallery 510 feet long under a salient of the Confederate position, and in this gallery 300 kegs of powder were stored. The explosion was set for three o'clock in the morning, July 30, 1864. Troops, trained for the assault and ready to rush in after the explosion, lay on their arms. At three o'clock the fuse was lighted. For an hour the army waited anxiously; but nothing happened. Then two men from the Forty-Eighth Pennsylvania Regiment, recruited in the anthracite coal regions, Lieutenant Jacob

Daugherty and Sergeant Henry Reese, volunteered to enter the mine and learn the cause of the delay. They crawled in on their hands and knees and relighted the fuse, and at sixteen minutes before five the mine was exploded, blasting a huge crater in the Confederate lines. That was superb bravery, bravery not in the light, under the sun, with thousands looking on and cheering, but all alone, in the darkness of the tunnel, knowing that at any moment there was a possibility of being blown to atoms.

A colonel of the Seventh Rhode Island Regiment in the War Between the States had become very unpopular with his men. The report reached him that in the next engagement his own regiment would take occasion to shoot him. When he heard that, he gave orders for the men to march out for the cleaning of their muskets; and, taking position on top of a bank of clay and facing the regiment, he gave the order, "Ready! Aim! Fire!" Any man could have killed him without the slightest risk of discovery; but every soldier admired his superb courage, and whoever was disposed to kill him refrained.

COURTESY

Coventry Patmore says somewhere that courtesy is the only virtue that will be practiced in heaven. I wonder if that is so? Courage? No, for there will be nothing to fear there. Hope? No, for our life will leave nothing to be desired. Charity? No, for then we shall hunger no more, neither shall we thirst. Sympathy? No, for there shall be no more crying. But there will still be room for the exercise of courtesy, the kindly greeting and salutation of one soul by another.

Immanuel Kant had a saying, "Always treat a human being as a person, that is, as an end in himself, and not merely as

means to your end." The personality of ourselves we feel very intensely and are outraged when others seem to ignore that personality in us, but the personality of others we do not sense so keenly.

COVETOUSNESS—see also AVARICE, MONEY

To a man who demanded that he should compel his brother to divide with him, Jesus said: "Man, who made me a judge or a divider over you? . . . Take heed, and beware of covetousness" (Luke 12:14-15).

I thought of that saying of Jesus when a man came to see me about a woman—his sister, who was a member of my congregation—and demanded that I should use my pastoral office to compel her to divide the inheritance with him. When I declined to do so, on the same grounds which Christ took in similar circumstances, the man said as he went out, "If there is a hell, she will go there!" But when I heard those words and saw the look on his face I thought to myself, Wherever his sister may go in the next world, this man already is in hell. And what put him there was the fact that he was thinking of this world only, and that to lose everything.

CREATION—see STARS AND GOD

CREATOR

A great masterpiece of literature, which shows in a most fascinating way how many things a man can contrive and put together and how many useful articles he can manufacture, even though never trained to it, is Defoe's tale of the shipwrecked Crusoe. He made his house, his clothes; he grew and prepared his own grain for food, and slew his own meat. He arrived at length at a state of affluence and luxury which every real boy has envied, and all that was the work of one poor, untrained, shipwrecked man. But Robinson Crusoe created nothing. Without the raw material he would have died.

Christian doctrine tells a man that with all his intelligence and cunning he could not have *made* the earth on which he lives—not to speak of himself. That there is an almighty though invisible God who has made him and his world is a truth that at once commends itself to the conscience of man. There is that in man, however he may play with ideas, which says, the moment this truth is presented to him: "That is true, that is as it ought to be, as it must be. 'It is he that hath made us, and not we ourselves'" (Ps. 100:3).

CREED

Sometimes we get a little impatient or discouraged with the slow progress of our creed. Thomas Carlyle and Bishop Wilberforce were one day walking together and speaking of a mutual friend who had died.

Suddenly Carlyle said, "Bishop, have you a creed?"

"Yes, and the older I grow, the firmer that creed becomes under my feet. There is only one thing that staggers me."

"What is that?" asked Carlyle.

"The slow progress that creed seems to make in the world."

Carlyle was silent for a moment, and then said, slowly and seriously, "Ah, but if you have a creed, you can afford to wait. You have a platform upon which you can stand, and no world convulsion can shake it down."

CROSS, THE—*see also* ATONEMENT, BLOOD OF CHRIST, CHRISTIANITY, CHURCH, FORGIVENESS OF SIN, RECONCILIATION, SIN (PREACHING IT)

—Eternal—It was on a visit to Macao in 1825 that Sir John Bowring, then gov-

ernor of Hong Kong, received the inspiration to write his great hymn, "In the Cross of Christ I Glory." At Macao the early Portuguese colonists erected as one of their first buildings a massive cathedral on the crest of a hill. Three centuries ago, under the assault of a violent typhoon, the cathedral fell, all save the front wall. The cathedral has never been rebuilt, and the ponderous façade has stood for three hundred years now as a monument to the past. On top of the façade is a colossal bronze cross silhouetted against the sky, defying rain, lightning, and typhoon. It was this cross, towering o'er the wreck of the past, that inspired Bowring to write:

In the cross of Christ I glory,
Towering o'er the wrecks of time.

As long as the Church is faithful to the Cross, as long as it holds up to a dying world Christ and him crucified, it will have power and glory, and the gates of hell shall not prevail against it.

—And forgiveness—When the penitent bows at the foot of the Cross, his sin becomes a different thing. In the beautiful memorial window of the Abbey Church at Elstow, the visitor can see in the mystic colors of ecclesiastical glass Christian kneeling at the foot of the Cross, while his dark and heavy burden rolls from his shoulders. Bunyan's immortal picture is as true and brief an answer as can be given to the question, "What is the result of forgiveness?" Christian said that he "saw it no more" —the burden was gone. This will always be true. It does not mean that the memory of transgression will pass, or that its shadow will never fall across our path; but that the sting and shame and pain which constitute its burden are gone.

—And life's mystery—In Turgenev's powerful novel *Fathers and Sons,* filled with so much that is tragic and inexplicable in the tangled and stained web of human lives, Pavel Petrovitch presents the princess, who once loved him but has left him and forsaken him, with a ring, on the stone of which is engraved a sphinx. What he meant in his hour of bitter grief and disappointment was that life is an enigma, as unanswering and silent as the Sphinx to all prayers and cries and tears and entreaties. After the princess died in Paris, he received back the ring. Over the sphinx on the stone she had drawn the rude lines of the cross, and with it the words that the solution of life's mystery and enigma is the Cross, and the divine love that suffered thereon.

—The offense of—There came recently to see me a young man who is contemplating the gospel ministry. Of evangelical family and inheritance, he passed with distinction through Harvard University. In Appleton Chapel he listened to a preaching of Christianity which he recognized as totally different from, and in contradiction to, the faith in which he had been reared. After a time he withdrew from these services and worshiped in a Cambridge church, where the preaching was more in harmony with his beliefs. Yet he recognized a certain attractiveness and appeal in the nonevangelical and modernistic preaching to which he had listened in the Harvard chapel.

Now, after two years in secular pursuits, he is contemplating the ministry; and he came to ask questions that were in his mind, as he wants to be sure of the ground upon which he will stand as a minister. One of his questions was this: Why is it that modernism and liberalism, if false and anti-Christian, are so popular and appeal to so many people? The answer that I gave him was the great answer of the Apostle Paul: "The offense of the cross" (Gal. 5:11). Modernism and liberalism, however much they talk about the Cross—and that now is very little indeed—leave out its offense.

Our indebtedness to—Winston Churchill paid a great tribute to the young men of the Royal Air Force, who mounted up with wings as eagles and with their sheltering wings guarded the land they love. He said, "Never in the history of mankind have so many owed so much to so few."

But when we think of the cross of Christ, and him who died on it, what we say is this: "Never in the history of the universe has mankind owed so much to one."

—The power of—In the *Journal* of David Brainerd, the great apostle to the Indians, who died in the home of Jonathan Edwards, the editor of the *Journal,* we have this striking testimony to the practical value of the Cross: "I never got away from Jesus and him crucified, and I found that when my people were gripped by this great evangelical doctrine of Christ and him crucified, I had no need to give them instructions about morality. I found that one followed—a sure and inevitable fruit of—the other."

One day early in the eighteenth century, a German artist, Stenberg, walking through the market place of his home town, was attracted by the face of a dancing gypsy girl. He invited her to come to his studio and sit for him, and with her as a model he painted his "Dancing Gypsy Girl." The little girl was much taken with what she saw in the artist's studio, and watched him with great interest as he worked on a painting of the Crucifixion.

One day she said to Stenberg, "He must have been a very bad man to have been nailed to the cross like that."

"No," the artist said, "he was a good man. The best man that ever lived. Indeed, he died for all men."

"Did he die for you?" asked the girl. That question set the artist to thinking, for he had not yet given his heart to Christ. One day he chanced to go to a meeting of the Reformers, who opened the Scriptures to him, showed him the way of salvation, and brought him to Christ. Then he went back to finish his painting of the Crucifixion, working this time not only with an artist's skill and technique but with the love that comes of a believing heart.

When the painting was finished it was hung in the gallery at Düsseldorf. One day a young aristocratic German count, wandering through the studio, paused before Stenberg's "Crucifixion." The painting moved him greatly, as did the words written under it: "This I did for thee; what hast thou done for me?" That set the young count to thinking about what he could do for Christ. The result was the founding of that noble pietistic and missionary brotherhood, the Moravians, for the young count was none other than Nicholas Zinzendorf.

—And preaching—The great Scottish preacher Chalmers, after having been, as it were, reconverted in the midst of his ministry—when he turned away from preaching mere morality and began to preach redemption through the Cross— confessed that all his former sermons about man's moral duty had not exerted a feather's weight of influence upon the conduct of his people. It was only when he brought them by his preaching near to the Cross that he was able to note any change in their lives.

One of my elders, writing from London, told me that he had worshiped in the most conspicuous nonconformist church in the world's metropolis and the capital of Protestantism. The preacher spoke on the Crucifixion. He gave a graphic description of the death of Christ. "But," said my friend, "as for the congregation and their relation to that event, he might have been preaching on the execution of Socrates."

—A refuge—In ancient Israel six cities were founded as cities of refuge. Thither for refuge could flee men who, without malice or premeditation, had taken the life of a fellow man. Once within the gates of the city of refuge, they could not be touched by any hand of vengeance or judgment. The rabbis have an interesting tradition that once every year the roads leading to these cities of refuge were carefully repaired and cleared of obstacles and stones, so that the man fleeing for his life would have no hindrance in his way. The Cross is God's great and eternal city of refuge from the penalty upon sin.

—And Satan's kingdom—When his spoilers called for mirth in the temple of Dagon, blind Samson, groping with either arm, laid hold upon the pillars of the temple and then, bowing himself, brought the Philistines and their idols and their temples down in ruin and death. So our great Champion, with his arms spread out on the Cross, seizing with one arm the pillar of sin and with the other the pillar of death—the two gigantic pillars upon which rests the kingdom of Satan, bowed himself unto death and brought that kingdom down into irretrievable ruin.

—And suffering—The religion of Benjamin Franklin as outlined by his statements and his published creed was far different from that of the evangelical Church. Nevertheless, when Benjamin Franklin came to die he directed that a crucifix, or picture of Christ on the cross, should be so placed in his bedroom that he could look, as he said, "upon the form of the Silent Sufferer."

—Trust in—Michelangelo was an incarnation of the art and learning and wisdom of the Middle Ages. Yet when he came near to the end of his life, all his art and culture and learning meant nothing to him. He put his trust in Christ and him crucified. He tells us this in his beautiful sonnet:

> *Now hath my life across a stormy*
> *　　sea,*
> *　Like a frail bark, reached that*
> *　　wide port where all*
> *　Are hidden ere the final reckon-*
> *　　ing fall*
> *Of good and evil for eternity.*
> *Now know I well how that fond*
> *　　fantasy*
> *　Which made my soul the wor-*
> *　　shiper and thrall*

> *Of earthly art, is vain: how crim-*
> *　　inal*
> *Is that which all men seek unwit-*
> *　　tingly.*
>
> *Those amorous thoughts which were*
> *　　so lightly dressed,*
> *　What are they when a double*
> *　　death is nigh,*
> *　　The one I know for sure, the*
> *　　　other dread?*
> *Painting nor sculpture now can lull*
> *　　to rest*
> *　My soul that turns to His great*
> *　　love on High,*
> *　　Whose arms to clasp us on the*
> *　　　cross were spread.*

CYNIC

"Let the man of learning," writes Theodore Roosevelt, "the man of lettered leisure, beware of that queer and cheap temptation to pose to himself and to others as the cynic, as the man who has outgrown emotions and beliefs, the man to whom good and evil are as one. The poorest way to face life is to face it with a sneer."

D

DANGER—*see* PRAYER AND DANGER

DAVID

—Fall of—We could almost wish that David had died before he fell into sin. O David, why didst thou not die, fall thyself in battle, before that dreadful night! The glory and the splendor of thy reign are past; now comes the eclipse and the night. If thou hadst died before thy double crime, thy name would have

come down to us unstained. But now, sufferings and misfortunes await thee. Never shall the sword depart from thy house. If only thou hadst died before thine eyes beheld Bathsheba, before thou didst write the letter that murdered Uriah, thou hadst never seen incest among thine own children, Tamar dishonored and Amnon murdered, the bloody dagger of Absalom pass like a curse before thine eyes! Never wouldst thou have forsaken thy capital, to hear the curses of Shimei, nor have cried out, there on thy face in the chamber over the gate, with the tears bathing thine aged cheeks: "O my son Absalom, my son, my son Absalom! would God I had died for thee, O Absalom, my son, my son!" (II Sam. 18:33.)

—**Psalms of**—According to an old rabbinical legend the harp of David hung over his couch. The night wind playing upon the strings made such pleasing music that David arose from his bed and, all through the night, till the morning came, united words to the music. This legend embodies the idea that in the Psalms of David we have all the music of which the human heart is capable.

—**Repentance of**—Now, Angels of Heaven—ye who hanged your harps on the branches of the Tree of Life when ye heard of David's fall, and have not struck a chord or sung a single note since—now, Angels, take down your harps, for once again you can sweep their chords as you sing that greatest of all songs, the song that tells the joy of heaven over one sinner that repenteth, for David has come back to God! And David himself, with his own harp, will sing with you as he forever teaches transgressors the ways of God.

DEAD, THE—*see also* CHURCH MEMBERS (DEAD)

Reading recently some of the prayers of Samuel Johnson, I came upon the prayer which he wrote just after his wife's death. In this prayer Johnson says: "O Lord, Governor of heaven and earth, in whose hands are embodied and departed spirits, if Thou hast ordained the souls of the dead to minister to the living, and appointed my departed wife

to have care of me, grant that I may enjoy the good effects of her attention and ministration, whether exercised by appearance, impulses, dreams, or in any other manner agreeable to Thy government; forgive my presumption, enlighten my ignorance, and however meaner agents are employed, grant me the blessed influences of Thy Holy Spirit, through Jesus Christ our Lord. Amen."

What is this influence of our departed friends? Is it only our memory of them? It is certainly that—but also, perhaps, something more than that. I believe that perhaps it is a conscious ministry of influence which they exercise on our behalf.

Schumann believed that the departed Schubert and Mendelssohn knew what he was composing, and that their spirits visited him in sleep and gave him a theme which he afterward wrote down.

The most devout of Christians have felt a kindling glow of love come over them when they read from the Bible those great words: "Seeing we also are compassed about with so great a cloud of witnesses, . . . let us run with patience the race that is set before us" (Heb. 12:1). Perhaps the best interpretation would make that passage mean only that we have the example of the great and the good to inspire us in our life. But the heart, which has a theology of its own, takes comfort in thinking that the spirits of our departed friends are often near us, fully conscious of all that we do.

DEAFNESS—*see* BLINDNESS AND DEAFNESS

DEATH—*see also* GOOD LIFE AND DEATH, IMMORTALITY, SOUL AND DEATH

—**Adventure of**—In the introduction to a sermon on the future life, Canon Liddon, the noted English preacher of a generation ago, told of an India army officer who had retired from the service and had come home to spend his last days in England. One day his friends persuaded him to give an account of his life and service in India. As he related his battles and sieges, ambushes and surprises, and his experiences in the Sepoy Mutiny, they listened in breathless interest. At the conclusion he said, "I expect to see something more thrilling than anything I have seen yet . . ." His hearers were surprised at that, for they knew he was well past seventy and had retired from active service. But after a pause he added, in an understone "—the first five minutes after death!"

—**Blessing of**—Azrael, according to tradition, was the angel of death. Here is a beautiful thought concerning Azrael—that the reason he casts such a shadow upon the soul in this world is that, although his feet are planted on the earth, his head is in heaven, aureoled with the splendor of God's light. That is why he casts a shadow over men when he stoops from the unfathomed height of heaven to lift to God those whom we call dead.

—**Conquered by Christ**—An old Greek legend told of the Sphinx at Thebes, which had the body of a lion and the upper part of a woman. It lay crouched on the top of a rock on the highway and propounded to all travelers a riddle. Those who failed to solve the riddle were slain by the Sphinx. None yet had been able to answer it. But when Oedipus came to the Sphinx she asked him the question: "What creature walks in the morning upon four feet, at noon upon two, and in the evening upon three?"

Oedipus replied, "Man, who in childhood creeps on hands and knees, in manhood walks erect, and in old age goes with the aid of a staff."

The Sphinx, mortified at the solution of her riddle, cast herself down from the rock and perished.

So for ages on the highway of human life crouched the cruel sphinx of death, propounding to all travelers its unsolvable and unanswerable enigma. No one was able to answer; all perished. Death reigned. But Christ solved the riddle and overturned the sphinx from her rock. He is the First and the Last, the one who was dead and is alive forevermore. He conquers death by his own death.

—**Courage in**—Our English Bible owes more to William Tyndale than to any other man. He is the musician who plays for us in psalms and prophecies, in Gospels and Revelation. In 1535, after he had published his translation of the Bible and smuggled it into England, he was treacherously arrested and confined in the castle of Vilvorde, near Brussels, whence he was taken out and strangled and burned. Before he died he wrote: "I entreat your Lordship that by the Lord Jesus, that if I must remain here for the winter, you would beg the Commissary to be so kind as to send me, from the things of mine which he has, a warmer cap—I feel the cold painfully in my head. Also a warmer cloak, for the one I have is very thin. He has a woolen shirt of mine, if he will send it. But most of all I entreat you and implore your kindness to do your best with the Commissary to be so good as to send me my Hebrew Bible, grammar, and dictionary, that I may spend my time in that pursuit."

—**Facing**—Louis XV, King of France, foolishly ordained and ordered that death was never to be spoken of in his presence. Nothing that could in any way remind him of death was to be mentioned or displayed, and he sought to avoid every place and sign and monument which in any way suggested death. Carlyle said of him: "It is the resource of the ostrich, who, hard hunted, sticks his foolish head in the ground and would fain forget that his foolish body is not unseen too."

There is no reason why a brave and sensible man should not face all the facts of life, and one of these—the ultimate fact, so far as this world is concerned—is the fact of death. Therefore, never let death take you by surprise.

—And faith—In almost the greatest book ever written, the two pilgrims, Christian and Hopeful, received their summons and came down to the river. But when they saw how deep and wide and swift and dark its waters were, they were stunned. They met two men whose raiment shone like gold, and their faces as the light. They asked them if there was no other way to get to the gate of the Heavenly City. Were there no boats, no bridges, no fords, no ferries? But the men said, "You must go through, or you cannot come at the gate." Then they asked the men if the waters were all of a depth and they answered—and that is almost the greatest thing in that great book—"You shall find it deeper or shallower as you believe in the King of the place."

Then they addressed themselves to the water, and when they entered, Christian began to sink. He cried out to his companion, "I sink in deep waters; the billows go over my head; all his waves go over me."

But Hopeful answered, "Be of good cheer, my brother: I feel the bottom, and it is good."

And with that Christian broke out with a loud voice, "Oh, I see him again; and he tells me, 'When thou passest through the waters, I will be with thee; and through the rivers, they shall not overflow thee.'"

Then they both took courage, and the enemy was after that as still as a stone until they were gone over.

In his *Newcomes* there is a splendid passage in which Thackeray describes the death of old Colonel Newcome. Just before his passing, at the usual evening hour the chapel bell of the school near by began to toll. The old colonel's hands, outside the bed covers, feebly beat time. Just as the last bell struck a sweet smile lighted up his face; and, lifting his head a little, he said, *"Adsum,"* and fell back. That was the Latin phrase for "present," which the boys had used when their names were called at school. Now the old colonel, his heart again that of a little child, had answered to his name as he stood in the presence of the Master.

So when life's day is over and our name is called, may we answer "Present," as we stand in confidence and faith before our Judge, who is also that one who loved us and gave himself for us?

—Fear of—As Bacon put it in his celebrated essay, "Men fear death as children fear to go in the dark." My own experience at many deathbeds has been to the effect that death is its own anesthetist and banishes fear in the minds of the dying. But because so many dread that last experience in life, it will be always true that cowards die many times. The Christian should be the last of all men to fear death.

—Of the first-born—The hour of midnight approached; and as it drew nigh, on every swart countenance there was a look of wonder and anticipation, from the octogenarian leaning on his staff to the little child in his mother's arms. Then at length it came—what they had been waiting for! Suddenly there arose a great cry—a long wail of woe, a tidal wave of lamentation that swept over the whole land. In his porphyry palace Pharaoh awoke with a sense of dread and called for his prince, only to learn that the prince of the realm, his first-born, was dead. Parents stirred uneasily, and anxiously called for their stalwart sons, only to find them cold in death. Mothers awoke in terror to find that the babes they clasped to their breasts were nothing but corpses. In the dungeon the prisoner shook his chains and turned over to find that his son at his side was dead. In the temples of Isis and Osiris the priests called in vain upon the gods to restore their dead offspring. And even the cattle in the fields moaned over their dead; for that night the angel of the Lord smote the first-born of Egypt, "from the first-born of Pharaoh that sat on his throne unto the first-born of the captive that was in the dungeon; and all the first-born of cattle." (Exod. 12:29.) Death reigned! Death! Death! Death! Death in the palace! Death in the cottage! Death in the temple! Death in the dungeon! Death on the river! Death on the highway! Death in the fields! Death! Death! Death! And everywhere a moan of anguish went up to Egypt's skies.

— — —

—Of the good—There was great sorrow in England at the death of Prince William, the only son of Henry IV—the atheling, as the English fondly styled the child of their beloved Queen Matilda. Returning from Normandy to England, the prince with a number of nobles took passage in the *White Ship,* which lingered behind the rest of the royal fleet. When the vessel finally swept out to sea, it struck a rock at the mouth of the harbor and went down with all hands, leaving behind it only a terrible cry echoing through the royal fleet. When the news reached the king, his father, he fell unconscious to the ground—and rose never to smile again. All England, too, shared his grief over the popular prince.

In ancient Israel all ranks and classes mourned for Abijah. Children were held up in the arms of their parents and told to imitate his life as his funeral cortege went by. In many a home there was sorrow as if for a child of their own. He had been so good and true and kind that when death struck him it was not to destroy him but only to spread abroad a fragrant memory of his beautiful character.

— — —

—Inevitable—What is the inevitable word? What is the word that to each man seems unnatural when applied to himself but natural when applied to others? What is the word that God never intended man to pronounce? What is the word that man began to speak only after he had pronounced the saddest word? What is the word that reduces all men to the same rank? What is the word that strips Dives of his millions and Lazarus of his rags? What is the word that cools avarice and stills the fires of passion? What is the word that men struggle not to pronounce, and yet all must pronounce—the prince and the peasant, the fool and the philosopher, the murderer and the saint? What is the word that none is too young to lisp and none too old or too weary to whisper? What is the word that frustrates ambition and disappoints hope—and yet has the power to solve all problems and heal all wounds of life? What is the word that men one day shrink from, and yet on another day, and in different circumstances, desire and seek after more than hid treasure? What is the word that men fear, and yet the word which, if men will listen to its voice, can teach them the meaning of all other words in life? That word is *"Death." "It is ap-*

pointed unto men once to die." (Heb. 9:27.)

———————

One of the stories told of Buddha treats of the shock and amazement with which men first look on death. The only child of the young mother Kisagotami was dead. The mother clasped the child to her breast and went about from house to house, seeking medicine that would cure him. Finally a Buddhist convert told her that Buddha might tell her of a medicine that would restore the child. When she approached the sage he told her he could cure the child, but that she must bring to him mustard seed secured from some house where no parent or husband or son or slave had ever died. Eagerly and hopefully she set out to get the mustard seed. But at each house, after she had been given the mustard seed and had asked if any had died there, the reply was always the same: "Lady! what is this that you say? The living are few, but the dead are many." At length she began to understand that all must die; and, leaving her child in the wood, she returned to the sage and, bowing to the impermanence of all things, entered the life of contemplation.

———————

Under the great dome of the Church of the Escorial, in Spain, is the high altar, with the kneeling figures of Charles V and his wives. There you look through the opening through which the dying Philip could glance with glazing eye toward the altar and the kneeling effigy of his great father. For fifty days he who had visited so much suffering upon men for conscience' sake lay dying in a little cell, suffering a living hell from the pains of a revolting disease, yet bearing it all with patience, fortitude, and Catholic faith. To his son and heir he wrote at this time: "I should have wished to save you this trial; but I

want you to see how the monarchies of this earth end. Behold! God has stripped me of all the glory and majesty of sovereignty, that they may pass to you. In a few hours I shall be covered only with a poor shroud and girded only with a coarse rope. The kingly crown has already fallen from my brow, and death will soon set it upon yours. The crown will fall from your head one day as it now falls from mine. You are young, as I have been. My day draws to a close; the tale of your life God alone can see, but it must end like mine."

———————

Visiting once the Pennsylvania cemetery where President Buchanan is buried, I saw on a grave this inscription (by Felicia Hemans):

Leaves have their time to fall,
And flowers to wither at the North
    wind's breath,
    And stars to set; but all,
Thou hast all seasons for thine own,
    O Death!

After we have learned the whole vocabulary of life, each one of us at length, at the appointed hour, must learn to pronounce the last and inevitable word, which is "death."

———————

—Loneliness of—She was a friend in the church who passed over the river last summer. A few days before she received her summons she said to her daughter, "You know I have been thinking about a text that I heard my minister preach on in Scotland when I was a girl."

"And what was it, mother?" asked the daughter.

"It was something about horses and the swelling of the Jordan. Yes, that's it! 'If thou hast run with the footmen, and they have wearied thee, then how canst thou contend with horses? and if in the land of peace, wherein thou trustedst, they wearied thee, then how wilt thou do in the swelling of Jordan?'" (Jer. 12:5).

"What a strange text!" said the daughter. "What could the minister ever get out of that text?"

"What could the minister get out of that text?" said the mother in her soft Scottish voice. "What could he get out of it but this—that when we take our friend, our father, mother, or little child, down to the river, that is as far as we can go with them. And when we ourselves go down, that is as far as they can go with us. Then it is you and your Saviour for it!"

———•••———

—And the materialist—In his autobiographical sketch one of the most notable of American writers, W. H. Hudson, author of *Green Mansions* and *Days in Patagonia,* tells of an incident of his early life in South America. The family dog Caesar had died and been lowered into a grave dug for him. The schoolmaster looked around on the boys assembled at the grave and said solemnly: "That's the end. Every dog has its day, and so has every man, and the end is the same for both. We die like old Caesar and are put into the ground and have the earth shoveled over us."

That is the materialist's view of death.

———•••———

—Mystery of—The last enemy, the final riddle, is death and the after death. In the Highland churchyards they used to play the plaintive ballad "The Flowers of the Forest":

*I have seen the smiling of fortune's
     beguiling,
I have felt of its favors and found
     its decay,
Sweet was its blessing and kind its
     caressing,*

*But now 'tis all fled, 'tis fled far
     away.*

*I have seen the forest adorned the
     foremost
With flowers of the fairest, most
     pleasant and gay.
Sae bonnie was their blooming, their
     scent the air perfuming,
But now they are withered and a'
     wede away.*

Yes, we know life's smiling, and then the smile passes. Life has much that is delightful and lovely, but it passes. Life is like an autumn scene, as you see it in the landscapes of Inness, rich and beautiful, but with the shadow of brevity falling over it—too beautiful to last. What about tomorrow? Science, knowledge, knows nothing of tomorrow. Its territory is yesterday. Pleasure knows nothing of tomorrow. Its territory is today. But tomorrow, what of that? The mind can state its reasons and fortify itself in a belief in life to come; and the heart, which hath reasons of its own, can put forth its hope; but man dieth and lieth down and giveth up the ghost, and where is he? Who shall tell the secret?

———•••———

After the wreck of his fortune and reputation, Aaron Burr still retained his most cherished joy and possession—his beautiful and accomplished daughter, Theodosia. In 1813 this daughter, who was the wife of Governor Alston of South Carolina, embarked at Charleston on a pilot ship sailing for New York. The ship never came to port, nor was it ever heard of again. Had we been in the vicinity of the Battery on almost any day in the years which followed the disappearance of the vessel, we might have seen a man—old and broken, but bearing still the unmistakable mark of distinction of mind—walk slowly down upon the Battery and stand for a long time gazing wistfully down the harbor at the incoming vessels, as if still "cherishing the faint, fond hope that his Theodosia was coming to him from the other side of the world."

So do the bereaved look out toward that ocean of mystery which has swallowed up their beloved, and wonder if no voice, no message, no form, though shadowy and but for a moment, will come to break the long, long silence and to comfort and assure their troubled hearts.

One of the finest passages in English poetry are the lines in Byron's "Cain" where he describes Cain standing over the body of the murdered Abel, astonished at death, then new in the world and now so old. The old, old fashion— and yet something which comes with new wonder and shock to the men of each new generation. Death in some other city, or in some other house down the street, is one thing; but when death invades our own house and family we are forced to look on it with the same awe and surprise and wonder which Byron so splendidly imagines in the mind of Cain.

—Ready for—On November 20, 1847, there died at Nice, France, a retired and long-time-ill Church of England curate, Henry Frances Lyte, who had worn himself out in charitable labors in the slums of London. At his death his family found the almost illegible manuscript of a poem he had written during those last days, now a hymn which has sung itself around the world. It was this:

> *Abide with me: fast falls the eventide;*
> *The darkness deepens; Lord, with me abide!*

> *When other helpers fail, and comforts flee,*
> *Help of the helpless, O abide with me.*

There was a man whose faith in Christ enabled him to get the best of death, and the hymn which he left behind has helped multitudes of other souls to gain that great victory.

Those who visit the chapel at Washington and Lee University, where the great Confederate captain lies buried, are conducted to his study. There everything is just as he left it when he went out of that office for the last time.

How are things in the office and study of your life? Is everything just as you would wish to leave it—leave it never to be changed?

As I look out over this vast congregation, I wonder just where and how death will come for you and for me. But somewhere, sometime, it must be—that last experience, that final scene. For some, the familiar chamber in the home; for others, a hotel room in a strange land; for another, a room or ward in the hospital; for some of the young men here today, perhaps—although we pray God to avert it—a field of battle; but *somewhere* each of us must go through this final experience of Christ, when our spirit shall bid farewell to this world and to this life. And when that hour comes, may you, because your trust is in the finished work of Christ, have the peace and calm and assurance of Christ, who said, "Father, into thy hands I commend my spirit" (Luke 23:46), and bowed his head and gave up the ghost.

The hour of death is appointed. It is written in God's book. We need not concern ourselves about that. Our duty s to live the right life and to put our faith in Christ. After the Battle of Bull Run, Imboden asked Stonewall Jackson, who had received a painful wound in the battle, "General, how is it that you can keep so cool and appear so utterly insensible to danger in such a storm of shell and bullets as rained about you when your hand was hit?"

"Captain," answered Jackson in a grave and reverential manner, "my religious belief teaches me to feel as safe in battle as in bed. God has fixed the time for my death. I do not concern myself about that, but to be always ready no matter when it may overtake me." Then, after a pause, he added, "That is the way all men should live, and then all would be equally brave."

On a dark afternoon in September, 1583, in a stormy sea near the Azores, the *Golden Hind,* commanded by Sir Walter Raleigh, sailed close to the *Squirrel,* a smaller vessel commanded by Sir Humphrey Gilbert. The captain of the *Golden Hind* cried out to Gilbert, who was sitting in the stern of his vessel with a book open in his hand, and urged him for his safety to come aboard the larger vessel. This Gilbert refused to do, saying he would not leave his companions in the *Squirrel.* Then Raleigh heard him call out over the waves, "Heaven is as near by sea as by land." At midnight that night those on the *Golden Hind* saw the lights on the smaller vessel suddenly go out, and in that moment Gilbert and his ship were swallowed up by the dark and raging sea.

Heaven is as near by sea as by land! That is a true Christian sentiment. That is what Paul meant in that great sentence of his, "Whether we live or whether we die, we are the Lord's." Live in that faith, and fear will no longer have dominion over you. And this will be the victory that overcometh the world, even your faith.

———————

—Sudden—One of the many dramatic incidents in the tragedy of the Ides of March was the dream of Calpurnia, Caesar's wife. Before and on the day of his assassination there were many events to warn Caesar of his fate. As Plutarch puts it in his sketch of Caesar, "Fate, however, is to all appearance more unavoidable than unexpected." When Caesar was signing some letters the day before his death, a question arose among his friends as to what sort of death was the best. Before anyone could speak, Caesar answered, "A sudden one!"

DECEIT—*see* SIN (DECEIT OF), WORLD (ITS DECEIT)

DECISION—*see also* CHOICE, OPPORTUNITY

An officer once came to Grant's headquarters and called his attention to the vast expenditure of money involved in an order he had given, and asked him if he was sure he was right. "No," said Grant, "I am not; but in war anything is better than indecision. We must decide. If I am wrong, we shall soon find it out, and can do the other thing. But not to decide wastes both time and money, and may ruin everything." Quick and powerful decision has been the gateway to success in every field of life. One of the secrets of Napoleon's great success as a military leader was the quick and firm, and sometimes terrible, decision which marked his early campaigns. But in the last chapter of his life Napoleon showed great indecision and vacillation, and in contrast with the decisiveness of his early career was often unable to bring himself to the timely decision. The campaign of Waterloo showed that. Men who hesitate and linger are left behind by the men who have decided and who bind what shall be to their will. Life is not a playground, but an arena where we must decide.

In the early days of his struggle toward the truth, Augustine made a prayer, "Lord, save me from my sins, but not quite yet." Then sometime after that he prayed, "Lord, save me from all my sins, except one." And then came the final prayer, "Lord, save me from all my sins, and save me *now!*" It was when he made that final decision against evil that the victory was his. There is no joy and strength and, for that matter, no peace, like that which visits the soul which has taken an unconquerable resolve against that which is evil.

Lincoln used to tell the story of a man who heated a piece of iron in the forge, not knowing just what he was going to make out of it. At first he thought he would make a horseshoe; then he changed his mind and thought he would make something else out of it. After he had hammered on this plan for a little while, he changed his mind and started on something else. By this time, he had so hammered the iron that it was not good for much of anything; and, holding it up with his tongs and looking at it in disgust, the blacksmith thrust it hissing into a tub of water. "Well, at least I can make a fizzle out of it!" he exclaimed.

It is better to concentrate on one thing than to dream about a hundred things. How often in old age is heard the echo of this sigh coming from the lips of men who have made no mark for themselves, "If I had only followed one thing!"

—For Christ—On Sunday night, October 8, 1871, D. L. Moody preached to the largest congregation that he had ye addressed in Chicago. His text wa "What shall I do then with Jesus whicl is called Christ?" (Matt. 27:22.) At th close of the sermon he said, "I wish yo would take this text home with you an turn it over in your minds during th week, and next Sabbath we will come t Calvary and the Cross, and we will de cide what to do with Jesus of Nazareth. Then Sankey began to sing the hymn,

> *To-day the Saviour calls;*
> *For refuge fly;*
> *The storm of justice falls,*
> *And death is nigh.*

But the hymn was never finished, fc while Sankey was singing there was th rush and roar of fire engines on th street outside, and before morning Ch cago lay in ashes. Moody to his dying da was full of regret that he had told th congregation to come *next* Sabbath an decide what to do with Jesus. "I hav never since dared," he said, "to give a audience a week to think of their salv tion. If they were lost they might rise u in judgment against me. I have neve seen that congregation since. I will neve meet those people until I meet them i another world. But I want to tell you one lesson that I learned that nigl which I have never forgotten, and th is, when I preach to press Christ upo the people then and there and try bring them to a decision on the spot. would rather have that right hand cut o than to give an audience a week no to decide what to do with Jesus."

When Antiochus of Syria invade Egypt, the Romans sent a herald, Por pilius, to order him to withdraw. Whe Pompilius delivered the message, Ant ochus read it and said, "I will consid the matter and answer soon. The hera then took his wand, the symbol of his office, and, marking a circle around Antiochus, said to him, "Consider and answer before you step out of this circle."

Would that the preacher could do that—draw a circle around the soul that has not yet decided for Christ and say to it, "Decide; give your answer before you step out of this circle!"

———•◆•———

Lying ill once in a New York hotel, I chanced to hear through the air these words of Moses spoken by a Portuguese rabbi: "Therefore choose life!" Coming suddenly in upon me out of the invisible places and the silence of the night, these words seemed unspeakably solemn and arresting. Life and death set before man, the voice of the prophet ages ago, and the voice of the preacher of today, calling upon men to choose life rather than death! So today I fling out this great text: "I call heaven and earth to record this day against you, that I have set before you life and death, blessing and cursing: therefore choose life" (Deut. 30:19).

DEEDS, GOOD—*see also* DOING GOOD, SAMARITAN (GOOD)

Over the door to the operating theater of one of the Philadelphia hospitals I used to read these words: "Think not the beautiful doings of thy soul shall perish unremembered. They abide with thee forever, and alone the good thou doest nobly, truth and love approve. Each pure and gentle deed of mercy brings an honest recompense, and from it looms that sovereign knowledge of thy duty done, a joy beyond all dignities of earth."

———•◆•———

Ecclesiastes 11:1 says, "Cast thy bread upon the waters: for thou shalt find it after many days." The Moslems have a proverb which is probably a comment on this verse: "Strew thy bread upon the surface of the water and on the dry land, and thou shalt find it in the end of days."

The caliph of Bagdad had a son who was drowned while bathing in the river. He offered a large reward to anyone who should recover the boy's body. After seven days a bather discovered the boy alive in a cavern in a precipitous mountain past which the river flowed. The caliph learned that the boy had been kept from starvation by cakes of bread floating on the water, on which cakes were stamped the name of a Moslem of Bagdad. The caliph summoned the Moslem and asked him what had induced him to throw bread into the water. He replied that he had done so every day for a year in order to test the truth of the proverb. The caliph thereupon rewarded him with five villages in the vicinity of Bagdad. The legend, which has all the elements of possibility in it, reiterates the truth of the proverb that deeds done unselfishly for others not only do good to the one for whom they are done but return in blessings upon the head of the doer.

———•◆•———

Kipling has a powerful poem called "Tomlinson." Tomlinson is summoned from his house in Berkeley Square and conducted by a spirit far down the Milky Way till they come to a gate in the wall, to which Peter holds the key. Peter says to Tomlinson, Stand up and answer loud and high

The good that ye did for the sake of
    men or ever ye came to die—
The good that ye did for the sake of
    men in little earth so lone!

When he hears that, the naked soul of Tomlinson grows "white as a rainwashed bone." He mentions a priest who has been his friend on earth and would answer for him if he stood by his side. But Peter tells him that he must answer for himself—that "the race is run by one and one and never by two and two." Then Tomlinson speaks of what he has read in a book—of what some man in Russia thinks—of what his own opinion or guess is. But Peter tells him that it's not what he's read, or heard, or thought, but what he has *done*—the good deeds he has done. Rejected at the gate of Heaven, Tomlinson is conducted to Hell Mouth Gate, where he is likewise rejected because they are not able to discover after the trial by fire that he has a soul in him at all. The devil sends him to the earth with the prayer that the God he took from the printed book may be with him.

DEITY—*see* CHRIST (DEITY OF)

DELAY

In one of the battles of the Civil War an officer rode up to his superior, General Longstreet, and said that he was not able to obey the order that had been given him to bring his men up to the line of battle.

"Very well," answered Longstreet with withering irony, "never mind. Just let them stay where they are. The enemy is going to advance, and that will spare you the trouble."

If you delay to make war against evil, remember that Satan does not.

DEMOCRACY—*see also* HOPE AND DEMOCRACY

"The question of the permanence of democracy resolves itself into the question of whether mankind is growing in wisdom and virtue, and with that comes the question of what religion will be in the future. Governments that have ruled by force and fear have been able to live without moral sanctions, or to make their subjects believe that those sanctions consecrated them. But no free government has ever yet so lived and thriven, for it is by a reverence of the powers unseen and eternal which impose those sanctions that the powers of evil, however imperfectly, have been kept at bay, and the fabric of society held together." [1]

DEMONS

It is said today that there is no such thing as a demon—and probably never was. The people in the time of Jesus—in their ignorance—thought an insane man was possessed of the devil, possessed by demons.

Yet I am not so sure that they were not right. When I read the morning paper and see what men and women, made in the image of God, have done, I am not certain that people today are not possessed of the devil. When I see what men do under the bondage of drink and lust, and hatred, and anger, and jealousy, I am not at all certain that the evil spirits no longer take hold of a man's soul.

———•◦•———

—**And Christ**—When Legion, the once wild Gadarene, arrives, it is like a city of the dead. But his daughter, looking out of the window, says to her mother, "It is Father! But he has his clothes on, and his face is not covered with blood, and there are no broken fetters on his arms and legs. Instead of leaping over the ditches and the dykes, he is coming down the pathway." The mother looks, too, and when Legion arrives before his home the mother and the children open the door and rush out and greet their father. Quickly the word is passed up

[1] James Bryce, *Modern Democracies* (new ed.; New York: Macmillan Co., 1921), Vol. II, p. 606.

the street, and one by one the doors and windows open and the people gather about Legion as he stands there in front of his house in the midst of his family, clothed and in his right mind. They listen to him as, ordained by the Son of God himself, he tells them the old, old story—of redeeming love, what great things Christ had done for him, and how he had compassion upon him.

Memory paints vivid pictures on the tablets of the mind. Here is one of them: Four boys on a camping expedition—up one river and then another. Supper by the campfire in a lonely ravine. At midnight a terrific thunderstorm. The boys take refuge from the storm in the haymow of a farmer's barn. Lying on the hay, safe now from the pouring rain, they hear—when the thunder is not speaking—loud, wild cries of a human voice. All through the night they hear that terrible shouting. In the morning, when they come down from the haymow, they learn the reason. The farmer's father is insane, a maniac; and he is locked up, like a dangerous bull or other animal, in one of the outbuildings of the farm. Still the cries of that man echo in the memory of one of those boys. . . . There were two storms that night: the storm of nature, the thunderstorm; and the storm of human nature, the storm of insanity in that poor man's mind and body.

Likewise there are two storms in the great story of Jesus' interview with a man who wore chains. First of all, the storm at sea, when Jesus and the disciples were crossing over and they awakened him, thinking they were going to perish. And Jesus rebuked the wind and said to the sea, "Peace, be still." Then, after that storm and the quelling of the tempest, came the storm in a man's soul, and the stilling of that tempest by the love and power of the Son of God.

DENIAL—*see* PETER'S DENIAL

DEPRESSION—*see also* DISAPPOINTMENT, DISCOURAGEMENT, OUTLOOK ON LIFE

Elijah was a man of like passions with us. The lark which had sung her song at the very gate of heaven sinks at last, wearied and voiceless, into the brown furrow. The height of the crest of one wave measures the depth of the trough of the next.

The devil was once informed by an angel that God was going to take away from him all but one of the temptations with which he tempted men.

"Which one is that?" asked Satan.

"Depression," said the angel.

At that Satan laughed and said, "Good! In this one gift I have secured all."

In time of discouragement it is well to remember others. A Friends minister of the eighteenth century, Luke Cock, very much depressed by his own spiritual life, was told by the devil that there was never another minister in such a state of mind as he. After this, Cock went to visit his friend and colleague John Richardson, a noted minister. When he asked him how he was, Richardson replied, "As to the body very well; as to the pocket, very comfortable; but if thou mean as to best things, I was never worse." At that Cock threw up his hat and shouted, "The devil is a liar, and I was a fool to believe him," and rode home rejoicing.

DETERMINATION—*see also* CHANCE AND DETERMINATION

In *Pilgrim's Progress,* the Interpreter conducted Christian to where he beheld a stately palace on the top of which were walking certain persons clothed all in gold. Around the door stood a great company of men desirous to go in, but who dared not. A little distance from the door, at a table, sat a man with a book and an inkhorn to take the name of him that would enter into the palace. In the doorway stood many men in armor to keep it, being resolved to do what hurt and mischief they could to anyone who tried to enter. All were starting back in fear, and Christian himself was in a maze, when he saw a man of stout countenance go up to him with the inkhorn and say, " 'Set down my name, sir'; the which when he had done, he saw the man draw his sword, and put a helmet on his head, and rush towards the door upon the armed men." After receiving and giving many wounds, he cut his way into the palace; and voices were heard of those who walked in gold raiment on top of the palace, saying,

"Come in, come in,
Eternal glory thou shalt win."

It is not enough merely to *wish* to go in. It is not enough to have the man with the inkhorn set your name down as an applicant. You must *fight* your way through.

DEVIL—*see* SATAN

DISAPPOINTMENT—*see also* ADVERSITY, DEPRESSION, DISCOURAGEMENT

I remember a visit I once paid to the coast of Devon and Cornwall. The land breaks off abruptly at the sea, and grim granite walls and huge boulders mark the dividing line between the dominions of earth and sea. Against those iron cliffs the waves of the Atlantic Ocean, rolling straight in from Labrador, hurl themselves with thunderous reverberation. At almost any place along that coast you can find pieces of broken ships that have been wrecked there. In the churchyards

under the gray towers there are never wanting the graves of seamen whose bodies have been washed up on the shore when the sea gave up her dead. Here and there the artistic figurehead of a gallant ship stands as a gravestone for the members of her crew.

So the shores of humanity are strewn with the wreckage of all kinds of ships —all kinds of hopes, desires, and ambitions. "They went not; for the ships were broken at Ezion-geber." (I Kings 22:48.) This is a fact of life with which religion must deal. You cannot ignore the broken ship, the wrecked argosy, the breakdowns and failures and disappointments of life.

• • •

At Ezion-geber, on the Red Sea, the two kings built their ships. At length all was ready. The kings, no doubt, were present to see the fleet sail. With a sound of trumpets, a flourish of banners, and the benediction of royalty, the anchors were hoisted, the sails set; and with a favoring wind the armada sailed out of Ezion-geber down the Red Sea, bound for far-off Ophir. But the ships went not. The storm arose and drove them on the treacherous rocks of the Red Sea. When the next morning dawned, the proud armada lay scattered on the rocks, a tangled mass of tinder and cordage; and those who had sailed on the ships were buried in the deep. That was the end of Jehoshaphat's expedition for gold. "They went not; for the ships were broken at Ezion-geber." (I Kings 22:48.)

That saying is the epitaph for many a hope and dream and ambition. It is the final sentence in many a story of the soul's adventure. The keels were laid, the ships were built, the seas were charted, the anchors hoisted, the sails set. But the ships went not. Expeditions of the head and of the heart, some for gold and gain, some for fame and power, and some for knowledge, some for the good of man, and some for love; but they never reached their goal. The ships went not.

------◆◆◆------

When the Confederate army under Hood was confronting Thomas at Nashville, Grant sent repeated orders to Thomas to go out and give battle. Thomas was willing to fight, but not until his army was ready. The administration became alarmed and Grant dispatched Logan to relieve Thomas, and finally started himself. But before either he or Logan could reach Nashville, Thomas and his army had won the most complete and crushing victory of the Civil War. Sherman, writing of the incident, says of Thomas, and the tragedy that almost befell him—to end his great military career by being cashiered—"He acted in time, gained a magnificent victory, and thus escaped so terrible a fate." That was the fate of Moses—to be removed just at the gates of victory.

Lord Kitchener for two years silently bore the burden of preparing Britain's armies, but just when those armies were about to launch their great offensive and strike mortal blows to the foe, ere the nation could thank him, the man who raised the hosts went down to his death off the lone Orkneys.

When Blake was coming home from victory on the seas, he prayed that he might live until he reached England; but just before the ship reached Plymouth harbor he expired.

------◆◆◆------

Charles Sumner, great senator from Massachusetts and eloquent pleader for the slaves and for the Union, drank a bitter cup of sorrow and disappointment in his domestic life. When he was struck with death, there lay on his table a volume of Shakespeare, this passage in *King Henry VI,* probably the last lines upon which his eyes ever gazed, marked with his own hand:

Would I were dead! if God's good will were so;
For what is in this world but grief and woe?

------◆◆◆------

—**Blessings of**—In a churchyard at Brighton, England, there is a garden plot which the workingmen of Brighton keep free of weeds and fresh with flowers. In the center of the plot is a monument to Frederick Robertson. His father served in the British army during the American war. His boyhood days were spent playing about the forts at Leith. By temperament and heredity he desired to be an officer in the British army. His name was on the commander in chief's list, but for some reason he was not granted a commission. He then matriculated at Oxford, and at lenth was ordained to the ministry. The boy's hopes were disappointed; but the whole Christian world rejoices today that the door into the army was closed, and that he became instead a good soldier of Jesus Christ and the great preacher who spoke to all classes, from professors to workingmen. Today the common people, who heard him gladly, make it always summertime about his grave.

------◆◆◆------

God disappoints us and baffles us sometimes in order to make us succeed. If Phillips Brooks had succeeded as a schoolmaster, he would never have stood in the pulpit to move men with his mighty ministry. If Frederick Robertson had got his commission in the British army, he would never have written the sermons which still throb with his great and yearning spirit. If Hawthorne had been retained at the custom house, he never would have written those wonderful studies in the deep places of human sorrow and love and sin.

————◆◆◆————

No author ever wrote of the family joys and sorrows and affections in such a tender manner, ever struck the lyre of domestic affections with such winning touch, as did Charles Dickens. Perhaps the fact that his own home was a desert had something to do with that magnificent expression of family hopes and joys and sorrows.

There may be gold for others in our own disappointments.

————◆◆◆————

Here is Paul on his second missionary journey. With his ever-burning zeal and immense energy, he is on his way first of all to Ephesus, the great city in that part of the world. What a place Paul thought to preach the gospel in—under the very shadow of the temple of Diana to proclaim the glories of the temple not made with hands! But the Holy Spirit forbade him to preach there. Then he turned northward to go into Bithynia, where along the Black Sea were great and populous cities. No doubt Paul was greatly discouraged and perplexed at the barriers which were flung up in front of him, and wondered at the detour which took him down through Mysia to Troas. But there he learned the reason, for it was there the man from Macedonia appeared and besought him to cross over to Europe and help them. Had he gone to Ephesus alone, or had he been permitted to go into the remote North along the Black Sea, Athens, Corinth, and Rome might not have heard the accents of the gospel from his prognostic lips.

————◆◆◆————

When James Buchanan, afterward president of the United States, was a student at Dickinson College, he suffered keen disappointment as to some college honor or prize. At that time his father wrote him a letter, in which was this fine passage: "Often when people have the greatest prospects of temporal honor and aggrandizement they are all blasted in a moment by a fatality connected with men and things, and no doubt the designs of providence may be seen very conspicuously in our disappointments in order to teach us our dependency on Him who knows all events, and they ought to humble our pride and self-sufficiency."

————◆◆◆————

One has well said: "Disappointment is like a sieve. Through its coarse meshes small ambitions and hopes and endeavors of the soul are sifted out relentlessly. But the things that are big enough not to fall through are not in the least affected by it. It is only a test, not a finality." The big things—faith, hope, love, courage in our own troubles, kindness in the troubles of others—disappointment cannot hurt; on the contrary, it discovers new charm and beauty and power in them.

————◆◆◆————

Jean François Millet, whose canvases present the almost perfect story of French peasant life, depicted in "The Reapers," "The Angelus," "Shepherds and Flock," and "Man with the Hoe," made his first appearance in the world of art with his "Oedipus Unbound." Before that he had presented at the salon "St. Jerome" in 1845. This picture was rejected. Millet was so poor he could not afford to buy more canvas for a new picture, and thus it was over the rejected canvas of "St. Jerome" that he painted his first successful picture, "Oedipus Unbound." Disappointment and failure served only to spur him to greater things.

DISCIPLINE—*see* HOME TRAINING, CHILDREN (TRAINING OF)

DISCOURAGEMENT—*see also* DEPRESSION, DISAPPOINTMENT

The devil, according to legend, once advertised his tools for sale at public auction. When the prospective buyers assembled, there was one oddly shaped tool which was labeled "Not for sale." Asked to explain why this was, the devil answered, "I can spare my other tools, but I cannot spare this one. It is the most useful implement that I have. It is called Discouragement, and with it I can work my way into hearts otherwise inaccessible. When I get this tool into a man's heart, the way is open to plant anything there I may desire."

The legend embodies sober truth. Discouragement is a dangerous state of mind, because it leaves one open to the assault of the enemies of the soul.

Leafing through a book in my library recently—*The Life of William Cowper,* by Goldwyn Smith—I came upon these lines which I had marked when the book was first read: "Let those whom despondency assails read this passage of Cowper's life and remember that he lived to write 'John Gilpin' and 'The Task.'"

Then I turned back to read the passage referred to. It was the story of Cowper's early discouragements and disappointments. He had received an appointment to a clerkship in the House of Lords, but as soon as he received the appointment he began to conjure up visions of the terrors of an examination and of hostility to him in the office where he had to study the *Journal,* until his mind was deranged. First, he tried to take his life with laudanum; then he resolved to fly to France, change his religion and bury himself in a monastery; then he turned again to self-destruction and, taking a coach, ordered the coachman to drive him to the Thames, intending to throw himself into the river. But once again he drew back. On the night before the day appointed for the examination before the Lords he lay for some time with the point of his penknife pressed against his heart, but could not bring himself to thrust the knife home. Then he tried to hang himself, but the rope by which he was suspended broke. Such is the history of the man who lived to write "John Gilpin" and "The Task"—and what is more than that, to live to write "God Moves in a Mysterious Way His Wonders to Perform."

Napoleon used to say of his famous marshal, Massena, that he had a remarkable reserve strength and that he was never himself till the tide of battle began to turn against him. He took new life from what to many would bring discouragement.

An old man with a bundle of sticks on his back sank down by the roadside and with a groan said he wished that he were dead. To his surprise and terror Death at once made his appearance and asked him what he would have. The old man said quickly, "My bundle on my back and my feet once more on the road." In his discouragement what he asked for was not really what he desired. That is true of many of our wishes in the hour of discouragement.

In the lives of the great men who have toiled for the true and lasting greatness of righteousness in themselves and in their fellows, we hear very often a note of defeat and failure. "The characteristic of waning life," writes Dean Farrar, "is disenchantment, a sense of inexorable weariness, a sense of inevitable disappointment. We trace it in Elijah, and John the Baptist; we trace it in Marcus

Aurelius; we trace it in Francis of Assisi; we trace it in Roger Bacon; we trace it in Luther. All in vain. We have lived, humanly speaking, to little or no purpose. We are not better than our fathers. 'Art thou he that should come, or do we look for another?'" (Matt. 11:3). They thought that they had failed, but this was because the desert and the juniper tree were poor places for vision.

A Negro hod carrier, sick of his job and weary of life, sighed audibly as he started up the ladder with his bricks, "I wish I was dead." Another worker high up in the building overheard his wish and, being of a mind to accommodate him, dropped a load of bricks on his head. When the Negro came to, he exclaimed, "Lord, I thought you could take a joke!"

It is a good thing that God *can* take a joke, or rather, that he does not take us at our word in the time of depression and discouragement.

DISILLUSIONMENT

A senator from one of the states on the Pacific Coast at a public dinner recently told of his boyhood ambition to become a United States senator. All paths led to the Capitol, and the Senate chamber was the land of all his dreams. At length, after long years of toil and waiting, his state sent him to Congress. He entered with fear and trembling, and when the doorkeeper brushed him unceremoniously aside he felt that he was never born for such high honor. But after a few days in the Senate, instead of wondering how it was that the people of his state had sent him to the august body, he fell to wondering how the others had ever got there. He had attained the goal of his early ambition— but it seemed dull and commonplace.

As a child coming home from some boyish expedition into the country, I used to like to stand near the graceful stone arch over which the railways passed and watch the through express to the West thunder past on its way to Chicago. The scream of the whistle, a rumble and roar, a flashing of lights through the windows, a trail of heavy black smoke— and it was gone, like a meteor. Chicago! The great city somewhere off there, beyond the hills where the sun went down. How wonderful a place a city must be! But the Chicago of expectation of childish wonder and the Chicago of actuality, seen with the eye of the body and not with the eye of the heart, how different they are!

We are always looking for some great city beyond the hills which one day we shall visit, and a wonderful city it will be. But when we get there it does not quite measure up to our expectations.

In one of her novels George Sand tells of a French marchioness who in her old age related the story of the one consuming passion of her life. As a mere girl she had married a rich, dissipated, and worn-out marquis; and she was left a widow at seventeen. She had many suitors, but only one love. One night at the *Comédie Française* she happened to see an Italian actor, Leilio, who played some of the parts of Racine and the other great French dramatists. The marchioness became passionately attached to this actor, whom she had never seen except on the stage. She rejoiced in his triumphs; and if in a given character he was put to death, she had to stifle her screams of distress with her handkerchief. Month after month this went on; but one night as she was leaving her private box by a side entrance she saw a stage carpenter remove his hat to an undersized man who was passing and salute him as M. Leilio. Instantly alert, she followed the cloaked figure to a restaurant and took a table not far from her idol. But alas, when she saw him eat, heard his rough language, and saw those who were his intimates, he was no longer Hippolytus, or any of the great characters of the stage, but just ordinary Italian Leilio.

———•—•—•———

One who comes much in contact with the official and social life of Washington recently said to me: "You have no conception of the tragedies of disappointment and disillusionment, and bitterness and cynicism, which are to be found here in Washington under the showy surface of political and social life." The nation's capital is a City of Disillusionment.

DOCTOR, THE

An old Southern doctor had his office over a drugstore. In front of the drugstore was a sign reading, "Dr. Riley is upstairs." When the old doctor died, after a long life of day-and-night service for mankind, he left no money even for his burial; and across account after account on his books they found the entry, "Paid off." When he was buried, his friends wanted to put up some memorial or stone on his grave. They had no money for an expensive stone or marker, so they set up over his grave the sign that was in front of the drugstore; and that was his beautiful epitaph: "Dr. Riley is upstairs."

———•—•—•———

In the Tate Gallery in London you may see the original of the familiar painting which adorns the offices of so many doctors and the walls of so many homes —"The Doctor," by L. Fields. The doctor, an earnest, thoughtful man, sits by the pallet of a little sufferer in a cottage room, his head resting on his hand, his eyes observing his patient. A shaded lamp burns on a stand where spoons and medicine glasses are ready for use. In another part of the room the mother has fallen forward on the table, with her face buried in her arms, the arrow of anguish and anxiety piercing her soul. At her side stands the peasant husband, his great hand resting lightly on the shoulder of his sobbing companion and his face turned in expectation toward the doctor.

That picture shows the doctor at his best—the friend of the meek and lowly, giving his time and his strength and his wisdom to save the poor man's child. What monetary reward could compare for a moment with the pleasure of seeing the light of hope come back into that broken-hearted mother's face?

———•—•—•———

Physicians are a happy race, because they, more than any other class of men, receive the tokens of human gratitude and thanks. Their worldly reward may not always be forthcoming, but from the eyes and lips and hearts of patients whose pains they have relieved and whose anguish they have soothed they receive those tokens of love and gratitude which mean so much more than fees and dollars and decorations. There are times in life when only the physician can be with us. He brings us into the world, and his is the last face we see as we push off the shores of time into the sea of eternity. When we are distressed with the hard rowing of life, when the storm of pain has broken upon us, then down from the mountains of science comes the beloved physician, walking over the sea of our trouble, clothed with the wonderful arts and secrets of his profession, and says to the winds and the waves, "Peace, be still" (Mark 4:39).

———•—•—•———

101

Right in the middle of the highway at Midlothian, Virginia, there is a singular monument to an old-time country doctor. He had done such service to the community that the people wanted to erect a memorial to him in the village while he was yet alive. But the doctor was too modest for that and said, "When I die, you all just bury me wherever I be." Shortly afterward, as he was driving his buggy on his way to a sick patient, he died there in the middle of the road; and there today, right in the middle of the road, so that you have to drive your automobile round it as you pass through the village, stands that singular monument.

———— • ———— • ————

Drumtochty's parish doctor was William Maclure. In the dark and in the light, in the snow and in the heat, without rest and without holiday, he did his best for man, woman, and child for forty years. Seated on his old mare Jess, with instruments and medicines strapped before and behind, the old doctor was a familiar figure in every part of the glen. When, as a last resort, the London specialist was to be summoned to save the life of Annie Mitchell, at a cost of one hundred pounds, he asked the laird to let him pay half of it, saying, "A' haena mony pleesures, an' a' wud like tae hae ma ain share in savin' Annie's life."

After he had saved the life of Saunders and, riding home by the kirk on the Sabbath, was cheered by the village folk and the minister himself, the doctor, talking with his horse, said, "Yon was oor reward. No mony men in this warld will ever get a better, for it cam frae the hert of honest foulk."

That is the physician's best reward—the unfeigned thanks and gratitude of those whom he has helped and healed. His favorite text ought to be, "The Son of man came not to be ministered unto, but to minister" (Matt. 20:28).

DOING GOOD—*see also* DEEDS (GOOD), SAMARITAN (GOOD), SERVICE

John Wesley had this for his rule of life:

> *Do all the good you can,*
> *By all the means you can,*
> *In all the ways you can,*
> *In all the places you can,*
> *At all the times you can,*
> *To all the people you can,*
> *As long as ever you can.*

Abraham Lincoln used to say that he always plucked a thorn and planted a rose wherever he thought a rose would grow. And how few places there are where a rose will not grow!

———— • ———— • ————

On Princes Street in Edinburgh, among the memorials of soldiers, poets, and scholars, one likes to see the monument to the great Scottish preacher, Thomas Guthrie. Taking refuge under his arm is one of the waifs of the great city, one of the street Arabs for whom Guthrie founded the Ragged Schools, and whom he sought to rescue from the maelstrom of the city's cruelty and sin. The favorite poem of Guthrie, the one which he liked to quote so often, was this verse by G. Linnaeus Banks:

> *I live for those who love me,*
> *   For those who know me true,*
> *For the Heaven that smiles above*
> *   me,*
> *   And awaits my spirit too;*
> *For the cause that lacks assistance,*
> *For the wrong that needs resistance,*
> *For the future in the distance,*
> *   And the good that I can do.*

———— • ———— • ————

John Keble used to say, "When you are quite despondent, the best way is to go out and do something kind to somebody."

This is a medicine that never fails to cure. To test it, try it. Your visit to the sick, the bereaved, the disheartened, and the lonely, will kindle fires of love and hope upon your own desolate hearth. Christ was faithful and cheerful, and one reason was that he "went about doing good" (Acts 10:38). Imprison yourself with your sorrow, and life will be a gloomy bondage.

Some years ago I received a letter, written of a friend after his death, in which was this sad sentence—yet not altogether sad, for it indicated that before he passed the friend had learned something of the real secret of life. This was the sentence: "I think his tragedy was that it took him a willful lifetime to see how to make life bless him and others through him."

I have no doubt whatever that the true secret of the way to bless your own life and, through your life, the life of others, is this, "Blessed are ye that sow beside all waters" (Isa. 32:20).

DREAMS—*see also* IDEALS

In the middle of the night of the fourteenth of March, Caesar awoke in his bed, and looking down upon Calpurnia, who lay sleeping in the moonlight by his side, he heard her utter in a dream indistinct words and inarticulate groans. When the day dawned, Calpurnia told Caesar how in her dream she had held him bleeding and dying in her arms. She besought him not to stir out of the house, but to adjourn the meeting of the senate fixed for the fifteenth, the Ides of March, to another day.

Caesar was impressed by this dream of his wife, and resolved not to go to the senate on that day. But the conspirators employed one of Caesar's closest friends, Decius Brutus—but not the famous Brutus—to persuade him to go to the meeting. This Brutus asked Caesar what his enemies would say if he sent a messenger to the senate telling them to adjourn for the present and meet again when Calpurnia should have a better dream. Caesar then changed his mind and set out for the senate. On his way through the street a friend who knew of the conspiracy thrust a paper into his hand saying, "Read this, Caesar, alone and quickly, for it contains matter of great importance which concerns you." Caesar thought it a petition and, without reading it, placed it among his other papers. Thus "the fate of the empire hung upon a thread, but the thread was not broken." Had Caesar heeded the dream of Calpurnia, the thread would have been broken and his life would have been spared.

There was another faithful wife who had a dream of immense significance. Pilate's wife, whose name we suppose to have been Claudia, sent a message to him during the trial of Jesus, in which she said, "Have thou nothing to do with that just man: for I have suffered many things this day in a dream because of him" (Matt. 27:19).

—Great—On a July day in 1491 the dean of the church at Seville assembled the chapter in the Court of the Elms and said, "Let us build a church so great that those that come after us may think us mad to have attempted it." The result of that dream was the glorious cathedral at Seville.

No great cathedral was ever reared except on the foundation of a great dream, and no great life was ever built except upon the foundation of a dream. Joseph dreamed greatly, and a great life was the result.

The highest and most beautiful dream of all is possible for all; for the Holy Spirit, through whom we reach the goal, is ready to help all and to guide all. What can compare with a Christlike man? What book can compare with the book of a good life? What speech is like the golden eloquence of a pure and Christlike heart? What Titian, or Rembrandt, or Rubens, or Velázquez, or Raphael, or El Greco, can hang alongside that masterpiece of the Holy Spirit, a true Christian life? That is the real goal, that is the high ambition. Dream of that. When we stand yonder by the throne, how poor and mean even the highest dreams of this world will seem in comparison. Here none dreams too late. Even your old men shall dream dreams. The thief dreamed that dream when he hung dying on his cross, and Christ told him that it was not too late. But do not wait till then! Dream now! Make God the chief end of your life.

—Lost—Whenever I take up Tennyson's "Locksley Hall," there comes to my mind a strong, stalwart, handsome young man in the Freshman Class at college; and I can hear his voice as he repeated in the course of his oration the lines,

For I dipt into the future, far as
human eye could see,
Saw the Vision of the world, and all
the wonder that would be; . . .
Till the war-drum throbb'd no
longer, and the battle-flags were
furl'd
In the Parliament of man, the Fed-
eration of the world.

He was a choice young man. All that was desirable was in store for him. Everybody predicted that he would make his mark in the world. But one day he was missing. Rumors were rife, and at length the sad story of his infamy and turpitude came out. Under some other name he fights out the battle of life, in a station far below his ability and talent. I doubt not that his mind often runs back to the old days at the college when his face was turned toward the sun and his heart beat high with hope and ambition, when men praised him and predicted for him a brilliant future; and as he goes back and lives those old days over again it must be bitterness and gall to him to contrast what he is—what he has become—with what he might have been.

How sad is the shipwreck of the vessel of one's honorable dreams! In his *Tale of Two Cities* Charles Dickens describes in unforgettable language the man who once had great and beautiful dreams, but was separated from them by his own follies and transgressions. Sidney Carton, the gifted barrister, who ended his life with a glorious act of self-sacrifice, taking the place of Charles Darnay at the guillotine, had wasted the substance of his gifted life in intoxication. Dickens describes him as he goes one morning at the breaking of the day up to his dismal lodgings, sodden with drink after an all-night carousal. "Waste forces within him, and a desert all around, this man stood still on his way across a silent terrace, and saw for a moment, lying in the wilderness before him, a mirage of honorable ambition, self-denial, and perseverence. In the fair city of this vision, there were airy galleries from which the loves and graces looked upon him, gardens in which the fruits of life hung ripening, waters of hope that sparkled in his sight. A moment, and it was gone. Climbing into a high chamber in a well of houses, he threw himself down in his clothes on a neglected bed, and its pillow was wet with wasted tears."

Shortly before the death of Senator Matthew Stanley Quay—not only one of the most powerful politicians that the American system has produced, but a man of genius—he was visited by Senator Beveridge from Indiana, a much younger man, opposed to many of the policies of Quay, but with great admiration for Quay's personality and the brilliancy of his intellect. Frail and haggard, Quay sat by the window in his apartment. As Beveridge rose to go, Quay, looking out of the window, said to him, "In a few months I shall be dead, and the papers will say, 'Matt Quay, boss, is dead.' Had I lived my life differently they would say, 'Death of Matthew Stanley Quay, statesman.' Take warning by me, young man."

Then, taking up a copy of *Peter Ibbetson,* he wrote upon the flyleaf the enigmatic words "Dream true," and gave it to Beveridge as a parting gift.

———•••———

—Of youth—To dream true, to hitch one's wagon to a star, is the first equipment for the battle of life. General Grant as a cadet at West Point hated the army, and when a bill was pending in Congress for the dissolution of the academy, the young cadet eagerly read the newspapers, hoping that he would find that the academy had been abolished. But one day he saw Winfield Scott, a lieutenant general of the army and the hero of two wars, ride by in a review at West Point; and when he saw that, he thought to himself, "How wonderful it would be if I one day were in Scott's place." Thus even the homesick cadet, weary with his military drill and duties, had his dream of future distinction.

Our dreams are the golden ladder by which we climb to heavenly places. They are the mountain peaks of vision whence we see afar off the country toward which we travel. They are the lantern by whose light we pass safely through dark valleys. They are the inner flame that gives us strength and energy for the struggle. They are the two-edged sword by which we cleave the steaming head of the dragon of temptation, and leave him dying at our feet.

DRIFTING

Where one Christian is lost to the Christian life through a particular and special assault of evil through one breakdown, there are a hundred who drift away from the life of worship and of faith. More drift out of Christian life than fall out of it.

Some years ago an American liner was wrecked off the Scilly Isles. The sea was calm; the weather was clear. But the ship was caught in a treacherous current which slowly but surely lured it out of its course.

In life there are treacherous currents which get the soul in their grip and slowly but surely carry it toward the shores of ruin and wreck. For every drift ends in a wreck. When one awakens to the fact that he has been drifting, that there is not the same moral resistance, not the same eager purpose, to know the truth and do it, then is the time to put a trumpet to the lips.

DRINK

Herodotus, the Greek historian, says that Cyrus attacked and took Babylon at night, when the king and the nobles were drunk. That was not the first nor the last kingdom to be lost when men were under the influence of strong drink.

In contrast with Belshazzar is the story which Xenophon relates of the young Cyrus. Cyrus as a youth was taught to shun the intoxicating cup. Once, on a visit to his royal grandfather in Media, Cyrus asked to be permitted to act as the cupbearer. Cyrus did everything to perfection, and was loudly applauded by the nobles present, who were delighted with his perfect mimicry of the cup-bearer, stepping so grandly and solemnly about. The king, too, praised him, but called his attention to one omission—he had neglected to taste the wine, as the cupbearer always did before he handed it to him. Cyrus said that the reason he had not tasted the wine was that he thought it had been poisoned. Asked why he imagined that, he answered, "It was poisoned the other day when you made a feast for your friends on your birthday. I knew by the effects. The things you do not allow us boys to do you did yourself, for you were very rude and noisy. You could not even stand erect and steady. So I thought that the wine which produced these effects must have been poisoned."

There is a sermon on liquor and strong drink which is unanswerable in its simplicity and in its power.

———————

A religious leader of note in our country, riding on a train toward Chicago, fell into conversation with a soldier. The question of drinking came up, and she asked him if he drank. At first he said No, and then he said that on several occasions with his fellow soldiers he had taken a few drinks. On his last furlough, on the way to Chicago he had been drinking with his companions on the train, and by the time he reached Chicago he was drunk. He had wired his fiancée to meet him at the station, and as the train pulled in he was hoping and praying that something might have kept her from coming to the station, so that she would not see him in that condition. But she was there, waiting at the gate, when he came staggering along the platform. When she saw his condition she called a taxicab, pushed him into it, gave the driver his home address,

slammed the door, and walked off. For several days afterward the young man tried ineffectually in his bitter remorse to get in touch with her. At length she relented, in so far, at least, as to write him a letter with the promise of another opportunity. But in the letter she said this: "I would far rather receive one of those telegrams from the War Department saying, 'Missing in action,' or 'Killed in action,' than ever again see you as I saw you that day at the station." Words that were wisely spoken. "Missing in action," "Killed in action"; in that there is no stain, no defilement, but honor rather than dishonor.

———————

There died recently at the age of eighty-five a man who was well known in London and throughout Great Britain as an apostle of temperance, partly because he gave up a fortune of six million dollars for conscience' sake and for the sake of his fellow man.

Frederick N. Charrington was out one evening making a night of it with a group of friends. Strolling down one of London's most notorious streets, they passed a gin palace. Suddenly a woman, ragged and pale, reeled out, her frail frame convulsed with sobs. She was clinging to a ruffian who was trying to shake her loose. "For God's sake," she cried, "give me a copper. I'm hungry, and the children are starving." But the man clenched his fist and struck her to the ground. Young Charrington and his friends rushed in to intervene and protect the woman. After the police had taken the couple away he happened to glance up at the illuminated sign over the saloon door, and there he read in letters of gold his own name—"Drink Charrington beer."

"The message," afterward wrote this young man, "came to me then as it had come to the Apostle Paul. Here was the source of my family wealth. Then and there I raised my hands to heaven, that not another penny of that tainted money should come to me, and that henceforth I would devote my life to fighting the drink traffic." He had a sudden awakening to his responsibility and his influence, and saw that the earth was being cursed for his sake.

"Wine is a mocker, strong drink is raging." (Prov. 20:1.) Oliver Wendell Holmes, physician and philosopher, told the whole truth about it when he said that strong drink "destroys men's viscera when they are alive and confers immortality on those parts when they are dead."

Sometimes Negro speakers—and white also, for that matter—get their words mixed up. This Negro meant to use a word which sounded very much like the one he did use, but was quite different. Nevertheless, his mistake enabled him to utter a profound truth, so far as strong drink is concerned. He had applied for a job and was asked if he ever used strong drink. He thought a moment, and answered, "I don't know that I do, and I don't know that I don't. But I do know that I don't drink to *success.*" Who ever *did* "drink to success"? To what do men drink? They drink to the failure to get a job when they apply for one; they drink to the loss of their job when they have one; they drink to the loss of their health, to the loss of honor and happiness, and the hope of heaven, but never *to success.*

DUTY

In George Eliot's great story *Romola* there is a chapter entitled "An Arresting Voice," which tells how Romola, fleeing from the difficulties and trials and sorrows of her life in Florence was met by Savonarola, who commanded her to go back, saying: "It is the truth that commands you, and you cannot escape it. Either you must obey it and it will lead you, or you must disobey it and it will hang on you with the weight of a chain which you will drag forever. You are seeking some other good than the law you are bound to obey. But how will you find good? It is not a thing of choice; it is a river that flows from the foot of the Invisible Throne, and flows by the path of obedience."

The old Russian army had a tradition that when a sentinel had been posted, he could be relieved or withdrawn only by the officer who had posted him, or by the czar himself. During the first World War there was the story of a Russian soldier who was posted as a sentinel in a dangerous position. The officer who posted this sentinel was killed in battle, and the soldier refused to leave his post until an order came from the czar himself.

In the old cemetery at Winchester, Virginia—that starlit abbey of the Confederacy—there is a monument to the unknown Confederate dead. On it are cut these two lines:

Who they were none knows,
What they were all know.

Look at that lonely figure silhouetted there against the evening sky. There where the bridge crosses the river, with his musket over his shoulder, he walks slowly up and down, hour after hour, through the long watches of the night. What is he doing? He is guarding a bridge that is a vital link in the line of communications from the army's base to the battlefield. Over that bridge must pass the trains laden with troops and munitions and supplies. The lonely sentry does not hear the sound of the guns;

the heavens are not illuminated at night for him by the flashing of the artillery. Nevertheless, his work of guarding that bridge is just as necessary and just as honorable as that of the soldier in the forefront of the hottest battle.

E

EDUCATION—*see also* CHRISTIANITY AND EDUCATION, MORALS AND EDUCATION, OPPORTUNITY AND EDUCATION, PARENTS SACRIFICING FOR CHILDREN

In a passage in McGuffey's *Fifth Reader* Lyman Beecher struck the note to which our nation has ever been loyal when he said: "We must educate, we must educate, or we must perish by our own prosperity. If we do not, short will be our race from the cradle to the grave. If in our haste to be rich and mighty, we outrun our literary institutions, they will never overtake us, or only come up after the battle of liberty is fought and lost as spoils to grace the victory and as resources of inexorable despotism for the perpetuity of our bondage."

EMOTION

The beauty of righteousness, and how in the long run it is infinitely better to live the humble Christian life—that comes home to every man. But the danger is that we are deceived into thinking that in that very wave of emotion or remorse or high longing there is saving grace and power. I come into church and the music and architecture and ordered worship lift and purify my thoughts. The strains of old hymns awaken echoes in the depths of my heart. I give assent to the sublime truths of the gospel as they are read and spoken, and I go from that religious exercise feeling better, thinking more about God, and having a greater desire to strip my soul of mean-

ness and envy and hatred and greed and pride and jealousy and self-worship.

Be not deceived. Balaam felt that way and gave utterance for all others who have felt that way—in words of music and beauty and grace. But how did Balaam die? He died just as he had lived —not as he had wished to die—an enemy of God. Oh, remember it is possible to have noble ambitions and heavenly aspirations and to agree to sublime truths —and yet to live, and, in the end, *die* unreconciled to God!

ENCOURAGEMENT

Few know how great a part General Grant's friends played in his great career. What, for example, his chief of staff, John Rawlins, the Galena lawyer, did to keep him from intemperance; or what Sherman did to keep him in the army. After the victories of Fort Henry and Fort Donelson, Grant was shabbily treated by the commanding general, Halleck, and was virtually under arrest for misconduct. When he was restored to his army, he won the great battle at Shiloh, in April, 1862. But after that victory General Halleck himself joined the army and Grant was reduced to a merely titular command. His position became intolerable, and he determined to resign from the army. He had his effects packed and was about to leave.

Sherman came to see him and, sitting down on one of the boxes, expostulated with him and pled with him to reconsider his resolution. There had been a day, he said, when he had felt just the way Grant did, but now all was prosperous with him. He was sure it would be so with Grant, if he remained with the army. Some happy event would come along and everything would be changed. Grant reluctantly agreed to stay in the army. In a few weeks the happy event turned up in the appointment of General Halleck to the chief command at Washington. This put Grant at the head of his army again, and the way was opened for him to carve out the great career with ponderous hammer blows at Vicksburg, Chattanooga, Missionary Ridge, the Wilderness, and Appomattox.

———•◦•———

One of the chief ornaments of American letters is Nathaniel Hawthorne. In the dedication of his *Snow-Image* Hawthorne writes to his college friend Horatio Bridges: "If anybody is responsible at this day for my being an author, it is yourself. I know not whence your faith came; but while we were lads together at a country college, gathering blueberries in study hours under the tall academic pines, or watching the great logs as they tumbled along the current of the Androscoggin, or shooting pigeons or gray squirrels in the woods, or batfowling in the summer twilight, or catching trout in that shadowy little stream, which, I suppose, is still wandering riverward through the forest—though you and I will never cast a line in it again—two idle lads, still, it was your prognostic of your friend's destiny that he was to be a writer of fiction."

———•◦•———

In Hawthorne's life there is a chapter which illustrates how another's faith, and particularly a woman's faith, can comfort and strengthen. On the day of his discharge from the customs house at Salem, Hawthorne came to his home a beaten and discouraged man. When he told his wife of the disaster which had befallen him, her answer was, "Now you can write your book." She put pen and paper and ink before him, and on that same afternoon he commenced his immortal tale, *The Scarlet Letter.* If he is the chief ornament of American letters, it is due, first of all, according to his own confession, to a schoolboy's faith in his future, and then to the unshaken confidence of his wife, the frail woman who marshaled and set in array his half-hesitating abilities, protecting him from the cruelty and hardness of the world, until he could speak of her as "that flower lent from heaven to show the possibilities of a human soul."

———•◦•———

"You will see now one day we shall shake hands across the brook. You, as first in literature; I, as first in divinity; and people will say, 'Both these fellows are from Annandale. Where is Annandale?'"

Thus, on one of their summer afternoon rambles by the shores of the Solway, or along the coasts of Fife, spake a tall young divinity licentiate to his taciturn and discouraged companion. It was a prophecy which was strangely fulfilled, for the day came when the young licentiate was the most renowned preacher in Britain, and his moody and dyspeptic companion the greatest of living writers of prophets. Both scaled the heights of fame; and both, especially the first, tasted the sorrows of Gethsemane. The young licentiate was Edward Irving, and the young student of literature was Thomas Carlyle.

"Life," wrote Carlyle long years afterward, of that period, "was all dreary, eerie, tinted with the hues of imprisonment and impossibility; hope practically not there. To all which Irving's advent was the pleasant contradiction and reversal, like sunrising to night, or impenetrable fog and its spectralities."

END OF THE AGE

The day had been dark and overcast since it dawned, with here and there an occasional gleam of sunlight. But as I drove into the country toward evening, the western sky was all glorious with great bars of red and gold. It was as if the sun had declared his splendor after the long day of cloud and wind and rain.

Humanity's day has been long and stormy. The bright and promising dawn soon changed to clouds and gloom, when man sinned and fell. Ever since, though sunlight here and there has broken through, clouds and darkness have been around the path of the race. But the western sky is bright with the splendid colors of a grand sunset. With the brush of inspiration prophets and apostles have painted for us the glory which shall be revealed, the sublime ending of the story of creation and redemption. No Christian has heard the greatest music of his faith till he has listened to this music of the great consummation. Nor has he exercised his highest privilege until he has stood upon the mountain peaks of divine inspiration and looked over the hills and valleys of time to the final triumph of the Kingdom of Jesus Christ.

ENDURANCE

I remember talking with one of the soldiers of the army of the Potomac who took part in the battle of Gettysburg. He belonged to the Sixth Corps, the corps that made the famous march from Manchester to Gettysburg, a distance of thirty-four miles. He said that march, with the clouds of dust, the perspiration, the blood of chafed limbs trickling down into his shoes, was the hardest experience of his whole long war service.

It is sometimes harder to march than it is to fight. The test of endurance is the long march. You have set out on a long march. You will meet many others who have gone part of the way and turned back. You will have by your side many others who are ready to quit and go back with you, if you will go with them. But always there are some who are going steadily forward and who have no idea of anything but enduring unto the end. "He that endureth to the end shall be saved." (Matt. 10:22.)

ENEMIES—*see* FORGIVENESS OF ENEMIES, PRAYER FOR ENEMIES

ENTHUSIASM

"Men of imagination," said Napoleon, "rule the world." We say the same thing when we say that men of enthusiasm rule the world. In speaking of some new rivers that he had discovered Livingstone wrote: "I find I wrote when the emotions caused by the magnificent prospect of the new country might subject me to a charge of enthusiasm, a charge which I deserved, as nothing good or great had ever been accomplished in the world without it."

Without enthusiasm no battles have been won, no Iliads written, no cathedrals builded, no empires founded, no religions propagated. The secret of success is enthusiasm. The men of victory have been the men who kept the fires burning on the altars of enthusiasm when other flames had sunk into cold, gray ashes of despair. The life of David Livingstone is one more monument to the power of enthusiasm.

ENVIRONMENT

The reign of Ahaziah was neither long nor illustrious, although it might have been both. He was the son of Joram, and both were kings of Judah, and wicked men. The sacred historian makes his own observations as he passes quickly over these wicked and forgotten kings. In both cases he traces the downfall of the kings to their evil environment. The father of Ahaziah was Jehoram and he was the son of the good king Jehoshaphat. But his marriage with Athaliah, the daughter of Jezebel, neutralized the good influences of his parentage. His son, Ahaziah, thus had a bad heredity on both sides. That might have ruined him in itself. But whatever chances he had to save his character from pollution were lost when he kept up a close friendship with the king of Israel, Joram.

———————

Voltaire's agnosticism and skepticism are by some traced to the influence of the Abbe de Chateuneuf, who, although a priest of the Church of Christ, sowed the seeds of deism in his youthful charge and introduced him to dissolute companions. With a different environment in youth he might have been as mighty for faith as he was mighty for unbelief. John Locke, the English philosopher, as a young man had for a friend and counselor Lord Somers, described by Horace Walpole as "one of those divine men who, like a chapel in a palace, remain unprofaned, while all the rest is tyranny, corruption, and folly." Such a friendship left its mark on Locke's character. At Oxford, John Wesley determined to have no companions save those which would help him in the life of faith and righteousness that he was trying to lead.

ENVY—*see also* JEALOUSY

Aristides the Just was present at the Athenian assembly when that body voted that he should be banished. An illiterate member from the country, not knowing who Aristides was, went up and asked him to write the name Aristides on his shell for him, meaning that he voted for

his exile. As Aristides obliged him, he asked the man if he knew Aristides, or had anything against him. "No," the man said, "I don't know him or know anything about him; but I get tired of hearing him spoken of as Aristides the Just."

EPITAPH

"Antipas was my faithful martyr, who was slain among you, where Satan dwelleth." (Rev. 2:13.) This is the greatest epitaph of the Bible. In the days of his flesh, Christ promised eternal life and eternal reward to those who are faithful to him. If they confess his name before the world, he will confess their names before his father in heaven. But Christ, speaking to John on Patmos, singles out and names one man as having been faithful unto death, and that one man is Antipas, his faithful witness, who died for Christ at Pergamos.

ESCORIAL

I had almost finished my tour in Spain, but I had not yet seen the Escorial. Leaving Madrid—that strange, artificial city built on a barren upland by Phillip II, today a heap of bomb-blasted ruins—we were soon out in the country, with the familiar landscape of Spain all about us. The yellow, treeless plains with the harvesters at work; the asses plodding along with their heavy burdens; the shepherds with their red blankets thrown over the right shoulder; the water wheels, reminiscent of Syria, turning slowly round; the ancient olive orchards; the red tile roofs of the farmers' houses; and always in the distance the gaunt and lonely mountains. Near the mountains we passed through some rugged pastures where herds of young black bulls were being raised for the cruel and bloody combat of the bull ring. Suddenly, as the train rounded a curve, high up

111

against the mountains I saw a gigantic yellow dome rising up to meet the sky, and under that dome a colossal gray-yellow structure, severe, forbidding, and melancholy as the naked wind-swept mountain which bent over it.

When you see the Escorial, you are looking at more than a building. You are looking at the Middle Ages, Roman Catholicism, the Inquisition, Spain, and world empire. More than any building on the face of the earth, it seems to gather up all those periods, ideas, systems, and kingdoms. It is a tomb for kings. But when you first see it, or last leave it, you feel that you are looking upon the tomb of an epoch, a system, an idea, an empire. It is as if Titans had carried away to burial the Spain of the sixteenth century, its world empire, its Inquisition, its Roman Catholicism, and buried all of them there together by the tomb of Charles V and Phillip II.

EVANGELISM—*see* SOUL WINNING

EVIL—*see also* MAN (GOOD AND EVIL IN), RETRIBUTION

—Overthrow of—A very impressive thing about history is the sudden, unexpected collapse of evil systems and evil tyrants and evil nations. We are familiar with Voltaire's satirical remark about God's being on the side of the heaviest battalions, and with Napoleon's remark that Providence is on the side of the last reserve. In 1812, when Napoleon seemed to be in the hour of his greatest power and influence, and his word was law from Sweden to the Mediterranean, he invaded Russia—mysterious, ominous, prophetic Russia. Today the pyramids of French cannon and cannon balls that you see piled up before the Kremlin at Moscow show the high-water mark of Napoleon's career of conquest. From Moscow to the Nieman his legions lay

scattered in the snow, frozen in the rivers, dead on the successive fields of battle. In a single campaign the greatest victories of history were suddenly succeeded by one of the greatest military disasters of all time.

To this day—at least until the godless Russian Revolution—the Russian people, realizing that in their deliverance there was something more than the genius of Kutuzov, and what they called "General Winter," celebrate that overthrow by chanting in their churches the great song which the Hebrews chanted when the hosts of Sennacherib, without an arrow shot against them, melted away before the walls of Jerusalem: "God is our refuge and strength. . . . The heathen raged, he uttered his voice, the earth melted" (Ps. 46:1, 6).

In his *History of the English People* Green relates the fall of Cardinal Wolsey, the man who, in Shakespeare's words, said:

Had I but served my God with half the zeal
I served my king, he would not in mine age
Have left me naked to mine enemies.

The career and fall of Wolsey is an example of how God permits wicked ambition to swell and advance until the hour of reckoning strikes. "Slowly," writes the historian, "the hand had crawled along the dial plate; slowly as if the event would never come; and wrong was heaped on wrong, and oppression cried, and it seemed as if no ear had heard its voice, till the measure of the wickedness was at length fulfilled. The finger touched the hour, and as the strokes of the great hammer rang out above the nation, in an instant the whole fabric of iniquity was shivered to ruins."

That hour struck for Cardinal Wolsey; it struck for Herod. It strikes for every doer of iniquity.

Opposite St. Philip's Church in Charleston is an old, ill-kept cemetery. One August day I passed through the gates, looking for the grave of John Calhoun. I soon came upon it, a great vault of brick covered with a large slab of marble with one word on it—"Calhoun." It was in 1850 that his friends laid him there, a time when it seemed that the Union was going to pieces and the principles that he advocated would prevail. There by that tomb of Calhoun, with the branches of the ancient elms and live oaks playing their shadows across it, is a good place for one to sit and think of this conflict that goes on between light and darkness.

When Charleston was occupied by troops from Sherman's army a service of jubilee was held in that cradle of secession and nullification. The editor of the *Liberator,* William Lloyd Garrison, was among those who attended the exercises. As he went out of the desolate city, sitting defiantly amid her ruins, he visited that same cemetery and stood by that same tomb and thought of that same conflict between good and evil, in one battle of which he had borne so great a part. Men naturally stood back and waited to see what Garrison would think and say about John C. Calhoun, who was the very soul of the institution against which Garrison had waged his long warfare. What he said, with one hand resting upon the marble slab, was this: "Down, into a deeper grave than this, slavery has gone; and for it there is no resurrection." The stars in their courses fought against slavery.

Man has no chance when the stars are against him. Sisera had on his side the vast host of the Canaanites and nine hundred chariots of war. But the stars were against him; hence he fell. The final end came by the hammer stroke of a woman who nailed him to the floor of her tent; but that had not been possible unless the stars had been against Sisera.

—Persistence of—In his vision John stood upon the sand of the sea and saw a beast coming up out of the sea. The monster had seven heads and ten horns. Upon the horns were ten diadems, and upon the seven heads names of blasphemy. The beast was a fearful composite of leopard and bear and lion. The power which he was able to exercise he owed to the dragon who sent him forth. On one of the seven heads of the beast there was the scar of a terrible wound; but his death stroke had been healed. And the whole earth wondered after the beast and worshiped the beast, saying, "Who is like unto the beast?" (Rev. 13:4).

The horrid scar on the beast's head—the death stroke that had been healed—suggests to us the perduring power of this antihuman and antidivine spirit of the world, and how, desperately wounded in one generation or one century, the beast returns with undiminished fury in another.

—For sake of others—Everywhere we are confronted by the tragic story of evil done just for the sake of those who sit at meat with us. Abraham Lincoln was a man of easy access, anecdotical and friendly. Yet there was one incident in his career to which he never permitted anyone to refer, and of which he was thoroughly ashamed, and that was his almost duel with Shields on an island in the Mississippi River.

On the roadway which traverses the

highlands between Weehawken and Hoboken, overlooking the Hudson River and the sky-reaching temples of mammon in New York, one can see a low stone monument on which are these words: "Here on July 11, 1804, Alexander Hamilton fell in a duel with Aaron Burr." When Burr challenged Hamilton to fight the duel, the first inclination of Hamilton was to refuse, for dueling was abhorrent to him as a man and as a Christian. But lest the refusal to fight should injure his future usefulness, just for the sake of pleasing a depraved public opinion, Hamilton accepted the challenge; and on the very spot where his son had fallen a year before he met his tragic and lamented end.

EVIL SPIRITS—*see* DEMONS

EXAMPLE

At a Pennsylvania bankers' convention one of the bankers related to me an incident in the life of a judge whom we both happened to know. In his college days this judge had been addicted to drink. Now he had a fine and promising son coming along, whom he had recently sent to college. Complaints soon reached him of his son's misbehavior, his drinking and general dissipation. The father called the son before him and remonstrated with him, telling him that he was ruining his prospects and that his conduct would break his mother's heart. Imagine his surprise when his son replied, "Why, Father, they tell me you did just the same thing when you were at college." This flash of retributive justice in the words of his wayward son was, in the providence of God, the means of a radical transformation in the life of that father.

According to an old Moslem legend, the death of Abel was at the direct instigation of Satan. Cain, according to this story, was filled with envy and hatred toward his brother, but did not know how he could destroy his life. "But one day Satan placed himself in Cain's way as he walked with Abel in the fields and, seizing a stone, shattered therewith the head of an approaching wolf. Cain followed his example, and with a large stone struck his brother's forehead till he fell lifeless to the ground."

Elijah was one of those few men "of whom the world was not worthy." (Heb. 11:38.) That such a man lived makes us rejoice in our common humanity. Carmel itself was not more rugged and more majestic than that prophet when he stood upon the mountain peak, his face flushed with the splendid victory over the howling priests of Baal. As eloquent Wendell Phillips said over the grave of John Brown, "Men will believe more firmly in virtue now that such a man has lived and died."

EXPERIENCE

The University of Experience is one in which we are all enrolled. The tuition is the highest that can be paid—sorrow and suffering. Therefore, to throw away experience and its lessons is to commit murder against the soul. Experience is what we make it. It does not run after us and plead with us, but it waits to see if we shall give heed to it and invite it to be our guide and companion. For some men, experience is only a graveyard, while for others it is the garden of inspiration.

"I want to see life!" This exclamation was made to me on a winter evening at the door of the church by a young woman who had sought my counsel.

The sound of those words, spoken with an accent of bravado, soon vanished on the night air. But their echo has often come back to me: "I want to see life." I wonder how much of life by this time she has seen, and how much, now that she has seen it, she thinks of it. What value does she place upon it? Does it seem now of so much greater reality and interest and power than the life which she had been living, and which seemed to her a life of drab color and dull limitations?

In his celebrated "Give me liberty, or give me death!" speech Patrick Henry said, "I have but one lamp by which my feet are guided, and that is the lamp of experience. I know of no way of judging of the future but by the past."

Experience is the lamp which guides the footsteps of man. Just as there is no progress without memory, so there is no wisdom and character without experience. Yet how many act regardless of, or in defiance of, experience.

When Walpole in the House of Commons accused William Pitt with the atrocious crime of being young, Pitt rejoined by wishing that he might "be one of those whose follies cease with their youth, and not of those who continue ignorant in spite of age and experience.

Ignorant, in spite of experience! Multitudes are in that condition. The full companies of the living and the regiments of the dead press forward to entreat men to be wise, to be taught by experience. But they continue to be foolish, as if they could rewrite the moral law and found a moral world of their own, a world in which folly is not punished and where sin is not followed by retribution. There are some for whom experience is like the stern light of a vessel. It gives no light in advance, but it does serve as a guide and a warning to those who follow.

—And faith—Imagine, if you will, a man in his old age—one who has drunk deeply of the cup of life and experienced much of its joys and sorrows, its shams and frauds, and its great and beautiful realities, too—returning to visit on a summer day the church of his childhood. The congregation that once worshiped there are now scattered, and of those that once filled the pews on the holy day, many now sleep in the quiet acre adjoining the church. It was there he listened to the preaching of the word of God, and was exhorted "to keep himself unspotted from the world," to love his fellow man, "to do justly, and to love mercy, and to walk humbly" with his God. Then it was all theory, but now he has had a chance to put these theories to test in the laboratory of life.

Sit down by his side in the pew, in the now empty and silent church, and ask him to tell you what his verdict is. Will he tell you that those rules and precepts of the Kingdom of God were not worthy, that time has proved their falsehood? Or will he not rather say, "I have learned by experience that these things are true. 'The judgments of the Lord are true and righteous altogether. More to be desired are they than gold, yea, than much fine gold. . . . Moreover by them is thy servant warned: and in keeping of them there is great reward.' " (Ps. 19:9-11.) Yes, after all other things have come and gone, that faith, hope, and love of which the apostles spake are the things that remain. Link your life to that which abides forever!

—Warned by—It was a saying of Terence, "This is a wise maxim, 'to take warning from others of what may be to your own advantage.' " Always these

115

danger signals are flashing in the lives of other men, letting us know when we draw near to some dangerous shore, inviting us to Stop, Look, and Listen. What flaming lessons! What stern and earnest teachers! Everywhere we see men and women getting ensnared, entangled, soiled, defiled, broken, wrecked. How can we hear of this, read of it, see it depicted on the printed page, or elsewhere, without being warned thereby?

If you have started just recently, or perhaps, who knows, have traveled far along the same path, be warned by what you see in the experience of others. O Life, what a teacher thou art! how generous with thy lessons! how patient with thy unwilling scholars! how plain and unmistakable thy instruction, line upon line and precept upon precept! How eloquent thy pleadings! How sad thy farewell to the soul that would not be warned. "Turn you at my reproof. . . . Because I have called, and ye refused; I have stretched out my hand, and no man regarded; but ye have set at nought all my counsel, and would none of my reproof: I also will laugh at your calamity; I will mock when your fear cometh." (Prov. 1:23, 24-26.)

The man was just out of the Maryland penitentiary. Talking to him, I learned that he had had a Christain training and background and had led a Christian life. But he became the accomplice of a fellow clerk who was playing the races, and together they robbed the bank. He was apprehended and sent to the penitentiary. I said to him, "You are an intelligent man. You must have read the newspapers and must have known what happened to other men who tried to do what you were doing. How did you think that you could prove an exception to the rule of exposure and punishment? Why did experience teach you nothing?"

He answered, "Well, I see that now, but like so many others I didn't think of it at the time."

———— ◆ ————

—And the world—Listen to the verdict of the great Apostle John. It is true that John was just a fisherman in his youth, but he had been in company with the greatest of teachers, and in the long years of his life at Ephesus, one of the world's greatest and richest cities, he had had good opportunity to see what the world can do for a man. You can see him there in some upper chamber of his home at Ephesus. In the distance rise the great columns of the world's grandest temple, the temple of Diana. Outside his chamber, perhaps the multitudes pass up and down the famous *Corso,* with its marble stones and its busts of the emperors and the gods.

John is dictating to his amanuensis the first of the three letters that bear his name. As he speaks, perhaps the wind, blowing in from the Aegean, carries with it the sound of the cheering of the multitude assembled in the amphitheater to enjoy its bloody spectacles. John pauses for a moment, as he and the others listen, and then he says: "Love not the world, neither the things that are in the world. . . . For all that is in the world, the lust of the flesh, and the lust of the eyes, and the pride of life, is not of the Father, but is of the world. And the world passeth away, and the lust thereof: but he that doeth the will of God abideth for ever." (I John 2:15-17.)

F

FAILING

—At the last—John Bunyan draws *Pilgrim's Progress* to a rather unexpected and alarming conclusion by giving us a picture of Ignorance fumbling at the gate of the city for his certificate and finding none. At the command of the King the two shining ones bound him hand and foot and thrust him through the door in the side of the hill. "Then I saw that there was a way to hell even from the gates of heaven, as well as from the City of Destruction."

FAILURE—*see* DISAPPOINTMENT

FAITH

In his great tale *The Christ of Flanders* Balzac describes the passage of a ship from the island of Cadzant to Ostend on the Flanders coast. Just before the ship cast off, a bareheaded stranger of plain attire boarded the vessel. The rich and fashionable passengers in the rear of the ship hastened to sit down so as to prevent the stranger from taking a seat in their midst. But the poor who sat in the bow of the boat moved along and made room for him.

The vessel had not gone far when the sea and the sky took on an ominous look and gave forth warning sounds and groans and murmurs, as of an anger that would not be appeased. In a moment a hurricane broke over them. Suddenly the clouds parted for a little above the vessel, and in that transient light all the passengers looked with amazement at the aspect of the late comer. His golden hair, parted in the middle on his tranquil, serene forehead, fell in many curls on his shoulders, and outlined against the gray sky was a face sublime in its gentleness and radiant with divine love.

Meanwhile all the passengers were in fear for their lives as the ship plunged in the storm. The young mother cried out, "Oh, my poor child, my child, who will save my child?"

"You yourself," replied the stranger.

And when the mother heard his sweet voice, she had hope in her heart. The rich merchant, falling on his knees cried out, "Holy Virgin of Perpetual Succor, who art at Antwerp, I promise you twenty pounds of wax and a statue if you will get me out of this."

But the stranger spoke, "The Virgin is in heaven."

The handsome young cavalier put his arm around the proud damsel and assured her that he could swim, and that he would save her. Her mother was on her knees asking for absolution from the bishop, who was blessing the waves and ordering them to be calm—but he was thinking only of his concubine at Ostend. The ragged old prostitute cried out, "Oh, if I could only hear the voice of a priest saying to me, 'Your sins are forgiven you,' I could believe him."

The stranger turned toward her and said, "Have faith, and you will be saved."

When the ship, almost in view of Ostend, driven back by the convulsion of the storm, began to sink, the stranger stood up and walked with firm steps on the waves, saying as he did so, "Those that have faith shall be saved. Let them follow me." At once the young mother took up her child in her arms and walked with him on the sea. Then followed the soldier, and the old prostitute, and the two peasants. And last of all came one of the sailors, Thomas, whose faith wavered, and who sank several times into the sea; but after three failures he walked with the rest of them. The merchant went down with his gold. The man of science, who had mocked, was swallowed up by the sea. The damsel and her lover, the bishop and the old lady, went to the bottom, heavy with their sins. But those who had faith followed the stranger and trod with firm, dry feet on the raging waters. At length they reached the shore, where the stranger led them to a fisherman's cabin, where a light flickered in the window. When they had all come in and were gathered about the fire, then the Saviour disappeared.

True and beautiful commentary on Christ and Peter walking on the sea: "Those that have faith, let them follow me!" Can you walk on the sea? Anyone can walk on the land; but can you walk on the *sea*? What is your sea? Is it a sea of sickness ? Is it a sea of loneliness? Is it a sea of disappointment? Is it a sea of pain? Is it a sea of sorrow? Is it a sea of temptation? You can walk on it if you will. Will you make Peter's prayer tonight,"Bid me come unto thee on the water" (Matt. 14:28)? And when you make that prayer, Jesus answers, "Come!"

In Tennyson's *Idylls of the King* a city is described as built to music, and therefore never built at all, and therefore built forever. So it is with the pillars of the city of our faith. They are there— although we cannot touch them with our hands. Ours is a city built to music, and therefore never built at all, and therefore built forever.

After Sir Walter Raleigh was beheaded in the tower they found in his Bible these true and striking lines, written the night before his death:

*Even such is time, that takes in trust
Our youth, our joys, our all we have,
And pays us but with age and dust;
Who in the dark and silent grave,
When we have wandered all our
        ways,
Shuts up the story or our days.
But from this earth, this grave, this
        dust,
My God shall raise me up, I trust!*

All the things of this world he had lost, but he had kept his faith; and faith spoke to him of a hope and life beyond the grave.

—In America—In the summer of 216 B.C. the army of Hannibal destroyed a great Roman army under the consul Terentius Varro. This came at the end of eighteen months of terrible battles with the conqueror from Carthage. In these battles the Roman armies had lost sixty thousand men. Yet the great disaster did not shake Rome. The Senate voted the defeated general, Varro, their thanks—"because he had not despaired of the commonwealth." When Hannibal encamped not more than three miles from the wall of Rome, the ground on which his army was encamped was put up for sale at Rome and brought its full market value. It was a magnificent tribute to Rome's confidence in herself and her future. In the Civil War, Lincoln never despaired of the Republic.

—A ferryboat—Some years ago, traveling in Asia Minor on the way from Ephesus to Miletus, crossing a vast plain we came suddenly upon a deep and wide and swiftly flowing river. It was none other than the classic Meander—now the Menderes—which, still true to its original name, meanders over the plain. Across the river we could see our goal and destination, the ruins of ancient Miletus, where Paul said farewell to the elders of the church at Ephesus, and rising above its ruins the still Greek theater. But the river was too wide and too deep and too rapid to ford or to swim across. There was no bridge and we had no boat. But presently we discerned a movement on the farther shore, and soon saw in the middle of the river a huge, cumbersome ferry propelled by broad sweeps. The ferry touched the shore where we were waiting with quite a group of natives who had assembled by this time, and all went aboard and were carried across the river; and when we had finished our explorations we were carried back again.

Standing on that ancient ferry, my mind reverted to the day when David crossed the Jordan on a ferryboat, and that ferryboat, no doubt, was just the same kind of craft on which we crossed the Meander. So across Life's wide and dangerous river there goes the ferryboat of faith. "There went a ferry over the river."

In his famous caricature of popular and easy religion, *The Celestial Railroad,* Nathaniel Hawthorne tells of the new and easy way by which one can travel today from the City of Destruction to the City of Life. On this journey the engineer of the train was Christian's old enemy, Apollyon. The Hill Difficulty had been pierced with a tunnel, and the Valley of the Shadow of Death had been illuminated with inflammable gas. Pilgrims were popular now at Vanity Fair, and Flimsy Faith ran the Castle of Giant Despair as a house of entertainment. When the train, with a loud blast of the engine, finally reached the river, Pilgrim hurried aboard the ferryboat, only to see

that his traveling companion and guide, Mr. Smooth-It-Away, was not going on board. Pilgrim cried out to him and asked if he was not going over to the Celestial City. "Oh, no," he answered. "I have come thus far only for the sake of your pleasant company. Good-by; we shall meet again." Pilgrim then rushed to the side of the boat, intending to fling himself on shore; but the wheels, as they began their revolution, threw over him a dash of spray so cold—so deadly cold, with the chill that will never leave those waters until death be drowned in his own river—that with a shiver and heartquake Pilgrim awoke.

The final test of a religion of faith or plan of life is, Can it get you over these rivers: the river of temptation, the river of trial and affliction, the river of sin and guilt, and that last river which we must all cross, the river of death? The ferryboat is still running. Despite the scoffings of the world, despite the proclamations that the ferryboat is now out of date, and fit only for the museum, it is still running. It is carrying across these dark and dangerous rivers thousands upon thousands in safety and in peace, and landing them safe at last upon Canaan's shore.

—Keeping—Eisleben is a small town, but one of the most interesting in the in the world. At one end of the town is the house in which on a November night in 1483 Martin Luther was born. The house was at that time an inn. Strange that the greatest man in the world, in the last ten centuries, should have been born in an inn, and died in one. At the other end of the town is the house where Luther died. He had come to Eisleben on a mission of reconciliation, and there his last days were spent in preaching the gospel and bringing men and women to Christ. On the night of the eighteenth of February, 1546, Luther awoke in great pain and cried out, "Lord God, how I suffer! I believe I am going to remain here in Eisleben where I was born and baptized."

Then he sank into a stupor and was roused out of it only when a friend said to him, "Reverend Father, do you stand firm by Christ and the doctrine you have preached?"

In a child's whisper he answered, "Yes."

Then those great deep eyes that all men had wondered at, and which sixty-three years before had opened on the world for the first time, now opened for the last time, and Luther was with his God, a sinner saved by grace.

—And life—Traveling in Norway, you sail slowly through the beautiful and silent fjords, with the grand mountains rising all about and beautiful cascades making sweet music as they hurry down the perpendicular cliffs on their way back to their mother, the sea. Standing on the deck of the vessel, you will see the channel in front narrowing until it looks like a blind end. You seem to be sailing straight into the mountain. A few hundred yards farther, and you are sure the prow of the steamer will strike on the iron cliffs. But just when progress seems inpossible the channel opens up and the steamer glides out upon another fjord of entrancing beauty.

So it is with the iron gates up to which we come on the pilgrimage of life, whether it be the iron gate of present and personal difficulty, or temptation, or sorrow, or sin, or death itself. In God's own way and in God's own time the gate will swing open and we shall pass out into the city.

Last summer I met a classmate of mine who had been passing through deep waters of affliction and trial. He told

me that in the midst of his troubles he said to his wife, "We've talked about it, and preached about it, and sung about it, and prayed about it; now, we'll see if it works!"

"It worked, didn't it?" I said to him.

"Yes," he answered, "it worked!"

Can you show in this church, in this city, in your home, in your place of toil of business, that the gospel "works"?

—Life without—Jeremy Taylor wrote a famous book of noble English prose whose second section bears the lugubrious title "Holy Dying." In the first chapter of the book, "On the Shortness of Man's Life," he gives the record, or epitaph, of Ninus, the legendary king of Assyria. "Ninus, the Assyrian, had an ocean of gold, and other riches more than the sand in the Caspian Sea. He never saw the stars; and perhaps he never desired it. But he was most valiant to eat and drink. This man is dead. Behold his sepulchre, and now hear where Ninus is: 'Sometimes I was Ninus, and drew the breath of living man. But now I am nothing, but clay. I have nothing but what I did eat, and what I served to myself in lust. I that wore a mitre am now a little heap of dust.' "

—Without sight—One of the romances of the heavens is the story of the discovery of the planet Neptune, the outermost of known planets as related by Professor Simon Newcomb. Up to that time the planet Uranus, discovered in 1781, had been regarded as the outermost of the planets. The study of Uranus by the astronomers revealed certain deviations and perturbations for which they could not account by any of the known laws and theories. Then they began to wonder if these perturbations might not arise from the action of another planet.

They got to work with their mathematics and their theories, and finally reached the conclusion that the disturbances which they had noted in Uranus must be due to the action of an unknown planet. Then they located on their charts the place in the heavens where that planet must be. Finally, after midnight on the morning of September 14, 1846, an astronomer student turned his instrument on the place designated, and the great planet swam into view. The theories upon which they followed· their investigations and finally discovered the planet were, of course, based upon observed data; nevertheless, it was faith in the laws of the universe, and in the fidelity of those laws, which led them to discover the great planet. The eye of the mind, the eye of faith, discovered it long before it was seen through the lens of the telescope.

—**The source of joy**—The orange trees, which now make the California landscape look like an inverted sky where the stars are golden oranges, must first of all receive the life giving waters, without which there can be only desiccation and death. The cool pure wind, blowing where it listeth, may sweep around the house where there is pestilence and disease, but it can enter and do its cleansing, reviving work only when the doors or the windows of that house are flung open. To try, then, to have joy and peace and hope without faith is like trying to produce fruit on trees without water, or cleanse a pestilence-stricken or tainted chamber without opening the doors or windows. Yet I wonder if a great number today are not trying that foolish experiment, trying to get something out of religious life, out of their church and Christian life, without that which is the condition and the source of all its blessings—faith?

—**Surviving by**—In the early days in the West the circuit-riding preachers had to swim their horses across the rivers. They tell us that when they were crossing swollen and overflowing rivers if they fixed their gaze upon the swirling waters around them they were likely to become dizzy and, falling from their seat, be swept away by the flood. But if they fixed their eye upon the trunk of a great tree on the bank, or upon some mighty rock, or upon the summit of a hill or mountain, they rode through in safety.

In the storms of life faith gives us balance and calm and safety, for we fix our eye, not upon the shifting scene about us, but upon the eternal God.

A town in England had been bombed one moonlit night by the Germans. When workers were clearing away the debris, they found on top of a heap of rubbish a sailor's prayer book, open at the Twenty-seventh Psalm, with the thirteenth verse marked: "I had fainted, unless I had believed to see the goodness of the Lord in the land of the living." The incident was widely commented upon in Great Britain, for it seemed to many that the verse noted in the open prayer book found amid the ruins of that town was the secret of Britain's magnificent endurance during the worst days of her trial. The victory was won, not by battleships and tanks and rifles and armed men alone, but by faith in God. Unless the Britons had believed to see the goodness of the Lord in the land of the living, unless they had believed in a great future for their country, they had fainted in despair.

The end tells the story. Coligny's statue in front of the *Oratoire* in Paris with the inscription, "He endured, as seeing him who is invisible" (Heb. 11: 27). Faith is the secret of endurance.

—The sword of—There is a tendency to discount the authority of faith and to prefer the evidence of things seen to the evidence of things not seen. I can imagine a youth being conducted through the armory where he is to arm himself for the battle of life. When he is offered the Sword of Knowledge, he accepts it. When he is offered the sword of Eloquence, he says, "I can use that; give it me." When he is offered the Sword of Wit, he is glad to take it. When he is offered the Sword of Personality and Charm, he eagerly lays hold on its hilt. But when he is offered the Sword of Faith, he turns away from it in disdain. "That weapon," he says, "was all right for my father and my grandfather and my great-grandfather, but it is of no use to me. It is completely outmoded, a weapon that is all right for the museum, but not for the battle of life."

How sad, and yet how common, a mistake that is; for faith is not the weakling's sword but a weapon that flashes and gleams like a meteor in the midst of the host when all other swords have snapped at the hilt and been trampled in the dust of the arena. When King Arthur had fought his last battle he handed his marvelous sword Excalibur to one of his knights and told him to hurl it into the sea. When he did so, a white and mystic arm seized the sword and, brandishing it aloft three times, drew it under.

It is a parable of life. He fights most enduringly and triumphantly in this far-flung battle line of life who fights with a sword that is bathed in heaven—the Sword of Faith.

—Triumphant—*Pilgrim's Progress* comes to a close with these words, as the weary but faithful pilgrim got safely across the river, "So he passed over, and all the trumpets sounded for him on the other side." That was what I was thinking of last Wednesday when, just as the sun was westering, we stood by my mother's grave on the wind-swept hilltop, the river beneath us flowing silently away like the river of a man's life. "And all the trumpets sounded for *her* on the other side!"

—And works—There is a legend of two knights who fell into a dispute over the composition of a shield which they saw flashing before a pavilion on a distant field. One declared that the shield was of gold, and the other vehemently asserted that the shield was of silver. There was no occasion for a quarrel. Both were right, for each man was looking on a different side of the shield. So "faith" is one side of the Christian shield and "works" the other.

Two men were once earnestly disputing the relative importance of faith and works when they came to a ferry over a river. As they started across they asked the ferryman his opinion on the subject. Was it faith by itself, or works by themselves, that was the Christian duty and the Christian hope? For answer the godly ferryman pointed to his two oars. "One," he said, "I will call faith, the other works. If I pull only on this one oar, the right oar, I get nowhere, but go round in a circle. Just so if I pull only on the left oar. But when I pull on both oars, then the ferry moves across the river." A very sensible explanation, describing the relationship of faith and works.

—Wreck of—Paul knew all about shipwrecks, having passed through that harrowing experience several times. But what he warns Timothy against is the shipwreck of faith. A wreck is always a sad and dismal sight—a sad sound, too, with the waves breaking over it with melancholy music. The wreck tells of lost good, abandoned hopes, frustrated ambitions, and perhaps lost lives. But saddest of all is the shipwreck of faith; for what cargo is so precious as the soul, and what port so glorious as heaven? Christianity had not been long in the world when Paul wrote this letter to Timothy; but long enough for a few wrecks to strew its shores. He gives him counsel of a nature to warn, encourage, and inspire him—sailing instructions, as it were, for the voyage of life. But everything he has to say is summed up in this word of exhortation, "Holding faith and a good conscience; which some having thrust from them made shipwreck concerning the faith" (I Tim. 1:19).

FALL

—Of great men—You sometimes hear it said of certain noted men that if they had only died at this or that point in their great career it would have been far better for their fame. If Arnold had died at Quebec, or Saratoga; if David had died when he brought the Ark to Jerusalem; if Solomon had died when the Temple was finished. So we are tempted to say in the case of Gideon. If Gideon had only died on the field of that grand victory over Midian, then his name would have come down to us without a stain. But God knows best. You can never tell by the brightness of the dawn or the noontide how the evening of the day will be. The brightest sun may go down in a dark and clouded sky.

—Of man—At Ephesus, or Pergamos on its towering mountain, or Baalbek on its sandy plain, I clamber over the ruins of palace and temple and theater and bath and library and market place; and I say to myself, "How wonderful and magnificent this all must have been before it was shaken down by war and earth-

quake, and fire, and the rough hand of time! What a place it must have been when the throngs of the great walked over those now grass-covered pavements, when the broken arch was complete, when yonder prostrate columns all stood erect, and when through yonder gate the worshipers passed into the temple to offer sacrifice and incense to their God!"

In like manner the ruins of the soul of man proclaim his original greatness. What a temple, what a palace, what a city it must have been, when will and reason and intellect and desire—instead of, as now, being in angry rebellion and opposition one to another—dwelt together in beautiful peace and harmony.

Here on the top of a mountain by the sea are the ruins of a once notable building. It must have been a temple where men worshiped their God and offered their sacrifices. Following the stones of the foundation, I discover that it was a building of noble dimensions; but now the walls are fallen, the very foundation stones themselves are sunk in sand and debris, amid which the lizard makes his den. The great columns lie in broken fragments across the temple's base. All that remains of the temple are two Corinthian columns which still support the central stone of the temple's door. Both column and frieze are cut and defaced with wind and weather, worn with time and covered with vegetation. On the stone at the archway some kind of inscription was once written. Many of the letters are missing, and the others are only half legible. But by careful study and supplying lost letters, I have been able to restore the inscription to its original form, which was this—"Thou hast made him a little lower than the angels" (Ps. 8:5). As I stand there in the bright sunlight, with the wind blowing across the promontory, surveying the ruins of this once great temple and reading the legend over its doorway, I seem to see a second inscription underneath the first, which reads, "O Lucifer, son of the morning, how art thou fallen!"

Such, then is man—in mind, body, and spirit, a noble temple, in the image of God himself, but now fallen, his faculties deranged, that which should be in command subordinate, and that which is subordinate now in control, his will perverted, his affections dislocated, his heart the prey of every wind of passion which sweeps across its chords.

———

There are few, I imagine, who have not read Stevenson's famous tale *Treasure Island*. Few books have the power to bid care be gone and sorrow vanish as that wonderous tale of treasure and adventure. One of the striking characters of the book is the poor castaway, Ben Gunn. He had been marooned for years on the lonely island with nothing but hidden treasure and the graves of his murdered comrades for companionship. The customs and the manner and the speech of humankind were beginning to leave him; there was gradual and natural degradation toward the brute; for it is not meant for man to be alone— he was made for human society.

When the lad Jim first met Ben Gunn in a remote part of the forest, he was running along the ground and leaping from tree to tree. But Jim's doubts were put to an end when the poor creature, after much advancing and retreating, now seized with terror and now animated with hope, at length came forward and fell at his feet and made supplication to him in the human tongue. The moment he saw that man, that lad from his own country, England, and heard his own tongue again, the years of isolation and solitude were blotted out and he saw life

as it ought to be lived and as God intended that he should live it.

Man has suffered shipwreck; he has fallen away from the life that God intended him to live; till our life at its best must be but a faint recollection of what it was, of what it might yet be. But the moment Christ appears before the human consciousness he presents to man the lost ideal of His being. Man looks upon Christ and says to himself, Yes, that is the life for me. That is my true speech; that is my true behavior!

———

The soul of man is like a ship that has started for its port across the seas, and on the way has been boarded by pirates who have locked the truth below, or thrown it overboard, and taken possession of the vessel. This is the gospel description of human nature. Is it false or is it true? It must be true, for wherever we open a book of history, wherever we look into the record of humanity, we find the mark and the trail of these evil passions.

FAME

A woman named Damaris! How strange a thing is fame! The names of all those philosophers in that distinguished congregation to which Paul preached on Mars Hill, save the one who believed in Christ, are forgotten. But here is a woman named Damaris, whose name is immortal because she heard Paul preach and found the Lord Jesus Christ. Here is a parable of life and immortality. Identity with Christ alone gives us permanence in a fixed place, and destiny amid the flying fragments of time.

FAMILY ALTAR—*see also* WORSHIP (FAMILY)

How many homes in this congregation have a family altar? Today many excuse themselves on the ground that the pace of life has been so speeded up that there is no time for family altars or devotion and prayer. No more insincere nonsense was ever spoken. The same person who says that will spend a whole afternoon every week, or several of them, on the golf course, and half the night at the moving picture theater; and yet he will claim that he is too busy, that life is too fast, for kneeling at a family altar!

A returned missionary, shocked at conditions in America, noted the fall of the family altar as one of the chief changes in American life: "My father gathered his family together each morning, and commended us to God's keeping before we separated for the duties of the day. On my return from India I found that he had given up the practice of family prayer entirely, and that my younger brothers and sisters were individualists who cared nothing for the moral and religious influence of the home. What is true of my father's household is true of many homes throughout the length and breadth of the land. The home is no longer a unit; family life, with its spiritual and moral training is very largely a thing of the past. This in my judgment is the explanation of the lack of moral earnestness and disregard for the rights of others so strikingly apparent to me after an absence of a comparatively few years."

FATALISM—*see* PREDESTINATION AND FATALISM

FATHER—*see* LOVE (A FATHER'S)

FEAR—*see also* COURAGE

At the siege of Khartoum, when someone suggested to that great Christian, General Gordon, that they stop up the windows of his headquarters with sand, he became angry. Putting lighted candles on the table he said, "When God was proportioning out fear to all the peoples in the world, at last it came to my turn, and there was no fear left to give me. Go tell all the people in Khartoum that Gordon fears nothing, for God has created him without fear.

Biologists say that fear is not only a universal emotion but the first of the emotions to be developed in man and beast. The whole creation is under the dominion of fear. Man comes into this world stamped with fear before he is born, and those fears are multiplied as he increases in knowledge and experience.

As a boy did you never catch a robin or an oriole and, holding the bird in your hand, feel the rapid, terrified beating of the little heart? The bird had had no experience or acquaintance with you or any other man. It had no reason to fear you but that of instinct. It was in dread of everything but its mother and its companion birds. As the creation is at the present time, the sense or the instinct of fear is a very necessary part of the equipment of beast and man.

—**Conquered by love**—There is a painting by Max Gabriel which has always seemed to me an illustration and representation of a great text of John's. You see copies in almost every gallery, the original of which is in the Louvre in Paris. It is called "The Last Token." It describes a scene in the days when to be a Christian meant persecution, suffering, or death. One of the Christians, a slender and beautiful maiden, is about to be torn by the beasts. At her side is the great stone wall of the amphitheater, rising tier above tier and crowded with the brutal multitude whom sin has brought to that fearful state. The iron grating into the den, or vivarium, of the beasts has been lifted, and a ferocious tiger, enraged by captivity and hunger, is stealth-ily creeping out of the cage toward his helpless victim, with the blood lust in his glaring eyeballs.

The maiden is clad in white, save for the dark mantle about her head and shoulders. She stands only a few feet from the opening out of which the tiger is coming. But she heeds not the beast, and seems to be oblivious to its nearness. At her feet lies a white rose, which some friend or lover or relative has thrown into the arena; and her upturned and fear-less eyes eagerly scan the benches above for the face of him who has cast the rose. The hate of man has condemned her to death, and the savage beast is soon to taste her virgin blood; but one single rose with one beating heart behind it has changed the whole scene. Now there are no beasts, no bloody sands, no jeering mob—only a white rose and love triumphant. Perfect love has cast out fear.

———

—Of God—A prominent physician said to me recently, "When I used to go to church as a young man I heard the preachers talk about the fear of God. Now I hear nothing but the love of God." The physician's diagnosis of the religious condition of our times is, on the whole, correct. Men hear all the time about the love of God, but almost noth-ing of the fear of God.

———

—And worry—Fear is man's greatest ad-versary. According to an ancient legend, a man driving one day to Constantinople was stopped by an old woman who asked him for a ride. He took her up beside him and, as they drove along, he looked at her and became frightened and asked, "Who are you?"

The old woman replied: "I am Chol-era."

Thereupon the peasant ordered the old woman to get down and walk; but she persuaded him to take her along upon her promise that she would not kill more than five people in Constantinople. As a pledge of the promise she handed him a dagger, saying to him that it was the only weapon with which she could be killed. Then she added: "I shall meet you in two days. If I break my promise, you may stab me."

In Constantinople 120 people died of the cholera. The enraged man who had driven her to the city, and to whom she had given the dagger as a pledge that she would not kill more than five, went out to look for the old woman, and meet-ing her, raised his dagger to kill her. But she stopped him, saying: "I have kept my agreement. I killed only five. Fear killed the others."

This legend is a true parable of life. Where disease kills its thousands, fear kills its tens of thousands. The greatest miseries of mankind come from the dread of trouble rather than from the presence of trouble. From the cradle to the grave fear casts its baleful shadow. Fear betrays man's spirit, breaks down his defense, disarms him in the battle, unfits him for the work of life, and adds terror to the dying bed.

FLAG

One of the most memorable of the oc-casions on which Bishop Simpson de-livered a certain lecture was on Novem-ber 3, 1864, in the Academy of Music in New York, just before the election when Lincoln defeated McClellan. At the close of his speech, laying hold of the shot-riddled flag of a local regiment, Simpson said, "The blood of our brave boys is upon it; the bullets of rebels have gone through and through it, yet it is the same old flag. Our fathers followed that flag. We expect that our children and our children's children will follow it. There is nothing on earth like that old flag for beauty. Long may these stars shine. Just now there are clouds upon it, and mists gathering around it. But the stars are coming out, and others are joining them, and they grow brighter and brighter; and so may they shine till the last star in the heavens shall fall."

FLOOD

Doré has given us a picture of the Deluge which, once seen in childhood, can never be forgotten. The anguish and woe of perishing men and beasts he describes with terrific and appalling power. Poets and orators have followed in his steps. But the thing is too vast, too great, too awful, for words to describe. We leave it just as the Bible leaves it: "The waters prevailed exceedingly upon the earth; and all the high hills, that were under the whole heaven, were covered. . . . And the mountains were covered. And all flesh died that moved upon the earth, both of fowl, and of cattle, and of beast, and of every creeping thing that creepeth upon the earth, and every man: all in whose nostrils was the breath of life, of all that was in the dry land, died." (Gen. 7:19-22.) Death! death! death! universal death.

FLOWERS

Why do people put a geranium, or a lily, in the window instead of a book, or a photograph, or an article of clothing? Why do people plant morning glories and lilac bushes and rosebushes in their meager yards? Why do men who have achieved a degree of independence and a competence buy a place in the country? What is there about the country which draws the majority of mankind like a magnet, even if all their days have been spent in the roar and dust and smoke of a great city?

The answer is found in the first book of the Bible. "And the Lord God planted a garden eastward in Eden; and there he put the man whom he had formed." (Gen. 2:8.) Man has never been able to throw off the influence of that early environment.

FORGIVENESS—*see also* ATONEMENT, BLOOD OF CHRIST, SIN (FORGIVENESS OF)

The language spoken in heaven by the angels and the redeemed is the language of forgiveness. It will be the only language spoken there. No other language will be understood. It will be spoken by the cherubim and the seraphim and the whole angelic host as they praise God, the author of forgiveness and of eternal salvation. It will be spoken by all the redeemed as they greet one another on the banks of the River of Life and gather round the throne of the Lamb and sing their song unto him who loved them and washed them from their sins. But no one can learn that language after he gets to heaven. It must be learned here upon earth—in this world, and in this life. That is what Jesus taught us when he taught us to pray, "Forgive us our debts, as we forgive our debtors."

———— • • • ————

In *The Rise of the Dutch Republic* Motley records a fine exhibition of the Christian spirit, under the most trying of circumstances, on the part of a persecuted Protestant: "An affecting case occurred in the north of Holland, early in this year, which, for its peculiarity, deserves brief mention. A poor Anabaptist, guilty of no crime but his fellowship with a persecuted sect, had been condemned to death. He had made his escape, closely pursued by an officer of justice, across a frozen lake. It was late in the winter, and the ice had become unsound. It trembled and cracked beneath his footsteps, but he reached the shore in safety.

The officer was not so fortunate. The ice gave way beneath him, and he sank into the lake uttering a cry for succor. There were none to hear him except the fugitive whom he had been hunting. Dirk Willemzoon, for so was the Anabaptist called, instinctively obeying the dictates of a generous nature, returned, crossed the quaking and dangerous ice at the peril of his life, extended his hand to his enemy, and saved him from certain death. Unfortunately for human nature, it cannot be added that the generosity of the action was met by a corresponding heroism. The officer was desirous, it is true, of avoiding the responsibility of sacrificing the preserver of his life, but the burgomaster of Asperen sternly reminded him to remember his oath. He accordingly arrested the fugitive, who, on the sixteenth of May following was burned to death under the most lingering tortures."

Instances like this shine like stars in the night of man's history since Christ came into the world to die for it. Nor does the fact that the hapless Anabaptist was fleeing the brutality of men who bore the name of Christian cast the least shadow over the beautiful Christianity of his fine act; but, on the contrary, it only serves to make it stand out in brighter glory. We read this narrative and we exclaim, "There is the Christian spirit!"

—Of enemies—During one of the persecutions of the Armenians by the Turks, an Armenian girl and her brother were pursued by a blood-thirsty Turkish soldier. He trapped them at the end of a lane and killed the brother before the sister's eyes. The sister managed to escape by leaping over the wall and fleeing into the country. Later she became a nurse.

One day a wounded soldier was brought into her hospital. She recognized him at once as the soldier who had killed her brother and had tried to kill her. His condition was such that the least neglect or carelessness on the part of the nurse would have cost him his life. But she gave him the most painstaking and constant care. One day when he was on the road to recovery he recognized her as the girl whose brother he had slain. He said to her, "Why have you done this for me who killed your brother?"

She answered, "Because I have a religion which teaches me to forgive my enemies."

During the Revolutionary War, at the town of Ephrata, beyond Harrisburg, there lived a very reputable and highly respectable citizen who had suffered an injury from a worthless and vile man in that town. This wicked man enlisted in the army, and there lived up to his evil record in civil life. Presently he was arrested for a very serious offense, convicted by a court martial, and sentenced to be hanged.

The news of his sentence got back to Ephrata. Then that citizen whom this convicted man had wronged set out for the army, walking all the way to Philadelphia and beyond. When he found his way to Washington's headquarters, he pled for the life of this convicted man. Washington heard him through, and then said he was sorry but that he could not grant the request. The sentence must be carried out and executed, first of all, because the man had committed a heinous offense, and second, for the sake of the discipline of the army. But seeing the disappointment in the man's face when he turned to go, Washington said, "Are you a relative of this man?"

The man said, "No."

"Then," said Washington, "are you his friend?"

"No," said the citizen, "that man was my deadly enemy."

———•—•—•———

In *Quo Vadis,* that great tale of early Christian history, Chilo, a man of all wickedness, the peripatetic philosopher, thief, slanderer, panderer, and betrayer of the innocent, had sold the wife and daughter of his friend Glaucus into slavery and tried to kill him for his faith in Christ. Glaucus was one of those Christians who were covered with pitch, fastened to pillars, and then set on fire in the Vatican gardens for the amusement of Nero. As he drove down the lines of this human agony, Nero had by his side this wicked Chilo. Presently they came to the pillar where Glaucus was burning, but still alive and conscious. As the wind blew the smoke away for a moment, disclosing the face of Glaucus, Chilo was seized with sudden compunction of conscience and bitter remorse. Stretching his arms up toward the agonizing martyr, he cried out, "Glaucus, in Christ's name, forgive me!"

At that the head of the martyr moved slightly, and from the top of the pillar was heard a voice like a groan, "I forgive."

Those who stood about saw a strange light come into the face of Chilo. Turning toward Nero and lifting an accusing finger, he cried out, "*There* is the incendiary."

In the excitement that followed Chilo encountered in the crowds St. Paul, who told him of the infinite forgiveness of Christ and baptized him into the Christian faith. The next day when Chilo himself was in the hands of Nero's torturers, who demanded that he retract his Christian confession, Chilo asked that he might die in the way the Christians died. When his torturers were binding him with ropes and piercing him with iron tongs, Chico kissed their hands with humility and forgiveness. Forgiven himself, he had learned to forgive—and he died in peace.

———•—•—•———

Joseph Parker as a young man used to debate in the mining fields of England, on the town green, with infidels and atheists. An infidel once shouted at him, "What did Christ do for Stephen when he was stoned?" Parker said the answer that was given him was like an inspiration from heaven. "He gave him grace to pray for those who stoned him." Stephen had the mind of Christ; and hearing him pray for those who did him wrong at once recalls the prayer of Jesus himself, under like circumstances: "Father, forgive them."

———•—•—•———

When the minister was examining Andrew Jackson as to his faith and experience, he asked him a question that probably not many ministers would have asked him. He said: "General, there is one more question which it is my duty to ask you. Can you forgive all your enemies?" The question was in view of the many feuds, duels, and personal bitternesses of Jackson's stormy career.

After a moment's silence, Jackson responded: "My political enemies I can freely forgive; but as for those who abused me when I was serving my country in the field, and those who attacked me for serving my country, and those who slandered my wife . . . Doctor, that is a different case."

The minister made it clear to him that none who willfully harbored ill feelings against a fellow being could make a sincere profession of faith. Again there was silence, until at length the aged candidate affirmed that he would try to forgive all his enemies. This done, his name was written upon the rolls of the church, and he received the Communion of the Body and Blood of Christ.

———•••———

As a child I used to hear read that verse from the book of Proverbs which is repeated by Paul in his letter to the Romans: "If thine enemy hunger, feed him; if he thirst, give him drink: for in so doing thou shalt heap coals of fire on his head" (Rom. 12:20). I wondered just what it meant. I saw a picture of a man with a coal scuttle full of burning coal taking the shovel and shoveling the coals onto the head of his enemy. But how did that fit in with feeding him, and giving him to drink? The wisest commentators today seem to know no more about that verse than did the child with his childish vision of the coal shovel and the scuttle. But whatever it means, it tells us that we get revenge upon our enemies by loving them, and not by hating them, by doing them good, and not evil.

———•••———

—God's—I can imagine a great convocation in heaven, when God announced to its inhabitants that man had fallen, that the new creation was stained with sin. From every quarter of the universe the great angels come posting in, riding upon the wings of the wind, to hear the dread announcement by the Almighty.

When God asks for a remedy and calls for volunteers to go down to earth and deliver man from the curse of sin, one great angel comes forward and says: "I will go down to earth. I will live a life of peace and truth and purity and love before man, and thus I will win his soul to the good. Thus I shall take away the stain of his sin."

But God answers him: "Thy way of life is good; but it will not turn man from his sin, neither can it take away the stain of his sin."

Then another angel comes forward and says: "I will go down. I will teach the truth to man. I will fill his mind with the precepts of righteousness; and thus, contemplating the truth, he shall be delivered from the stain of sin."

But again the almighty Father answers: "Thy precepts are good, and thy statutes are right; but they cannot deliver man from sin or wash away the stain of sin. They will only remind him of what he has lost, and whence he has fallen. Thy precepts are efficient, but not sufficient."

Then a third angel comes forward, and he says: "I will go down to earth and I will tell man of a great hope. I will allure him out of his sins by the music of the hope of a future life that shall be sinless. Thus he shall arise and follow after righteousness, and thus he shall lose the stain of his sin."

But once more God answers: "Mighty spirit, sweet is the music of hope; but the hope about which you will sing to man cannot save him. It will only sadden his heart with the difference between what he is and what thou tellest him he may become."

For a time there is silence in heaven. Then comes the Son, in whose face is the brightness of the glory of God, and before whom angel and archangel, cherubim and seraphim, bow down in reverence. Then speaks the Son:

"Eternal Father, I will go down. By the power of the Holy Spirit I will take man's nature; by the power of the Eternal Spirit I will offer myself on the cross and shed Immanuel's precious blood. My blood will cleanse man from his sin!"

And all the host of heaven rejoiced at that saying, and cried together with a voice like the sound of many waters, "Eternal Son, go down! Thou only canst redeem man! Thy blood alone will cleanse him from his sin."

—Of sin—One hardly knows where to commence when he launches out upon this ocean of truth, the death of Christ for sinners. Here are two wills. The one was filed in May, 1564, at Geneva. The testator was a scholar and minister of Christ whose property amounted to thirty-two dollars, a few books, and a few old chairs. In this will, the testator says: "With my whole soul, I embrace the mercy which He has exercised to me through Jesus Christ, atoning for my sins by the merits of His death and passion, that in this way He might satisfy for all my crimes and faults, and blot them from His remembrance. I testify also and declare that I suppliantly beg of Him that He may be pleased so to wash and purify me in the blood which my sovereign Redeemer has shed for the sins of the human race, that under His shadow I may be able to stand at the Judgment Seat."

The second excerpt is from the will of a man who died at the beginning of the twentieth century, and who, at the time of his death, was probably the richest man in America. The first paragraph of his will is as follows: "I commit my soul into the hands of my Saviour in full confidence that having redeemed it and washed it in His most precious blood, He will present it faultless before the throne of my Heavenly Father, and I entreat my children to maintain and defend at any cost of personal sacrifice the blessed doctrine of the complete Atonement for sin through the blood of Jesus Christ once offered, and through that alone."

These two wills were made by men differing in race—one a Frenchman, the other an American; one living in the sixteenth century, the other in the twentieth century; one a scholar and a minister, the other a banker and financier; one a poor man, the other a rich man.

Yet they were alike in the confidence which the testators reposed in the redeeming work of Jesus Christ on the cross. Calvin did not plead his poverty, and Morgan did not plead his riches. Both put their trust in the precious blood of Christ.

Both of these testaments are alike in that they declare that man's greatest need is the forgiveness of sins, that Christianity's greatest blessing is the bestowal of forgiveness, and that the forgiveness of sins is secured for us by the shed blood of Christ, the death of the Son of God upon the cross.

In a Highland village there was a shepherd who had a little daughter. He would take her with him when he went out over the moors to tend and fold the sheep. Most of all the daughter liked to hear her father call the sheep with the shepherd's call, sounding free and beautiful down the wind, over the moors.

By and by the little girl became a beautiful young woman and went off to the great city, Edinburgh or Glasgow, to take a post. At first her letters came regularly every week. Then the intervals between them grew longer, and finally the letters ceased altogether. There were rumors, too, in the village, that the shepherd's daughter had been seen in gay company and in questionable places. At length a lad from the village who knew her well saw her one day in the city and spoke to her, but she pretended that she had never seen him before. When the shepherd heard this, he gathered a few things together and, clad in his shepherd's smock, with a shawl wrapped around his shoulders and his shepherd's staff in his hand, set out for the city to seek and find his lost daughter.

Day after day he sought her in vain, on the avenues and in the slums and closes of the city. Then he remembered how his daughter loved to hear him give the shepherd's call. Again he set out on his quest of sorrow and love, this time sounding, loud and free, the shepherd's call. Passers-by turned with astonishment to look on the shepherd in his smock and with his staff as he went up and down the streets sounding the shepherd's call.

At length, in one of the degraded sections of the city, his daughter, sitting in a room with her gay companions, suddenly looked up with astonishment in her face. There was no doubt about it! It was her father's voice! The shepherd's call! Flinging wide the door, she rushed out upon the street, and there was her father, who took her in his arms and carried her with him to the Highland home, and there loved her back to decency and to God.

* * *

Not far from New York there is a cemetery where there is a grave which has inscribed upon its headstone just one word—"Forgiven." There is no name, no date of birth or death. The stone is unembellished by the sculptor's art. There is no epitaph, no fulsome eulogy—just that one word, "Forgiven." But that is the greatest thing that can be said of any man, or written upon his grave, *"Forgiven."*

FREE WILL—*see* PREDESTINATION

FRIEND

—In adversity—Among a great many of Paul's friends who were frightened and ashamed, and made shift to break their relationship with him, there was one upon whom he could count. The world's scorn and contempt, the probability of being thrown to a beast or covered with pitch and set on fire to illuminate the driveway of the emperor by night, never caused Onesiphorus to falter. It wasn't easy to find Paul, but he persisted in the

search until he found him. There was no excuse which he could make to his conscience for not finding his old friend and ministering to him. Paul says, "He oft refreshed me"—literally, "made him cool," as if he had poured cold water on his fevered head and feet.

* * *

In *Great Expectations* Charles Dickens tells how Pip went to visit for the last time his benefactor, Magwitch, the dying ex-convict, who had been condemned to be hanged. The convict took Pip's hand and said, "You've never deserted me, dear boy. . . . And what's best of all, you've been more comfortable alonger me, since I was under a dark cloud, than when the sun shone. That's best of all." Yes; it is not when the sun is shining, but when the clouds gather, and darkness comes down, that friendship has its real test.

* * *

If Onesiphorus could have asked for an epitaph, I am sure it would have been this—"Here lies the friend of Paul!" And Paul might have said, in these lines of unknown authorship:

Timotheus, when here and there you go
Through Ephesus upon your pastoral round,
Where every street to me is hallowed ground,
I will be bold and ask you to bestow
Kindness upon one home, where long ago
A helpmate lived, whose like is seldom found;
And when the sweet spring flowers begin to blow,
Sometime, for me, lay one upon his mound.
Thus Paul, long since from out his Roman cell,

132

*As from the past he saw a face
   arise—
Fit picture of the veteran who surveys
His yester years, waiting for the
   evening bell,
While Hesper shines within his
   quiet skies,
And memory fills with cheer his
   lonely days!*

———◆◆◆———

In the great hall of one of the old-time mansions of the Shenandoah Valley there hangs the portrait of a broad-shouldered cavalier, and written in his own hand are the words, "Yours to count on—J. E. B. Stuart."

———◆◆◆———

It is written, "A friend loveth at all times, and a brother is born for adversity." (Prov. 17:17.) But there are a great many friendships which are not born for adversity. Adversity is the wind or the fan which separates the chaff of flattery from the grain of solid friendship.

The Shadow once said to the Body: "Who is a friend like me? I follow you wherever you go. In sunlight or in moonlight I never forsake you."

"True," answered the Body, "you go with me in sunlight and in moonlight. But where are you when neither sun nor moon shines upon me?"

The true friend is one who is faithful in adversity and who abides with us in the darkness of the night.

———◆◆◆———

A man in adversity is like a ship which has been driven on the shore and wrecked. The ship needs extensive overhauling and repair before it will be ready for sea again. So is it with the friend who has met with troubles and disaster. He needs the ministry of his friends. There are two beautiful examples of that in the Bible, one in the Old Testament and one in the New. When David's fortunes were at the lowest ebb, when he was pursued day and night by the relentless hatred and jealousy of Saul, and when, apparently, his own hope was sinking and his faith in God declining, then that faithful friend Jonathan, whose love to him David said was "wonderful, passing the love of women," went to him at night in the wood of Ziph and strengthened his hand in God.

———◆◆◆———

Years ago in Philadelphia a prominent bank failed. Even those officers and employees who had been innocent were looked upon with suspicion. One of these men who was innocent of wrongdoing felt bitterly the new attitude of old friends toward him. But one day in the mail he received a letter which had in it just a single sheet of paper. On the paper there was drawn a man's hand, and underneath was the signature of his friend. There was a man, a friend, who was not ashamed of his chains.

In the olden days in Greece the symbol of a true friend was a young man upon whose garments were written the words "Summer and winter."

This Friend of friends about whom I am trying to tell you, you can trust in winter as well as in summer.

———◆◆◆———

—Christ the true—Napoleon was a man who had many courtiers but few friends. Indeed, he boasted once that he loved no one living, not even his own brothers. But he was attached in a way to one of his marshals, Duroc. In the Battle of Bautzen in 1813 Duroc received a fatal wound from a cannon ball. When the army had bivouacked, Napoleon went to see him. The duke grasped his hand and kissed him. The emperor, putting his right arm around the marshal, remained a quarter of an hour, with his head resting on his left hand, and in complete silence.

At length the marshal said, "Ah, Sire, leave me. Such a sight as this must pain you."

Whereupon the emperor left, unable to say more than these words, "Good-by, my friend."

He then returned to his tent and admitted no one that night. After the Battle of Waterloo, when he had hoped to find asylum in England, Napoleon expressed the desire to assume the name of his old friend, and be known merely as General Duroc.

You have a Friend, your friend forever, who permits you to bear his name —the name which is above every name, and the name which God delights to honor.

When Bishop Beveredge was dying, one of his closest friends said to him, "Bishop Beveredge, do you know me?"

The bishop asked, "Who are you?" And when the name was mentioned he said, "No."

Then they said to him, "Don't you know your wife?"

"What is her name?" he again asked.

His wife came forward and said, "I am your wife, do you not know me?"

"No, I did not know I had a wife."

The old man's mental machinery was breaking down. Then one knelt by him and whispered in his ear, "Do you know the Lord Jesus Christ?"

At that the dying man's face lighted up, and he answered, "Yes, I have known him for the last forty years, and I can never forget him."

Ah, yes; when memory's cords are all snapping, and the mind wanders in a maze, still the name of this Friend, the name of Jesus, will sound with sweet meaning in the believer's ear. The cord of memory that binds to Christ will still

hold, and along it will flash messages of cheer and strength which shall establish your soul in the last darkness.

—A faithless—The man appeared daily at the noon hour at the Brooklyn city hall, holding to the rails of the iron fence with hope and expectation in his face, looking up toward the clock in the tower as it struck the hour. Then he would wait—ten, twenty, thirty minutes. Then the light of hope and joy faded from his face. He became an old, beaten man, and shuffled off in dejection. It was the tragedy of a broken promise. He had been a man of affairs in the city, and in a time of financial difficulty a friend had promised to meet him at the city hall and hand him a large sum of money. But the friend did not keep his promise. Disappointment broke the man's heart and upset his reason. Every day after that he came and looked wistfully at the clock, waiting for it to strike, and looking in vain for the friend who promised he would come. But we have a Friend who always keeps his promise. "He is faithful that promised." (Heb. 10:23.)

—Of God—The youthful Ian Maclaren, visiting his uncle in the Highlands, looked with wistful admiration on a white-haired elder in the kirk who passed the sacred cup at Communion. When he saw him the next day breaking stone on the road, he was amazed, and asked his uncle how it was that the bearer of high office yesterday, today should be laboring on the highway. His uncle told him that James was an elder in the kirk because he knew more about God than any other man in the village. He was a friend of God.

—A true—Henry James in his life of Nathaniel Hawthorne gives no little prominence to the influence of his friendships. When he was a student at Bowdoin in the early twenties Hawthorne formed a warm attachment for a college mate, Franklin Pierce. In 1857 General Pierce became president of the United States and appointed Hawthorne consul general to Liverpool. It was more than a recognition of one whose works were the chief adornment of American letters. It was a gracious tribute to personal friendship; and to Hawthorne, then fifty years of age, it was the dawning of the new day of hope and happiness. When he resigned the consulship in 1857, he went to live in Rome, and there his spirits suffered an eclipse. His future was uncertain, and his eldest daughter was near to death with a malady which he speaks of as a trouble that "pierced his very vitals."

At this time it was that his old friend and recent benefactor, Franklin Pierce, then traveling in Europe, came to see him, and the Notebooks of the period contain beautiful allusions to the help and comfort of that friendship. He writes, "I have found him here in Rome, the whole of my early friend, and even better than I used to know him; a heart as true and affectionate, a mind much widened and deepened by the experience of life. We hold just the same relationship to one another as of yore, and we have passed all the turning-off places, and may hope to go on together, still the same dear friends, as long as we live." The hope was fulfilled, for when Hawthorne took sick in the spring of 1864 it was this old friend, Franklin Pierce, who proposed that they should take a tour among the mountains of New Hampshire. But they had only reached the little town of Plymouth, when General Pierce, going one morning into the room of Hawthorne to call him, found that he had been called by Another. They were pleasant and lovely in their lives, and at death

they were not divided. Hawthorne had a friend.

———◆◆◆———

There is a Bible verse which says, "There is a friend that sticketh closer than a brother." (Prov. 18:24.) That is saying a great deal, for a good brother will stick through thick and thin.

In a battle in Scotland there were two brothers in the same regiment. Their army was beaten and was leaving the field. One of the brothers lay on the ground desperately wounded; but the other brother, also wounded, was still able to walk. Disregarding the entreaties of his brother that he leave him to die and flee with the others, he stooped down and lifted him to his back and thus left the field. By and by the warmth of the body of the brother who carried him revived the spirit and strength of the unconscious one; but the brother who carried him, when he had reached a place of safety, staggered and fell dead beneath him. One brother had given his life for another. Yet we are told that there is a friend that sticketh closer than a brother.

———◆◆◆———

When Fox, the founder of the Friends, or Quakers, was lying in a filthy dungeon at Lancaster, a Friend went to Oliver Cromwell and offered himself, body for body, to lie in the prison in his stead, if Cromwell would accept the substitution and let Fox at liberty. Cromwell was so struck with the offer that he said to the great men of his council, "Which of you would do as much for me if I were in the same condition?" Although he could not accept the friend's offer, because it was contrary to law, yet the power, he said, and truth of this generous offer "came mightily over him."

FRIENDS

It has been said that the test of friendship is the number of friends one would desire to see in heaven. This is indeed the test of our friendship with Christ. If we have not loved him and followed him as our Redeemer here, there is no reason why we should desire to see him hereafter. The Christian's keenness of desire for life to come will depend upon his love for the Lamb of God which died for him on the cross.

—Choosing—Test your friendships. What is the attitude of your friend toward that which you, as a Christian, hold sacred—honor, purity, the Bible, the home, the Church, and Christ? In *Faust* the beautiful and chaste Margaret confessed that when Faust was present she was unable to pray. What is the influence of an evening with your friend? Does it make it easier or harder for you to pray?

—Lack of—John Randolph of Virginia was one of the greatest men produced by the Old Dominion, a brilliant and, in many respects, a wonderful man. Nothing in American history is more pathetic than the death of Randolph in the hotel in Philadelphia, where he compelled his physician to remain with him up to the very end because the Virginia law required that when a man manumitted his slaves those who witnessed the will had to be present at his death. Therefore he had the servants lock the door, and the physician had to remain with him until the end. Thus did Randolph, recognizing the injustice of slavery, make sure that his own slaves should be freed and well provided for.

But together with these noble characteristics he had a bitter, cantankerous, vindictive spirit and tongue. Men found it difficult to live with him. What could be more touching than Randolph's own account of himself mounting his horse

and sitting for half an hour motionless, trying to make up his mind where to go or with whom to speak. His great plantation, his well-stocked library, his eminent public services—what were all these when what the heart longed for was friendship and the human touch?

Right kind of—One cannot always choose his vocation or surroundings in the world. But one *can* choose his friends. The philosopher Antisthenes used to wonder that men would examine carefully an earthen vessel which they were about to buy, worth just a few cents, to see if there were any cracks or flaws in it, and yet the same men would exercise no thought or care in the choice of friends. When John Wesley was a student at Christ Church, Oxford, he made the resolution that he would have only those friends that would help him on the road to heaven.

—Value of—General Grant's chief of staff, the Galena lawyer John A. Rawlins, was closer to Grant than any other during the war. It was to Rawlins that Grant gave his pledge that he would abstain from intoxicating liquors. When he broke that pledge Rawlins went to him and with great earnestness pleaded with him, for the sake of himself and for the sake of the great and holy cause of the nation, to refrain from strong drink. Faithful were the wounds of that friend. In front of the Capitol at Washington today there stands the magnificent monument of General Grant, sitting his horse in characteristic pose and flanked on either side by stirring battle scenes. But at the other end of Pennsylvania Avenue, a little to the south of the avenue, is Rawlins Park, where there stands a very ordinary, commonplace statue of Rawlins. Whenever I stand before the great monument of

Grant on his horse there in front of the Capitol, I think of that other monument. I think of that faithful friend who kept Grant on his horse.

———•◆•———

—**Wrong kind of**—Frequently I used to go down to the penitentiary to visit a man who was serving a life term. This was how it happened: He had not long been in this country. He went out one evening with a group of men who had invited him to accompany them. The first thing he knew they were robbing a store. In the shooting which ensued the woman in the house was fatally wounded. Sometime afterward the young man, who did not even know that a murder had been committed and who actually had nothing to do with it, was picked up and interrogated by the police, whom he frankly told that he had been out that night with a group of young men. He was tried and sentenced to death, for murder, and legally so, as he was in the company of those who had committed the crime. Just one night of thoughtless, careless friendship—and a life was all but ruined!

———•◆•———

A gentleman once came to see me about a friend in whose welfare he was interested. For some time this friend had been on the downgrade. I remember that the gentleman said of him, "He has contracted a dangerous friendship. The first thing we must do is to break that friendship." Mirabeau, writing to a friend, said of Talleyrand: "I am hoping this man is not known to you. Through the history of my misfortunes I was thrown into his hands." There are thousands of people who are in their graves, at least so far as the nobler and better part of them is concerned, and whose epitaph might well be, "He had a friend." There are thousands going with heavy hearts through the labor of life who look back with sorrow and pain and poignant regret to the hour when they met a certain friend, and say of that hour and of that friend, "Oh, if I had never met him! If I had never known him!"

———•◆•———

Heraclea in ancient Greece was noted for its honey. Beyond all other honey it was sweet to the taste and exhilarating to him who ate it. But this was because it was poisoned by the juice of aconite. So there are friends who entertain and thrill and excite—but, like Heraclea's honey, have deadly poison in them.

In the life of Robert Burns we can trace the evil influence of the wrong kind of friends. At the age of nineteen he fell in with some rough, fast, young men in a near-by town. There was one unprincipled youth in particular who exerted a strong fascination over Burns. Burns said of him, "He was the only man I ever knew who was a greater fool than myself when woman was the presiding star. But he spoke of lawless love with a levity which hitherto I had regarded with horror."

———•◆•———

Amnon had a friend! That was his epitaph. It is the true epitaph of many a broken life. That brief sentence tells the story of many a man who has disappointed his own hopes and the prayers of those who loved him and dreamed for him. It tells the secret of the bitterness of many a sad and heavy-hearted person who today goes mechanically about his work, his mind all the while turning with bitterness back to the ill-starred day when he met the friend who slew him. In many a person that once followed Jesus Christ and honored him as Saviour and King, but who now has no faith and no hope, or is following some of the gods made by the fancies and desires of men, that is the secret of the backsliding and apostasy—he had a friend.

FUTURE OF MANKIND

Clouds and darkness are round the world today, but the better day will come. The light of the prophetic morning shall dawn; the peace and the beauty of Apocalyptic dreams shall one day paint the new heavens and the new earth with a glory compared with which the brightest day that has yet dawned upon the earth, or that has yet entered into the mind of man, is but the shadow of darkness; for one day he who paid the price of the world's redemption shall come to reap the fruit and harvest of his crimson sowing, to see the travail of his soul, and to claim his Kingdom. Then war, and the memory of war, shall be forgotten; for wars and all that caused wars shall have passed away. Men shall beat their swords into plowshares and their spears into pruning hooks, and love shall paint the unclouded horizon of a world redeemed.

FUTURE PUNISHMENT—see also HELL

Jesus Christ is our one great teacher and authority on the subject of future punishment. "The most uncompromising revelation of this awful truth, which no rationalizing sophistry can effectually obscure, issued from the lips of the Incarnate Word himself." If it is the Lamb of God who is represented as inflicting men with his wrath in the great day of his wrath, let us remember that it is this same Lamb of God—he who bore our frame, he who took little children up into his arms and blessed them, he from whose lips fell the imperishable sentences of mercy and pity, he who sighed over the dumb boy and poured out his tears at the grave of Lazarus and wept over the doom of Jerusalem. It is he, the Lamb of God, who is our one great

teacher on this solemn theme of future retribution.

It would seem almost that he anticipated the difficulties this doctrine would occasion, the stumbling block it would be, and the objections which would be brought against it, and therefore made it forever clear that he whose word is truth is our authority for the teaching. You can pick and choose what you like or do not like in the gospels, but no one who takes Jesus as a teacher of truth can deny that he taught future punishment and warned men to flee from the wrath to come.

The great dramas and novels all have running through them the strain of punishment, not disciplinary and reformatory punishment, but burning and consuming penal and vindicatory punishments, punishments to satisfy the law, to avenge the spirit of justice, and not to reform the evildoer. Would it be possible to have a great book in which this note had not been struck?

Take George Eliot's *Romola*. The great tale reaches its climax when the wronged and betrayed and disowned old father and guardian, Baldasarre, wanders by the river, waiting, waiting, all the light of reason quenched by his wrongs and sufferings, save the one elemental instinct of justice and revenge. The body of Tito, escaping from the mob on the bridge, is cast up on the bank at the old man's feet. Like a panther he leaps upon the half-conscious man, fiercely clutching his throat. Thus they die together. Justice had brought Tito to the bar. The reader heaves a sigh of satisfaction, for he realizes that what something deep down in his heart demanded as the proper sequel to the tale had come to pass. The chapter concludes with these words: "Who shall put his finger on the work of justice and say,

'It is not there'? Justice is like the Kingdom of God—it is not without us as a fact; it is within us as a great yearning."

In *Confessions of an English Opium Eater* De Quincey tells of a relative of his who almost drowned in a river, and how her whole life in its minutest inci-dents appeared arrayed before her simultaneously, as in a mirror. De Quincey says he feels assured from his opium experiences that no such thing as forgetting is possible to the mind. Accidents will rend away the veil which other accidents and incidents have interposed between us and the past.

G

GARDENS—*see* FLOWERS

GETHSEMANE

Some years ago I had occasion to change trains at a railroad junction in the southern part of Texas. It was a wretched, straggling town, the streets mere gashes through the red loam. There were several warehouses and a collection of general stores, with mules and horses tied at the rail in front. On top of a barren hill was the courthouse; and scattered about, without any semblance of order, depressing in their location and appearance, were the houses of the inhabitants. There was a brick Baptist church, not more attractive than the other buildings. But as I passed by I could make out in the large stained-glass window the figure of Christ kneeling in Gethsemane. The glass was cheap and the window poorly executed, but cheap glass and poor execution could not altogether destroy the majesty and pathos of Christ kneeling in his agony for the salvation of souls. The miserable hamlet seemed to take on a certain dignity and worth now, because one realized that he who was represented there as entering into his agony in Gethsemane had suffered and died for you, for me.

GOD—*see also* HISTORY (GOD IN), RIGHT (TRIUMPH OF), SUFFERING AND GOD

—First—An Oriental king once summoned into his presence his three sons and set before them three sealed urns—one of gold, the other of amber, and the third of clay. The king bade his eldest son to choose among these three urns that which appeared to him to contain the greatest treasures. The eldest son chose the vessel of gold, on which was written the word "Empire." He opened it and found it full of blood. The second chose the vase of amber, whereon was written the word "Glory"; and when he opened it he found it full of the ashes of men who had made a great name in the world. The third son chose the vessel of clay, and on the bottom of this vessel was inscribed the name of God. The wise men at the king's court voted that the third vessel weighed the most, because a single letter of the name of God weighed more than all the rest of the universe.

There is a legend of St. Theresa that she once saw an angel holding in one hand a curtain and in the other a shell filled with water. When she asked the angel what these were for, he answered that the curtain was to hide heaven and the shell filled with water to put out the flames of hell, so that men would choose and praise God for himself. That is what Christ invites us to do in the first petition of the Lord's Prayer. It is the keynote of all that follows. Before the prayers for the necessities of our life, and for deliverance from sin, and for others, is the great petition that God's name shall be hallowed.

—Good-by to—At Princeton there is a tradition about Aaron Burr: how one night, when the college was shaken by a revival, he shut himself in his room, saying that before the night was over he would decide the matter of his relationship to God. Late at night the students living near him heard his shutters thrown open and a loud exclamation, "Good-by, God!"

The echo of this cry is heard in many quarters today, and with more or less enthusiasm. Those of us who are of the household of faith are reluctant to admit the sweep and range of the present anti-Christian movement. It proceeds under two forms: first, open and avowed atheistic propaganda, or the worship of No-God; second, and much more dangerous and subtle, the cowardly compromise with unbelief on the part of religious leaders of our day.

—And history—In 1847 Frederick Douglas, the eloquent fugitive slave, was addressing an antislavery convention just over the Ohio line at Salem. His own sufferings and those of his people, and the slow progress that the great reform was making, had somewhat depressed him; and a certain bitterness was manifest in the speech which he was making. In the midst of that speech he was suddenly interrupted by sojourner Truth, the aged Negress, who was a unique and powerful figure in the antislavery crusade, who cried out, "Frederick, Frederick, is God dead?"

No, God is not dead! God was not dead in the days of Gideon; he is not dead in our day; and blessed are they to whom is given the instinct to tell that God is on the field when he is most invisible!

—In our lives—For the special benefit of young men or young women who may have been listening to the present-day gospel of revolt and of self-expression, let me quote these words which Thomas Wentworth Higginson once wrote to his son: "He can think as he pleases about religion; but he has got to live with other people, and he cannot get rid of God. The world and we are all made so, and the boy who sees it clearly and lives accordingly is best off."

—Knowledge of—The richest man in the world, Croesus, once asked the wisest man in the world, Thales, What is God? The philosopher asked for a day in which to deliberate, and then for another, and then for another, and another, and another—and at length confessed that he was not able to answer, that the longer he deliberated, the more difficult it was for him to frame an answer. The fiery Tertullian, the early Church Father, eagerly seized upon this incident and said it was an example of the world's ignorance of God outside of Christ. "There," he exclaimed, "is the wisest man in the world, and he cannot tell you who God is. But the most ignorant mechanic among the Christians knows God, and is able to make him known unto others."

—Mercy of—Riding over the desert early one morning last winter, I saw a beautiful sight. There had been a slight rain in the morning, and a rainbow appeared on the western horizon. If it had been a flat country the rainbow would have arched itself only against the horizon. But here it cast its marvelous and iridescent bridge against the grim and rugged mountain. The predominant colors of the rainbow—green, violet, orange, and blue—made a lovely picture against the barren and yellow mountain, just as barren and yellow as the mountains of Patmos where John saw his vision. The rainbow touched the mountain with heavenly splendor and softened its severity and ruggedness. As I looked upon it far across the desert I said to myself, There is the rainbow of the Apocalypse, the rainbow which St. John saw when a door was opened for him into heaven. And he beheld a throne set in heaven and "there was a rainbow round about the throne." (Rev. 4:3.)

There was the mountain, towering, massive, severe, and forbidding, but suffused and softened now with the colors of the rainbow. And in St. John's vision is the throne of God's judgment and righteousness, the throne of his government and his sovereignty. But round about the throne, completely encircling it, is the rainbow of his love and mercy. Here, then, in this vision of the throne and the rainbow, we have set forth the truth of God's justice and righteousness, and also the truth of his mercy and his love.

—**Our strength**—The world knows something of Charlotte Brontë and her famous *Jane Eyre;* not so much of another of the sisters, Emily, the author of a powerful book, *Wuthering Heights.* The promise of this book was not fulfilled, for death cut short Emily's career. When the family opened her desk after her death and looked over the papers—those papers always impressive because written by a hand that is now forever still—

they found no begun or half-finished novel, but a poem which is fit monument to the woman's heroic spirit. One of the stanzas runs thus:

> *No coward soul is mine,*
> *No trembler in the world's storm-*
> *troubled sphere.*
> *I see Heaven's glories shine,*
> *And faith shines equal, arming me*
> *from fear.*

> *Oh God within my breast,*
> *Almighty, ever-present Deity!*
> *Life—that in me has rest,*
> *As I—undying Life—have power in*
> *Thee!*

"I used to lean upon my own strength . . ." The man had been speaking to me about his troubles and his burdens. I waited for him to add another, a concluding, clause or sentence. But that was all he said. He left that for me to do. I was to draw my own conclusions. He used to lean upon his own strength; but now he was leaning somewhere else, upon some other strength. The sentence marked an epoch in his spiritual history. There had been a complete change in the plan of his life. He had had bitter experience of the weakness of his own strength. It was only a reed which bent beneath the weight, or pierced the hand that reposed upon it. Now he had found something better. He had come to lean upon God. God was his refuge and his strength, a very present help in the time of trouble.

—**Presence of**—One of the most interesting of London's ancient cemeteries is Bunhill Fields. There rests the dust of Charles Wesley, Isaac Watts, and Daniel Defoe, the author of *Robinson Crusoe.* The cemetery is sometimes spoken of as the "Westminster Abbey of Nonconformity." Directly across from this ancient graveyard is the chapel of John Wesley, and the house in which he lived and died, and the monument which has been reared to his memory. Just before his death on March 2, 1791, John Wesley opened his eyes and exclaimed in a strong, clear voice, "The best of all is, God is with us!" Yes, best of all, and last of all, God is with us.

—Proof of—A great French thinker said, "I think, therefore I am." His argument was that he must exist, else he could not have thought of himself. In the same way we are justified in our faith concerning God. The idea of God is certainly in the minds of men throughout the world today, and has been in the minds of man throughout all ages. The question is, How did this idea of God arise? We must choose between two answers. One is that man's cogitation and meditation resulted in the idea of a God. The other is that God exists, and that his existence accounts for the idea of God in man's mind. Certainly the latter answer is rational and simple. Some have said that clever priests invented the idea of God to further their selfish ends. But where did those priests get such an idea? Others have pointed out the low and gross conceptions of God which prevail among heathen people, or among the pagans of antiquity. But where did the heathen and the pagan get their idea of God, even such base and low thought of God? Others there are who vehemently assert that there is no God. But even the man who asserts that he is an infidel is an argument for the existence of God, for before he could deny that there is a God he had to have the idea of a God in his mind.

There may be times when you could wish for more striking signs of God's presence and power in the world and in your own life: a bush that burns and is not consumed, like that which told Moses that God was nigh; a fleece that is wet with dew on the rock that is dry, like that which let Gideon know that God was speaking to him; the shadow going back on the face of the dial, like that which assured Isaiah that his life would be spared fifteen years. But when you stop to think of it, this longing is without reason. What more striking evidence could you have that there is a God and that God is in the world, that God has dealings with you, than conscience within your soul? How could God have made himself more real to us than by conscience?

When a first-year student in the theological seminary at Princeton, I went out to preach one Sunday in a New Jersey town. In the home where I was entertained there was a man, well along in years, who was, or claimed to be, an infidel. His argument was as follows: "If a man tells me that he has a horse which can trot a mile in three minutes, I tell him to bring out the horse and prove it. If you tell me that there is a God, I ask you to produce God and prove his existence."

No Christian claims to know God, nor would want to know him, in that way. By that kind of searching we cannot know the Almighty to perfection. The Christian believer does not say, "I know God," or "I see God," or "I think there is a God," but "I *believe* in God."

—And temptation—The author of a drama dealing with Joseph and his temptation in the house of Potiphar represents Potiphar's wife as answering the objection of Joseph that he could not sin against God by taking her skirt and throwing it over the bust of an Egyptian god which stood in her chamber. "Now," she said, "God will not see."

But Joseph answered, "My God sees."

———◆———

—Works of: telegraph—Almost thirteen centuries before the birth of Christ the prophet Balaam stood on Pisgah's summit and surveyed the encampment of Israel. Having had his eyes miraculously opened to the grandeur of the destiny of the people of God, he exclaimed, "It shall be said of Jacob and of Israel, What hath God wrought!" (Num. 23:23.)

Thirty-one centuries passed. In the chamber of the Supreme Court in the Capitol at Washington, Samuel Morse, an American painter who had turned inventor, tapped out a message on a new device. The message was received and recorded by those who were waiting in a room in Baltimore. The telegraph, which since that time has transmitted so many thousands of messages of joy and sorrow, of birth and death, of war and peace, was an accomplished fact. May 24, 1944, was the hundredth anniversary of the sending of the first message. Again that first message—the exclamation of that eloquent seer on Pisgah's height—was flashed over the wires, sounding this time around the world: "What hath God wrought!"

GODLINESS—*see* FRIEND OF GOD

GOOD—*see also* MAN (GOOD AND EVIL IN)
—Out of evil—I cannot think, as some have, that Jesus' plea from the cross was meant only for the Roman soldiers, who were merely carrying out their commands, and that the Pharisees and scribes and Sadducees were excluded from the mercy of that prayer. I wonder if he meant, when he said, "Father, forgive them; for they know not what they do" (Luke 23:34), not merely, They do

not understand that they are crucifying the Prince of Glory and the Son of God, but this: Father, forgive them, for in their malice and blindness they cannot see what eternal blessings are to come to mankind through my death upon the cross? Yes, so far as the providence of God is concerned with the dark and wicked things of this world, the Cross of Christ is the great answer; for that was the most wicked, the most dreadful act that ever stained the earth, and even the sun blushed when it was done, and hid its face, and the earth groaned when its Maker died. Yet see what came out of that most wicked deed—blessings abound forever because Christ was crucified on the cross.

———◆———

It took a year of defeat and disappointment to bring the government to a state of mind where it was ready to proclaim the emancipation of the slave. Horace Greeley—the great editor of the *Tribune,* who ran in the masthead of his paper the slogan "On to Richmond!"—was fiercely critical of what seemed to be the blundering failures of the government. But when he came to write his reminiscences, after the war was over and slavery had been destroyed and the Union preserved, Greeley saw clearly the hand of God in that early history of the war. "Had Napoleon or Jackson," he wrote, "been in Scott's place in 1861, the rebellion would have been stamped out ere the close of that year. But slavery would have remained to scourge us still. Thus disaster is overruled to subserve the ends of beneficence. Thus the evil of the moment contains the germ of good that is enduring."

That was a great sentence by Greeley: "Thus the evil of the moment contains the germ of good that is enduring."

GOOD DEEDS—*see* DEEDS (GOOD)

GOOD LIFE

On the Cornish coast of England, on a jutting crag with the waves of the Atlantic rolling in and breaking upon it in thunderous refrain, are the ruins of the legendary castle of King Arthur. It was near that same Tintagel that King Arthur fought his last battle. When he was dying he gave his famous sword, Excalibur, to one of his knights, with the command to cast it into the sea. The sword had been drawn by the boy Arthur from the miraculous stone by the church door—a feat which caused the people to proclaim him king. When Sir Bedivere hurled Excalibur back into the sea, an arm clothed in white, mystic and wonderful, caught the sword by the hilt, brandished it three times aloft, and drew it under.

This is a parable of the truth that the righteous life girds a man with power. By your own life you forge the Excalibur with which you will win your victories. There is no other sword like that. May everyone be able to say, as David said about the sword of Goliath the Philistine, "There is none like that; give it me" (I Sam. 21:9).

—**Blessings of the**—I think the most beautiful of all the creations of Dickens was the lovely child Nell. The victim of misfortune from the beginning of her life, faithful to her aged grandparent in whose breast burns the flame of the gambler, Little Nell wanders to and fro over England, often homeless, fireless, cold, coming in contact with coarse and rude men—gypsies, gamblers, bargemen, furnacemen, and showmen—and yet, wherever she went, by the sweetness and kindness of her disposition awakening kindness in others and speaking to that better angel which sleeps in every human breast. "When I die," was her request, "put near me some thing that has loved the light, and had the sky above it always."

"She was dead. Dear, gentle, patient, noble Nell, was dead. . . . And still her former self lay there, unaltered in this change. Yes. The old fireside had smiled upon that same sweet face; it had passed, like a dream, through haunts of misery and care; at the door of the poor schoolmaster on the summer evening, before the furnace fire upon the cold wet night, at the still bedside of the dying boy, there had been the same mild lovely look. So shall we know the angels in their majesty, after death."

Every heart responds to that beautiful passage in *The Old Curiosity Shop,* for whoever looked upon the still, calm face of the godly dead and felt that their life had been in vain, or that godliness was not profitable for this life as well as for the life to come?

—**And death**—Perhaps the greatest of all Christmas stories is that masterpiece of Charles Dickens, *A Christmas Carol.* When the third phantom, the Ghost of Christmas Yet to Come, arrived at the door of Scrooge, the hard-as-flint miser who had accumulated so much silver and gold, he conducted him to a low, beetling pawnshop in one of the poorer districts of London.

There he saw an old hag bring in a bag and empty it on the floor, and he was horrified to discover that the articles had been stripped from his own chambers. Then the phantom touched him, and he found himself in his own bedroom.

On the bed lay a still, sheeted form. Scrooge dared not lift the sheet to look upon the face. Then said the phantom, "O cold, cold, rigid, dreadful Death, set up thine altar here, and dress it with such terrors as thou hast at thy command: for this is thy dominion! But of the loved, revered, and honored head, thou canst not turn one hair to thy dread purposes, or make one feature odious. It is not that the hand is heavy and will fall down when released; it is not that the heart and pulse are still; but that the hand WAS open, generous, and true; the heart brave, warm, and tender; and the pulse a man's. Strike, Shadow, strike! And see his good deeds springing from the wound, to sow the world with life immortal!"

When the Master of Abbotsford, Sir Walter Scott, lay dying, he called for his son-in-law and biographer, Lockhart, and said to him, "Lockhart, my dear sir, be a good man. Be virtuous, be religious, be a good man. Nothing else will give you any comfort when you come to lie here."

GOSPEL—*see also* PREACHING THE GOSPEL, WITNESSING

—Comfort of the—In the historical sketch of an Ohio Church I read with interest how a Bible with raised letters was presented in 1863 to the blind organist, Walter L. Campbell. In the words of presentation, spoken or written by the pastor of the church, I found expressed the following pious wish: "May the precious truths of the gospel of Christ be your comfort in life, your support in death, and your portion in eternity." How well and truly was that spoken! The gospel of Christ, to him who believes it, and who humbles his heart and mind before the majesty of Christ's atonement for sin, is our comfort in life, our stay and support in death, and in eternity our sure and everlasting portion.

—Divine origin of the—When I stand on the coast of Cornwall and see those tremendous granite cliffs against which the waves, rolling in clear from Labrador, are flinging themselves in their fury, I know that man's hand did not cut those mighty niches in the rock. When I see the sun setting in the west, as I saw it tonight—a beautiful center of red and about it a border of blue, just fading here and there into grey—I know that the hand of man did not paint it. When I look upon the gospel with its great answer, with its marvelous remedy, with its satisfactions for the whole nature of man, I know that it came from God— "Master, no man can do the work thou doest except God be with him." Man with his sins and wanderings is the problem. Christ is the solution. Man with his needs is the question. Christ is the answer. "Lord, to whom shall we go? thou hast the words of eternal life." (John 6:68.)

—Fits man—An African woman who had heard for the first time, from a missionary, the story of Christ and the Cross, exclaimed, "I always knew that there must be such a man as that!" When we speak of the witness of humanity to Christianity, that is what we mean: that Christianity must be true because it is adapted to man—ancient, medieval, modern, man wherever he has appeared in the past, man in whatever state we can imagine him to exist in the ages to come.

—Fits man's soul—When Marshal Soult returned from a sojourn in Spain he brought with him to Paris a copy of Murillo's "Virgin and Child." When he came to examine the painting he discovered that only the center of the picture was genuine, that the border was meretricious and of inferior work. Some years after, Lord Overstowe while traveling in Spain was attracted by a painting which had a very inferior center but the border of which was superb—angels and clouds, the sort of thing in which Murillo excelled—and for the sake of the border he bought the picture. Then at the sale of Soult's effects he purchased the picture which Soult had brought from Spain, and on examining the two in his gallery he discovered that Soult's picture contained the center for the picture which he himself had brought from Spain, fitting exactly not only in detail of mechanism but in tone and color.

The Christian religion is a glorious border that fits man's soul. The soul of man comes from God, therefore the religion which fits it, which answers his utmost need, must also come from God.

———◆◆◆———

—Love for the—Deep in the heart of the Virginia mountains stands an ancient gray stone church. In the quiet acre alongside, close to the wall of the church, as if craving in death the fellowship of God's house which they enjoyed in life, sleep the pioneer forefathers who conquered that wilderness with rifle, ax, and psalm book. In a stone over the portal of the church are cut these words: "This church was built by God-fearing inhabitants of this place as a token of their love for the holy gospel of our Lord Jesus Christ."

———◆◆◆———

—Preaching the—A minister well known in England was called once late at night to visit a dying woman in one of the poorest sections of the city. After climbing the stairs up to her wretched apartment, he sat down beside the woman and tried to comfort her by speaking of courage, and patience, and hope, and that sort of thing—the themes that had been the tenor of his preaching in the church. But the woman interrupted him saying, "All that's true, but it's not for the likes of me. Just tell me how a poor

sinner can get in." Then the minister remembered what he had never forgotten, although he had ceased to preach it, and told her the Bible's simple story of repentance and salvation through the death of Jesus Christ. . . . "I got her in," he said, afterward, "and what's more, I got myself in, too."

———◆◆◆———

—The social—The Swedish novelist Selma Lagerlöf, in her tale *The Miracles of Antichrist,* tells of a wonder-working image of Christ as a child, which was enshrined in a monastery on Capitol Hill at Rome and greatly venerated by the monks. The image was adorned with costly jewels and wore a crown of gold. An Englishwoman of great wealth who came to pray in the chapel where the image stood was greatly taken with it. But when she asked the monks to sell it to her, they told her that if she were to give them a pile of gold as high as the Capitol Hill they would not part with it.

Then she contrived to secure the image by craft and deceit. She had a workman produce an image of the same dimensions, yet made of cheap wood. It was furnished with a crown, but only of tinsel, not of gold. When it was finished, it looked just like the genuine image—so much so that, in order not to be confused herself by the resemblance, she had the workman scratch upon the tinsel crown with the point of a needle, "My kingdom is only of this world." Then one day while praying before the real image she pretended to faint, and when the attendant went off for a glass of water she exchanged the images and secreted the true image under her cloak.

For a time worship went on in the chapel just the same as before. No one detected that a false image had been substituted for the genuine. But one night at midnight the monks heard a loud knocking at the door of the monastery.

When they opened the door, lo! there stood their true image of Christ! In amazement they carried it up to the chapel; and then, carefully examining the other image, they discovered the fraud and read the inscription written with the needle point on the crown of the false image: "My kingdom is only of this world." Whereupon they set the true image in its place and in anger hurled the false image down the steps of the Capitol. There it was recovered by the woman who had had it made.

Wherever she went on her travels through Europe with that false image, in some mysterious way the Church and the gospel seemed to lose their power. At length, in one of the riots of the Commune in the streets of Paris, the workmen who had recovered the false image from the baggage of a wrecked carriage set it up on their barricades. There it was seen by a philosopher and thinker, who read the inscription, "My kingdom is only of this world." That legend he adopted for the gospel of socialism which he proclaimed.

Today there is proclaimed in the world a gospel, popular in many churches, which looks like, and sounds like, the real thing. But if one looks closely, he will see written across its brow that inscription, "My kingdom is only of this world."

———— • ————

—**Tests man**—Hugo Grotius has written, "It is the will of God that those things which He would have us believe, so that faith should be accepted from us as obedience, should not be so very plain, as those things we perceive by our senses, and by demonstration; but only so far as it is sufficient to procure belief, and persuade a man of the thing, who is not obstinately bent against it, so that the Gospel is, as it were, a touchstone to try men's honest dispositions by."

GOSPELS, THE FOUR

Browning's "A Death in the Desert" is the poet's imagination of what John might have said, or ought to have said, when he was dying. On the whole the poem does gross injustice to him who spake so clearly and wrote so simply, and for lucidity of thought and simplicity of style Browning had studied John to no purpose. But here and there he makes John say something sensible and comprehensible. One instance is where John refers to his great age and how when he dies the last eyewitness will be gone:

If I live yet, it is for good, more love
Through me to men: be naught but ashes here
That keep awhile my semblance, who was John,—
Still, when they scatter, there is left on earth
No one alive who knew (consider this!)
—Saw with his eyes and handled with his hands
That which was from the first, the Word of Life.
How will it be when none more saith, "I saw"?

———— • ————

Anyone who has done historical writing or investigation is familiar with the variant accounts of any historical event. Take, for example, the Gettysburg speech of Abraham Lincoln. From those who ought to have been in a position to know the facts as to the composition and delivery of this famous speech we get the most irreconcilable accounts. But the thing about the Four Gospels in their narrative of the death and resurrection of Jesus which sets off this event from all other events is their grand agreement as to the one great fact—that Christ, who predicted his resurrection, was crucified, dead, and buried, and that he rose again the third day.

GOSSIP

How easy it is to pass on an ill report with such phrases as this, "Have you heard?" "Do you know?" "They tell me," "Keep this to yourself, but—" "I don't believe it's true, but I heard so-and-so say"; or that ancient and familiar word of defamation, "They say." That was the word with which Sanballat came to Nehemiah when he tried to threaten him with the anonymous report that he was plotting rebellion against the king of Persia.

* * *

When Aaron Burr at the end of his long life, during which he had tasted the cup of honor and distinction and also drained the dregs of bitterness and humiliation, lay dying in a boarding house at Port Richmond, Staten Island, a friend who was waiting upon him in reporting to him some rumor commenced by saying, "They say." At that Burr interrupted her and said, "My dear, never use that word. It has broken more hearts than any other."

* * *

There is a kind of gossip that is good and profitable. A turning point in the early life of John Bunyan was when he chanced to hear three or four poor women sitting at a door in the sun, talking about the things of God. If they had been talking about their neighbors or rolling some morsel of scandal under their tongues, who knows that it might not have been altogether different in the future with John Bunyan. But what he heard them talking about was the new birth, the work of God in their hearts, and how they were comforted and refreshed by the love of Christ. As he went about his work as a tinker, mending the pots and pans of the neighborhood, "their talk and discourse went with him."

GRACE, DOCTRINE OF—*see* AUTHORITY

GRACE OF GOD

In heaven there was once a great debate as to who was the greatest monument of God's grace. All breasts were bared and all secrets were told as the redeemed sought to pay tribute to the grace of God. One after another related the sin or transgression out of which Christ had delivered him. At length the choice seemed to be settling down upon one man who apparently had committed all sins. Iniquity after iniquity he related as he turned over the ghastly pages of his autobiography. And then he related how on his deathbed Christ came and saved him as he had saved the thief on the cross.

But just before the vote was taken another of the redeemed stepped forward and asked to tell his story. It was this: He had come to know and love Christ as a child and had followed him all the days of his life, and by his grace he had been kept from the sins and transgressions of which the others had spoken. Then the vote was taken; and it was not the drunkard, the thief, the adulterer, the perjurer, the murderer, or the blasphemer, but the man who had followed Christ all his days and had been kept by his grace who was selected as the greatest monument to the grace of God.

GRATITUDE

Dean Swift thought ill of the education given him by a charitable uncle. "Yes," he once said when asked if his uncle had not educated him, "he gave me the education of a dog."

"And you," replied his interlocutor, "have not the gratitude of a dog."

Like a sudden glow of sunlight appearing through the black clouds at the close of a stormy winter's day is the last act in the tragedy of King Saul. When Saul had fallen on Gilboa's mount, the Philistines cut off his head and stripped the body of armor. Then they sent messengers to all parts of the Philistine country to carry the good news of their victory over the great foe. Saul's body they nailed to the wall of Beth-shan.

At length the tidings came to Jabesh-gilead, away across the Jordan, the town that Saul had saved out of the hand of the Ammonites when first he was made king. No other city in all Israel raised a finger to save the dust of Saul from desecration; but these men of Jabesh-gilead remembered the service Saul had done them years before, when he was himself, and not at war with man and God. In gratitude for that past service these men, taking their lives in their hands, went all night to the Philistine stronghold. They took the body of Saul and the bodies of his sons down from the wall of Beth-shan, carried them to Jabesh, and burned them there; then they buried the dust under the tamarisk tree and fasted for seven days.

When General Grant arrived in New York in 1854, after he had resigned under a cloud from the army in California, he was without funds and still far from his Ohio home. In this difficulty he went to call on a West Point friend and comrade in the Mexican War, Simon Bolivar Buckner. Buckner generously supplied him with funds, so that he could reach his home in Ohio. Eight years afterward, when Grant captured Fort Donelson in that great victory in February, 1862, the surrender was made by General Buckner, the other officers having fled.

In a speech delivered at a Grant birthday dinner, Buckner told what happened there at Fort Donelson: "Under these circumstances I surrendered to General Grant. I had at a previous time befriended him, and it has been justly said that he never forgot an act of kindness. I met him on the boat (at the surrender), and he followed me when I went to my quarters. He left the officers of his own army and followed me, with that modest manner peculiar to him, into the shadow, and there he tendered me his purse. It seems to me that in the modesty of his nature he was afraid the light would witness that act of generosity, and sought to hide it from the world."

When Robinson Crusoe was wrecked on his lonely isle he drew up in two columns what he called the evil and the good. He was cast on a desolate island, but still alive—not drowned, as all his ship's company were. He was divided from mankind and banished from human society, but he was not starving. He had no clothes, but he was in a hot climate where he didn't need them. He was without means of defense, but he saw no wild beasts, such as he had seen on the coast of Africa. He had no soul to speak to, but God had sent the ship so near to the shore that he could get out of it all things necessary for his wants. So he concluded that there was not any condition in the world so miserable but there was something negative or something positive to be thankful for in it.

GREAT MEN—*see also* LONELINESS OF THE GREAT

—And their age—Great men are to a certain extent the product of their day and generation. They are thrust out upon the arena of some crisis. At any other period of America's history than the Revolution, George Washington would

149

have been just a well-to-do Virginia planter. At any other period than that of the great dispute over slavery and union, Lincoln would have been a successful country lawyer, or if by any chance elected to the presidency, just another one of the presidents. The same is true of the great men of the Bible. Moses appears when Israel needs a deliverer out of Egypt. Elijah appears when all but seven thousand in Israel have bowed the knee to Baal. Likewise Gideon. He appeared as a deliverer when the whole land was groaning under the hand of the Midianites.

————

—And their backers—The biographies of great men reveal how, in almost every instance, back of the great man, hidden in the shadow, stood some wise friend who comforted him in trouble and counseled him with precepts of virtue and wisdom. Alexander the Great had his Clitus, his friend in youth, the savior of his life at the battle of Granicus—who fell at Alexander's hand in a drunken quarrel. David was no exception to this rule, for he had a Jonathan whose love to him was wonderful, "passing the love of women" (II Sam. 1:26), and who, at a critical hour in his life, renewed his courage and his faith.

————

—And unknown helpers—How often it has been true that great men have been aided and put forward by others who are little heard of. Grant would never have lasted through his first campaigns had it not been for two men—one his chief of staff, John A. Rawlins, who kept him from intemperance; and the other Washburne, congressman from Illinois, who was Grant's spokesman at court. And going back into the history of the Church, there is its greatest figure—Paul, who when in obscurity and unable to get a hearing as a preacher of the gospel, was vouched for by Barnabas and introduced to his great work at Antioch. At first it was Barnabas and Paul, then Paul and Barnabas. After a little Barnabas disappeared altogether.

In the Church there are just a few Pauls and Peters and Luthers, Knoxes and Wesleys and Whitefields, Chalmers and Beechers—but back of them is the great army of the humble, inconspicuous, but faithful workers and witnesses: ministers, most of whom toil in obscure places; elders; Sunday school workers; and teachers. Paul always went out of his way to recognize those faithful friends and workers who helped him to do his work, and he is proud to speak of them as his yokefellows and fellow soldiers of Christ: Epaphroditus, whose name means "charming," and who brought the gift of the church of Philippi to Paul when he was in prison at Rome; and all the others, whose names, Paul says, are in the Book of Life, written there as clearly and distinctly and as indelibly as the name of Paul himself.

GREED—*see* AVARICE, MONEY

GUARDIAN   ANGELS—*see*   ANGELS (GUARDIAN)

H

HAPPINESS

—Complete—There is no ideal state in this life. That was the ruling idea of Samuel Johnson's famous tale *Rasselas*. The Abyssinian prince, although all his wants were supplied and he lived in peace and luxury, became dissatisfied with his closed-in valley and, escaping from it, roamed the world in search of those who were altogether happy. To his surprise he discovered that such a person did not exist, and disillusioned he returned to his mountain home in Abyssinia.

—And death—After his defeat on the plains, Croesus took refuge in the citadel of Sardis. According to Herodotus, Meles, a former king of Sardis, had carried his son Leon, whom his concubine bore him, around the walls to render them impregnable. But he omitted to carry his son about that part of the wall opposite to Mount Tmolus. There the soldiers of Cyrus made their assault and took the city. According to the cruel custom of the day, Croesus was condemned to the flames. As the fire was about to be lighted, he pronounced three times the name of Solon. Hearing the name, and having great respect for Solon, Cyrus released him and delivered him from death.

Years before, Solon had paid a visit to Sardis. After he had shown him the vast depositories of his wealth, Croesus said to him, "My Athenian guest, the voice of fame speaks loudly of your wisdom. I have heard much of your travels. I am hence induced to inquire of you what man of all whom you have beheld seemed to you most happy." Croesus was much disappointed when, instead of naming him, Solon named an obscure Athenian patriot who had died for his country. When Croesus expressed surprise that Solon thought so meanly of his wealth and prosperity, Solon gave his famous answer, "Call no man happy till you know the nature of his death."

It was that sentence that came to the mind of Croesus on that day when in the sudden reversal of his fortunes he stood bound on the funeral pyre.

—The highest—In 1791 the Academy at Lyons offered a prize for the best essay on the subject "What Truths and Sentiments Is It Most Necessary to Impress upon Men for Their Happiness?" Among the contestants was a young man of whom the world would shortly hear much, the young Napoleon. Napoleon's essay is full of truth and elevated ideas, and particularly interesting is what he has to say about ambition—how it caused Alexander the Great to conquer and ravage the world without being able to satisfy it; how it guided Cromwell to rule England, but tormented him with all the daggers and furies; and how the ambitions of Charles V, Philip II, and other rulers, were, like all disordered passions, a violent, unreflecting madness which only ceased with life, a conflagration fanned by a pitiless wind which did not end till it had consumed everything. There Napoleon the youth pleads with Napoleon of the future.

As for happiness, he commences his essay by saying that happiness is the enjoyment of a life which is most suited to our organization. But our organization is twofold—animal and intellectual. This is a very sound definition. The gratification of the natural desires is good for man, for they are a part of his organization; but man is more than body. He therefore cannot have happiness without enjoying the life that is best fitted for the soul, the highest part of his nature. Since man is a moral being, the effort after happiness must not violate the conditions of man's moral nature, for when that is done, misery follows. This being the case, life is rather a place of preparation for the highest happiness than a place for its enjoyment, and in this life our chief business is to seek first the Kingdom of God.

—Hunters of—In a certain sense all men are gold hunters, Argonauts. They seek the gold of happiness and content. The pathos of life is that men seek for happiness and satisfaction where they can never be found. The Spaniards who followed Ponce de Leon toiled through wildernesses where no gold could be found. Men are as ignorant of moral geography as the Spaniards were of physical geography. They struggle on in their quest for the gold of happiness, ever seeking, never finding, ever disappointed, ensnared by the pestilential passions that rise out of the low places of human nature, deluded and deceived by the mirage of their imagination, tracked by remorseless misfortune, till death puts a "thus far and no farther" to their journey.

In the museum of the State House of Mississippi I once saw an old rusty breastplate and halberd. They were relics of the first expedition of the Spaniards to Florida and the lands to the west. The lure of gold drew them to that fabled shore; but they found only monotonous stretches of sand, melancholy fir trees, venomous reptiles, poisonous insects, malarial savannahs, wild beasts, and wilder men. They were seeking for gold; but the farther they wandered into the wilderness the farther away from gold they went. The story of these hapless Spanish adventurers, wandering about in the swamps and jungles, now despairing and now feverish with hope born of some tale of treasure just beyond them, seeking for the yellow metal that so often strikes men blind when they find it—is not this a parable of life?

All men are seeking for gold. I suppose that if a poll were taken of this congregation, it would be discovered that more than one person has even invested in a gold mine. But when I speak of gold, I mean the gold of satisfaction and happiness. The drunkard on the street, the thief in the sleeping household, the pale student at yonder window where the midnight lamp is burning, the businessman at his desk, the mother in her home, the throngs in the playhouse, the worshipers in the church of Christ—all of them are on the quest of gold.

—The right to—As soon as I heard his story I knew that there was no hope; but the manifest anguish of the man moved me to say that I would go and speak with his wife. I was courteously and even kindly received. After a somewhat delicate and difficult interview I asked her if I might offer a prayer on her behalf. To this she readily assented. I prayed that she might be guided in the path of right and duty. When I was about to leave she thanked me for coming, but with great decisiveness affirmed her determination to have no reconciliation whatever with her husband, for whom she had neither love nor respect. "I believe," she said, "that everyone has the right to be happy, and I propose to claim that right."

When I had gone out, I found the husband pacing up and down the street in front of the house. I told him that the best thing for him to do was to accept the inevitable, that his wife's affection for him was dead, and, so far as I could see, there was no hope of a resurrection. Instead of permitting himself to be broken and distracted, I counseled him to patience, forgiveness, and faith. But as I left him and went my way, the sentence kept repeating itself in my mind, "I believe everyone has the right to be happy." And then I would say to myself, *"Has* he?" *"Has* she?"

Months afterward, riding on a train to New York, a member of the family with whom for a time she had taken refuge, and in whose house I had interviewed her, handed me a clipping from one of the New York papers. There in brief words was the ending of the chapter, and a sad ending, too, in one of the New York hospitals. At once there flashed back to me her words, "I believe everyone has the right to be happy." Her golden apple had turned out to be only an apple of Sodom, and had crumbled to ashes at her touch.

—Source of—A kind and virtuous mother, let us imagine, has two sons— one of them kind, obedient, thoughtful; the other, unfilial, cruel, and vicious. The mother falls ill, and messages are sent to the absent sons. The dutiful and obedient son is at a great distance, and during the long journey to his mother's bedside he is racked by the pains of suspense. The train is filled with interesting people and passes through lovely country. But the man is distressed and unhappy because he is fearful lest his mother should die before he reaches her side to receive her blessing. In memory he dwells upon her thousand kindnesses and shrinks from facing that hour when he will mourn as one that mourneth for his mother. Great, I say, is that man's unhappiness. But it is not so great as that of the unworthy son, whose mind as he stands by his mother's side is tortured, not by the pains of suspense, nor by the fear of bereavement, but by a remorse which cuts him like a knife as he looks down upon the face that his follies have helped to line with care, and the hair his sins have whitened. He, too, is unhappy, but his unhappiness is the harder to endure because it is a moral unhappiness, the unhappiness issuing from guilt and sin. Perhaps we might say that while one was unhappy, the other was miserable.

Pascal, author of the celebrated *Thoughts,* has a profound thought when he says that happiness is not in ourselves but in God. There are, indeed, by-streams of happiness, such as affection for others and from others, doing good to others, doing creative work, entertaining hope for the future, sitting in the sunlight of pleasant memories of the past. But these are only by-springs. The real fountain and source of happiness is a state of life and soul that is right with God, and, therefore, right with man.

HATE—*see also* FORGIVENESS, REVENGE

Leonardo da Vinci was one of the outstanding intellects of all history, for he was great as a draftsman, an engineer, and a thinker. Just before he commenced work on his "Last Supper" he had a violent quarrel with a fellow painter. So enraged and bitter was Leonardo that he determined to paint the face of his enemy, the other artist, into the face of Judas, and thus take his revenge and vent his spleen by handing the man down in infamy and scorn to succeeding generations. The face of Judas was one of the first that he finished, and everyone could easily recognize it as the face of the painter with whom he had quarreled. But when he came to paint the face of Christ, he could make no progress. Something seemed to be baffling him, holding him back, frustrating his best efforts. At length he came to the conclusion that the thing which was checking and frustrating him was the fact that he had painted his enemy into the face of Judas. He therefore painted out the face of Judas and commenced anew on the face of Jesus, and this time with the success which the ages have acclaimed.

That is a profound parable of the Christian life. You cannot at one and the same time be painting the features of Christ into your own life, and painting another face with the colors of enmity and hatred.

———•—•———

Aaron Burr is an instance of a gifted and able man who permitted hatred to get the best of him. When he and Jefferson were deadlocked in the House of Representatives for the presidency, it was the influence of Alexander Hamilton, who likened Burr to Cataline, that led to Burr's defeat for the presidency. Again, in 1804, it was the influence of Hamilton, who wrote letters disparaging the character of Burr, that played a prominent part in Burr's defeat for the governorship of New York. After these two overthrows Burr was possessed of hatred toward Hamilton, and he eventually killed him in the fatal duel on the tragic shores of Weehawken. But the pistol shot which took the life of Hamilton also took the political life and the national reputation of Aaron Burr. Long afterward, he confessed that it would have been wiser for him had he taken the sensible view that the world

was big enough for both Aaron Burr and Alexander Hamilton.

———•—•———

There are two ways of dealing with your enemies—the wrong way, the way that Haman took toward Mordecai; and the right way, the way that Joseph took toward his brethren who had sold him into slavery. Let us consider the wrong way, or how *not* to get the best of our enemies.

Haman built a gallows fifty cubits high on which to hang his enemy, Mordecai. In the early morning light, passers-by in the city of Shushan saw a body dangling from a gallows fifty cubits high, and the vultures already circling around it. But it was not the body of Mordecai, for whom Haman had built the gallows, but the body of Haman himself. He was a victim of hate and revenge—not another's, but his own. A dismal and terrible sight, that body dangling there with the vultures wheeling around it. Yet it is not without profit that you pause to look upon this sight; for since every soul can hate, every man has in him the making of a Haman.

———•—•———

—And the Holy Spirit—Among the particular sins which quench the fire of God's Holy Spirit are envy, jealousy, anger, hatred. A well-known public woman in her autobiography says of a woman who, she thought, had wronged her, "I hate her now; I hated her then. I have often hoped the feeling would leave me. It never has."

What a terrible confession! Hannah More once well said, "If I wished to punish my enemy, I should make him hate someone." What a punishment it is for a man to hate another! And the worst kind of punishment is the risk of the withdrawal of the Holy Spirit.

I may be speaking now to someone who has deliberately reserved in the temple of his life a chamber to which God's Holy Spirit is not admitted, and where the soul bows before an altar of implacable hatred. How can God's Holy Spirit do his work and bestow his blessings in such a life as that? This must be the reason why we are told over and over again in the New Testament to forgive one another freely from the heart, even as God for Christ's sake hath forgiven us. We are reminded, too, that there must be a serious question as to the reality of our love of God, whom we have not seen, if we hate our brother whom we have seen.

HEART

—Its music—You have sat in the public hall listening to the performance of a company of skilled musicians as they render the works of some of the masters of music. With sudden and abrupt beginning, or with low harmony, the musicians take up their theme; and the great audience follows them patiently through all their crescendos and diminuendoes, their sudden and fearful crashes, with blaring trumpets and rumbling drums and noisy cymbals, and their whispered cadences, almost too faint for the keenest ear to catch. Then the manner changes and we follow the composer into some delightful bypath of sweetest melody—it may be an aria that all have known and hummed to themselves, or one that invokes the memories of the long, long ago and brings back faces long since faded from view and voices that for long years have been still. Amazement, perplexity, patience, or pretended or professional attention gives place now to rapt expectation; a holy hush falls all over the house; and breasts heave deeply but quietly, and every ear and every eye is attentive as the thousands who hear feel within them the vibrations of immortal song.

What happened? what wrought the change? The orchestra had touched one of those melodies which awaken immediate response in the universal heart.

—Its secret life—One of the interesting aftermaths of the great flood which recently inundated Pittsburgh was the revelation of the underground life and structure of a great city. Passing along the streets, one looked down into manholes, sewers, trenches, chambers, and boxes. One was amazed at the depth, the intricacy, and the extent of these catacombs of a modern city. Under normal conditions they are hidden from view, and we think little about them. Only the excavations and openings for the repair of the damage wrought by the flood revealed this subterranean world; and yet there were lodged and hidden the power lines, the gas, the electricity, the telephones, the water mains, without which the great granite buildings which raise heavenward are but cold, dark, and useless shells.

Like a great city, man has an underground life. It is not visible as the surface man is; yet the hidden man of the heart, as Peter calls him, is a real man. He is, indeed, the hidden man.

—Right with God—When Sir Walter Raleigh was led to the block, his executioner asked him if his head lay right. Raleigh answered, "It matters little, my friend, how the head lies, provided the heart is right." Here in the presence of God, here before him through whom are revealed the secrets of all hearts, here before the Cross of mercy and of love, what does your heart speak, how does your heart lie?

HEAVEN—*see also* HOME (HEAVENLY), IMMORTALITY

"One world at a time," was the reply Henry Thoreau made to Parker Pillsbury when the latter asked Thoreau, who was not far from the other world, what his thoughts about that world were. But that is hardly the natural answer, nor is it an answer that satisfies. Everyone knows this couplet from Pope's "Essay on Man":

Hope springs eternal in the human breast—
Man never is, but always to be, blessed.

But who knows the next two lines:

The soul, uneasy and confined from home,
Rests and expatiates in a life to come.

The three great questions of life are Whence? What? and Whither?— Whence have I come? What is my duty here? and, Whither am I going? Christian faith answers all three.

In that most peculiar and unusual book, *Religio Medici*, Sir Thomas Browne writes that when we begin to talk about the life after death we are like two infants in the womb discussing with one another the nature of this present life. We might infer from that that the difference between our present knowledge and apprehension of life to come, and the knowledge we shall possess when we awake in His likeness, will be no less great than that which exists between an unborn babe and a man in the strength of his days. When men enter with rash feet this field of the future life and begin to relate in detail its activities, there always rises before me that ridiculous picture of Thomas Browne, the two unborn babes telling each other about the world into which they are shortly to be born.

—And Christ—Think of what Bartimaeus saw when he received his sight! Think of the wonders of seeing for the first time a crowd of human beings just like himself, the walls and palm-tree groves of Jericho, the sky, so blue above him, and the hills of Moab in the distance. But that was not the first thing that he saw. The first thing that he saw was the face of Jesus, the face of the one who had healed him. And for you and me, too, that will be the greatest of all sights. When we awake from the dream men call life, when we put off the image of the earthy and break the bonds of time and mortality, when the scales of time and sense have fallen from our eyes and the garment of corruption has been put off, when this mortality has been put on immortality and this corruption has put on incorruption, when we awaken in the everlasting morning, that will be the sight that will stir us and hold us. Oh, I am sure there will be many wonderful sights there—the sea of glass mingled with fire; the great white throne; the river of the water of life; and the tree of life, that yielded her fruit every season; and those marvelous twelve gates, every gate a pearl; and those marvelous foundations of the walls, garnished with all manner of precious stones; and the faces of the patriarchs and the prophets, the apostles and the martyrs; and the faces of those we have loved long since and lost awhile. But most wonderful of all will be that face into which Bartimaeus looked that morning outside the gate of Jericho, after his eyes had been opened—the face of him who loved us and redeemed us, and washed us in his own precious blood.

When Jesus went to call Lazarus back from the grave, he wept. Some have wondered why he wept. The Jews must have thought it was from sorrow, because they said, "Behold how he loved him" (John 11:36). Yet we wonder why he wept, if he was going to call him back to life. Some have fancied that Jesus wept because for his present purposes it was necessary to call Lazarus back from the joys of heaven. When we mourn for the dead, it is sometimes a check to our grief to remember that they are with Christ. "They shall hunger no more, neither thirst any more." (Rev. 7:16.) They are ever with the Lord. They shall reign forever and ever.

———

At a funeral I heard a minister say, "I cannot tell you anything about the life to come. I cannot prove it to you, for I have never been there. But I have a Friend who has, and I trust that Friend."

That sums it all up. We believe in the resurrection of the body and the life of the world to come because of the testimony of that friend, Jesus Christ. My hope of life after death, and a great and blessed life, depends altogether upon faith in that friend, Jesus Christ. When we turn our faces toward the unseen world we walk by faith and not by sight.

———

—Friends in—There is a lyric, "A Song of the Camp," by Bayard Taylor, which tells how before a charge was to be made by the British soldiers at Sevastopol the soldiers in the trenches, thinking of loved ones at home, were singing "Annie Laurie." Each soldier was thinking of a different woman, but the thought was expressed in one common song.

They sang of love, and not of fame;
Forgot was Britain's glory:

Each heart recalled a different name,
But all sang "Annie Laurie."

As we gather here today we each think of different names, we behold different faces. Some see the faces of little children, babes, "flowers no sooner blown than blasted"; others see young men and young women; others, men and women in the midst of days; and still others, the dear, tired faces of fathers and mothers, faithful unto the end. Each heart recalls a different name; but we all sing the same Creed, "I believe in . . . the communion of saints, . . . the resurrection of the body, and the life everlasting."

———

—Joys of—Izaak Walton on the banks of the Itchen, hearing the birds sing, exclaimed, "If thou, Lord, hast provided such music for sinners upon earth, what hast thou in store for thy saints in heaven!" The supreme disclosure of God's love and power will be sacrificial love. The lights of the heavens—sun, moon, and stars—can all be put out, for the Lamb is the Light thereof.

———

In the Middle Ages a monk, Brother Thomas, went out from the monastery to gather sticks in the forest. As he was engaged in this task, he heard the singing of a bird, and ceased from his labors, entranced with the music. Such singing, he thought, he had never heard before. After a little the bird stopped singing, and the monk, taking up his bundle of fagots, returned to the monastery. When he rang the bell at the gate the brother who opened the door asked him who he was. "Why," said the monk, "I am Brother Thomas."

"But," said the other, "there is no Brother Thomas in this community."

"But," protested the monk, "I left the

monastery not more than an hour ago to gather sticks in the wood."

Then, carefully scrutinizing him, the brother at the gate said, "I now recall that when one of our aged brothers died many years ago, he told us of a certain Brother Thomas who had gone out into the woods to gather sticks and had never returned. They supposed that he had been devoured by the wolves."

What Brother Thomas, entranced with the singing of the birds, supposed to be just a few minutes was a hundred years. So will it be with the music and the joys of the heavenly life.

—**Known in part**—Standing upon a lofty mountain in South Carolina this last summer, I asked one who stood by my side to point out to me the grounds and the mansion of the most beautiful and costly of American estates. I looked in the direction he indicated, but at first was able to discern nothing. If the mansion was there I was not able to distinguish it from the drifting clouds and the patches of forest. But upon a second effort I was able to make it out, like a great fortress, facing toward the South, flanked by broad meadows and gardens and sentineled by the everlasting hills. But that was all I could see. The composition of the walls and the adornments of the builders I could not know at that distance. If there were flowers blooming in the gardens I could not mark their colors; if there were men at work and women and children at play, I could not even discern their forms, still less see their faces or hear the sound of their voices. All was distant, silent, in dim and shadowy outline. Nevertheless, I clearly saw that there was a mansion in the distance, and that it was magnificent in its proportions, a pleasing spectacle, even though the mists and the haze concealed the details of its form and the color and sound of the life which inhabited it.

To me that is the way Christianity unfolds its doctrine of the future. It leaves us in no degree of doubt as to a future, and the general facts of that future it makes plain. But there it stops, and he who goes beyond that general outline is wise above that which is written. We know in part.

The Manx poet T. E. Brown writes of a lighthouse off the Calf of Man. From the shore of the Calf a long slope runs off to the crest of the island. Near the top of the slope are the cottages inhabited by the families of the lighthouse keepers, their doors opening directly toward the lighthouse, which is separated from the mainland by a stretch of stormy sea. For months at a time the keepers cannot visit their families; but on a clear Sabbath, when the sun shines brightly, they solace themselves by looking through a powerful telescope at their wives and children gathered in front of the cottage doors.

Between us and the company of the beloved dead there stretches a sea which we may not cross till God bids us come. But there are days when, as it were, the fog lifts and the mists are dispelled, and by the aid of the glass of faith we behold them as they gather in the unclouded sunshine about the everlasting doors of our Father's house.

—**Occupations of**—Imagination need not tarry over the question of what the labors and enterprises in heaven are to be. But truly, they will be great and glorious. What do you suppose Elijah, mighty Elijah, has been doing ever since he went up to heaven in the pillar of fire? Has David never taken down that lyre to sing again the praises of God, whose mercy endureth forever? Did Isaiah finish his work when he painted those masterpieces of Christ as Redeemer and King; and what of Peter and John; and what has Paul been doing ever since, there by the Pyramid of Cestius, the headsman's ax flashed in the sun and he put on immortality?

In his *Castilian Days* John Hay, describing a picture of Vandyke in the Prado at Madrid, and regretting that Vandyke died so young, tries to imagine what he would have accomplished had he lived to the ripe age of Titian or Murillo, and says: "We are tempted to lift the veil that hides the unknown, at least with the furtive hand of conjecture, to imagine a field of unquenched activity where the early dead, free from the trammels of the lower world, may follow out the impulses of their diviner natures —where Andrea has no wife and Raphael and Vandyke no disease, where Keats and Shelley have all eternity for their lofty rhymes, where Ellsworth and Koerner and the Lowell boys can turn their alert and athletic intelligences to something better than war."

—Our home—Sometimes, when the way gets a little rough and steep, and heavy clouds hang over my road, I grow weary and wonder just what it all means. At such times I get an increase of faith by traveling back along memory's path to the old home, which stood on the brow of a hill above a winding river, facing the college where my minister-father was a professor. The most precious recollections of that home are not those that center about the vast attic, where I used to lie by the hour and pour over old numbers of the one pictorial magazine which came into our home, nor the cavernous cellar, where with red-hot poker we used to bore holes in our sleds, nor the drawing room, scene of many a happy party, but the dining room, where family worship was held every morning and evening. Once again I see the united family circle as father led us in worship. That family circle is broken now, some in heaven and some on earth. But the benediction of that family altar will, I am sure, follow me through this life and up to the gates of heaven. There was a sentence with which father used to conclude his prayer, and with that petition I finish, for it sums up my own wish for myself and for others: "May we all get home at last." Yes, heaven is our home, our Father's house.

When the ten thousand Greeks fought their way out of Persia the one hope that sustained them and made them brave in battle and enduring on the march was the thought of reaching the sea toward which they were marching, for when they reached the sea they knew they would not be far from home. The blue sea was the hope that like a banner floated before them as they fought and marched. Let the thought of the soul's true home be often in your mind. Think of its social joys, its multiplied powers, its grand enterprises, its fountains of knowledge, its unclouded felicity, its absolute harmony with the soul's deepest desires; think of catching up the broken threads again and finishing what we here began; think of its innumerable company of angels, its spirits of just men made perfect, its Lamb upon the throne, its thrilling reunions.

O then what raptured greetings
On Canaan's happy shore,
What knitting severed friendships up
Where partings are no more!
—HENRY ALFORD

Let Jerusalem be in your mind!

Heaven will be *home,* our eternal home. During the Civil War, when Moody was working with the Christian Commission, he was going down the Tennessee River after the bloody Battle of Shiloh with a cargo of the wounded. Everywhere the cry that went up from the wounded men on the decks was, Water! Water! Moody gave them water, but he also told them of the Water of Life. At length he came to a soldier who made no answer when he spoke with him. When he called the surgeon's attention to this soldier, he said the wounded man could not recover because he had lost so much blood. Moody said, "I can't find out his name, and it seems a pity to let him die without knowing who he is. Don't you think we can bring him to?" At the doctor's direction Moody gave him a little water and brandy. As he was doing this he asked another soldier standing by if he knew the boy's name. He answered that he did, that he was his chum, that he had a widowed mother living, and that his name was William Clark. Presently the boy opened his eyes, and Moody said to him, "William, do you know where you are?"

The lad looked around for a moment in a daze, and then said, "Oh, yes, I am on my way home to mother."

"Yes, you are on your way home," Moody said; "but the doctor says you won't reach your earthly home. I thought I'd like to ask you if you have any message for your mother?"

At that the boy's face lighted up, and he answered, "Oh, yes, tell my mother that I died trusting in Jesus."

That is the way to live! That is the way to die! And when God calls us from our earthly home, Christ will receive us into our heavenly home, the house of many mansions.

—A place—I drove recently across my own state of Pennsylvania and wondered anew at the marvelous panorama of broad rivers and forest-clad mountains and wide sweeping valleys and fields. Pennsylvania itself would make a suitable heaven, if everyone who lived in it had a heavenly mind. Personally, I have no objection to thinking of heaven as a place as well as a state.

—Powers of—On the walls of the Temple were engraved the mysterious figures of the cherubim with the faces of the ox, the eagle, the lion, and the man. These mysterious creatures have sometimes been taken as the symbol of man's resurrection life. The redeemed and purified soul in the glorified body, all the powers of creation now vested in man, and all the beautiful harmony—the strength of the ox, the daring of the lion, the eagle's mastery of space, and the intelligence of man.

—Recognition in—Even a great scholar like Haeckel has repeated the stale jest of the Sadducees. In his book *The Riddle of the Universe* he asks what Henry VIII will do when he gets to heaven? Whose husband will he be? Catherine of Aragon's, Anne Boleyn's, Jane Seymour's, Ann of Cleves's, Catherine Howard's? Thus we soil the heavenly existence by carrying over into it the kind of life we now live. *Now* we are the children of *this* world; then we shall be children of the Resurrection. Now we bear the image of the earthy; then we shall bear the image of the heavenly. Marriage is a relationship of the earthly and the physical nature, and none the less honorable for that. But in the heavenly state such a relationship can have no place. Marriage is of the earth, earthy. And if this seems to some to deny the future union and blessedness of noble men and women who have lived together on earth, all that I can venture is, that as our souls will be purged of the earthly and made to inhabit a spiritual body, we cannot but think that there will be a fellowship and union and blessed recollection without any of the embarrassments which our present state would intimate. Marriage, and the union of marriage, we need not think of as the highest state for pure souls. God may have something else in store, and that advanced state shall be one of joy unspeakable.

———◆◆◆———

I know it is said, and rightly said, that the great thing the Bible emphasizes about the dead is the beatific vision, the presence of God. But this need not preclude the joy of meeting and knowing our friends. Even the pagans believe that much. Homer's Ulysses came upon the heroes of the Trojan war in the other world and recognized them; Vergil's Aneas found and embraced with great joy his father, Anchises. Certainly the Christian faith gives us as much to look forward to as did the pagan.

And what about children? Are they still children there? I think they are. Why not? If a child is, as Christ said, the best description of heaven—"for of such is the kingdom of heaven" (Matt. 19:14) —why should there not be children in heaven; if children add so much to the joy and life of this world, why not in the world to come? Let us look forward, then, to the life to come and to reunion there with the beloved dead, and to all the joy and love of fellowship here infinitely expanded and multiplied there.

———◆◆◆———

In a celebrated passage in Shakespeare's *King John* Constance, the mother of Arthur, gives expression to the fear that she will not know her child when she meets him in the court of heaven.

*When I shall meet him in the court
of heaven
I shall not know him: and therefore
never, never
Must I behold my pretty Arthur
more.*

But all that we know and love in Christ gives us ground for the hope and expectation that on the eternal shore old friends shall meet once more. And as for problems and difficulties of personalities and relationships of this life transferred to the eternal world, like that foolish difficulty about the seven times married woman which the mocking Sadducees submitted to Jesus, all that we can leave to the solution of infinite power and infinite love.

———◆◆◆———

In the winter of 1862 Lincoln's son William, a lad of twelve, sickened and died. It was the great sorrow of a sad life. For a number of weeks Lincoln observed the Thursday on which the child died as a day of seclusion and mourning, and was with difficulty persuaded to give up the dangerous practice. Some months afterward he was at Fort Monroe. In a moment of leisure he was reading his favorite author. Calling his aide into the room, he read to him passages from *Hamlet, Macbeth,* and then the passage from the third act of *King John,* where Constance, whose boy has been imprisoned by his uncle, King John, expresses to her confessor the fear that she may not know her boy in heaven. When he had finished reading the lines, Lincoln turned to his aide and said, "Colonel, did you ever dream of a lost friend, and yet have a sad consciousness that it was not a reality? Just so I dream of my boy Willie." And with that he bowed his head on the table and sobbed aloud.

161

—Reunion in—Thomas Carlyle wrote concerning the death of James Carlyle, his father: "And now, beloved father, farewell for the last time in this world of shadows! In the world of realities may the great Father again bring us together in perfect holiness and perfect love! Amen."

Last week when I alighted from a train at a station in Wisconsin, I saw a young woman come rushing down the platform. Turning in the other direction, I saw a young man in the uniform of the navy of our country come hurrying up the platform. He was back on furlough, perhaps safe from the peril and death of the Coral Sea, or the battle at Midway. I stood and watched them in the joy and ecstasy of their reunion, which was but for a day, or a few days, and then back to the peril of battle and wounds and death.

That other reunion will be an everlasting reunion. They shall go no more out and come no more in.

—A vision of—As a young man William Tennent was preparing for his examinations before the presbytery of New Brunswick, and intense application had affected his health. He was conversing one morning with his brother when he fainted away and apparently expired. After every test of death had been applied his body was prepared for burial, and the day set for the funeral. The people had assembled for the funeral, when the body suddenly opened its eyes and gave a dreadful groan. After vigorous restoratives had been resorted to, his resuscitation was effected. For many weeks he was in an extremely weakened condition, but slowly he began to mend. He had no recollection for a time of any transaction previous to his sickness, and had to be taught his letters again as a child. But one day his memory came back to him, and his knowledge of the past was that of any normal man.

Although very reluctant to speak of his experience, he related on several occasions what had happened. In an instant he had found himself in another state of existence under the direction of a Superior Being who bade him follow him. Thus conducted, he beheld an ineffable glory and an innumerable company of happy beings in the midst of this glory. He, too, thrilled to their great joy and besought his conductor to permit him to join them. But his guide told him that he must return to earth. He heard and obeyed the sentence with the sorrow of despair. "Lord, must I go back?" was his expostulation. The shock of his disappointment made him faint, and he saw his brother and the doctor disputing over his inanimate body.

In his visit to the heavenly world he saw glorious and happy beings, but no bodily shape or representation in the glorious appearance. So deep was the impression made on his spirit that the ravishing sounds of the music he had heard faded not out of his ears for the space of three years.

—What it is like—Two monks were once discussing the life to come. One insisted that it would be *taliter*—like this life; the other that it would be *aliter*—unlike it. Finally they agreed that whichever of the two died first should communicate with the brother left on earth. In the course of time one died and was buried. True to his pledge, he visited his brother on earth in a dream and this was his message: *Nec taliter, nec aliter, sed totaliter aliter!*—Not as thou thoughtest, nor as I thought, but altogether different. There will indeed be surprises for us in the life to come, but our ignorance as to the minutiae of the life is no excuse for shutting our eyes to what God hath revealed.

———◆———

—What it is not—If you were going to describe to an untutored native of the Arctic regions some tropical land, you could hardly give him an idea of it by mentioning some of the things that are there. What would palm trees mean to a man who had never seen anything but Arctic berries and snow and ice? What would the flash of brilliantly plumaged birds mean to one who had never seen any bird but the penguin? What would the elephant or the lion mean to one who had seen only the floundering seal? You would have to begin the other way. You would have to describe that land by telling him what was not there—that there was no snow, no ice, no polar bears. To a certain extent that is the method the Holy Spirit employs in telling us about the life beyond the grave. It tells us, first of all, the things to which we are accustomed here that are not found there.

———◆———

It is a sad comment on the stability and the content and satisfaction of the things of this world that when the New Testament writers come to describe the things of the spiritual and the heavenly world, in every instance they must use a negative—that is, the joys and satisfactions of the spiritual and heavenly world are in this or that respect *not* as the things of this world. So Peter describes the Christian inheritance in three great negatives. In the first place it is incorruptible—literally, not corruptible.

———◆———

—Wonders of—Marco Polo, the famous Venetian traveler of the thirteenth century, when he lay dying, was urged by his attendants to recant—to withdraw the stories he had told about China and the lands of the Far East. But he said, "I have not told half what I saw."

Whatever heaven is and wherever it is, this much is certain—we shall never be able to tell, not a half, but a hundredth part, of what it is like.

HELL—*see also* FUTURE PUNISHMENT, JUDGMENT, REMORSE, RETRIBUTION

To one who claimed to have got rid of hell, Voltaire replied, "I congratulate you, for I have not been able to do that myself." Someone has said that if there were no hell we should have to invent one. However that may be, if there were no word that carried with it the implication of our word "hell," we should be compelled to coin some word which would fit the facts of the heart; for without such a word as "hell," one of the deepest, strongest sentiments and convictions of the heart would have no equivalent in expression. Words are only the pictures, or symbols, of reality.

———◆———

—And memory—The open book of which John speaks in Revelation will be to every man the solemn apocalypse of his own entire past life. In that apocalypse—that sudden, but full and faithful vision of all that we have thought, said, imagined, done, and of the attitude we have taken toward the Redeemer whom God sent to save us—in that there will be sufficient material for judgment.

———◆———

—Napoleon in—In the gallery of Antoine Wiertz, at Brussels, there is a collection of the most astounding and overwhelming paintings that one will see anywhere in the world—most of them exposing the brutality and horror of war and the cruelty of conquerors, but some of them heralding the Empire of Peace and the triumph of Christ. Walking down the hall where these extraordinary paintings hang, one is suddenly brought to a halt by a great painting which is entitled "A View of Hell." With folded arms and familiar cocked hat on his head, there stands the figure of a man. There is no name given; but there is no need, for he is at once identified as Napoleon Bonaparte. On his shadowed but remarkable face there is a look of amazement, astonishment, with just a trace of dread and fear, as he beholds what is about him.

By the light of the flames of hell burning all about him you can see back of him the serried ranks of the slain in battle. Little children stretch out clenched fists at the emperor; and mothers, with agony on their countenances, surround him, holding up the bleeding, amputated arms and legs of the slaughtered. One woman has the head of her husband in a sack, and another carries the torso of a dead and mangled body; a raw and bloody arm, severed at the shoulder, is thrust close to the face of Napoleon. Over there is a naked body, upheaved, with a sword plunged into the abdomen. On the faces of the children, the wives, and the mothers are depicted rage, horror, anger, hate, and infinite pain and sorrow. This is terrible, horrible, you say. Yes, and that is just what Wiertz meant it to be—it is Napoleon in hell!

—**Reality of**—"I believe I am going to hell." The sentence shocks you. It has a dread echo to it. But if such is the effect upon you, hearing it repeated by me, how much more solemn and impressive it must have been had you heard it as I heard it when it fell, not from the lips of one who repeated it and reported it, but from the lips of the very person whose soul was upheaved.

It takes an internal explosion and upheaval to know what people are really feeling, thinking, or believing. Explosions beneath the surface of a lake or river bring to the surface dead bodies and hidden objects. So in the breast of man great convulsions of grief, pain, fear, and remorse hurl hidden things to the surface, and the beholder stands aghast at what he has seen or heard. Then the question of sincerity sinks out of sight; and the truth, whether it be glorious or terrible, reveals itself.

It was such an explosion that I saw and heard when the troubled soul before me hurled up from its depths that sentence of fear and woe, "I believe I am going to hell."

HERITAGE

A Presbyterian minister of long and honorable service, who died sometime ago, concluded his last testament and will with this final bequest: "I desire also to bequeath to my children and their families my testimony to the truth and preciousness of the gospel of Jesus Christ. This heritage of the Christian faith, received in unbroken line from exiled and persecuted Huguenots and Scotch Covenanters as ancestors, is of infinitely more value than any house, land, or barns. I hereby bequeath and devise it to them."

The greatest thing that parents can bequeath to their children is an interest and fortune in the Kingdom of God.

HEROES AND HEROINES

There are real heroes and heroines among the sick. How much I have learned from them! How many beautiful and inspiring examples of undaunted fortitude and unfaltering hope I have found in them!

I asked a certain sick woman how long it had been since she was taken ill. She named the length of time—more than two years. Immediately I thought of all the journeys I had taken and all the places I had been in two years. I had seen the Danube rolling toward the Black

Sea. I had passed through the rugged mountains of Macedonia. I had scaled the mountains of Asia Minor. I had seen the sun rise on the Aegean. I had visited the Isle of Patmos, where a door was opened for John into heaven. All these places came back to me when I thought of what this woman told me; and I contrasted my journeys with her journeys of the past two years—from the bed to the window and from the window back to the bed, yet with no complaint, with no fault to find with man or God.

HISTORY—*see also* BIBLE (CIVILIZATION AND THE), GOD AND HISTORY, PROVIDENCE AND HISTORY, RELIGION AND NATIONAL MORALITY, RIGHT (TRIUMPH OF)

—**God in**—God must be in this terrible chapter of the world's history through which we are passing today. Otherwise one would have to exclude God from a great part of history. In his powerful description of the battle and the battlefield of Sedan, where the German army conquered the French in 1870, Victor Hugo says, "In the midst of the terrible plain I saw thee, O Thou Invisible One." The Invisible One is always present. The history of the world is the judgment of the world, and as a great history maker, Cromwell, put it, "What are all our histories but God throwing down and trampling under foot whatsoever He hath not planted?"

————•◦•————

At the very hour of his greatest power and influence, Napoleon, against the advice of his wisest counselors, was tempted to invade Russia. Today the pyramids of French cannon and cannon balls that one sees piled up on the courtyard at the Kremlin at Moscow show the high-water mark of Napoleon's career of conquest. From Moscow to the Niemen his legions lay scattered in the snow, frozen in the rivers, dead on the fields of battle. In a single campaign the greatest victories of history were suddenly succeeded by one of the greatest of military disasters in the history of mankind. To this day—at least until the Russian Revolution—the Russian people, realizing that in their deliverance there was something more than the genius of Kutuzov, the snow, the wolves, and the Cossacks, celebrate that overthrow by chanting in their churches the great psalm which the Hebrews chanted when the hosts of Sennacherib, without an arrow shot against them, melted away before the walls of Jerusalem: "God is our refuge and strength. . . . The heathen raged, the kingdoms were moved: he uttered his voice, the earth melted" (Ps. 46:1, 6).

————•◦•————

One of the striking things about God in history is the way in which evil systems and evil causes begin suddenly to wither and crumble just when to the view of man they seem to be at the very zenith of power and worldly strength and pomp. The Spanish Armada, arrogantly called the "Invincible Armada," sailed out of Lisbon down the Tagus, bound for the coast of England, to crush that Protestant power; and invincible indeed it seemed, with its huge ships and its multitudes of soldiers and sailors and weapons of destruction. But he that sitteth in the heavens laughed. He held them in derision. The wind blew, and the Invincible Armada was scattered on the rocky coasts of the British Isles. The great conspiracy had come to naught. On the medal which was struck at that time the English stamped the words of the song of Moses after the overthrow of Pharaoh and his chariots in the Red Sea, "Thou didst blow with thy wind, the sea covered them" (Ex. 15:10).

————•◦•————

—**And judgment**—One of the most eloquent of all books is Volney's *Ruins,* the book which almost made an infidel out of Lincoln because of its effort to put a fool's cap upon Christianity and all other religions. Yet in his account of the fall of ancient kingdoms Volney agrees with the Scriptures. They fell through their own sins and follies. Sitting one moonlight night on the shaft of a pillar and viewing the rows of columns at Palmyra of the Desert, Volney invokes the phantom of the past, the genius of the tombs, who rebukes the mortal for complaining against heaven, declaring the destruction of the civilizations of the past was due to man's folly and sin. "I will ask," says the mortal to the phantom, "the ashes of legislators by what secret causes do empires rise and fall." The Bible makes plain to us the reason for the fall of empires. There is a moral law at work among the nations, for nations are made up of men. "Whatsoever a man soweth, that shall he also reap" (Gal. 6:7); and whatsoever a nation soweth, that also shall it reap. As the great historian of Rome, Mommsen, put it, "God makes a Bible out of history."

HOLY COMMUNION—*see* LORD'S SUPPER

HOLY SPIRIT—*see also* CHURCH AND THE
HOLY SPIRIT, HATE AND THE HOLY SPIRIT,
OPPORTUNITY AND THE HOLY SPIRIT

The golden candlestick with its seven lamps was a part of the furniture of the tabernacle and the temple of Solomon. It appears here in this vision of the prophet Zechariah, and again in the vision of John "in the isle that is called Patmos" (Rev. 1:9); where the seven golden candlesticks are the seven churches. It must have been regarded with peculiar reverence by the Jews as one of the sacred glories of the temple, for to this day, on the arch of Titus at Rome, where are depicted incidents in the siege of Jerusalem, one can see the great candlestick borne aloft in triumphal procession by the victorious soldiers of Titus. From what the angel said to Zechariah in the vision, it is clear that the candlestick with its seven lamps fed by the oil from the olive trees is a symbol of the Church illuminated by divine grace.

———•———

According to legend Memmius was a spy in the days of the last and worst of the persecutions, that under Diocletian. It was his work to spy out the Christians in their secret places of worship and bring them before the judges and the persecutors. Memmius was engaged in this infamous task, and was creeping stealthily along one of the narrow passages, when suddenly, at a turning of the passage, he came upon a little chamber where some Christians were met together. The candles were burning before the crucifix, and the priest was standing before the altar. For a moment a divine indulgence was granted Memmius; and if he had been capable of it, he might have bowed and received the everlasting light. But he hardened his heart, and those candles, symbols of the everlasting light, bewildered him with darkness; and the cross itself was stamped upon his heart as a sign that it should never open to conviction. Henceforth Memmius wandered through the catacombs seeking for some unwary visitor to take him by the hand and lead him from the darkness into the light.

———•———

—**Grieving the**—A great preacher, Pusey, once said that one of the greatest surprises of heaven will be our amazement at the number of ways in which we insult the divine grace and grieve the spirit of God.

166

—Quenching the—Floating one summer night down one of America's rivers, my companion and I sought vainly for the sign of a human habitation where we could spend the night, or a place along the steep bank where we could pitch our camp. At last, wet and cold and exhausted, we drew up our boat on a sand bar. There, groping in the darkness, we gathered together a few pieces of driftwood, and after several ineffectual attempts, succeeded in lighting a fire. How carefully we tended that fire, brooding over it until we were certain that it was going to burn; and when, at length, it began to burn briskly and brightly, illuminating our dismal surroundings and warming our cold and weary bodies, we realized as never before what a friend fire is to man.

The metaphor used by the apostle when he says, "Quench not the Spirit" (I Thess. 5:19), is that of putting out a fire.

------•◆•------

—Resisting the—Telling me one day last week of his religious history, a man who has reached the allotted three score and ten related how when a youth at boarding school his heart was touched by a message which he heard in the chapel, and he resolved to give his heart to Christ and become his disciple. It brought to him a joy, he said, which the long stretches of his life had never repeated. But it was a joy that was short lived, for when he found that his school fellows made him the object of their ridicule and jest, he promptly abandoned the new life he had chosen. "Now," he said, "I pray, I go to church, but the old feeling never comes back to me." Will it ever come back? Who knows? There are strange mysterious laws at work in the spiritual world, and none can violate them with impunity.

HOME—*see also* CHILDREN, FAMILY ALTAR, HEAVEN (OUR HOME), WORSHIP (FAMILY)

"When Joseph came home." There is the word that strikes a universal chord! In the early spring of 1863 the Union and the Confederate armies lay encamped along the Rappahannock River near Fredericksburg, the Union army on the northern bank of the river, and the Confederate on the southern. In the evenings, when there was a lull in the fighting, the soldiers of both armies would sing their favorite songs. On the Union side the band would play "We Are Coming, Father Abraham," or "The Girl I Left Behind Me," or "The Battle Hymn of the Republic"; and the Union soldiers would raise a great cheer. And on the Southern side the band would play, "The Bonnie Blue Flag," "My Maryland," or "Dixie"; and then the Confederate soldiers would raise a great cheer. At length the band on the northern side played "Home Sweet home"; and when it was finished, both armies sent up a great cheer. "Home Sweet Home" struck a universal chord which knew no union or secession, no North or South.

------•◆•------

Observing any great throng of people at the close of day, waiting about the gates of a railway station, or on the street corner for a car, and looking into their faces, you may have asked them, mentally, "Where do you live?—In the town, or the village; in the city, or in the country; in a flat, an apartment, or a single house? Who is at home waiting for your return? Will the sound of your footsteps on the porch or on the stairway cause little children to run from their books or their toys to fling their arms about you and kiss you? Or will the sound of your coming strike an arrow of dread through some unhappy heart? Do they expect a caress and a smile; or a scowl, a frown, a repulse? Are you going to a house that is silent and lonely, and is this the reason that you walk less rapidly than the others, because you almost dread to go to that silent home where silent rooms, vacant chairs, unused garments, unlifted books, open sorrows, recent wounds, make you wonder why you call it home when all that makes home is gone?"

—**A godless**—The only place to bring up a family is in a Christian church. A well-known minister went to a home to conduct a funeral service for the daughter of the home. It was the home of a successful businessman—but a thoroughly worldly and godless home. On one side of the coffin sat the father, on the other side the only other person present besides the minister, the father's intimate friend. Suddenly the father broke into speech, talking to himself more than to any other: "There is nothing in these things. You and I have been living for a good time and success. We have got everything we could during the week. We have been good poker players on Saturday night. We have spent our Sundays in the automobile and in social pleasures. We have put the club and the bank first, and my son has disgraced me with his shameless marriage, and my daughter is dead. I tell you there is only one place in which to bring up a family, and that is a Christian church. There is only one way to use Sunday for children, and that is to take them to church. What with money and wine and poker and pleasure all day Sunday, and parties all Sunday night, my family has been ruined. People don't know what the result of this kind of living will be until the end comes. But I know."

—**Heavenly**—Years ago a number of skylarks were imported from England and set loose in one of the eastern sections of the country, where they soon were at home and began to breed. One day a student of birds was listening with great interest to the song of the emigrant birds in the American landscape. But as he was listening to their song he saw an Irish laboring man, who had heard the larks sing in Ireland, suddenly stop, take off his cap, and turn his face skyward, a look of surprise and joy and memory on his face as he listened entranced to the song of the bird that he had heard sing in his youth. For the bird expert it was only a scientific observation, but for the Irishman it was the listening of recollection and remembrance, of affection and of hope.

So through the gospel of Christ there come to us those songs which tell us of our heavenly home, the homeland of the soul.

—**Love of**—Out of the heart are the issues of life; the thoughts and emotions which center about home declare the preeminence of the heart life. Abd-er-Rahman was the first caliph of Cordova in Spain. There, thousands of miles from his native haunts along the banks of the Euphrates, the Moslem prince set up his kingdom and ruled over the conquered Spaniards. But always he was homesick for Mesopotamia. He had a palm tree brought him and planted in the courtyard of the palace at Cordova, in order that it might remind him of his home; and never could he gaze upon that palm tree without bursting into tears. Patriotism is only an enlarged and exalted kind of love for home.

Toward the end of his life Sir Walter Scott, in ill-health, took a trip to Italy. One day in a bookshop he happened to see a lithograph of Abbottsford, his beautiful home on the Tweed in Scotland. Bursting into tears, he hurried from the shop and started at once for Scotland. When he reached London he was unable to stand, but he insisted that he be carried to the steamer for Leith. On the journey to Tweedside he lay unconscious in the carriage; but when the carriage entered the valley of Gala, he began to look about him, and presently to murmur a name or two: "Gala Water, surely!" "Buckholm!" "Torwoodly!" And when the towers of Abbottsford came into view, he sprang up with a cry of delight.

—**Loyalty to**—Into the life of Charles Lamb there came a deep attachment to a woman, but he willingly forewent marriage when he saw the need of his own family. Brother, son, and husband, he became the guardian angel of that home, and especially of his sister Mary, who was at times mentally deranged. After she had stabbed her mother to death in one of her mad moments, Charles Lamb stripped himself for his sister Mary as Jonathan stripped himself for David; and for eight and thirty years he watched over her with a tender solicitude. A friend tells how he would sometimes see the brother and sister walking hand in hand across the field to the old asylum, both their faces bathed in tears. A sad story, and yet a grand story. Charles Lamb had his place in his home, and it was never left empty.

—**Memories of**—This will be my last Sabbath in the old home. Years ago I used to try to imagine what it would be like—when father and mother were gone to their long home, the children scattered far abroad and living in homes of their own, and the homestead fallen into the hands of aliens from its rich memories. What was then foreseen only in a dreamy, vague way has now come to pass. This final Sabbath has dawned. I say Sabbath because this was a religious home, and Sabbath fits it more than Sunday. The home has been consecrated by the prayers of religious parents, and almost every window opens toward Jerusalem.

Strange, is it not, how brick, stone, timber—things made with hands as well as growing and living things—take hold upon one's life and seem to become a part of it? Yet so it is, and even in its semiswept and semigarnished state, the house is redolent with memories; and every room and window and door has some story to tell. This house has known life's winter and summer, its seedtime and harvest, its "each perplexing path." It has been decorated with orange blossoms and with the ensign of death. Children's feet have raced over its halls. Its history is a cross section from life. Sorrow, affliction, sickness, death, anxiety, and perplexity this home has known; but the darkest shadows, the shadows of dishonor and disgrace, thank God it has never known. Now that the book is closing, there is no chapter that we dare not open.

Prosperity sometimes makes a man forget his home and his family. But not so Joseph. They put Pharaoh's gold collar around his neck and gave him an Egyptian name, but they could not change his heart. The heart of Joseph was ever in the highlands of Canaan. There were times when his ministers of state would come before him and ask him a question, and be amazed because he never answered, but stared straight ahead into the distance. The reason he never answered was that he was asking himself questions: "Jacob, my father? and Benjamin, my brother? Do they still live? And the ten brothers who sold me into Egypt? Have their hearts changed? Do their consciences smite them?" There were days, too, when his beautiful wife, the daughter of the Priest of On, put her arms about his neck and said, "Joseph, what means that far-away look? Withdraw your wandering thoughts. Are not my love and the love of your two sons, Ephraim and Manasseh, enough for thee?" No! Joseph did not forget his shepherd home. There were days when the colossal pyramids, the rigid lines of saluting soldiers, the splendors of his palace, the fountains climbing the ladder of the sun, the red sandstone columns, enwound with fierce birds and serpents, the pillars bursting at the top into lotus flowers, his gleaming, golden chariot—all faded from his view, and in their place he saw the live oak trees and the black tents and the flocks of Hebron, and the faces of Jacob and Benjamin and his brothers.

> 'Mid pleasures and palaces though
> we may roam,
> Be it ever so humble, there's no
> place like home.
> —JOHN HOWARD PAYNE

—And mother—In 1886 the New England Society held a dinner in New York. Among the speakers was the great popular preacher, T. De Witt Talmage. In his address Dr. Talmage described the return home to the North of a Union soldier after the Civil War. Then a young man on the staff of the *Atlanta Constitution* arose to speak. In simple pathos he described the Confederate soldier as he came back, ragged and wasted, in his faded gray uniform, to his ruined and desolate home in the South. The next morning Henry W. Grady awoke to find himself famous. Everybody wanted to hear him speak. Eulogy and flattery poured in on him like a flood from all parts of the nation.

One day he closed his desk at the office of the *Constitution* and, telling his associates that he was not sure when he would be back, disappeared. No one saw him or heard of him for a week. He had gone to the Georgia farm where his mother still lived. When she met him at the door, he said, "Mother, I have come back to spend some time with you. I have been losing my ideals out in the world where I am living. I am forgetting the things I learned here in the old home, and God is getting away from me. I have come back to you, Mother, to live for a little while." The famous orator was a boy again with his mother, the two wandering together over the fields, talking, praying, singing together. Then he went back to the city, refreshed and strengthened, ready to face the temptations of life.

—Religion in the—A man who had traveled far in the world went back to visit his native village. Everything was changed: there was not a street, store, or house which he could recognize. Even the fields and the trees were different. But there was one thing which was just the same, and that was the spring out of which, as a thirsty, barefoot boy, he used to drink.

An early religious training is a fountain which never ceases to flow and to which the world-sated and time-weary soul returns to quench his thirst.

HOME TRAINING—*see also* CHILDREN (TRAINING OF), MOTHER (INFLUENCE OF)

There was a time when every well-regulated Scottish household had in it a taws. We had one in our own home. It hung always in the appointed place—and was used when occasion demanded. I looked recently in the dictionary, and could not even find "taws" in it; but I knew where it was—where it hung in our house, on a nail just by the kitchen stairs. It was an instrument of persuasion, which, on occasion, we were required to fetch. "Albert! Clarence! Bring the taws!" We brought it—and then we *got* it! Unless children today no longer go astray from the womb, as the Bible says they do, and unless the human race has suddenly become saintly, then every home has need of the taws, either mental or in leather, for the safeguarding of the home.

One of Aaron Burr's uncles speaks of Burr when he was a child as being under a "maple-sugar government." We had maple sugar now and then, indeed, tapped a tree or two ourselves; but we had no maple-sugar *government!*

Everything good, in fact or in principle, is found in the Bible. Away back in Deuteronomy (22:8), even before the people settled in Caanan, we have "safety first." In the building regulations of Moses is this law, "When thou buildest a new house, then thou shalt make a battlement for thy roof, that thou bring not blood upon thine house, if any man fall from thence." The houses in that part of the world, then as now, had flat roofs; and the climate being semitropical, the roof of the house was much frequented. To leave it without a coping or balustrade would endanger the life of the members of the family and any visitor who might come in. This ancient law makes us think of the safeguards of the home.

HOMESICKNESS

William D. Howells, the well-known American author, in an autobiographic sketch tells how as a boy he once left his Ohio home and went with an older brother to take a job in a near-by town. His brother got him settled in his lodgings and then went back to the station to take the train home. But when the train came in, William was there, too; and together they went home, as if from a far country and after a year's absence. It was a winter afternoon when he turned up at the station, and the sky was apple green. All through his life, Howells said, he could never see a sky that color in the winter without experiencing the same feeling of homesickness and desolation that came over him that wintry day in the long ago in that Ohio town.

HOPE—*see also* STAR OF THE MORNING

Of all the galleries I have visited, among all the masterpieces I have viewed, the picture that stands out most clearly now is one which I went to see again in the Tate Gallery in London—Frederic Watts's "Hope." All that one sees is a beautiful female figure seated upon a globe—and yet he can never forget that figure. She is blindfolded, and in her hand she holds a lute, of which all the strings but one are broken. The blindfolded girl is touching that one string with her hand, and her lovely head is bent toward it in the closest attention, earnestly waiting to catch the note of that one wire. So it was that Frederic Watts conceived of hope, triumphant over the world's sin and sorrow, surviving its pain and disaster. In this simple, and yet profound, study there is infinite pathos and tenderness. Eternal hope! Perhaps one reason why I remember that painting more clearly than many of the descents from the cross, or transfigurations, or entombments, is that I came back this summer with a deep impression that our world today stands in sore need of a revival of hope.

When Jupiter sent woman down to earth endowed with every charm, he named her Pandora—"the gift of all the gods." In the hand of Pandora the immortals had placed a casket which she was forbidden to open. Overcome by curiosity, one day she lifted the cover of the box and looked in. Forthwith there escaped from the box every conceivable plague for man's body and his mind, and immediately they scattered themselves far and wide throughout the earth. Pandora hasted to replace the lid of the box, but only one thing was left—hope. That was the ancients' way of giving pre-eminence to hope.

Lord Byron in "The Bride of Abydos" said of hope:

Be thou the rainbow to the storms of life!
The evening beam that smiles the clouds away,
And tints to-morrow with prophetic ray!

———•◦•———

—**An anchor**—No one who knows what can happen at sea would go to sea in a vessel that carried no anchor, even though it were the greatest and most modern liner afloat, for circumstances might arise when the hope of the ship and all her company would depend, not on the captain or the crew, the engines, the compass, or the steering gear, but on the anchor. When all else has failed there is hope in the anchor.

———•◦•———

—**And death**—Come with me, and we will turn away for a little from the present world with its glory and its shame, its noise and its confusion, and pass into that silent, buried, and forgotten world of the Roman catacombs, where the early Christians buried their dead. We follow the flickering candle of our guide; and, descending the steps which have been cut out of the soil, we find ourselves in one of the almost innumerable narrow passages which undermine for miles in every direction the Roman *Campagna*. On either side of these narrow passages

are the niches into which the bodies of the dead were pushed; and on the stone or cement which more than a millennium and a half ago sealed the bodies, we can still read in Latin and Greek the names of the dead and sentiments of faith or sorrow which were inscribed with the point of the trowel upon the mortar. Among the inscriptions are ones like these: "Alexander is not dead, but lives above the stars"; "To dear Serichas, sweetest son, mayest thou live in the Holy Spirit"; "Victoria, in peace and Christ"; "Gordian, the courier from Gaul, strangled for the faith. Rests in peace." Whose heart would not grow soft and tender reading these pathetic inscriptions of sorrow and of hope?

Rudely written, but each letter
Full of hope, and yet of heartbreak,
Full of the tender pathos of the here
And the hereafter.
                              —Author unknown

Now we come to one of the chambers where services for the dead were held and where we can see inscribed on the walls and ceilings scenes from the Old Testament and the New Testament. Among the most frequent are Noah and the ark, Jonah and the whale, the sacrifice of Isaac, and Christ the good shepherd, with the lamb in his arms.

Here, too, are the ancient symbols of Christianity—the cock, with its reminiscence of the fall of Peter, admonishing the believer to watch and pray; the phoenix, as a symbol of the resurrection of the body; the vine, the symbol of the believer's union with Christ; the palm branch, the symbol of the Christian's victory through faith which overcomes the world; the fish, because the first three letters of the Greek word for fish formed an acrostic for Jesus Christ, the Son of God; and here, too, is one of the favorite symbols, the anchor, which was the symbol of hope.

Even in the pagan world the anchor had been the symbol of hope, because there were times when it was the last dependence and the last resource of the storm-tossed sailor. It was easy for the Christians to take over this ancient symbol and baptize it with a Christian meaning, for the very form of the anchor suggested the cross, and in the letter to the Hebrews the Christian faith was explained and illustrated by the metaphor of the anchor.

—**And democracy**—How significant are these last words of James Bryce, the words with which he concludes his book *Modern Democracies*: "An Eastern king, with an uncertain temper, desired his astrologer to discover from the stars when his death should come. The astrologer, having cast the horoscope, replied that he could not find the date, but had ascertained only that the king's death would follow immediately upon his own. So may it be said that democracy will never perish till after hope has expired." [1]

—**The heart of man**—When John Adams asked his old friend Thomas Jefferson if he would agree to live his seventy-three years over again, Jefferson replied, "Yea, I think with you that it is a good world on the whole. My temperament is sanguine. I steer my bark with hope in the head, leaving fear astern." Hope is the pillow for weary heads, the heart's ease for weary hearts. When hope is gone, what is left? We say of this one or that one, "He has lost heart." What we really mean is that he has lost *hope*. When hope dies, then the heart goes out of man.

[1] Vol. II, p. 609. Used by permission of the publishers, The Macmillan Company.

—**Is not an argument**—A man despairing of happiness in life had climbed up on the parapet of the Brooklyn Bridge and was about to leap into the river when a policeman laid an arresting hand upon him and drew him back. But the man protested to the policeman, saying, "You do not understand how miserable I am and how hopeless my life is. Please let me go."

The kindhearted officer talked with him and said, "I will make this proposition to you. You take five minutes and give your reasons why life is not worth living, and then I will take five minutes and give my reasons why I think life is worth living, both for you and for me. If at the end of the ten minutes you still feel like jumping from the bridge I will not stop you."

The man then took his five minutes, and the officer took his five minutes. The result was that at the end of the ten minutes they joined hands and both leaped from the bridge.

Hope is not an argument. Hope is a great instinct of the soul.

—**Living**—In the letter of Peter we have a great description, or inventory and survey, of the Christian's inheritance. He describes it, first of all, as a "living" hope. That is in striking contrast with the hopes of this world, for the worldly hope men set their hearts upon fail them. We know a great deal about "dying" hopes and "dead" hopes, hopes that wither; but here is a living hope. California for many years has had a higher percentage of suicides than any other state. At first that seems strange when one reflects upon its beautiful scenery, its blue skies, and bright sunlight. Life, one would think, ought to be easier there than anywhere else. Why, then, so many suicides? The reason ascribed is that many have gone to California with what has been a last hope, either as to their health or their personal fortune; and when this hope failed them, life held nothing for them. But Peter says the believer has been begotten, born into, an inheritance of a *living* hope.

———◦———

—**For mankind**—Writing of the tumult of the French Revolution and how men hoped amid its darkness for an unspeakably better society, Carlyle breaks into the apostrophe to hope: "O blessed Hope, sole boon of man: whereby, on his strait prison walls, are painted beautiful far-stretching landscapes, and into the night of very Death is shed holiest Dawn! Thou art to all an indefeasible possession in this God's world."

HUMILITY—*see also* PRIDE

All men are tempted to take a census —that is, to number their own virtues, graces, accomplishments, resources, and thus draw the heart away from God. But what ground can there be for our counting or for our pride? Are we proud of our talents? But what have we that we have not received from God? Are we proud of our wisdom or knowledge? A brick falls on our head, a machine strikes us on the street, and then where is the vaunted knowledge of the mind? Are we proud of our beauty? A wasting sickness smites us, and then where is beauty? Are we proud of our riches? A revolution breaks out in the country, and then what are our riches?

As we take a census of our virtues, let us remember these lines of William Knox, which were so often upon the lips of Abraham Lincoln:

Oh, why should the spirit of mortal be proud?
Like a swift-flitting meteor, a fast-flying cloud,

A flash of the lightning, a break of the wave,
He passes from life to his rest in the grave.

———◦———

It is said that the angels were once moved by the godly and beautiful life of a saint on the earth who, wherever he went, diffused goodness as a flower diffuses the sweetness of its odor. Greatly interested, they came down to investigate the secret of his power. So impressed were the angels with the life of this saint that they summoned him to them and offered him the gift of miracles. By the touch of his hand he would be able to heal the sick or raise the dead. But the saint declined the gift, saying that God alone could heal the sick. Then they offered him the power to convert sinners and turn men unto repentance. Again the saint declined, saying that only the Holy Spirit could work the grace of repentance in human souls. The angels then offered the saint the power to become a model of goodness, so that men might be drawn to him by the virtue of his life. But this, too, the saint declined, declaring that if men were drawn to him they might be estranged from God. Perplexed, the angels then asked him what he desired. The saint answered, "That I might have His grace, so that I might do good to men without knowing it." Then the angels decreed among themselves that wherever the shadow of this saint fell where he himself could not see it, the shadow should cure disease and heal broken hearts and wipe away tears.

———◦———

On one occasion Lincoln called at McClellan's home to consult him about a military matter. The general had gone to a reception. Lincoln waited for a considerable time, and finally the general returned. He walked down the hall and ascended the stairs to his bedroom, although word had been given him as to his visitor. After some minutes a second message was sent. Word came back that General McClellan had gone to bed.

Lincoln never spoke of that incident, but he did not call again on McClellan until the great crisis of September, 1862, when he and Halleck went to McClellan's house and asked him to take charge of the defeated and disorganized army of the Potomac, which Lee had defeated in the second Battle of Bull Run. When Lincoln's friends expostulated with him because of his toleration of the attitude of McClellan, Lincoln said, "Why, I would be willing to hold McClellan's horse, if only he will give victory to our army."

--- • ---

The world does not commonly associate humility and courage. It likes to listen to the man who gives himself out to be somewhat, and it discounts the humble man. Yet how often, when it comes to taking a stand for principle, and enduring the taunts and ridicule of the people, it is the meek and unassuming man who surprises us with the greatness of his courage. In some pathway through a deep glen of the forest you have come upon a jutting rock, covered with green moss, and through it there trickles a tiny cascade. Nothing on earth is softer than that moss, but when you tear away the moss you come upon the cold, naked rock. So underneath John's humility was the cold, naked, adamantine rock of incorruptible and indomitable courage.

HUNGER

Hunger is one of the elemental appetites—with thirst, the strongest appetite of the body. Under the mad craving of hunger men have thrown off every consideration and refinement of civilization. The Bible tells us the story of two mothers of Samaria who, when that city was besieged by Benhadad, made a pact to kill and eat first the babe of one mother and then the babe of the other.

High up in the Sierras I once visited Donner Lake, a peaceful body of water nestling there under the mountains. But it was the scene of one of the most terrible tragedies in the history of the frontier. It was there that the stranded Donner party, on its way to California, was trapped in the mountain snows. These people, coming from the state of Illinois, represented the best American life; but under the terrible drive of hunger they devoured one another.

In one of the tales about our aviators floating in the Pacific on a raft the narrator relates how they discussed the question of whether, if one of them expired, the others should eat his body.

These facts show you the power of hunger.

--- • ---

I once heard a survivor of Andersonville prison relate how hunger gradually stripped from the starving prisoners the principles of honor and chivalry and humanity which obtain under ordinary circumstances. He related how two men who had been bosom friends and comrades during the war, and within the terrible prison stockade, lay side by side growing weaker and weaker, each eagerly waiting for the other to die so that he might seize his handful of beans and bread. Impatient, the one whose strength was a little greater choked his comrade to death, only to expire himself within a few minutes.

HUSBAND—*see* LOVE FOR HUSBAND

HYPOCRISY

A friend brought up on a western Pennsylvania farm was telling me how the best of dogs will sometimes be taken with the fever of sheep killing. The killing is always done at night. The guilty dog will always endeavor to tempt other dogs to go with him and, if possible, lay the blame at their door. When this madness of sheep killing is on him, the dog will assume during the day, at the house and around the barn, an unusually genial and friendly air. Thus even animal natures seem to share in the hypocrisy which has invaded human natures.

I

IDEA, POWER OF AN

The most powerful thing in this world is an idea. It may be powerful for good, it may be powerful for evil—but always it is powerful. The world has been blessed, from the standpoint of comfort and well-being, by the application to daily life and its problems of the discoveries of science. Imagine our world today without the electric light, the steam engine, the wireless, the wheel. How did all this come about? Through the power of an idea. Watts saw steam lift the lid of the kettle—and had the vision of power in industrial life through the energy of that steam. Franklin saw the play of lightning—and had the idea of its power. Marconi had the idea of a message transmitted through the air, and now wherever at sea a vessel is in distress half a hundred ships will hurry to the rescue, called by the mysterious voice of the wireless. An idea is power.

IDEALS—see also DREAMS (GREAT; OF YOUTH), YOUTH (IDEALS OF; OPPORTUNITIES OF)

Andrea del Sarto was spoken of in Italy as the "faultless painter." Yet, like every great worker, he realized that he fell far short of his ideals and ambitions. He took that falling short, that failure, however, as evidence of life to come. So Browning makes him say:

Ah, but a man's reach should exceed his grasp,
Or what's a heaven for?

———•—•—•———

—Fidelity to—As a mother once sat by the cradle of her child, five spirits approached her and proffered her a gift for the child. The first said, "I am health, and whom I touch shall never know pain or sickness." The second said, "I am wealth, and whom I touch shall never know poverty or want." The third said, "I am fame, and whom I touch shall have immortal fame." The fourth said, "I am love, and whom I touch shall have a friend in life's darkest hour." But the fifth said, "Whom I touch shall be forever faithful to his dreams and his ideals." When the wise mother heard the fifth spirit, she laid hold upon his garment and besought him to touch her child.

But that is only a dream, a legend. There is no one, outside of ourselves, who can touch us and make us faithful to our dreams and our ideals. The only one who can do that is ourselves.

———•—•—•———

—Lost—As in some old ruin you will come upon the fragments of a delicately traced capital or massive archway which proclaims the original beauty and splendor of what is now but a heap of rubbish, so in the life of the worst sinner or criminal, where now only sin and bestiality reign, you may discover the fragments of a different kind of man—a man who measured up to the best that you yourself know, a man who entertained hopes just as radiant as your own, who set before him aims just as high as your own, who hung high the golden shields of a pure and honest life and promised that he would reverence them to the end.

--- ◆ ---

Brass for gold! That tells the story of the decline of Judah. It tells the story, too, of what so often happens in the kingdom of a man's life. One day the walls of the palace of his soul, like those of the House in the Wood, are hung with bright shields beaten out of the pure gold of honorable ambition and lofty principles. Then comes the struggle of life, the invasion of sordid motives, the temptations to ease and self-indulgence,

The hardening of the heart that brings
Irreverence for the dreams of youth.

--- ◆ ---

The Danish theologian and philosopher Kierkegaard has a parable of a wild duck. With his mates this duck was flying in the springtime northward across Europe. On the flight he happened to come down in a barnyard in Denmark where there were tame ducks. He ate and enjoyed some of their corn, and stayed—first for an hour, and then for a day, and then for a week, and then for a month, and, finally, because he liked the good fare and the safety of the barnyard, stayed all summer. But one autumn day when his wild mates were winging their way southward again they passed over the barnyard, and their mate heard their cries. It stirred him with a strange thrill of joy and delight; and, flapping his wings, he rose in the air to join his old

comrades in their flight to the land of summer.

But, alas, he found that his good fare had made him so soft and heavy that he could rise no higher than the eaves of the barn. So he sank back again to the barnyard, and said to himself, "Oh, well, my life is safe here and the fare is good." Every spring, and again every autumn, when the wild ducks flew over his barnyard and he heard their honking cry, his eye gleamed for a moment and he began to lift his wings and would fain have joined his mates. But at length the day came when the wild ducks flew over him and uttered their cry and he paid not the slightest attention to them.

What a parable that is of how the soul can forget its high ideals and standards and be content with lower things!

--- ◆ ---

When the bill for "local option" came up in the assembly of one of our states, among the speakers for the liquor interests was a former governor of the state, who was also a former attorney general of the United States. There he stood, with brewers, saloon keepers, vicious representatives of organized iniquity, laying his great gifts—cold, incisive logic, satire and irony, imagination and scorn—upon the filthy altar of rum. Fifty thousand dollars, they said, was his retainer.

One summer I was worshiping in the Presbyterian church in a little county seat in the mountains of southwestern Pennsylvania. After the service I shook hands with one of the elders, the prothonotary of the court. When he learned where I was from, he asked me if I knew this former attorney general and governor. They had been classmates at college back in the seventies. He said that the man who had since risen to such places of eminence gave full promise of his future when in college. Then he asked about his religious life, about his activity in the Church of Christ. I told him what I knew: that when he had first come to that city he had been the teacher of a Bible class in the First Presbyterian Church, but that his Sabbaths were now spent on the golf course. He said he was sorry to hear that it was so; for when they were in college a revival swept through the student body and this man was converted, and in prayer meeting, in student rooms, on the campus, his voice and his life spoke for the Lord Jesus Christ.

Oh, the sorrow of it! There is the young man of college days, gifted, anointed with oil, giving his heart to Jesus Christ, rising to places of great honor and trust in state and nation. Now behold him, for fifty thousand dollars pleading for perpetuation of that traffic which has damned more souls, and broken more hearts, and destroyed more happiness, than any curse that ever came out of hell.

—Sacrificing for—In one of the galleries of Paris there stands a notable statue. The sculptor, like so many great artists, was a very poor man, and lived and did his work in a garret. One night the beautiful statue was finished. The sculptor surveyed it in pride and affection for a time, and then lay down to sleep upon his bed. But that night a killing frost fell over Paris. The sculptor awoke in his chilly room and thought of the statue he had just finished—how the water would freeze in the pores and destroy the dream of his life. With that thought, without a moment's hesitation he got up from his bed; and, taking the bed clothes, he draped them carefully about the statue. In the morning the sculptor was dead, but the statue lives on. Some things must die if we are to be faithful to our standards and our ideals and keep our shields of gold.

IMAGINATION

One has written of the soul as a palace where reason is a noble hall, memory a spacious library, imagination a picture gallery, while hope is an observatory where the watchers of the night are always looking toward the stars. Let us think, then, of the decorations of the house. The fashion now, I believe, is to have bare walls in the new houses. That never appealed to me. I do not think it would appeal to anyone, save on the ground of following the fashion of the crowd.

Imagination is the painter and the artist, the interior decorator, of our homes. The fancies of the mind are the pictures on the walls. "The soul," said Marcus Aurelius, "is dyed the color of its thought." What about the color of your thought? In the excavated houses of Pompeii, buried centuries ago beneath the lava, there are rooms which have most beautiful decorations. The color and form are there just as they were when first painted by the decorators. But there are other chambers where people are not permitted to go, where the decorations are not fit to behold. The chambers of imagination are not unlike those houses of Pompeii.

In an old Grecian myth, Gyges had a ring which enabled the possessor of it to be invisible to all. Many would wear the ring of Gyges if they could; and if they did, their lives would be quite different from what the world sees. In the subterranean chamber of imagination, what do you worship? Before what pictures do you bow? Do you do in the mind and imagination what you fear to do in the flesh? Are words spoken there which you dare not speak with the lips? There do you scorn and ridicule one whom you publicly praise or flatter? In this realm do you ever wish another out of your way? What are the pictures on the walls of imagination?

———•—•—•———

The earth began to take form when the Spirit brooded upon the deep. So it is with the chaos of thought. Imagination broods upon thought and the world of thought takes form—its light and darkness, its day and night, its dry land and seas. The glory of imagination is when thought takes a pure and noble form—holy aspirations, generous purposes, courageous resolves, pure desires. The shame of the imagination is when thought takes ignoble form—impure pleasures, hateful and vindictive purposes, contemptible desires.

———•—•—•———

—Evil—A celebrated Italian scholar spent his days and nights in his library among his precious volumes. One morning he was found dead in his chair. The light still burned in his student's lamp. There was no wound or mark of violence, no sign of struggle. The cause of the scholar's death remained a mystery until, upon drawing back the sleeve of his robe, his friends saw on his wrist a tiny spot of red. Then they understood the cause of his death. The red mark told of the bite of an asp. The scholar had opened an old volume in which the small but venomous creature made its home, and it had stung him to death. What happened to that scholar in actual life often happens, figuratively, to those who defile the imagination with an evil book.

———•—•—•———

Through unrestrained indulgence of thought and desire men are led into wickedness and sin. Before an evil thing is done in the visible world, it is always done first in the realm of the heart. The world sees the outer fall, but not the inner fall, which long antedates the outer. Evil thoughts and imaginations, secretly indulged in, work silently, like miners sapping a wall, and give no intimation of their approach to the fortress of the soul. When men are overthrown by a given temptation, it is not so much this particular temptation that has overwhelmed them, as the things which led up to and prepared the way for that temptation.

A few summers ago I visited Lake Trasimeno, where in 217 B.C. Hannibal, invading Italy, overwhelmed the Roman army sent against him. It was not so much the assault of the Carthaginian army in the gray mists of that fatal morning which accounted for the overthrow of the Roman legions, as the steps and maneuvers taken by Hannibal to get the Roman army in that dangerous position between the mountains and the sea, where escape was impossible.

So is it with the disasters which overtake the soul: the real damage is wrought before men see that anything is wrong.

———•—•—•———

What a strange mystery is the mind of man! It has upper stories of the Hall of Fantasy, where we hold converse with the celestial regions, and gloomy subterranean chambers where we communicate with the regions infernal. If it is thought injurious to one's soul to visit certain places, and go with certain people, then how can it be thought harmless to visit those places in imagination and feast the eye of the soul on those scenes? The best part of you, the immortal part, the heavenly part—your mind, your soul—has gone and has looked, and has been tainted thereby.

IMMORTALITY—*see also* HEAVEN

On a bright July day some years ago I was resting at a posthouse on a journey across the mountains of Norway. The village was but a cluster of cottages, and most of the inhabitants were standing about the door of one of the cottages.

Presently men came out of the house carrying a rude coffin. It was laid on the flat bed of a low wagon, and the procession started for the place of burial. Down the steep hill rumbled the wagon, followed by the company of mourners and neighbors. At the foot of the hill they took a road to the left which led them through fields sweet with new-mown hay. After a moment's pause at the gate of the churchyard they passed through and came to a stop before the door of a white Lutheran church. The body was carried into the church, the men and women and children filing in after it. In the space of half an hour they came out again into the clear sunlight and gathered about the open grave.

For a little time there was quiet and silence, like that which brooded over the Sabbath fields of hay and the deep fiord, across whose placid face lay silver cascades and the shadow of the mountains. Then the company broke up and went their several ways, each waiting his time —until for him, too, the little episode of life would be over, and he would take the same journey, down the hill, through the meadow, into the church, and then to the grave, while the bell in the tower tolled a sad, yet sweetly sounding, requiem.

As I saw them come slowly up the hill again, I thought of the question that was in my own mind, and in the minds of those honest, hard-working, yet life-loving peasants, a question to which their noble mountains and peaceful fields and deep mysterious fiords could give no answer: "If a man die, shall he live again?"

One question, more than all others,
From thoughtful minds implores reply,
It is, as breathed from star and pall,
What fate awaits us when we die?

When the early Christian missionaries came to England in the sixth century they went as far north as Northumbria. Ethelbert, the king of Northumbria, uncertain whether to permit the preaching of this new religion or not, called a council of his lords and nobles. At the council some thought it would be dangerous to permit this strange doctrine to be preached. In the midst of their deliberations, which were held at night, a swallow flew in a window at one end of the great hall and then flew out a window at the other end. One of the aged chiefs arose and said, "You have seen this swallow fly through the hall. Out of the darkness it came, and after a brief moment in the light it passed out again into the darkness. Even so is the spirit of man. It comes out of the darkness and then passes again into the mysterious darkness. If these men with their new religion can tell us whence the soul of man comes, or whither it goes, then let us hear them."

Traveling once in Russia, my brother and I arrived late at night at the station in Petrograd. Unable to speak a word of the country's language, or even to read the signs which we saw here and there, we had to depend altogether upon the good will of those with whom we tried to communicate our ideas by falling back upon the universal language of signs. A rather villainous-looking droshky driver got us into his carriage, and we showed him a slip of paper with the name of our hotel written upon it. After a long and circuitous drive through the rambling town, with the light of the northern summer beginning to fade from the huge, tawny buildings, we at length drew up before a hotel. It was not the hotel that we had named, but our driver mumbled something that seemed to imply that the other hotel was closed. We therefore alighted; and after supper we were conducted to two bedrooms, like everything else in Russia, enormous.

The feeling of remoteness from our own land and language and people—indeed, from anything with which we had been familiar—the new manners and customs and tongue, and the strange silence of the vast hostelry where we were established, produced in me something akin to uneasiness; and a cloud of depression crept over me. Before I closed my eyes I struck the wall at my side several times with my hand. At once there came back answering knocks from my brother on the other side of the wall. I knew then that all was well with him, and he knew that all was well with me.

Pilgrims together, my friend and I take the long and winding path through life. By and by the shadows of the night come down and the pilgrims are separated, and one is left to be brave alone. Between us death uplifts its dark wall and heavy barricade. Then what? It is not strange that I should wonder how it fares with him, nor is it strange that I should wonder if he is "conscious or not of the past."

—**And analogy**—Man saw the beetle emerge from his filthy bed of corruption —and in his temples he hung up the golden scarabaeus as the symbol of life to come. He saw the butterfly come out in radiant glory from her dark bed— and on his tomb he carved the butterfly as a symbol of the resurrection. When the ice and the snow began to melt, and the south winds began to blow softly, and spring blew her clarion o'er the dreaming earth, man saw the dead branches bud and put forth new leaves— and in the great change of the springtime he saw the sure token of the revirescence of man after death.

In a hundred different forms man has liked to repeat the myth of the phoenix

—how that fabled bird, after subsisting for five hundred years, loads his wings with spices and, flying to the temple, is burned to ashes upon the altar; and out of the ashes there emerges the new bird, which salutes the priest and flies away. Therefore, in his temples man set up the phoenix as the symbol of life everlasting.

These analogies, of course, prove nothing; for the beetle, the butterfly, and the tree only *seem* to be dead; yet the appeal of man to these processes in nature show how deep is his instinct for immortality.

—**Belief in**—In certain respects the *great* article of the Apostles' Creed is the last: "I believe in . . . the resurrection of the body, and the life everlasting." Without that article, the other great affirmations have no meaning. Suppose one were to say, "I believe in God the Father," but not in life everlasting; or, "I believe in . . . Jesus Christ his only Son," but not in the life everlasting; or, "I believe in the Holy Ghost," but not in the life everlasting; or, "I believe in . . . the holy catholic Church, the communion of saints," but not in the life everlasting. All those affirmations would be meaningless without the great chord that is struck in the final sentence of the Creed :"I believe in . . . the life everlasting." Without that affirmation, the Creed would be like a great cathedral wrapped in gloom and the darkness of night. But with that affirmation the Creed is like a great cathedral illuminated by the sun and showing all the glory of architect, sculptor, and painter.

One day, realizing that he was not long for this world, Moody said to a friend, "Someday you will read in the papers that D. L. Moody of Northfield is dead. Don't you believe a word of it. At that moment I shall be more alive than I am now. I shall have gone up higher, that is all—out of this old clay tenement into a house that is immortal, a body that sin cannot touch, that sin cannot taint, a body fashioned like unto His glorious body. I was born of the flesh in 1837; I was born of the Spirit in 1856. That which is born of the flesh may die; that which is born of the Spirit will live forever."

Bismarck, speaking with Andrew White, our ambassador to Germany, said of immortality: "I do not doubt it, even for a moment. This life is too sad, too incomplete, to satisfy our highest aspirations and desires. It is meant to be a struggle to ennoble us. Can the struggle be in vain? I think not. Final perfection, I believe in, a perfection which God has in store for us."

Both reason and affection, then, bear witness to the desirability and possibility of future recognition.

After giving many reasons why death is not to be dreaded by a good man, Cicero concludes with this justly celebrated passage: "From this life I depart as from a temporary lodging, not as from a home. For nature has assigned it to us as an inn to sojourn in, not a place of habitation. Oh, glorious day! when I shall depart to that divine company and assemblage of spirits, and quit this troubled and polluted scene! For I shall go to my friend Cato, than whom never was better man born, nor more distinguished for pious affection; whose body was burned by me, whereas, on the contrary, it was fitting that mine should be burned by him. But his soul, not deserting me, but oft looking back, no doubt departed to those regions whither I saw that I myself was destined to come: Which though a distress to me, I seemed patiently to endure: not that I bore it with indifference, but I comforted myself with the recollection that the separation and distance between us would not continue long: For these reasons, O Scipio, old age is tolerable to me, and not only not irksome, but even delightful. And if I am wrong in this, that I believe the souls of men to be immortal, I willingly delude myself: nor do I desire that this mistake, in which I take pleasure, should be wrested from me as long as I live: but if I, when dead, shall have no consciousness, as some narrow-minded philosophers imagine, I do not fear lest dead philosophers should ridicule this my delusion."

It does not follow that the breaking up of the form of life destroys life itself. When you burn a bit of coal you apparently destroy it. To the eye, only ashes remain. Yet we know that these particles of fossilized wood were not destroyed, but that they merely entered into the atmosphere in gaseous form. You might take a hammer and shatter the Venus of Milo into a thousand pieces, and then grind the pieces into the most impalpable dust; but not a single particle of the marble image upon which the hungry generations have gazed with awe and wonder has been lost. The crystal drop which flashes with beauty on the rose leaf when the sun first dawns has vanished long before the sun has reached the middle station; neither touch nor taste nor eye can detect it. Yet it has not been destroyed; it has but changed its form, and persists as vapor. If these atoms and particles—dust, iron, and lime—are indestructible, are we to think that annihilation comes only to that which we associate with spirit and with soul?

—Endless earthly life—The idea of living on, forever and forever, the kind of life that we now live in the flesh is indeed very dreadful. In his famous satire Jonathan Swift brings Gulliver to the island of Luggnagg, where he has an interview with the Struldbrugs, a race of men born immortal, but not endowed with immortal youth. Gulliver is very anxious to see them and talk with them, but is sadly disappointed when they tell him of their misery. "When they came to fourscore years, which is reckoned the extremity of living in this country, they had not only all the follies and infirmities of other old men, but many more which arose from the dreadful prospect of never dying."

The same terrible idea of immortality appears in the Grecian myth of Tithonus. Tithonus, the son of the king of Troy, was beloved by Aurora, who persuaded Jupiter to confer upon him the gift of immortal life; but she forgot to have youth joined in the gift, and soon perceived that Tithonus was growing old, yet could never die. When his hair was white she left him alone in the palace, and finally she turned him into a grasshopper.

Sir Edwin Arnold records a legend of the East in which it is related that King Solomon sat once upon his throne on a great mountain west of the Indus. All creatures were gathered about him, and in his hand he held an emerald cup full of the water of life. The intimation had come to him that if he drank of it he would be young forever. In order to get their advice, Solomon called before him representatives of all created things. All advised him to drink of the cup, "Drink, O King! Live forever!" Then Solomon inquired if all creatures were present, and learned that the dove had not yet appeared. When he asked the dove, she said, "O King, if my mate died I should die, too. What good will immortal youth

do you if you see everything to which you are attached perish around you?" Taught by the voice of affection, Solomon poured out, untasted, the water of endless life for himself alone.

—And faith—It was when he saw the wagons from Egypt that Jacob believed Joseph was alive. It takes more than reasons, more than argument, to inspire the hope and faith of immortal life. And that we have, the great fact that meets and masters all other facts—the resurrection of Jesus Christ from the dead. There, indeed, is God's wagon rolling out of Egypt, proclaiming to us the fact that Christ is "risen from the dead, and become the firstfruits of them that slept" (I Cor. 15:20). Upon the empty grave of Christ, the eternal Son of God, who died for our sins and rose again for our justification, we build the structure of our faith and hope; and we defy death with all its sting and the grave with all its victory to shake it or overthrow it.

The ancient thought and hope for life to come is supposed to have reached its high-water mark in that beautiful passage of the *Phaedo* where Plato, after rehearsing the arguments and intimations for immortality, makes Socrates say that from all these reasons and arguments you must select that which you think is the best, until there comes some sure word of prophecy or revelation upon which, as upon a ship, you can take your journey across the angry seas.

But when this same great man, Christlike before Christ, came to die, he said to his friends: "And now we go our different ways, you to life and I to death. Which is better God only knows." With this farewell to life and salutation of life to come compare the words of the Christian philosopher, who declared that life and immortality had been brought to light, their secret told and revealed in the gospel. He, too, is standing where the Athenian philosopher stood, near to the gates of death. What does he say? What does he think? Does he answer, "I have a desire to depart and to be with Christ, which is very far better"? Far better! And there we leave our dead. They shall walk with him in white. "They shall hunger no more, neither thirst any more; neither shall the sun light on them, nor any heat. For the Lamb which is in the midst of the throne shall feed them, and shall lead them unto living fountains of waters: and God shall wipe away all tears from their eyes." (Rev. 7:16-17.) Far better!

———

—Hope of—A few days before his death Thomas Jefferson told his dear daughter Martha that in a certain drawer, in an old pocketbook, she would find something for her. It was a piece of paper on which he had written eight lines, "A Death-Bed Adieu to Martha Jefferson from Thomas Jefferson." These lines had in them no classical reference or philosophical speculation, but the simple statement of his hope that on the shore "which crowns all my hopes, or which buries my care, I will find awaiting me two seraphs, long shrouded in death." The two to whom he referred were his wife and his daughter Maria.

The hope expressed by Jefferson as he was about to enter the unknown world is the hope of normal man. Just as man does his work and makes his plans with the expectation, although not the proof, that the sun will rise tomorrow, so we live in the general expectation of life beyond the grave. We hope that after the sunset here today there will be daybreak elsewhere. It would be a poor life, indeed, if through the cypress trees we could not catch a glimpse of the shining stars of hope.

—Influence of belief in—The Russian novelist Dostoevski in his famous story *The Brothers Karamazov* makes his characters discuss the subject of the life to come. Dmitri says, "Is that really your conviction as to the consequences of the disappearance of the faith in immortality?"

"Yes," answered Ivan, "that was my contention. There is no virtue if there is no immortality."

The same idea is expressed by Renan in his *History of the People of Israel.* "Let us not deceive ourselves," he says; "man is governed by nothing but his conception of the future. Any nation which en masse gives up all faith in what lies beyond the grave will become utterly degraded. An individual may do great things, and yet not believe in immortality. But those around him must believe it, for him and for themselves."

It will give us strength for the battle of today and for the unknown things of tomorrow if we feel upon our brow the cold, energizing wind which sweeps in upon the valleys of this life from the high places of the life to come.

———

James Bryce has an impressive passage in which he describes a great American city and wonders what would be the effect upon its life and manners if all who dwell there should lose all interest in and all faith in a life to come. "Would men," he asks, "say, 'Let us eat and drink; for tomorrow we die' [I Cor. 15:32], or would custom and sympathy, and a perception of the advantages which stable government offers to citizens as a whole, and which orderly self-restraint offers to each one, replace supernatural sanctions and hold in check the violence of the masses and the self-indulgent impulses of the individual? History, if she cannot give a complete answer to this question, tells us that hitherto civilized ociety has rested on religion, and that ree government has prospered best among religious peoples."

In the conclusion of his famous work of the seventeenth century, *The Saints' Everlasting Rest,* Richard Baxter, a master of English prose, has a beautiful passage in which he speaks of the influence of the heavenly mind upon man's life in the midst of the trials of this world: "Thou wilt be as one that stands on the top of an exceeding high mountain; he looks down on the world as if it were quite below him; fields and woods, cities and towns, seem to him as but little spots. Thus despicably wilt thou look on all things here below. The greatest princes will seem but as grasshoppers; the busy, contentious, covetous world, but as a heap of ants. Man's threatenings will be no terror to thee; nor the honours of this world any strong enticement; temptations will be more harmless, as having lost their strength; and afflictions less grievous, as having lost their sting; and every mercy will be better known and relished."

Huxley somewhere protests against the great words of Paul read by an English rector at the funeral of his child: "If the dead rise not? let us eat and drink; for to morrow we die" (I Cor. 15:32). He took the position that even if there is no after life, there is opportunity for nobility in this life. But as a matter of fact Paul is right, and Huxley is wrong. The very idea of nobility in this life is a by-product of the world's faith in life to come. If this life is all, then, "eat, drink, and be merry"; get the most you can out of it, in that animal, sensual way, for that is your real existence. But if this life is the training place for another life, then the wise man will live not for time but for eternity.

Danton, a leader of the French Revolution, on his way to the guillotine, said to his companions on the scaffold, "Our heads will meet in yonder sack." That is the outlook on life if there is no resurrection of the dead. But because Christ is risen, and because the dead rise, the Christian believer as he lays the body of his beloved in the grave can say, "Our souls will meet in yonder heaven."

—Man's instinct for—When Columbus was sailing toward the unknown continents of the west, he saw, floating in the sea, leaves and branches which told him he was drawing near another world; and in that faith he sailed ever on, until the sands of the Bahamas shone white in the moonlight. The tides, the winds, and the waves carry man, the "lonely and sublime Columbus of creation," across the ocean of existence. He cannot see the land toward which he is going, nor is he permitted to speak to any ship that has sailed thither; for they who have reached that land return no more. But in the affections and longing of his heart, in the instincts of his being, in the processes of nature that serve as a picture of what it might be like to live and die again, and in the too-evident brevity and incompleteness of earthly existence, he can see portents and intimations, reminding him that the sea of life washes the shores of eternity.

A woman in Germany, who had no faith in immortality, in keeping with her convictions and unbelief caused herself to be buried in a sepulcher of heavy masonry covered with a heavy stone slab, on which was inscribed her declaration that for her this was the end. But in some way a seed found lodgment in the mortar and, feeding upon her body, grew to be a tree that burst asunder her stone coffin. In like manner man's instinct bursts asunder the stone coffin of doubts and arguments with which it sought to deny the fact and hope of immortality.

———•◦•———

In Toledo in Spain I went to see the paintings of the great artist who is known to fame only by his nationality —El Greco, "the Greek." In the cathedral you see his apostles and saints. Some of them are just bare, unfinished sketches. He planned to finish them, but death overtook him; and now one looks on the mere outline of a face or a hand. Whether we think of those who had little opportunity in life, who did little in the vineyard because no one hired them, or of those who were the most gifted, who found their place and their niche and for whom the gate of opportunity was flung wide—always there is a shadow of incompleteness. Man seems to come to an end as Moses died on Nebo's lonely mountain—just on the borders of the land which he desires to enter. There is something in him that is greater than the brief span of time in which he lives. His intellectual and moral endowments are on a scale immeasurably larger than the needs of this present life.

Among the essays of Bacon there is one called "Of Fame." It is only a fragment. At the end of the essay we read in brackets, "The rest was not finished." How true that is of man and his works in this world!

Thomas Chalmers said, "Man feels an interminable longing after nobler and higher things which naught but immortality and the greatness of immortality can satiate."

———•◦•———

—Man's need for—Toward the end of his life—on his seventieth birthday— Victor Hugo wrote: "Winter is on my head, but eternal spring is in my heart. The nearer I approach the end, the

plainer I hear around me the immorta symphonies of the worlds which invit me. For half a century I have been writ ing my thoughts in prose, verse, history philosophy, drama, romance, tradition satire, ode, song—I have tried all. But feel that I have not said the thousandt part of what is in me."

Or, to quote the words of the eloquen French preacher Saurin, "Such is m soul. But where is it lodged? It inhabi a world of vanity and nothingness. can discover no object capable of fillin my capacious desires. I ascend th thrones of sovereigns; I descend into th beggar's dust; I walk the palaces o princes, I lodge in the peasant's cabin; retire into the closet to be wise; I avoi recollection, choose ignorance and in crease the crowd of idiots; I live in soli tude; I rush into the social multitude but everywhere I find a mortifying void In all these places there is nothing satis factory." Since God has put eternity i man's heart, the world can never satisf him. Only the greatness of immortalit can meet the hunger of man's soul.

———•◦•———

One of the most striking and impres sive things ever said on the subject o immortality, and man's need for it, wa what Hortense, daughter of Napoleon' Joséphine and mother of Napoleon III wrote to her son when he was for a brie time in America. He was seriously ill and she did not expect to meet him again in this life. But she wrote: "Be lieve that certainly we shall meet again Have faith in this consoling idea. It i too necessary not to be true."

IMPURITY—*see also* TEMPTATION

In the national gallery in Stockholm there is a remarkable, almost terrible painting. I do not know that it has a name, but it needs no name. A path winds in and out among the rocks along the side of a mountain. Just above the path there is the opening to a cave in the rocks. At the entrance stands what seems at first to be a beautiful woman. It is a woman's head and face, but the head is set on the lithe and sinewy body of a lion. Below this beast with the woman's face are torn robes, and the rocks are splashed with blood. The cold, steel eyes in the beautiful face are turned toward the path, along which may be seen approaching another victim. Whoever painted the picture preached a great sermon. Many a young man would do well to get a copy of that painting and hang it on the wall of his room; and underneath it let him write the words of Paul, "If any man defile the temple of God, him shall God destroy" (I Cor. 3:17).

INDECISION — *see* DECISION

INFIDELITY

There is a story that Voltaire when in the midst of an atheistic discussion with some of his friends got up from his chair and closed the door into the room where his valet was, saying as he did so that he did not want his valet to cut his throat. If all the declarations of avowed atheists and infidels, and their more dangerous allies who wear the garb of religion, were taken seriously, there would be a vast amount of throat cutting among men.

INFLUENCE — *see also* SIN (INFLUENCE OF), TEMPTATION

The word "influence" occurs only once in the whole Bible, and that is in a sublime passage from the book of Job in which the Almighty asks Job unanswerable questions. Among the questions is this one (Job 38:31): "Canst thou bind the sweet influences of Pleiades, or loose the bands of Orion?" The Pleiades are a cluster of stars in Taurus, one of the constellations of the heavens. We of today know a good deal about refrigerators and radios and automobiles, but the ancients knew more about the stars; and I am not sure that their knowledge is not to be preferred. Little is known about the Pleiades; but the intimation here is that they exert an influence—perhaps on other celestial bodies, perhaps upon our world, its life, and its climate. Whatever that influence is, it was thought of by this inspired author as benign, powerful, silent, irresistible. "Canst thou bind the sweet influences of Pleiades?" A beautiful idea that, for the influence, not only of the heavenly bodies, but of the lives of men one upon another. There is an influence and a power which goes forth from one life to another.

—Evil—A man once dreamed that he was in hell. When asked to give an account of what he had seen—if there were flames there, and suffering there, and wrecked and malign creatures with whom he had to associate, and if the place resounded with oaths of blasphemy —he said, "Yes, but there was something far worse than that: I was compelled to face my influence. I knew that I deserved punishment, for I had scorned and rejected Jesus Christ; but my sorest pain was to see what the effect of my life had been upon others."

He was a young man who undoubtedly belonged to Christ. But only in the last part of his life had he given himself to Christ. When he came to die, he was filled with regret that he had done so little for Christ, and with remorse that he had done so much against him. His dying request was this, "Bury my influence with me."

There is a story that Alexander the Great once sent to a certain province a beautiful maiden whose breath was like the perfume of richest flowers. All her life, however, she had lived amid poison, inhaling it until her body was full of poison. Flowers presented to her withered on her breast, and if she breathed on a bird it fell dead.

The legend embodies the truth that there are lives in whose presence nothing pure or beautiful can thrive, and whose moral breath is corruption and death.

* * *

We live in a world of echoes. Be careful then how you speak. Thomas Hughes in the introduction to *Tom Brown's School Days* describes the character of the famous master of Rugby, Thomas Arnold, and tells how the great teacher took pains to remind the boys under his care of the effect of their influence. "He taught that in this wonderful world no boy or man can tell which of his actions is indifferent and which not; that by a thoughtless word or look we may lead a brother astray!" How easily, alas, this can be done!

* * *

One of the most gifted preachers and poets of the early seventeenth century was John Donne, who at his death was dean of St. Paul's. His last sermon, "Death's Duel," preached shortly before his death, is a remarkable discourse in which with beautiful and moving sentences he points the sinner to Christ on the cross. The sermons of this great preacher, of whom Walton said, "He was a preacher in earnest, weeping sometimes for his auditory and sometimes with them; always preaching to himself, like an angel in the clouds," are always published in the same volume with his poems. Those who have patience to go through much dross and elaborated ob-

scurity will find in the book real gems of poetry to reward them. There is much, however, in the verses written in the early manhood of Donne which seem a very strange accompaniment to the sermons in the close of the volume. One wonders how the man who wrote these earnest sermons and delivered them with such sincerity and eloquence could be the same man who wrote the erotic poems.

Men who heard Donne preach always noted in him a vein of sadness and melancholy; in truth, as Walton said, "like an angel out of the cloud" he preached unto himself, for he was shadowed and haunted by the recollection of the licentious poems which he had written with all the great talent which God had bestowed upon him, poems calculated to sow the seeds of licentiousness and immorality in other lives, and which he could never recall. Henceforth he had to face the fact that he must influence the world not only as a preacher of the everlasting gospel but as the author of amatory and lust-filled verses.

* * *

—Good—In Pittsburgh I often hear of a character of the frontier days in this then western country, a man called Appleseed Johnny, who went down the Ohio Valley planting apple trees. Today, in many a valley and on many a hillside, that man's wise thought and beneficent practice is bearing its fruit. I love a tree about as well as anything on earth, and whenever I drive up an avenue of ancient elms, or locusts, or eucalyptus, and see the farmhouse or the mansion at the end of the shaded lane, I think of the man now long in his grave who planted those trees and realized that long after he was in his grave, they would be lifting their arms to heaven and speaking peace and rest to the sons of men.

* * *

Speaking once at the commencement of an Indiana university, I heard frequent reference to a man spoken of as Samuel Morris, "the angel in ebony." I asked the students to tell me who this Samuel Morris was. This was his story:

Samuel Morris was a black boy, son of an African king, who escaped from the neighboring tribe which captured him and, making his way to the coast, came to a Christian mission, where he heard the gospel and gave his heart to Christ. He stowed away on a sailing vessel bound for America, and after great hardships and cruelties reached New York, where a man whose name had been given him sent him across the country to this Indiana college. Soon after he arrived, and under his influence, the college was swept by a revival.

The boy planned to go back to his African country and tell his people the story of the gospel. He would describe to his fellow students how he planned to gather his people about him on the sand and tell them of the way of salvation. But God had another plan for him.

The severe American winter was too much for this black boy—he was stricken with consumption, and after a brief illness died. It was a strange providence to those who had followed his marvelous career, but a providence which was soon vindicated. Three young men who stood at his grave gave themselves then and there to the work of Christ in foreign lands, to do what this boy had planned to do. Thus the power of his spirit-filled life was carried in every direction. His influence and his death became the chief endowment of that university. Students came from all parts of the world, drawn by his story; and out of the large class which I addressed on that commencement day three fourths of them were going into the service of Christ in foreign lands. The grave of that black boy in the cemetery at Fort Wayne, Indiana, is the most visited grave in all that city; and when a monument recently was erected there, almost forty years after the boy's death, hundreds of citizens came from far and near to wonder at his grave and to give thanks to God.

——◆—◆—◆——

One summer, going up a street along the shore of Lake Geneva, I saw a low, dim building on which were written the words, "Here John Calvin lived and died." At once there came to my mind the conclusion of the great eulogy on Calvin by Bancroft: "And so he continued, year after year, solitary and feeble, toiling for humanity, till after a life of glory, he bequeathed to his personal heirs a fortune in books and furniture, in stock and bonds, not exceeding two hundred dollars, and to the world a purer reformation, a republican spirit in religion, and the kindred principles of republican liberty."

——◆—◆—◆——

After Bishop Simpson, the great Methodist preacher, returned from college he attended a camp meeting in Cadiz, Ohio. There he took an interest in a group of young men, and was anxious that they should be preserved from the temptations to which they were exposed. At the evening meeting he observed some of these young men go forward to the altar. Deeply moved, he was regretting that he, whose life had been so guarded by Christian influences, should not experience the same emotions that they were undergoing. He saw standing near the railing a young man who was not a professed Christian. The thought occurred to Simpson that while he himself was not being benefited, this young man might be. He laid his hand on his shoulder and asked him if he would like to go forward for prayer. The young man said he would go if Simpson would go with him, and together they went to the altar and knelt down. It was after this that Simpson became a member of the Church and dedicated himself to Christ.

* * *

Left motherless at a tender age, Beecher had for a companion an old Negro, Charles Simms, who used to saw the wood for his father and do odd chores about the place. Beecher makes frequent allusion to this Negro and the influence he exerted upon his life. They occupied the same room, and Beecher pays a beautiful tribute to the Negro's character and piety: "Every night he would set the candle at the head of his bed, and pray and sing and laugh, and I bear record that his praying made a profound impression upon my mind. I never thought whether it was right or wrong—I only thought, How that man does enjoy it! What enjoyment there must be in such prayer as his. I gained more from that man of the idea of the desirableness of prayer than I ever did from my father or mother. My father was never an ascetic. He had no sympathy with anything of a mawkish tendency. Yet this poor man, more than he, led me to see that there should be real overflowing gladness and thanksgiving in prayer."

When we see Henry Ward Beecher standing in his pulpit, dramatizing the horror of auctioning off a slave, or hurling his thunders against the fugitive slave law, we must remember that picture of the lad lying in his bed and watching the old Negro at his prayers.

* * *

When Charles Dickens was passing one day through the streets of York an unknown woman accosted him saying, "Mr. Dickens, will you let me touch the hand that has filled my house with many friends?"

—Loss of—In the seminary there was a man in the class above me who was converted and brought into the ministry by an unusual experience. After leaving college he became the secretary to a United States senator from a near-by state. A party had gone with this senator on a campaign through his state. There was plenty of whiskey and champagne and all that goes with it. In all this the young secretary was a willing participant. One night they were in their room in the hotel, and their life that evening had been in keeping with what had been going on before. Preparing for bed, this young man was surprised to see one of his fellow secretaries kneeling in the attitude of prayer at the side of the bed. The group had heard him mock and had seen him drunk, but never before had they seen him pray. They thought he was just mocking, putting up a joke on them. One of them gave the kneeling man a push with his foot, whereupon the unresisting body fell limply to the floor, with wide-open eyes staring up at the ceiling. The man was dead. The incident shocked this other young man into sobriety, and turned his steps toward the Church. If you got down to pray, are there those who would conclude at first that you were mocking?

* * *

—Resisting evil—One of the most successful preachers of Scotland, Ambrose Shepherd, writes thus of his youth: "I have already alluded to my experience in a hard school. Indulge me if I return to it for a moment. My earlier years were spent in a Lancashire cloth mill. In it I wrought from morning to night side by side with youths of my own age and men who were older. For the most part, young and old, they were practiced in almost every conceivable coarse and brutal way of casting their existence as rubbish to the void. But I think I can truthfully say that, while I tried to be loyal to the conditions of contract, and as a comrade in the ranks was not unpopular, yet they knew that neither within those grim walls nor without them was I of their world."

Have your own world! Have the courage to stay in that world and breathe its pure air.

———————•———•———

Years ago, when I was a junior in the theological seminary at Princeton, the venerable Dr. William Paxton was just closing his career as a professor. He told us one day of an incident which I have never forgotten:

On Sabbath evenings in his Pittsburgh church he had noted a young man of fine appearance sitting in one of the galleries and giving careful and reverent attention to the preacher. Shortly before a Communion season this man called at Dr. Paxton's home and said he wished to make a confession of his faith and unite with the Church. After the conversation was over and the arrangement had been made, just as the man was leaving, Dr. Paxton asked, not out of curiosity, but as a matter of courtesy, what his business was. He was surprised when the man told him that he was a liquor dealer, and gave the name of one of the best-known liquor firms in Pittsburgh. Dr. Paxton asked him to sit down again, and expressed his sorrow that such was the case, explaining to him that with the convictions he held he could not conscientiously receive him into the membership of the Church. But he told him that there was then no church law on the subject, that it was his own personal judgment in the matter, and that there were other ministers, whose opinions he did not judge, who took a different view of the matter. The young man replied heatedly that he considered the minister's attitude a personal affront. His father and

his grandfather before him had been in the liquor business, and he had always regarded it as an honorable calling. With an air that told plainly that he was through with churches and ministers, he took his hat and walked out.

Dr. Paxton never expected to see the man again. He was therefore much surprised when one morning several months afterward the same man came to his study and said, "Dr. Paxton, when you refused to receive me as a member of your church I felt angry and outraged, and resolved in my heart to have nothing more to do with churches. But when I was leaving you told me that it would be a good thing if I would see what my business was doing in the city. The other day I took your advice. I followed one of our wagons about over the city. I watched it as it went into the private home, the mansion of the rich, the hovel and the tenement of the poor, the rich man's club, the dance hall, and places of amusement and of crime. Now I know what you meant. You were right and I was wrong. I honor and respect you, sir, for refusing to receive me into the membership of your church. But now that I have seen the evils of this business, I have given it up and, confessing my sins, I desire to be received into the Church."

———————•———•———

—Unconscious—A Pittsburgh lawyer, desperately ill, was sent as a last resort to a sanatorium. He was so weak that he had to be carried to the train on a stretcher. On the night of his arrival the physician who examined him, alarmed at his condition, told him that he must have a stimulant at once, and prescribed whisky. The lawyer, who had been a total abstainer all his life, said he would not take it. The physician then had a private interview with the man's wife, saying that unless her husband took the stimulant he could not answer for his being alive on the morrow. The wife answered, "You might as well try something else; you will carry him out of the hospital dead before he will take a drink of whisky." Another kind of stimulant was prescribed, and in the course of a week or ten days the sick lawyer was on his feet and on the road to recovery.

The physician who was attending him was the brilliant son of a brilliant father, also a physician. The son had been highly educated and had started in his profession with great promise; but, disappointed in a love affair, he had taken to drink, and had gone to the very depths. After some years of this sort of life he had a meeting with his former fiancée, who held out hopes of marriage if he could prove to her that he was free from the dominion of strong drink. With this as an animating and inspiring motive, the man pulled himself together and reestablished himself as a reputable and highly regarded physician.

In one of his visits to his now convalescent patient, he said to him, "Sir, I owe you a great debt of gratitude. At intervals the old appetite for drink comes back upon me with terrible power and threat. It just happened that I was in one of those dangerous periods when I was first called in to see you. I was on the point of surrendering again to my old enemy; but after I heard your steadfast refusal to take the whisky I had prescribed, even though I told you your life was in danger if you did not take it, I said to myself, 'If that man at the very point of death can hold to such a resolution, certainly I can resist the craving for drink that is now upon me.' The crisis soon passed, and I was myself again. I thank you, sir. You did not know it, but when you refused to take that whisky you were holding me back from another fall and disaster. Your refusal saved me."

A striking and dramatic illustration of the power of unconscious influence!

———◆◆◆———

Passing through the corridors of a great hospital, I saw sitting on a bench a minister whom I had known. He was a man well advanced in years, now broken in health, who for some time had given up his church, where he had been in unhappy disputes with members of his congregation. I turned to speak with him, expecting to hear from him some word of melancholy reminiscence or present gloom; but I received a pleasant surprise. He told me that a woman going by had just turned to speak with him and had told him that long ago a word spoken by him in the pulpit had been the means of bringing her to Christ. He was happy in the knowledge that his shadow had once pointed the way to Jesus Christ.

INGRATITUDE

In *Gulliver's Travels* Jonathan Swift gives us his opinion of ingratitude to friends and benefactors when he thus describes the laws of the Lilliputians: "Ingratitude is reckoned among them a capital crime; for they reason thus, that whoever makes ill return to his benefactors must needs be a common enemy to the rest of mankind, from whom he hath received no obligation. And, therefore, such a man is not fit to live." Though severe, the reasoning is sound: If a man does ill to one who has helped him, how much more will he do to those who have not helped him in any way?

———◆◆◆———

On one occasion Tallyrand, being told that a certain public officer was saying evil things against him, exclaimed, "That surprises me; I have never done him a favor."

When the ministry of Robert Walpole fell, and a hostile vote was being taken in the House of Commons, Walpole, watching those who voted against him, said to the one who sat near him, "Young man, I will tell you the history of all these men as they come in: That fellow I saved from the gallows. And that one, from starvation. This other one's son I promoted."

The most common sin is the sin of ingratitude. In a newspaper magazine section a number of years ago I saw a full-page illustration entitled "Ingratitude." In the center stood a colossal image, across the breast of which was written the word "ingratitude." Around the image was assembled a great crowd of men, each one of whom was hurling a stone against the image of Ingratitude. But when you looked more closely, you saw that every one of those men who was hurling stones at the image of Ingratitude was holding in his own left arm a small image on which was written "ingratitude." The cartoonist thus gave expression to the sentiment that, although all men detest ingratitude manifested in others, they have more or less of it in their own hearts.

—Filial—Even the Saviour himself was hurt and wounded by ingratitude; and if he, who then can be insensitive to its wounds? Some think that Shakespeare sounded the depths of mortal sorrow and suffering in that tremendous scene in *King Lear,* where the aged king and father, cast out by his unnatural daughters, wanders on the gloomy heath at night and utters his apostrophe to wind and rain, thunder and lightning. He had learned

How sharper than a serpent's tooth
it is
To have a thankless child!

Ingratitude in all its degrees is an ugly thing, but most loathsome it is when it shows itself in a child.

Ingratitude,   thou   marble-hearted
fiend,
More hideous when thou show'st
thee in a child
Than the sea-monster!

—To God—When Colonel Gardiner, whose remarkable conversion is related by Philip Doddridge, was suddenly arrested on his path of evil and turned to God, he felt himself doomed to eternal punishment. But the thing which troubled him most of all, he said, was not the thought of that punishment, but the realization that he had been such a monster of ingratitude to the God of holiness, who had loved him and given his Son to die for him. Those two elements, then, fear of the judgments of God and fear of that self-judgment which is even more severe, if that be possible, act as restraining influences upon man's conduct. That was what Joseph meant when in his hour of temptation he cried out, "How then can I do this great wickedness, and sin against God?" (Gen. 39:9).

INNOCENCE—*see* CHILDHOOD

INTOLERANCE—*see also* TOLERANCE

There is an old legend of Abraham which teaches its lesson of toleration. Sitting one day at the door of his tent, he was visited by a stranger. Abraham asked him within and they sat down to break bread together. Unlike Abraham, the stranger did not pause to ask a blessing. Abraham inquired the reason why, and he told him that he worshiped the sun. Angry with him, Abraham drove him out of the tent.

Afterward the Lord called and asked where the stranger was. Abraham replied, "I thrust him out because he did not worship thee."

Then said the Lord: "I have suffered him and his ancestors for hundreds of years, and couldst not thou endure him for one hour?"

When we grow angry with those who differ from us, impatient of differing sects of Protestants or loud-mouthed bigoted unbelievers, or indignant with Germans and Japanese and wish them eliminated from the families of the earth, let us remember that God has suffered them, yea, that he has suffered generation after generation of sinners upon the face of the earth. We can afford to be as tolerant as God.

When James and John wished to bring down fire and lightning upon a Samaritan village which had been inhospitable to Jesus, Christ rebuked the sons of thunder, and said, "Ye know not what manner of spirit ye are of." (Luke 9:55.) There are few hymns which we like to sing more than "Rock of Ages," by Toplady, and "Jesus, Lover of My Soul," by Charles Wesley. John Wesley had a most bitter dispute with Toplady, the author

of "Rock of Ages." Wesley grossly caricatured Toplady's Calvinism as amounting to this:

"One in twenty of mankind are elected; nineteen in twenty are reprobated. The elect shall be saved, do what they will: the reprobate shall be damned, do what they can. Reader, believe this, or be damned. Witness my hand, A— T—"

To this stinging satire Toplady responded with a pamphlet calling Wesley a perverter of the truth and saying that under different circumstances a similar forgery would have landed him in Virginia or Maryland.

Of the same nature was a dispute between Newman Smith and Robert Hall. Smith was the author of a widely read and useful pamphlet, "Come to Jesus." In his controversy with Hall, Smith wrote a bitter pamphlet, and unable to think of an appropriate title, he submitted the article to a friend on whose judgment he relied and asked him to suggest a title. His friend read the fierce pamphlet, and then said to Smith, "I would name it 'Go to Hell,' by the author of 'Come to Jesus.' "

J

JEALOUSY—*see also* ENVY

Hawthorne was a man well qualified to take hold of that great study in psychology, the character of King Saul. We regret that he never did so. But in his tale "The Bosom Serpent" he illustrates the power of jealousy to destroy a soul. The man, who had been separated from his wife because of jealous suspicions, would sometimes hold his hand to his bosom and exclaim, "It gnaws! It

gnaws!" For this reason he was known to the people in the town as the man with the snake in his breast. Sometimes he would create great consternation and alarm when he stopped other men on the street and asked them how their serpent was. At length, after all kinds of remedies had been tried, his wife appeared and pleaded with him to forget himself and show his love for her. At that the man fell on the ground, and there was the sound like the passing of a serpent through the grass, and a tinkle was heard as if it had dropped into the fountain. Thus the man was cured of the bosom serpent of jealousy.

What about the serpent in thy breast? Oh, beware of the bosom serpent of jealousy!

I sat not long ago in the office of a doctor and talked with him of a victim of cancer now lying near death, the dread enemy conquering portion after portion of the body. "If two years ago that person had submitted to an operation, she would now be walking about and doing her work." But, instead of that, soothing measures were taken; and the virus spread through the system. Jealousy is like cancer: it must be dealt with in its incipient stages; when fully developed there is no surgery or medicine which can remove it.

Is there, in all the world, a single person whom you fear might divide with you the kingdom of your affection and love? Then beware of jealousy. You are not too refined, too educated, too sensible, too Christian to avoid destruction. The flame is there in your heart, and unexpected breezes of a tempting occasion may cause it to break forth in devastation that now would appall you.

The counselors of Florence asked Leonardo da Vinci, then Italy's most celebrated artist, to submit sketches for the decorations for the grand hall at Florence. One of the counselors had heard of a young and little-known artist who had done good work, Michelangelo, and asked him to submit sketches also. The sketches of Leonardo were superb, in keeping with his genius, but when the counselors saw the sketches of Michelangelo there was a spontaneous expression of wonder and enthusiasm. News of

this reached Leonardo. He also heard that one of the counselors had said, "Leonardo is getting old." He was never able to get over the eclipse of his fame by Michelangelo, and the remaining years of his life were clouded with gloom and sorrow.

The quarrels and bitternesses among men of ability and education—statesmen, artists, musicians, scholars, and even clergyman—are too notorious to call for more than passing comment. Jealousy is the spur with which the devil will ride the noblest tempers. There are men of the finest parts, of splendid disposition and character in other areas of their life, who cannot bear to hear another man praised, especially if the man's activities lie in the same field of endeavor.

One of the great artists stood one day before the work of a greater contemporary, one whose talents were far superior to his own. But, instead of being depressed, or filled with envy or bitterness, he exclaimed, as he surveyed the beautiful work which expressed so fully ideas which he himself had not been able to realize, "I, too, am a painter!"

But there are few like him.

JOB, BOOK OF

Everybody ought to read at least one great book before he dies and enters into the presence of the Truth himself. There are many great books, but the consensus of human opinion seems to be that the book of Job is the greatest of all. When you take up Job, you have no need for Shakespeare, Milton, Plato, Homer. In Carlyle's beautiful tribute in *Heroes and Hero Worship,* "Here in this book is sublime sorrow, sublime reconciliation, oldest choral melody, as of the heart of mankind, so soft and great as the summer midnight, as the world with its seas and stars."

JOHN THE BAPTIST

Once on a bright June day I stood
upon a summit of the Blue Ridge Mountains. To the north and to the south
stretched the mountains, their mighty
shoulders draped with a haze of infinite
blue. In front of me lay the Cumberland
Valley, well watered, like the garden of
the Lord. I could see the fields and orchards with their alternate hues like
checkered squares, the white ribbons
which marked the fine highways along
which half a century ago might have
been seen the eager soldiery of Lee as his
army marched into Pennsylvania, the
enormous red barns, the white towers of
the hamlet churches, the gray stone farm-
houses, and man going forth to his labor
until the evening. I had often passed
through that valley, but it was only when
I stood upon the summit of the mountain
that I was able to see it in all its length
and breadth.

There are times when it is good for us
to get above the smoke and dust and
confusion of our everyday existence and
look at life from some great eminence,
where the winds blow fresh and clear
and the view is unobstructed. And what
better place to stand than upon the shoulders of one of God's great men?

JOHN AND JESUS

John, we know thou wilt not mind if
we ask thee to move over and make room
for us, too. Let me share that breast,
John, with thee. Let me, too, John, have
a claim to that proud title, "Now there
was leaning on Jesus' bosom one of his
disciples, whom Jesus loved" (John
13:22).

JORDAN RIVER

Hail, sacred river! Thou art not
mighty among the rivers of the earth:
the Nile is longer; the Euphrates wider;
and the Tiber and the Thames flow past

statelier buildings. Yet art thou first
among the rivers of the world. Thou art
not wide; and yet to cross from one
bank to the other is to pass from Abraham to Christ. Thou art not long, yet,
standing on thy banks and watching the
flow of thy dark waters, I seem to follow the course of the stream of redemption until it loses itself in the "river of
water of life."

I saw the river Jordan once on a summer day when it was a stream hardly
wider than this room, flowing peacefully
between its banks, the branches of the
plane trees reflected in its clear and placid
face. As I looked upon it there came back
to my mind all the great memories of the
Jordan. That day when the priests, bearing the Ark of the Covenant, stepped
down into the water, and immediately
the waters of the river stood up in a
wall to the north and flowed away to
the south, and the people passed over
dry shod. And that day when the soldiers
of Jephthah held up the fleeing Ephraimites at the fords of the Jordan and asked
them to say, "Shibboleth," and if they
could not pronounce it, put them to the
sword. And that day when there went
a ferry over the river, carrying David
back to his kingdom after the rebellion
of Absalom had been repressed, leaving
his father's heart buried there with the
desecrated body of Absalom under the
pile of stones in the Wood of Ephraim.
And that other day when David's greater
Son came down into the Jordan and was
baptized of John, and then of the Holy
Spirit. All these memories came back to
me then.

But I had been looking at the river.
Then I looked up, and lo! at an incredible height, on the very tops of the trees,
I saw the sticks and the stones, the rubbish, the flotsam and the jetsam, which
showed where the Jordan rolled when it

overflowed its banks. There it was. The swelling of the Jordan!

And in like manner life's placid stream can suddenly become flooded and tempestuous. And that was what Christ said in the climax of the greatest sermon ever preached, how one house looked just like the other house and in fair weather was just as good to live in, but when "the rain descended, and the floods came, and the winds blew, and beat upon that house; . . . it fell: and great was the fall of it" (Matt. 7:28). What we must have is a faith that will serve us well when the floods come and the rains fall and the winds of adversity blow and beat upon the house of our soul.

JOY

In one of the Reformed churches in France, in the chancel back of the pulpit there are three panels. The first is for the law, and the inscription on it is, "Thou shalt love the Lord thy God" (Matt. 22:37). The second is for the gospel, and the inscription upon it is the great verse from John (3:16): "God so loved the world, that he gave his only begotten Son, that whosoever believeth in him should not perish, but have everlasting life." The third panel is for the psalms, and the verse written upon it is that from Psalm 118 (14): "The Lord is my strength and song, and is become my salvation."

—Of battle—The Jews have a tradition that when Lucifer was cast out of heaven he was asked in hell what he missed most out of his former life, and replied, "I miss most the sound of the trumpets in the morning." Does anyone here tonight miss the note of the trumpet? Is the old spirit ebbing and the strong purpose declining? Then, dauntless, put the trumpet to the lips and answer all your doubts and all your wavering and all your fears with a magnificent "Thou!"

JUDAS

"And as to Judas Iscariot, my reason is different. I would fain see the face of him who, having dipped his hand in the same dish with the Son of Man, could afterwards betray Him. I have no conception of such a thing; nor have I ever seen any picture (not even Leonardo's very fine one) that gave me the least idea of it."

So, according to William Hazlitt in his essay "Persons One Would Wish to Have Seen," spake Charles Lamb. And so say we all. Could we see his face, we might get some idea of the man and some understanding of his crime. Judas is the man of mystery among the Twelve.

Centuries ago in Italy, an artist about to paint a picture of the Madonna and the Child after long search found a beautiful young peasant woman with a lovely child at her breast. He selected them for his model, and the picture was painted and hung in one of the galleries. Long afterward he was at work on a New Testament scene which brought in Judas. He searched through the criminal quarters of the city and among the baser elements of the population, and at length in one of the jails he found a desperate, wicked man sentenced to death for his crimes against mankind. He chose this evil, sinister face as his model for Judas Iscariot. Day after day he went down to the prison and sketched the face of this criminal. Working on the painting in his studio one day, he saw something about the face that made him wonder. Day after day he puzzled over the matter, and at last the secret flashed upon him—it was the same face that he had painted long ago as the infant Jesus!

Judas represents one of the strange mysteries of life, the capacity for good and the capacity for evil which resides within every human breast. It is because we have those two possible men in us that we must ever do what Christ warned us to do, "Watch ye and pray, lest ye enter into temptation" (Mark 14:38)—and betray the nobler self within us.

I imagine a vision of the New Jerusalem in all its splendor. I ask the angelic guide about the light, the absence of the temple, the open gates, the streets of gold, the twelve gates with the names of the twelve tribes, the twelve walls or foundations with the precious stones— jasper, sapphire, chalcedony, emerald, sardonyx, sardius, beryl, topaz, chrysoprase, jacinth, amethyst. The angel reads the names on the foundations—the names of the apostles of the Lamb— Peter, Andrew, James, John, Philip, Bartholomew, Thomas, Matthew, James, Simon the Canaanite, Judas, not Iscariot. When I ask the angel why one stone has no name on it, he tells me that stone was for Judas. Judas raises deep questions. Always the sense of tragedy, of something lost, of what might have been.

JUDE, BOOK OF

There is a melody that I can hear vibrating even in the midst of storm and whirlwind. You have seen summer days which broke with heavy skies and intermittent winds. All day the clouds drifted to and fro, now and then collecting their forces and pouring a deluge upon the earth; now and then there was the rumble of thunder; and here and there in the heavens the lightning came out of the east and shone fiercely even to the south. It was a day of storm and of gloom. But just before the night fell the sun came out in his strength, the rainbow let down from heaven his iridescent ladder, the grass and the leaves of the trees and all the pastures were dressed in glorious sheen and sparkled with a million diamonds.

The conclusion of the stormy book of Jude is as such a sunset: the clouds pass, the sun pours out his radiance, the rainbow of promise spans the heaven; and as we listen we hear the music of a great ascription, "Now unto him that is able to keep you from falling, and to present you faultless before the presence of his glory with exceeding joy, to the only wise God our Saviour, be glory and majesty, dominion and power, both now and ever. Amen" (Jude 24-25).

JUDGMENT—*see also* BLOOD OF CHRIST, HELL, RETRIBUTION

—Day of—Writing in the *Spectator,* Number 26, on Westminster Abbey, Addison said: "When I see kings lying by those who deposed them, when I consider holy men that divided the world with their contests and disputes placed side by side, I reflect with sorrow and astonishment on the little competitions, factions, and debates of mankind. When I read the several dates on the tombs, of some that died yesterday and some six hundred years ago, I consider that great day when we shall all of us be contemporaries and make our appearance together.

—Divine—Daniel Webster, when secretary of state under President Fillmore, was dining once with twenty gentlemen at the Astor House in New York. Unusually reticent and aloof from the course of conversation, he sank into a reverie. In order to draw him out, one of the men asked him this rather unusual question for a dinner table, or anywhere else: "Mr. Webster, will you tell me what was the most important thought that ever occupied your mind?"

Webster passed his hand over his forehead and said in a low tone to one next to him, "Is there anyone here who does not know me?"

"No," said the man, "all are your friends."

Then Webster said aloud so that all could hear, "The most important thought that ever occupied my mind was that of my individual responsibility to God." He discoursed upon this theme for twenty minutes, and then rose from the table and retired to his room.

———•••———

Have you ever been at Pompeii? Then you have some idea of what Sodom must have looked like when God rained his judgment upon it. The fiery lava transfixed and sealed the people in whatever act or attitude it found them—at the theater, the baths, the kitchen, the market place, or in the haunts of sin. Hearts that had burned that day with unholy flame were now forever still, and pulses that had throbbed eagerly with sinful expectation had now forever ceased to beat.

———•••———

The teachings of Christ are not unlike a river that flows for a long time smoothly and noiselessly between its banks, and then suddenly takes the tremendous plunge of the cataract. In the utterance of Jesus about the coming of his Kingdom we have the cataract note of his preaching. The same lips which pronounced the Beatitudes and spake the quiet parables of growth and development, tell of the coming of his Kingdom and the great and terrible day of the Lord.

———•••———

—False—In a log cabin in the woods, after Bull Run, General Bee lay dying.

His only words were "Find Imboden! Find Imboden!" Imboden had blamed his superior officer, Bee, and cursed him bitterly for leaving him and his battery unsupported. The dying Bee had learned of this and wished to tell Imboden with his own lips that he had given orders for his relief. All through the night the men were scouting the fields and the woods, riding up and down the country roads, searching for Imboden. At length they found him and brought him to the cabin where Bee was dying. Full of regret now, and remorse, too, that he had so mistaken the action of his superior officer, Imboden took Bee by the hand and called him by name. No curses now; he spoke softly, fondly, filially. But there was no answer! Too late now, dying Bee, to make your explanation! Too late now, fierce-looking Imboden, hereafter much to be heard of in this war between the brothers, to take back your reckless and mistaken curses.

———•••———

In *The Stickit Minister* Samuel Crockett gives a pathetic instance of the cruelty of false judgment. The people thought that the older brother was a blockhead, and that that was the reason he had left the university and given up the ministry. Hence they dubbed him the "stickit minister." But if they had known the facts, how different would have been their estimate of him, for then they would have learned how he had left the university, given up the scholar's dreams and renounced the high and holy calling because, discovering that he was in poor health and that the death of the father had not left sufficient funds for the education of both sons, he, although the elder, had magnanimously made way for the younger. They would have known that the hard, uncongenial toil in the fields was not the labor of one who had failed but the splendid heroism of a magnanimous soul.

—The last—Justice Gray of the Supreme Court once said to a man who had appeared before him in one of the lower courts and had escaped conviction by some technicality: "I know that you are guilty and you know it, and I wish you to remember that one day you will stand before a better and wiser Judge, and that there you will be dealt with according to justice and not according to law."

—Rash—Among the innumerable legends that come down to us about Professor Blaikie is the story of a student who rose to recite in his classroom and held his book in his right hand. Blaikie told him to take the book with the other hand, but still the student read on with the book in his right hand. Again the angry professor thundered at him to take the book in the left hand. "I cannot, sir," answered the student, as he brought an empty sleeve from behind his back. The students hissed, but the next moment they cheered when the famous Grecian made his earnest apology.

Lips that move and do not speak, sleeves that have no arm within them, this is life; yet we pronounce our rash judgments, the falsity of which would fill us with humiliation and sorrow could we but know the facts.

At beautiful Grassmere Lake in the Lake Country of Cumberland County, England, the haunts of the English poets, there is a jutting promontory called Point Rash Judgment. One day Wordsworth, his sister, and Coleridge were taking a walk along the shore of the lake. In a boat some distance from the shore they saw a man fishing. It was the harvest season, when all able-bodied men were toiling in the fields. They said one

to another, "How improvident for this man to be spending his time here fishing when he ought to be at work in the fields." But when they came nearer to him they saw that he was an aged and decrepit man, unable to work in the fields, and that he was doing the best he could. Struck with the falsity and unkindness of their rash judgment, they named the promontory "Point Rash Judgment."

In his diary a lieutenant colonel of a Northern regiment relates this incident which took place near Berryville, Virginia, during the Civil War. In the gathering darkness, while the battle was still raging, the colonel saw three men going toward the rear and leaving the battle, two of them supporting the companion that limped between them. This was a favorite dodge of cowards to pretend that they were carrying a wounded comrade to the rear, and so escape the perils of the battlefield. Convinced that this was another case of pretended injury and wounds, the angry colonel stopped the three men and ordered them to go back to the firing line. The man who was being helped protested that he was wounded, and badly wounded. But the angry colonel said to him, "You are not wounded; are trying to sneak out of the fight in the dark. Go back to your regiment."

The wounded soldier then said, "Give me your hand, Colonel." Not knowing just what he meant, the colonel put out his hand, whereupon the man took it and thrust it into a hole in his shoulder while the warm blood spurted up the arm of the skeptical colonel. Shocked and overcome, the colonel exclaimed, "You poor fellow! You poor fellow! Forgive me; go back to the doctor, quick." The man took a step forward and fell dead. He had given his life for his country; but in the moment of supreme sacrifice he had been mistaken for a coward and a deserter.

The first reason why we should be slow and careful in the judgments we pass upon our fellow man is our too frequent ignorance of the facts. A fragment of anything is apt to be deceptive, and all that we mortals show to one another is but a fragment of our true selves. How little we know! "Judge not according to the appearances" (John 7:24), said Jesus; but that is often all the data that we have to go on.

Eli looked on the outward appearance, and judging by outward appearance a drunken woman had come into the tabernacle and deserved to be put out and rebuked. What he did not know was the bitterness of her soul, the taunts which the polygamous household had heaped upon her, her unseen strivings in prayer, the holy, mysterious woman's hope that beat within her breast. His motive in judging, his zeal for the purity of the house of God, no fault could be found with that; but his knowledge was imperfect.

K

KINDNESS—*see also* CONTROVERSY AND KINDNESS, SYMPATHY

Charlotte Brontë's life was short, her married life just a brief break in the clouds that had settled about her; but when they laid her beneath the snow in the churchyard, there stood by the grave a lonely woman who had been seduced and cast out, but loved and cherished by the gentle author, and another, a blind girl who begged neighbors to lead her over the wet, snowy roads that she might shed her tears over the grave of the woman who had been eyes to the blind. These two were but the representatives of a large class who had known the kindness of Charlotte Brontë.

God wanted a deliverer to lead the Negroes out of bondage, and for this work he called the kind and honest country lawyer from the black soil of Illinois. The youth who on a journey had seen a nest blown from the beach by the winds, and its helpless inmates scattered over the grass, and then growing anxious about the birds, walked back for several miles and put the nest high, where the serpents might not get at it, and the birds back into the nest, was father to the man who was to take a helpless, abused, despised race, and lift it to its feet, amid the execration of half a continent, and lead it out of the house of bondage.

—To a child—Sometimes men are awakened out of mere creatural existense through the breath of kindness. Henry M. Stanley's early life is a story that moves the hardest heart. Never knowing his father, disowned by his mother, in the Asaph workhouse surrounded by misery and cruelty, he used to hear the hear the lesson read from John 4:4, 7: "Little children, . . . love one another," and wondered what it meant. His childish heart was ready and yearning for love, but none gave love to him; and he began to think the sweetest parts of the Bible were wholly inapplicable to actual life. He had come, even at early years, to disbelieve in love.

Then one day the fugitive boy who had run away from the ship at New Orleans stood in front of a kind, grave gentleman who had taken him into his store and then into his home. The man took a basin of water, made the sign of the cross on his brow, gave him his own name, Henry M. Stanley, and then took him in his arms and kissed him. His senses whirled about him, and tears, which no amount of cruelty could ever have forced from him, poured in a torrent under the influence of that simple embrace. "The golden period of my life began from that supreme moment."

* * *

—**Of God**—Henry Drummond used to say, looking back over a more than ordinarily distinguished life, that the things which stood out in this retrospect as of abiding worth and value were the four or five times he had reflected to others the kindness of God.

* * *

—**Of Jesus**—That sycamore tree into which Zacchaeus climbed that spring day at Jericho so that he might see Jesus has become one of the greatest pulpits in the history of the Church. It preaches, first of all, a sermon on the power of kindness. That was how Christ won Zacchaeus. Suppose he had paused under that tree and, looking up at Zacchaeus, had called out to him, "You child of the devil! You who grind the face of the poor and turn orphans and widows out on the streets, how shall you escape the damnation of hell?" Now Jesus knew how to condemn and how to be severe, and in language far beyond that which I have just imagined him speaking, he denounced and excoriated and anathe-

matized the evildoer. But here was a man who was still capable of being won for God. If Jesus had denounced him in those words I have just used, you and I would never have heard of Zacchaeus. Instead of that, he spoke kindly to him and called to him to come down, and went to his house as a guest.

You know that old fable of the wind and the sun. They once had a debate as to which first could make a man take off his cloak. First the wind tried it. It stormed and raged and blew. But the man only wrapped his mantle the closer about him as he cowered before the blast. Then when the wind had given it up the sun shone kindly and warmly upon the man, until, heated by its rays, he divested himself of his garment. We can all take the method of the sun. We can all take the method of the Savior that day when he dealt so kindly with the outcast publican and brought out the best that was in him, and made the name Zacchaeus—which means "pure," but then was so soiled and darkened and obscured by sin—stand forth again in its original meaning.

* * *

—**To the living**—I wonder what Joseph and Nicodemus felt as they were carrying that loved body through the garden down into the grave. Were there pangs of regret and remorse? Yes, I am sure there must have been. These two men must have regretted those lost years, when, knowing the truth and believing in Christ, they had not openly confessed him. Beautiful is their devotion now. But a clean linen cloth, and sweet-smelling spices, and a costly sepulcher are no substitutes for devotion and service to the living. That is true of our friends. A costly bier and sweet-smelling flowers for the dead cannot atone for neglect of the living soul. Bring your spices to the living, not to the dead.

KINGDOM OF GOD—*see also* CHURCH

"Thine is the kingdom." (Matt. 6:13.)

The proud king Robert of Sicily, brother of one of the popes, appareled in magnificent attire, was listening on St. John's Eve to the priests as they chanted the Magnificat. He caught at one particular phrase which the priests were chanting in Latin, and asked the clerk what it meant. When the clerk told him the words were these: "He hath put down the mighty from their seats, and exalted them of low degree" (Luke 1:52), King Robert muttered scornfully, " 'Tis well that such seditious words are sung only by priests and in the Latin tongue; for let it be known that there is no power can push me from my throne." With that he leaned back and fell asleep.

When he awoke, it was already night and he was alone in the empty church. When he succeeded in having the door of the cathedral opened, he rushed through the night to the banqueting room of his palace, but there on the dias sat another king, wearing his robes, his crown, his signet ring. It was an angel, although a hidden angel whom none recognized. When Robert claimed his throne, saying that he was the rightful king, the king on the throne, or the angel, told him that he was but the king's jester and commanded him to wear the jester's bells and cape, and to lead an ape through the streets.

So the years passed with the ex-king performing the wretched office of a jester. But one day during Holy Week the angel-king summoned the jester-king before him, and said, "Art thou the king?" Whereupon the penitent Robert confessed his sins and acknowledged that the angel was the king. With that the angel vanished. When the court attendants appeared, they found Robert appareled again in splendor as in days of old, but kneeling on the floor near his throne, absorbed in private prayer.

So the legend, enshrined in noble verse by Longfellow, taught the great truth that God is the only King, that he putteth down the mighty from their seats, and exalteth them of low degree.

———◆◆◆———

I stood once on little Patmos, that brown gem in the Aegean Sea. But all that I saw was the brown mountain, the turquoise sea; and all that I heard was the gentle washing of the waves and the soft chiming of the bells of St. John's Monastery. I did not see what John saw there, the star Wormwood falling from heaven, the four horsemen going forth, the woman clothed in the sun, Satan bound for a thousand years, and then finally cast into the abyss. I did not see the white horse and his rider going forth to conquer, as John saw it; nor did I hear the blast of the trumpets of revelation and judgment. I did not see the new heaven and the new earth, nor the New Jerusalem coming down from God out of heaven, like a bride adorned for her husband. Yet Christ said, "Blessed are they that have not seen and yet have believed" (John 20:29)—they that have such faith that they never doubt the victory of righteousness and truth, never doubt the glorious consummation, compared with which the brightest day that has dawned upon the world is midnight and the fairest splendors which have invested it but the shadow of darkness.

———◆◆◆———

—Victory of the—There is no city like Damascus, which is the oldest of cities built by man. There, as everywhere in the Near East associated with great events in the birth of Christianity, one is oppressed and depressed by the dominance of a fierce anti-Christian religion, for Damascus today is one of the sacred places of the Moslem world. What was once the great church of St. John the Baptist has now for centuries been a Mohammedan mosque. Standing in the shadow of the dome of the tomb of Saladin, the great Moslem conqueror, one can hear the muezzins call the faithful to prayer from the minarets of the mosque that once resounded with hymns of praise to Christ. Reflecting upon that, and hearing that strange music, one's faith needs to be strong. On one side of mosque, where evidently there was an entrance to the ancient church, there are still to be seen, unobliterated by the Mohammedans, some words carved into the stone. Climbing up to read them, one finds these words—and takes new hope and courage for the future of Christ's kingdom—"Thy Kingdom, O Christ, is an everlasting Kingdom!"

—Worth of the—In a famous tale, "The Necklace," Maupassant tells of a beautiful young French woman who, because she had no dowry, married an ordinary government clerk. Ofttimes she lamented the fact that with her charms and her personality she was barred from the great social world. But one day her husband brought home with great joy an invitation asking him and his wife to be guests at a reception of one of the high departments of the French government. But to his surprise his wife showed no elation. "How can I go?" she said. "I have no dress to wear." He asked her how much a proper dress would cost. She answered, "About 500 francs." He winced a little at that, but having laid aside 400 francs with which to purchase a rifle so that he could shoot on holidays, he said he would get her a dress. The day before the reception the dress came, and she tried it on. It was most becoming—a fine framework to display her beauty. But she said, "I cannot wear the dress without any ornament." He suggested flowers, but that idea was dismissed. Then he said, "Why don't you ask Jeanne to lend you some of her jewels?" Jeanne was an aristocratic school friend of Mathilde. She said "Yes, that is the thing, the very thing." Off she went to the home of her friend, who gladly opened to her all her treasures. She tried one piece of jewelry after another, and finally came upon a beautiful necklace. Holding it up against her breast, she looked into the mirror with great delight. When her friend said she might take it she flung herself on her neck with kisses of joy, and then hurried off to her home.

On the great night of the reception she appeared in her beautiful gown, with the handsome necklace flashing on her neck and bosom. Wherever she moved the eyes of men and women followed her with admiration. Everyone craved the privilege of a dance with her. After the reception they walked part of the way home, and then found a dilapidated cab which carried them to their apartment. The husband was half undressed and his wife was standing in front of the mirror starting to undress when she gave a cry of horror. The husband asked what the trouble was. She answered, "The necklace! The necklace is gone!" They searched through the apartment and down the stairway. The husband went off and walked over the route which they had taken on their way home. But at seven in the morning he returned, but with no necklace.

At the dictation of her husband Mathilde sat down and wrote a note to her friend saying that she had broken the clasp on the necklace and sent it to the jewelers to be repaired. Then they set out to find another like it. At length in a shop on the *Palais Royale* they found one which closely resembled the lost necklace. They could have it for 36,000 francs. The husband received a bequest of 18,000 francs; then by borrowing 500 francs here and 100 there, and 50 somewhere else, he managed to get together the 36,000 francs. The necklace was put in the original box and returned to the friend who had lent it. Then began the terrible task of making good the debt, for they had signed away their life for years to come. They dismissed their servants and took a cheap garret apartment under the roof in a poor quarter of the city. The husband slaved at night when his work in the office by day was over, copying manuscripts and doing odd jobs. Mathilde did her own marketing, scrubbed her own floors, grew stout and red in the face, talked loudly like the women about her. But sometimes when her husband was away she would sit by the window and think of that wonderful night of her triumph when she wore the beautiful necklace.

Ten years passed, and the debt was paid. One day Mathilde was walking along the bank of the Seine when she saw a beautiful young woman coming along with a child in a carriage. Recognizing her as her friend of old days, she stopped and greeted her. The woman looked upon her with surprise, and said with some haughtiness, "I am afraid you have a mistake."

"No," the other replied, "I am your old friend Mathilde."

"O Mathilde," she exclaimed, "how you have changed."

Then Mathilde told her of her struggles. "You remember the necklace you lent me?"

"Yes, what of it?"

"It was lost."

"But how was it lost, you returned it to me?"

"No, it was another that I returned, one just like it, for which we paid 36,000 francs."

The woman looked at her in astonishment and in pity, and then said, "Do you mean to say you paid 36,000 francs for that necklace you brought back? The one that I lent you was paste, and worth, at the most, 500 francs!"

The prophet asked, "Wherefore do ye spend money for that which is not bread? and your labors for that which satisfieth not?" (Isa. 55:2). For the paste diamonds and pearls of this world men seek far and wide, and spend all they have; but they pass by in contempt the pearl of great price, which is the Kingdom of God. "Seek ye first the kingdom of God." (Matt. 6:33.)

KNOWLEDGE

Sometimes the more one has eaten of the tree of knowledge, the more quickly wither his hopes. The most informed men have seldom been the happiest. John Morley, looking down on the great library of Lord Acton, described it as the most pathetic sight of wasted labor that ever met the human eye, the most impressive of all testimony to the vanity of life.

L

LAMB OF GOD—*see also* ATONEMENT

In Germany many years ago a man was working high up on the steeple of a church. Suddenly he lost his footing and fell headlong to the ground beneath. Grazing on the grass in the churchyard was a lamb. The body of the man fell on the lamb, and thus his fall was broken. The lamb perished, but the man was saved. As a token of his gratitude he carved in one of the stones over the doorway of the church the figure of a lamb.

Every true church of Christ has that lamb, as it were, carved in the stones of its wall. "Behold the Lamb of God, which taketh away the sin of the world." (John 1:29.)

LEBANON—*see* CEDARS OF LEBANON

LIBERTY

Samuel Johnson said, "I would not give half a guinea to live under one form of government rather than another. It is of no moment to the happiness of the individual." In commenting on that utterance John Morley wrote: "The strange undying passion for the word 'republic,' and all the blood and tears that have been shed in adoration of that symbolic name, give the verdict of the world against him."

However it may be with the forms of government, and I am inclined to think that Morley has the best side of the argument, there can be no doubt about the passion of men for independence. However long they have been in subjugation, however inured to its restrictions and limitations, races and nations have a strange undying passion for independent existence, both as individuals and as groups. William Cowper wrote:

'Tis liberty alone that gives the
  flower
Of fleeting life its luster and perfume,
And we are weeds without it. All
  constraint,
Except what wisdom lays on evil
  men,
Is evil.

LIFE—*see also* BLOOD, OUTLOOK ON LIFE

Crossing the Allegheny River recently, I paused in the middle of the bridge and leaned over the parapet, watching the interesting scene which was displayed before me: the sun setting beyond the steep hills, the smoke rising from engines and factory, the steamboats pushing their barges up or down the river, the houseboats clustering along the banks of the river, and the river itself flowing rapidly away like the river of a man's life. As I stood gazing down the river, with the stream of humanity passing behind me, I suddenly heard a voice say: "If I had my life to live over again—" I turned quickly to get the rest of the sentence and to see who the speaker was. He was a man well advanced in years, who had reached that period of life when men are governed more by memory than by hope. But, in spite of my keenest attention, the conclusion to his sentence was lost in the roar of traffic. I thought of hurrying after him and asking what the end of the sentence was. But, failing to do that, I asked myself: What was there in the man's life that he would have changed? What things did he miss which he would secure if he had his life to live over again? What things has he done that he would not have done? What things has he left undone that he would have done?

Men say, "I have my own life to live." So far as responsibility is concerned, that is true. But not so far as duty, relationship, and opportunity. Our life is not our own. All that makes it great is borrowed, like the ax of the son of the prophet. Life is short—but it is long enough for all of us to learn its worth before Death lifts his hammer to strike the passing of the hour of time.

In one of his tales James Barrie writes: "The life of every man is a diary in which he means to write one story and writes another, and his humblest hour is when he compares the volume as it is with what he vowed to make it." There is always a difference between the reach and the grasp.

—Battle of—In the countries where conscription now prevails, men of certain ages, or certain occupations or physical conditions, are exempted from the service. And when men who have been drafted and have fought in the ranks have been wounded seriously or have been weakened by disease and exposure they are relieved from further military duty. But in this great warfare of life none are exempted from service. All are conscripted and all must serve, nor do the wounds or length of service and gallantry of action permit one to retire. "And there is no discharge in that war." (Eccles. 8:8.) The child that did but yesterday suspire and the nonagenarian are both in the ranks. Some of us are but raw recruits. All we know about the battle is the manual of drill and the mechanism of the guns. Our banners are untorn and our uniforms are new and unstained with blood and dirt. But others are in the forefront of the hottest fight, giving and receiving a multitude of wounds and blows, with no thought and no sound but that of war and conflict. Still others are near the end of the fight; they bear the scars of many a conflict, and soon for them will sound the trumpet of release and recall. Yet all are born to the warfare.

In *Tom Brown's School Days* Thomas Hughes speaks of the influence of Arnold of Rugby over the boys at that school, and how he impressed on their minds the fact that they were entering life as a battlefield ordained from of old. "And so, wearily and little by little, but surely and steadily on the whole, was brought home to the young boy for the first time the meaning of his life, that it was no fools' or sluggards' paradise into which he had wandered by chance, but a battlefield, ordained from of old, where there are no spectators, but where the youngest must take his side, and the stakes are life and death. And he who roused this consciousness in them showed them at the same time by every word he spoke in the pulpit and by his whole daily life how that battle was to be fought, and stood there before them, their fellow soldier and the captain of their band."

The great masters of imagination, like Edmund Spenser or John Bunyan or Paul, have thought of life under two metaphors, a pilgrimage and a battle. Sometimes it seems more like a pilgrimage, and at other times more like a battle. In this warfare some of us are only raw recruits. All we know about the battle is the music of the bands, the cheering of the populace, and the waving of the banners in the sunlight. Our uniforms are new and unstained, and our step is eager and elastic. Others are in the midst of the strife, standing in the forefront of the hottest battle, their uniforms stained and torn, their faces blackened with powder, their dreams of anticipation changed into a desperate reality. Others, again, are nearing the end of the battle, their armor well hacked and dented with the blows of the foe, and their visage marred, and soon for them will sound the trumpet of recall. But for one and all, life is a battle. When a royal infant is born, his name is at once inscribed on the roll of one of the regiments of the army. In like manner man is born to a place on the battlefield. Is there not a warfare appointed unto man? The puzzle of life begins the moment we forget that it is a struggle and a battlefield, not an end in itself, but a battle where, by the conflict we are trained and tested and put on probation for the life which is to come.

—Changes of—Floating down the Potomac River one summer, we frequently passed through what they call there the "riffles," or rapids. For miles the river would flow peacefully and quietly between grassy banks, or gently caressing the roots of the sycamore and oaks and willows that in turn gave it a blessing as it left them, the river, the while, hardly making a sound as it made its way seaward.

Then, where the cliffs became precipitous—where aeons before the river had broken its way through the mountains—the hitherto placid stream suddenly changed into a turbulent and angry river, foaming and leaping over the rocks, and requiring skill, courage, and steadfastness on the part of the boatman. Then again the rapids were left behind and the river, forgetting its anger and distress, flowed quietly seaward till once again the noise of distant waterfalls, borne to us on the evening wind, warned us that the river was once more entering the rapids.

This is not a bad description of life: the peaceful stretches and the boiling rapids are always following each other in quick succession. You look ahead, as a man drifting down the river might look, but you cannot tell what is coming any more than he can.

—And death—One of the most thrilling tales of disaster by air and by sea was that related by the three aviators who took off some years ago in Portugal for the United States, and were rescued from an ocean grave after having clung to their plane in the sea for six days. In the account given by the pilot, he tells how, some distance west of the Azores, they detected a faltering of their motor. Eagerly they listened and watched the working of their engine, for they knew that it meant life or death for them. "It was a matter of life and death. A hackneyed, wearied phrase, that—but we knew its truth then only too well." A worn and familiar phrase suddenly became living and powerful because of the experience through which they were passing.

—Definitions—Life is a long campaign, and day by day we fight its battles. The Bible has many metaphors to describe life. Now in its brevity it is a mist that appears for a little, like the mist which hangs over a river at autumn and then, when the sun is risen, is gone. Now it is a swift ship rapidly disappearing on the horizon. Now it is a caravan winding its way across the desert. Now it is the weaver's shuttle threshing to and fro. But the most easily understood of all the metaphors of the Bible for life is when the Bible calls life a warfare and a battle.

Life is a book of three volumes. A great number never get past the first volume. A still larger number never go beyond the second volume. And to only a few is it permitted to live and write the third and final volume.

— — —

—Greatness of—Michelangelo came one day into the studio of Raphael and looked at one of Raphael's early drawings. Then he took a piece of chalk and wrote across the drawing *"Amplius,"* which means "greater," "larger." Raphael's plan was too cramped and narrow. God looks down on our plan of life today, and knowing what is in man, writes over that plan *"Amplius"*— Greater! Larger!

— — —

—Hidden sources of—The hidden man of the heart is the source of power and influence. We see a great building which rises toward heaven and which houses hundreds or thousands of people, but we do not see its foundations. Yet without those foundations the building is nothing. We see the great river that flows through our city, which once in fifty or a hundred years does damage to the city, but which day after day and year after year carries the commerce of the city and supplies its people with water, but we do not see the small contributory and source streams which form the river. If those streams,—the Youghiogheny, the Kiskiminetas, the Conemaugh, and streams like them—should dry up, if the fountains which feed them should go dry, the great river would cease to flow through the city. Likewise, on a spring day we can behold in the country a noble tree lifting its arms to heaven. The birds of the air make their home in its branches, and the beasts of the field take shelter in its shade, and its fruits will rejoice the heart of man. But the tree lives by its roots, and the roots are unseen.

It is not otherwise with human life. Prayer, meditation, study, aspiration, determine life. They all belong to the unseen world, yet they are decisive. A man is just as strong as his heart. "As a man is, so is his strength." (Judg. 8:21.) That is, a man is as strong as the hidden man of his heart.

— — —

—Meaning of—One of the earliest recollections of my youth is that of going on a Friday night to attend the meetings of one of the two literary societies of the college where my father was a professor. And there, permitted to come as a child because I was the child of one of the professors, I listened with wonder to the essays and orations and debates which at that time formed one of the most important features of college life.

The speeches I have long since forgotten, but not the legend, or motto, of the society painted in great letters of gold and black across the wall at the back of the stage, *Ars longa, vita brevis.* I was told that the translation was "Art is long, but time is fleeting." But, of course, it was not until long afterward, that I began to realize the deep and impressive meaning of that motto on the wall: that life, our term of existence, is always brief, ever fleeting, shortened by every exhalation and inhalation, but that the art of living—true, godly, Christian living— goes on forever; it is as long as eternity.

— — —

Solomon did not ask for a long life, but for a good life. Philip James Bailey expressed a similar thought in *Festus*:

We live in deeds, not years; in
* thoughts, not breaths;*
In feelings, not in figures on a dial.
We should count time by heart-
* throbs. He most lives*

Who thinks most, feels the noblest,
acts the best.

———◆◆◆———

The great Battle of Blenheim was fought at the village of that name on the Danube, August 13, 1704. The commander of the British and Austrian armies, which defeated the French and the Bavarians, was the Duke of Malborough, an ancestor of Mr. Winston Churchill. Many years after the battle, as related in Southey's famous poem, a little lad brought to his grandfather, Caspar, a round, smooth object which he had found near the brook by which he had been playing. The old man exclaimed to the lad that this was the skull of a soldier who had fallen in the Battle of Blenheim. The boy wanted to know about the battle, and the old man took him on his knee and told him the story of the battle. When he was through with his tale, the lad questioned the old man:

"But what good came of it at last?"
Quoth little Peterkin.
"Why, that I cannot tell," said he;
"But 'twas a famous victory."

Often in life there comes to us that thought which startles, alarms, and haunts us. What if our labor should be in vain? What if no good came out of the long struggle of life? That is a question that goes to the very roots of existence. For answer we have Paul's great statement, based upon the sublime truths which he has just been declaring, the Atonement, the resurrection of Christ, the life to come, and our own personal immortality: "Therefore, my beloved brethren, be ye steadfast, unmoveable, always abounding in the work of the Lord, forasmuch as ye know that your labor is not in vain in the Lord" (I Cor. 15:58).

—Monotony of—When Jesus told the disciples to launch out into the deep and let down the nets, Peter said, "Master, we have toiled all the night, and have taken nothing." (Luke 5:5.) Yet it was in those same waters that they made the great haul of fish.

We are sometimes inclined to think that if we could have a different line or net, get into a different place, have a new environment, all would be different with us. But remember what Jesus said to those disciples, in the same waters, with the same burdens, the same temptations, the same occupation, the same trials— there or nowhere must be our victory.

———◆◆◆———

—Reality and shams of—In the mountain country during the summer months you have awakened in the morning to find the horizon a wall or curtain of mist and fog, hiding the whole landscape. Then after an hour or two the curtain of vapor began slowly to lift and rise, disclosing the realities, the abiding things— trees, fields, the river flowing melodiously away, the everlasting hills. So it is in life that the thought and vision and reach of man are often centered on those things which are but vapor and mist, and which veil the great realities of our existence.

———◆◆◆———

—Transiency of—At Bangkok, in Siam, the Buddhists have a celebration on the river in which they set adrift miniature illuminated ships laden with thank offerings. As the flaming ships drift down with the current, the priests chant, "Short is the life of mortals and full of pain— a flame launched upon a deep sea, drifting to the inevitable dissolution; for whatever has origin also has an end."

So far as the transiency of life is concerned the flaming ship, drifting with the tide and soon extinguished in the darkness, is a true figure of our life. But it is not a true figure of the meaning and the length of life summed up, not in years, but in character, in faith and hope and love.

Edwin Booth once wrote to Adam Badeau, Grant's secretary and biographer, "Be brave and struggle, but do not set your heart on anything in this world. If good comes to you, take it and enjoy it; but be ready always to relinquish it without a groan."

That is sound advice. It is wise for us to recognize clearly the transiency of human life and that our relationships in time are but for a little. Our stay here is brief and our hold on life is fragile. Edward Young in *Night Thoughts* said,

*The spider's most attenuated thread
Is cord, is cable, to man's tender tie
On earthly bliss; it breaks at every
breeze.*

—As a trial—If I were to be banished to a lonely island and could take with me just a few books, one of them would be that book which Napoleon used to read amid the crash and thunder of his campaigns, and to which Humboldt used to turn when his mind wearied with reading the starry manuscript of the heavens, Saint-Pierre's *Paul and Virginia*. I would choose it not merely for the music of its diction and the way in which it touches the deep and tender chords of the here and the hereafter, but because it would help me to be reconciled to my lot and teach me to have faith in the wise decree of providence. All this is beautifully summed up in the words which Virginia is imagined to address to her distracted lover, Paul: "Life is only a trial. I have been found faithful to the laws of nature, of love, and of virtue. Heaven found my probation sufficient. Now at the source of all beauty, whence flows all that is de-

lightful upon earth, my soul sees, hears, tastes, touches what before she could only feel through imperfect organs. O my friend, raise your thought towards the infinite that you may support the pains of the moment."

Paley contrasts the lot of a West Indian slave of his day with that of the slave's lord and master: "A West Indian slave who, amid his wrongs, retains his benevolence, I, for my part, count as among the foremost of human candidates for the rewards of virtue. The kind master of such a slave, that is, he who, in the exercise of inordinate authority, postpones in any degree his own interest to his slave's comfort, is likewise a meritorious character."

What he was getting at was that, although there is great and sad inequality among men as to this world's possessions and places and stations, yet, after all, as to the greater purposes of life there is a grand equality, that, since virtue is infinitely various, infinitely various are those conditions of life which afford opportunity for the production of virtue in the lives of men. This being the case, the particular arena of our trial, the order and method and nature and agency of it, are of secondary interest. As my mother used to say to her sons, quoting Pope's "Essay on Man," "Act well your part, there all the honor lies."

—Weariness with—When John Knox lay dying in his house in Edinburgh, weary of his long, hard battle, he said, "I heartily salute and take my good night of all the faithful of both realms earnestly desiring the assistance of their prayers, that without any notable slander to the evangel of Jesus Christ, I may end my battle, for as the world is weary of me, so am I of it."

I do not mean that from this valedictory of Knox we are to conclude that his faith in the Kingdom of Jesus Christ had suffered eclipse. No, not that. But the old man was weary of the hard warfare, and longed for his discharge, realizing that the battle is the Lord's and that he has seven thousand other prophets and agencies through which he can work his sovereign will. Elijah must have realized that when he cast his prophetic garment about the shoulders of Elisha. God never quits the field.

—**Work for all**—God has something for everyone to do. This legend is inscribed on the Brashear Home, in Pittsburgh: "Somewhere under the stars there is a work waiting for you that no one else in the world can do but you."

LINCOLN—*see also* COMPASSION (LINCOLN'S)

Standing on the oak-covered hillside at Springfield on a bright May morning in 1865, Bishop Simpson delivered a noble eulogy. In this oration Simpson revealed the fact that Lincoln had frequently said to him, "I never shall live out the four years of my term. When the rebellion is crushed, my work is done." In the concluding paragraph, Simpson said: "Chieftain, farewell! The nation mourns thee. Mothers shall teach thy name to their lisping children. The youth of our land shall emulate thy virtues. Statesmen shall study thy record, and from it learn lessons of wisdom. Mute though thy lips be, yet they shall speak. Hushed is thy voice, but its echoes of liberty are ringing through the world, and the sons of bondage listen with joy. Thou didst not fall for thyself. The assassin had no hate for thee. Our hearts were aimed at; our national life was sought. We crown thee as our martyr, and Humanity enthrones thee as her triumphant son. Hero, martyr, friend, farewell."

—**His loneliness**—In his great oration delivered at the unveiling of the Lincoln Memorial at Hodgenville, Kentucky, President Wilson said of Abraham Lincoln:

"I have read many biographies of Lincoln; I have sought out with the greatest interest the many intimate stories that are told of him, the narratives of nearby friends, and sketches at close quarters, in which those who had the privilege of being associated with him have tried to depict for us the very man himself 'in his habit as he lived'; but I have nowhere found a real intimate of Lincoln's. That brooding spirit had no real familiars.

"I get the impression that it never spoke out in complete self-revelation, and that it could not reveal itself completely to anyone. It was a very lonely spirit that looked out from underneath those shaggy brows and comprehended men without fully communing with them, as if, in spite of all its genial efforts at comradeship, it dwelt apart, saw its visions of duty where no man looked on."

—**His unbelief**—Ward Lamon, Lincoln's bodyguard, said: "It is very probable that much of Mr. Lincoln's unhappiness, the melancholy that 'dripped from him as he walked,' was due to his want of religious faith. When the black fit was on him, he suffered as much mental misery as Bunyan or Cowper in the deepest anguish of their conflicts with the evil one. But the unfortunate conviction fastened upon him by his early associations, that there was no truth in the Bible, made all consolation impossible, and penitence useless. To a man of his temperament, predisposed as it was to depression of spirits, there could be no chance of happiness if doomed to live without hope and without God in the world. He might force himself to be merry with his chosen comrades; he might 'banish sadness' in mirthful conversation, or find relief in a jest; gratified ambition might elevate his feelings and give him ease for a time; but solid comfort and permanent peace could come to him only through 'a correspondence fixed with heaven.' The fatal misfortune of his life, looking at it only as it affected him in this world, was the influence at New Salem and Springfield which enlisted him on the side of unbelief. He paid the bitter penalty in a life of misery."

LITERATURE—*see* BOOKS

LONELINESS

"Now I am all alone." I sat with the physician in his library, speaking the usual words of sympathy and condolence. He gave me a brief history of his sister's illness, their past fellowship, and then concluded with these words, "Now I am all alone." On the desk was the framed photograph of a beautiful woman. I lifted it and, glancing at it, said to him, "Another sister?"

"No," he answered, as the shadow of another and an earlier, perhaps deeper, sorrow came over his face. Then again he said, "Now I am all alone."

His words followed me to the vestibule, down the steps, around the corner, down the avenue, and back to my own home. Sometimes as I pass down the crowded street and see some face shrouded with loneliness—and how many such there are in the great city with its teeming thousands!—or as I have spoken a word of encouragement and sympathy to one who has been left to be brave alone, those words of that physician spoken to me as he sat there, with his pale face lighted up by the lamp of his library, have come back to me, "Now I am all alone."

Man was made for man, and it is not meet for him to be alone. It has been well said that he who loves solitude—that is, permanent, unbroken solitude—must be either a beast or a god. Once in the mountains of Kentucky I stayed in a mountain home with a man and his wife who perhaps for half a century had not been out of that little valley. Once, indeed, they told me, they had started westward with other neighbors to settle in the bluegrass country; but they had not gone far when a longing came over them for their own people. As they put it in their mountain way, "We didn't like to be so far away from the graves of our kin."

———————

—Of the city—There is the loneliness of the midnight hour, and the loneliness of the desert and the uninhabited isle, and the heavy, depressing solitude of the mountains. But the worst loneliness of all is the loneliness of the crowd—the solitude of the city. You pass up and down the busy highways, and look into the windows of thousands of homes, and pass thousands of men and women hurrying hither and yon on their respective errands. They are men like yourself, of the same passions, hopes, fears, capacities for joy and sorrow. Multitudes, multitudes of faces! Yet your heart grows sick within you when you reflect that beyond the ordinary ties of humanity you are nothing to those thousands of persons, and they are nothing to you. If you have joy, you cannot share it with them; if you are bearing a heavy load of anxiety or care, they will not help you with it. You could lie down on the sidewalk and breathe your last, and not a heart among all those thousands of hearts would beat more rapidly, and not an eye would be suffused with tears. "No man cared for my soul" (Ps. 142:4) is the appalling realization that suddenly grips your mind.

———•◦•———

At the summit of Crampton Gap, where a battle was fought two days before Antietam, is the picturesque mountain home of one of the most celebrated of the war correspondents; and not far from his home is a noble archway erected as a memorial to the correspondents of the Civil War. Some years ago a friend saw this famous correspondent at the depot in New York, hurrying for a train. The friend halted him and asked him whither he was bound. His response was "I'm going down to my home in the mountain in Maryland. It's too lonely here in New York."

———•◦•———

—Of conscience—There is a noble loneliness of the soul, the loneliness that sometimes comes in the path of duty, the loneliness that comes as the price of conviction, the loneliness of dissent from what is sinful. I imagine that Vashti, the queen of Ahasuerus, was lonely after she had been deposed from her high office and separated from the Persian court because she refused to expose herself on the night of that drunken banquet, when Ahasuerus entertained a thousand of his lords. But it was a queenly and honorable and immortal loneliness, because it was the loneliness which was the price of honor and of self-respect. Far better to be lonely with a good conscience than to be in gay company with a bad conscience!

———•◦•———

—Of the great—Some years ago some friends and I climbed the highest mountain in southern California. When we reached the summit we found nothing but a heap of rocks and trampled sand. Not a tree, not a blade of grass, not a stump or shrub, not a living creature. There absolute silence reigned, a solemn,

awe-producing silence, which seemed to carry one clear back to the dawn of creation. On the mountain peak there was only solitude. The people and the noises of the world were far below us, where we could neither see them nor hear them.

So it is in life; the higher you climb the lonelier you become. Elevation of soul separates from the crowd. The very elevation of a man's character, no matter how social and humanitarian he himself may be, and how noble his efforts for mankind, that very elevation of soul may repel men as well as attract them. The conviction men have that here is an incorruptible soul, one who will not compromise with iniquity, serves to separate that man from them. The grandest men of history have been the loneliest. Men like Moses, on the mount alone with God; Elijah, standing alone for God in a wicked and corrupt generation; Jeremiah, appointed to stand as an iron pillar and a brazen wall against a whole nation; John the Baptist, letting the thought of God take hold of him in the desert; Paul, after his glorious life for mankind, deserted and forsaken in the prison at Rome.

———•◦•———

—Of sorrow and suffering—The strange and mysterious capacity of man to suffer in body and in spirit is an index to his greatness and immortality. The winepress of suffering, man must tread alone. Always I am struck and awed by the revelation of an unexpected and unguessed burden of trouble or sorrow which someone about me is carrying. When the starving woman, during the siege of Samaria, disclosed the fearful pact which she had made with another mother to devour their children, the horrified king of Israel rent his garments, and lo, there was sackcloth within, upon his flesh! Hitherto he had carefully concealed the tokens of grief and sorrow. When a sudden wind lifts the outer garments of peace and prosperity, we are sometimes surprised to see that underneath is the coarse sackcloth of trouble and suffering.

LORD'S PRAYER

The daughter of an atheist once said to a friend, "I was brought up without any religion. I do not believe in God." Then she added a little wistfully, "But the other day in an old German book I came across a German prayer, and if the God of that prayer exists I think I could believe in him."

"What was that prayer?" her friend asked. Then she repeated slowly, in German, the Lord's Prayer.

The Lord's Prayer is indeed one of the proofs of the existence of God. How could there be such a thought of God, so sublime and beautiful, of man's relationship to him, of the coming of God's Kingdom, unless God existed? The fact, too, that men for so many ages have prayed "Thy kingdom come" is a proof that one day his kingdom will come.

LORD'S SUPPER

When I was about twelve years of age, there came a Communion season; and most of the boys whom I knew united with the Church. Before we did so we were told to search our hearts and find out if we loved Him. We thought that we did; and, having answered many questions about what he had done for us, we were received at the communion table. I had often watched from our pew the congregation march slowly up the aisle to the table singing the Forty-fifth Psalm (13)—how the "King's daughter is all glorious within." At one end of the table stood a hunchbacked elder, dressed in broadcloth, with a grave, friendly face. He took our tokens as we passed to our seats at the table. Then one of the ministers delivered a short discourse, after which, amid profound silence, the elders passed the bread and the wine. There was something overwhelmingly solemn about the service. I felt that I was sitting in a shadow of an awful tragedy and mystery, yet at the same time something inexpressibly sweet and tender. The words which impressed themselves upon me were those pronounced by the minister, "This is my body, broken for you: this do in remembrance of me." That taught me that I had offended God, but that this friend had saved me by dying for me, and therefore I must always love him and remember him.

LOVE—*see also* MOTHER'S LOVE

Recently I read a remarkable letter written by John Brown to his family just before he was hanged at Charles Town, Virginia. Among the many excellent things he says in that memorable letter is his statement to his children that he has found the highest joy in life in loving and in being loved. Man is made for love. But in the image of the earthy there are many shadows and many difficulties in the way of loving and being loved.

———————

—Of Christ—I read in the papers one day a curious will in which the mother left to her son chiefly good advice and counsel. At the end of the will she said that she wanted to thank him for his kindness and affection, because his love had made the last twenty-five years of her life well worth living. Contemplating the end of this earthly life, the woman testified that the love of her son had made life worth living.

Even in the human sense, this is true. No one who loves has lived in vain. But whatever may be the fortune or misfortune of human relationships, the love of

Christ and the love for Christ will always make life worth living.

In the Jewish temple and tabernacle there burned a lamp, a light of sacrifice that never went out. Day and night, summer and winter, it shed its soft and mystic glow within the holy place. In the temple of the life of our Lord and Saviour Jesus Christ there was a lamp, a light that never went out. The oil that supplied it was never exhausted. No scorn, no hostility, no hatred could ever quench it. It was the light of love. "Having loved his own . . . he loved them unto the end." (John 13:1.)

—A father's—Absalom had denied David, but when the father heard that his son was dead, his father's love covered all the boy's faults. Great love always does that, for love hopeth all things and believeth all things. I recall a very distinguished clergyman who had a son, handsome and gifted like Absalom, but who, following his father into the ministry, brought reproach to the cause of Christ and immeasurable anguish to his father. The son was deposed from the ministry. Years afterward the father appeared before the synod of the church and pleaded with his brethren to restore the son to holy office. Those who were present describe the scene as the most moving and dramatic they had ever witnessed. The theologian, the wise counselor, the man who took thought for the church, the guardian of the honor of the cause—all these were gone, or forgotten for the moment, and only the father stood there pleading for his beloved son.

O love, love of fathers for sons, love of frail creatures of the dust for passing shadows like themselves, love that wilt not let any go without a tear, a sigh, a lamentation, by thine ever-burning flame thou dost teach us to read the noble characters which are writ large in human nature and, reading them, to think more highly of ourselves and hope more firmly in God!

—For husband—The sacraments of human love are being celebrated about us all the time. What is more common than this? A woman is married to a man who turns out to be, in the common saying, "no good." He is unfaithful, he is intemperate, shiftless, at times cruel, the very caricature of husband and father. All that he means to the woman is want, shame, dread, and pain. His irregularities reach their climax in some criminal act, and the man forfeits his liberty for a season and is confined within the walls of the penitentiary. To the world, outside of that woman, he ceases to exist. His own brothers and sisters disown him and only hope never to set eyes upon him again. His old friends forget him. The years slip by. The term of imprisonment is ended. He is discharged. The penitentiary gates open for him as he steps back into the world on a bleak winter's day; and there, like an angel of mercy, stands his wife, with open arms, to welcome him back to life again.

How can you account for it? Only thus: she loves him. Marvelous, august, enduring love! Love that beareth all things. Many waters of adversity cannot quench it, neither can all the raging floods of sin drown it.

—Opportunity for—In George Eliot's *Scenes from Clerical Life* there is a passage where she describes the grief of the rector, Amos Barton, over his departed wife. So keen was his distress that he felt as though her passing must be only a dream: "Oh, the anguish of that thought that we can never atone to our dead for the stinted affection we gave them, for the light answer we turned to their plaints or pleas, for the little reverence we showed to that sacred soul that lived so close to us and was the divinest thing that God had given us to know!"

— — —

—Reviving power of—In George Eliot's great book *Silas Marner,* the wounded, rebuffed, and finally embittered and God-rejecting old miser, coming into his cabin and mourning the loss of his hoard of gold, was stooping to push the logs together—when to his blurred vision it seemed as if there were gold on the floor in front of the hearth. He thought his gold had come back again. It *was* gold; but when he put out his hand to seize the metallic treasure, his hand touched the soft golden curls of a little child who had crawled from its dead mother's arms in the snow outside to the light of the fire. At first Silas thought it was his sister—whom as a child he had carried about in his arms, in the long ago—come back to him. "He had a dreamy feeling that this child was somehow a message come to him from that far-off life; it stirred fibres that had not been moved for many a year, old quiverings of tenderness, old impressions of awe at the presentiment of some Power presiding over his life."

The golden-haired child had come—as many another child has come and will come—to lead the gloomy man out from his false self and back to his real self. He came to himself. But a little child led him. Do you wonder that when God came to seek and to save the lost, he came as a little child?

— — —

—Sacrificial—"Greater love hath no man than this, that a man lay down his life for his friends." (John 15:13.) I remember having once seen these words writ-

ten on a memorial tablet on the wall of a home where I was staying. The home was without an earthly father, and this verse told the reason why. With his wife and children the father had been sailing on a lake. One of the children fell overboard, and the father leaped to his rescue. The child was saved; the father was lost. There was nothing exceptional about the sacrifice; many another has risked the same for one who was not his child, but a stranger. Yet the father gave all that he had for the child—his life. Now the child, coming to manhood, looks upon the tablet in that home and every day is reminded how his father laid down his life for his sake. "Greater love hath no man than this, that a man lay down his life for his friends." The son ought to be a better and more honorable man because he realizes that his being spared to live cost the life of another.

— — —

—For wife—A great character was that man of storm and thunder, Andrew Jackson. Perhaps no man in American history ever received so much adulation and so much execration and malediction. When at length he retired to the Hermitage, near Nashville, to end his days, he had back of him the memory of the great victory over Wellington's veterans at New Orleans and his two terms as president of the United States. Yet, in those sunset days at the Hermitage, these were not the things of which he was thinking, nor were they the things which brought him comfort and consolation. Visitors at the Hermitage who entered his room relate how they would find the old man sitting before the fire, in one hand his Bible and in the other hand a miniature of his beloved Rachel. On her tomb, near the Hermitage, on a bright spring morning when the trees were white with blossoms and the mockingbirds sang in their branches, I read the inscription which Jackson composed, his beautiful tribute to the companion of thirty-five years: "Here lie the remains of Mrs. Rachel Jackson, wife of President Jackson, who died the twenty-second of December, 1828. Age 61 years. Her face was fair, her person pleasing, her temper amiable, her heart kind. A being so gentle and so virtuous, slander might wound but could not dishonor. Even death, when he bore her from the arms of her husband, could but transport her to the bosom of her God."

What the old warrior took comfort in was not the huzzas of the multitude after his marvelous victory at New Orleans, nor the recollections of his eight years of absolute power at Washington, but rather the affections and devotions of his beloved Rachel. There, in the realm of the heart, and not in the realm of things, are to be found the abiding satisfactions of life.

—For woman—On the third day of the Battle of Gettysburg, when the Union artillery had ceased firing, creating the mistaken impression among the Confederates that the Union guns had been silenced, the Confederate chief of artillery, Alexander, sent a message to Longstreet, who commanded the corps from which Pickett's division was taken for the famous charge. As soon as this message was received, Pickett sprang to his feet, and, looking toward Longstreet, said, "General, shall I go forward?" Unable to speak the order which he was convinced must end in disaster, Longstreet grasped Pickett by the hand and bowed his head. The next moment Pickett was on his horse and off at a gallop. But in a few minutes he came riding back to Longstreet and handed him a letter addressed to his fiancée at Richmond. On the back of the envelope he had written in pencil, "If Old Peter's [Longstreet's sobriquet] nod means death, good-by, and God bless you, little one."

As he went to the head of his lines again, Wilcox, another commander, rode up to him and, taking a flask from his pocket, said, "Pickett, take a drink with me. In an hour you will be in hell or glory." Pickett refused to drink, saying: "I promised the little girl who is waiting and praying for me down in Virginia that I would keep fresh upon my lips, until we should meet again, the breath of the violets she gave me when we parted. Whatever my fate, Wilcox, I shall try to do my duty like a man; and I hope that, by that little girl's prayer, I shall today reach glory or glory." Thus "for her sake," without the smell of whisky upon him, Pickett rode to glory.

Who can tell how much evil has been refrained from and how much good has been done for the love of a noble woman?

During the Civil War, Charles Sumner, commenting on the assault made on him by Preston S. Brooks in the Senate in 1851, said, "When I was assaulted in the Senate chamber in 1851, no one thought I would live. In the weary months of illness that followed, my thoughts were much on my unfinished fight against slavery. But in the midnight watches, my keenest heart-gnawing regret was that, if I were called away, I never had enjoyed the choicest experience of life, that no lips responsive to my own had said, I love you."

—Of the world—In his tale *Mare Nostrum* the Spanish novelist Ibáñez makes the action center about an unworthy woman whose better nature has been aroused by the affection of her lover. She shows the awakening of her better self by an endeavor to avoid him and to persuade him to set his affections upon one more worthy. So the mistress of this world has, as it were, moments of compunction and conscience, when she repels men from her embrace and tells them to set their affections higher—to seek first the Kingdom of God. This is a truth, beautifully stated in the First Epistle of John (2:15, 17), and also echoed and confirmed in the experience of mankind: "Love not the world, neither the things that are in the world. . . . The world passeth away, and the lust thereof: but he that doeth the will of God abideth for ever."

LOYALTY TO CHRIST

There is a fine passage in *Tom Brown's School Days* which tells of a boy who had the courage to stand up against ridicule. A new boy had come to the school, and on his first night, in a room where there were twelve beds and boys, he knelt down to say his prayers. Tom Brown's head was turned just in time to see a heavy slipper flying through the air toward the head of the kneeling boy. When the lights went out a little later, Tom Brown thought of his own mother, and the prayers that she had taught him to say, but which he had never said since he came to Rugby. Then and there he made a decision that the next time he went to bed, he, too, would say his prayers. When that next night came, the other boys in the room, ready to laugh and scoff at this newcomer who said his prayers, were amazed to see Tom Brown, whom they all respected and feared, kneel down at the side of his bed and pray. That boy's courageous prayer, in spite of ridicule, at length won him the respect of all his companions—and he rose to be one of the most distinguished men of the Church of England.

LYING

An incident comes back to me out of my young manhood which illustrates how good men are tempted to lie, and to do it in a way that does not altogether commit them on the record. The man whom I have in mind was a rancher in Colorado. He was a godly man, and a good and kind man, a man who had family prayers with his "help" on the ranch every morning. At the end of the season, which had been a very bad one, I drove with him with a colossal load of alfalfa hay to a near-by town. The hay was what was called "third cutting," and therefore inferior. When the bales were being hoisted into the barn, the purchaser pulled out a few wisps and, examining them exclaimed, "This is not first cutting, as I have given instruction!"

The rancher looked at him with a look of injured integrity and exclaimed, "That is what you ordered, isn't it?" conveying the impression that as an honorable man he would deliver to the purchaser only the hay which he had ordered, which was first cutting.

I can recall the deep silence after the man thus spoke—for all three knew that it was a falsehood.

That night, as we stood on the road, the man paid me off before I started east to return to college. His conscience evidently troubled him, for as he handed me the gold pieces that meant so much to him, and for which I had worked so hard, he said, calling me by the name they gave me on the ranch, "I didn't tell that man it was first cutting, did I?" Literally, of course, he had not; *actually,* he had.

———————

There are those who hold that it is never permissible for a Christian to state what is false, even to save a life. The classic example of that is Jeanie Deans in *The Heart of Midlothian*.

Effie Deans was on trial for her life, charged with the murder of her infant. The sister Jeanie was put on the stand. A single word, "No," in answer to the question of the attorney for the defense, would have saved the life of her sister. But Jeanie Deans would not lie. She said "Yes," and her sister was condemned to death.

It was not for lack of love for her sister that Jeanie Deans refused to lie; for after her sister had been sentenced to be hanged, Jeanie walked all the way to London to petition the king for a pardon, which was granted. Jeanie Deans is said to have had a counterpart in real life, a woman named Helen Walker, to whose memory Scott erected a monument with this inscription: "This stone was erected by the author of *Waverly* to the memory of Helen Walker, who died in the year of God, 1791. This humble individual practiced in real life the virtues with which fiction has invested the imaginary character of Jeanie Deans, refusing the slightest departure from veracity, even to save the life of a sister."

M

MAN—*see also* SIN, SOUL

In what a competent judge has called the greatest passage in French prose, Pascal wrote: "Man is but a reed, the feeblest thing in nature. But he is a reed that thinks. It needs not that the universe arise to crush him. An exhalation, a drop of water, suffices to destroy him; but were the universe to crush man, man is yet nobler than the universe, for he knows that he dies, and the universe, even in prevailing against him, knows not its power."

I wish to speak this morning about that in man which is greater than the universe in which he lives.

———•◆•———

Life is so common, it has such sordid aspects, there are so many souls about us, that we forget the wonder and the glory of man. Men are being killed by so many thousands upon thousands on the fields of battle that we are tempted to account men as little more than sheep for the slaughter. But if you were cast upon a desert island, and had for your companions only the hot sands and the undulating seas, or at the best, crawling reptiles and chattering tropical birds, and beasts that fled at your approach— if you had been living thus for a number of years, and then one day discovered in the sands, as did Defoe's hero, the footprint of a man made in your image, how it would thrill you and stir you, what waves of emotion would surge over your soul! In that exalted moment you would realize what a piece of work man is.

———•◆•———

—**Divine nature of**—In a recent address a Yale professor, Chauncey Brewster Tinker, said: "The disease of the world today is a loss of faith in the moral nature of man. What we have lost is a conception of the dignity of life and of the imperial position of man in nature. Instead of thinking of the august character and destiny of man, we have been preoccupied with him as one of the highest order of primates. Man has been found to be a speaking animal. The view that he is also the son of God was an amiable, but deluded, notion of our ill-informed ancestors." In the search for the origins of man's physical life we seem to have forgotten altogether something far more important—the meaning and the objectives of man's life, not only whence came he, but whither is he going.

———————

—And environment—In his wild dream of Gulliver's travels Jonathan Swift predicted some of the social and scientific changes which have taken place since the eighteenth century. But by depicting the vices and follies of the inhabitants of the countries which he visited—the Lilliputians, Brobdingnagians, Lagadonians, Struldbrugs—all under different conditions and social machinery, he showed how man can be low and contemptible under any form of government or manner of life.

What we need, then is not a New Athens, or a New Oceana, or a New Atlantis, but a *new man.*

———————

—Good and evil in—Victor Hugo in one of his poems wrote, "I feel two worlds struggling within me." I remember seeing once in the Metropolitan Museum of Art a sculpture by Carpenter which illustrated that saying. Out of the central block of marble emerge two persons, or personalities—the one intellectual, refined, spiritual, desperately struggling to get free; the other of the earth earthy, animal, sensual, cruel. There, in extreme form, in the sculptor's thought and creation is expressed what goes on beneath every human breast.

———————

When Charles Spurgeon was once being shown through the library of Trinity College, Cambridge, he stopped to admire a bust of Byron. The librarian said

to him, "Stand here, sir, and look at it."

Spurgeon took the position indicated and, looking upon the bust, remarked, "What an intellectual countenance! What a grand genius!"

"Come, now," said the librarian, "and look at it from this side."

Spurgeon changed his position and, looking on the statue from that viewpoint, exclaimed, "What a demon! There stands a man who could defy the Deity!" He asked the librarian if the sculptor had secured this effect designedly.

"Yes," he replied, "he wished to picture the two characters, the two persons —the great, the grand, the almost supergenius that he possessed; and yet the enormous mass of sin that was in his soul."

———————

—Greatness of—"What a piece of work is a man! how noble in reason! how infinite in faculty! in form and moving how express and admirable! in action how like an angel! in apprehension how like a god!" Shakespeare's description of man is true of him as the Eighth Psalm (4-8) describes him. There is man, with the crown of reason on his head, endued with conscience and moral freedom, "a little lower than the angels"—literally, a little lower than God. "Thou madest him to have dominion over the works of thy hands." This world—and not only this world, but the universe—is for man. The sun shines in heaven for his candle and lamp. The energies of the earth are stored up for his furnace. The fields and the harvests and the flocks and the beasts are for his sustenance and his clothing. The oceans are his pathway around the world. The laws of space and matter are for his convenience. The beautiful panoramas of sky, and sea, and earth are for his delight. God gave it all to man, created it for him and said, "All this is for you. Have dominion over it."

—Greatness and fall of—Man is like one of the old Greek temples, whose ruins—like those of the temple of Neptune at Sunium—arouse our interest and admiration and make us wonder what the perfect temple must have been. Although the roof, the walls, the pillars are fallen, and the stones covered with rubbish and earth, yet one can trace the outlines of the temple and see where the walls went up and where the mighty columns, so exquisitely carved, cast their long shadows.

It matters not what has happened to man, the foundation of his greatness is clearly to be discerned. I can never give up the Christian and biblical idea of man. The "growing brute" theory fits not nearly so well the facts of human nature as the Bible theory of a great city, fallen and desolate, but still capable of restoration and redemption. I am still ready to say, with Robert South, that Aristotle was but the wreck of an Adam, and Athens but the rubbish of an Eden.

—Nature of—Rousseau, whose *Confessions* testify in such an amazing way to the sinfulness of the human heart, how corruption can be lodged side by side with noble and philanthropic motives and kind and generous deeds, was a prophet of those who hold that man is not inherently evil by nature, but only by association, custom, and environment.

There is much sense in what Napoleon said about this theory: "I used to think highly of Rousseau and his theory, but since I have visited the East and seen human nature there, I do not have any use for Rousseau." My only comment on that biting sentence is this, that one hardly needs visit the East and see human nature there to know there is nothing in this theory of environment and association.

If the environment and association are poison, it is because they have issued from a poisoned fountain. The sinfulness of man's nature is not due to a bad example. A bad example might incite me to sin and cause me to walk in evil ways, but unless I had in myself the sinful nature or the bad example, the seductive temptation could have no effect upon me.

Plato said that if it were true that children learn evil only by example, as birds learn to sing, to make them good it would only be necessary to seclude them. But suppose you did seclude them and isolate them? Take the offspring of parents who are heirs to the best and the highest our civilization and religion have to offer and put them down on an uninhabited island. Five centuries hence—yes, within a few generations—you would have in the human society which sprang from those two persons everything which today occasions our regret and our amazement. Why? Because man's nature itself is productive of sin.

MANKIND, FUTURE OF—*see* FUTURE OF MANKIND

MARKS OF CHRIST

After his conquests in Persia and in India, Alexander the Great, at Opis, announced to his veteran army that the wars were over and that those who had served him so well, many of whom were wounded, homesick, and enfeebled, would be sent back to their homes in Macedonia. He planned to change his Macedonian and Greek army to one of foreign and Persian complexion.

At this announcement a storm of protest interrupted the words of the king. "You have used us up, and now you cast us aside. Take your barbarian soldiers! Will you conquer the world with women? Come, let us all go. Keep all or none. Why don't you get your father Ammon to help you?"

Stirred by this mutiny, Alexander leaped from the platform where he was standing and put several of the ringleaders under arrest. Then, returning to the dais, he faced the sullen, turbulent army and made them a speech which showed that he was great not only as a soldier but as an orator.

He said: "Will anyone say that while you endured privation and toil, I did not? Who of you could say that he has suffered more for me than I for him? Come now, who of you has wounds? Let him bare himself and show them, and I will show mine. No member of my body is without its wound; there is no kind of weapon whose scars I do not bear. I have been wounded by the sword, by the arrow from the bow, by the missile from the catapult. I have been pelted with stones and pounded with clubs, while leading you to victory and to glory and to plenty, through all the land and sea, across all the rivers, and mountains, and the plains."

Thus, by the wounds and scars on his body, Alexander the Great proved to the soldiers of his army his courage, patriotism, and devotion.

So Paul could lay back the folds of his garment and say, "I bear in my body the marks of the Lord Jesus" (Gal. 6:17).

———————

A missionary to the Arabians told of an Arab of standing in his community who sought him out late one night with a burden on his soul. He told him that he had learned to see that Christ was the Son of God and his Saviour. The missionary reminded him that the next step was confession. The man then told him that this would mean either death or being driven out on the hills like a wild animal. He could endure such a fate for himself, but he felt he ought not to bring such suffering upon his young son. The faithful missionary reminded him

of the words of Christ, "He that loveth father or mother . . . son or daughter more than me is not worthy of me" (Matt. 10:37). Looking out of his window afterward, the missionary caught a vision of the man kneeling beneath a tree, in an agony of prayer—praying, no doubt, that he might be given strength to drink this cup and confess Christ before the world.

The missionary had no doubt that he had stated the terms of Christian discipleship according to the words of Christ himself. But, telling the story before a church gathering in this country, he said: "When I see the easy, selfish lives of Christians here, and see them come to the Lord's table without any thought or purpose of real denial or self-sacrifice, and then think of that Arabian kneeling beneath the trees, I begin to feel that I made the terms too hard for him."

MARK'S, ST.

One of the great churches of the world is St. Mark's in Venice. According to a rather untrustworthy tradition, Mark's body was transported in the ninth century from Alexandria, where he died, to Venice, where a great church was built as a resting place for his dust. Venice rose in all its splendor and beauty out of the marshes and lagoons of the Adriatic coast. The marsh became a great city. So Mark, at first weak, unreliable, and unstable, finally emerges in the last part of his New Testament history a pillar of strength, a finished character, all his past failures overcome by perseverance, faith, and the grace of God. He is one of those who "out of weakness were made strong" (Heb. 11:34).

MARRIAGE—*see also* HOME, LOVE, WIFE

I might put my advice about marriage in the form of five "don'ts," for some people can remember a negative more easily than a positive assertion.

First, to the young man:

1) Don't marry a woman who does not pray.
2) Don't marry a bad-tempered or jealous woman.
3) Don't marry a woman who loves the moving pictures and the matinee more than the home.
4) Don't marry a woman who drinks. It is bad enough when a woman marries a man who drinks, infinitely worse when a man marries a woman who drinks.
5) Unless you have plenty of money, or she has plenty of money, so that you can employ someone to do it for you, don't marry a woman who cannot cook or cannot learn to cook.

To the young woman:

1) Don't marry an unbeliever.
2) Don't marry a man of bad habits.
3) Don't marry a coffin man, that is, a man with room for himself and no one else.
4) Don't marry a peacock man, a conceited man.
5) Don't marry a man of low moral standards.

———•••———

Rebekah said, "I will go." (Gen. 24:58.) How that answer has echoed upon the lips of thousands and thousands of the sisters of Rebekah! "Wilt thou go?" And back has come the answer, "I will go"—earth's sweetest music, no doubt, to those who hear both sentences!

"I will go!" And she has gone—although it meant the crossing of broad seas; a hut in a land of savages; a rude frontier settlement; one room in the third story back, which must serve as bedroom, living room, and kitchen.

"I will go!" And she has gone—although it has meant separation, loneliness, childbearing, sickness, grief, sometimes disappointment, sorrow, and tragedy.

Yet the world keeps on going, because men ask, "Wilt thou go?" and women still answer with radiant eye and tremulous voice, "I will go."

———•••———

When William Jennings Bryan went to call on the father of his prospective wife and seek the hand of his daughter in marriage, knowing the strong religious feeling of the father, he thought to strengthen his case by a quotation from the Bible, and quoted the proverb of Solomon: "Whoso findeth a wife findeth a good thing" (Prov. 18:22). But to his surprise the father replied with a citation from Paul to the effect that he that marrieth doeth well, but he that marrieth not doeth better. The young suitor was for a moment confounded. Then with a happy inspiration he replied that Paul had no wife and Solomon had seven hundred, and Solomon, therefore, ought to be the better judge as to marriage.

———•••———

Young men and young women must not be too disturbed by the alarming prevalence of divorces. Even if there is one divorce in every six marriages, think of the millions of happy homes where men and women and their children live together in loyalty and in love. A happy home is as near to heaven as we ever come in this world. The medieval knights had a saying that no knight was properly fitted for battle unless the hand of a woman had buckled on his armor.

———•••———

—And good disposition—Marry a woman of good disposition. That is advice that I would put almost first of all. Remember the comments of Solomon,

224

whose wide experience certainly qualified him to speak on the subject of marriage. One day, irritated by one of his numerous wives, Solomon took refuge on the roof garden of his house. Looking down on the tenements of one of his subjects, he saw a man sleeping contentedly on his mattress in a corner of the housetop; and, taking up his quill, Solomon wrote this proverb: "Better to dwell in the corner of the housetop, than with a brawling woman" (Prov. 25:24). On another day, a day when it did nothing but rain, hearing the dripping of the rain, Solomon had another idea; and, taking up his quill, he wrote another proverb: "A continual dropping in a very rainy day and a contentious woman are alike" (Prov. 27:15).

—And religion—The marriage of Mark Twain with Olivia Langdon is an illustration of how unbelief in a husband affects a believing wife in the marriage relationship. His wife was a simple and devout Christian. In their first married days they had grace at meals and read a chapter from the Bible every day. But this was soon abandoned. At length the young wife confided to her sister that she had given up some of her religious convictions. Her travels in Europe with her husband, the philosophies she had listened to from friends of her husband, and from her husband, also, and the hordes of people she had seen in her travels—all these had shaken her faith in the providence of God. At a time of sore bereavement Mark Twain said to his wife, "Livy, if it comforts you to lean on the Christian faith, do so."

She replied sadly, "I can't, Youth (always her name for her husband); I haven't any."

The thought that he had destroyed her faith, even though to him it was an illusion, frequently came back to him and troubled him in the days which were to come. The highest and purest and happiest relationship is where there is a unity of heart and faith in love for God.

MARTYRS—*see also* CHRIST SUFFERING FOR MARTYRS

—Early Christian—Imagine a warm spring afternoon at Ephesus toward the close of the first century. The city's great avenue, the *Corso,* paved with white marble and lined with the busts of the emperors, is filled with a great throng moving toward the arena where the games are to be held. Soon the great bowl, with its tiers of stone benches rising toward heaven, is filled with a vast multitude hungry for the bloody shows of the arena. Here and there a fountain is playing, and clouds of sweet incense go up to cancel the disagreeable odor of blood and death. Under a purple canopy sits the Roman governor and his staff. One by one the shows are put on—by boxers, javelin throwers, and those who fight with the net and the sword. Then the arena is cleared again, and a great shout goes up, "The Christians to the lions!" That is the chief spectacle, the climax of the shows, for which the pleasure-loving multitude has been waiting.

As the thousands are shouting, a door is opened under the last tier of seats; and a small company of men, women, and children is led out to the center of the arena. One is an old man, not far from the grave by nature's path even if he had not been condemned to die in the arena. Another is a handsome young man, strongly muscled, to whom life must have been dear; another a young woman in the bloom of beauty and youth; another a mother with a little child in her arms. Gathered close together, their eyes sweep the stone benches above them, looking in vain for a face of sympathy or of deliverance. Then, while the mob cries for their blood, they kneel together on the sand, and the old man lifts his hands in prayer. When the prayer is finished, they rise from their knees and, standing close together, begin to sing. When the roar of the mob subsides you can catch a few words of their hymn. It is this (II Tim. 2:11-12):

It is a faithful saying:
For if we be dead with him,
we shall also live with him:
if we suffer, we shall also
reign with him: if we deny him,
he also will deny us.

Then a gate on the farther side of the arena is pushed open; and the lions, starved for a week, rush out into the arena and, beholding the helpless Christians, with fierce roars leap upon them and tear them to pieces. A few bloody relics are dragged to a corner of the arena, and more of those who "loved not their lives unto the death" (Rev. 12:11) have won the martyr's crown.

In the shadows of the evening I walk about the walls of the Colosseum. In this dark dungeon did some Christian lie, some aged man or woman, some noble youth, some lovely maiden, or worse, some mother with her babe at her breast? And did they hear through the watches of the night the roars of the ravening beasts waiting for their human prey? Just a few grains of incense on the pagan altar, just a word of veneration for the image of the emperor, and the dungeon gates would open for them—for them again the dear light of the sun and of the sky, the embrace of friends and relatives instead of the fetid breath of the wild beast.

Did any of them wonder why they chose the darkness rather than the sunlight, the dungeon rather than the sky, the gory mane of the lion rather than the embrace of friends, Christ rather than life? What did they think? What did they say as they were led forth into the blinding glare of the arena, and heard the roar of the oncoming beast? Was it the words of David: "The Lord is my shepherd; I shall not want. . . . Yea, though I walk through the valley of the shadow of death, I will fear no evil" (Ps. 23:1-4)? Or was it the word of God through the prophet: "When thou passest through the waters, I will be with thee" (Isa. 43:2)? Or this: "The young lion and the dragon shalt thou trample under feet" (Ps. 91:13)? Or did the awful cry of Christ himself echo at times through the arena: "My God, my God, why hast thou forsaken me" (Matt. 27:46)?

Now their sufferings are long past. They overcame through the blood of the Lamb; they loved not their lives even unto death. These are they of whom the world was not worthy. Now, having washed their robes and made them white in the blood of the Lamb, they walk with him in white.

—**Forty wrestlers**—The forty wrestlers were Christian soldiers in one of the legions of the Roman army. The army was on a campaign in the high mountains of Armenia, in Asia Minor, and it was bitter winter. The emperor had issued a decree to the generals of all his armies that on a given day the soldiers must march past the statue of the emperor, do obeisance, pour out a libation of wine, and drop incense on the fire.

At the appointed time the trumpets blew and the army marched past the emperor's statue, where all bowed and poured out the wine and offered the incense, as if to a god. But the forty wrestlers, these Christian soldiers, refused to pay the emperor's statue divine honors. They were renowned for both their prowess on the field of battle and their athletic triumphs in the amphitheater. Their general, who thought highly of them, besought them, for his sake and their love for him, to obey the decree. For a moment they hesitated, as they thought of the sweetness of life and of their families at home—but it was only for a moment. Then they answered their general and said, "For Rome we will fight on any field and under any sky. In the service of the emperor, if necessary, we will die. But we worship no one save our Master, Jesus Christ." Then with great sorrow and reluctance the general pronounced the sentence of punishment decreed for those who refused to worship the image of the emperor.

The forty soldiers were stripped of their armor, which they had honored so in many a hard-fought campaign. Their helmets and breastplates and shields and spears and swords were taken from them. Then they were divested of their undergarments and their sandals, and, stark naked, were driven out into the subzero weather upon the frozen lake. The night had come down, and as the soldiers of the legion sat about the campfires in their bivouacs they could hear the voices of the forty wrestlers as they sang, "Forty wrestlers wrestling for thee, O Christ, claim for thee the victory and from thee the crown."

As the night passed, their song grew fainter and fainter, as man after man succumbed to the cold and fell lifeless on the ice. At length only one survivor was left. Naked and trembling and shivering, he appeared before the tent of the general and said to the sentinel, "I will drop the incense and pour the wine." But the sentinel, who, although a pagan, had been moved by the heroic faith of the forty wrestlers, answered, "Since thou hast proved a coward, I will take thy place." With that he stripped off his armor and his clothing and went out in the night upon the ice to take his stand among the thirty-nine who had fallen.

For a time the soldiers about the campfire heard his voice singing as he caught up the chant of those who had fallen: "Forty wrestlers wrestling for thee, O Christ, claim for thee the victory and from thee the crown." At length he, too, fell dead upon the ice. When the morning sun rose over the bleak Armenian mountains, that was what it looked down upon—the forty wrestlers who had died for Christ, and from whom they had received the crown.

———•·•———

—John Huss—On a summer Sabbath afternoon I sat on a bench under the trees on Rhadcany Hill and looked out over the ancient city of Prague. Perhaps there is no city in Europe which brings back more vividly the Medieval Ages. To my left was the cathedral and the monastery. Below them the modern town, then the winding Moldau, dotted with green islands and spanned by the Charles IV Bridge with its massive towers. On the other side of the Moldau lay the ancient city, with its towers and gables, spires, red roofs, and turrets. Now and then I could hear faintly the chiming of a church bell, sounding like an echo out of the long-vanished past. In front of the town hall is the magnificent monument to Bohemia's most celebrated citizen, John Huss. A magnificent monument it is; with his head thrown back and a look of exultation on his countenance, Huss appears like the incarnation of heroic defiance of man and unfaltering trust in God.

As I gazed upon that monument, my mind ran back five centuries and more, to a July day in 1415, when in a pleasant meadow near the shores of Lake Constance a pale, thin man of mean attire was chained to a stake and burned to ashes, amid the hooting and execration of those who stood about. Now in the heart of his nation's capital stands the bronze figure of the martyr. So it has ever been. One generation, one century, execrates and burns. The next century, or a fifth century afterward, builds monuments to the martyr's name.

- - - ◆ ◆ ◆ - - -

Under the guard of a thousand armed men, and followed by a vast throng of people, Huss was escorted to the place of execution, the Devil's Place, a pleasant meadow near the lake. As he walked to the stake he recited Psalm 51, and Psalm 31 (1, 5): "In thee, O Lord, do I put my trust; let me never be ashamed. . . . Into thine hand I commit my spirit: thou hast redeemed me, O Lord God of truth." His arms were fastened behind his back and his neck was secured to the stake with a chain. Then the straw and wood were heaped about him up to his chin, and rosin was sprinkled over them. Offered one last chance to recant, he said, "I shall die with joy in the faith of the gospel which I have preached." His face being turned toward the east, bystanders came up and brutally turned it toward the west. Then the torch was applied. As the flames leaped up, Huss repeated the prayer of the liturgy:

> O Christ, Son of the Living God,
>   have mercy upon us;
> O Christ, Son of the Living God,
>   have mercy upon me;
> Thou who wast born of the Virgin
>   Mary—

Then the wind blew the flames into his face, and his voice was stilled forever. But, like him who first died for Christ, being full of the Holy Ghost, he looked up steadfastly into heaven, and saw the glory of God, and Jesus standing on the right hand of God.

- - - ◆ ◆ ◆ - - -

As Huss stood chained to the stake, his persecutors prepared for him a triple crown of paper with painted devils on it. Seeing this, Huss said, "My Lord Jesus Christ for my sake wore a crown of thorns. Why should not I, then, for his sake, wear this like crown, be it ever so ignominious? Truly I will do it, and that willingly."

When the crown was set on his head, the bishop said, "Now we commit thy soul to the devil."

"But I," said Huss, lifting up his eyes toward heaven, "do commit my spirit into thy hands, O Lord Jesus Christ."

MARY OF THE "SISTINE MADONNA"

I have never read any comment on it, but I take it for granted that Raphael's great painting of Jesus and his mother in the Dresden gallery is an attempt to describe the thoughts and emotions of the mother at the presentation of her child in the temple. Mary, listening to the words of Simeon, presents, and yet holds back, her child; and her unfocused eye seems to be filled with wonder and awe as she sees, far in the distance, the strange destiny of the child who rests in her arms.

MEMORIAL DAY

On a spring afternoon I left the Virginia highway and made my way through the woods to the bluffs on the south bank of the Potomac, where I had seen the flag of the nation waving over the tops of the trees. There in the midst of the forest solitude I came upon a lonely cemetery, the smallest of all our national cemeteries. Within that little enclosure sleeps the dust of fifteen soldiers who fell there in the all-but-forgotten Battle of Ball's Bluff, October 21, 1861.

As I stood there by the forgotten, seldom-visited, but not neglected, graves of those fifteen men of the California regiment, with the vagrant wind of the springtime sighing through the tops of the pine trees and the Potomac flowing silently and rapidly away like the river of a man's life, my mind reverted to the half a million graves of those who fell in the same great conflict—some of them far beneath the waves of the ocean, some sunk in the sands of the Mississippi or the Arkansas rivers, some interred in the woods of Shiloh, or the solitudes of Chickamauga, or the pleasant meadows and fields of Antietam and Gettysburg, or in the tangled thickets of the Wilderness and the Peninsula, and in a thousand village cemeteries, east and west, north and south.

Today, with cheers for the living—a mere handful of survivors of the 1,700,-000 of the Grand Army of the Republic; just 389—and with tears for the dead, we visit these multitudinous graves and think of those who gave their lives for America, and for the government of the United States, whose bodies rest in peace but whose name liveth forevermore.

———•••———

Memorial Day strikes the chord of memory. In the words of a poet of the South, Father Ryan, in *Poems*: "A land without ruins is a land without history. A land that wears a laurel crown may be fair to see; but twine a few sad cypress leaves around the brow of any land, and be that land barren, beautiless, and bleak, it becomes lovely in its consecrated coronet of sorrow and wins the sympathy of the heart and of history. Crowns of roses fade—crowns of thorns endure. Calvaries and Crucifixions take deepest hold of humanity. The triumphs of might are transient, they pass and are forgotten —the sufferings of right are graven deepest on the chronicles of the nations."

MEMORY—*see also* CONSCIENCE, HELL, IMMORTALITY, REMORSE

—Childhood—Among the clearest and most pleasant recollections of my boyhood home is the memory of the locust trees where we used to hitch the family horse. It was a pleasant spot between the house and the barn, well shaded by the branches of the trees. Perhaps it was only an association of names, but, as I remember, it was there in that locust tree on the long summer afternoons that I heard the song of the locust. Even the child's heart, untried and untainted yet with life's experience, caught a note of something that was sad and melancholy in the music of the locust. When we heard that song we knew that summer was waning and that winter was on the way.

———•••———

—Desire to be remembered—Man craves the knowledge and the sympathy of the Eternal. During a lull between the charges at the second Battle of Cold Harbor, in June, 1864—the only battle that Grant said he regretted fighting—officers going through the Union ranks saw the men, sitting on the grass under the trees, or in the thickets, sewing their names on the sleeves of their coats.

Why were they doing that? It was because they expected to die in the ensuing charge, and shrank from the oblivion of a nameless grave. They wanted someone in the hills of western Pennsylvania, Vermont, New York, Wisconsin, to know how they had died and where and when, and where their bodies rested. Yes, the human heart wants to know if there is any ear to hear, or any eye to witness, its sorrows, its conflicts, and its struggles.

———•••———

Some time ago I went to visit the first important battlefield of the Civil War, Rich Mountain, in the mountains of West Virginia, where in July, 1861, General George B. McClellan defeated the Confederate troops under General Robert Garnett. The battlefield, the name of which once rang throughout the country, is in the midst of a wild mountain solitude. On one of the outcropping rocks on the farm where the battle was fought, you can read the name "Powell." The story is that a certain soldier, mortally wounded, asked by his comrades if there was anything that they could do for him, answered, "No, only knock the cap off this rock." When they had done so, he asked for his bayonet. Taking the bayonet in his hand, he cut upon the face of the rock with the point of the bayonet the letters of his name. He did not wish to die in that mountain desolation unremembered and unnoted. It was a beautiful and pathetic tribute to man's desire to be remembered, and to his instinct for immortality.

—Of the just—In all cities of the world there are to be seen stately and magnificent monuments and cenotaphs which memorialize the dead of the first World War. In front of these monuments and under these triumphal arches have been kindled ever-burning fires, to signify that the memory of the dead shall never pass from the mind of man. But there is something more wonderful and more beautiful than that—the invisible monuments, more precious by far than those of stone or marble or bronze or granite, which loving and grateful hearts have reared to the memory of the righteous dead.

Few falser words have ever been spoken than those which Mark Antony is reputed to have uttered over the body of Julius Caesar (Shakespeare):

> *The evil that men do lives after them;*
> *The good is oft interred with their bones.*

There is a sense, of course, in which evil goes on leaving its blight and shadow, even when the man who put it into operation has passed out of this world. But the inference from those words of Shakespeare, that the good which men do has but a brief memory and influence compared with the evil they do, is altogether false.

Once in the beautiful Protestant cemetery at Rome, which stands just near the Pyramid of Cestius, hard by where Paul was beheaded, not far from the graves of Shelley and Keats, I came suddenly upon the grave of a distinguished professor of Latin whom I had known in my university days. Not long afterward, reading a memorial article about him in the alumni magazine, I came across a sentence from Tacitus which this professor used to quote to his classes—to the effect that it is the duty and obligation of every man "to leave behind him a pleasant memory of himself."

—And retribution—The ancients fancied that there was a river called Lethe in the Elysian Fields, from whose waters the souls of the dead drank oblivion of their past life. But in the command to Dives to remember his life on earth we have the very opposite. Instead of drinking of the stream which brings oblivion of the past, Christ shows us that the souls of men must drink of the stream which makes the past live again. Son, remember!

—Of sins—How strange, and yet how terrible, is the vitality of sin! You may have changed, life may have changed, but your sin comes back unchanged.

> *What is this power*
> *That recollects the distant past,*
> *And makes this hour,*
> *Unlike the last,*
> *Pregnant with life,*
> *Calling across the deep*
> *To things that slumber, men*
> *   that sleep?*
> *They rise by number*
> *And with stealthy tread,*
> *Like a battalion's tread,*
> *Marshal our dead.*
>
> *This is the gift*
> *Men cannot bargain with nor*
> *   shift;*
> *Which went with Dives*
> *Down to hell,*
> *With Lazarus up to heaven;*
> *Which will not let us e'er forget*
> *The sins of years,*
> *Though washed with tears.*
> *Whate'er it be,*
> *Men call it "Memory."*
>
> —Author unknown

—**To be desired**—John Locke once said that memory was the only paradise out of which man cannot be driven. There is a world of truth in the statement. Not only is memory a paradise out of which man cannot be driven, but, when he has been cast out of some paradise, memory is the highway that will lead him back into it.

In his gripping tale "The Haunted Man," Charles Dickens tells of a chemist who sat before the fire troubled with unhappy memories. As he sat there in dismal reverie, a phantom appeared and offered the haunted man the opportunity to have his memory destroyed. He immediately closed with the offer, and thenceforth he was a man not only without any memory but also with the dread power to strip other men of their memories. But the gift was a disappointment. So great was his misery, and so great the misery that he inflicted upon others, that he besought the phantom to restore to him his memory. The tale comes to a conclusion with the man's grateful and earnest prayer, "Lord, keep my memory green."

Vergil shows Dante two streams as they emerge from purgatory and enter the forest of the terrestrial paradise. One of these streams, Eunos, had the power to bring back remembrance of every good deed in the past. The other, Lethe, had the power to take away the remembrance of every offense, and all that was unpleasant. This fancy, borrowed from ancient mythology, is a tribute to the power of memory. What memory brings back, both pleasant and unpleasant! It is only in fancy, however, that memory can be purged of the unpleasant. No such stream as Lethe flows through human life, and it is probably for our good that it does not. There is profit and warning in what memory brings back of the unpleasant or the unworthy, as well as of the pleasant.

MINISTER—*see also* PREACHING

Since the minister in a sense belongs to everybody, everybody has something to say about his work and how it ought to be done; and what they have to say will recall the answer of Christ to the scribes and Pharisees: "We have piped unto you, and ye have not danced; we have mourned unto you, and ye have not lamented" (Matt. 11:17). The people of that day didn't like John, because the stern ascetic came neither eating nor drinking; and when Jesus came eating and drinking, they said, "Behold a man gluttonous, and a winebibber, a friend of publicans and sinners" (Matt. 11:19). Human nature has not changed since then. But still preaching is justified of her children.

If the minister has no wife, he certainly needs one. If he has one, he must have been handcuffed and blindfolded when he picked her out. If his wife knows how to dress, she is worldly. If she goes about in the style of the gay nineties, she is a disgrace to the congregation. If she speaks in the missionary society, she is trying to run the church. If she sings in the choir, she has a voice like a magpie.

If the minister is quiet, dignified, and reserved, he is cold. If he goes about slapping men on the back and telling stories, he ought to have been a traveling salesman or president of the Kiwanis Club. If he preaches without notes, he is not deep enough. If he reads his sermons, he is too deep, and dry. If he preaches on the great doctrines, he ought to preach practical sermons. If he preaches practical sermons, he ought to go down deeper and get hold of the great doctrines of the gospel. If he calls on the rich, he is a snob. If he calls on the poor, he is playing to the galleries.

But still preaching will be justified of her children.

—**Character of a**—John Milton has a great passage in which he gives us his idea of what the character of a poet ought to be. He says: "He who would not be frustrated of his hope to write well ought himself to be a true poem—not presuming to sing high praises of heroic men and women or famous cities, unless he have in himself the experience and practice of all that which is praiseworthy."

—**And his adversary**—In one of his visions the prophet Zechariah saw God's judgment throne. Before the angel of Jehovah stood the high priest Joshua. At his right hand, ready to accuse him, stood Satan. The high priest was clothed in a filthy garment. At the command of the angel of Jehovah the filthy garment was taken from him and a clean robe put upon him, this act typifying his purification and forgiveness. Then the angel of the Lord said to Joshua: "Thus saith the Lord of hosts; If thou wilt walk in my ways, . . . then thou shalt also judge my house, and shalt also keep my courts, and I will give thee places to walk among these that stand by." (Zech. 3:7.)

The judgment scene in Zechariah is to me a parable of the hindrances and obstacles in the way of the minister's complete consecration to the will of his chosen Lord and Master. As Satan, the adversary, stood at the right hand of Joshua the high priest to oppose his consecration and bring accusation against him, so at the right hand of every young minister about to commence his work there stands an adversary. Satan hath desired to have him that he may sift him as wheat.

—**Loyalty to your**—Dr. David J. Burrell related a story of Norman Macleod. A woman of his parish in Glasgow was fallen sick with a most grievous and contagious sickness. Instead of calling in her own minister she called in the minister of a neighboring parish. After a few moment's conversation, he learned that the woman belonged to Dr. Macleod's parish. In surprise and with a little annoyance he said, "Why in the world did you not call Dr. Macleod?"

The answer was one that only a loyal Scottish parishioner could ever give: "Hoots! mon; we canna spare Normie."

If you love and cherish your minister after that manner, all will be well.

———•••———

—Mother of a—Waiting for God's leading, Bishop Simpson went once to a prayer meeting, thinking in his heart that he ought to speak at the meeting. To his surprise his uncle said to him, "Don't you think you could speak to the people tonight?" That night he made his first Christian address. At once men saw his ability, and he was invited to preach; but still he declined. He was restrained partly by the consideration that he was the only one at home with his widowed mother, and he could not bear the thought of leaving her. But one day he ventured to introduce the subject to his mother. With a smile on her face, and tears in her eyes, his mother said, "My son, I have been looking for this hour ever since you were born."

Simpson used to relate this incident, and always with moving and telling effect, when he was at the height of his fame as a minister.

———•••———

—And prayer—I remember the day an honored servant of God, a well-known minister of Philadelphia, came to see me. He was a man of great devotion and of the highest integrity. But a slanderer always loves a shining mark, and a cruel and altogether false charge had been made against his character. The thing that I recall from that conversation is his saying to me, "I have prayed every day that God would keep me from doing anything that would bring reproach upon Christ or dishonor upon my ministry." A good prayer that, not only for ministers, but for all who profess the name of Christ.

———•••———

—Rewards of a—The poet who wrote the book of Genesis tells how a river went out of Eden to water the garden, and from thence was divided into four heads, and how the first "compasseth the whole land of Havilah, where there is gold; and the gold of that land is good" (2:11-12).

You are going out today into the land of Christian ministry, "where there is gold." You will have to search for it, and dig for it, and toil for it, and suffer for it; but *the gold is there*— "and the gold of that land is good."

———•••———

—And temptation—I think it was Bengel who, at the end of the long day of study, would close his books and say aloud, before going to bed, "Lord, we are on the same old terms." That is the great thing: to keep on terms of intimacy with our Lord and Saviour. That companionship must be the fountain of all our influence. Keep on good terms with Jesus Christ. No minister who does that will fail. Someone, somewhere, both here and hereafter, will rise up to call his name blessed.

MINORITIES

Minorities, since time began—
Have shown the better side of man.
And often in the lists of time
One man has made a cause sublime.[1]

MIRACLE

—The true—Archbishop Trench tells how, in 1690, an agave plant was brought over and planted in the gardens of Hampton Court Palace by Queen Mary. The last ten years of the seventeenth century passed, and the plant gave no sign of flowering. The whole of the eighteenth century passed, and never a bud did the plant put forth. Eighty-eight years of the nineteenth century passed, and still no sign of a flower. But in 1889 the venerable plant burst into blossom.

[1] Paul Laurence Dunbar. Used by permission of the publishers, Dodd, Mead & Company.

Several generations of men might have watched that plant and written learned books about it, and said it was not of the flowering species and that it could never blossom. "And yet they would have been wrong. The blossoming potency was there, latent, slumbering, deep-hidden in its core. It was no miracle, but a long-delayed fulfillment of the law of its being, when it burst into blossom."

The great miracle is God himself. If you grant that, then all is possible.

Admit a God—that mystery supreme!
That cause uncaused! All other wonders cease;
Nothing is marvelous for Him to do;
Deny Him—all is mystery besides.
                    —ARCHBISHOP TRENCH

MIRACLES

—And evidence—Traveling once in a train from Moscow to Warsaw, I fell into conversation with two Americans, one an editor of the Boston *Transcript,* the other a young physician from the state of Washington. The physician happened to refer to an act passed by the legislature of Washington. To me and my companion it seemed an altogether unlikely, and even inconceivable, thing that any legislature should pass such an act; and we insisted that he must be mistaken. When we returned to America, however, we found that the physician was correct—the legislature *had* passed such an act. The fact that I thought the act inconceivable, that it could not have been enacted by any legislature, had nothing to do with the real record of the case. It was a matter of evidence, not of preconceived opinion as to whether the thing was possible or not.

So it is in regard to what we call miracles. Whether you believe, with David Hume, that no miracle has happened, or can happen, or whether you would like to say with Tertullian that there are not difficulties enough for your faith to vanquish and conquer, neither affects the fact of miracles. It is a question of record and evidence.

—And gospel—A long time ago, before the word "modernist" had yet been invented, a celebrated modernist, Jean Jacques Rousseau, made a character in "The Vicar of Savoie" say: "Remove the miracles, and you will have the world at the feet of Jesus Christ." Our liberal friends have reached the conclusion that you cannot preach a supernatural Christ to college students of the "modern mind," and therefore you must build up some theory by which the miracles can be deleted from the Four Gospels. In other words, the liberals, like Rousseau in his day, would bring the world to the feet of Christ by abandoning his miracles.

But you cannot discard the miracles without at the same time destroying the moral authority of Christ as a teacher. The only Christ who existed was the Christ who worked miracles.

—And nature—What is a miracle? Millions of people listened to the voice of King George VI speaking in the venerable Westminster Abbey in London as he took the vows of kingship and promised to uphold the law of the realm and defend the Protestant faith. No doubt many said to another during that day, "The radio is a wonderful thing, isn't it? A miracle." But is the radio—your hearing in Pittsburgh the voice of a man speaking in Westminster Abbey in London—a miracle? No. It is something that takes place by man's using and obeying in the strictest way the laws of nature—the atmosphere, electricity, call it what you please. Many of the things that are popularly spoken of as miracles are things done in strictest obedience to physical laws.

What, then, is a miracle? Here is a good definition of it: "A miracle is an event occurring in the natural world, observed by the senses, produced by divine power, without any adequate human or natural cause, the purpose of which is to reveal the will of God and to do good to man." A wonder, such as the radio or wireless photography, however little the layman may be able to explain it, is an event occurring in the natural world and observed by the senses, and produced by natural causes; whereas the miracle is without natural cause and is produced by the power of God.

—Seeming—We cannot be dogmatic about what may have happened, or what can happen, beyond our field of observation. The Zulu chief would not believe it when his men told him they had come back from England in an iron ship. Who ever heard of iron floating in the water? If fifty years ago a minister standing in a pulpit had made the prediction that within half a century one of his successors would stand in the same pulpit and preach not only to the people gathered together in the church but at the same time to people in New Jersey, Delaware, New York, and even as far away as New Hampshire, Wisconsin, and California, that those people far off could even hear the congregation sing the hymns—if he had said that, had predicted such a thing, his people would have thought him a fit candidate for a madhouse. Yet that very thing, by means of the radio, many preachers are doing any Sunday night.

MISSIONARY

Some years ago the Class of 1876 of Yale presented a building to their alma mater. On that building was to be placed a tablet, and on the tablet was to go the name of that member of the class who, in the judgment of his classmates, best symbolized and embodied their aspirations and ideals. It was a distinguished class. On its roll was William H. Taft, then president of the United States. Among the number were chief justices, merchant princes, heads of railroads and financial institutions, presidents of colleges, poets, and authors. But whose name, think you, was chosen to go on that tablet? It was the name of a member of that class who immediately upon his graduation went out to China as a missionary of Christ, and there in that darkness held up the light of Christ and him crucified.

My mother's church in Great Hamilton Street, Glasgow, had for a church missionary a young man of great industry and great zeal. He had worked his way through the university and the theological seminary, and had also taken a course in medicine. So successful was he in his work that his mission developed into a church where hundreds of young men and young women gathered as early as seven o'clock in the morning to hear him teach the Bible.

One day, at a meeting of the assembly of the Reformed Presbyterian Church of Scotland, the degelates, disappointed at their inability to secure a missionary to join one who had already gone out to the South Seas, cast lots. The result was so indecisive that no one was chosen. But this young student heard a voice saying, "Since none better qualified can be got, rise and offer yourself." Through his last years in the divinity hall the young man had said, "I continually heard the wail of the perishing heathen in the South Seas." So now he resolved to go. All his friends besieged him with their opposition. His minister told him that he had been blessed in his work in Glasgow, and that if he went out to the South Seas he "might fail to be useful and only throw away his life among cannibals." To this he answered that he had only once to die and was content to leave the time and place and the means in the hands of God.

One of his parishioners always ended his protesting arguments by saying, "The cannibals. You will be eaten by cannibals." To this the young man answered, "I confess to you that if I can but live and die, serving and honoring the Lord Jesus, it will make no difference to me whether I am eaten by cannibals or by worms; and in the Great Day my resurrection body will arise as fair as yours in the likeness of our risen Redeemer."

The young man was John G. Paton.

⁂

Here is the testimony of Dr. M. S. Culbertson when he was dying in China in 1862. He had passed through West Point with distinction and had drilled many of the noted officers of the Civil War. Two of his friends told him that if he were now at home he might be a major general commanding great armies. His reply was: "No doubt I might. Men I drilled are in that position. Among these are Sherman, Thomas, Rosecrans. But there is not one with whom I would be willing to exchange. There is no post of influence on earth equal to that of a man who is permitted to give the word of God to four hundred million of his fellow men."

MISSIONS

I want to tell you about the man from Macedonia. He wears every kind of clothing. He has all degrees of education, or the lack of it. Sometimes he is a man of high estate, sometimes a man of low estate. Sometimes this man of Macedonia is a Greek, sometimes a Roman or a Jew or a Frenchman, a German or an Englishman, sometimes an African, sometimes an Indian, sometimes a Korean, a Japanese, a Chinese, a Malay. Some who hunted and searched for the man from Macedonia found him to be a white man; others found him to be a black man; some, a yellow man, and some, a red man. This man from Macedonia speaks every language under the sun. But wherever and whoever he is, whatever his color and whatever his speech, there is one thing about him that is always the same—he is a man who needs help; he needs Christ. Although he speaks so many languages, he has just one speech. Sometimes it is his conscious need which pronounces that speech, sometimes the bitter hostility to Christ and his message; sometimes his sins and follies and crimes pronounce the words. But, wherever you find him, the sentence is the same: "Come over . . . and help us" (Acts 16:9).

⁂

An Englishman who boasted that he did not believe in God once visited the Fiji Islands. As he saw the natives going to church with Bibles in their hands, he exclaimed, "The Bible is no good. Your religion about Christ is false."

To this a simple native teacher answered, "It is a good thing for you that we left our heathenism and cannibalism and took to our Bibles and Christianity, else you would be clubbed, cooked in a native oven, and eaten."

⁂

A few years ago a young graduate in medicine, having finished a postgraduate course in surgery, was offered a position in Philadelphia which meant his successful establishment and his freedom from worry about the support of his wife and two small children. He had made up his mind to accept the offer. But not long afterward, as he was on his knees saying his prayers before he got into bed, he had a vision. Out of what seemed to be a map of Africa there was stretched the arm and hand of a leper, covered with sores and hideous to behold. It was clear to him that the hand was held out for him to clasp. Overcoming his natural loathing and repugnance, he put out his hand to take the hand of the leper.

Instead of settling down in Philadelphia, the young doctor went to Ethiopia and opened a hospital for lepers.

* * *

One St. Thomas Day, on a bridge in London, an unwanted babe was picked up by a kindhearted man. The child was named Thomas Bridges, because he had been picked up on a bridge on St. Thomas Day. After he was educated, he went out as a missionary to Tierra del Fuego. Charles Darwin on his scientific expedition to study the beetle saw what Bridges was doing for the savages and sent him a contribution, saying he formerly had little use for missions, but having witnessed the transformation in the lives of the natives wrought by Thomas Bridges, he was glad to have a part in the work.

* * *

I remember a great many things that my mother told me, but nothing more than this: When she was troubled by the thought of the world's sorrow and pain, and by the thought of so many persons dying without the knowledge of the truth and entering into a Christless eternity, the word that came to her was always this, as if Christ were speaking to her soul: "I gave my life for the world. What are you doing for it?"

MISUNDERSTANDING—*see* JUDGMENT (FALSE)

MONEY—*see also* AVARICE, BEAUTY AND MONEY, COVETOUSNESS

Money has been defined as that something which buys everything but happiness and takes a man everywhere but to heaven. But money used in the right way can confer a great deal of happiness and be the means of starting many a person on the path to heaven. When Saladin died he left directions that his empty hands should be on view outside his coffin. By this he meant to teach that, of all his vast wealth and conquests, he could take nothing with him.

* * *

A man once came to visit Robert Hall, the famous English preacher, to take some exception to a statement the preacher had made in his sermon. Hall saw that the man was in the bondage of love of money. Having sized the man up, Hall took a half sovereign out of his pocket and, opening the Bible, pointed to the word "God."

"Can you see that word?" he said to the man.

"Certainly, I can see it."

Then Hall laid the half sovereign over the word. "Can you see it now?" he asked.

There was no need for the man to answer. It was an unforgettable sermon: Money, the love of it, can hide from the soul of man even the face of God.

MORALS—*see also* RELIGION AND NATIONAL MORALITY

—And education—Edwin Stanton, famous secretary of war under Lincoln, when living in Steubenville, Ohio, refused to let his son go to a night class to which his tutor had invited him, on the ground that his son's morals were paramount to all the education that he could receive. To educate the mind without the heart is to do men more injury than good. It is like putting a repeating revolver in the hands of a savage.

MORGUE

I suddenly found myself in the chamber of the dead. Here, beneath the glass covering, lay the sheeted dead, the real "unknown" dead, but with no poetry or flag, or art of oratory, to commemorate their death. The rolling, tossing sea of humanity and mortality had cast them up on the city's shores. Save that they belonged to the human race, no one knew who they were.

As I stood there I thought, What woman awaited thy coming with a thrill of expectation? And thou, what arms embraced thee in thine infancy? And thou, what ambitious plans were sketched for thy career? What if that father's pride could have seen thee here? And thou, what love was lavished upon thee, and what kisses were bestowed on these now marble lips? Tell me something of your journey. What tempter led thee astray? What infidelity stabbed thy heart? What bitterness made thee life's enemy and life thine enemy? What fair ideals once decorated the chambers of thine imagination? What tears of regret have stained these cheeks? What sighs of remorse once heaved thy now passionless breast? Now, life for thee, in this world, with all its hopes and tears and transient joys, its sins and crimes, is all forever past, and the world looks upon thee through a window of glass.

The very place seemed to mock at life and all its sacred significance; but as I turned, with a cloud of depression upon me, to leave the place, I saw a printed sign on the wall which read as follows: "Gentlemen will remove their hats."

All sorts of people, but most of them from the lower ranks of life, and even from the submerged life of the city, entered that chamber of mortality in search of a friend or an acquaintance. All of them, when they entered, removed their hats. Why? Was it a tribute to these nameless ones—outcasts, criminals, perhaps? No! Not a tribute to them, but a salutation to life and its sacredness. Even these melancholy ruins were sacred, because they were the fallen temples of the human spirit.

MOTHER—*see also* PARENTS, REMORSE AND PARENTS, SORROW (2nd entry)

—A godly—When General Grant's mother died at Jersey City in 1883, he said to the minister who was to officiate at the funeral: "Make no reference to me. She owed nothing to me, to any post I have occupied or any honors that have been paid me. Speak of her just as she was, a pure-minded, simple-hearted, earnest Methodist Christian."

—Gratitude to—Passing through Lancaster recently, I thought of her two most distinguished citizens, men so different in their capacity and characters, James Buchanan, whose beautiful home, Wheatland, is still to be seen, and Thaddeus Stevens, the iron ruler of Congress during the Civil War, who is buried in a cemetery where Negroes can be buried, for the reason, as his epitaph declares, that he might bear witness even in his death to those principles which he had advocated through a long life. Somewhere about Lancaster, too, is the grave of Stevens' mother, who did so much for him when he was a boy in Vermont. As a youth Thaddeus was feeble and lame. His mother resolved that he should not be handicapped in the race of life, and with great sacrifice she gave him the means of an education.

Thinking of what his mother had done for him, Thaddeus Stevens once wrote: "I really think the greatest pleasure of my life resulted from my ability to give my mother a farm of 250 acres and an occasional bright gold piece, which she loved to deposit in the contributor's box of the Baptist church which she always attended." In his will he established a sum, the income of which was forever to be used to plant each springtime "roses and other cheerful flowers" upon her grave. If you should visit that grave on one of these spring days, you would no doubt find blooming there those "roses and other cheerful flowers."

—**A guardian angel**—There is an old tradition that the angel who let Peter out of prison was his mother. Certainly, if such a task is assigned to those who have passed from this world into the world to come, a good mother would qualify for it better than anyone else. And we like to think, at least, that our mothers compass us about and follow us with their prayers, rejoicing over our successes and grieving over our hurts and wounds—grieving most of all when we yield to temptation and turn away from Christ.

—**Influence of**—Napoleon, whose mother, Madame Mere, was one of the strongest of women, said: "My opinion is that the future good or bad conduct of a child depends entirely on its mother."

Let me say to all mothers: Think not that your work and toil and prayers are in vain. They abide with your sons forever. I was reading recently a pamphlet, written by my own mother, called "Mother's Influence." She invokes a spirit which conducts a mother from generation to generation, so that she may behold the influence for good or evil which has come out of her life. Most mothers when they think of their influence on the future stop with the first

generation. But that is just the beginning of it. It goes on from age to age and from generation to generation. At the close of this series of visions, she quotes the words of Peter (II Pet. 3:11): "What manner of persons ought ye to be in all holy conversation and godliness?"

When Alexander the Great entertained the kings and nobles at the court of Persia, he appeared wearing only those garments which had been woven for him by his mother, Olympias, who was the daughter of a chieftain, the wife of a king, and the mother of a conqueror. Long ago we discarded the garments that were made for us by a loving mother's hands; and yet, in a certain sense, as to life and character, we are all still wearing the garments that were woven for us by a mother.

Ian Maclaren—Dr. John Watson—when a boy lost his mother, for whom he had a deep devotion. When she was on her deathbed he made with her some mysterious pact or covenant which he was to keep till they met again in the other world. He used to tell his friends how that sacred treaty and covenant between his mother and himself had often kept him safe when assailed by the temptations of life.

"Since his mother died, he is a different sort of man. I have never known him to pray before, but since his mother died, he kneels down and prays every night."

That sentence, spoken to me by a man's wife, lingered long in my memory. Often, hurrying along the street, or in the quiet of the study, I hear again its echoes; and there rises before me the picture of that unknown man kneeling in prayer. Since his mother died! Before his mother died the man never prayed. Not since he had knelt as a little child at his mother's knee in the long, long ago had he prayed. He had been the manager of hotels where the sporting fraternity resorted, and the world and its ways had won him far from prayer. Not the prayers of his own mother, nor the ups and downs that come to all of us in life, had taught him to pray. But one day his mother died. Since then the man prays. Prayer now seems to be the most natural and most sacred thing that he can do.

There was a woman who had wandered very far from the teachings and example of her Christian home. She was seated at the dinner table, arrayed in the most fashionable and costly style and surrounded by gay and altogether worldly companions, when the butler came up bearing a salver with a note on it. The woman took the note, read it, and immediately excused herself. Presently she came back arrayed in the garb of a waitress—a black dress with white collar and cuffs. Her guests thought that this was a new and novel means of entertainment; but their jokes and laughter soon turned to silence, for the woman said, "I am going home. My mother is dying. She thinks I am a waitress." Then, sweeping the company with scorn, contempt, and remorse, she added, "And would to God I were!"

Said Henry Ward Beecher concerning the influence on him of the sorrows and sufferings of his mother: "Now you may put all the skeptical men that ever lived on the face of the earth on one side, and they may plead in my ears. And all the scientists may stand with them, and marshal all the facts of the universe to disprove the truth of Immanuel, God with us; and yet, let me see my mother, walking in a great sorrow, but from the surface of which sorrow reflecting the

light of cheer and heavenly hope, patient, sweet, gentle, full of comfort for others —yea, and showing by her life as well as her lips that with the consolation wherewith she has been comforted, she is comforting others—and that single instance of suffering is more to me, as an evidence of the truth of Christianity, than all the arguments that the wisest men can possibly bring against it."

—Inscriptions for—I once received a telegram from a committee in charge of erecting in their church a memorial window to the memory of my mother. The telegram asked me for a suitable inscription. Without a moment's hesitation I telegraphed this inscription—"Her children arise up, and call her blessed" (Prov. 31:28).

What could surpass the beauty and tenderness of the sentence which Thomas Gray wrote for the resting place of his mother? In the old churchyard at Stoke Poges, hard by the elm and yew beneath which Gray wrote the matchless "Elegy," you can read today these words: "In the same pious confidence, beside her friend and sister, here sleep the remains of Dorothy Gray, widow, the careful and tender mother of many children, one of whom alone had the misfortune to survive her."

On the grave of Phillips Brooks's mother is the verse put there by her sons: "O woman, great is thy faith: be it unto thee even as thou wilt" (Matt. 15:28).

—Memory of—In his *Journal,* in the entry for February 28, 1854, soon after his mother's death, Carlyle tells of a vision he had of the old home, Main Hill, with mother, father, and the others getting dressed for church: "They are all gone now, vanished all their poor bits of thrifty clothes, their pious struggling efforts, their little life—it is all away, it has all melted into the still sea, it was rounded with a sleep. Oh, pious mother, kind, good, brave, and truthful soul, as I have ever found, and more than I have elsewhere found in this world, your poor Tom, long out of his school days now has fallen very lonely, very lame and broken in this pilgrimage of his, and you cannot help him or cheer him any more. But from your grave yonder in Ecclefechan churchyard you bid him trust in God, and that also he will try, if he can understand, and do."

I stood one day in sanctifying memories by the grave of my sainted mother. Suddenly I was conscious of the presence of another. Turning about, I saw a stranger standing near. As he seemed to be waiting for me to speak, I said to him, "Friend, who art thou? And why dost thou intrude upon my sacred memories and reflections?"

At that he answered, with a note of impatience in his voice, "Do you not know me? I am the king of terrors!"

"The king of terrors? I see nothing terrible about thee."

"No, you see nothing terrible about me; for where men and women live and die as this woman lived and died, there I have no terrors at my command. My authority has vanished. But where men have lived in selfishness, or impurity, or strife and hatred, where they have lived for this present world and for the things of this world, and where they have lived without God and without hope, there it is that I rear my throne and dress it with such terrors as are at my command. But here I have no power and no terrors. Mortal, blessed and happy in thy memories of the sainted dead, I leave thee in peace."

—Prayers of—A well-known minister once told me how one of his classmates at Yale, also a well-known minister, came to enter the ministry.

When they were students at Yale a great revival broke out, and many were taking a stand for Christ and the Christian life. This one man appeared to be untouched by the sacred influence; he made no profession of faith and showed no interest in the revival. Long after they had both become ministers, his friend asked him how it was that he had gone into the ministry, especially since he was one of the few students who had not been moved by the revival which swept the college when they were at Yale.

His answer was the story of a mother's prayers. He related how he had been greatly affected and moved by the revival, but steeled himself against it, chiefly on the ground that if he yielded and confessed his faith he would likely become a minister. After he left Yale, he went south to Georgia and entered the law office of a noted Southern lawyer. He tried to put out of his mind all thoughts of the Christian life and the Christian ministry. He progressed so well in his law studies, and was so highly thought of, that his employer proposed to take him abroad for a trip, and when they returned to have him enter his office as his partner.

But one day the young lawyer received a letter from his father far off in New England, telling him that his sister and his mother had died, and that when his mother died her last request was that the father should tell their son that she died praying for his conversion. When he got this letter he went out into the pine forest and, sitting down beneath a tree there, fought his lonely battle. The issue was that he determined to confess his faith in Christ and enter the Christian ministry. He gave up his bright career in the law, returned to the divinity school at Yale, and shortly afterward was ordained as a minister. Before he was ordained, however, there was a baptism to be administered in the little church which he was serving. He had a friend, an ordained minister, come over to take that part of the service which he was not yet licensed to perform. As this old man, his friend and a friend of his father and mother, stood before the parents and their babe, he said: "I am thinking today of a scene long ago. I see a handsome man and a beautiful wife coming up the aisle with their babe in the father's arms. As I prepared to ask the questions and administer the sacrament, the mother handed me a card on which was written the name of the child, the date of his birth, and underneath, 'Given to God and to the gospel ministry.' That child," he concluded, "is now your minister."

———————

Cardinal Vaughn, one of eight sons to enter the priesthood, brother of three sisters to enter holy orders, used to say that his mother in her prayers for her children never once asked for them a temporal blessing, but always spiritual blessings—the prosperity of the soul, not the prosperity of this world.

———————

Men come near to God when they pray for others. A well-known minister of the last generation said that his mother and two other mothers in the vicinity of his boyhood home made a pact that they would meet together on one day of every week and pray for the salvation of their children. One by one, those children came into the Kingdom of God, until this afterwards distinguished minister made his confession of faith and completed the number. What sacred objectives for intercession do fathers and mothers have set before them!

———————

She has long since gone to her reward; but my mind now runs back to the old home on the banks of the river, and I can see the room which was her trysting place with God, where at a certain hour of the forenoon she was wont to kneel in intercession for the salvation of her children.

Truly our mother's works do follow her, now that she herself rests from her labors; and not the least potent and the least blessed among those works is the daily influence of her prayers on our behalf. No rude clamor of the world can altogether dim the sweet reverberation of her prayers in the minds of her children; and if the base solicitations of the world should ever be heeded and obeyed by her children, it will be in spite of, and not because of, a mother's earnest prayers.

———————

Dr. McCosh, president of Princeton, had a custom of praying with members of the senior class ere he bade them farewell as they went out into the world. When he asked a certain young man to kneel and pray with him, the man responded that he did not believe in God and did not believe in prayer. Hurt and astonished, the president shook hands with him and bade him farewell.

Some years afterward Dr. McCosh was delivering a course of lectures in Cincinnati. Before going to the lecture hall he was sitting in the exchange of the hotel. A man came and sat down beside him and said, "What is this, Dr. McCosh, I hear about your turning out infidels at Princeton?" Surprised, Dr. McCosh asked him what he meant? The man then gave the history of the student who had refused to pray with Dr. McCosh, saying that he had advanced to an important post in the schools of Cincinnati, and that everywhere he was sowing the seeds of unbelief and infidelity.

"But," the man added, "he has a godly, praying mother, and I believe that in the end she will win."

A year or two later Dr. McCosh was in his study at Princeton when a young man appeared with his wife. He said to Dr. McCosh: "You do not remember me, but I am the student who refused to let you pray with him. I thought that I was an unbeliever, and wherever I could I sowed the seeds of unbelief; but all the time my godly mother was praying for me. Her prayers have won. I am here in Princeton to enter the theological seminary, and before I go I want you to kneel down with me and offer that long-postponed prayer."

—**Stepmother**—I had tried often to find him but had always failed. No address . . . Out of town . . . Moved . . . I had about given him up as one of those persons on your church roll that you never get to know or even to see, who are lost in the vast crowd of the city. This winter night I was passing his latest number. I thought to myself, I will try once more. The maid who answered my ring took my name and said she would see if he was in, but she thought not; he was always out of an evening. The same old story, I thought to myself. But soon I heard a man's footsteps on the stairs, and we stood face to face, each with a look of nonrecognition on his face. I introduced myself.

"Will you come up to my room?"

"Thank you."

I followed him up one, two, three flights of stairs. He was well on in years, and I noted that he breathed heavily. I went slowly and pretended to be exhausted myself, lest I should cause him to overtax his strength. On the top floor we entered his room, a large, well-lighted front room, more like a living room than a bedroom, with photographs on the wall—all faces of education and refinement. There were pieces of furniture that evidently did not belong to that house, but must have come from his own home of former days.

We sat together for a little, and soon he began to tell me about his daughter and his son in the army in France. He showed me their photographs. Something led me to speak of his parents and his place of birth, trying hard, as ministers always do, to get the man placed, environed. Rising from his chair, he went to the wall and, taking down a small framed photograph, handed it to me. I carried it over to the lamp on the desk that I might have a better view. It was the picture of an elderly woman, in the simple garb of the Friends—kind, strong, faithful, intelligent, and, above all, Christian.

"Your mother?"

"No, my stepmother, but the only mother I ever knew."

Then, after silently looking at the picture, he said, "That woman had no faults."

—**Tribute to**—Among the royal tombs of Westminster there is one tomb of unusual interest. It is the costly sarcophagus of Mary, Queen of Scots, of tragic memories. When her son James—James I of England and James VI of Scotland—came to the throne, one of the first acts of his reign was to exhume the body of his beheaded mother and give it the resting place of a queen among the tombs of the Abbey.

—**Wesley's**—The real power in the Wesley household was the remarkable mother, now forever famous as "The Mother of the Wesleys." A review of the great reformers shows that some of them had weak or indifferent fathers, but that all of them had strong, God-fearing, and, in some cases, gifted mothers. To his mother John Wesley owed his logic, piety, and orderliness. If somewhat lacking in feminine grace and affection, she was a woman of dignity, determination, and intellect. She was the twenty-fifth daughter of Dr. Annesley, the "St. Paul of Nonconformity."

Her system of educating her many children was unique. At one year they were taught to fear the rod and to cry softly. Speech, play, work, habits—everything in the child's life was carefully regulated. She believed that the first thing to be done with a child was to conquer its will. At five years the child was taught its letters, and the next day it commenced to read the first chapter of Genesis.

MOTHERHOOD—*see* MARY OF THE "SISTINE MADONNA"

MOTHER'S BIBLE

There are those among you who recall godly fathers and mothers. Yet you never think of them in terms of money, whether they left you much or little, or nothing at all. If they left you the imprint of their character and their prayers, and the memory of their daily godly life, that is an inheritance incorruptible, undefiled, that fadeth not away. The money which they left you may have disappeared long ago, but the influence of their godly example is an ever-present reality and power.

Once, in a Virginia church, I saw an aged minister hold aloft a little black book and tell the congregation that all the money in the world could not purchase that book. It was not the book itself that was so valuable, for it was an inexpensive volume, and its contents could be had in thousands of similar books throughout the world. What made it priceless to him was the fact that it was the Bible that his mother, now in heaven, had put into his trunk when he left home to go to college. Silver and gold she had none, but she had left him the memory of her faith and her prayers.

MOTHER'S LOVE

An officer of the Confederate army tells in his *Recollections* of how, on his way home after the sunset at Appomattox, he saw, sitting in the seat across from him, a frail, withered, hard-worked woman dressed in faded calico, with a sunbonnet on her head. She held by the hand a young man who had lost his sight from a wound received in battle. Not only was the light of the eye quenched—the light of the mind was also quenched. From her home away down in Texas the mother had come to Virginia to take her now sightless and idiotic boy back home. She had sent him forth full of energy and hope and enthusiasm. And the war had returned to her—a sightless idiot. But he was her son.

A noble example, that, of the mother's love that many waters cannot quench, neither can the floods drown!

No one ever read Victor Hugo's *Notre Dame* without being moved and purified and cleansed in heart at that marvelous scene where the demented mother, who has been searching over all Europe for her child, long years before stolen by the gypsies, matches the shoe she carries with the shoe the maid has carried all the years about her neck, and discovers her long-lost child. The heavenliness of her joy, and the terribleness of her anger and grief when her daughter is again dragged from her, exhibit perhaps as well as anything that was ever written the strange and awful powers of human love.

God sent an angel down from heaven to find the most beautiful thing on earth and bring it back to heaven. When the angel saw the flowers at springtime he said, "These must be the most beautiful things on earth"; and he gathered them up to take with him back to heaven. Then he met a child of wondrous beauty and golden hair and lovely smile. When he saw the child he said, "This must be the most wonderful thing on earth. Nothing could be sweeter than the smile of that innocent child."

But farther along, in a remote valley, he came to a humble cottage where a mother sat in the doorway with her little babe on her lap. As he watched her tender and beautiful care for the little babe, he said, "This must be the fairest thing on earth. I will take that mother's love back with me to heaven."

When he reached the portals of heaven the flowers had faded and were dead, the smile on the child's face had changed into a scowl—but the mother's love was unchanged.

MUSIC—*see also* HEART (ITS MUSIC), WORSHIP (SINGING IN)

On a visit to Bergen in Norway I saw in a park a monument to the great Norwegian violinist Ole Bull. The great minstrel stands playing his violin while a savage holding a lyre bows before him. The statue is meant to symbolize the fact that "music hath charms to soothe a savage breast." Ever since the days of Jubal, the father of all who handle the harp and the organ, mankind has felt the power of music. Are not the great chapters of man's life opened and closed with music? There is music when he is born, when he is married, and even at his death.

N

NAPOLEON

On the banks of the Seine, in the very heart of Paris, beneath a gilded dome rest the ashes of the restless Napoleon. Old banners, yellow with age, grimy with the smoke of battle, and rent with shot and shell, stand like sentinels about the tomb of him whose conquests they proclaimed. The names of his battles are cut in the marble walls which surround the sarcophagus—Marengo, Austerlitz, the Pyramids, Lodi, Jena. Men from all nations come and go and look with awe upon the box of stone which contains the dust of him whose armies overran the world. Through heavy windows of yellow glass the sunlight streams in upon the silent chamber as if to represent the effulgence of immortal fame.

But there is a light that never shines there, a light that never shone in the face of him whose dust reposes there. You look down upon him and think of the only woman who loved him and sacrificed to his ambitions; you think of the company of his admirers and flatterers and satelites, but not of his friends.

You think of him standing on his lone rock in the waters of the south Atlantic and wondering if anyone in the world loves him. You think of the trail of blood and bones which marked his advance and retreat over Europe, Africa, and Asia. The light of power, the light of military genius, the light of adulation; but not a ray of that only light which, when all other lights have gone out, abides to cheer and bless. No light of the Lamb, no light of self-sacrificing love, shines over that marvelous tomb.

But I could take you, and you could take me, to some quiet acre of God where beneath a modest stone, with no wondering throngs pressing to gaze upon it, sleeps the dust of one whose influence is unending, whose companionship abides forever, and whose light never goes out—because it was a life that followed in the footsteps of the Lamb.

Napoleon was himself a prophet of the passing away of his own empire and of the perpetual reign of Christ. Standing on his rock prison in the Atlantic, and contemplating his approaching end, Napoleon thus soliloquized:

"I die before my time. My body will be given back to the earth to be done with as men please and to become the food of worms. Such will be the fate of him who has been called the Great Napoleon. What an abyss between my deep misery and the external Kingdom of Christ, which is proclaimed, loved and adored, and is extending over the whole earth!"

NATIONS—*see* HISTORY AND JUDGMENT

NATURE—*see also* FLOWERS, SPRINGTIME

In his life of David Hume, Huxley has an eloquent passage in which he describes Hume's tomb on the eastern slope of Calton Hill, looking down on Edinburgh, where, he says, "one may meditate undisturbed upon the epitome of nature and man, the kingdoms of this world spread out before him." "Surely," he continues, "there is a fitness in the choice of this last resting place by the philosopher and historian who saw so clearly that these two kingdoms form but one realm, governed by uniform laws and alike based on impenetrable darkness and eternal silence."

We reject both Huxley's and Hume's conception of the universe, but there is something in what Huxley says about the silence of the natural world as to God. Perhaps the best that we can do, as far as God and the natural world are concerned, is to say, with always deep, original, and helpful Pascal, that "the world only gives indication of the presence of a God who conceals Himself."

On a hot summer afternoon or evening, worn with the burdens of the day and weary of the noise and grind and dust and odors of the city, you may have gone out into the beautiful country which lies like a lover's arm around the smoking and distraught city.

What a new and different world it is! As you enter it the soul seems to come to its own once more. Like great billows of the ocean after the storm has subsided, the hills rise and fall and roll away to the distant horizon as far as the eye can range. On the summits, and extending down the sides of these hills, are the oak forests with their deep green; and in the valleys, the fields sweet with new-mown hay, or here and there the tender green of winter wheat, or oats or rye; in the meadows, knee-deep in daisies, the cattle graze, and here and there sheep rest under the shade of the trees; even black, unpainted barns look not unsightly in this sea of green.

On some hilltop there is the tower and spire of a church; and, here and there, with a pine tree or two in front of it, a square brick house facing the world as honestly as did the godly pioneers who once dwelt there, and whose industry and piety made this country great. Over all is a veil of blue haze, soft as God's mercy—a symbol of infinity. Here the soul comes to its own. Here it is easier to forget the injury, to dry the tears of sorrow, to face our troubles and temptations, and to hunger and thirst anew after the Kingdom of God.

NEW YEAR—*see* TIME (NEW YEAR)

NIGHT

I have noticed in reading of the disasters which befall airplanes that the great majority of them happen by night, in spite of intricate instruments and signals flashing along the route of the plane. If a survey were made of the lives of those who have met spiritual and moral shipwreck, it would undoubtedly show that the great majority of them commenced their downward course in the night. They, too, were victims of the night.

Midnight on the St. Lawrence River. In the darkness, barge after barge loaded with British soldiers floated silently down the broad river. As they were nearing their destination, the commander of the army, Wolfe, recited to the officers of his staff these lines of Thomas Gray:

The curfew tolls the knell of parting day,
The lowing herd winds slowly o'er the lea,
The plowman homeward plods his weary way,
And leaves the world to darkness and to me.

When he had finished the stanzas, he told his officers he would rather be the author of that poem than win the battle with the French on the morrow.

By a mountain path the army made its ascent in the darkness from the river to the Plains of Abraham. When the sun began to shine the morning of September 13, 1759, its rays were reflected upon the bayonets and cannon of the English army. The French army fought well and courageously all that day; but their courage and their heroism, and that of their gallant commander, Montcalm, were all in vain. The battle had been irrevocably lost by night. An empire, a kingdom, the dominion of North America, had been lost by night. It was not the first, and not the last, time that a battle and a kingdom were lost by night.

Belshazzar lost his kingdom at night. He fell a victim to the sins of the night. One night did the fatal business for this young king of Babylon. One night has done the fatal business for many another young man.

In Philadelphia sometime ago the courts had a peculiar case of a man who was adjudged sane by day but insane by night. That would seem to be true of not a few in the world about us today. Sometimes the mistakes and errors of the night suggest and demand the sins of the day. Lawless acts of the day are committed to cover up and meet the demands of the sins of the night.

Night life has played its part, and a chief part, in the downfall of many a trusted employee. The stealings and dishonest transactions of the day are carried out to cover up the losses of the night. God knows there are enough sins by day, but many of them are the lineal descendants of the sins of the night. The true epitaph for many a man who has made shipwreck of his career, and cast away his kingdom, and who now lies dissceptered and uncrowned, is this: "In that night he was slain." Every night, in every city, immortal souls, made for fellowship with God, made for the purple robe of honor and the scepter of right and the throne of influence, are stained, marred, broken, slain, lost. O night watchman! O policeman! O physician! O nurse! O priest! O minister! O magistrate! O father or mother! O sister or wife! What if thy lips could open and tell of the tragedies of the night!

NO

Some time ago the editor of one of our magazines which specialize in word study asked a small number of distinguished writers to answer the following questions:

1. What word to you in English seems the most beautiful in sound?
2. What English word seems to you the most useful in the language?
3. What word to you seems the most annoyingly used or misused?

In answer to the first question, seeking the most beautiful word, some of the old favorites were given, among them the musical word "Mesopotamia." This is the word the great English actor Garrick wished he could pronounce the way the famous preacher George Whitefield pronounced it. Nearly all agreed that the most misused word is "Yes," and nearly all voted that the most useful word in the language is "No."

The late United States senator from Massachusetts, and one of the noblest characters the Senate has known, George F. Hoar, in his *Autobiography* tells of his college days at Harvard in the early forties. He pays a high tribute to one of the faculty, Dr. James Walker, who frequently preached in the college chapel. He says that the ticking of the clock in the chapel was inaudible when the chapel was empty, but it ticked out clear and loud upon the strained ears of the students as they waited for the next sentence from the preacher.

Among the sermons which Hoar recalled after sixty years was one which he says no hearer could forget to the day of his death. It was on the text, "Thou shalt say, No." I can hardly hope for a like impression. I can hardly dare to expect that fifty years from tonight this text will sound in the memory and conscience of some young man or woman who hears the sermon tonight. Yet it may be that the easily remembered words of this text will be used of God to strengthen and fortify a life and to turn a soul back from temptation.

General Grant, describing his able and faithful chief of staff, General John Rawlins, says of him that to a request he felt should not be granted he knew how to say No in such a manner that the request was never repeated. To be able to do that is an important equipment, not only for a staff officer in war, but for all of us in the battle of life.

NURSES

In his recital of the adventures of Martin Chuzzlewit, Charles Dickens gives us a picture of the nurse of his day in the person of Sairey Gamp:

"She was a fat old woman, this Mrs. Gamp, with a husky voice and a moist eye, which she had a remarkable power of turning up, and only showing the white of it. Having very little neck, it cost her some trouble to look over herself, if one may say so, at those to whom she talked.

"She wore a very rusty black gown, rather the worse for snuff, and a shawl and bonnet to correspond. In these dilapidated articles of dress she had, on principle, arrayed herself, time out of mind, on such occasions as the present; for this at once expressed a decent amount of veneration for the deceased, and invited the next of kin to present her with a fresher suit of weeds; an appeal so frequently successful, that the very fetch and ghost of Mrs. Gamp, bonnet and all, might be seen hanging up, any hour in the day, in at least a dozen of the second hand clothes shops of about Holborn.

"The face of Mrs. Gamp—the nose in particular—was somewhat red and swollen, and it was difficult to enjoy her society, without becoming conscious of a smell of spirits. Like most persons who have attained to great eminence in their profession, she took to hers very kindly, so that, setting aside her natural predilections as a woman, she went to a lying-in or laying-out with equal zest and relish."

That is a great scene in *Middlemarch* where the dying miser, Peter Featherstone, makes a vain effort to destroy one of two wills which he had drafted—the one which was unjust to those he left behind him. He asks the woman attending him to take his key and open the strong box and burn one of the wills. Deaf alike to coaxings and to threats, she refuses to touch his key or his money. The morning light comes through the window and finds the old man dead on the pillows, his bony hand clutching the key. At the last he wished to write a new will and destroy the old, but death intervened and made that forever impossible. In the court the unjust will was filed for probate.

Behind us here and in front of us yonder, in the hands of the judge, we leave when death comes a disposition of heart and a record of thoughts and deeds which cannot be mended or altered in the least degree.

O

OBEDIENCE

I can recall my father sometimes saying, when he wanted the lawn mowed or the horse harnessed, that if he had one son instead of four he might get something done around the place.

We judge from the parable of our Lord that a disobedient son was a very ancient trial. The father in the parable had a vineyard. The time had come to irrigate it, to cultivate it, and to prune it. So he said to one of his sons, "Son, go work to day in my vineyard." (Matt. 21:28.) He answered, All right, father; I'll go. But he went not. Then the father said to the second son, "Son, go work to day in my vineyard." He answered, I will not! I have done my share of work in that vineyard. Let my older brother take his share of it! I am through with

the vineyard. And with that, he jammed his hat on his head, slammed the door, and walked out on the street.

OFFENSE, TAKING

In the book of Judges we have the story of Gideon's pursuit of the routed army of the Midianites, clear across the fords of the Jordan. In the heat and excitement of the campaign, for some reason the Ephraimites who dwelt on the other side of the Jordan had not been called. They had taken only a minor part in the campaign. When Gideon returned from his great victory, instead of saluting him for delivering Israel out of the hands of the Midianites, the men of Ephraim chided him sharply, and said, "Why hast thou served us thus, that thou calledst us not, when thou wentest to fight with the Midianites?" (Judg. 8:1.) Fortunately, Gideon was a man of self-control, and knew the wisdom of, "A soft answer turneth away wrath" (Prov. 15:1); so he said to the men of Ephraim, "What have I done now in comparison of you? Is not the gleaning of the grapes of Ephraim better than the vintage of Abi-ezer?" In other words, "The part that you have played in this campaign is just as important as the part that I have played."

How true that bit of Old Testament history is to present life! How modern it is! In every campaign, and especially in the life of the Church, there are always men of Ephraim who have to be pacified, who take unwarranted offense, whose feelings are hurt, whose pride is offended, when no offense is meant.

OLD AGE—*see also* CONVERSION IN OLD AGE, COURAGE IN OLD AGE

I saw in an illustrated English paper the drawing of one of the charges of the British troops. It shows the men rushing forward, amid the smoke and bursting shell, over the shell craters and through the wire. In the foreground lies a wounded officer. But he has lifted himself on his elbow and with his free arm is cheering his comrades on to victory. He is out of it, done for, but he thinks not of that; he thinks of the foe, of the cause, of victory.

Happy are the aged who, when time carries them off the field, can leave with a cheer for those who with unabated strength are pressing on to meet the foe. These are they of whom the psalmist sang, in the old Scottish version:

And in old age when others fade,
They fruit still forth shall bring;
They shall be fat and full of sap,
And aye, be flourishing.

OPPORTUNITY—*see also* DECISION, RECONCILIATION, REPENTANCE

—And affection—In the nave of the Abbey Kirk at Haddington you will see a grave with this inscription over it: "In her bright existence she had more sorrows than are common but also a soft invincibility, a capacity of discernment, and a noble loyalty of heart which are rare. For forty years she was the true and loving helpmate of her husband, and by act and word unweariedly forwarded him as none else could in all of worthy that he did or attempted. She died at London, 21st April, 1866, suddenly snatched from him, and the light of his life as if gone out."

It is the inscription upon the grave of Jane Carlyle. In truth she was the light of Carlyle's life; but, if we are to judge by the pathetic entries in his diary, he never realized that fact until she was snatched from him and the light of his life was as if gone out. In all literature there is nothing more moving than these words of Carlyle taken from his diary after a visit to the grave of his wife: "Cherish what is dearest while you have it near you, and wait not till it is far away. Blind and deaf that we are; oh, think, if thou yet love anybody living, wait not till death sweep down the paltry little dust clouds and dissonances of the moment, and all be at last so mournfully clear and beautiful when it is too late.

———

There is a very old and very impressive story of a youth greatly beloved who died. In the next life he besought the gods to let him return to this world for just one day, a day that was one of the least notable, one of the most ordinary, days of his past life. The gods granted his request; and he appeared again, just as he had been at the age of fifteen, in his old home. As he entered the living room his mother passed him, engaged upon some household task. Then he stepped out into the yard; and his father, busy with some work and carrying tools in his hand, gave him an indifferent glance and passed on. Then the youth awoke to the fact that we are all dead, that we are only really alive when we are conscious of the treasure we have in our friends and loved ones. A piercing parable of truth! And if that is so, that we are only really alive when we are conscious of our treasures, then how often we are dead!

Acts of kindness, words of appreciation, ministries of affection, have their Now, their Today; and to say, "When I have a more convenient season" to these great opportunities is to bid them depart from you.

> *I did not know how short your day*
>   *would be!*
> *I had you safe, and words could*
>   *wait awhile—*
> *And yet . . . your eyes begged ten-*
>   *derness of me,*
> *Behind their smile.*
>
> *And now for you, so dark, so long,*
>   *is night!*
> *I speak, but on my knees, un-*
>   *heard, alone—*
> *What words were these to make a*
>   *short day bright—*
> *"If I had known! Ah, love—if*
>   *I had known!"* [1]

—**And education**—I got off a train at Baltimore one night to send a telegram. The operator had a copy of the *Iliad* lying beside his telegram pads; and, be-

[1] Ruth Guthrie Harding, in *A Lark Went Singing and Other Poems.*

tween the periods of sending dispatches of business and sorrow and joy and love and death over the wires with deft fingers, his eyes perused the Greek words, and he was hearing across the seas and continents, yea, across the ages—it may be before Shamgar judged in Israel— the music of the great voice, the winged words of Homer, the shock of his battles, the thunderbolts of his gods, the cries of his heroes, the roar of his ocean.

—**And the Holy Spirit**—On the walls of the Sistine Chapel in Rome, together with the prophets and the apostles, you can see the sibyls which Michelangelo painted there to show the preparation for the coming of Christ in the pagan world.

The sibyls, like the prophets in the Old Testament, were supposed in the pagan world to have the power of predicting the future. One of the sibyls offered her nine books for sale to the proud Tarquin, legendary founder of Rome, when he consulted her. Tarquin refused the offer. Whereupon, the sibyl burned three of the books and offered him the six that remained. Again Tarquin refused. The sibyl then destroyed three more books and offered Tarquin the remaining three.

Alarmed that the three had been offered him at the same price as the six and the nine, Tarquin consulted the augurs. At their advice he purchased the remaining books, which were put in a chest of stone and kept underground in the capitol, forever guarded. These books became the guide of Rome. But priceless information had been lost with the books which had been rejected and destroyed.

There is profound spiritual truth in that legend of Tarquin and the sibyl. Not a legendary sibyl but the Holy Spirit of God offers us in our time those things which belong to our peace. Every rejection shortens the day of opportunity, and with every refusal man's heart becomes less responsive.

———— • • • ————

It was shortly before America entered the first World War. I took the text, "An Angel's Chance" because I deemed it an appropriate theme for the New Year. At the close of the sermon, in which I expressed the hope and confidence that there was at least one present who would be influenced by the sermon, I announced that we would have a brief aftermeeting in the chapel.

Quite a company went from the church into the chapel, among them a distinguished professor in the law school of the University of Pennsylvania, his wife, and a friend of the family who was visiting them. He was a young man whose parents were honored missionaries in the Balkans. He was a graduate, not many years before, of Princeton University; but he had never made a confession of his faith.

His friends were quite surprised when he expressed a willingness to go with them into the chapel for the aftermeeting. I, too, was somewhat surprised to see him there. Alas, how often we preachers are of little faith! But when, after a brief period of prayer, I gave the invitation, and asked if there was anyone present who desired to make use of the Angel's Chance and start the year with Christ, this young man was the first to rise up. Today he is at the head of an important Christian school in Greece.

———— • • • ————

As a boy I used to like to read the story of Ali Baba and the Forty Thieves —how the man who had the mystic words "Open sesame" got into the cavern filled with treasure, and then went from one door to another and from one chamber to another. So the open door that Christ sets before us leads to other doors and to higher chambers of usefulness.

When we obey God and open the door that he sets before us, then he will open another door unto us.

———— • • • ————

—Lost—Hartley Coleridge was the gifted son of the great poet. He had an unfortunate career at Oxford, where he lost his fellowship. Once on a visit to his home at Grassmere he chanced to pick up a schoolbook that had been given him long before. He glanced through it, and then wrote on the fly leaf: "Only seventeen years have passed over me since this book was given to me. Then all looked forward with hope and joy to what I was to become. Now every mother prays that her lamb, every father hopes that his boy, will never be what I have become."

———— • • • ————

Once after the evening service, as I was passing down the steps of the church to the street, I saw quite a group assembled on the sidewalk, as if waiting for me. When I drew near to them, I noticed that whenever one of them moved there was the sound as of the clanking of fetters. When one put up his hand to his hat to greet me, again I heard the clank of fetters. In amazement I asked them, "Who are you? And what mean these clanking chains on your arms, on your ankles?"

Then one of them answered, "We are the souls in prison—some chained with the chain of fear, some with the chain of doubt, some with the chain of hatred, some with the chain of anger, some with the chain of unbelief, some with the chain of lust and unclean desire. But there was a time when in the church we saw a light, and heard a Voice, and the Angel of God smote us and said, 'Arise, and follow me!' But we did not heed his light, or his blow, or his voice. Our hour has passed, our opportunity disappeared. Still, tonight, we who might once have been free are in the prison and wear these chains and fetters."

—And preaching—Driving down the Georgia coast a few years ago, without any particular reason for doing so I turned aside from the main highway and, driving through the marshes celebrated in the songs of Sidney Lanier, crossed over to St. Simon's Island, an enchanting spot washed by the waves of the Atlantic and shaded by immense live oaks. I had heard that John Wesley had preached beneath an oak tree on this island when he was in Georgia. Remembering that the oak was in the old churchyard, I entered the quiet acre so that I might stand beneath that historic tree. Walking along the path by the graves, I was suddenly arrested by the sight of a familiar name. I stopped in surprise and read the name and dates again, to make sure. But there was no mistake. There it was —Lucien Lamar Knight, one of my classmates in the seminary. Long after the time when most men enter the ministry he felt the urge to preach the gospel, gave up a lucrative post as associate of the celebrated Henry Grady on the *Atlanta Constitution,* and entered theological seminary. There his notable gifts were remarked by all, and everyone predicted for him a brilliant and useful career in the ministry. But an unfortunate marriage wrecked his career as a preacher and led him to resign from the ministry. He gave himself to historical studies, and was for a time state historian of Georgia. On his grave was an eloquent epitaph which he himself had prepared, speaking not of himself but of his desire to sleep in those beautiful and historic surroundings, which recalled to me the accents of his silvery tongue as I remembered him preaching in his seminary days.

To me there was something deeply moving, stirring, and arresting in my coming suddenly upon the grave of a classmate on the lonely and remote island. It seemed as if the hand of Providence had turned me aside from the main road and the beaten highway southward and brought me to this island grave of my old friend under the shadow of the mournful oaks. Standing there, I thought of the eloquent tongue now stilled in that grave, and these words came to me: "There is . . . a time to keep silence, and a time to speak" (Eccles. 3:7). I did not think of them in the way they are usually taken—a time when speech is silver and silence is golden. What I thought was that there is a time when we *can* speak, when we *ought* to speak, and also a time when we cannot speak even if we would. My friend and classmate had come to a time when, so far as this life was concerned, he could speak no longer. It was not strange, then, that this sudden coming on his resting place on that lonely island should have filled me with a new desire to speak more earnestly in the great accents of the gospel while I have the opportunity and while it is called Today.

—And reconciliation—In one of the galleries of the Louvre there hangs a double painting which appeals to far more eyes and hearts than many a far-famed Ascension or Transfiguration. In the first painting is an outraged father with uplifted hand, ordering the wicked son from the paternal door. In the background cower the weeping mother and the sisters and brothers. The second scene shows the same cottage and the same humble room and the same father and mother and brothers and sisters. But the father lies still upon the bed, the aloofness of death upon his face. At the side of the bed, with her face buried in her hands, kneels the mother with her children. The cottage door has just been flung open, and the returning prodigal stands with his foot on the sill and his hand on the door, as if he has been smitten into stone. He has come too late. Both father and son have waited too long. Now the father cannot speak the words of forgiveness and the son can find no place for repentance, though he seeks it carefully and with tears.

—And repentance—"Arise, let us be going!" (Matt. 26:46.) The three disciples had failed miserably in the task assigned to them: when they might have watched with Christ they had slept, and that hour was gone forever. But then Christ spoke, not of the past, but of the present and the future. There was still a duty which could be done, still an opportunity to serve him; poorly as they had prepared themselves for it, there was yet a chance for them to do something for Christ.

The words of Jesus, "Sleep on" (Matt. 26:45), are words of condemnation. They speak of the irrevocable past! But his words, "Arise, let us be going" are words of invitation and of opportunity. God in his grace and mercy, although he shuts doors in the past, opens new doors for us in the future. Had he said only "Sleep on," hopeless would be our condition. But he said also "Arise." What if God let us depart from him and never called us back to him again? What if he let us sin, but did not call us to repentance? What if he said "Sleep on" concerning the duties, the responsibilities of the past, and opened no door of hope with his great "Arise"? But in his love and mercy, God gives us another chance.

One of the old Saxon kings set out with an army to put down a rebellion in a distant province of his kingdom. When the insurrection had been quelled and the army of the rebels defeated, the king placed a candle over the archway of the castle where he had his headquarters and, lighting the candle, announced through a herald to all who had been in rebellion against him that those who surrendered and took the oath of loyalty while the candle was burning would be spared. The king offered them his clemency and mercy, but the offer was limited to the life of the candle.

Every great offer of life and of time has its candle limitations. This is true of the offer of fortune and prosperity, or knowledge, or health, or affection. There is a limited period of time in which to make use of the offer and the opportunity. This is true most of all of the greatest offer ever made to man—the offer of eternal life through Jesus Christ his Son.

The Parthenon at Athens had a gateway, the Propylaea, the ruins of which show it to have been of almost equal splendor with the virgin's temple itself. So the door of repentance and faith is in keeping with the splendor of the house and temple of heaven. At what a cost that door was opened! The stars halted to admire it, the angels wondered in sore amazement at the cost of opening; and nature groaned and the sun veiled his face while He the great Redeemer died. What a door opened for sinners!

Strange that with that door open men should choose any other door. The door has stood open through the ages. So long has it been open that it does not seem that it could ever close. But at length, when Christ comes again, when the whole earth shakes with the cry, "Behold, the bridegroom cometh" (Matt. 25:6), the door will close for the whole human race.

But *now,* long before that, and for men in this life, that door is always closing. While there is life there is hope; but when the door is shut, and the acceptable day is passed, it opens not again. Prayer we think of, and rightly so, as the mightiest weapon that man can use. But we have it on the authority of Christ himself that there comes a time when prayer itself is without power. "Lord, Lord, open to us." (Matt. 25:11.) Those who had permitted the door to close against them prayed, but the door opened not.

—Seizing—Deep in the heart of Texas, a rancher was brought to the hospital desperately ill. For days he lay in a coma. Then one morning, revived a little, he asked his nurse what time of the year it was. The nurse answered, "Why, it is springtime."

"Springtime!" said the man. "Then I can't die now, for it is plowing time!" Make use of your plowing time!

In the Bible we have the history of men like Herod, Felix, Agrippa, and the rich young ruler—men who had sincere interest in Christ and were visited with conviction. But, just as ships at sea will sometimes emerge for a moment from the shadows as they cross the pathway of the moon and then are lost again in darkness and gloom, these men appeared for a moment in the light of conviction and opportunity and then disappeared forever. The only time to which God binds himself is *Now*. Great things can be done in a moment of time; but tonight you have just 10,080 fewer minutes of time than you had at this hour a week ago, and 524,162 fewer minutes of time than you had before you on this day last year.

Once on the rocky coast of Scotland a man was lowered by a rope from the top of a cliff to a ledge in order to gather the eggs of wild sea fowl. In a careless moment he let the rope slip away from him. Realizing his great peril, and seeing the rope come swinging toward him

again, and knowing that its second swing would be shorter than the first, he waited till it reached the end of the swing and then leaped to seize it—and was drawn up the cliff to safety. In a moment of time he had to choose and act. That will often be so in the destiny of the human soul.

One of the best-known figures in American public life half a century ago, an able lawyer and statesman, and an eloquent orator, was William M. Evarts. In his last years in the Senate he suffered from an affliction of the eyes which made it impossible for him to read or to recognize any but the most familiar faces. On a trip to Europe he went to consult an eminent physician, who told him there was not the slightest hope. Darkness would certainly, though gradually, settle down upon him. Evarts received the sentence with composure. But he said he had long wished to see Raphael's famous Virgin at Dresden, and that he would go to Dresden to see it before the night set in and it was too late. This he did, and the face of the lovely Virgin was no doubt a consolation to him in the long darkness. While he had the light he walked in it.

One summer evening I was walking through Monterey Gap in the South Mountains. The sun had already disappeared behind the mountains, leaving only the twilight; and the shadows were falling rapidly over forest and field and valley and hillside. Far up on the mountainside there was a clearing, and in this field a farmer was plowing. I could see his white horses against the brown of the field and the green of the neighboring forest. The field was almost finished, and he was calling to his horses and urging them on as he sought to complete the work before the shadows stole farther down the mountainside. In half an hour it would be dark, and he could plow no more.

———————

Some years before his death I was driving across Chicago with William Jennings Bryan. On our way we passed near the coliseum where he delivered the great speech at the Democratic Convention of 1896, the speech which made him three times the candidate of his party for the presidency, and which concluded with the famous peroration, "You shall not press down upon the brow of labor this crown of thorn. You shall not crucify mankind upon a cross of gold." I said to him, "Mr. Bryan, I suppose many times before you had made just as able a speech as that, and it was never heard of."

"Yes," he said, "I suppose that is true. But that convention was my opportunity, and I made the most of it." Then he was silent for a moment, as his great head rested against the cushion of the taxicab, and the light of reminiscence and retrospection came into his eyes. After a moment he broke the silence with these words: "And that's about all we do in this world—lose or use our opportunity."

———————

The astronomers tell us of those heavenly bodies whose orbits draw them nearer and nearer together, until they approach the point of closest approximation and then turn away, and every second, every hour, every day, every year, every century, every aeon, finds them farther and farther apart.

There is something like that, too, in the destiny of a human soul. It may be that there are those here tonight who are near to Christ, and from now on will come nearer and nearer—or from now on will drift farther and farther from God.

———————

Today is the key that opens the door to the chamber of success. Today is the ladder by which men climb to fame and power. Today is the sunlight by which men follow the path that leads to happiness. Today is the sword with which men smite temptation. Today is the vision in the light of which men follow their dream. Today is the voice that calls men out of fatal slumber. Today is the word that is written over the gates of heaven, flaming with jewels—the ruby, the topaz, the jacinth, the chrysoprase, the emerald, and all the precious stones. Today is the word that on the lips of the redeemed in heaven blends with the other word, Eternity.

———————

—True—John Morley on a holiday in the Highlands met with a well-educated and unusually able young minister. The minister expressed regret to Morley that he was isolated in this bleak region, far from libraries and the stimulus of London. But Morley encouraged him by saying that London or the Highlands made little difference in his intellectual life, as a minister depended upon what he did in his own study. "Here, or nowhere, is thine 'America,' he said to him, quoting the expression of Goethe when he rebuked restless souls in Germany who thought that they could change all their life by migrating to America.

"Here, or nowhere, is thine America." It is not the country but the man, not the sword but the man behind the sword. Your true America, your land of opportunity, is in your heart. As a man "thinketh in his heart, so is he." (Prov. 23:7.)

OTHERS—*see also* PRAYER FOR OTHERS

In one of the frontier countries a settler's child was lost in the wilderness, which was still infested by wild animals. The father took his rifle and set out to find his child. Presently he came to a cabin, and in the woods near the cabin he saw prowling leopards. He knew that those leopards threatened the life of any children who might live in the cabin, but his heart was wild with anxiety about his own child. "Why should I stop and shoot these leopards and save these unknown children, when my own child is yonder in the wilderness in peril?" So he started to press on. But his kindlier feelings got the better of him, and he stopped and shot the leopards about the cabin. He then entered the cabin, and lo, there was his own child!

When you act for others you act for yourself—your highest and noblest self, your eternal self.

In Scott's *Heart of Midlothian* we meet the beautiful character Jeanie Deans, who walked all the way to London to seek a royal pardon for her wayward and fallen sister. Jeanie Deans, who had done all for her unfortunate sister Effie, is the author of that fine saying, "When we come to the end of our life, it is not what we have done for ourselves, but what we have done for others, that will be our help and comfort."

On the bells of one of our New England universities are inscribed these words:

For him who in art beautifies life, I ring;
For him who in letters interprets life, I ring;
For the man of science who widens knowledge, I ring;
For the philosopher who ennobles life, I ring;
For the scholar who preserves learning, I ring;
For the preacher of the fear of the Lord, I ring.

But the one legend which more than any other strikes the major chord of the true purpose of a college and of life, is that on the first bell:

For him who in any station seeks not to be ministered unto, but to minister, I ring.

One of the poets of the South, Sidney Lanier, sings of the journey of a Georgia river, the Chattahoochee, from the hills and the mountains down into the plain. As the river starts on its journey, the waterweeds try to hold it in thrall; the rushes and the little reeds cry and sigh, "Abide, abide"; the chestnut, the oak, the walnut and the pine, overleaning the river, beseech it not to pass by their deep shades and manifold glades. The stones of the brook, ruby, garnet and amethyst, do what they can to bar the way and lure the river from its goal. But the river does not yield to these temptations; it goes on to water the plains far below.

. . . I am fain for to water the plain.
Downward the voices of Duty call—
Downward, to toil and be mixed with the main.

Everywhere life will tempt you, as Sidney Lanier fancied that river was tempted, to stop with yourself; but life's true destination is to help and to bless others. Paul is the most influential man in the New Testament, and Abraham, perhaps, in the Old Testament. And it was to Abraham that God said, "Thou shalt be a blessing" (Gen. 12:2).

OUTLOOK ON LIFE

In the *National Geographic Magazine* sometime ago I read a description and saw pictures of the strange towerlike houses built somewhere in the Caucasus. The peculiarity of these odd structures is that they have no windows. As long as they are in the house the people live in darkness. A house without windows is a dismal place—a dungeon rather than a house, a prison rather than a home. Too many persons live with nothing but an "inlook"; they contemplate their own troubles and dwell with their own petty schemes until they become morbid, disagreeable, like an unsunned chamber.

With the music of his inimitable prose John Bunyan tells us, "The pilgrim they laid in a large upper chamber, whose window opened toward the sunrising. The name of the chamber was Peace." We must have chambers opening toward the sunrising. In an address made to the students of the University of Edinburgh, Viscount Haldane said, "The way to escape from the depressions incident to the numerous reverses of life, and that deeper depression which arises from no external cause, is by acquiring a large outlook."

P

PARENTS—*see also* HOME AND MOTHER, LOVE (A FATHER'S), MOTHER, REMORSE AND PARENTS

—Respect for—John Ruskin, after his farce marriage to the future wife of Millais, went home to his father and mother. They were severe religionists, but the son submitted to the discipline of that home. On the Sabbath this man of middle age, now famous in Europe, acceded to the rule that his beloved Turners should be screened. He could look at them for six days. What mattered one day, if it pleased his parents to have them veiled on the Sabbath?

His father died at seventy-nine and was buried in Shirley Church, Surrey. His son inscribed upon his tomb this remarkable epitaph: "He was an entirely honest merchant, and his memory is to all who keep it dear and helpful. His son, whom he loved to the uttermost, and taught to speak truth, says this of him!" Seven years later, at the great age of ninety, the mother followed the father, and what Ruskin wrote for her was but the reflection of his life: "Nor was dearer earth ever returned to earth, nor purer life recorded in heaven."

—Sacrificing for children—Daniel Webster was the son of godly Captain Ebenezer Webster. On the New Hampshire hills the father toiled for the sake of his children. On a hot day, in the last year of Washington's administration, Webster tells us, he was making hay with his father when a man rode by who had just been elected to Congress. When he was gone, Ebenezer Webster called his son Daniel and said, "My son, that is a worthy man. He is a member of Congress. He goes to Philadelphia and gets six dollars a day, while I toil here. It is because he had an education, which I never had. If I had had his early education, I should have been in Philadelphia in his place. I came near to it, as it is, but I missed it, and now I must work here." Webster relates how he, the boy, cried when his father said this. His father then went on to say, "My child, it is of no importance to me. I could not give your elder brothers the advantage of knowledge, but I can do something for you. Exert yourself and prove your opportunities, and when I am gone you will not need to go through the hardships which I have undergone, and which have made me old before my time."

When we stand in the hall of Congress and listen to the great speeches of Daniel Webster, we should remember that godly father who sacrificed for his son.

* * *

—Tribute to—At Blantyre, near Glasgow, is the quiet acre where sleep the father and mother of David Livingstone. The words which he prepared for that grave are words which every one of us might take to heart: "To show the resting place of Neil Livingstone and Agnes Hunter, his wife, and to express the thankfulness to God of their children, John, David, Janet, Charles, and Agnes, for poor and pious parents."

A friend insisted that he change the wording to "poor *but* pious"; but he kept it as he had written it, "poor and pious," a tribute of love to parents who were both poor and pious.

PAST, THE
—Conquering—When Dr. Andrew B. White, once ambassador to Germany and formerly president of Cornell University, commenced his teaching career at the University of Michigan, he was greatly annoyed by an able but impudent and disorderly student in one of his classes. He managed to win the friendship of this student, who, however, was dismissed from the university for participation in a disgraceful escapade in which one of the students was killed. Before he left the university this student came to see Dr. White to thank him for what he had tried to do for him. As he was leaving he said, "I'll make a man out of myself yet." The Civil War was just break-

ing out, and the expelled student enlisted in a Michigan cavalry regiment.

On the third day of the Battle of Gettysburg, in the new uniform of a brigadier general, to which rank he had just been promoted for fidelity and gallantry, an officer was ordered by General Kilpatrick to charge the right wing of the Confederate army. It was a mistaken order; but, leading his men in a magnificent, if hopeless, charge, the young officer fell gloriously within the Confederate lines. He was General E. J. Farnsworth, the student who had been expelled from the University of Michigan. He had made good his promise that he would make a man of himself.

No matter what the mistakes or failures or blunders, there is the possibility of noble and honorable success, if the will and the purpose are there.

* * *

I speak of the kind of heroism which is rarest and greatest. I had marked a certain woman and her beautiful daughter in the church where I commenced to preach. One day she came to see me. I addressed her as Mrs. ——. "But," she said, "I am not Mrs. ——; I am just Margaret ——."

Like many others more sinned against than sinning, she had taken captivity captive. With her child she had come from Scotland and toiled daily as a weaver in the silk mill. Rarely have I known such faith and courage and beauty of character. Yet the battle that she fought so courageously and won so triumphantly was not to the waving of banners, or with the blare of trumpets. She had taken captivity captive and had come off conqueror and more than conqueror through Him that loved her.

* * *

A man who once applied for a position with a manufacturer began to refer with apology to some unhappy incident in his past. The manufacturer said, "I don't care about the past. Start where you stand."

Start where you stand and never
    mind the past;
  The past won't help you in be-
    ginning new.
If you are done with it at last,
  Why, that's enough. You're done
    with it, you're through;
This is another chapter in the book,
  This is another race that you have
    planned.
Don't give the vanished days a back-
    ward look—
  Start where you stand.

The world won't care about your old
    defeats.
  If you can start anew and win
    success,
The future is your time, and time
    is fleet,
  And there is much of work and
    strain and stress;
Forget the buried woes and dead
    despairs.
  Here is a brand-new trial right at
    hand;
The future is for him who does and
    dares—
  Start where you stand.

Old failures will not halt, old tri-
    umphs aid;
  Today's the thing, tomorrow soon
    will be;
Get in the fight and face it, unafraid,
  And leave the past to ancient his-
    tory.
What has been, has been; yesterday
    is dead,
  And by it you are neither blessed
    nor banned;

Take courage, man, be brave and
    drive ahead—
  Start where you stand![1]
      —BERTON BRALEY

British army bulletins of 1918 tell of a certain Colonel Elkington, who in the early part of the war was cashiered from the army for conduct unbecoming an officer. The public dispatches do not state the nature of this misconduct, but the inference is that it was cowardice in the face of the enemy.

The disgraced man, with his name dropped from the rolls of the British army, went back to Paris, assumed another name, and enlisted in the Foreign Legion. Wherever the men of the Legion went into action, this man was conspicuous for his daring and gallantry. After one of his feats of heroism he was decorated by the government of France. In some way his real identity was disclosed, and the facts were brought to the attention of the British government. His commission was given back to him; and, resuming his name and title, he again joined his old regiment at the front. By wounds and daring and fidelity he won back the honors and the rank that cowardice had forfeited him.

—**God of**—Frederick Maurice wrote of Carlyle that he believed in a God who lived up to the time of the death of Oliver Cromwell. From the conversation of some men, you would gather that they believe in a God who died when they were boys or who lived in the time of their great-grandfathers, or in the age of Lincoln or Washington. There were giants in the earth in those days, but now all we have is a race of pygmies.

—**Redeeming**—In one of the cathedrals of England there is a beautiful window

[1] Used by permission of the author.

through which the sunlight streams. It displays the facts and personalities of the Old and New Testament and the glorious truths and doctrines of the Christion revelation. This window was fabricated by the artist out of broken bits of glass which another artist had discarded.

On a hill outside Florence, in a park ... the ... s the ... slay- ... e of ... oung ... stone ... t out ... artist ... away ... akes, ... ower, ... put ... able ... fair ... *Old Mortality* Sir Walter Scott tells how the schoolmaster was wont to seek relief on summer evenings from the tedium of the schoolroom by walking to a lonely glen where was a deserted burial ground. The monuments, half sunk in the earth, were overgrown with moss. Daisies and harebells, deriving their nourishment from the dew of heaven, hung over the graves. Some of the tombs were imposing. One bore the effigy of a knight in his hood of mail, with his hands clasped on the hilt of his great sword. On another was the miter and pastoral staff of a bishop. But underneath two stones slept the dust of Covenanters who had perished in that glen by the hand of the troopers of Charles II.

Approaching the deserted mansion of the dead on a certain summer evening,

the strolling schoolmaster was surprised to hear sounds other than those which he had been accustomed to hear there— the gentle chiding of the brook and the sighing of the wind in the boughs of the gigantic ash trees. It was the clink-clank of a hammer. Going nearer, the schoolmaster saw an old man seated upon the monument of the martyred Presbyterians, deepening with his chisel the letters of the inscription, which, in the language of the Bible, pronounced the blessings of heaven upon the slain and anathemas upon their murderers. A blue bonnet of unusual dimensions covered the gray hairs of the pious workman. It was none other than Old Mortality, that singular character who wandered up and down Scotland seeking out on remote moors and in wild glens the graves of the martyred Covenanters, renewing with his chisel the half-defaced inscriptions and repairing the emblems of death with which the tombs were adorned.

So it is fitting that with the chisel of historical reminiscence and investigation we should renew the inscriptions upon the graves of those honored ones of the past who have contributed to the great and honorable history of mankind.

PATMOS

As the ship sails out from the Gulf of Smyrna you can see high up on the top of the mountain that overlooks the bay the cypress trees which mark the grave of one of John's disciples, Polycarp, who on that spot made his grand testimony to Christ and, refusing to say that Caesar was lord instead of Jesus, was burned at the stake. The picturesque city of Smyrna becomes just a dim blur on the eastern horizon, and soon the ship is over against Chios. Then night comes down, and the mainland and the islands are hid from our view.

At four o'clock in the morning we are

summoned on deck. Almost noiselessly the ship glides into a land-locked harbor and then, with the rattling of anchor chains, comes to a standstill. In front of me a dark mass is rising out of the sea. In the heavens above, the brilliant stars are still shining; and I think of the seven stars, or the seven churches, which one like unto the Son of Man held in his right hand.

A small boat puts off from the side of the steamer, and we are rowed into the landing place. Now the stars are beginning to pale, and the sun rising in the east gilds the placid sea and touches with light the tops of the mountains. Soon the white buildings of the monastery of St. John are discernible on the top of the mountain.

Absolute silence reigns. Silence on the sea, silence on the land. That deep silence —silence like that which was in heaven for half an hour ere John saw the wonders of revelation—was a fit introduction to Patmos, for that is where we were standing, on the "isle that is called Patmos" (Rev. 1:9).

PATRIOTISM—*see* HOME (LOVE OF)

PAUL

Yes, Paul is ready! Come, cruel, sensual, debased, satanic, abominable Nero, thou beast of Rome, come with all thy tortures. Flash, headsman's ax; thou canst not touch Paul's soul! Thou canst not bind or limit the world-wide and age-long reach of his influence. Thou canst not stain or dim the majesty of his life! Strike, shadows, strike! All that thou canst do is to crown his earthly life with glory and admit him to Christ's everlasting Kingdom!

In the conclusion to his homilies on the Letter to the Romans, Chrysostom says that of all the cities he loves Rome most because there Paul died, there his dust reposes, and there he will be raised up to meet the Lord. In his enthusiasm Chrysostom prays that he might be permitted to throw himself about the body of Paul and be riveted to his tomb, to see "the dust of Paul's body that sowed the Gospel everywhere; the dust of that mouth which lifted the truth on high, and through which Christ spake the great and secret things, and greater than in his own person; the dust of those hands off which the serpent fell into the fire and through which the sacred writings were written; the dust of those feet which ran through the world and were not weary; the dust of those eyes which were blinded gloriously, but which recovered their sight again for the salvation of the world; the dust of that heart which a man would not do wrong to call the heart of the world, so enlarged that it could take in cities and nations and peoples, which burned at each one that was lost, which despised both death and hell, and yet was broken down by a brother's tears."

PERSEVERANCE—*see also* COURAGE

A number of years ago I picked up in London a two-penny pamphlet biography of Joseph Chamberlain, the famous English statesman. It told how he had been in his youth a Sunday school teacher at Birmingham, and how his favorite verse in the Bible was this sentence from Genesis 12:5: "They went forth to go into the land of Canaan; and into the land of Canaan they came." It was a verse well suited to a man of his ambition, iron will, determination, and perseverance.

There are two qualifications for success in life. One is to have a goal for which we start—"They went forth to go into the land of Canaan." The second is to keep on going after we have started— "Into the land of Canaan they came."

Coming into New York from New Jersey, in the days before the tubes were built, I found never-ending delight in standing on the upper deck of the ferry-boat and watching the craft of all descriptions going up the North River to their docks.

There go the ships—ships from all parts of the world! There is the stately bark or brigantine laden with silks, or teas, or spices, that has slipped down some river in Siam or China, has sailed through the typhoon-infested China Sea, skirted the coral islands of the South Pacific, turned the stormy and dangerous Horn, then through the South Atlantic and the tempestuous North Atlantic to New York, and now is being towed by a tug to her berth in Hoboken or Staten Island. There is the one-funneled fruiter that comes from Panama and Colón and Havana, whose twelve manner of fruits will in a day or two be sold on the streets of New York, Boston, Philadelphia, Pittsburgh, and Chicago.

There is the private yacht, trim and white; and yonder the tramp steamer laden with the merchandise of Britain or Germany; and here the low-lying battleship with its military masts and its signals flying, and its naked guns peering out with wicked eye. Passing on this side is the great four-decked liner from Liverpool or Hamburg or Havre, its sirens sounding a hoarse warning, bearing its cargo of thousands of human lives, some returning home again, others coming from the steppes of Russia, or the Mediterranean lands, looking with hope and wonder on the far-famed city of the New World, with its towers of Babel reaching heavenward.

There go the ships! Through mist and fog and snow and rain and calm and gale; through seas that were chill with icebergs and others that were as blue as heaven's vault. From Europe, South America, Asia, the West Indies, the Pacific Coast, these ships have come; and as they move up the river they seem to say to the world that is waiting for them, "I have finished my course" (II Tim. 4:7).

Sometimes in a museum you see one of the old prairie schooners on which the pioneers crossed the continent. If they had stopped to contrast each day the distance they had traveled with the vast stretches of the continent before them, they would never have reached their goal. But day by day the oxen plodded on; night by night the wagons were halted, the cattle watered, and the fires lighted. Thus, by going on, day by day, they crossed plains and mountains and reached the lands on the Pacific. It is not doing something brilliant or striking that wins you the victory and brings you to the journey's end, but keeping everlastingly at it, sailing on from port to port, island to island, this day and then the next day. The ministers of the old time used to ask in their prayers that we might be granted an "honorable through-bearing." A fine phrase that, signifying perseverance up to the very end.

In Grecian myth Orpheus, with his lyre, went through the infernal regions in quest of his lost wife, Eurydice. As he passed, Tantalus ceased for a moment from stooping to quench his thirst, Ixion's wheel stood still, the vulture ceased to tear the giant's liver, the daughters of Danaüs rested from their futile toil, Sisyphus sat on the rock to listen, and even the cheeks of the Furies were wet with tears, so compelling was the music of Orpheus mourning for his lost companion.

Pluto consented that Orpheus should take his wife with him to the upper air, upon one condition—that he would not look on her until they reached the regions above. All hell held its breath as they passed on their way to the light. One by one the dreadful perils were passed. But just as they were on the verge of the upper world Orpheus looked back, and all his labors were in vain. Eurydice had vanished.

So it was with this man of God who was slain by the lion after his heroic witness against the altar of Jeroboam (I Kings 13:1-30). Almost to the very close of the chapter he is magnificent in his courage, steadfastness, and faithfulness to the word of God. But at the last he looked and was lost.

The Athenians used to have a race in which the runners carried lighted torches. The victors who were crowned were those who arrived at the goal with their torches still burning. May you come to your goal, reach the end, with your torch still burning! The highest tribute, the highest reward, you can ever receive is to have said of you, "He was a true, a consistent, man clear down to the end."

PETER

Men speak of the paintings of the Greek-Spanish artist known as El Greco, and how his heavy strokes tell you that what you are looking at is one of El Greco's paintings, in whatever gallery you may see it. So Peter is always Peter—whether in a state of nature or a state of grace, whether before or after he became a follower of Christ, whether during the days of his discipleship or the days of the founding of the Church, whether pulling in nets on the Sea of Galilee or with Christ in the desert place when he asked the disciples who he was, or listening to Christ talk with Moses and Elijah on the Mount of Transfiguration, or sitting with Christ at the last supper, or even in his dreams. You can't miss him or mis-

take him for any other. No matter where you put Peter down, he will always speak and act like Peter.

PETER'S DENIAL

One of the most dramatic scenes in literature is that sketch of George Eliot's in *Romola* where the selfish and attractive young Greek, Tito Melema, confronted at the banquet by his foster father, Baldassare—who had toiled and sacrificed for him and when they parted had given him the jewels with which to purchase his freedom from the pirates who held him a slave—coldly said that he had never seen the man before, that he must be some poor lunatic.

That was a great scene. But what can compare with the scene when Jesus and Peter met face to face? All the angels who had been watching turned away their faces in sorrow when they heard Peter swear. He said he had never known Christ. If we could have put our minds into the mind of Christ, perhaps this is what we would have heard him saying to himself: "Peter says he never knew me! Me, who called him that day by the Sea of Galilee; me, who told him he would become a rock; me, whom he confessed as the Son of God; me, whom he said he would never permit to wash his feet; me, whom he said he would follow to prison and to death!"

PEW, THE EMPTY

The empty pew, your vacant place at the church, is a vote with the world and against the Christ. The world that is opposed to Christ asks nothing more from you in its enmity to Christ than that you do what Thomas did—stay away.

"I am an Empty Pew. I vote for the world as against God. I deny the Bible. I mock at the preached Word of God. I rail at Christian brotherhood. I laugh at prayer. I break the Fourth Commandment. I am a witness to solemn vows broken. I advise men to eat, drink, and be merry, for tomorrow they die. I join my voice with every atheist and rebel against human and divine law. I am an Empty Pew. I am a grave in the midst of the congregation. Read my epitaph and be wise."

PILATE

Everyone who goes to Rome pays a visit to the *Scala Santa,* or the Sacred Stairs of the judgment seat of Pilate. It can hardly be credited that the actual marble stairs of Pilate's judgment seat were brought to Rome, although such a thing is within the realm of possibility.

Roman Catholic superstition bestows a special merit and grace upon the devout pilgrim who ascends those stairs on his knees. It was when he was in this act of devotion that Martin Luther, a pilgrim in Rome from Germany, heard the words sounding in his ear which afterward became the watchword of the Reformation—"The just shall live by faith!"

However one dismisses the likelihood of the stairs upon which he is looking being actually those of Pilate's judgment seat, it is not possible to stand there without thinking of Pilate and of Christ. Those two figures rise before you—the heavy-headed, large-bodied Pontius Pilate, sitting at the head of the stairs, perplexed as to his prisoner; and Jesus, standing on the marble flags at the foot of the stairs, his head crowned with thorns, a purple robe about him, the blood from his recent scourging making a crimson stain upon the white marble of the steps.

———•◆•———

—And Jesus—In his tale *The Procurator of Judea* Anatole France imagines Pon-

tius Pilate meeting at a fashionable watering place on the Bay of Naples an old friend, Lamia, who had been exiled from Rome and had spent much time in Syria. The two men sit down together and have pleasant conversation about the events of thirty years before.

Pilate tells Lamia of his troubles with the Jews and incidents of his administration as procurator, and chides Lamia for his licentious habits and his failure to marry and give children to the state, as every good citizen ought to do. But Lamia's attention has been drawn to a group of Syrian dancers who are performing near by. As he looks eagerly upon them, he tells Pilate how he once knew a Jewish dancer at Jerusalem, who, with her loins arched, her head thrown back, dragged down by the weight of her heavy red hair, her eyes swimming with voluptuousness, eager, languishing, and compliant, would have made Cleopatra herself grow pale with envy. He tells how he followed this fascinating dancer wherever she went and spent much time in her company. But one day she disappeared and he saw her no more. He sought for her in all sorts of disreputable alleys and taverns, but it was only by chance, and long months afterward, that he learned that she had attached herself to a small company of men and women who were followers of a young Galilean healer.

"His name was Jesus," said Lamia, "and he came from Lazareth. He was crucified for some crime, I don't know what. Pontius, do you remember anything about the man?"

Pontius contracted his brows, and his hand rose to his forehead in the attitude of one who probes the depths of memory. Then, after a silence of some seconds— "Jesus?" he murmured, "Jesus—of Nazareth? I cannot call him to mind."

Lamia remembered the Jewish dancer

Mary of Magdala, but Pilate could not remember Jesus of Nazareth!

PITY

In George Eliot's great tale *The Mill on the Floss* Maggie Tulliver was reproached by her brother Tom for what seemed to him wayward and dangerous conduct. Maggie reminded him how he had always enjoyed punishing her, even when she was a little girl who loved him better than anyone else in the world, and how he would let her go crying to bed without forgiving her. "You have no pity," she said. "You have no sense of your own imperfection and your own sins. It is a sin to be hard; it is not fitting for a mortal—for a Christian."

Yes, that is true; it is a sin to be hard. For a mortal, subject to temptation, it is not fitting; and, above all, it is wrong for a Christian, whose hope for eternal life depends upon the forgiving love of God in Christ.

PLACE, THE EMPTY

In speaking once of officers who had fallen in battle fighting against the flag of their country, General McClellan referred to Marino Falieri, the doge of Venice, who after great services to his country as a soldier and statesman was convicted of treason and put to death. On the wall of the doges' palace at Venice where the portraits of the rulers hang, in the place which belonged to Falieri, instead of his portrait, there is an empty space covered with a black canvas.

POPULARITY

This is a sermon from life. A girl just finishing high school, and going off to college in the fall, was asked by one of her teachers if she was popular with the students. She answered, No.

"But why are you not popular?" asked the teacher.

"Because I will not pass around my examination papers to be copied."

"Oh," responded the teacher, "you will never be popular if you don't do that."

The girl answered, "Am I, or am I not, my brother's keeper?"

Hearing of this incident, I had first of all a feeling of sorrow that any teacher should so speak to a scholar and degrade her high office by seeming encouragement to do a dishonest thing, and then a feeling of pride that this young woman was a member of my church. Her final reply, "Am I, or am I not, my brother's keeper?" showed that she had not only a high regard and reverence for her own self and her own soul but a high sense of her responsibility toward others. She could not conscientiously, and therefore would not, assist others in dishonesty and deceit.

Shall I be popular or shall I be right? That was the question this girl answered. She answered it in the right way. Our first duty is to be right, and let popularity care for itself. The incident has a special bearing on school and college life, but is applicable to all people, especially young people, in every circumstance of life.

———◆·◆·◆———

In his *Spirit of the Age* William Hazlitt, writing of Wilberforce, the great foe of slavery, says of him: "He does not seem greatly to dread the denunciation in Scripture, but rather to court it—'Woe unto you, when all men shall speak well of you!' [Luke 6:26.] We suspect he is not quite easy in mind because West Indian planters and Guinea traders do not join in his praise. His ears are not strongly enough tuned to drink in the execrations of the spoiler and the oppressor as the sweetest music. He is anxious to do all the good he can without hurting himself or his fair name."

PRAYER—*see also* MOTHER (PRAYERS OF), WAR AND CHRISTIANITY

One of the most beautiful things that I ever read on the subject of prayer is a verse I found in a Norwegian novel, *The Wind from the Mountains,* by Trygve Gulbranssen. Adelaide hands to old Dag, who amid his sorrows and difficulties is struggling toward the light, the bishop's Bible, with these lines on the flyleaf:

> *Our human thoughts and works are not so mighty*
> *That they can cut a path to God, unbless'd,*
> *And so from Him the gift of prayer is sent us*
> *To hallow both our labor and our quest.*
> *Over life, and death, and starlit spaces*
> *The highroad runs, that at His word was laid,*
> *And reaches Him across the desert places;*
> *By prayer it is our pilgrimage is made.*[1]

How true that is! Over life and death and starlit spaces runs for us the highroad of prayer, and by prayer our pilgrimage is made.

What a friend we have in prayer! What a protector! And how little use we make of it! When the Atlantic cable was laid in 1850, there were great celebrations and rejoicings on both sides of the Atlantic. But what is the Atlantic cable, with the messages of war and peace, of nations in commotion and sore

[1] Used by permission of the publishers, G. P. Putnam's Sons, New York.

travail, which flash across it, compared with the heavenly cable of prayer, whereby the tempted and tried man communicates with the God of heaven, and receives messages and messengers of encouragement from heaven just as Jacob did at Bethel when he saw a ladder set up on earth, the top of which reached to heaven, and the angels of God ascending and descending.

When Grant was fighting his last campaign with cancer at Mount McGregor, General O. O. Howard, who had honestly won the title "The Christian Soldier," came to call on him. He spoke for a time to Grant about some of the battles and campaigns of the war in which both men had played so illustrious a part. Grant listened for a time and then, interrupting him, said, "Howard, tell me what you know about prayer." Face to face with death and the unknown, the question of prayer was of greater interest to the dying soldier than the reminiscences of his battles.

—Benefit of—In the diary of his prison experience at Fort Warren, in Boston Harbor, Alexander Stephens thus describes the close of his prison day: "He undresses and stretches himself on his bunk. Here with soul devout he endeavors through prayer to put himself in communion with God. To the Eternal, Prisoner, in weakness and full consciousness of his own frailty, commits himself, saying from the heart, 'Thy will, and not mine, be done.' With thoughts embracing the well-being of absent dear ones, and all the world of mankind besides, whether friend or foe, he sinks into that sweet and long sleep from which he arose this morning."

A medical missionary captured by bandits in China, informed that he was to be shot at a spot ten minutes' distance away, tells how a terrible fear and help-lessness came over him at the thought of such a death so far away from his native country, from his friends and his family. But he had strength enough to pray. This was his prayer: "My Lord God, have mercy on me, and give me strength for this trial. Take away all fear, and if I have to die, let me die like a man." Instantly, he said, his terrible fear began to disappear. By the time he had reached the gorge where he was to be shot he felt perfectly calm and unafraid. At the last moment, however, the bandits relented and his life was spared. In the days which followed, full of danger and suf-fering, the memory of this experience was cherished more and more. "My own will had failed in the most critical mo-ment of my life. But the knowledge that I could depend on a power greater than my own, one that had not failed me in that crisis, sustained me in a wonderful way to the very end of my captivity. What ingratitude it would be in me not to proclaim this power."

It was an unusual thing when a cer-tain man, well advanced in years, of high professional standing as a lawyer and high social standing, publicly confessed his faith in Christ and united with the Church. One of the reasons he gave for taking this step was for the sake of his influence upon others. Among those of whom he was thinking was a young man associated with him in his law practice. He had made a brilliant record in the law school and had marked ability; he was married and had two charming chil-dren. But he was the victim of an evil habit, indulgence in strong drink. Speak-ing of this young man and his prospects and his temptation, his uncle told me one day how, when he had been coun-seling him and expostulating with him,

he had said to the young man, "Do you ever pray about it?"

Do you ever pray about it? The ques-tion which that fine Christian gentleman addressed to his nephew when speaking with him about his besetting sin has always remained in my mind. It sug-gests to me the way in which prayer helps us in our temptations, in our battle with sin.

Harold Dixon, one of the three men on a raft who drifted for thirty-four days a thousand miles in their rub-ber raft, eight feet by four, with no food and no water, speaking of the prayer meetings which they held every night, said: "There was a comfort in passing our burden to someone bigger than we in this empty vastness. Further, the com-mon devotion drew us together, since it seemed we no longer depended entirely upon each other, but could appeal simul-taneously to a Fourth that we three held equally in reverence."

That reference to a "Fourth" with them in that raft makes one think of those three Hebrew lads in the fiery furnace who prayed to God and put their trust in God, and how, when Neb-uchadnezzar came to look into the fiery furnace to see what had happened to them, he saw that they were unharmed by the flames, and lo, in the midst of them, he saw the form of a Fourth, like unto the Son of Man! That is one of the great blessings of prayer. It puts you into fellowship with the form of a Fourth—with God, with Jesus Christ, the Saviour of men.

—**And danger**—There was once a god-less seaman who was in a boat fishing with his companions when a storm came up which threatened to sink the ship. His companions begged him to offer a prayer; but he demurred, saying it was years since he had prayed or entered a church. But finally, upon their insistence, he made this prayer: "O Lord, I have not asked you for anything for fifteen years, and if you deliver us out of this storm and bring us safe to land again, I promise that I will not bother you again for another fifteen years!"

There is no doubt that many of those who pray earnestly in time of great distress, afterward, when the storm is over and the danger is past, forget God. But that in no way invalidates the fact that in their distress and danger they realized that there was a higher power than themselves and turned to that power in earnest supplication.

—**For enemies**—Madame Chiang Kai-shek, who is a product of Christian missions and whose father and mother were devout Methodists, relates how her mother would spend hours in prayer in a room on the third floor of their home. At the time of the Manchurian invasion Madame Chiang said one day to her mother: "Mother, you are so powerful in prayer, why don't you pray that God will annihilate Japan by an earthquake or something?"

Her mother looked gravely at her and said: "When you pray or expect me to pray, don't insult God's intelligence by asking Him to do something which would be unworthy of you, a mortal."

"After that," said Madame Chiang, "I can pray for the Japanese people."

—**Hindered**—Few persons, I suppose, have read the sequel to Robinson Crusoe's story of his captivity on the lonely island—*Serious Reflections*—in which Crusoe tells how he revisited the island and endeavored to convert to Christianity the mixed colony of English and natives. Most notorious among these islanders was the wicked and profligate seaman

Will Atkins. After his conscience had been reached and it was suggested to Atkins that he and his companions teach their wives religion, he responded, "Lord, sir, how should we teach them religion? Should we talk to them of God and Jesus Christ, and heaven and hell, it would make them laugh at us." In his ever charming style Defoe describes Atkins sitting by the side of his tawny wife under the shade of a bush and trying to tell her about God, occasionally going off a little distance to fall on his knees to pray, until at length they both knelt down together, while the friend who was watching with Crusoe cried out, "St. Paul! St. Paul! behold he prayeth!"

In Coleridge's "Rime of the Ancient Mariner" we have the poetic conception of how sin hinders prayer. After the Ancient Mariner had killed the sacred albatross, in his distress he tried to pray. But his lips could not pronounce the words:

I looked to Heaven, and tried to pray
But ever a prayer had gusht,
A wicked whisper came, and made
My heart as dry as dust.

It was only after his repentance, and when the spell of judgment had been lifted, that he found himself able to pray, and set out on his pilgrimage from land to land, to teach by his own example love and reverence to all things that God made and loves. The great poem comes to a conclusion with the Ancient Mariner telling his delight in going to the church with the goodly company to pray.

—**Intercessory**—When Senator Penrose, of Pennsylvania, stricken with his last sickness, was being wheeled about in a chair, his once gigantic frame shrunken and haggard, Penrose said to his faithful

Negro valet, "William, I want you to tell me the truth, not what the doctors tell me, but the truth. Do you think I'm getting better?"

With tears in his eyes, the Negro answered, "Senator, I will tell you the truth. You are not far from the end. Amen."

With that Penrose lifted a once mighty hand and said, "Then, William, when you go to church tomorrow, put up a prayer for me."

—**For others**—A woman once said to me that there was no one in the world who prayed for her. If that was so, it was all the more reason why she needed to pray for herself. Certainly it was true that she had been prayed for at one time, when she came into the world, and a father's and a mother's love blended in spoken or unspoken prayer. There is not a person for whom someone—in heaven, on earth, perhaps in hell—has not prayed. This fact invests life with a sacred interest.

In Dick's *Philosophy of a Future State,* the book which converted David Livingstone, there is preserved a beautiful prayer made by a Mrs. Sheppard, a lady of Somersetshire, for the conversion of Lord Byron. In the prayer she referred to him as one as much distinguished for his neglect of God as for the transcendent talents God had bestowed upon him. She prayed that he might be awakened to a sense of his danger and led to seek peace and forgiveness in Christ.

After the woman's death her husband forwarded the prayer to Byron. It took him in one of his best moods; and he responded, "I can assure you that not all the fame which ever cheated humanity into higher notions of its own importance would ever weigh in my mind against the pure and pious interest which

a virtuous being may be pleased to take in my behalf. In this point of view, I would not exchange the prayer of the deceased in my behalf for the united glory of Homer, Caesar, and Napoleon."

The head of an insane asylum for the inebriate in New York testified that those who were sent there by their relatives or neighbors or by the state simply to get rid of them and to restrict their liberties never recovered. The ones who recovered were those who had some loved one, father or mother, or wife or child, or sister, praying for them. Suffering love has the power to restore. So the suffering love of God in Christ can restore the sinner.

What could be finer than that final touch which Thackeray gives to the beautiful character of Amelia in *Vanity Fair*: "No more fighting was heard at Brussels. The sound of battle rolled miles away. Darkness came down on the field and city, and Amelia was praying for George, who was lying on his face dead, with a bullet through his heart." Sorrow, anguish, battles, wounds, darkness, and death; but shining in that darkness the calm star of a faithful woman's intercession!

—**Physical attitude in**—Even the very posture in prayer is important. The most reverent attitude, I think, is that of the worshiper standing with bowed head, as one sees him in public worship in Scotland and as I witnessed it among the Waldensians in Italy one summer. But whether kneeling or standing, in public or in private, the body should speak the reverence of the soul.

David Livingstone in his diary relates how careful he was in the wilds of Africa, removed from all that he had known and seen, to observe the reverent attitude in prayer. Even till death he was faithful in this, for he died upon his knees. A weak, fever-stricken, dying man might have been excused from the physical effort of prostration, but this man left his cot and died upon his knees.

—————

—Power of—Here is a great modern cannon, one of those big guns about which we have heard so much. Here is the long and graceful barrel of the gun pointing toward the foe. But there is nothing in that barrel by itself. Birds could nest in it. And here is the wheel that elevates and lowers the gun. But there is nothing in that wheel itself which could strike against the enemy. And here is the range finder, a delicate and beautiful instrument. And here is the shell, or cartridge, with the powder back of it, ready to be hurled against the foe. But there is nothing in that shell of itself which can injure the enemy. And back of the gun is the gunner, ready to do his work with strong mind and trained hand. But in himself there is nothing, no power, that can hurt the enemy. It is only when the spark of fire is applied to the powder that that great cannon with its intricate mechanism and its death-dealing shell and its trained gunners becomes an instrument of power and destruction.

So prayer is the spark that brings the power of man into action.

—————

—Reality of—Doctor Charles Parkhurst, distinguished preacher and reformer of New York, in an address in which he dealt with his early religious life related how he had often heard his father pray in the church, at the family altar, and at the family table. But it was only when he heard him praying aloud on his knees in the barn that he knew the reality of prayer and the deep reality of the religious life.

—And temptation—I was once consulted by a student who had been urged to take a course of conduct that was wrong— not only wrong, but shockingly wrong. Amazed that one should feel it necessary to consult a minister, or anyone else, as to the right or wrong of the suggested action, I said, finally, "How does it seem to you when you pray about it?"

"Oh, then," came the quick answer, "it seems to be wrong."

That is the great thing about prayer. It strips the mask from the face of temptation. A temptation to succeed, at least in the beginning, must wear some disguise or mask. But prayer tears away that disguise and reveals evil in all its hideous features.

Look at the suggestion or the temptation in the light of prayer; bring it into contact with holy thoughts and desires. If wrong, it cannot stand that light, for prayer will no more direct the temptation-beset soul in the wrong direction than the North Star will direct the tempest-tossed mariner in the wrong course on the sea.

—————

—Unanswered—While I was buying a ticket in a station in New York, in the first days of my ministry, the ticket agent, learning that I was a minister, asked me if I believed in prayer. It was in no querulous or bitter tone, but in earnestness and humility, that the question was asked. Then he went on to tell about the long illness of his wife, and how year after year he had made futile prayers, or rather unanswered prayers, for her recovery.

I could not tell him then why his prayers were not answered. I could not tell him now. But the question that he asked has often come to mind in the thirty years which have passed since then. We must continually face what seems to be the absence of God, just when we need him most. How many strange providences there are, things that are past our comprehension!

------•◆•------

In his *Confessions* Augustine relates how he set out for Rome from Carthage against the prayers and entreaties of his godly mother, who was praying earnestly for his salvation. Augustine deceived her when she was weeping over him by telling her that he was merely going on board to see a friend who was sailing for Italy. When his mother refused to go home without him, he persuaded her to pass the night in a memorial chapel of the martyr Cyprian. But that night while his mother Monica was praying in the chapel, beseeching God to prevent him from going, Augustine set sail.

This departure of her son must have seemed to Monica at that time the refusal to grant her prayer; yet in the providence of God the journey to Italy was to be the means of Augustine's conversion. The denial of the mother's prayer was in the end a great answer to her prayer for the salvation of her gifted son. "But Thou," says Augustine, "in Thy hidden wisdom, didst grant the substance of her desire, yet refused the thing she prayed for in order that Thou mightest effect in me what she was ever praying for. . . . She loved to keep me with her as mothers are wont, yes, far more than most mothers, and she knew not what joy Thou wast preparing for her out of my desertion."

Here we have a striking and beautiful illustration of how God sometimes answers a prayer for the salvation of a soul after what seems, to the one who prays, a long delay.

------•◆•------

There are answers beyond our answers—that is, beyond what seems to us an answer. David lay on the ground all night and prayed for the recovery of

that child of love and sin; but the prayer, as he asked it, was not answered. The child died, but David did not cease to pray and to believe in prayer. He comforted himself and said of the child, "I shall go to him, but he shall not return to me" (II Sam. 12:23).

Paul prayed earnestly, if ever man did. He besought the Lord three times that his grievous and painful thorn in the flesh be taken from him; but his prayer, in that form, was not granted. The thorn remained to pierce and harass him to the end of his days. And yet at the same time God answered him when he prayed, and this was his answer: "My grace is sufficient for thee" (II Cor. 12:9). Paul found that to be the answer to his unanswered prayer.

------•◆•------

I once visited a man who had been bedridden for many months with a painful affliction. After I had prayed with him, he said, "Yes, this morning the pain was terrible; and I said, 'Father, if you are willing, take away this pain.' But he didn't do it; the pain grew worse."

When you can't answer, it is always best frankly to say so. I told him I did not know why God had not answered his prayer and relieved him of his distress. Then I told him of Paul's prayer that the thorn might be plucked out of his flesh—how the prayer was not answered, but how the Lord said to Paul, "My grace is sufficient for thee: for my strength is made perfect in weakness" (II Cor. 12:9).

------•◆•------

—Wrong kind of—On the wilderness journey the people had been saved from starvation by the manna which fell for them from heaven. But they began to weary of it and lusted for the fleshpots of Egypt, saying: "Who shall give us flesh to eat? . . . Our soul is dried away; there is nothing at all save this manna to look upon" (Num. 11:4, 6). The answer of the Lord to this complaint and ingratitude was to give them as a judgment that for which they asked. A wind blowing in from the sea covered the ground about Israel's camp with quails. For a night and two days the greedy, flesh-lusting people gathered the quails and ate them; but while the flesh was yet between their teeth God smote the people with a great plague. The place where the victims of the plague were buried was called the Graves of Lust. God let them have the quails for which they asked, but with them he sent the plague. The psalmist's inspired comment on that bit of Hebrew history is this: He gave them the desire of their hearts, but sent leanness into their soul (Ps. 106:15).

PREACHER—*see* MINISTER

PREACHING—*see also* BIBLE (PREACHING AND THE), THE CROSS AND PREACHING, GOSPEL (PREACHING THE), OPPORTUNITY AND PREACHING, SIN (PREACHING IT)

If you are going to preach, you want to preach with enthusiasm, with power, with authority—not the varying authority of personal experience but the authority of heaven itself. In that most searching book, *Mark Rutherford's Deliverance,* Rutherford tells how his friend McKay had an idea that he could regenerate the submerged masses by quick spiritual means instead of by teaching and progress, and wished that he might speak from a pulpit. Rutherford asked him what he would say, and then told him how he himself had once been in St. Paul's Cathedral, excited at the thought of speaking to three or four thousand of his fellow men, but in a minute or two discovered that his sermon would be very much as follows: "Dear friends, I know no more than you know; we had

better go home." Without a "Thus saith the Lord," the preacher knows no more about it than anyone else.

———————

Every morning on my way down to the church study I used to walk across a bridge over the Schuylkill River. Looking over the parapet of the bridge, I could tell the state of the tide by the condition of the river banks. When the tide is at flood the river clings high up against the piers and close to the grass that grows along the banks. But when the tide is out a dirty scum is left on the stone piers, and the lower reaches of the banks are oozy and beslimed, altogether unlovely and unattractive.

There are flood tides in the work of the ministry, and there are low tides. There are days when the minister feels himself carried along by the great momentum of centuries of Christian history: he is standing in the long succession of teachers, preachers, prophets, and disciples of Jesus Christ; he is a citizen of the only kingdom that the convulsions of time and human passion have not shaken down. He feels confident of the ground of belief upon which he stands; his heart is warmed by the knowledge that this or that person has been helped and strengthened by the preaching of the gospel; he knows that his own heart and life have been uplifted and purified by the great truths of redemption which he has declared to the people; and in his own church there is pleasant unity and Christian harmony. This is the flood-tide experience, and it is then that the minister magnifies his office above any other office among the sons of men.

But the very next day may come the low tide. He has preached more earnestly than ever before, yet a Communion season approaches with fewer than ever coming forward to signify that those truths have gone home and produced the fruits of conviction and repentance and faith in Jesus Christ.

—**Beecher's**—His great English contemporary Charles Haddon Spurgeon called Beecher the "most myriad-minded man since Shakespeare." Whoever reads the sermons or speeches of Beecher is amazed at the spontaneous discharge of his mind and soul. As Theodore Parker said of him, "Other preachers have tanks, barrels of rain, well-water, but on their premises is no spring, and it never rains there. A mountain spring supplies Mr. Beecher with fresh living water." In this respect America has never produced a preacher like him. Perhaps in all its ages the Christian Church has never produced a preacher of such spontaneous and overwhelming power as Henry Ward Beecher.

—**After the benediction**—One of the most solemn and tender parts of a church service is when the benediction has been pronounced and the congregation starts for the door. Standing in his pulpit and looking over the throng, the minister may wonder what has been accomplished. Where has God's Word not returned unto him void? How many lives have been impressed, but only for a moment, and tomorrow will go back to their old ways and to their old sins? Where are the hearts which are like the stony ground upon which the seed has fallen, and tomorrow the birds of the air, the thoughts and pleasures of the world, will gather up the precious seed. And where are the hearts to which the seed has fallen only to be choked tomorrow by the cares of this world? And where are the hearts which have been permanently impressed and will obey God's voice and bring forth fruit unto Eternal Life? God only knows. Like the great Preacher and the great Sower himself,

the best the preacher can do is to scatter far and wide his seed.

If God speaks to your heart, if the least impression has been made upon your soul tonight, do not let it go unused. Tonight God speaks. Only man, only the world, says Tomorrow. But when the Spirit of God speaks to our hearts he never says Tomorrow but always Today! Tonight! Today, if you will hear his voice, oh, harden not your hearts!

—**And comfort**—A young English preacher speaking one day to the celebrated Dr. Dale was telling him how necessary it was that ministers should preach to the times, meaning by that that he should serve the ordinary menu of social and ethical discourses. Dale responded, "Go thou, young man, and preach to broken hearts, and you will preach to the eternities."

—**And conversion**—Very early in my ministry I read in the *British Weekly*, then the most widely read of religious journals, an article by the editor, Sir Robertson Nicoll, in which he related his experiences in visiting churches of the south of England during a period of convalescence after a long illness. He spoke of the sober order and dignity of the church services, and how all the preachers were sincere and well-educated men who delivered thoughtful and well-prepared sermons. But at the end of the article he said, "Not a single one of the sermons I heard would have converted a titmouse."

That sentence of indictment has often come back to me in the many years that have passed since I read that article. Not one of them would have converted a titmouse! How many of our own sermons, if the truth were to be told, would have that indictment written across the last page!

—Courageous—It takes little courage to stand upon a platform and denounce at long range the sins of what we call "high society." It took real courage to do what John did. He marched into the palace itself and there, in the presence of the adulterous pair, said to Herod, "It is not lawful for thee to have her; you are breaking God's commandment and God will judge you." That sermon cost John his life. Oh, if John had been mobbed by the people, assassinated by the soldiers, or torn by a wild beast in the midst of one of his desert reveries, that, we think, had been a death in keeping with his life. But to think that he had to die at the whispered wish of a vindictive adulteress! The greatest man that ever lived, and here is his head on a silver charger to please the whim of a half-naked dancing girl! And the sun still smiles, the earth does not yawn to swallow up the authors of this infamy!

But wait! The evangelist tells us that when John was dead his disciples came and took up the body and buried it, and went and told Jesus. John had friends, disciples; and I have no doubt that they wrapped his body in as clean a linen cloth as that which enwound the body of the Lord, and women anointed him with their tears. Perhaps in Jerusalem they buried the body, perhaps by Jordan's flood, and rolled a great stone to the door of the sepulcher and departed. *It* not *him;* the body, not John! They could not bury John. Time has not been able to bury him; the ages have not been able to engulf him. No wonder guilty Herod, when he heard of the preaching of Jesus, stricken in conscience, cried out in fear and remorse, "John whom I beheaded is risen from the dead!" The soul of John the Baptist marches on; still cries his voice in the wilderness—every word that he uttered a battle, and his name an army with banners!

Bourdaloue was the court preacher of Louis XIV. Wishing to rebuke the king for his profligate life, he drew in general terms a picture of a great sinner and the doom upon such a trangressor, hoping that the king would recognize the portrait. But perceiving that the pleasure-loving monarch was undisturbed, Bourdaloue suddenly cried out in a voice of thunder, as Nathan had once done to King David, "Thou art the man" (II Sam. 12:7)! Afterward he said to the startled monarch, "Your majesty must not be angry, for in the pulpit I have no other master than the King of Kings."

"In that night was Belshazzar the king of the Chaldeans slain." (Dan. 5:30.) This was one of the great, tragic, and unforgettable nights of the Bible. One thing I learn from this night is the value and the power and the influence of a fearless preacher. Tempted by the huge reward offered him, or fearful of the king's vengeance, Daniel might have hedged a little on the interpretation of what was written upon the wall. He might have said, as did the prophets of Babylon, that he was unable to read it; or he might have given it some other meaning than the true meaning; or he might have read only a part of it, and left out the pronouncement of death and doom.

But Daniel was a true and fearless preacher. With Belshazzar and a thousand wine-inflamed lords and nobles for his congregation, the grand old Hebrew prophet declared unto them the "whole counsel of God." The majesty of an earthly king and kingdom was nothing to Daniel, compared with the majesty of the King of Kings!

—Earnest—In *Confessions of an English Opium Eater* Thomas De Quincey describes the preacher to whom he listened as a boy in Manchester as "sincere, but not earnest."

Sincere, but not earnest! How could a man be sincere, but not earnest? De Quincey did not manhandle words but used them to express a very definite idea. What could be the idea that lay back of this distinction between a sincere preacher and an earnest one? Light was thrown on the subject by what he said about this preacher's starting from the low ground of such themes as the benefits of industry, the dangers of bad companions, the importance of setting a good example, or the value of perseverance. More light shone on the matter when I read a little farther and came upon this: "By mere accident I heard quoted a couplet which seemed to me sublime. It described a preacher such as sometimes arises in difficult times, or in fermenting times—a son of thunder that looks all enemies in the face and volunteers a defiance even when it would have been easy to evade it. The lines were written by Richard Baxter. As a pulpit orator he was perhaps the Whitefield of the seventeenth century—the Leucononmos of Cowper. And thus it is that he describes the impassioned character of his own preaching—

"I preached as never sure to preach again,

"(Even that was telling; but then followed this thunder peal):

"And as dying man to dying men.

"This couplet, which seemed to me equally for weight and for splendor like molten gold, laid bare another aspect of the Catholic Church, revealed it as a church militant and crusading."

Putting these two paragraphs together, that about his preacher's unimpassioned and desultory themes, and this about Richard Baxter, who described himself as one who preached as "a dying man to dying men," I began to see what De Quincey meant when he said of this preacher, whom he loved and respected, that he was sincere, but not earnest. Much of the best preaching of our day is sincere, but not earnest. It is not earnest because it does not lay hold upon what Chalmers in his regal manner called the "grand particularities" of the Christian religion.

———•◄►•———

—First attempts at—At the close of my seminary course the members of the village church I had served for two happy summers invited me to become their pastor. It was hard to refuse the invitation of these fine, loyal souls; and, although my lot was cast elsewhere, I have never forgotten them—can never forget them. There I first learned to love and appreciate the noble calling of the Christian ministry; there for the first time I formed those habits of study which have never been broken; there for the first time I stood the "reverend Champion" in the house of pain and sickness; and there for the first time I marveled at the aloofness of death, and repeated the grand music of David and Paul over the open graves in the quiet, white-fenced cemetery, where the shadows of the elms played to and fro on the rich grass, as if to remind the mourner of the shadow brevity of human life.

I visited the village twelve years later, and found the same white cottages and clambering vines; but many of those who had sat under me in the little church, and for whom I had tried to break the bread of life, were not there to greet me. Their names and their years were graven on the tomb.

Ofttimes in the midst of my labors in the other churches where I have been permitted to labor that little square-towered church rises before my eyes, and I can hear the sweet music of its bell calling me to my sacred task, and then floating off toward the hills along the river, flowing swiftly and silently away like the river of a man's life. As I sit at my desk in the study I can at times inhale the fragrance of the lilac bushes which grew near the window of the church manse. I would not be altogether frank unless I confessed that to think of that village church and those village friends ofttimes brings to my lips the sigh of David when he beheld afar off the well of Bethlehem and said, "Oh that one would give me drink of the water of the well of Bethlehem, which is by the gate!" (II Sam. 23:15).

—**First sermon**—David Livingstone was sent one Sunday evening to preach in the village of Stanford Rivers, where the tradition of Livingstone's first effort at preaching is still cherished. The raw, somewhat heavy-looking Scotch youth, to whom public speech was always a difficulty, gave out his text "very deliberately." That was all the congregation got—the sermon composed on the text had fled, owing to the nervous embarrassment produced by a handful of people in a village chapel. "Friends," said the youth, "I have forgotten all I had to say" —and, hurrying out of the pulpit, he left the chapel.

—**The gospel**—The center of the preacher's message is always Christ. St. Bernard said that one Sabbath he preached himself, and all the scholars came forward to praise him. The next Sabbath he preached Christ, and all the sinners came up to thank him. To be worthy of the thanks of sinners, not the praise of men, is the ambition of the true minister.

On the northwest tower of St. Paul's in London hangs the great bell known as "Great Paul." The bell bears this inscription from the Vulgate (I Cor. 9:16): *"Vae mihi si non evangelisavero"*— "Woe is unto me, if I preach not the gospel!" Those words had, I am sure, a double meaning for Paul—not only that he felt he must preach but that he dreaded the woe upon him who stands to preach and yet preaches something other than the gospel.

I read recently a book of sermons, selected sermons, preached by a distinguished minister before university congregations. From beginning to end there was not a sermon or a paragraph or a sentence which proclaimed Christ as the Savior from sin. One could say of them what Dr. McCosh once said of the sermons of the minister who baptized him: "They are gracefully written, in short and well-constructed sentences, and they have fine sentiment; but they do not contain one sentence of gospel truth, that is, of Jesus set forth as the Redeemer of sinners."

A young preacher went to David Swing, the poet-preacher of Chicago, many years ago and asked him what he should do to get a congregation on Sunday. He said, "I have tried history, biography, literature, poetry, book reviews, politics—but the people won't come. What shall I do?"

Swing responded, "Suppose now you try the gospel!"

—**And great themes**—A noted Russian musician and composer visiting in England was taken by his host to church, where he heard a little sermon on a little subject. When the next Sabbath came around his host asked him if he wished to go again. He said, "Yes, I will go if the preacher will ask me to do something great."

This morning I ask you to do something great—to address your mind and to fix your faith upon the providence of Almighty God.

—From the heart—Dr. McCosh describes the extraordinary and sustained popularity of the famous preacher of Scotland, his uncle by marriage, Thomas Guthrie. Critical hearers said he was not logical and that he was not profound. "But," says McCosh, "the people thronged to hear him because they knew he would warm their hearts. Man longs for that. He likes a friend who has a real interest in him. He likes to go to a church where he believes the people and the minister are interested in him and where his heart will be warmed by the message of the love of God."

—Responsibility of—Delayed once for several hours in the town of Dijon in France, I went into the venerable cathedral there. What I remember now about that cathedral is the finely wrought stone pulpit, and just beneath it the figure of a recording angel, holding a tablet in one hand and a pen in the other, with face upturned toward the pulpit, waiting to hear and to record what the preacher says.

Always that angel stands below our pulpits. He is not waiting to put down things which the congregation might like to record—in pleasure or displeasure—but whether or not the words of the preacher are true to the gospel with which he has been entrusted.

—Results of—Percy Ainsworth, had rooms with the village wheelwright in

Sussex. He often wished that he could see the results of his work as the wheelwright could view his finished product. But all his preaching and praying—what effect was it having upon the rough country and town lads? Was it guarding them from evil, lifting them up into the likeness of God's children?

Many others who fish in the deep and mysterious sea of character, seeking to win from men and for them the fruits of the spirit—love, joy, peace, long suffering, gentleness, goodness, faith—must wish at times that their fidelity and energy might have its visible reward, as in other kinds of work done by men. But that is denied them, and often it may seem to them that they too have toiled all night and taken nothing. They who thus labor must themselves have that faith which they commend to others, and endure as seeing Him who is invisible.

Stephen Grellet, the noted Friend, once felt a burden on his heart and the leading of the Holy Spirit to preach the gospel to men in an American lumber camp. But when he arrived at the camp he found it deserted, for the men had gone farther into the forest. Feeling, nevertheless, that he had been sent there by the Holy Spirit, he stood up in the empty mess hall and delivered his sermon, heard, as he thought, only by the board walls of the building and the lofty trees of the forest.

Years afterward, crossing London Bridge in the evening gloom, he was somewhat rudely stopped by a man who accosted him and said, "You are the man I have been looking for all these years. I have found you at last."

"There must be some mistake," said Grellet. "I have never seen thee."

"No," said the man. "But did you not preach at a lumber camp in the American forest?"

"Yes, but there was no one there."

"I was there," responded the man, "and I heard the sermon."

Then he went on to relate how he had come back from where the men were working to get a saw that had been left behind, when he was startled and alarmed at hearing the sound of a man's voice. Approaching the building, he looked through a chink of the logs and saw Grellet standing by himself preaching the sermon. He listened to the preacher, was convicted of sin, got hold of a copy of the Scriptures, learned the way of life, was saved, and brought others with him into the Kingdom of Heaven.

* * *

Spurgeon went one day into Albert Hall, where he was to preach on the coming Sabbath. In order to test out the hall with his voice, he mounted the platform and repeated the text, "The blood of Jesus Christ his Son cleanseth us from all sin" (I John 1:7). Not long afterward he received word that the repetition of that text had borne rich fruit. A painter, at work in some part of the great hall, was startled when he heard the voice of Spurgeon repeating in the empty hall that great sentence of John's. The words so impressed him that he was converted and brought to Christ.

—Reward of—A minister, buffeted and weary of the world, after confessing that he was afraid he had not brought a single soul to Christ, died and was buried. It was a cold, dismal, rainy day. Only the undertaker, the gravediggers, the officiating minister, and one other man were at the grave. When the benediction had been pronounced, the minister noted that the solitary attendant was in tears. He walked around the grave, and, taking the man by the hand, said to him, "Were you his relative?"

"No."

"A member of his congregation?"

"No."

"Were you his friend?"

"No. I was not his relative, nor his friend, nor a member of his church. But that man saved my soul!"

* * *

—To the sinner—Every Sabbath morning and evening in a small New England church there was seen among the few worshipers a man whose great head and cavernous eyes were in keeping with his great distinction. Someone who knew him in Washington asked him how it was that there in the village he was so regular in going to the small church and listening to the ungifted minister, whereas in Washington he paid little attention to great churches and distinguished preachers. The man with the great head and the wonderful eyes answered: "In Washington they preach to Daniel Webster the statesman and the orator. Here in this village this man preaches to Daniel Webster the sinner."

* * *

—Thrill of—Who going up the steps of a pulpit would not feel the mystery and the awe of any congregation? It is that which makes the pulpit what Spencer called it, "this awful place." What sorrows, what hopes, what fears, what anxieties, what prejudices, what sins, what temptations, and what despairs, are all present before him! Thinking of that, who would not say, "Who is sufficient for these things?" Yet here the people are, waiting to hear what he will say!

PREDESTINATION—*see also* SUFFERING AND GOD

Side by side with the conviction of our freedom and responsibility there goes the evidence of something, or Some One, beyond our own life and its choices. In the great railroad stations you can see a metallic pencil come out and write in huge characters on the wall the time of the arrival or departure of the trains. The metallic pencil seems to write of itself; but we know that, hidden in an office somewhere, the mind and hand of a man are operating the pencil. So in our own life we note our own deliberations and choices and decisions, and yet in the fabric of our destiny there seems to be other strands—strands not of our own weaving.

<hr>

Contrary to the opinion of those who held that Abraham Lincoln was fortunate in his death, Horace Greeley thought him most inapt for the leadership of a people involved in a great struggle for self-preservation but that few men were better fitted to guide a nation's destinies in time of peace.

Greeley says: "I sat just behind him as he read his inaugural on a bright, warm, still March day, expecting to hear its delivery arrested by the crack of a rifle aimed at his heart. But it pleased God to postpone the deed, though there was forty times the reason for shooting him in 1860 that there was in 1865, and at least forty times as many intent on killing him or having him killed. No shot was then fired, however, for his hour had not yet come."

In that sentence, "His hour had not yet come," Horace Greeley gives us his philosophy of history. Lincoln was not assassinated in 1861, because his hour had not yet come.

<hr>

In the first book of Samuel we have a curious, and in some respects a very extraordinary, story of how the people of a nation and of a city made an experiment to see whether or not God was in their national life and in the disasters that had befallen them. The Israelites had been defeated in a great battle into which they had taken the Ark of the Covenant with the hope that its presence would insure victory over the Philistines. But in the battle the army of Israel was beaten and the Ark was carried off in triumph by the victorious Philistines.

But wherever the Philistines took it or set it up, in the Temple of Dagon or elsewhere, the presence of the Ark was accompanied by grievous disasters and plagues. The leaders resolved to get rid of the Ark, but in doing so they determined to ascertain, if possible, whether the disasters which had fallen upon them had anything to do with the Ark of Israel and Israel's God. This was the plan they devised: The Ark was placed on a cart to which were hitched two cows whose calves were in the stalls. The cows were started along the road northward leading in the direction of Israel. If, obedient to the strong, maternal instinct of all animals, the cows turned backward toward their offspring, the conclusion would be that the misfortunes which had fallen upon the Philistines just happened by chance and that there was nothing really dangerous about the Ark. But if, on the other hand, going contrary to their natural instincts, the cattle went on northward, disregarding the calls of their offspring, the conclusion would be that what had happened to the Philistines in connection with the Ark was a judgment of God.

The whole population turned out to watch the experiment and to see what would happen. Instead of turning around to go back to the stalls where their calves were, the cows went lowing along the highway straight in the direction of Israel. The Philistines knew that what had had happened to them was not chance but the judgment of God.

<hr>

In his anxiety to know whether or not he had faith, John Bunyan was tempted to work a miracle; and one day between Elstow and Bedford he was about to say to the puddles that were in the horse path, "Be dry," and to the dry places, "Be you puddles." If he had faith he ought to be able to work miracles. But just as he was about to speak, this thought came into his mind: "Go under yonder hedge and pray first that God would make you able." When he had prayed he concluded that he had better not try the experiment, because if he failed he would have to look upon himself as a castaway. "Nay," thought he, "if it be so, I will not try yet, but will stay a little longer."

This incident reminds one of what Rousseau says in his *Confessions* about his anxiety concerning election. He determined to decide the matter as to whether or not he was of the elect by throwing an apple at a tree. If he missed, he was doomed to be lost. If he hit the tree, he was of the elect. He tells us that he hit the tree—but confesses that he had chosen a tree of considerable diameter!

John Burroughs, the famous naturalist, said of predestination: "It was an iron-clad faith, and it stood the wear and tear of life well."

This generation is too light and frivolous for such a heroic creed; the sons of the old members are not men enough to stand up under the moral weight of Calvinism and predestination.

———

—And fatalism—On the lips of thousands of soldiers in training camps or in the forefront of the hottest battle there are words which confess to their belief in predestination—that is, in the sense of the time for their death being appointed. "Fatalism," a friend said to me when I spoke to him along this line.

"No," I rejoined, "not fatalism, but predestination."

"What is the difference?" he asked.

"The difference," I answered, "is all the difference that there is between a Turk and a Presbyterian elder in America."

It is easy to throw dust into the air and try to confuse fatalism with predestinationism, but "by their fruits ye shall know them" (Matt. 7:20). What mean these noble letters that Christian lads have written home to their parents in Scotland and England and Canada and America, telling their loved ones not to worry about them, nor greatly to grieve over them when they have "gone west," for their times are in God's hands and they yield gladly to his plan in their lives and in the life of the world? It means that the sufferings and hazards of the battlefield have brought to the front again that grand old belief in the eternal purpose of God.

———

—And free will—When the ship on which Paul was traveling to Rome was nearing the rocks off Malta, the seamen, under cover of paying out the anchors, were lowering the boats, intending to desert the ship. Without their help the necessary subsequent navigation of the ship was impossible, and Paul said to the centurion, "Except these abide in the ship, ye cannot be saved" (Acts 27:31). With that the soldiers drew out their swords and cut the ropes which held the boats. Yet only a little while before the angel had definitely informed Paul that everybody on board would be saved. Paul believed that, but his belief did not make him so great a fool as to neglect the ordinary precautions in a shipwreck. The decree of God was that the ship's company should be saved, and the decree took in the free and courageous and skillful activity of the seamen. Their freedom and responsibility were not curtailed by God's decree.

PRIDE—*see also* BEAUTY

After summarizing the vices of mankind in the biting satire of the voyage to the Houyhnhnms, Dean Swift concludes by saying: "My reconcilement to the Yahoo kind in general might not be so difficult, if they would be content with those vices and follies only which nature hath entitled them to. I am not in the least provoked at the sight of a lawyer, a pickpocket, a colonel, a fool, a lord, a gamester, a politician, a whoremonger, a physician, an evidence, a suborner, an attorney, a traitor, or the like; this is all according to the due course of things: but when I behold a lump of deformity and diseases both in body and in mind smitten with pride, it immediately breaks all the measures of my patience; neither shall I ever be able to comprehend how such an animal and such a vice could tally together."

———————

Dombey and Son, by Dickens, is a powerful study of the lasting and devastating effects of pride. Dombey's whole interest centers in his business firm. When Paul is born he changes the name of the firm to Dombey and Son, and his fierce and colossal pride invites the natural enemy of pride—adversity. This is the theme of Dickens to show how terrible pride is, and yet how low all its powers can be laid.

The birth of Paul, which made possible Dombey and Son, was to Dombey more than a compensation for the mother who died as the child began to live. But, driven too rapidly at school by the impatient father, Paul sickens and dies. Then the father, lured by the bait of wealth, marries a woman who is very beautiful, but as proud as himself. His humiliation of her leads to her humiliation of him by running off with his chief clerk; and when Dombey's love-starved daughter, looked upon with scorn because she cannot command the love of others, attempts to console the dishonored father, he strikes her down in his fury. She flees the house, leaving Dombey alone.

Then comes the final calamity—Dombey and Son fails. We see the ruined and desolate man sitting alone in the house which on the morrow he must leave. In that powerful passage Dickens describes the desolate and lonely man going about from room to room on the last night with a candle in his hand. At length he goes up to the little room where the little bed had been and there throws himself down on the floor and lets his tears flow as they will; and yet he is still a proud man who, if a kind hand could have been stretched out or a kind face could have looked in, would have risen up and turned away and gone down to his cell.

The way to companionship, fellowship, and happiness is the path of humility.

———————

Some of the proudest families in the country are, in the North, descendants of Jamaica rum merchants, owners of slave ships, and, in the South, descendants of ticket-of-leave convicts from Old Bailey in London. Upon such a platform as this does pride exhibit its Punch-and-Judy show!

PRINCIPLES—*see also* CONSCIENCE (LOYALTY TO), DREAMS (GREAT; LOST; OF YOUTH), IDEALS

In the battle of Hampton Roads the dreaded ironclad *Merrimac* swept down the Union line, passed unscathed through their fire, and drove her iron beak crashing into the wooden sides of the *Cumberland.* As she backed from the wound the angry waters rushed in and the old frigate, stricken a mortal blow, lurched to larboard and sank beneath the waves. But look! As her keel touches the bottom she rights, her masthead reappears, and there, above the surging waves and through the lurid smoke of battle, *there streams triumphant the Stars and Stripes!*

The ship may go down, and the cannon's roar may be hushed in the hissing seas; but the Principle is immortal and must prevail!

Shortly before the Civil War a young lawyer came down from Vermont and settled in Adams County, Pennsylvania. There he saw the fugitive slaves escaping from bondage, and as a conductor on the Underground Railroad he helped them to liberty. The iron of the thing entered into his soul and he gave himself with all his powers to combat that evil and to deliver all oppressed. When the great crisis, to which all those events were pointing, had broken over the nation, Thaddeus Stephens was perhaps the most powerful influence in the government of the United States. When he came to die, his only attendants were two Negro preachers. Today in the very midst of Lancaster, in a shabby cemetery, you can see his tomb, and on the tomb these words: "Finding that other cemeteries were restricted as to race by charter rights, I have chosen to lie in this humble spot, in order that I might testify, even in my death, to those principles which I have advocated through a long life."

PROFANITY

When St. Paul's Cathedral was being built, its famous architect, Sir Christopher Wren, had posted in different parts of the structure this notice: "Whereas among laborers and others that ungodly custom of swearing is so frequently heard to the dishonor of God and to the contempt of His authority, and to the end that such impiety may be utterly banished with these works which are intended to the service of God and the honor of religion, it is ordered that profane swearing shall be a sufficient crime to discharge any laborer that comes to the call."

To the builder of St. Paul's and those other noble temples associated with his name, profane words spoken by the builders desecrated and profaned the holy place. If that is true of the temple made with hands, how much more is it true of that most wonderful temple of all, the temple not made with hands—man himself!

William Cowper has a satirical piece in which he imagines a Persian listening to an Englishman swearing and, mistakenly thinking that he must be worshiping and praying, since he uses the name of God so frequently, asks him for an interest in his prayers.

A Persian, humble servant of the sun,
Who, though devout, yet bigotry had none,
Hearing a lawyer, grave in his address,
With adjurations every word impress,
Supposed the man a bishop, or at least,
God's name so much upon his lips, a priest;
Bow'd at the close with all his graceful airs,
And begg'd an interest in his frequent prayers.

A heathen coming to America and hearing people "pray" might get the idea that we are a much more devout and religious people than we are!

Woodrow Wilson liked to speak of his godly ministerial father, Dr. Joseph R. Wilson, for many years a distinguished Presbyterian minister in the South. Among the anecdotes he related of him was this: "He was once in a company of men where they were having a heated discussion. In the midst of it one let out a profane expletive. Then, seeing Dr. Wilson there, he offered him an apology, saying, 'Sir, I had forgotten that you were present. Please pardon me.' Dr. Wilson's reply was, 'It is not to me that you owe your apology, but to God.'"

PROGRESS

Agassiz used to illustrate progress by the three stages of growth: first, the seed stage, which is the slowest of all; then the blade, which is faster; then the fruit, which is the fastest stage of all.

In the blessings of our society today we see the flowering of a seed that was planted centuries ago and had to wait long in the cold and darkness of the earth before even the blade began to appear, and still more centuries before the fruit. As for other regenerative forces, we may be living only in their seed stage. It will be long generations before the fruit will appear to bless the children of mankind. God is never in a hurry. One day with him is as a thousand years, and a thousand years as one day.

———————

—In Christian life—A plane is made to go forward and upward. Between an airplane and every other form of locomotion and transportation there is one great contrast. The horse and wagon, the automobile, the bicycle, the locomotive, the speedboat, and the great battleship—all can come to a standstill without danger, and they can all reverse their engines, or their power, and back. But there is no reverse about the engine of an airplane. It cannot back. It dare not stand still. If it loses its momentum and forward drive, then it crashes. The only safety for the airplane is in its forward and upward motion.

What a parable that is of the Christian life! The only safe direction for the Christian to take is forward and upward. If he stops, or if he begins to slip and go backward, that moment he is in danger.

———————

—An illusion—The great French entomologist Fabre writes: "To what an ideal height will this process of evolution lead mankind? To no very magnificent height, it is to be feared. We are afflicted with an indelible taint, a sort of original sin. We are made after a pattern, and we can do nothing to change ourselves. We are marked with the mark of the beast, the taint·of the belly, the inexhaustible source of bestiality."

That, then, is what science sees through its glass. It beholds progress of a kind, but no victory of good over evil. The idea of a natural, inevitable, unstoppable progress, culminating in the abolition of wrong and the victory of right, is contrary not only to revelation but also to reason and experience and common sense.

Prolong life as it may, can science stop men from dying? Can progress restrain men from sinning? Can knowledge heal the broken heart or wipe away the tear? A few simple questions such as these, and this gorgeous phantasmagoria of a natural and inevitable progress and evolution fades and vanishes; and we are left on the dusty plains where we stood before, and the pompous human eloquence which has accompanied this theory of the world movement is exposed as tinkling cymbal and sounding brass.

———————

—And the soul—Once the newspapers had much to say about a dog who happened to come into a room of experimentation at Schenectady and bark into the microphone with which its master was experimenting. In three seconds the bark of the dog, which had gone to Australia and clear around the world, was distinctly recorded on the loud speaker in the room.

But who cares whether a dog heard its own bark carried clear around the world in three seconds? Or who cares whether or not man's bark is heard around the world? What occasion for jubilee is there in that? Much of our celebrating and self-congratulation and boasting is like the commotion that was made over a dog's barking clear around the world. Our great skyscrapers, our engines of destruction and locomotion, our mighty bridges, our enormous factories—all this development of the external and the mechanical and materialistic side of life is in reality no occasion for boasting or for celebration. All these are far from God's idea of memorable events.

But when a soul turns from its pride and self-love, when it gets up from among the swine where it has been lying and says, "I will arise and go to my father" (Luke 15:18); whenever love conquers hate; whenever pity subdues anger; whenever faith conquers despair; whenever a soul gives itself in penitence and love to its Redeemer—that, says Jesus, is something worth celebrating.

PROPHECY

Eighteen centuries ago a young scholar of philosophy from the Roman colony near ancient Samaria was taking a solitary walk along the shores of the Mediterranean Sea. Thirsting after truth as the one great possession, he had drawn water out of every well of ancient learning and philosophy, only to thirst again. He had gone the rounds of the Stoics, the Platonists, the Peripatetics, the Pythagoreans, and yet had not come to satisfaction and peace. But on this morning walk by the seaside he met a venerable Christian. They engaged in conversation,

and that conversation changed the course of Justin Martyr's life. This unknown friend showed him how the philosophers reasoned about the truth, where as the Hebrew prophets spoke of truth as men who had been witnesses. He pointed out to him how the prophets had foretold the coming of Christ, and how their predictions were fulfilled in his life and work. Taking the old man's advice, Justin commenced the study of the Old Testament prophecies and their confirmation in the Gospels. This convinced him of the truth of Christianity, and he became a Christian and one of the greatest defenders of its truth and most heroic of its martyrs.

PROSPERITY

Prosperity sometimes makes men forget the friends of their humble origin. I dined once with a distinguished lawyer. I did not know it at the time I dined with him—for forty years had passed since I had seen him—but he lived not far from my boyhood home and I knew his family and their exceedingly humble surroundings. The man knew where I had come from, but never once in the course of the evening's conversation did he refer to his home town or his early surroundings; evidently he did not want to be reminded of that.

PROVIDENCE—*see also* CHANCE, DEATH (READY FOR, 4th and 5th entries), GOD, HISTORY, PRAYER (UNANSWERED), PREDESTINATION

Sometimes you hear people speaking of how by a kind providence their life was spared in some accident. They were saved from injury and death either because they did not take the train or the plane or the ship that met with disaster, or because in some unaccountable way the shaft of death missed them. But what about those who did take the ship, or the train, or the plane, and were killed? Shall we exclude providence from their death?

John Bunyan was drafted as a soldier in the Civil War in England, to take part in the siege of Leicester. As he was just about ready to go forward with his company, another requested to go in his place. "He took my place; and, coming to the siege, as he stood sentinel he was shot in the head by a musket bullet, and died." That providence saved John Bunyan for his mighty labors for the Kingdom of God. But there was a providence, also, in the death of the soldier who took his place.

— And adversity—We owe a great deal of our knowledge concerning the birds of our country to the celebrated American ornithologist Audubon. He spent part of his early life in Kentucky; and when Abraham Lincoln, a gangling country youth, went to the country store to buy calico, or buttons, or groceries for his cabin home, he was, no doubt, waited upon by the young clerk Audubon.

The journal of Audubon is a document of deep human interest. In it we have a recital of the sufferings and hardships and discouragements through which he passed when the world to him was a blank; and yet he writes: "Through those dark days I was being led to the development of the talents I love. One of the most extraordinary things among all these adverse circumstances was that I never for a day gave up listening to the song of our birds, or watching their peculiar habits, or delineating them in the best way that I could; nay, during my deepest troubles I frequently would wrench myself away from the persons around me and return to some secluded part of our noble forests, and many a time at the sound of the wood thrush's

melodies have I fallen on my knees, and there earnestly prayed to God. This never failed to bring me the most valued thoughts, and always comforted me."

— And conversion—This is an unpublished incident in the life of Hudson Taylor. He came to the city of Hangchow. The next day, with a bag of books over his shoulder, he started an evangelistic tour of the city. Great crowds followed him about. At night, weary, he sat down to rest at a tea house in the suburbs on the way to his boat in the river. As he sat at the table he saw peering at him though the gathering gloom an elderly Chinese. The man was evidently seeking someone.

"Are you a foreigner?"

"Yes, I am an Englishman."

"Are there books in that bag on the table?"

"Yes, there are."

"Are you a teacher of a foreign religion?"

"Yes, of the Jesus religion."

The Chinese then told Taylor that he had been an earnest seeker after truth for many years, but could find no religion which could take the burden of guilt from his soul. A few nights before, he had had a vision: a man in white had told him to go to Hangchow, that he would find there a foreigner sitting in an inn, with a bag of books on the table before him. He had visited the inn but had found no such person. Finally, hearing of this inn in the suburbs, he had as a last hope come thither. He asked Taylor to tell him the truth, whereupon he preached the gospel and gave him a New Testament. Two days later Taylor visited his house and found he had destroyed all his idols and was rejoicing in Jesus Christ. Taylor left the man adoring God not only for his power to save, but also for his marvelous and miraculous ways of leading souls to the messenger and the message of the gospel.

* * *

—In daily life—Dr. John Witherspoon, signer of the Declaration of Independence and president of the College of New Jersey, which became Princeton University, lived at Tusculum, a country seat at Rocky Hill, about two miles from the college, and drove every day to his duties as teacher and president. One day a neighbor came excitedly into his study at the college and said, "Dr. Witherspoon, you must join me in giving thanks to God for his extraordinary providence in saving my life, for as I was driving from Rocky Hill the horse ran away and the buggy was smashed to pieces on the rocks, but I escaped unharmed!"

"Why," answered Dr. Witherspoon, "I can tell you a far more remarkable providence than that. I have driven over that road hundreds of times. My horse never ran away, my buggy never was smashed, I was never hurt."

* * *

—God's plan—It is a cold, bleak, dark night on the Pennsylvania Canal; the *Evening Star*, a towboat, is gliding along through the dark waters. As the boat approaches one of the locks a bugle is sounded and a boy in his teens awakens out of his sleep and, pulling his jacket about him, comes to the deck to take his turn at the bowline. As he is uncoiling the line, the slack of the rope catches in a crevice on the edge of the deck. The boy, half asleep, gives it one pull, then another, but it does not yield. Then a harder pull, and it comes loose; but the strength of the pull on the rope throws him backward off the deck into the water. As he sinks beneath the water he has a feeling that only a miracle can save him. Instinctively he clutches at the rope that has fallen with him into the water. Once again the slack of the rope catches

in the crevice on the deck, and holding to the rope the boy is able to pull himself on deck, hand over hand. As he sits there, cold and dripping, reflecting on his escape, he is convinced that only a miracle has saved him.

To prove this he takes the same rope and tries to fling it into the crevice where twice it had caught, once to throw him into the water, the second time to pull him out of his grave. As many as six hundred times, he tells us, he tried to throw the rope into the crevice. But not a single time out of the six hundred did it catch. Ten times six hundred, he calculated, would be six thousand; therefore the chance of his being saved was one to six thousand. Convinced that God had saved his life, he felt, therefore, that his life must be worth saving; he resolved to go home, get an education, and be something else than a hand on a towboat.

He left the boat and started for his mother's cabin home in the woods of Ohio. It was evening when he arrived; and, looking through the window, he saw his mother before the fire, with her Bible on her knee. She was not reading the words, but rather repeating them, and the words which he heard were these: "O turn unto me, and have mercy unto me; give thy strength unto thy servant, and save the son of thine handmaid" (Ps. 86:16). The boy entered the cabin and told his mother what had happened, that he had given himself to God, and that he proposed to make a man of himself.

Years pass, and the young boy has become the president of a college. The drums of the Civil War are beating. He has a wife and children, and is not sure whether it is his duty to go to the front. To decide the matter, he takes his Bible and goes apart. At the end of that watch with God he comes out to say that he

287

regards his life as belonging to his country, and goes off to the front, where he becomes a distinguished soldier and a major general.

The war is over; but rejoicing has been turned into sorrow, all the stars of hope have been obscured by the clouds of a great calamity. The president whose patience and gentleness and forbearance and unshaken faith in justice and truth have led his country through the terrible years of war has fallen by the assassin's bullet. In the narrow street in front of the Exchange in New York a great crowd has assembled. Passions are running high, and the mob is getting ready to vent its wrath upon the property and lives of all those who have opposed the administration.

At that moment a man steps out between the great pillars and, waving what seems to be a telegram in his hand, cries, "Another telegram from Washington!" The crowd becomes quiet to hear what the message is. But instead of reading a telegram, this is what he said: " 'Clouds and darkness are round about him: righteousness and judgment are the habitation of his throne' (Ps. 97:2). Fellow citizens! God reigns, and the government at Washington still lives." The speaker is the boy whose life had been saved by the rope catching in the deck of the towboat—James A. Garfield.

⁂

At thirty-two years of age William Cowper passed through a great crisis in his life. He tried to end his life by taking laudanum. Then he hired a coach and was driven to the Thames, intending to throw himself into the river; but some power seemed to restrain him. The next morning he fell upon a knife, but the blade broke and his life was saved. He then tried to hang himself, and was cut down unconscious but still alive. Then one morning, in a moment of strange cheerfulness, he took up his Bible and read a verse in the Letter to the Romans. In a moment he received strength to believe, and rejoiced in the forgiving power of God. Some years later, after he had passed through a rich Christian experience and had written many beautiful hymns, Cowper sat down one day and summed up his faith in God's dealings with him, and with other men, in the great hymn on divine providence:

> *God moves in a mysterious way*
> *His wonders to perform;*
> *He plants his footsteps in the sea,*
> *And rides upon the storm.*

> *Deep in unfathomable mines*
> *Of never-failing skill,*
> *He treasures up his bright designs,*
> *And works his soverign will.*

⁂

Suppose that I go down to the navy yard and find there a ship in process of construction. I know nothing of the purpose for which the ship is being built, whether it is to be a vessel of war, or pleasure, or to carry passengers, or to sail the seas with the wares of the world. What right do I have to say to the builder and designer, "Why do you not do it thus?" or "Why is this put in this place instead of yonder?" The builder need not answer my objections; he can tell me to wait until the ship is finished and launched to do the work for which it is being built.

Only God sees the consummation; and until you and I see that consummation divine of God's glorious plan, the mystery hid from the foundations of the world, we can claim no right to find fault with what has been done.

⁂

Over the desk of Dr. E. C. Norton, for many years professor of Greek at Pomona College, California, there hung a curious decoration. Framed under glass were the burned fragments of a cuff, carefully pasted together upon a piece of cardboard. During his senior year at college Norton was hitching a team to a tree when lightning struck the tree and killed both the horses, felling him to the ground and burning his arm and hand so that for a time they were paralyzed. Commenting on that narrow escape, he said, "I guess the Lord must have had something for me to do."

The framed fragments of the cuff on the wall of his office were a constant reminder that God had something for him to do.

———•◦•———

Columbus, on his way back to Italy disheartened and discouraged, leading his boy by the hand, stopped one day at a convent not far from Granada and asked for a drink of water. The monk who gave him a drink and heard his story was the man who intervened on his behalf with Queen Isabella, and out of that request for a glass of water came the discovery of America.

John Calvin on his way to Italy, the regular road being closed because of the war between France and Italy, had to pass through Geneva; and there he met Farrel, who with fiery eloquence demanded that he stay at Geneva and lead the work of God there.

Abraham Lincoln, rummaging in a barrel of rubbish that someone had left in his store at Salem, came upon a copy of Blackstone's *Commentaries;* and of that chance discovery were awakened the ambitions and desires which were to play so great a part in American history.

George Whitefield, greatest of all preachers, employed as a drawer in the Bell Inn, was unable to get along with his brother's wife; and that led him to give up his employment and go to Bristol, and then, step by step, to Oxford, and

then to his apostolic career in the ministry. Whitefield used to say that the difference he had with his brother's wife was God's way of forcing him out of the public business and calling him "from drawing wine for drunkards to draw water out of the wells of Salvation for the refreshment of his spiritual Israel."

———•◦•———

Only a cradle of bulrushes, daubed with slime and pitch—yet never did loving maternal hands put more of a mother's soul and a mother's heart into the making of a cradle for its little occupant. By night she carried the babe and his cradle down to the river Nile. Never was a child more tenderly laid in his cradle than was Moses that night by the hand of his faithful mother. When the rising sun made it dangerous for her to linger longer, she gave her babe a last kiss, took a last look at him, and then went back to the city, leaving Miriam, the sister, to watch and see what might happen.

How much of the world's hope was vested in that frail cradle rocking there in the waters of the Nile, with the infant looking up at the lotus flowers which bent over it! Only that ark of bulrushes between the child and the river, only the lotus flowers along the banks to screen him from the murderous hand of Pharaoh! And yet the child was safe, because he represented the great purpose and plan of God.

———•◦•———

The true attitude toward life, together with the hopelessness and inadequacy of any other view of life, is well set forth in Wordsworth's poem "The Excursion." The Wanderer and the Poet meet in a lonely glen an aged hermit. The Solitary tells them the cause of his melancholy and distaste for life. Full of life's joys and hopes, he had brought his young bride to a cottage in this glen. For a time it was always summer. Then came two children, upon whom rested all the parents' hopes and joys. Then came the sudden change in their souls' weather. First the daughter died, then the son— and then the mother, his beloved wife.

From the first paroxysm of his grief the Solitary was roused by the outbreak of the French Revolution; and in the great ideas of liberty, equality, and fraternity he sought to forget his sorrow. But with the excesses of the Revolution he found that he had worshiped liberty and, as Brutus did with virtue, had found it but a shade. Next he sought relief and new engagement in the great republic of the West—America.

But there, too, he was disappointed, and found only "big passions strutting on a petty stage." Westward he took his way to the wild and virgin forests. But instead of the pure archetype of human greatness he found the savage, "squalid, vengeful, and impure." In disgust he came back to his English glen, without hope; and he is now patiently, yet listlessly, waiting for the stream of his life to find the unfathomable gulf of the grave.

To this indictment of life and hope the Wanderer thus responds:

> *One adequate support*
> *For the calamities of mortal life*
> *Exists—one only; an assured belief*
> *That the procession of our fate,*
> * howe'er*
> *Sad or disturbed, is ordered by a*
> * Being*
> *Of infinite benevolence and power;*
> *Whose everlasting purposes embrace*
> *All accidents, converting them to*
> * good.*
> *—The darts of anguish* fix *not where*
> * the seat*
> *Of suffering hath been thoroughly*
> * fortified*
> *By acquiescence in the Will supreme.*

In December, 1852, the president-elect of the United States, Franklin Pierce, traveling with his family on a train, was wrecked at Concord, New Hampshire. Several of the passengers were killed, among them the young son of the president-elect, a fine lad of ten years, who died in his mother's arms. The accident was thought to be due to dereliction of duty on the part of an intoxicated brakeman; and some of those who had received injuries, or whose relatives had been killed in the disaster, brought suit against the railroad company. But Mrs. Pierce, a devout Christian, would not permit the president-elect to become a party to the suit; on the contrary, she had him secure the services of the famous lawyer Benjamin Butler to defend the railroad, on the ground that she regarded the disaster and the great personal sorrow that it had brought to them as a special providence better to prepare the president-elect for the high office to which he was shortly to be inaugurated.

—God's touch—On February 26, 1844, occurred one of the major disasters in the history of our navy. The *Princeton,* the most powerful warship of that day, commanded by Captain Stockton, was taking members of Congress and government officials down the Potomac. On board were the president of the United States, and the secretaries of state and navy. For the entertainment of the guests the great gun on the *Princeton,* called the Peacemaker, was fired. At the second discharge the gun burst, killing the secretary of state, the secretary of the navy, and a number of others.

Just before the gun was fired, Senator Thomas Benton of Missouri was standing near it, when a friend laid a hand on his shoulder. Benton turned away to speak with him, when, much to his annoyance, the secretary of the navy, Gilmore, elbowed his way into his place. At that moment the gun was fired and Gilmore was killed. That singular providence had a great impression upon Benton. He was a man of bitter feuds and quarrels, and recently had had a fierce quarrel with Daniel Webster. But after his escape from death on the *Princeton* Benton sought reconciliation with Webster. He said to him, "It seemed to me, Mr. Webster, as if that touch on my shoulder was the hand of the Almighty stretched down there, drawing me away from what otherwise would have been instantaneous death. That one circumstance has changed the whole current of my thought and life. I feel that I am a different man; and I want, in the first place, to be at peace with all those with whom I have been so sharply at variance."

Benton answered that "touch of God" on his shoulder. God has many ways of touching your shoulder, many ministries by which he speaks to your heart; and when he does, then is the time to act. Resist not that touch.

———————

—**A guiding hand**—One bleak autumn day a lad from New England was making his way westward—leaving home, starting out in life, facing the world. He felt lonely and homesick and sad and troubled about his future. Just then he happened to see a waterfowl winging its way southward. That waterfowl, guided by its wonderful instinct, preserved and upheld by its Creator, made young William Cullen Bryant think of God's care for his own life, and so he wrote:

> He who, from zone to zone,
> Guides through the boundless sky
>   thy certain flight,
> In the long way that I must trod
>   alone,
> Will lead my steps aright.

—**And history**—We see the hand of God in the rise and spread of nations. Paul was talking to a group of philosophers on Mars Hill at Athens, giving them the true and only philosophy, when he made that memorable statement that God had made of one blood all nations of men for to dwell in all the face of the earth, and had "determined the times before appointed, and the bounds of their habitation" (Acts 17:26). This means not merely that God presides over the destinies of nations and overrules their crimes and their follies to hasten forward that one far-off and divine event toward which the whole creation is moving but that he has actually willed and decreed the rising of nations, the exact length of time they shall endure, and the limits of their boundaries.

Calvin, exposing a halfway view of God and his providence in the world, writes that some people think of God as if he sits hidden in a watchtower on the battlefield of time, waiting anxiously to see if what men and nations do will fit in with his plan and purpose. Thus, God's plan would be contingent upon what men and nations do. But the Scriptural truth and teaching is far more than that—God acts before the nations act; he has determined from the beginning the course of their history.

———————

Napoleon had a saying, "Providence is always on the side of the last reserve." What he meant was that the army which in the midst of desperate struggle can call at the critical moment—those few minutes which decide victory for one side or the other—upon a reserve regiment or brigade, will win the battle. His own last great battle demonstrated the truth of that Napoleonic epigram. All day long on that nineteenth of June, 1815, Napoleon had been hammering, with artillery and cavalry and infantry, at the English lines. Evening had come, Blücher was up with the Prussian army, but Grouchy with the French reserves had not yet put in an appearance. With one mighty stroke Napoleon had planned to break the English lines and re-establish himself as the despot of Europe. To deliver this blow he had called upon the flower of his army, the Imperial Guard. Now, on they came in the gathering gloom, every battalion commanded by a general, and all of them led by the heroic Marshal Ney. The attack was directed at the right center of the English lines, where lay the fine troops, the Guards, under General Maitland. These troops had been lying on the ground while the fire of the French artillery plunged over them; and when the advance of the French column were within fifty yards of the crest of the ridge all the Frenchmen could see was a group of officers, one of whom was Wellington. Then suddenly they heard a voice cry out, "Up, Guards, and at them!" It was the voice of Wellington. The troops of Maitland sprang to their feet, and, rushing upon the Imperial Guard, tore it to pieces. Napoleon was vanquished, and the history of the world was changed.

Napoleon was right—Providence was on the side of the last reserve.

"Their rims, they . . . were full of eyes." (Ezek. 1:18.) This is a sentence from Ezekiel's great vision of the "four living creatures," the wheels, and the throne of God. By the banks of the Chebar Ezekiel saw emerging from the whirlwind and the amber cloud the four living creatures, with four faces—the face of a man, a lion, an ox, and an eagle. The living creatures, which ran with outstretched wings and returned as the appearance of a flash of lightning, were attended by four wheels. These wheels moved with the living creatures,

not only forward, but backward and to either side, and the rims of the wheels, high and dreadful, were full of eyes. Above the living creatures was the likeness of a sapphire throne, and upon the throne was the appearance of a man, which was the appearance of the glory of the Lord.

This magnificent vision has always been taken to express not only the majesty and the glory of God but also the sovereignty of God, his activity in history, and his rule among men and nations.

The rims of the wheels were full of eyes. This expresses God's perfect knowledge and the absolute wisdom and justice of his doings. At first glance the history of the world seems to be—and sounds just like—a rush and roar and clash of wheels of events, getting nowhere, guided by no intelligence, accomplishing no great end. We seem to see nothing but the monotonous cycle of war and invasion, the rise and fall of empires, one crowding another down into its grave. But when we look at history in the light of the truth of God's government, we discern something more than chaos and confusion; we discover that these everturning and ever-flashing wheels of the world's events are full of the eyes of intelligent purpose, and that just as the movement of the four living creatures and the four wheels was sometimes backward and sometimes to either side, yet ever straight forward, so the chariot of divine providence moves ever on to its great goal.

A thought which impresses one as he ponders the history of Napoleon Bonaparte is the fact of providence in his life. Jesus Christ came into the world, Paul said, in "the fullness of the time" (Gal. 4:4). So did Napoleon. He was not an accident. He came at the appointed time and to do an appointed work in the world, cruel, evil, and sacrilegious though he was. That is the Bible view of history. Another famous soldier, General Gordon, used to take up the morning newspaper and say, "Let us see what God is doing in the world." When you read your morning newspaper and hear of Hitler and Hirohito, read it in the light of the Bible, and say to yourself, "What is God doing in the world?" Even the worst of men God uses to fulfill his purposes. Cyrus, he said, was his rod. So was Napoleon. Surely, as Psalm 76:10 says, God makes the wrath of man to praise him, and the residue he will restrain.

In 1815 Queen Louise, the Prussian queen, wrote a great letter about Napoleon to her father. In this letter she said: "It were a crime to say that God is with the French Emperor; but he is manifestly an instrument in the hands of the Almighty to bury out of sight the old order, for which He has no further purpose." Whether men execrate or admire Napoleon, they must all acknowledge that he broke down the barriers between men and nations, that he, like Cromwell, shook down in the dust what God had condemned. He told his soldiers that every soldier carried in his knapsack a marshal's baton. He was therefore the preacher and herald of the popular movements that have swept the world since then, sometimes for good, sometimes for evil. He preached a terrific sermon on the text that the nations that forget God shall be cast into hell. He proclaimed, unconsciously, perhaps, the supremacy of the moral order; and even by his own flaming fall, like that of the star Wormwood out of heaven, was a witness that righteousness and judgment are the habitation of God's throne.

In his chapter on the adoption of the Constitution of the United States, Bancroft throws out this suggestion: "Do nations float darkling down the stream of the ages without hope or consolation, swaying with every wind, and ignorant whither they are drifting? Or is there a Superior Power of intelligence and love which is moved by justice and shapes their forces?" The Bible has a plain answer to that question, for it tells us that God is the Supreme Actor of history, and that the great men and the great nations and the great movements are but the brief embodiment and transient realization of his desires.

On the night before the eighteenth of June, 1815, there was heavy rain in Belgium. So heavy was the rain and so soft were the roads that Napoleon, who had won his battles with his artillery, was not able to get his guns into position until eleven o'clock in the morning. Had it not rained, he could have had his guns up by seven in the morning, instead of eleven; and by two o'clock the battle would have been won—three hours before Blücher and the Prussians put in their determining appearance. "A cloud traversing the sky out of season sufficed to make a world crumble."

The words "I girded thee, though thou hast not known me" (Isa. 45:5) are spoken of Cyrus, conqueror of Sardis and of Babylon, when he diverted the Euphrates from the walls of the city. One of the first acts of this monarch when he overthrew Babylon was to issue a proclamation permitting the captive Jews to return to their own land. Cyrus was a nobler sort of heathen and gained a legendary renown as a paragon of all virtues, but he was a heathen and knew nothing of the true God. Yet he was an agent in the hands of God; and over a century before he appeared on the stage of history he was called by name, and the part that he was to play in the destiny of God's people was predicted. He was to be God's "shepherd" in bringing the people back from captivity. "I girded thee, though thou hast not known me." This gives us not only the doctrine of God in history, but God working in history with a wise and beneficent purpose.

———•◆•———

In the first days of September, 1862, the Confederate armies, flushed with victory over the armies of McClellan and the armies of Pope at the second Battle of Manassas, crossed the Potomac into Maryland and set out on the first invasion of the North. At Fredericksburg, Lee divided his army, sending sections of it to take the Federal garrisons at Martinsburg and Harper's Ferry, and then join the main army at Hagerstown on the way into Pennsylvania. By one of the chances of war a copy of Lee's orders to his generals was left behind in Fredericksburg, wrapped about a package of cigars.

When the Union army came cautiously into Fredericksburg, a Union man put the orders in the hands of McClellan. Lee's brilliant plan of campaign was in the hands of his adversary. The bugles sounded in the blue ranks, and at the double-quick the Union army marched for the passes of South Mountain to overtake Lee. They drove his army through the passes before he could call back his other divisions, and on September 17, the bloodiest day of the Civil War, defeated it at the fords of the Antietam.

When the baffled army of Lee had crossed the Potomac back into Virginia, Lincoln told his advisers how he had covenanted with God that if the North was victorious in the struggle in Mary-land he would show his gratitude by freeing the slaves. A careless staff officer wrapped Lee's order about his tobacco, and the plan of the campaign was in the hands of the adversary; surprise was impossible, defeat certain; the North was freed from invasion, and the Proclamation of Emancipation was issued. And all due, as Thomas Nelson Page puts it in his life of Lee, to "one of those strange events which, so insignificant in itself, yet under Him

Who sees with equal eye, as God of all,
A hero perish or a sparrow fall
[Alexander Pope]

is fateful to decide the issue of nations."

———•◆•———

—A lottery—The author of *The Decline and Fall of the Roman Empire*, Gibbon, writing of his life and achievements, says that he was fortunate in drawing a high number in the lottery of life. On the surface of things life does sometimes look just like a lottery. Men are born into families, circumstances, and conditions of life which seem to determine to a large degree their place and their work in life. But every now and then we are conscious of some startling exception to that, and even one exception is enough to make us wonder if the lottery theory of life is the true one.

———•◆•———

—The shadow of—There are many shadows that fall across the earth—the shadows of floating clouds, of trees swaying in the wind, of smoke ascending from chimneys, of birds on the wing, and the shadows of great rocks on mountainsides. But the deepest and longest and kindest shadow which falls over the earth is the shadow of divine providence.

—Sorrowful—God's providence is universal. It takes in all events. "All His creatures and all their actions," as the definition of the Catechism puts it. On the wall of the first church where I preached there was a memorial tablet to a devout Sabbath school teacher who had met a sudden and, it seemed to her friends, an untimely end. The inscription spoke of how she was suddenly removed by a "sorrowful providence." I have often pondered over that phrase, "a sorrowful providence." It was indeed sorrowful to her friends and her family, yet they had faith to understand that there was a providence in her taking off.

———•◆•———

—Trust in—On the morning of one of the great battles of the Civil War a soldier awoke hearing the intense firing of the pickets, and there came to him the conviction that there was going to be a great battle and he was not ready in his soul or in his heart for what the battle might bring. He therefore knelt down, confessed his sins, and committed his soul to the keeping of God, realizing that if it was well with his soul it mattered little what happened to his body.

And that is exactly what Christ said in connection with the verse, "Fear not them which kill the body" (Matt. 10:28). Now that the soldier had committed his soul to God and left his body to the incidents and laws of the battlefield, all fear and anxiety left him, although hundreds were falling at his right hand and ten hundred at his left hand. "Commit thy way unto the Lord; trust also in him." (Ps. 37:5.)

PUNISHMENT—*see* FUTURE PUNISHMENT

PURITY

In his life of John Locke, Fowler quotes this sentence of Horace Walpole about one of Locke's friends, Lord Som-

mers: "Lord Sommers was one of those divine men who, like a chapel in a palace, remain unprofaned while all the rest is tyranny, corruption, and folly." We cannot choose the surroundings and environment of our work. We cannot even choose the home into which we have been born. If there are those who feel that the Christian life is one of great difficulty for them, but that if only they had a different environment and atmosphere they could be better Christians, let them remember that there were saints in Caesar's household, and saints at Satan's seat in ancient Pergamos. Them Christ salutes and commends.

PURPOSE—*see also* AMBITION, DETERMINATION, PERSEVERANCE

I always liked that poem of Browning's "Childe Roland to the Dark Tower Came." The dark tower was his goal. Men tried to warn him, to turn him back, but he pushed on—through deserts and over raging streams, past terrible places and through marshes, past grim enemies —until he reached the tower; and there his enemies stood ranged along the hillside in a sheet of flame:

> *And yet*
> *Dauntless the slug-horn to my lips*
> *I set,*
> *And blew. "Childe Roland to the*
> *Dark Tower came."*

———•◆•———

The heavenly lanes are open to airplane travel in every direction. Likewise the lanes of life are wide open to him who would attain unto the highest life, for we are called, as Paul so splendidly puts it, unto nothing less than "glory and honor and immortality" (Rom. 2:7), or again, "unto a perfect man, unto the measure of the stature of the fullness of Christ" (Eph. 4:13). How loyal are you to your purpose? How faithful are you to your goal? Is your motto that of Paul, "This one thing I do" (Phil. 3:13)? How faithful are you to the man you meant to be?

PYRAMIDS

A little after four one morning I arose and joined a party which was to climb the great pyramid and witness the dawn. My Arab guide, anxious to have me the first up, took me up the huge steps at a pace which almost finished me. Halfway up I became quite dizzy and wished I had not started, but to start down seemed worse than to go up; so on to the top I went. My guide left me to pant on a rock by myself; and, going to the edge of the pyramid, he went through his devotions, bowing down and prostrating himself toward Mecca.

When I was sufficiently recovered, I stood up to take in the panorama. To the west lay the desert, not flat, but waving billows of sand, ruddy now in the reflection of the Orient sun. To the east the long barrier of red which ran across the sky suddenly changed to the shape of the oncoming sun; and distant domes, minarets, palm trees, and villages began to take shape and color and form, while to the south flowed the lordly Nile. Even when you cannot see the river, you know where it flows by the belt of green vegetation which follows it. I thought of that verse from Ezekiel's vision of the sacred stream: "Everything shall live whithersoever the river cometh" (Ezek. 47:9).

R

REALITY

Peter Cartwright, the famous circuit rider and Lincoln's opponent for election to Congress, once stayed overnight with a skeptical physician who claimed that the only reality was what the senses discerned. The physician said to him, "Did you ever see religion?"

"No."

"Did you ever hear religion?"

"No."

"Did you ever smell religion?"

"No."

"Did you ever taste religion?"

"No."

"Did you ever feel religion?"

"Yes."

"Now, then," said the doctor, with apparent triumph, "I have proved, beyond a doubt, by four respectable witnesses, that religion is not seen, heard, smelled, or tasted; and but one lone, solitary witness, namely, feeling, has testified that it is an experimental fact. The weight of evidence is overpowering, sir, and you must give it up."

Cartwright then said to the doctor, "In pretending to relieve pain in the human system, you have been playing the hypocrite, and practicing a most wretched fraud on the gullibility of the people."

To the doctor's indignant protest Cartwright said, "Well, sir, did you ever see a pain?"

"No, sir."

"Did you ever hear a pain?"

"No, sir."

"Did you ever smell a pain?"

"No, sir."

"Did you ever taste a pain?"

"No, sir."

"Did you ever feel a pain?"

"Certainly I did, sir."

"Then," said Cartwright, "four respectable witnesses have testified that there is no such thing as pain in a human system."

Taking advantage of the doctor's discomfiture, Cartwright fell on his knees and commenced to pray. In a short time the great deeps of the man's heart were broken up; and, after a brief period of anxiety and spiritual agony, he found the Lord with a shout of triumph. His slaves he sent at his own expense to Liberia; and he himself became a preacher of the gospel, with many seals to his ministry.

REAPING—*see* SOWING AND REAPING

RECONCILIATION—*see also* ATONEMENT, BLOOD OF CHRIST, THE CROSS, OPPORTUNITY AND RECONCILIATION

If Christ came to reconcile the world to God, then there must be a state of separation, alienation, estrangement. One would not speak of reconciling two loyal and trusting friends; one would not speak of reconciling two casual acquaintances; one would not speak of reconciling a man in San Francisco and a man in New York who had never seen one another. But one does speak of reconciling a father and son who have become estranged, a mother and daughter who have become alienated, a husband and wife who have become separated. Reconciliation can take place only between parties who have a close relationship one with another, and that is true of man in his relationship to God. Man ever has to do with God. No sinning, no wandering, no rebellion can break the eternal tie of his relationship with God; fallen, stained, and rebellious though he may be, he is by creation a member of God's family. This, then, is the condition which exists between God and man. As Isaiah expresses it (59:2), "Your iniquities have separated between you and your God, and your sins have hid his face from you."

One of the greatest and most beautiful things man can do is to reconcile, and make friends, those who are enemies. Both Martin Luther and John Bunyan brought their great lives to a close in an attempt to reconcile men: Luther, two brothers; Bunyan, a father and a son. Likewise, if we may say it, the greatest and the most beautiful act of God is his working out a plan of reconciliation of man with God by the precious blood of Christ.

Years ago in a Western city a husband and wife became estranged, and finally separated. They left the city and resided in different parts of the country. The husband one day chanced to return to this city on a matter of business. He went out to the cemetery to the grave of their only son. He was standing by the grave in fond reminiscence when he heard a step behind him. Turning, he saw his estranged wife. The first inclination of both was to turn away. But they had a common, binding interest in that grave; and instead of turning away they clasped hands over that grave of their son, and were reconciled one to another. It took nothing less than death to reconcile them! It takes nothing less than death, the precious blood of Christ, to reconcile man to God. The pronouncement, the proclamation, of that is the gospel message. We have, the great proclaimer of it said, "the message of his reconciliation." (II Cor. 5:19—Moffatt.)

—With God—A noted minister of a former generation bore testimony that his whole life was deeply influenced and impressed by a word spoken to him by an aged Christian woman. It was this: "Be ye aye in wi' God, Duncan, for He's aye right."

Yes, God is always right. Are you right with God?

REDEMPTION—*see also* SOUL (SALVATION OF)

On a hot August day in Florence, after visiting the great *Duomo,* where Savonarola thundered against the iniquities of the city, and the beautiful St. John's Church, with its marvelous gateway, I sought out a Protestant place of worship. It was an evangelical church of no great dimensions, in an obscure part of the city. The service was one familiar to all Protestants; and, although I did not understand much that he was saying, I could tell that the preacher spoke in simple earnestness to his people. On the wall over his head were the words: "There is one God, and one mediator between God and men, the man Christ Jesus" (I Tim. 2:5). However neglected this idea may be in popular teaching and preaching, however lost sight of in popular Christianity today, no one can read the New Testament without having presented to him the fact that the Kingdom of God is a kingdom of redemption and of mediation, and that the Mediator, the one who stands between man and God and reconciles man to God and God to man, is the eternal God-man, Christ Jesus.

* * *

Some of the most moving stories of the ancient and the medieval world center around the redemption of those taken captive and held in slavery. On a tombstone in Corsica is an inscription which the person buried there wrote before her death. It reads: "Seafarer from the North, whoever you be, tell Wilhelm Lowenstern in Stralson that you have seen the grave of his wife who was sold into slavery in Africa and then released,

and who died here in June, 1698. My son is still in slavery there. Let his father come to deliver him. If he passes by this place, he will find the remains of his Euphrasia."

Later excavation revealed another inscription: "Whoever you be that look within this grave, I know that G. Wachtendonk brought me news of my Euphrasia. I sought my son in Africa and found him dead. I have buried his remains here beside those of his beloved mother."

* * *

The medieval theologians, glorying in it, were wont to say that a single drop of the blood of Christ would have sufficed to redeem the whole race of mankind; and that is true, even if love had not driven mercy to the great extreme of the Cross. But this also is true—that if only one soul had been lost, Christ would have given himself and shed all his precious blood to redeem that one soul.

RELIGION—*see also* MARRIAGE AND RELIGION, REALITY

Among the memories in Livingstone's life there are few if any that he cherished more than the thought of his old Sunday school teacher, David Hogg, who sent for him as he lay dying and said, "Now lad, make religion the every-day business of your life, and not a thing of fits and starts, for if you don't, temptation and other things will get the better of you."

* * *

—Blessedness of—Not only was Ezekiel given the assurance of God's power and glory in the events of the world, but he was given a vision of the future blessedness which is to descend upon mankind. This vision took the form of a great city and a great temple. Accompanied by a heavenly guide, Ezekiel in his vision saw a stream of water issuing from the foundations of the temple and flowing eastward. A short distance from the temple the angel measured the waters, and the waters were only to the ankles. Still farther on he measured them again, and the waters were up to the knees of Ezekiel as he passed through them. Again he measured them, and the waters were up to his loins. And then a final measure, when he found a river too deep to ford, a river to swim in.

As he followed the course of the river he marked the many trees with their greenness and shade which grew on either side of the river. Wherever the river flowed there was vegetation and life. He could follow the river as it flowed eastward by the trail of green, here dark and deep, and there fresh and tender, which it left behind it. "Every thing shall live whither the river cometh" (Ezek. 47:9); even the Dead Sea, that monster among inland seas, heavy with salt, more than a thousand feet below the level of the ocean, with no outlet, and its bituminous waters scarcely tolerating any forms of life, was healed by the temple-born river which emptied a pure, life-giving stream into its bosom.

This is a vision. It is hardly a real river which Ezekiel is describing, but a river which in its origin, its gradual increase, its universal benediction, is a symbol of the power and blessedness of true religion.

—And national morality—In his Farewell Address, Washington said: "Religion and morality are the indispensable supports of political prosperity. Let us with caution indulge the supposition that morality can be maintained without religion. Reason and experience both forbid us to expect that national morality can prevail in exclusion of religious principle. Morality is a necessary spring of popular government. Who, that is a sincere friend to it, can look with indifference upon attempts to shake the foundation of the fabric?"

There are not a few today who evidently believe that we can have national morality without religion. You might as well expect to have a stream without a fountain, or a tree without a root. Mere philanthropy, altruism, or expediency, will never suffice to uphold society or the state. All moral sanctions go back to belief in God and the higher law.

REMEMBERING THOSE WE LOVE

When Ulysses, during his wanderings through those seas and among those islands about which we heard much in connection with the fighting between the Greeks and Italians, was leaving the enchanted isle where Calypso lived, Calypso came down to the beach as Ulysses was departing on his raft and said to him, "Say good-by to me, but not to the thought of me."

Christ was soon to be separated from his disciples, but he told them not to say good-by to the thought of him. He would not be forgotten by his friends—not merely, like the enchantress, for the sake of being remembered, but also for their good from age to age.

REMORSE—*see also* ANGER (DANGERS OF), CONSCIENCE

Fears may die, but not remorse. John Randolph, when he was dying in Philadelphia, kept repeating, "Remorse! Remorse!" He demanded that a dictionary be brought so that he could study the meaning of the word; and, when no dictionary could be found, he had the physician write it out for him on a piece of paper—"Remorse."

If hell were just the invention of pale-faced theologians, long ago the race would have cast the idea overboard. But it still remains, because it is not the invention of men who write books or uphold systems of thought, but is the deep affirmation of the human heart.

Remorse is like the ground swell in the ocean after a storm. The storm has subsided, the sky is blue, the air is balmy, there is not a whitecap to be seen; but the ship heaves and tosses and leaves the traveler in misery because of the mighty swell that has remained after the original commotion has subsided. So remorse heaves the soul as the tides heave the ocean. Or, to change the figure, it is like a bell buoy, incessantly and dismally tolling because of the unrest in the sea. To sin is to say farewell to peace.

———•◆•———

A number of years ago I visited Ravenna, where the great king of the Ostrogoths, Theodoric, reigned in splendor for thirty-three years. His reign was one of glory and happiness for Italy, but his last years were saddened by his remorse for the crime of putting to death Boethius and Symmachus. Gibbons relates how the noble Boethius was strangled with a cord around his neck, until his eyes almost started from their sockets. He goes on to tell how after his life of virtue and glory, Theodoric, now descending into the grave with shame and guilt, was justly alarmed by the condemnations of conscience. One evening, when he had been served with the head of a large fish at the royal table, he seemed to behold in the head of the fish the angry countenance of one of those whom he had murdered, his eyes glaring fury and revenge and his mouth armed with long, sharp teeth which threatened to devour him. Theodoric retired to his chamber, where, trembling with anguish and cold though under a weight of bed clothes, he expressed to his physician his repentance for the murder of Boethius and Symmachus. His malady increased, and in three days he expired.

In the magnificent monument erected by his daughter, from the center of the dome rise four columns which support in a porphyry vase the remains of the great Gothic king, surrounded by the brazen statues of the twelve apostles.

———•◆•———

George Romney, the great English portrait painter, at the age of nineteen impulsively married a young woman who had nursed him through a fever. Then, having heard Sir Joshua Reynolds say that marriage spoiled an artist, he deserted his wife and two children and went to London to pursue fame as an artist. He scarcely saw his wife again till the end of his life, when old, nearly mad, and quite desolate, he went back to her, and she received him and nursed him till he died. "This quiet act of hers," writes Edward Fitzgerald," is worth all Romney's pictures, even as a model of art, I am sure."

The one who inspired the painting of Romney and whom he painted into a score or more of his characters, such as St. Cecilia, the Magdalene, and Joan of Arc, was the beautiful but notorious Emma Hart, afterward Lady Hamilton, the one at whose feet Lord Nelson cast away his honor and his fame. In "Romney's Remorse" Tennyson represents a friend trying to comfort Romney with the thought that although he has played a base part in the world he at least has won the painter's fame:

Take comfort, you have won the
*   Painter's fame!*

But Romney answers:

The best in me that sees the worst
*   in me,*
*   And groans to see it, finds no com-*
*   fort there.*

———•◆•———

When Andrew Jackson was preparing for the duel in which he shot and killed Dickinson, an old friend at Nashville asked him if he was ready to bear the responsibility of taking the life of a fellow being. He reminded Jackson of his friend Aaron Burr, and how Burr had had no ease of mind since he killed Hamilton. Thus conscience bestows its severest penalties in the shape of remorse —remorse for the thing done, and, strange to say, as I have sometimes witnessed it, an even more poignant remorse for things that have been left undone.

———

In brief, this was her story: Unloved by her husband, she had fallen in with the son of a well-known man, had gone off to the city where I saw her, and there had lived in sin. So as not to bring pain to her mother, and to hide the real situation, she wrote and received her letters at the Young Women's Christian Association. Then came days of loneliness and nights of silent weeping. Then an invincible desire and purpose to confess and return. The way of transgression had suddenly become hard. Its flowers had withered, and the streams along which it ran had dried up. Now conscience awoke with a stab and a start. The woman sought the nearest church and the nearest minister. At the end of the interview she promised to return to her home, her children, and her mother. "Oh, how could I ever have done it!" I hear her cry now as plainly as you hear my words. In that cry there seemed to be more of the pain of remorse than in any other cry I have ever heard.

———

—Hopeless—Reading an English book some time ago, I came upon this sentence: "If you have ever seen it, you will never forget it—the agony of hopeless remorse, when the sense of sin, of evil done, or evil, the consequences of which have slipped out of control, haunts and scourges the soul into an agony of despairing pain." Several times, and each time never to be forgotten, I have seen this agony of hopeless remorse.

———

—And parents—Look at that old man standing bareheaded in the market at Uttoxeter, the rain beating upon him, the cold winds smiting him, the children and the hoodlums jeering at him. Who is he and why does he stand there? The old man is Samuel Johnson, on every hand sought after and praised. But he stands there in the market place exposed to the bitter weather because fifty years before, when he was a student at Oxford, his sick father asked him to take his place in the bookstall, and his pride made him refuse. Half a century has passed, with its fleeting joys and sorrows, but the memory of that single act of filial disrespect remains to rankle in his breast; and by that act of public penance the old scholar hopes—but vainly—to atone for his deed of dishonor.

———

From his grave beneath the stone pile in Ephraim's wood the mutilated Absalom calls to his father with reproach and judgment, saying: "You might have saved me from this awful end, but you gave me nothing but kisses and caresses. You never told me that the way of the transgressor is hard, that the eye that mocketh at his father and refuseth to obey his mother the ravens shall pluck it out. A little less indulgence, a little less leniency with my faults, and I might have been saved from this lonely grave of guilt and shame."

———

James IV stood in arms against his father. In after years, as a penance, he wore beneath his purple robes an iron belt; and to that belt he added a link with each new year. Do not forge for yourself that heavy chain of woe!

REPENTANCE—*see also* CONVERSION, OPPORTUNITY AND REPENTANCE, PRAYER

By his investigations and meditations and calculations the great Polish mathematician Copernicus revolutionized the thought of mankind about the universe. His famous treatise *The Revolution of the Heavenly Bodies* was printed just in time to be placed in his arms as he lay dying on his bed in May, 1543. Yet this man who had given to the race a new conception of the universe, before God saw himself not as an astronomer or a scholar but as a sinner.

Today on his grave at Frauenburg you can read the epitaph which he chose for himself: "I do not seek a kindness equal to that given to Paul; nor do I ask the grace granted to Peter; but that forgiveness which Thou didst give to the robber—that I earnestly pray."

Imagine Lazarus suddenly appearing in the hall where the five brothers of Dives, their hypocritical grief for him forgotten, sit arrayed in purple and fine linen, faring sumptuously, with some other beggar now at the gates, his sores licked by the same dogs. You can see their faces blanch at his sudden entrance into their midst. The glasses fall from their nerveless grasp, and are shattered on the pavement, as Lazarus says to them: "Your brother is in hell. He has sent me to warn you, and to tell you to repent." Such a visitation, such an apparition, you think, would break down the wall of any man's heart and bring prompt and full repentance. But He who knows the heart to its depths said No: "If they hear not Moses and the prophets, neither will they be persuaded,

though one rose from the dead" (Luke 16:31).

Many an old church has a cemetery near it; but in the sense in which I mean it now, every church has a cemetery right up against its walls—the cemetery of convictions and divine impressions and holy purposes and desires which were awakened within the walls of the sanctuary, but which were never acted upon. Chief among these buried impulses to action is the feeling of repentance—the holy desire to go to the Father. The heart was touched, the mind was convinced; but the man never arose to go unto his Father.

On the stormy southwest coast of England there is a church whose towers are silent. No bells ring for the living or toll for the dead. There is a legend that a ship was once beating its way along that shore, having on board bells designed for this church of Bottreaux. A sailor lad, hearing the neighboring bells of Tintagel sounding over the sea, thanked God for the favor that would soon bring them safe to port.

But the godless skipper told him to thank the steersman, the good ship, and the ready sail. As if in answer to his blasphemy, the sea rose and the waves dashed the ship and its godless master on the rocks. Now they say that the bells which went down with that ship may be heard above the surge of the ocean as it breaks on the iron cliffs, pealing out the invitation of the Church, the invitation of God, the coming of death, and after death the judgment.

For you tonight the bells of grace and mercy still peal and ring. Not yet have they become a dirge or knell.

When the prodigal son finally struck bottom, finally found himself among the swine, and even envied them their diet of corn husks, what would it have profited him to soliloquize thus: "Swine, as ye are now, so I was once; but long ago, aeons upon aeons ago, I passed through the swine stage. Now I have arrived at manhood. Yet I trace my origin back to you and to the beasts from whom you descended. All that is in me—of mind, of thought, of purpose, of hope, despair, and remorse—came ultimately from you, and through you from other beasts before you. In your dull brain are the rudiments of my own brain; in your hideous form are the outlines of my own form and body; and in your dull, stupid, brutish gaze I see as in a mirror all the elements of my own personality."

Would that have helped the prodigal? Would that have lifted him out of the mire—to have reflected on his kinship with the beast, how far he had ascended from them, and how far he had come back to them? No. The thing that brought the stab of poignant pain and shame to the prodigal's heart was the thought of how far he had wandered. When he remembered his father's love, his father's hopes for him, and contrasted his rags and filth and shame with what his life had been in his father's house, then it was that he came to himself, to his true, divine, immortal self, and said: "I will arise and go to my father, and will say unto him, Father, I have sinned against heaven, and before thee, and am no more worthy to be called thy son: make me as one of thy hired servants" (Luke 15:18-19).

—**Ashamed of**—The wise and sensible thing for a man to do is to repent. In the opening chapter of *Robinson Crusoe* Defoe relates how, in spite of the protest of his father and the tears and entreaties of his godly mother, he ran away from his home at York and went to sea. On his first voyage he was wrecked off Yarmouth and barely escaped with his life. He now saw the folly and the evil of the course he had taken, but was afraid and ashamed to go back to his home, lest some of his old companions should make sport of him. So, writes Defoe, men are not ashamed to sin, but are ashamed to repent; not ashamed to do that of which they ought to be ashamed, but ashamed to do that which is their only hope and rescue.

—**And forgiveness**—In *The Silence of Dean Maitland* the author tells how the dean fell into sin, and then committed one sin after another to cover up his first sin;—and, worst of all, permitted an innocent man to be punished and imprisoned in his stead. All kinds of temporal adversities broke over him. He lost his wife and children, his home became a wilderness, yet he would not repent. He said, "I cannot, I will not, I dare not, I must not repent." But at length the man who had spent a great part of his life in prison for the other's crime wrote him a letter telling him of his forgiveness. It was that letter that broke his heart and brought him to repentance. "God called to me," he said, "through many years, by many judgments; but I repented not until I was forgiven."

—**And prayer**—If you have read Victor Hugo's *The Man Who Laughs*, you will remember how the sailing vessel whose company have abandoned the disfigured child on the shores of England is overtaken by a storm on its way across the Channel to France, and is about to sink in the treacherous waters off the Channel Islands.

As the doomed company gather on the deck, the doctor calls to them, "On your knees! Repentance is the bark that never sinks. You have lost your compass? You are wrong! You still have prayer."

The waters have now risen to the decks, and at the words "Let us pray" they kneel in the darkness and repeat, each in his own tongue—the doctor in Latin, the Provençal in French, the Irish-woman in Gaelic—the petitions of our Lord's Prayer. By the time they reach the last petition the ship sinks, and the remorseless waves cover them, until the sea gives up its dead and the grave hers.

Yes, prayer is the highest resource of the soul. Do not fail to draw on that great resource now.

———•—•—•———

—Rewards of—The records of wars sometimes tell of officers who lost their rank and were dropped from the rolls of the regiment in disgrace, but afterward by heroic conduct won back their lost rank. There is always in the soul that possibility of reclaiming and regaining the honors and the righteousness it has lost.

No matter how deep into the far country the son has wandered, there is always a path that leads back to the Father's house. There is a robe kept in readiness for you, O wandering son! There is a ring that will never be put on any finger but yours, O wandering daughter! There is a welcome for you, O hardened sinner! Christ receiveth sinners! He likes to go out and meet them on the way back. He delights in remaking them and redeeming them.

Let cynics smile, let believers argue, this is the glory of Christianity—that it is able to save unto the uttermost all who come unto God by Jesus Christ. "Though ye have lain among the pots, yet shall ye be as the wings of a dove covered with silver, and her feathers with yellow gold." (Ps. 68:13).

———•—•—•———

An old man once dreamed unhappily about his past. He saw before him a long list of things in his life which were wrong, and for which he was sorry and ashamed. In his dream he was about to seize a sponge and rub these things out of his biography, when, to his amazement, he discovered that wherever there were deeds of gold shining through the story of his life they had been wrought there by regret and sorrow over past transgression, and that if he wiped out those wrong acts he would at the same time destroy whatever of nobleness or beauty there was in his character.

Thus it is that even our sins and follies, repented of, can be made stones in the walls of a godly life.

———•—•—•———

In the laboratory of the great chemist Faraday a workman accidentally dropped a very valuable silver cup into a tank of strong acid. He and the other workmen stood over the tank mournfully watching the quick disintegration of the cup. But Faraday, seeing what had happened, poured a chemical into the tank. The silver was precipitated to the bottom and recovered, and the shapeless mass was sent off again to the silversmith to be refashioned into its former likeness.

So the grace of repentance and of faith can recover what has been lost and restore it to its former usefulness and beauty.

———•—•—•———

Two brothers were once convicted of stealing sheep and, in accordance with the brutal punishment of that day, were branded on the forehead with the letters *S T,* which stood for "sheep thief." One of the brothers, unable to bear the stigma, tried to bury himself in a foreign land. But men would ask him about the letters on his brow, and what they meant. Thus he wandered from land to land, and at length, full of bitterness, died and was buried in a forgotten grave.

But the other brother, who repented of his misdeed, did not go away from his home. He said to himself: "I can't run away from the fact that I stole sheep, and here I will remain until I win back the respect of my neighbors and myself." As the years passed by he established a reputation for respectability and integrity. One day a stranger in the town saw the old man with the letters *S T* branded on his forehead and asked a native what they signified. After thinking for a little time the villager said: "It all happened a great while ago, and I have forgotten the particulars; but I think the letters are an abbreviation of Saint."

Yes, that is it! The wonderful grace of God in the penitent and believing heart is able to change and transform the odious marking and scarring of sin into a badge of honor and beauty.

———

—**Value of**—The last time I was at Baalbek, that most imposing and stupendous monument of the ancient world, I recalled Hood's story "Paradise and the Peri." The peri had been promised that she could get back into paradise if she brought to the gates of heaven that which was most precious to God. All over the world she searched for that treasure. She brought first the last drop of blood from a dying patriot's heart, and then a maiden's kiss of sacrificial love implanted on the brow of her dying lover. But the gates of heaven opened not. Her gifts were refused. Then, near the ruins of Baalbek, she saw a child kneeling in prayer by a fountain. As the child was praying a man rode up on his horse and dismounted to quench his thirst at the fountain. On his face was stamped all manner of iniquity and coarseness and crime. But as he stooped to lift the water to his lips, he saw the child kneeling in prayer. In a flash the hard face softened and changed, and a tear flowed down his cheek; for he recalled the day when he, too, was as innocent as the child and prayed for himself as the child was now praying. It was that penitential tear that opened the gates of paradise to the lost spirit.

———

The divinest thing in man is repentance, and great was the repentance of David. Voltaire is said to have attempted to write a profane parody of Psalm 51—David's psalm of repentance after his great sin—but he was overcome with shame and confusion and abandoned the blasphemous project.

RESERVES OF GOD

"Hast thou entered into the treasures of the snow? or hast thou seen the treasures of the hail, which I have reserved against the time of trouble, against the day of battle and war?" (Job 38:22-23). It is as if God had said, "Hail is one of my reserve battalions." At the time of the French invasion of Russia, the Russians had a saying that winter was their chief general. There is one historic instance in the history of Israel when God called upon the reserves of the hail. It was during the war of the conquest of Canaan, when Joshua and his army fought against the five kings of Canaan and won the victory which determined the destiny of Palestine. In that decisive battle a storm of hail fought on the side of Joshua. "The Lord cast down great stones from heaven upon them . . . and they died: they were more which died with hailstones than they whom the children of Israel slew with the sword." (Josh. 10:11.)

This allusion in the book of Job to the reserves of God opens up grand forest avenues of thought. In every time of trouble it is good to remember that God has reserves upon which he has not yet called.

RESPECT—*see* PARENTS (RESPECT FOR)

RESPONSIBILITY—*see also* JUDGMENT (DIVINE)

I remember once going through an Eastern penitentiary and talking in the cells with a number of prisoners. The strange thing was that not one of the men in prison acknowledged that he deserved to be there. Each one blamed someone else, or blamed circumstances. He felt himself not guilty of the crime of which he had been convicted. This is a trait of human nature which is writ large both without and within the prison walls.

In an airship the authority is somewhat divided between the captain, the first officer, and the flight dispatcher at the landing field. And the second officer can relieve and take the place of the first officer when he so desires. But in the flight of the soul through time there is only one person in authority—and that is thyself.

One sign which I read frequently on a cross-country automobile trip was this—"Travel at your own risk." Sometimes it was introduced by another statement—"Road under construction," or "Bridge condemned." By posting these signs the commissioners not only warned the traveler to be cautious and careful but also absolved the county or state of responsibility in case of accident on that part of the road so designated. If the traveler came to harm on the road, he could bring no suit for damages. He was traveling at his own risk.

"Travel at your own risk." In the long journey of life which we are all taking, every man travels at his own risk. You are the responsible party. Your friends, your neighbor, your parents, the community in which you live, your schools, your teachers, your relatives are not the responsible ones, but you yourself. You do the traveling, and you incur the risks, whatever they are. A proverb expresses this truth in familiar language: "Every man has his own life to live."

Daniel Webster, asked what was the greatest thought that had passed through that wonderful brain, answered "My accountability to God." Life is a great journey, with wonderful goals which flash through cloud and fog and mist their glorious invitations. But we must travel carefully and live as accountable to God. Not in the sense in which William Henley meant his well-known lines from "Invictus," but in the high and solemn and scriptural sense,

I am the master of my fate:
I am the captain of my soul.

See to it that you command your battle well. Do not expect that anyone else can fight or pray or suffer for you. Make the man of today the friend, and not the foe, of the man of tomorrow.

RESURRECTION
—**Of the body**—During the Revolutionary War a young officer in the British army, before embarking for this country with his regiment, became engaged to a young lady in England. In one of the battles of the Revolution the officer was badly wounded and lost a leg. He accordingly wrote to his affianced bride, telling her how he was disfigured and maimed, and so changed from what he had been when she had last seen him and they had plighted their troth that he felt it his duty to release her from all obligation to become his wife. The young

lady wrote an answer not less noble than that which she had received from the young man. In this letter she disavowed all thought of refusing to carry out the engagement because of what had happened to her fiancé in battle, and said that she was willing to marry him *if there was enough of his body left to hold his soul!*

———·•◆•·———

James Russell Lowell once remarked that a fitting epitaph for him would be: "Here lies that part of James Russell Lowell which hindered him from doing well."

Sometimes the body is not only a handicap but also an enemy of the spirit, for "the flesh lusteth against the Spirit" (Gal. 5:17). A weak back, a dim eye, a poor voice, has often opposed and interfered with the expression of the spirit. But the image of the heavenly shall be an image emancipated from the bonds of the flesh. It shall be perfectly adapted to the spiritual life, just as the body in this life was perfectly suited to man's physical and intellectual life. That, I am sure, is what Paul meant when he said of the body at death, "It is sown in weakness; it is raised in power: it is sown a natural body; it is raised a spirtual body." (I Cor. 15:43-44.) Then a corruptible body shall have been turned into an incorruptible, a mortal body into an immortal one. Then no great act or labor or desire shall be unattempted or left unfinished for the lack of strength. Then no sickness shall waste our strength or lower the wing of our aspiration, and no cry of anguish and pain shall break the silence of the night or mar the beauty of the day; for there shall be no more pain.

———·•◆•·———

In the old cemetery of Christ Church, at Fifth and Arch streets, Philadelphia, the passer-by can see through the iron railing the grave of one of America's greatest men and one of the world's most versatile geniuses. If you have made a pilgrimage to that quiet acre of the dead, walled off from the city's roar and traffic as if to comment upon the vanity of it all, you will have observed that the flat stone over Franklin's grave bears no trace of the epitaph which he composed. It was as follows:

Like the cover of an old book,
Its contents torn out,
And stripped of its lettering and
*   gilding,*
Lies here food for worms;
But the work shall not be lost,
For it will (as he believes) appear
*   once more*
In a new and more elegant edition,
Revised and corrected by the Au-
*   thor.*

———·•◆•·———

—Of Christ—No statement in the great and beautiful narrative of the Resurrection so brings out the majesty and the completeness of Christ's victory over death as that sentence from the Gospel of Matthew (28:2): "The angel of the Lord descended from heaven, and came and rolled back the stone from the door, and sat upon it." The angel rolled away the stone and sat upon it! Death was conquered! The grim and sinister powers of evil and darkness were routed by the powers of heaven.

———·•◆•·———

Some years ago a popular English novelist wrote a book called *When It Was Dark*. The story centers about the efforts of a wealthy unbeliever to discredit Christianity. He endeavors to do this by attempting to discredit the Resurrection. In that respect his logic is sound, for if the Resurrection can be discredited Christianity is overthrown. This man hired venal archaeologists to fake a discovery of the body of Jesus in the neighborhood of Jerusalem. On the tomb was an inscription testifying that the owner of this sepulcher stole the body of Jesus and hid it there. The novel then goes on to describe the ultimate effect of such a discovery, if accepted as truth, upon the Christian world, upon the Christian Church, and upon civilization in general. In powerful passages he shows how, gradually, the Christian Church crumbles and collapses; how men and women go back to lust, cruelty, and animalism; and how the flame of hope dies out in every human heart.

Had the body of Christ ever been found, or a grave in which it could be proved that his body had been placed, other than that of Joseph of Arimathea, the Church would indeed disappear and the sun of human hope would set in the darkness of an ever-ending life. But thanks be to God, now is Christ risen from the dead! On that empty tomb is the epitaph written by the angels, the epitaph that ends all other epitaphs— "He is risen; he is not here: behold the place where they laid him!" (Luke 16:6).

RETRIBUTION—*see also* CONSCIENCE, EVIL, HELL, JUDGMENT, SIN

A French peasant standing over the body of the murdered Robespierre at the time of the Reign of Terror, exclaimed, looking down upon him, "Yes, Robespierre, there is a God!"

————— • ◦ • —————

When the barbarians of Malta saw a viper hanging to Paul's arm as he brought up faggots for the fire which they had built to give warmth and cheer to those who had escaped from the shipwreck, they cried out to one another, "No doubt this man is a murderer, whom, though he hath escaped the sea, yet vengeance suffereth not to live" (Acts 28:4). They were mistaken as to the character of Paul; but they were not mis-

taken in their great conviction that sin will be punished, not only in this world, but in the world to come.

————— • ◦ • —————

Anne of Austria once said to Cardinal Mazarin: "My lord Cardinal, God does not pay at the end of every week; nevertheless he pays."

————— • ◦ • —————

He sat before me, a young man in the early twenties. But I needed to look at him for only a moment to see that he was scarred with the markings of sin. A few inquiries sufficed to open up the way for him to tell me his story. It was a dark story of transgression and sin. Both body and mind were reaping the consequences of his sin. Sometimes the payment of sin is long deferred, until men think the debt will be outlawed; and sometimes, as in this case, the demand of the creditor follows hard upon the bargain.

He had come to me for counsel and for help. But what could I do or say? Moral laws and the laws of inexorable nature were speaking and acting. Who could silence their speech? Who could stop their movement? When he was through with his tale, I sat dumb with silence, solemnized at the recoil of the broken law. At length the young man himself broke the silence which on both sides had followed the recital of his transgression. What he said was this: "If I had only known then what I know now!" For a moment his face was lighted up as if hope had flashed once more before his eyes a vision of what had once been and might be once again. Then the light died out of his face, and once more we sat in silence. "If I had only known then what I know now."

————— • ◦ • —————

"The way of transgressors is hard." (Prov. 13:15.) This man knew now that it was. He had no doubt about it. He had found out experimentally that the way of the transgressor is hard. It was the hardness and the difficulty of that way which brought him to me.

After conversation with me, and prayer, he signed a pledge to abstain from the use of intoxicating liquor, for that was his difficulty. He was married, the father of two children, and still was able to hold a good position. I said to him, "You are an intelligent man. How did you get into this habit? You must have known what it does to people. Did you think that you could indulge in this habit and not receive hurt?" His answer was: "You never think it will hit you the way it hits the other fellow."

———•••———

In Carlyle's *Past and Present* he tells of a proud and cruel prince, Henry of Essex, who profaned the shrine of St. Edmund, and shamefully used a certain Knight Gilbert, causing him to wear out his life in chains and imprisonment. Years afterward this prince was in a deadly battle with a knight on an island in the Thames. Giving way for a little, he glanced to one side, and lo! at the rim of the horizon he saw marching toward him an armed knight whose stature was gigantic. It was the wronged Sir Gilbert, and at his side marched St. Edmund. With that, Henry's sword fell from his hand, and he was soon vanquished. "Thus does conscience project itself across whatsoever of knowledge or imagination, understanding or natural disposition, a man has in him, and like the light through colored glass, paint strange pictures on the rim of the horizon. Justice and reverence are the everlasting laws of this universe and to forget them is to have all the universe against you, God and one's self for enemies, and only the Devil and the Dragon for friends!"

———•••———

One of the most powerful and moving scenes in all fiction is that in *Romola*

where George Eliot describes the retribution that befell the pleasure-loving Greek, Tito Melema, who had wronged two women and publicly denied and repudiated as a man he had never seen before the foster father who had brought him up and given him the jewels with which to purchase himself out of slavery. Tito has escaped from the angry mob in Florence by leaping into the Arno from the parapet of the bridge. At length, exhausted and almost unconscious, he is flung by the tide of the river up amid the reeds on the bank, where the old foster father, his mind reeling under the shock of the denial by his son, is waiting and hoping for vengeance. The old man has reason enough left to recognize Tito and strength enough left to clutch him by the throat with infinite satisfaction. At the close of that powerful scene, George Eliot writes, "Who shall lay his finger upon justice and say it is here? It is not without us as a fact. It is within us as a great yearning."

———•••———

—In history—In his *Autobiography* Andrew D. White tells of a visit he made to Columbia, South Carolina, some few years after the Civil War. Visiting the state legislature, he saw the presiding officer, a mulatto, order a white gentleman, a gentleman of the Old South, to take his seat. "To this it had come at last. In the presence of this assembly, in the hall where disunion really had its birth, where secession first shone out in all its glory, a former slave ordered a former master to sit down and was obeyed. I began to feel a sympathy for the South, and this feeling was deepened by what I saw in Georgia and Florida; and yet, below it all, I seemed to see the hand of God in history, and in the midst of it all I seemed to hear a deep voice from the dead. To me, seeing these things, there came reverberating out of the last century that prediction of Thomas Jefferson, himself a slaveholder, who, after depicting the offenses of slavery, ended with these words worthy of Isaiah—divinely inspired if any ever were—'I tremble when I remember that God is just!'"[1]

When American troops entered the city of Cologne, they found the majestic seven-century-old cathedral still standing, structurally unhurt. But the spires of the cathedral looked down upon a vast desolation. The great Hohenzollern bridge over the Rhine, its back broken, lay half submerged in the river. In the city itself factories, mills, shops, banks, theaters, churches, art galleries, railroad stations, mansions of the rich, and homes of the poor lay reduced to ashes and rubble. It was an abomination of desolation whose description would require the pen of Isaiah when he wrote of the overthrow of Babylon, or the pen of Ezekiel when he described the doom of Tyre, or the apocalyptic pen of St. John when he pictured the desolation of the Babylon of this world.

All that remains to complete the desolation at Cologne is for St. John's mighty angel to take up a stone like a great millstone and cast it into the Rhine, saying, "Thus with violence shall that great city Cologne be thrown down, and shall be found no more at all" (Rev. 19:21).

If they could preach, those majestic spires of Cologne, of what would they preach? They would preach of divine retribution. They would speak of the horror and devastation which Germany brought down upon defenseless cities— Warsaw, Rotterdam, Belgrade, Athens, Coventry, Plymouth—and they would

[1] Used by permission of the publishers, D. Appleton-Century Company.

say, O Cologne! O Germany! "The judgments of the Lord are true and righteous altogether" (Ps. 19:9).

—And judgment—The highest conception of justice and retribution requires not only that evil be punished but also that guilt be made public. Both elements of retribution appear in the punishments of the future. Once on a visit to the Channel Islands I thought of Victor Hugo's powerful tale based on those islands and the waters around them, *Toilers of the Sea*. The wicked Clubin had defrauded and cheated and murdered, and yet had evaded justice. "He had kicked Rantaine into space, Leithiery into ruin, human justice into the darkness, opinion into error, all humanity away from himself. He had just eliminated the world."

He had purposely wrecked his vessel on the rocks and sent all the ship's company off in a longboat, with the impression that he was dying like a hero, remaining with his ship, according to the tradition of the sea. Then, with his ill-gotten 75,000 francs in a leather belt about him, he was going to swim to the Man Rock, hail a passing vessel, and leave behind him forever the scene of his crimes. He dived from the deck of the vessel into the sea, struck bottom, and then struck out for the surface again. At that moment he felt himself seized by the foot by a cold, clammy, and yet steel-like arm. It was the octopus!

Clubin had been punished, but his sin and punishment had not yet been uncovered before man. Months afterward, when the tide was low, the heroic Gilliat, seeking to salvage the wreck, slew the octopus which seized him in the cavern and after his desperate battle, looked about him. Lo, he beheld a grinning skeleton encircled by a moldy leather belt, and on the belt the brass box, bright with the name of Clubin, containing the stolen money. What had been discovered in the abyss of hypocrisy and evil was brought to the surface. "There in the inexorable gloom what might be called the encounter of hypocrisies, those two existences made up of waiting and of shadow, had come into violent collision; and one which was the beast had executed the other, which was the soul. Sinister justice!"

—In kind—Adoni-bezek was a prince who ruled in one of the strongholds of the Canaanites, a stronghold as yet untaken at the time of the death of Joshua. This monster amused himself with the savage mutilation of the princes whom he conquered in battle, cutting off their thumbs and their great toes, thus rendering them unfit for military service. To cruelty and mutilation he added insult and degradation by compelling them to grovel about his table in his palace, where he threw crusts of bread to them as if they were a pack of dogs. But at length his day came. Simeon and Judah and their men at war took his stronghold and put his people to death. But Adoni himself they reserved for a more poetic justice and grim retribution. They dealt with him just as he had dealt with the princes who were unfortunate enough to fall into his hands. They mutilated him just as he had mutilated his own victims. When he had suffered this mutilation, Adoni exclaimed, "As I have done, so God hath requited me" (Judg. 1:7).

The incident is a striking example of the judgments of God.

In his history of the French Revolution, Carlyle tells of a minister of the Crown, Foulon, who, when his finance scheme raised the question, "What will the people do?" exclaimed, "The people may eat grass!" When the people rose, he was hanged from a post, "and his mouth after death was filled with grass, amid sounds as of Tophet from a grass-eating people. Surely, if revenge is a kind of justice, it is a wild kind. They that would make grass to be eaten, do they now eat grass in this manner? After long, dumb, groaning generations, has the turn suddenly become theirs?"

There is an old legend of a clock tower which was erected ages ago in one of the kingdoms of Europe. It was the highest achievement of a world-famous architect. For the clock he designed an intricate mechanism for striking the hours on a great bell: a bronze figure was to glide up noiselessly and strike the hours on the bell. When the metal for the bell was being poured into the mold, one of the workmen made a mistake which might have ruined the bell; and in his anger the architect took a hammer and struck the workman dead. A piece of the man's skull flew into the metal and left a flaw there which the architect did not discover until the day the tower was to be dedicated.

On the appointed day and at the appointed hour the king and his court and all the people were assembled on the plain beneath the tower waiting for the bell to strike the hour of one. As the time approached, the crowd became still. It counted the minutes and then the seconds. But when one o'clock came, there was no sound—only a dull thud, and then silence. After waiting for a time the people went up the stairs of the tower and found the artist dead beside his bell. He had been working feverishly in an effort to repair the flaw which had been made in the bell by the fragment from the skull of the man whom he had slain, and which he had just now discovered. Intent on his work he had not noted the time; and sharply at one the bronze figure which he had designed with his genius came noiselessly forward and, lifting its heavy hammer, smote. But instead of striking the bell, it struck the head of the architect.

———•◆•———

There is a law of retribution working in the universe. There is not only retribution but retribution in kind. Pharaoh has murdered the male children of the Hebrews by casting them into the river Nile. Now the angel of death flies across his own kingdom to smite through death the first-born of every Egyptian home. As Maxim Gorky puts it: "Life has its wisdom; its name is accident. Sometimes it rewards us, but more often it takes revenge on us. And just as the sun endows each object with a shadow, so the wisdom of life prepares retribution for man's every act. This is true, this is inevitable, and we must all know and remember it."

REVELATION

I visited some time ago the Luray Caverns in Virginia. As we stood in one of those marvelous chambers beneath the earth, the guide extinguished the light. We were in a darkness like that of the ninth plague, a "darkness which could be felt"—palpable, oppressive, overwhelming. We seemed to have passed into another form of existence, in which eyes had no use and no meaning. We looked into a wall of blackness; we could feel only the beatings of our hearts and the dim murmur of some subterranean waters far beneath us. As suddenly as the guide had put out the light, he turned it on again, and from the world of blackness we passed into one of beauty and glory. The chambers were like the abodes in which the gods might have lived in the fabled ages. Stalactite and stalagmite met together, massive pil-

lars of limestone upheld the roof, and the drippings had made of the walls exquisite tapestries of blue and purple and gold. Through millions of years nature had been carving there her matchless works in silence and fashioning them in thick darkness, as if to keep the secret from the unfit eyes of man. Now the light was let in, and we beheld with wonder the angels, and men and women and little children, and birds and beasts, and fluted columns and rounded domes, the altars, thrones, castles, palaces, cathedrals.

Life without the knowledge of God in Christ Jesus is like living in the unlighted chamber—just a dark cave where men tumble together like beasts in a meaningless struggle. But when God comes into the heart of man, he commands a new creation, "Let there be light!" (Gen. 1:3).

REVENGE—*see also* FORGIVENESS, HATE

I have no little admiration for William Tecumseh Sherman. I think the wreath that the sculptor represents as resting on his brow in that noble statue at the entrance to Central Park in New York rests there deservedly. He was not only the planner and executor of remarkable campaigns but a man of quick and scintillating intellect, not only a prophet of the times but a principal actor. But there is one incident in his life that I always read with sorrow. On May 24, 1865, the victorious Union armies paraded through Washington. After Sherman, attended by Howard and all his staff, had ridden past the reviewing stand, Sherman dismounted and went upon the stand. He shook hands with the President, General Grant, and each member of the Cabinet save one. When he approached Stanton, the secretary of war extended his hand—and Sherman publicly refused it. And worse than that, he records the incident with evident delight in his *Memoirs.* He had been aggrieved at Stanton's treatment of him after the surrender of Johnston. In this way he sought to humiliate him. But the only person he really humiliated was General Sherman.

Jules Verne in his *Twenty Thousand Leagues Under the Sea* was the prophet of the submarine, with its cruel devastation and destruction. Possessed with hatred of mankind, Captain Nemo ranges the seas in his submarine, the *Nautilus,* and takes fearful and titanic vengeance upon the human race. The book comes to a close with the description of the sinking of a man-of-war, with the swarm of seamen, like an ant heap overtaken by the sea, struggling in the waters and clinging to the hull of the sinking ship, until the dark mass disappears and is sucked down into the depths.

A seaman, a prisoner on the *Nautilus,* viewing the tragedy, turned to look at Captain Nemo: "I turned to Captain Nemo. That terrible avenger, a perfect archangel of hatred, was still looking. When all was over, he turned to his room, opened the door, and entered. I followed him with my eyes. On the end wall, beneath his heroes, I saw the portrait of a woman still young, and two little children. Captain Nemo looked at them for some moments, stretched his arms toward them, and, kneeling down, burst into deep sobs." Then he heard the captain exclaim, "Almighty God! Enough! Enough!" And with that the *Nautilus* was sucked down into the maelstrom.

The anguish and solitude of Captain Nemo are a powerful parable of the wages of hatred, of what happens to man when he tries to get the best of his enemies by hating them and destroying them.

REVERENCE—*see also* PRAYER (PHYSICAL ATTITUDE IN)

—For self—In a great passage, one of the noblest in English prose and one of the most inspiring for young men, John Milton said that he was kept back from the vices and immoralities which stained the lives of his fellow students at Christ College, Cambridge, because he had "a just and pious reverence for his own person." In another passage he gives two reasons why a man ought not to sin against God and against himself. The first is the dignity of God's image upon him by creation, and the second the price of his redemption. "He thinks himself both a fit person to do the noblest and goodliest deeds, and much better worth than to defile with such a debasement and pollution as sin is, himself, so highly ransomed and ennobled to a new friendship and filial relation with God."

REVIVAL, THE GREAT

On a November day in 1802, at a sacramental celebration at the church at Upper Buffalo, Washington County, Pennsylvania, John McMillan turned to Elisha McCurdy and asked him to preach a sermon while the Communion was being administered to a part of the great multitude. McCurdy ascended the wagon pulpit with fear and trembling, not knowing what he should say. After a hymn and a prayer, he opened the Bible at random and his eye fell on the Second Psalm—"Why do the heathen rage?"

The Whisky Rebellion and the terms of amnesty offered by the government were still fresh in the memory of the congregation. McCurdy startled his hearers by announcing that he would preach a sermon on politics. He said he had just received a letter from the government, informing him that an insurrection had taken place and that measures had been taken to suppress the rebellion, and amnesty had been proclaimed to all who would return to their duty. Since many of the rebels were present in his congregation, he said he would read them the proclamation of the government.

He then read the Second Psalm as describing the condition of sinners and announcing the terms of amnesty offered them in Christ (v. 12): "Kiss the Son, lest he be angry." During the sermon which followed, many fell to the ground, crying out in their anguish that they had been rebels against God. The scene was like the close of a battle in which every tenth man had been wounded.

This sermon on the Second Psalm, famous as McCurdy's War Sermon, played a mighty part in the Great Revival, which swept the country in the first decade of the nineteenth century and left behind it the missionary society, the prayer meeting, and the agitation against slavery and strong drink. Meditation upon God's Word, upon any part of his revealed truth, is never without profit; for it is only when God's truth begins to work upon individuals and in society and among nations that great results follow.

RICHES

—Of Christ—Some years ago men celebrated the centennial of mining in the anthracite coal region. Visiting there, I asked a man familiar with the mines about the possible exhaustion of these great deposits laid down through incalculable ages of time. I was surprised to have him tell me that one hundred years of mining had touched only the outermost fringe of those great fields of coal.

For over nineteen centuries, uncounted thousands of believers have been taking away, each for his own need, the riches of Christ. Theologians, philosophers, preachers, hymn writers, artists, and sculptors—all have taken the riches of Christ as their theme. But the vast deposit has hardly been touched, for these riches are unsearchable, inexhaustible.

———————

Thus read the will of Patrick Henry: "This is all the inheritance I can give to my dear family. The religion of Christ will give them one which will make them rich indeed."

———————

—Earthly—Whatever happens to our earthly inheritance during our lifetime, death is sure to take it from us. When Sir Walter Scott, broken in fortune and compelled to relinquish portions of his vast estate, took up his pen again, in order to pay off huge debts, and began the composition of *Woodstock,* he put this down in his diary: "I feel neither dishonored nor broken down by the bad, now truly bad, news I have received. I have walked my last in the domains I have planted—sat the last time in the halls I have built. But death would have taken them from me if misfortune had spared me." That will always be true of the earthly inheritance. Misfortune may spare it, but death is certain to take it from us.

———————

After the first World War there was a man of great wealth in New York who, anxious to do with his vast fortune something which should benefit mankind, employed a professor of Columbia University at a high salary to suggest some useful way of disposing of his fortune. But then the depression came, and when he died his fortune had been so reduced that one would never have guessed that he once found it necessary to employ an expert to make suggestions as to how to dispose of it. That earthly riches take to themselves wings is not just a rhetorical expression of the Bible; it is a truth that you and I have seen demonstrated many times—and will see many times again.

— • • • —

—True—On the grave of a man whose life had been an ornament to his country and a benefit to his fellow men was this epitaph: "My wealth consists not in the abundance of my possessions, but in the fewness of my wants." This man evidently had not been unmindful of the words of our Lord, that "a man's life consisteth not in the abundance of the things which he possesseth" (Luke 12:15).

— • • • —

Sitting in the dining salon of a steamer one summer, I chanced to overhear two American businessmen who were sitting near me speak of a classmate in the long ago at Princeton. He happened to be one of the most distinguished Christians of our day.

"How much do you think he is worth?" one said to the other.

"I don't think he's worth anything," the other replied.

From the standpoint of things, he was probably not far from the truth; but when it came to the soul, when it came to relationship with God and to doing good toward his fellow men, the man was rich indeed!

RIGHT, TRIUMPH OF

Nebuchadnezzar had seen in his vision a huge image, a colossus whose head was of fine gold, his breast and arms of silver, his belly and thighs of brass, his legs of iron, his feet of iron and clay. The mighty colossus seemed invincible; but a stone cut without hands smote the colossus on his feet of clay and brake the image to pieces, while the stone that smote the image became a great mountain and filled the whole earth.

That is a timeless parable, and the only true philosophy of history. No matter how formidable wickedness may seem, or how polished the silver and gold and brass of its material show and splendor, it stands upon feet of clay, and the uncut stone of God's justice and holy decree at length will smash it to fragments and cast it into the dust.

— • • • —

The hope which beats within the breast of man has ever pictured a great and a good end to the long process of history.

> *Ah, there is something here*
> *Unfathomed by the cynic's sneer,*
> *Something that gives our feeble light*
> *A high immunity from Night.*
>
> . . . .
>
> *A conscience more divine than we,*
> *A gladness fed with secret tears,*
> *A vexing, forward-reaching sense*
> *Of some more noble permanence;*
> *A light across the sea,*
> *Which haunts the soul and will not let it be,*
> *Still beaconing from the heights of undegenerate years.*
> —James Russell Lowell

— • • • —

There is a noble expression of confidence in the triumph of right found in a letter written by the Prussian Queen Louise in 1818, to her father, when Napoleon overran Europe: "It were a crime to say God is with the French emperor; but he is manifestly an instrument in the hands of the Almighty to bury out of sight the old order, which has no further purpose. I do not believe the Emperor Napoleon Bonaparte is firm and secure on what at present is so dazzling a throne. Only truth and justice are steadfast and at rest; he is politic, that is, cunning, and he guides himself, not according to the eternal laws, but according to circumstances as they are just now. Consequently, he stains his rule with much injustice. I believe steadfastly in God, and therefore also in a moral ordering of the world. This I do not see in the reign of violence, and so I entertain the hope that better days will succeed the present evil ones."

RIGHTEOUS, DEATH OF THE—*see* BALAAM

RIVER OF DEATH

Driving down to the bank of the Ohio, we saw an old-fashioned ferry come lazily over the river to ferry us across. It was a frail-looking platform for such a heavy machine, but soon we were safe on the farther side. I thought of a verse from Scripture: "There went over a ferryboat to carry over the king's household" (II Sam. 19:18).

Yes, at the end of life's pilgrimage we come to the river—deep, wide, swiftly flowing. Many roads here and there, but all coming down at length to the river's bank! Who shall ferry us over?

O Christ, thou divine boatman, whether it be early in the morning, when the dew is yet fresh upon the grass by the river's bank, that we come down to the ferry, or at high noon, when the sun burns down upon the broad waters and the cattle in the near-by meadows seek the shade of the willows, or late at evening, when shadows are hastening down like an army of giants to conquer the realm of light—whatever hour it be that we reach our utmost bound, do thou be there to greet us and fetch us over. Let us hear thy cheerful hail. As earth's shores recede and time for us ceases to be, let thy presence go with us and crown the journey's end.

RIVER OF LIFE

A river of water of life! How full of meaning that is to a traveler in the East! There you have sharp contrasts—arid deserts, bare hillsides, yellow mountains; but where the river flows, there is shade, coolness, greenness, fruits and flowers. Even the very sound of flowing water falls with pleasant music on the ear. Egypt is the "gift of the Nile," a garden bounded by a desert. Damascus is an oasis in the desert created by the Abana (now Barada) and Pharpar rivers flowing from the snows of Hermon. There the desert gives way to orchards and groves, laden with fruits and exhaling sweet odors.

Along the way to Antioch bare mountains yield to pleasant groves, where the waters of Daphne tumble over the rocks and where the great wheels lift the waters of the full-flowing Orontes into the gardens. But perhaps it is at Tarsus that one best understands how the river is the giver of life. To the north are the bare, rugged Taurus Mountains. Here in front of you lies the mean, dry, dusty, yellow, windswept town. But to the south, toward the sea, where the waters of the Cydnus are taken up by the great water wheels, you behold a very paradise of deepest green, where trees bend in the wind and gardens fill the air with sweet incense.

S

SABBATH

The Pilgrim Fathers, according to the old hymn, left England, first for Holland, and then for America, for "freedom to worship God." But freedom to have a *day* of rest and worship was one of the chief motives of their migration. King James had decreed that Sunday was a day for sports, and issued his *Sports Book*. The Pilgrim Fathers desired to build their families, and their civilization, upon another basis. Hence they came to America. From the very beginning, in all the colonies, observation of the Sabbath was part of the law of the land. There is no doubt, either, that their observance of this day made a mighty contribution to the moral stamina and spiritual well-being of the nation, as well as to its material and economic prosperity. The Sabbath gave the people a chance to know the Bible, the fountain whence have flowed the noblest streams of influence in the religion, education, and politics of the nation.

———•◆•———

Man is a seven-day machine, designed so by the Great Artificer. The greatest blessing ever conferred upon man as a toiler and a laborer is the Sabbath. Henry George said, "Moses was the first labor reformer, and the Sabbath was his chief labor reform." John Bright, speaking to the toiling miners of Lancashire, used to quote the lines of George Herbert:

*Without Thy light, the week were
    dark;
Thy torch doth show the way.*

———•◆•———

Walking once over the ruins of the best preserved of all Roman colosseums, that at Nimes, in the south of France, I came upon two gentlemen from Cincinnati. The colosseum at Nimes was to be used on the following Sunday for a bullfight. These men had just come out of Spain. I asked them if they had ever attended a bullfight in Spain. One of the men said that the others in his party had, but that he himself had not gone, although the excitement and the unusual spectacle tempted him sorely. But he was the teacher of a Sunday school class in a church in Cincinnati. He said, "I would not think of going to a ball game in Cincinnati on Sunday. Now, simply because I am in Spain and away from friends and acquaintances and from the routine of Christian duties, I will not go to a bullfight on the Lord's day." That was well said and well done. It had its influence upon me. It must have had its influence upon the others of his party.

SAINTS—*see* COMMUNION OF THE SAINTS

SALVATION—*see also* BOOK OF LIFE, SOUL (SALVATION OF THE)

At Tunbridge, England, there is a monument erected to the memory of a group of gypsies. Gipsy Smith, the noted evangelist, tells us the meaning of that monument: thirty gypsies, workers in the fields of hops, were driving rapidly and carelessly, singing and laughing, across a bridge over the Medway, when the wagon crashed into the railing and wagon, horses, and gypsies were thrown into the river.

One young gypsy seized a horse drifting downstream and, mounting him, watched earnestly and anxiously for his mother. At length he saw her and laid hold upon her; but she struggled in such a way that he was not able to save her. When the gypsies were being buried in the churchyard, the boy who had tried in vain to save his mother knelt down in the trench containing the coffins of those who had perished, and cried out, "Mother! Mother! I tried to save you; I did all a man could do, but you would not let me!"

So Jesus said on one occasion, "Ye will not come to me, that ye might have life" (John 5:40). Christ himself cannot save us unless we are willing to be saved.

———•◆•———

—Rejected—When Julius Caesar, after the Battle of Pharsalus, landed in Africa, whither the defeated Pompey had fled before him, the head of Pompey was flung at his feet. Looking at that gruesome trophy, Caesar exclaimed, "Alas, he would have it so!"

That, in effect, is what Jesus said when, at the end of his great lament over Jerusalem, he cried out, "And ye would not!" (Matt. 23:37).

SAMARITAN, GOOD

A great principle of Christ—that it is wrong to omit doing what we ought to do—is taught in the famous story of the good Samaritan. "A certain man went down . . . to Jericho, and fell among thieves." (Luke 10:30.) His nationality, his race, his religion are not noted. All that Christ says is that he was a man. He represents humanity. On that dangerous, and still dangerous, journey, through the bleak and barren gorge, down to Jericho, this man fell among thieves who assaulted him and robbed him and left him for dead. Presently there came down a priest who saw the man lying on the ground, but passed by on the other side.

No doubt he had plenty of good excuses to make to himself. "The man is either dead or so far gone that nothing I can do can help him. Too bad, but these things happen in life." Or, he may have said to himself, "This has been a recent attack and the robbers are still in the neighborhood. Perhaps lurking behind yonder rock. It will not be safe for me to stop and try to do anything for this unfortunate man. Moreover, if he is dead, it will be pollution for me to touch him; and my priestly duties would be interfered with." So he passed on.

Then came the Levite, another public exponent of religion, another man bound by his office. But he, too, passed by on the other side. No doubt he made the same excuses to himself that the priest did, and with this in addition. He probably said to himself, assuming that the priest and the Levite were not separated by a great distance, "If the priest did not stop, then I am sure that there is no necessity for me to stop."

Then came the Samaritan. For Christ to choose a Samaritan as the hero of his story would be like a speaker in Germany today before a Nazi holding up a Jew as the hero for his story, or address. And yet that is what Christ did. He did not mean to teach that all priests and Levites were heartless men, or that all Samaritans were good men, for just recently he had been turned out of a Samaritan village. But the compassion and humanity that he wishes to praise, he finds in this unlikely source.

The Samaritan could have made to himself the same excuses that the priest and the Levite made to themselves. Moreover, if the victim of the robber was a Jew, it was quite in keeping with custom that a Samaritan should feel no obligation to do anything for him. Yet this man stopped at once, ministered to the bleeding, wounded victim of the robbers, put him on his beast, brought him to the inn, and made himself responsible for his expenses there as long as was necessary for his recovery.

SATAN—*see also* BIBLE (DEVIL AND THE)

A murderer and a liar! That ought to settle the much-debated question as to the personality of Satan. You could hardly call an influence, an idea, an imagination, a figure of speech, or a personification, a murderer and a liar. But that is what Jesus called Satan. He said he was "a murderer from the beginning," and that he was "a liar, and the father of it" (John 8:44). Either Christ himself was a great deceiver or Satan is a personal power in rebellion against God, although under the government of God, and the great and subtle tempter and adversary of men's souls.

If Christ was not too great to be tempted of Satan, neither are you and I. The devil is often voted out of existence today; but someone certainly is doing his work, sowing tares where the wheat has been sown, mixing the fatal draught that palsies the heart and brain of man, dogging the steps of the toiling saints and digging pits for his feet, blighting the land with his fiery breath. A French priest was once addressed by a young man who said to him, "I suppose you no longer believe in a devil?" "Yes," said the priest, "I do; for if I did not believe in the devil, I would have to believe that I was my own devil."

This fact, taught by Christ and the Bible, that man is the object of a hostile interest on the part of the prince of evil himself lets us know that man is assailed not only by evil motives and desires but by the great spirit of evil himself, who goes about seeking whom he may devour. In the literal translation the Lord's Prayer reads, not "Lead us not into temptation, but deliver us from evil" (Matt. 6:13), but "Lead us not into temptation, but deliver us from the *evil one.*"

SCIENCE

Science, the knowledge of the natural world, does not hold the key. Men once hoped that it did and that, all else having failed, the key of science would turn the lock and admit mankind into the palace of peace and learning. But that, alas, was only an illusion. Science blesses with one hand and smites with the other; it leads mankind up to its Ebal and Gerizim, the Mount of Cursing and the Mount of Blessing. Today the world waits and trembles to see what new terrors science will unloose in war.

When Mary Shelley, the poet's second wife, was in Switzerland with Shelley and Byron in 1816, a proposal was made that members of their party should write a tale dealing with the supernatural. The result was Mrs. Shelley's famous tale, *Frankenstein.* Frankenstein was a young Swiss student of chemistry at Ingolstadt. In his laboratory experiments he became engrossed in the subject of life and death. What is physical life? And whence does its principle proceed? And what is death? And how does it work against life? In the pursuit of this subject he conceived the idea of creating life and producing an adult man. At length he became convinced that he was capable of bestowing animation upon lifeless matter. Day and night he toiled in his laboratory or haunted the charnel houses and the vaults and mortuaries, where he observed the gruesome inroads of death upon the human system.

Finally, one fateful day, he saw the body which he had constructed open its eyes and become a living creature. But immediately, now that he had achieved his purpose, he was filled with disgust and loathing for the monster he had created; and he fled from him in terror. Henceforth the creature haunted and pursued the creator, and took revenge on him by murdering his brother, his dearest friend, and his bride on their marriage night.

So man's genius and research, his mastery of the physical laws of the universe, have created a monster which today has turned upon its creator. Never can I look upon one of those huge, monstrous tanks of the modern battlefield, and see man, made in the image of God, lying dead and broken alongside of it, without thinking of the pathos and tragedy of it. Man was never made to be pursued by, to face or meet in combat, such a monster. And yet that monster is the creature of his own hands.

———————

There certainly is nothing in the future of learning or science which promises to disarm man's last enemy, which is death, and make him

> *Forego the scent which for six thousand years,*
> *Like a good hound he has followed.*
> —Author unknown

In Campbell's "Last Man," the survivor of a dying world expresses this idea of the inability of nature, progress, and science to heal the deepest wounds or quench the deepest thirst of man:

> *Thou dim, discrowned king of day;*
> *For all those trophied arts,*
> *And triumphs that beneath thee sprang,*
> *Healed not a passion or a pang*
> *Entailed on human hearts.*
> —Thomas Campbell

SEA

The earth has lost its mystery, but not so the sea. The ocean is still the home of mystery. Hast thou entered into the springs of the sea? The earth has been explored and her wildernesses conquered, but no man has entered into the springs of the sea. The earth changes; the sea sweeps on the same.

> *Unchangeable save to thy wild waves' play—*
> *Time writes no wrinkle on thine azure brow—*
> *Such as creation's dawn beheld, thou rollest now.*
> —George Gordon Byron

There is the mystery of its distance. Not on the mountain nor on the plain do we get such a conception of infinite space as on the sea. There is the mystery of its depths. Think of the monsters that come out of its slime; think of the golden treasures that strew its floors; think of the ships that sailed but never came to port; think of the fleets of war and merchandise that rot and crumble in its depth; think of the uncounted thousands of mariners and adventurers who sleep in its dark caverns and have "suffered a sea change into something new and strange." What makes its waters salt? What makes its tides roll up and down the shelf of the continent? The sea is still the home of mystery.

———————

On a long summer evening I once walked among the graves of the Clovelly churchyard. On stone after stone I read the words, "Lost at sea," "Perished at sea," "Drowned at sea." Loving hearts in Devon had raised these memorials. Far below me I could hear the booming of the surf as the waves of the Atlantic beat on the ironclad coast; but in the shelter of the church, under the shade of the evergreens and elms, the weary sailors slept in peace; and the accents of the Apocalypse seemed to echo sweetly through those grassy aisles: "There was no more sea" (Rev. 21:1). On one of the headstones I read these words, which breathe the hope, not only of simple seafaring folk, mourning for those who have gone down to the sea in ships, to do business in great waters and have never returned, but the only hope for all of us who sail through the mists and storms of life—the hope that by the way of faith and repentance this life of trial and probation leads to a life of satisfaction and reward.

SECOND CHANCE—*see* CHANCE (SECOND)

SECOND COMING

In Sherman's march from Chattanooga to Atlanta and from Atlanta to the sea, the Confederate government, impatient with the Fabian tactics of General Joseph E. Johnston, removed him from command and gave his army to the impetuous General Hood. Hood at once marched to the rear of Sherman, threatening his communications and base of supplies at Chattanooga and Nashville. An important link to these communications was Allatoona, which commanded the pass through the mountains. This post was at once attacked by Hood's army. Sherman sent an order to one of his lieutenants, Corse, to proceed to Allatoona. He himself went back as far as Kenesaw Mountain, and from that eminence on the clear October day could see plainly the smoke of the battle and hear the faint reverberation of the cannon. His flag officer at length made out the letters which were being wigwagged from the garrison at Allatoona, "Corse is here." This was a great relief to Sherman, who then heliographed his famous message, "Hold the fort. I am coming."

Among the soldiers in Sherman's army was a young officer, Major Whittle, who related the incident to P. B. Bliss, the famous evangelist. Taking this incident in the campaign for his inspiration, Bliss wrote the once well-known hymn, "Hold the Fort, for I Am Coming!"

The hymn thus inspired has genuine Christian truth in its lines. The Church is to *occupy* until Christ comes. It is assailed and besieged by the world and by the enemies of the truth. But Christ has not left it without a promise, a promise which means deliverance and victory. From the ramparts of heaven he waves to us the message that he is coming. Confident in that great appearance, the Church will occupy till he comes.

———

The Jacobites of Scotland never met one another on the mountain paths, never sat down to a table of council and conference, without lifting a cup to pledge the return of their king and prince, Charles. At length Charles came back, but only to bring to Scotland defeat, disaster, and suffering. In every celebration of the Lord's Supper, since that last and first night in the Upper Room, the followers of Christ have lifted the sacramental cup as a token of their faith that their King shall come. That is the meaning of those words which we hear so often that we forget their deep import: "As often as ye eat this bread, and drink this cup, ye do show the Lord's death till he come." Till he come! And when he comes he shall come not to bring pain and suffering, as did King Charles to unhappy Scotland, but to bind up all wounds, to set at liberty all the captives of sin, to wipe away all tears from all eyes.

———

Canon Liddon once said: "If Christ is not coming, we might as well lock the west door of this cathedral and throw the key into the river." In other words, Christianity would be proved false and all its lights and hopes would have faded, its great music quenched.

One day I paid a visit to an abandoned mining town in Nevada, near the California line. Around the town were great heaps of ore and refuse at the forsaken shafts. Through the town ran one broad street, flanked by the stores with their typical high board fronts. It was weird and almost uncanny to walk through the silent place and try to picture it as it must have been when it was a thriving, prosperous, and wicked mining town. Grass was now growing on the street and between the planks of the boardwalks in front of the shops and stores. The signs which told of boarding house, meat shop, drug store, saloon, and bank were still there; but what they had advertised had long since vanished.

On each side of the town stood a church, as empty and silent as the saloons and gambling dens whose evil influence they had sought to counteract. Only the cemetery was inhabited, and its inhabitants were unable to speak of the life they had once known in that now silent place.

I thought of the ambitions, the joys and sorrows, the hatreds and the affections, which once had surged in the hearts of those who dwelt there. What now had become of that population? Not all of them, probably very few of them, were dead, for the town had been abandoned only a few years. But all of them were gone elsewhere. What once in this town had engrossed their interest and their desire now meant absolutely nothing to them. Their life and all their interests were elsewhere.

To one familiar with the sayings of Christ about his second advent, this si-lent, empty, and deserted town spoke of the abandonments and evacuations and separations of the last great Day. It seemed to be a perfect picture of how in that great day all the values of this world will lose their significance, as meaningless as the empty shops and untenanted shanties of the mining town, and how all that which now engages our thought and our energy, and is the object of our desire, will become as nothing.

—And the Church—One of the great epics of classic literature tells of a woman who was separated from her husband. He had gone off to a foreign war. The months and the years had passed by, but no word had come of the missing Ulysses, tossed up and down on the waves of the ocean and tempted by sirens. The multitude of suitors pressed about Penelope, as she sat surrounded by her maids "laying her hands to the spindle and holding the distaff," and urged their claims upon her; but she was faithful to her absent lord—in Stephen Phillips' words,

> True to a vision, steadfast to a dream,
> Indissolubly married to remembrance.[1]

At length Ulysses himself in the guise of a beggar appeared one day among the suitors, took his own great bow and bent it, and thus revealed himself as the lost husband; and the fidelity of Penelope was rewarded.

To me that is a picture of the Church in the world. She is the blood-bought Bride of Christ, and all about her is the multitude of tempters and suitors who

[1] From "Ulysses," in *Collected Plays*. Used by permission of the publishers, The Macmillan Company.

would shake her loyalty to her Lord and master.

—And judgment—An unwritten saying of Christ preserved by Justin Martyr is an excellent summary of Christ's teaching as to the meaning of his return for each one of us: "In whatsoever employment I may surprise you, therein also will I judge you."

SELF—*see also* SOUL

Every man produces one masterpiece —himself. Day and night, year in and year out, in conscious and unconscious moments, his words and deeds, his secret desires, what he permits or refuses, every hope, every fear, every purpose—all are strokes of the brush, all help to produce the painting. One day the canvas is finished. Death frames it and puts it on exhibition. Then not a line can be erased or changed, not a feature retouched or altered. The work is finished. There is the masterpiece, a masterpiece because it is absolutely true to life.

Matthew Arnold once wrote a poem called "The Buried Life." He likens this life in man to a buried subterranean river which is ever flowing on its course, yet the sound of whose waters is seldom heard. It is only when men are still, when they lie quietly upon the earth, when they are detached from the noise and confusion of their daily work, that they catch the sound of this deeper river, the subterranean stream that flows quietly and swiftly away. We live a busy life amid the cares and the pleasures of the world; and only at rare intervals do we come to a realization that we have a soul within us, that we are made in the image of God. The whole course of our life is of a nature to hide this inner life and muffle the sound of its voice. Yet now and then, as if by accident, we stumble upon it, we hear for a moment the sound of this buried river:

Yet still, from time to time, vague and forlorn,
From the soul's subterranean depth upborne
As from an infinitely distant land,
Come airs, and floating echoes, and convey
A melancholy into all our day.

—Our better—There is a master touch in this incident in Charles Kingsley's *Hypatia*: Philammon goes to the old witch, Miriam, for a charm with which he can bring Hypatia to do his will. "The witch draws from her bosom a broken talisman, at which she looked long and lovingly, kissed it and wept over it, and fondled it in her arms as a mother with a child. Her grim, withered features grew softer, purer, grander, and rose ennobled for a moment to their long lost might have been, to that personal ideal which every soul brings with it into the world, which shines dim and potential in the face of every sleeping babe, before it has been scarred and distorted and encrusted in the long tragedy of life. Sorceress she was, pander and slave dealer, steeped to the lips in falsehood, ferocity and avarice, yet that paltry stone brought home to her some thought, true, spiritual, impalpable, unmarketable, before which all her treasures and all her ambitions were as worthless in her own eyes as they were in the eyes of the angels of God." The broken talisman had brought before the wicked woman's mind the vision of another—an earlier and an innocent—self.

In one of his tales Dickens, describing a low, coarse woman, says of her that, after going through many narrow passages, and up winding stairs, and down narrow hallways, you come at last to a door upon which is written the word "Woman." What he meant to say was that even in the lowest and worst of women there is something that is noble and womanly. So within every life there is the capacity of greatness. Underneath every covering of the rubbish and sin and defilement of life, you come at length upon a door on which is engraved that most wonderful of words, "Soul"—that soul that is yours by virtue of your creation in the divine image, that soul that sin has marred and defiled and fettered and choked, but can never destroy, that soul for the redemption of which Christ shed his precious blood on Calvary's tree.

—**Our chief foe**—Once in his dream a man was haunted and thwarted by a mysterious veiled figure. As soon as he had gained a fortune, the veiled form snatched it away from him. When he was about to enter into peace and joy, the veiled figure attacked his mind with fear and anxiety. When he was hungry and sat down to eat, the veiled figure snatched his food away from him. When he was overcome with slumber and lay down to sleep, this enemy of his life filled his mind with thoughts which banished sleep. When he had won fame, the veiled figure took away his reputation. When he stood at the open door of a great opportunity and was about to enter, the hand of the veiled one suddenly closed the door against him. When he stood at last at the marriage altar, and was about to give his sacred avowal and take the hand of his bride in wedlock, the veiled one strode forth, and, lifting up his hand in protest, said, "I forbid the banns!" Enraged, the unhappy man cried out to his adversary, "Who art thou?" and, stretching forth his hand, seized the veil and ripped it from the

face of his tormentor; and lo, the face that he saw was his own!

This dream sets forth the great truth that man is his own chief adversary and foe. If he is his own best friend, he is also his own worst enemy. Men make or ruin themselves. Our fault is not in our stars, but in ourselves, and we are the ones, and the only ones, who make or mar our destiny.

In talking with one man I asked him, in a kindly way, what his trouble was. He answered at once, "No trouble, sir, but myself."

How often that phrase has echoed in my memory: "No trouble, sir, but myself." The deepest and most dangerous troubles which afflict man's life come from within, not from without. Man's soul, that great fortress of Bunyan's imagination, fell only when there was treason within. The enemy entered through a gate that had been opened from within. The outside dangers and temptations of the world have no power over us *until* they receive the co-operation and help of the foe within our own souls.

Alcibiades, the gifted but unscrupulous Greek, was noted as an unhappy man. Someone asked Socrates why it was that Alcibiades, who had traveled so much and had seen so much of the world, was still an unhappy man. The sage answered, "Because wherever he goes, he always takes himself with him."

The chief foe and adversary of life is our own self. A great preacher, and a great winner of souls too, said: "I have had more trouble with myself than with any other person I ever knew." Very often men are reluctant to admit this. They like to blame the stars, outside circumstances, other people, for their difficulties and hardships, their lack of success in life. But now and then you hear a striking confession which confirms the truth that man is the architect of his own destiny. I once asked a husbandless mother, who had come to plan for her child, how she managed to get into this difficult circumstance, for if she told me, I said to her, on the ground of her experience I might be able to help someone else. Her answer was brief and to the point: "I have no one to blame but myself."

———

—The unknown—I was told some time ago of a Shakespearean scholar who said that several times in the year he read through *Macbeth*, not for scholastic purposes or literary investigations, but because the reading did him good, warning him and instructing him, because it showed the danger of ambition and the menace which lurks in the secret pool of imagination and desire. *Macbeth* is an illustration of the evil man in us and the loosing of him through the meeting of evil desire and opportunity. As the loyal soldier is returning from the wars in Norway, the spirits salute him as thane of Glamis, thane of Cawdor, and then as the future king. "All hail, Macbeth, thou shalt be king hereafter!" The spirits have hardly left him when messengers arrive to tell him that he has been elevated to the rank of thane of Cawdor. Why should not the third prophecy be fulfilled also? His companion warns the excited Macbeth against even entertaining such a desire:

And oftentimes, to win us to our harm,
The instruments of darkness tell us truths,
Win us with honest trifles, to betray's
In deepest consequence.

At that time Macbeth would have scorned the slightest suggestion that he gain his ambition by treason or murder. But when he reached his home he found that the king had come to visit him. In that moment his ambition and the opportunity to fulfill it were married, and the issue of that marriage was crime and sin.

SELF-APPROVAL

God help me so to live each day that at the close of the day I may have a high opinion of myself. The man to look at is the man in the looking glass. So careful we are, so thoughtful or anxious, about the other man, about what he thinks or says; but the one to look at is *thyself*—the man in the glass.

Just go to the mirror and look at yourself
And see what that man has to say;
For it isn't your father, or mother, or wife,
Who judgment upon you must pass.
The fellow whose verdict counts most in your life
Is the one staring back from the glass.

—Author unknown

If the one staring back from the glass does not approve, if he does not say, "Well done," then the praise and recognition and approval of others means nothing. Look, then, at the man in the glass, and see what he has to say.

SELF-CONFIDENCE

Margaret Slattery, in her *Living Teachers,* tells of a community in which a stranger came to settle and to engage in the practice of law. He immersed himself in his legal work; and when he was sometimes seen walking at the eventide, he walked alone, with his head down, and with the look of mental distress upon his face. One day he confessed to an artist who had a studio in the town that he had made one sad and terrible mistake in his life. The artist said nothing, but parted from him and went into his studio. Weeks afterward, he invited this melancholy and dejected lawyer to come in and view a portrait which he had finished, telling him that it was his masterpiece. The man was surprised and pleased that his judgment should have been sought by the artist, but when he went into the studio to view the portrait, he was surprised to see that it was a portrait of himself, only now he stood erect, with his shoulders thrown back and his head up, ambition, desire, and hope written on his face. Regarding it in silence for a few moments, the man said, "If he sees that in me, then I can see it. If he thinks I can be that, then I *can* be that man; and, what is more, I will be."

When Rear Admiral Du Pont gave to his superior officer, Farragut, the explanation of why he had failed to take his ships into Charleston Harbor, Farragut heard him through to the end and then said, "Admiral, there is one explantation which you haven't given."

"What is that?" asked Du Pont.

"This. You didn't believe that you could do it."

That lack of confidence has been the secret of failures not only in the field of war but also in this greater warfare of the soul.

SELF-CONTROL

A ship or an engine or a horse or a fire, out of control, is a dangerous thing; but most dangerous of all is a man out of control.

The words "He that ruleth his spirit [is greater] than he that taketh a city"

(Prov. 16:32) were written at a time when to take a city and sack it was the greatest of human achievements. The page of history abounds in accounts of the conquest of cities, telling how, either by process of slow siege or by sudden assault, the invading army stormed the walls and entered the city, leaving death and devastation in its trail. Then the conqueror made his triumphal entry into the city, mounted on his war charger or swaying in his gilded chariot. Through the broken walls he entered, to pass along streets flanked by profaned temples and smoking homes; and as he passed, the cheers of the conquerors made a dismal antiphony to the groans of the vanquished. This was what it meant to take a city. It was the utmost of human endeavor, the most renowned and distinguished of the exploits of man.

But even at that remote age, when the conqueror of a city was the greatest figure on the human horizon, there were those who saw that there was a still greater victory and conquest—the conquest of self. The greatest and most imperial city is that city of the human spirit, whose walls and towers, gates and turrets, are to be found beneath every human breast. He who takes this city and rules it in the interests of reason and faith is the greatest of all conquerors. He that ruleth his spirit is greater than he that taketh a city!

In front of the temple under whose auspices the Corinthian games were held ran a beautiful avenue. Along its sides were marble tablets, on which were the names of the winners of prizes at the games in past years. The great ambition of every athlete of Greece was to have his name inscribed on one of those tablets. Distinction in athletics then did not bring financial reward, as in the case of the notable athletes of our day. What the athlete strove for was to have his name inscribed along that avenue of fame and to wear upon his head the laurel crown. To secure that distinction he subjected himself to the most arduous discipline and training and abstinence for a period of ten months. At the end of that period, trained to the moment, he entered the arena and strove for mastery. It was that training that Paul had in mind when he spoke of the discipline and training to which the athletes subjected themselves, saying that all those who strove for mastery exercised "self-control in all things" (I Cor. 9:25).

In St. Petersburg—now Leningrad— I saw in the square, in front of St. Isaac's Cathedral, the magnificent equestrian statue of Peter the Great, with his hand uplifted, pointing his nation onward and eastward toward the sea. Peter was the maker of modern Russia. In many respects he well deserved the name "great." But he was subject to maniacal outbursts of fury and anger, in one of which he killed his own son. Toward the end of his reign Peter the Great once remarked, "I have conquered an empire, but I was not able to conquer myself."

Looking upon the immobile, impassive face of George Washington, as reflected in the portraits of Peale and Stuart, one would not imagine that under that calm and even surface there blazed a fiery spirit. Yet on two historic occasions—when he cursed Charles Lee for his insubordination on the battlefield of Monmouth, and then when he broke out in a volcano of wrath when word was brought to him at Washington of the defeat of St. Clair by the Indians near Fort Wayne, November 4, 1791—Washington showed that he had strong passions and was capable of great anger. But that spirit within him was ruled and controlled for the good of his country and for the ends of justice and righteousness. Not the least among the great traits of Washington was his mastery of himself.

If a man sleeps and nods, even for a second of time, when he is at the wheel of an automobile, the automobile will be wrecked. If when a plane is taking off or landing, the pilot loses control, even for the fraction of a second, the wreck of the plane and the death of the passengers will be the result. It is not otherwise with a man's life. A moment's carelessness, a moment's loss of self-control, may wreck his happiness and lay him in the dust.

SELF-RESPECT

James A. Garfield was elected United States Senator from Ohio in 1880, just before he was nominated for the Presidency. In an address to the Legislature, accepting the election, he said; "I have represented for many years a district in Congress whose approbation I greatly desired. But though it may seem perhaps a little egotistical to say it, I yet desired still more the approbation of one person, and his name was Garfield. He is the only man I am compelled to sleep with, and eat with, and live with, and die with; and if I could not have his approbation I should have bad companionship."

SERVE

Queen Victoria said to Gordon of Havelock, "When can you start for India?"

He answered, "Tomorrow."

That is the key to useful and successful and influential lives. When the call came they were ready—ready to make use of opportunity, to resist temptation, to answer the call of duty, of country, of God.

SERVICE—*see also* DEEDS (GOOD), DOING GOOD

In the Tate Gallery in London you will see one of the last and most notable of the paintings of Frederic Watts, his *"Sic Transit Gloria Mundi."* A shrouded form lies upon a bier in the middle of the room. On a table near by is an open book, and against the table leans a voiceless lyre. In one corner of the room is the rich mantle of a nobleman and in the other corner a lance and shield and divers pieces of armor, with roses strewn over them to show that the arts and tastes of life were mingled with the sterner duties. But now all is over. The still form cannot read the book, nor seize the lance, nor touch the lyre, nor don the mantle, nor catch the odor of the roses. On the wall in the background are three sentences of a German proverb: "What I spent I had. What I saved I lost. What I gave I have." Whatever you give in the ministry of your profession—of your hopes, your enthusiasms, your tears, your labors— that and that alone is yours, and yours forever.

The great enemy of the slave trade, the one who above all others accomplished its outlawry in Great Britain, was Wilberforce. After Parliament had passed the bill, a member, referring to Wilberforce, said that the pillow upon which he could rest his head at night, and know that the slave trade was no more, was a greater throne of splendor and glory than that of his contemporary, the Emperor Napoleon. Wilberforce was rich in what he had done for mankind.

SHEPHERD, GOOD

The only time that I remember seeing a sheepfold was a number of years ago on a visit to the Highlands of Scotland. Far out on the lonely moor which lay at the foot of the mountains, their tops covered with mist and their slopes with heather, I came upon this sheepfold. They who have traveled in both countries tell me that the sheepfolds of Scotland and those of Palestine are much the same. This one consisted of an enclosure walled off by stone walls about four feet in height, with a wooden gate for the entrance. Thither the sheep came from their grazing places, in the evening, and were shut up for the night, protected from the cold winds or the driving rain and safe from prowling beast. Keep that picture in your mind, and you will see clearly the meaning of the allegory of Jesus about the sheep, and the shepherd, and the fold.

SILENCE

In one of the Essays of Elia, writing of a Quakers' meeting, Charles Lamb says: "The Abbey Church of Westminster hath nothing so solemn, so spirit-soothing, as the naked walls and benches of a Quakers' meeting. Here are no tombs, no inscriptions.

. . . Sands, ignoble things
Dropped from the ruined sides of
kings.

But here is something which throws Antiquity herself into the foreground— Silence—eldest of things, language of old Night, primitive Discourser—to which the insolent decays of mouldering grandeur have but arrived by a violent, and as we may say, unnatural progression."

The Temple at Jerusalem was built in silence. How much noise does the river make as it flows swiftly and deeply to the sea, bearing the burden which it is to lay down in the river's mouth and thus sow the dust of continents to be? We look and fear and tremble at the boisterous works of nature, and foolishly think that then the world is doing its work. But the boisterous works of nature are just as unimportant as the boisterous works of man. It is not the storm of a century, tearing down beach and cliff, but the soft and gentle, almost imperceptible, lapping of the waves from hour to hour, and week to week, and year to year, that is building a new continent and submerging an old one. Whoever heard the flow of the subterranean waters that keep the world's heart fresh? How silently the snow falls, and how silent is the fierce griping of the frost. Whoever heard the soft procession of the early morn? The sun goes forth to run his race, but we never hear his panting or catch the sound of his footsteps; and night comes down to "blind with her hair the eyes of day," but no one hears her coming. Sleep is a dwelling place of silence; and death, mightier by far than all the vaunted strength of life, is just another name for silence. The Old Testament speaks of the dead as they "that go down into silence" (Ps. 115:17).

The forest has many voices with which it can speak to man. But it is not when the hunter or woodsman is crashing through the undergrowth, with the leaves and the fallen branches breaking beneath his foot, that he hears what the forest has to say. But when he leans his gun against a tree and sits down on a fallen log, then he can hear the voice of the forest—the grinding of one limb against another, the fall of a nut, the flitting of wings, the scamper of a rabbit,

the drumming of a woodpecker, in the tops of the trees the gentle stirring of the wind, like the sigh of a soul that has found its peace. The forest says, "Be still, and you will hear my voice."

The most musical voices of nature are heard only when man himself is still. It is then that "she speaks a various language." High up on the mountainside, where the Potomac and the Shenandoah mingle their floods to roll together toward the sea, there is a tilting rock known as Jefferson's Rock. According to tradition, it was when he was standing on that rock that Jefferson received inspiration for the description of that grand and beautiful country in his "Notes on Virginia." Far beneath you, toward the south and east, the beautiful Shenandoah flows over shelves of rock. The waters of the Shenandoah make noble music; but if you are speaking or laughing on the rock you cannot hear that music. It is only when you are still that you hear the voice of the river.

There is nothing so impressive as silence. I like to wander into some great cathedral and, standing alone in the nave, listen to the silence of the immense pillars, the soaring arches, the angels and saints carved upon the pillars or looking down upon you from the windows.

Nature, too, has great silences. The sea is magnificent when it is broken and driven by the lash of the wind. But it is still grander and more mysterious when it lies under your ship without a wave, motionless as a sea of glass. The mountains are noble in their silence, and so is the forest when not a leaf stirs beneath the wind. The cedars of Lebanon, with their gigantic arms like vast harps, sometimes respond to the breath of the wind, and throw out music like the breaking of waves on a distant shore. But still more impressive are they when they stand silent and motionless, the sad and lonely survivors of the generations which have passed over them.

• • •

We often associate noise and bustle with great undertakings. We like to hear the confused murmur about a new building or a new bridge—the songs of the workers, the rattle of machinery, the sound of the hammer and the saw. Ever since the tongues were confused at Babel, every great building operation has been a babel of tongues and labors and sounds. But the temple was built in silence: "It rose like an exhalation."

> *No hammers fell, no ponderous axes*
> *rung,*
> *Like some tall palm the mystic fabric*
> *sprung.*
>
> —HEBER

"There was neither hammer nor ax nor any tool of iron heard in the house, while it was in building." (I Kings 6:7.) Economy of time and convenience of transport may have been reasons why the timbers were cut and the stones hewn before they were brought up to the hill on which the temple was rising. But as it stands, the record would seem to tell us that all unnecessary noise and work was avoided at the temple because it was a place and a building dedicated to the worship of God. Silence was the highest tribute the workmen could give to God.

• • •

When Samuel informed Saul that God had chosen him to be king of Israel, he said to Saul, "Bid the servant pass on before us, . . . but *stand thou still* a while, that I may show thee the word of God" (I Sam. 9:2). God has great things to say to man, but if he would hear them man must be still. When Eliphaz had his great vision of God's majesty and power,

the record of it in the book of Job reads thus (4:16): "There was silence, and I heard a voice." It is when we are silent to God that we hear the things that are worth hearing.

SIN—*see also* FORGIVENESS OF SIN, SOUL AND SIN

The darkest fact in man is sin. The grandest fact in God is forgiveness. John Chrysostom, Christianity's most eloquent preacher, used to say, "There is only one calamity—sin."

• • •

In the introduction to his *Confessions* Rousseau commences with these striking words: "Such as I was I have declared myself to be; sometimes vile and despicable; at others, virtuous, generous, and sublime. Even as thou hast read my inmost soul, Power Eternal, assemble round thy throne an innumerable throng of my fellow mortals. Let them listen to my confessions, let them blush at my depravity, let them tremble at my sufferings, let each in his turn expose with equal sincerity the failings, the wanderings of his heart, and, if he dare, aver, I was better than that man." Who cares to accept that challenge?

• • •

The first temptation in the history of the human race took place in a garden, and with man at peace with the whole animal creation. The temptation of Jesus, the second Adam, took place in a wilderness, where he "was with the wild beasts" (Mark 1:13). That contrast between the first temptation and the temptation of Jesus, one in a garden, the other in a desert, is a picture of the ruin which had been wrought by sin.

• • •

Sailing past Mount Etna or Mount Vesuvius, by ship in the sea or by airship in the heavens, you can see by day the clouds of smoke pouring from the crater of the volcano, and by night the red glow of the fires that burn within. Only on occasion does there come the great explosion of internal fires and gases, when the volcano pours out ruin and death upon the people and cities at its feet.

So also is it with mankind, with the heart of the world. There come, as at the present time in this great World War, vast explosions of man's sin and corruption and rebellion against God. But that takes place only because ever smoldering beneath the surface of human society is the iniquity in man's heart.

—Beginning of—On the campus of the theological seminary at Princeton are many ancient, stately, and beautiful elm trees. Every spring I used to watch the tree surgeons at their work of pruning and trimming and cutting away the dead limbs and branches, and pouring their black cement into the holes and spaces where decay and corruption had commenced.

It is not otherwise with the tree of one's life and character. Where there is a hole, repair it, or it will lead to something worse.

—Besetting—A besetting sin, even one unnoted by ourselves, will check and retard the spiritual life. The first time I saw the ocean was at San Pedro. When I saw the great ocean, I felt as Balboa must have felt when he looked on the vast Pacific. And here at San Pedro were the ships with their tall masts, for sailing ships were still plentiful. What a thrill it was to look upon them as they lay at anchor in the harbor! With my brother I got into a rowboat and started to row across the harbor to Dead Man's Island, now vanished, but once a well-known landmark, familiar to all readers of *Two Years Before the Mast*. Halfway to the

island our boat began to move very slowly; it took the combined push of four oars to move it at all. Finally we looked over the edge toward the keel of the boat and saw that a small strip of iron had become bent and protruded down into the sea, and that a mass of sea weed had accumulated about it. That was why it was difficult for us to move the boat. So it is with a single besetting sin. It may gather such a mass of objects and hindrances as will stop completely the onward progress of the soul.

A Scottish writer tells of being with a deer stalker on the northwest coast of Scotland. Sitting down to rest on the hills of Quoich, he was entranced with the lovely view of the islands and the sea, and said to his companion, the deer stalker, "A man might sit here forever, and in peace."

But his companion answered, "You know the old true word of our race: 'Though a man have no foeman without, within there is always one.'"

Yes, this is true! Within there is always a foeman, and every soul has its own ladder down to hell.

Because of the dragging back, and dragging down, power of one besetting sin in a man's life, we see what the apostle means when he says that in this race for eternal life we must lay aside every sin.

In one of the famous battles of the Old Testament, the king of Judah, Jehoshaphat, and the king of Israel, Ahab, went up to fight against the fortress of Ramoth-gilead, in possession of the Syrian army under the command of Benhadad. Before the battle was joined, the king of Syria called together his thirty-two captains and gave them instructions: "Fight neither with small nor great, save only with the king of Israel"

(I Kings 22:31). They knew that when Ahab was killed or driven from the field the victory would be won, for he was the heart and center of the confederacy against Syria. Knowing that he would be the object of special attack, Ahab had disguised himself in the garb of a common soldier. But he could not avoid the shaft of judgment and retribution. A certain man drew a bow at a venture and smote the king of Israel between the joints of his harness. Mortally stricken, Ahab turned his chariot out of the battle and died at the going down of the sun. His death was soon followed by the defeat and rout of his army. The fallen king meant a fallen cause.

There is a parable for the warfare of life! Make war on the besetting sin! "Fight neither with small nor great," save only against your besetting sin; and when you do that, you make war against all the evil that is in your life. When that besetting sin is conquered, then you are on the road to victory.

The Arabian chieftain Ben Achmet, in the confines of a desert, amid sterile and almost inaccessible rocks, led a life of austerity and devotion. Roots and fruits, and the fountain at the foot of the cliff, supplied all his needs. Formerly he had been a priest in the mosque, but disgusted with hypocrisy and injustice, he took himself to the desert, where he lived as an anchorite. As the years passed by, the fame of his sanctity spread abroad. Akaba, an Arabian robber, who had lawless men under his command, many slaves, and a treasure house filled with his ill-gotten gains, smitten in conscience and arrested by the sanctity of Ben Achmet, went to visit him. He said to him, "I have five hundred cimeters ready to obey me, numerous slaves, and a treasure house full of riches. Tell me how to add to

these the hope of a happy immortality."

Ben Achmet led him to a neighboring cliff that was steep, rugged, and high, and, pointing to three large stones, told him to lift them from the ground and follow him up the cliff. Laden with the three stones, Akaba was unable to move. "I cannot follow thee," he said, "with these burdens."

"Then cast one of them down and hasten after me!"

He dropped one stone, but still was unable to proceed. "I tell thee it is impossible. Thou thyself couldst not proceed a step with such a stone."

"Let go another stone, then."

Akaba dropped another stone, and with great difficulty clambered the cliff for a while till, exhausted with the effort, he again cried out that he could go no further. Ben Achmet directed him to drop the last stone, and no sooner had he done this than he mounted with ease and stood with his conductor on the summit of the cliff.

"Son," said Ben Achmet, "thou hast three burdens which hinder thee in the way of the better world. Disband thy troop of lawless plunderers, set thy captive slaves at liberty, and restore thy ill-gotten wealth to its owners. It is easier for Akaba to ascend this cliff with the stones that lie at its foot, than for him to journey onward to a better world with power, pleasure, and riches in his possession."

The sea, which has been the path of empire, is also the path of sorrow. Again there is sorrow on the sea as great nations struggle for its dominion.

One of the most famous naval battles of history was the Battle of Actium, fought September 2, 31 B.C., between the fleets of Mark Antony and Cleopatra on one side, and the fleet of Octavian, afterward Augustus Caesar, on the other. In the midst of the engagement the war galley of Cleopatra withdrew from the battle, and the infatuated Antony deserted his fleet to follow the Queen of the Nile. Thus the empire of the sea and of the world passed to Octavian. There is a tradition that in the midst of the battle Mark Antony's war galley unaccountably slackened its speed, and then, in defiance of hundreds of slaves bending at the oars and of a strong wind in its sails, the ship came to a standstill. A diver went down to examine the hull, and brought up a little fish, which, according to the belief of even the scientists of that day, such as Pliny the Elder, had the power to bring a great ship to a standstill merely by adhering to it. To us this idea is an idle and foolish superstition. But, however it may be with ships and marine life, it is a true parable of the moral life. One single besetting sin, adhering to the life of a man, can arrest his spiritual development and bring his soul to disaster.

—Breaking with—"I can't let her go!" It was his answer to my suggestion and advice, which he had sought. The words were spoken, not defiantly or impetuously, but slowly, quietly, and sadly. "I can't let her go." It was not so much the words that impressed me as the way he uttered them. It was the expression in his face, the accent of his voice.

It was one of those tangled webs which human love and human sin are always weaving. He had conceived an infatuation and established a relationship which was wrong—contrary to the laws of man and forbidden by the laws of God. It could have no other eventuation than guilt and misery. Indeed, the misery was already apparent. That was why I told him that there was but one thing for him to do—break off the relationship and abandon the companionship. To this proposal he made answer, *"I can't let her go!"*

—Burden of—"It is not a matter of mere theorizing or intellectual assent to certain facts. It is the struggle of a soul that sinned specifically, and reaches out for Christ as a drowning man does for a life preserver."

This was the message which came to me from one who had to say with the psalmist, "My sin is ever before me" (Ps. 51:3). Writing on the fact of sin, Emerson says somewhere, "The less we have to do with our sins the better." Commenting on this, John Morley says, "Emerson has little to say of that horrid burden and impediment on the soul which the churches call sin, and which, by whatever name we call it, is a very real catastrophe in the moral nature of man."

—Compromise with—If you have had some encounter with a besetting sin, or evil habit, don't be content to let it go with compromise. God told Saul to destroy the Amalekites. Saul thought he was wiser than God and let some of them escape. Years passed by, and Saul, lying self-wounded on the field of Gilboa, called to a man, "Stand . . . upon me, and slay me." "So I stood upon him, and slew him, . . . and I took the crown that was upon his head, and the bracelet that was on his arm" (II Sam. 9, 10). And that man was an Amalekite. That is the natural history of sin when we spare it, and treat it lightly. One day it comes back to find us weak, and it stands upon us and takes the crown of manhood from our dishonored brow.

—Confession of—A young student once asked the discoverer of the anesthetic property of chloroform, Sir James Simpson, what he considered his greatest discovery. The man of science and the man of God answered, "The greatest discovery I ever made was when I discovered that I was a great sinner and that Jesus Christ is my Saviour."

———————

At the close of his eventful life Father Matthew, the apostle of temperance, went to reside at Queenstown, where he was often seen loitering about the town. A friend calling to see him one day found him at his devotions. The friend offered some apology for disturbing him at such a time; but the eloquent priest answered, "You must join me in my prayers to God; pray for me."

"For you, sir?"

"Yes, I was praying that God would prepare me to leave this world and would forgive me for the sins I have committed."

"But what necessity is there for my praying for you, Father Matthew? You who have done so much good for mankind?"

"No. I have done nothing, and no one can be pure in the eyes of God. Oh, who can be pure in the sight of God? Kneel with me and pray with me to the Father of mercy."

———————

Emperor Francis Joseph of Austria was buried in the gloomy crypt of the Church of the Capuchin in Vienna, where sleep all his fathers of the house of Hapsburg. At the entrance to the vault the procession was halted by a voice from within: "Who is there?"

The reply was: "His most serene majesty, the Emperor Francis Joseph."

The challenger then said, "I know him not. Who is there?"

A second reply was made: "The Emperor of Austria and Apostolic King of Hungary is outside."

Again the challenger answered, "I know him not. Who is there?"

This time the voice without replied, "A sinful man, our brother Francis Joseph."

Then the portal was opened and the king was laid to rest among his fathers.

———————

In his *Seven Great Statesmen* Andrew D. White tells of the death of Hugo Grotius. It is a recital that touches the deep places of the heart. On his way back from Sweden Grotius was shipwrecked on the Pomeranian coast. Battered by the elements, he managed to get as far as Rostok; and there the famous scholar lay down to die. The beacon light that had illuminated the darkness of his age was soon to be quenched in the smoke of death. The pastor of the Lutheran church, learning of his presence, came in to see him. He made no effort to wrestle with the great statesman, but simply read to him our Saviour's parable of the publican and the pharisee, ending with the words "God be merciful to me a sinner!" (Luke 18:13). At that the dying sage opened his eyes and exclaimed, "That publican, Lord, am I!"

Until we are ready to make a like confession Christianity is a closed book, a forbidden garden. Grotius, the poor publican, wicked David, stainless Paul—all made that prayer, and making it, passed into the City of Forgiveness and Peace. Without that prayer, Christianity may be a history, a philosophy, a code—but not a religion that saves.

———————

One of the most eloquent and powerful of American Colonial preachers was James Waddel, the blind preacher of Virginia, whose eloquence is celebrated in one of the most beautiful pieces of American prose, William Wirt's *British Spy*. When this blind Boanerges lay dying, one of his friends, when he was about to leave him after a visit, expressed the wish that when *he* came to die he would have back of him, for his own comfort in such an hour, the record of a godly life like that of Waddel. At that, Waddel lifted his hand in protest and declared that if his only comfort were the thoughts of the life which he had lived, he would be wretched indeed. Instead of that his comfort was in the fact that the Lamb of God taketh away the sins of the world.

The battleship *Victory* was rolling in the sea where the thunders of the guns of the British fleet were yet reverberating in the great triumph of Trafalgar Bay. Down in the dark cockpit of the *Victory* Lord Nelson, shot through the back and dying, said to his captain, who stood over him: "Kiss me, Hardy. I have not been a great sinner."

Of what was Nelson thinking in that hour? Perhaps of the one great transgression that had shadowed his life and done such deep and cruel wrong to Lady Nelson. But whatever it was, his estimate was wrong.

From the worldly standpoint, Paul had lived, as he claimed he had, a highly moral life. Facing the foes who falsely accused him with gross sin, Paul said what you and I would hesitate to say, "I know nothing against myself" (I Cor. 4:4). But when he saw Christ crucified, when he knelt before the Cross, this was all he had to say, "Christ Jesus came . . . to save sinners; of whom I am chief" (I Tim. 1:15).

The sooner we are ready to make a like confession, the sooner we shall enter into the power and joy of the Christian life.

When old Dr. Maclure was dying he asked his friend Drumsheugh to read a bit from the Bible. The laird opened at the fourteenth chapter of John and commenced at the familiar words, "In my Father's house are many mansions." But the dying doctor stopped him, saying, "It's a bonnie word, but it's no for the like o' me."

Then the laird let the Bible open of itself at the place where the doctor had been reading every night for the past week, the passage where Jesus tells us what God thinks of a penitent sinner: "And the publican, standing afar off, would not lift up so much as his eyes unto heaven, but smote upon his breast, saying, God be merciful to me a sinner" (Luke 18:13).

Yes, that is the passage for doctors and for ministers, for lawyers and for bankers, for soldiers and sailors, for all the sons of men, who, when they come to finish their lives, have nothing to say for themselves. "God be merciful to me a sinner."

—Conquered—There is an idea which both Longfellow and Tennyson have made very familiar by their poetry, but the original author of it was Augustine; for it was he who said that by trampling our sins and vices under our feet we frame a ladder by which we rise on our dead selves to higher things.

There is no grander spectacle in the universe than when a soul lays hold upon that golden ladder and commences the ascent from the depths to the heights. The battlements of heaven are crowded with spectators when that happens.

—Conquest of—In *The Four Horsemen of the Apocalypse* the Russian sage and prophet, looking upon the ravages of war, despairs of the death of the beast. The beast, he says, never dies. He is the eternal companion of man. He hides spouting blood for fifty or a hundred years, but eventually he reappears. But Christianity has a different horoscope for the world. The beast has received his fatal wound. Both death and hell will be cast into the lake of fire.

———•—•—•———

—Deceit of—I remember a tale that our mother used to tell us. It was of an army officer in India who had a tiger cub for a pet. The cub was an affectionate and playful animal, and was much with its master. It had grown to size and strength, and one day the officer was sitting in his library reading. As he read he fell asleep. The young tiger, which was lying by his chair, began to lick the hand of his master, which hung down near him. There was a slight abrasion on the hand; and as the tiger licked the wound he tasted blood, and with the blood he became more and more ardent, until the officer, awakening, found himself looking into the blazing yellow eyes, not of a playful tiger cub, but of a ferocious beast that had tasted his blood and now sought his life. Just in time, he seized his pistol and shot the tiger.

That story left a great impression upon me; and, so far as its figurative meaning in the realm of morals and temptation is concerned, the experience with life has only served to confirm that early impression. The wrong relationship, which today seems only pleasant and delightful, tomorrow may be the tiger thirsting for your blood.

———•—•—•———

The great vision or parable of the Apocalypse sets forth the power of evil in men's lives. The locusts had crowns of gold on their heads, but stings in their tails. Under the crowns of gold was soft hair, the hair of a woman; but their teeth were as sharp and cruel as the teeth of a lion. This is a true and timeless account of the working of evil in the world. Like these locusts, sin wears a crown of gold and presents a soft and easy appearance. But under all this are the iron teeth of retribution and the remorseless sting of suffering.

———•—•—•———

—Finds us out—Twenty years! "Surely," Jacob thought to himself, "that is long enough to dull Esau's memory of what I did to him. He has now become a great man, and will have forgotten the mean trick that I did to him." And yet Jacob knew that he himself had not forgotten. No. The one sinned against might forget, but not the one who sinned. Sin and remorse are not subject to time. They are ageless. The sin that a man commits today, twenty years from today—yes, fifty or seventy years from today, when conscience and memory bring it back to him—will be as fresh as it was twenty years after he committed the sin. "Be sure your sin will find you out!" (Num. 32:23.)

———•—•—•———

She had been more sinned against than sinning. Suffering and religious devotion had chastened and purified her character till it was one of rare Christian grace and beauty. She was telling me of a sermon she had heard in Scotland in her childhood on the text of the morning, "Be sure your sin will find you out." The divisions of the sermon as she remembered it after the long lapse of years were these: In Time, In Conscience, In Eternity. There could be no better arrangement made for a sermon on this text. Let us, therefore, follow those heads and see how sin finds men out—in time, in conscience, in eternity.

———•—•—•———

—Forgiveness of—Goethe brings *Faust* to a conclusion with a beautiful passage in which Margaret, against whom Faust had sinned, meeting him in heaven, asks and receives permission to become the spiritual guide and instructor of Faust in eternal life.

Incline, O maiden
With mercy laden, in light unfad-
ing
Thy gracious countenance upon my
bliss.
My loved, my lover,
His trials over,
In yonder world returns to me in
this!

The spirit choir around him seeing,
New to himself, he scarce divines
His heritage of new-born Being.
Vouchsafe to me that I instruct
him.
Still dazzles him the Day's new
glare.

Then answers the *Mater Gloriosa*:

Rise, thou, to higher spheres! Con-
duct him,
Who feeling thee, shall follow
there.

So great is the power of forgiveness that even past sin can become a minister for Christ. There is an old legend that sometimes when Peter was preaching he would hear the crowing of a cock, and for a moment he would be overcome with embarrassment and confusion. Then he would recover himself and preach with a new and more burning zeal and earnestness and tenderness.

—Influence of—He was a prosperous building contractor whom I had never seen in my church. His sister was a faithful member, and through her he made frequent and generous contributions to the work of the church. This I regarded as a desire to please his sister, rather than any personal interest in the church. When my ministry in that city was coming to a close, I was therefore surprised when this man called to see me and expressed his appreciation of the ministry of the church and the message which had been proclaimed. He said, "I suppose you wondered why I never came to church. It was not because I do not believe in the church or the gospel, for I do. I would like to take an active part in the work of the church as one of its members, but I don't dare to." Then he went on to relate a sad and unfortunate incident in his life. Should he now come forward and make a public profession of his faith and engage in the work of the church, he felt that accusation would be brought against him, and that the unfortunate incident and transgression of the past would be dragged into the light, to his own distress, to the distress of others, and to the injury of the church.

—Loneliness of—In the year 1602 there appeared in Europe at Leyden a pamphlet telling of a Jew who had taunted and struck Jesus as he passed on his way to the cross, shouting at him, "Go quicker!" Jesus paused and answered, "I go. But thou shalt wait till I return."

This story of the eternal, or the wandering Jew, met quick and popular acceptance everywhere, and in scores of works of fiction and poetry, and in paintings, the story has been told of that Jew who struck Jesus and was condemned to wander homeless, a fugitive on the face of the earth, until Christ shall come again.

This legend, which took so powerful a hold upon the thought and fancy of mankind, sets forth the solemn truth of the loneliness of sin. We read that when Cain slew his brother Abel he "went out from the presence of the Lord" (Gen. 4:16). Sin always drives a man out—out from his friends, out from his better self, and out from his God.

One hour before his fatal duel with Alexander Hamilton, Aaron Burr, sitting in his library at Richmond Hill in New York, wrote to his beloved daughter Theodosia, "Some very wise man has said, 'O fools, who think it solitude to be alone.' This is but poetry. Let us therefore drop the subject, lest it lead on to another on which I have imposed silence on myself." Already, even before the fatal shot was fired and the bloody deed was done, he felt the loneliness of his sin. In a few hours he was a fugitive from the sudden and deep abhorrence of his fellow citizens, his political career was over forever, and his great ambitions wrecked. Henceforth, like Cain, he was a fugitive and a vagabond on the face of the earth. For the rest of his life, until he died in poverty and obscurity and utter loneliness in the very city where he had risen to so great renown, Aaron Burr was a man without a country—almost without a friend. It was the bitter truth he uttered, when, informed of the death of his beautiful daughter Theodosia, he said, "I am severed from mankind." There are lonely people in this city tonight, and thousands who carry heavy and difficult burdens of grief, anxiety, pain, and disappointment. But the loneliest soul of all is the man whose transgression has raised up a wall, not of brick or mortar or stone, but nevertheless terribly real and solid, between him and his fellow men. Yes, sin separates us from our friends.

—Of omission—An eminent judge once appeared at the gate of heaven and, having been a fair and honorable judge on earth, expected easy admittance. But to his surprise Peter held him up and be-

gan to question him. He finally said to the judge that he was sorry he could not admit him. "Your record in most respects is admirable," Peter said, "but there is this against you. You pretended you were deaf."

"When?" asked the judge.

"Continually," said Peter, "in court. You told witnesses you could not hear them when you could."

"Is that fatal?" said the judge.

"Yes," said Peter, "it is fatal here. You knew how unhappy they were and you did not help them. That is the charge against you. You pretended to be deaf."

One of the most interesting of books, and, in some respects, one of the greatest, is the *Confessions* of Jean Jacques Rousseau. It is an extraordinary revelation of self. The man we see is just as Rousseau describes himself, sometimes noble and admirable, sometimes low, base, and despicable. Rousseau sums up his own character when he says, "Indolence, negligence, and delay in little duties to be fulfilled have been more prejudicial to me than great vices. My greatest faults have been omissions. I have seldom done what I ought not to have done, and, unfortunately, it has still more rarely happened that I have done what I ought."

—Original—In his "Gold Hair" Robert Browning relates the story of the beautiful maiden so esteemed for purity of heart and heavenly conversation that she was buried inviolate, her wonderful hair coiled about her head in the very space by the altar. Years afterward, when the pavement was being repaired, workers came upon the crumbling coffin, and lo, all about the head lay pieces of gold! She who had been thought so stainless loved gold so eagerly that she took it down to the grave with her, hidden in the tresses of her luxuriant hair. And then Browning concludes:

> The candid incline to surmise of
> late
> That the Christian faith proves
> false, I find.
> . . . .
> I still, to suppose it true, for my
> part,
> See reasons and reasons; this, to
> begin:
> 'T is the faith that launched point-
> blank her dart
> At the head of a lie—taught Orig-
> inal Sin,
> The Corruption of Man's Heart.

Thus we see that the condemnation of the Cross is in keeping with the facts of human nature.

—**In others**—Just as some loathed disease is less tolerable when seen in another than in ourselves, so sin looks worse in my neighbor than it does in me. Men are like Swift's Yahoos who hated one another more than they did any different species of animals; "and the reason usually assigned was the odiousness of their own shapes, which all could see in the rest, but not in themselves." As Jesus put it, "Thou hypocrite, first cast out the beam out of thine own eye; and then shalt thou see clearly to cast out the mote out of thy brother's eye." (Matt. 7:5.)

—**Preaching it**—When Marcus Whitman, the pioneer whose missionary work in Oregon was commemorated by a centennial celebration, preached to the Indians the Cross with its true implications, they would often protest and ask him to give them instead "good talk." "Tell us that we are good men, brave

men." The untutored Indians' resentment of the condemnation of the Cross is common to the human heart, whether he be an Indian in the Oregon forest or a professor in one of our modern universities.

—**Ruin of**—One of the scholarly old commentators made painstaking search through all available records to discover in actual history something comparable to the damage wrought by the army of locusts described in the book of Joel. Finally he came to the conclusion that to find a parallel to what is described there he needed to go no farther afield than his own heart. "Joel's locusts, I see now and am assured," he writes, "are not so far away as Arabia or Palestine. For all Joel's locusts in all their kinds and in all their devastation are in my own heart." Thus the best commentary on the book of Joel is our own heart.

—**Scars of**—One of the most powerful, yet saddest, warnings that I have ever read is the statement of that man who, with his marvelous eloquence, made war on the liquor traffic, John B. Gough: "Saved as I may be, so as by fire, yet the scar of fire is on me. The nails may be drawn, but the marks are there. . . . A man can never recover from the effects of such a seven years' experience, morally or physically. Lessons learned in such a school are not forgotten. Impressions made in such a furnace of sin are permanent. The nature warped in such crooked ways must retain, in some degrees, the shape. Lodgments are made by such horrible contacts and associations that nothing but the mighty Spirit of God can eradicate. Young men, I say to you, looking back at the fire where I lay scorching, at the bed of torture where the iron entered my soul—yes, looking back at the past, standing as I trust I do under the arch of the bow, one base of which rests on the dark days, and the other, I hope, on the sunny slopes of paradise—I say to you in view of the awful evil spreading around you—beware! Tamper not with the accursed thing, and may God forbid that you should ever suffer as I have suffered, or be called to fight such a battle as I have fought for body and for soul."

—Secret—Nathaniel Hawthorne wrote of himself: "A cloudy veil stretches across the abyss of my nature. I have, however, no love of secrecy and darkness; I am glad to think that God sees through my heart, and if any angel has power to penetrate into it, he is welcome to know everything that is there."

That must have been written in one of those serene moments which come upon the soul. Even so, we rather wonder at his confession.

In his powerful tale "The Black Veil" Nathaniel Hawthorne told a sad truth about human nature. The congregation had assembled in the New England church to greet their new minister. What was their amazement when their pastor appeared in the pulpit veiled in black! Some conjectured that his face was marred with disease, the ravages of which he would thus hide from his people; others, that he was bearing the burden of a recent bereavement; and others, that it was a token of penitence for sin.

Thus passed the weeks, the months, and the years of a long pastorate, and never once was the black veil lifted from the countenance of the minister. At length his summons came, and he lay dying on his bed. A neighboring minister, who had come in to pray with him, besought him to lift the veil from his face, that its secret might not go down with him into the grave. At that, the dy-ing man raised himself in bed and said, "Why do you tremble at me alone? Tremble also at each other. Have men avoided me, and women showed no pity, and children screamed and fled only from my black veil? What, but the mystery which it so obscurely typifies, has made this piece of crepe so awful? When the friend shows his inmost heart to his friend, the lover to his best beloved, when man does not vainly shrink from the eye of his Creator, loathsomely treasuring up the secret of his sin, then deem me a monster for the symbol beneath which I have lived and died. I look around me, and lo, on every visage a black veil."

The mystery which the black veil was supposed to typify was the mystery of secret and hidden sin.

In his vision Ezekiel saw the glory of God. He beheld a likeness as of the appearance of fire. Out of this appearance of fire came forth a hand which transported the prophet in the visions of God to Jerusalem, to the doors of the inner gate that looketh toward the north. Near the door of the inner court of the Temple he saw a hole, or opening, in the wall. At the direction of his angelic guide, Ezekiel digged in the wall until the opening was large enough for him to pass through. When he had passed the first wall he came to a second, and by a door in that wall he entered a hidden chamber. In this chamber he saw every form of creeping things and abominable beasts, and all the idols of the house of Israel portrayed, painted or carved, upon the walls of the room. Before these filthy pictures, loathsome objects, the inventions of depraved minds, stood the seventy elders, representatives of the people, mumbling their heathen incantations and waving the censers filled with incense. Then said the angel to the prophet, "Son of man, hast thou seen what the ancients . . . do in the dark, every man in the chambers of his imagery? for they say, The Lord seeth us not; the Lord hath forsaken the earth (Ezek. 8:12).

The vision of Ezekiel was true of the spiritual condition of Israel at the time of the exile. There was a formal adherence to the religion of Jehovah, outward temple and altars, but in their hearts they served other gods. In their secret chambers of idolatry and imagery they bowed down before the grinning images of Baal and Moloch.

* * *

Hawthorne came near to the truth when he said: "In its upper stories are said to be apartments where the inhabitants of earth may hold converse with those of the moon, and beneath our feet are gloomy cells which communicate with the infernal regions, and where monsters and chimeras are kept in confinement and fed with all unwholesomeness." Maeterlinck, too, is talking on the level of our own experience when he asks, "Where is there a soul that is not afraid of another soul?" What would happen, let us say, if our soul were suddenly to take visible shape and were compelled to advance into the midst of her assembled sisters, stripped of all her veils and laden with her most secret thoughts, dragging behind her the most mysterious, inexplicable acts of her life? Of what would she be ashamed? What are the things she fain would hide?

* * *

—Sense of—The sense of sin is keenest in Christianity, for the law of Christ reveals sin in the heart of man. When Amfortas drew near to the Holy Grail his flesh quivered. So the proximity of the believer to Christ gives him a sense of his own need and sin.

—Separation of—In his "Two Rabbis" Whittier tells how

The Rabbi Nathan, twoscore years and ten,
Walked blameless through the evil world, and then
Just as the almond blossomed in his hair,
Met a temptation all too strong to bear,
And miserably sinned. So, adding not
Falsehood to guilt, he left his seat, and taught
No more among the elders, but went out
From the great congregation girt about
With sackcloth, and with ashes on his head.

In his penitential grief Rabbi Nathan thought of his old friend Rabbi Ben Isaac, and resolved to go to Ecbatanna, where Ben Isaac dwelt, and lay his sins before him. One day at sunset, kneeling in a desert tomb, the Rabbi Nathan greeted kindly a kneeling stranger. It turned out to be the Rabbi Ben Isaac; and the two old friends clasped each other in their arms, praising the providence that had made their paths meet. Then, suddenly, Nathan remembered his sin and tore himself from the embrace, telling his friend that he had sinned and was not worthy to touch him.

This is a true picture of how sin separates friend from friend. These two friends, each discovering himself a sinner and asking the other to pray for him, at length found mutual forgiveness, and saw God's pardon in the other's face. Unfortunately, that happy sequel does not often follow, and man is severed from man by his transgression.

* * *

Sin separates man from his friends. It is not meant for man to be alone. But sin drives man out, breaks his contact and union with his fellow man. That is the history of sin in the Bible and in the human race. Cain killed Abel and went out from the presence of the Lord. Jacob deceived Esau and had to flee and go out into a strange land. Gehazi lied to Elisha and went out from his presence a leper white as snow. The prodigal son rebelled against his father and went out into a far country. Peter denied his Lord and went out and wept bitterly. Judas betrayed his Master, and went out and hanged himself. Always out! Sin has never had any other effect in the history of the human heart.

——————

—Sequence of—Balaam thought he could turn back at will, whenever his road got uncomfortable; and when he saw the angel standing with a drawn sword, he cried out, "I will get me back again" (Num. 22:34). But the angel said, "Go with the men!" And further and further he proceeded in his journey of equivocation and deceit and guile, until he lay among the dishonored dead upon the field of battle. Oh, dreadful hour, when having been beguiled by sin, having scorned the pleading of conscience and the warning of God, a man arrives at that place in his evil course where evil has ceased to please him, where clouds of retribution and judgment are gathering over his head, when the angel of remorse and woe stands before him with drawn sword, and he would fain turn and go back, but finds that he cannot, that he dare not, that a stern voice bids him march on the path that he has chosen for himself.

——————

In Victor Hugo's great tale *The Toilers of the Sea,* laid on the Channel Islands, we have that thrilling story of the battle between a man and a devil-fish. Searching in the sea grotto, the man thrust his arm into a crevice to draw out a crab; and at once he felt the arm seized by something living, slimy, adhesive, cold as ice, but solid as steel. It wound in spirals about his arm, and furrowed under the armpit. As he struggled to break its hold, lo, a second, a third, a fourth, a fifth tentacle shot out from the darkness and wound itself in excruciating pain about his chest and waist and limbs.

Evil is armed like that. The cruel tentacle of one transgression is quickly followed by others, if the first is permitted to get a grip upon its victim. Sin is like the octopus; out of its dark center come forth not one cruel, abominable, and adhesive arm but many, which seek to draw man down to destruction and death.

——————

In the days when tyrants did their will one of these despots ordered a man into his presence and asked him what his calling was. When he told him he was a blacksmith, he ordered him to go to his forge and make a chain. The man soon returned with a chain in his hand. "Go and make it longer," was the order of the tyrant. He soon appeared again, this time with a longer chain. "Go and make it still longer," was the order of the despot. This was repeated a number of times; and when finally the perplexed blacksmith appeared with a long chain in his hand, the despot gave the order to wrap the chain about him and cast him into the fire.

So men by repeated indulgence are forging an ever-lengthening chain with which they are to be bound and cast into the furnace of retribution and judgment.

——————

The way to avoid the second edition and the third edition of sin is not to publish a first. How true those words which Stephen Phillips puts into the mouth of the guilty Herod, "The first step lies with us. The rest belongs to fate." It is the first step in iniquity which tears the veil of innocence which the Creator has put about the soul as a safeguard. When that has once been rent, the second and the third attack are far more difficult to resist.

———•◦•———

Tito Melema, George Eliot's creation in her story *Romola,* is one of the best illustrations of how men do evil to avoid something hard and unpleasant. This cultured and naturally good-natured and lovable Greek had no positive purpose or sinister desire to do wrong. Yet he proceeded from one sin and cruelty to another, because always he sought to avoid that which was difficult and unpleasant. Thus he became involved in a net of hypocrisy, treachery, falsehood, disloyalty, and crime. "He had spun a web about himself which he was incapable of breaking. The web had gone on spinning itself in spite of him, like the growth over which he had no control."

———•◦•———

—**And suffering**—Until we realize the seriousness of sin, and that it deserves punishment, we are not prepared to receive the forgiveness of the Cross. In his great story of sin, *The Scarlet Letter,* Hawthorne brings this out in a striking manner. When Hester bent over the dying Puritan minister, who had bade her farewell, she said: "Shall we not meet again? Shall we not spend our immortal life together? Surely, surely, we have ransomed one another with all this woe. Thou lookest far into eternity with those bright dying eyes. Then tell me what thou seest."

"Hush, Hester, hush," said he with tremulous solemnity, "the law we broke, the sin here so awfully revealed, let these alone be in thy thoughts. I fear! I fear! It may be that when we forgot our God, when we violated our reverence each for the other's soul, it was thenceforth vain to hope that we could meet hereafter in an everlasting and pure reunion. God knows; and he is merciful. He hath proved his mercy most of all in my afflictions by giving me this burning torture to bear upon my breast, by sending yonder dark and terrible old man to keep the torture always at red heat, by bringing me hither to die this death of triumphant ignominy before the people. Had either of these agonies been wanting, I had been lost forever. Praise be his name; his will be done. Farewell!"

In that magnificent climax to his great tale Hawthorne showed his wonderful appreciation of the deep things of the human soul. Strong as was the minister's affection for Hester and his desire to be with her in eternity, stronger yet was his sense of his sin and his complete submission to the judgment of God. There are things in human life so deep that nothing can answer them or meet them but the deeps which are in the Cross of Christ.

———•◦•———

—**Universal**—An old Welsh poem tells how the Creator once held a review of the heavenly bodies. One by one sun, moon, stars, and all the host of heaven passed by, and as they passed by, their august Maker greeted them with a smile. But when the earth passed, God blushed!

Yes, it matters not how fair the beginning of life, or how unclouded its early sky, every man comes at length within that shadow which is as eternal as human history, the deep, deep shadow of sin.

———•◦•———

343

—Unpardonable—A man once wrote me: "Once in a rage I said, 'Damn God and all his attributes!' Have I committed the unpardonable sin? Is that the reason why my prayers are not answered?" It was easy to tell him that he had not. Not a few times I have had to deal with those who have had to reproach themselves for some particular transgression. Sometimes it was a word of blasphemy; sometimes an act of unkindness, or a word of unkindness to a loved parent; sometimes an act of unchastity. These cases testify in a sad and impressive way to the fact that the way of the transgressor is hard and that even a forgiven sin leaves its scar. But there are unpardonable sins.

A woman involved in a sad triangle, when apprehended, took an oath to her husband on the Bible that she was innocent. Later this perjury began to haunt her; and, because she had thus lied with her hand on the Word of God, she began to look upon herself as beyond the reach of pardon and condemned to everlasting punishment. Another said to me, when invited to confess Christ as Saviour and unite with the Church, "There are some things for which one can never be forgiven."

These unfortunate cases show a total misapprehension of the forgiving mercy of God in Christ Jesus. If there were any one sin which the death of Christ could not atone for, and which his precious blood could not wash away, then Christ would be a limited Saviour, and his Cross would have limited power. But the promise of God's Word is that the blood of Jesus Christ his Son cleanseth us from *all* sin. There is not a single sin which is inexpiable, or beyond the power of Christ by his death on the cross to forgive.

———

William Cowper, after his unsuccessful attempts at suicide, was seized with religious horror. He began to ask himself whether he had been guilty of the unpardonable sin—and began to feel that he had. Fortunately, contact with evangelical faith brought him out of that abyss, and he received strength to believe: "I saw the sufficiency of the Atonement He had made, and my pardon in His Blood."

John Bunyan in the first days of his Christian life was constantly beset by the devil, who urged him to "sell Christ." One day, after he had answered many times to this temptation, "No, no, not for thousands, thousands, thousands of worlds," wearied with his battle, he exclaimed, "Let Him go if he will!" After that he began to feel he had committed a sin too great for pardon. He compared his sin with that of David and Peter and Judas, and always to his own disadvantage. His sin, he said, was "point-blank against my Saviour, . . . bigger than the sins of a country, of a kingdom, or of the whole world."

———

—Wages of—A pagan artisan once manufactured a goblet in the bottom of which there was fixed the model of a serpent. Coiled for the cruel spring, a pair of burning eyes in its head, its fangs ready to strike, it lay beneath the ruby wine. The cup was of gold, and chastely wrought without. Never did the thirsty man who lifted the cup to quench his thirst and quaff the delicious draught suspect what lay below, till, as he reached the dregs, that dreadful head rose and gleamed with terror and menace before his eyes. It is not when you look on the brimming cup of temptation and sin that you see its power to hurt you. It is when the cup is empty that the serpent of remorse, guilt, despair, and punishment rises with its ghastly menace upon the astounded soul.

* * *

In his interesting reminiscences of his early life former President Calvin Coolidge describes his companions at Amherst College, most of whom, he says, were earnest, thoughtful young men who had come there not for the sake of going to college but for the sake of getting an education. He said there were a few dissipated men, but they had little standing and did not last long in the race of life. "A small number became what we called sports, but they were not looked on with favor, and they have not survived. It seems to be true that unless men live right they die. Things are so ordered in this world that those who violate its laws cannot escape the penalty. Nature is inexorable. If men do not follow the truth, they cannot live."

* * *

The way of the transgressor is hard, and no one has yet discovered a way to make it easy. Even sin forgiven must bear its temporal penalty.

> *Wounds of the soul, though healed,*
>   *will ache,*
> *The reddening scars remain*
> *And make confession;*
> *Lost innocence returns no more;*
> *We are not what we were*
> *Before transgression.*
> — Author unknown

SINS

—**Little**—All of us are likely to have at least some property holdings in Zoar—the "little" mountain, as Lot called it. A man will not steal, but he will overwork his employees. A man will not lie about his neighbor, but he will take up an evil report against the president of the United States and slander his name without the slightest compunction of con-

science. A man will not be guilty of open cruelty to his fellow man, but he will in his own home be unkind and thoughtless. A man will not defile the temple of the Holy Ghost with impurity, but he will let his temper run wild and think nothing of it. A man will not take the name of God in vain, but he will act in a churlish, unchristian manner when he finds his pew filled in church—and his conscience never trouble him. But our distinctions are not God's. In the quaint sentence of Matthew Henry, "There is no sin little, because there is no little God to sin against."

* * *

In the Battle of the North Sea, Admiral Beattie, because of a pierced pipe on the *Lion,* had to transfer his flag to a torpedo boat; and when he came up with the fleet it had withdrawn from the action. So a mighty and costly and precious mechanism of moral influence may be rendered useless by one little act or word.

* * *

—**Of Youth**—In geology there is a term "fossil rain." On the stratum of old red sandstone are to be seen the marks of showers of rain which fell ages ago, and yet so clear and perfect that they show which way the wind was blowing and the slant of the rain when it fell. So in manhood and age the marks of youthful sins are traced upon the tablets of the soul.

SLANDER—*see also* GOSSIP

On the table of the great Augustine there lay a distich to the effect that whoever attacked the character of the absent was to be excluded.

Mark Twain, who was not the most reverent man in the world, used to say that there are a hundred different ways of lying, but that the only kind of lying that is flatly forbidden in the Bible is bearing false witness against our neighbor.

There are three gates through which we ought to require an evil tale to pass before we pass it on. In the first place, Is it true? In the second place, Is it necessary? In the third place, Is it kind? There are few evil reports which can stand the test of those three gates: Is it true? Is it necessary that it be repeated? Is it kind? Christ says that in the day of judgment we shall all give an account of the words that we have spoken. How careful, then, we ought to be, and how we ought to take heed to our ways, that we sin not with our tongue. Who wants to know, in the day of judgment, that instead of helping another he hurt him and wounded him?

In the bitter political campaign of 1884 James G. Blaine was attacked as a corruptionist and Grover Cleveland as an immoral man. In the midst of the campaign the great American preacher Henry Ward Beecher took the stump in behalf of Cleveland. The reason was that, having suffered himself so deeply through slander, Beecher had resolved to defend, if he could, any man who was assailed in like manner. At a great meeting at the Brooklyn Rink on October 22 Beecher said: "When in the gloomy night of my own suffering I sounded every depth of sorrow, I vowed that if God would bring the daystar of hope I would never suffer brother, friend, or neighbor to go unfriended should a like serpent seek to crush him. This oath I will regard now because I know the bitterness of venomous lies. I will stand against infamous lies that seek to sting to death an upright man and magistrate." Thus Beecher found honey for others in the carcass of slander.

—Causes of—Sometimes slander is born of revenge, as when Joseph was slandered in the house of Potiphar. Sometimes it comes out of pride and hate and the innate selfishness of human nature, and sometimes it appears as a dreadful trait of human nature without any reason for a parent save the depravity of human nature.

In an essay on slander in the *Spectator* Addison tells of a fabled creature called the ichneumon, which makes it the business of his life to hunt and break the eggs of the crocodile, of which he is always in search. This instinct is all the more remarkable because the ichneumon never feeds upon the eggs he has broken. So there are those who prey upon the reputation of others, not for the sake of any real or imagined benefit they derive from it, but solely out of the delight of a fallen nature in the laceration of character and the massacre of reputation.

—Of Christians—A great preacher, Bishop Simpson, speaking on the theme of slander, and especially the slander of Christian men, once said, "I would rather play with the forked lightning, or take in my hands living wires with their fiery currents, than speak a reckless word against any servant of Christ, or idly repeat the slanderous darts which thousands of Christians are hurling on others to the hurt of their own souls and bodies." Then he goes on to say that the reason why Christians sometimes are not filled with joy, are not blessed and prosperous in their life, may be that "some dart which you have flung with angry voice, or in an idle hour of thoughtless gossip is pursuing you on its way as it describes a circle which always brings back to the source from which it came every shaft of bitterness and every evil and idle word."

—And half-truth—On a sailing vessel the mate of the ship, yielding to a temptation, became drunk. He had never before been in such a state. The captain entered in the log of the ship the record for the day: "Mate drunk today." When the mate read this entry he implored the captain to take it out of the record, saying that when it was read by the owners of the ship it would cost him his post, and the captain well knew that this was his first offense. But the obdurate captain refused to change the record and said to the mate, "This is the fact, and into the log it goes."

Some days afterward, the mate was keeping the log; and after he had given the latitude and longitude, the run for the day, the wind and the sea, he made this entry: "Captain sober today." The indignant captain protested when he read the record, declaring that it would leave an altogether false impression in the minds of the owners of the vessel, as if it were an unusual thing for him to be sober. But the mate answered as the captain answered him, "This is the fact, and into the log it goes." This is a good example of how, by an accuracy of statement, but by misrepresentation of circumstances, one can injure the character of another.

In the presidential campaign of 1864 opposition newspapers said that when Lincoln went down to visit General McClellan a few days after the Battle of Antietam, when the dead were still unburied, he asked his bodyguard, Colonel Lamon, to sing a comic song, "The Picayune Butler." But General McClellan raised his hand in protest and said, "No, Mr. President, not now. Anything but that here."

Lincoln was greatly pained and distressed at the slander, and took the trouble to write a long account of what actually happened on the visit. This was to go as a letter from Lamon to one who had inquired as to the truth of the slander. Lincoln determined at last, however, to make no reply. But the letter tells what actually took place. On the visit to Antietam, the President, riding in an ambulance with McClellan and other officers—not a day or two after the battle, but two weeks afterward, and where there was not a grave that had not been rained on since it was dug—in one of his melancholy moods asked Lamon to sing a little ballad called "Twenty Years Ago," the singing of which Lamon said had often brought tears to Lincoln's eyes as he listened to it on the circuit in Illinois or at the White House. The song commences

> I've wandered through the village,
>   Tom,
> I've sat beneath the tree.

The ballad then goes on to relate the feelings of a man who returns to his native village after an absence of twenty years and finds everything changed and all his friends gone. This was the song for which Lincoln had asked. But at the conclusion of it, in order to lift him out of his melancholy, Lamon, at his own initiative, did sing the comic, but altogether harmless, song "The Picayune Butler."

These were the facts; yet thousands believed that Abraham Lincoln was the sort of man who would call for a comic and indecent song when driving past the bodies of the men who had fallen in battle for the maintenance of the Union.

—Making amends for—Slander is an injury which it is hard to undo even when one might desire to do so. A peasant had slandered a friend, only to find out later that what he had said was not true.

Troubled in his conscience, he went to a monk to seek advice. The monk said to him, "If you want to make peace with your conscience, you must fill a bag with feathers and go to every dooryard in the village and drop in each of them one feather." The peasant did as he was told and, returning to the monk, announced that he had done penance for his sin. "Not yet!" said the monk sternly. "Take up your bag, go the rounds again, and gather up every feather that you have dropped."

"But," exclaimed the peasant, "the wind has blown them all away by this time!"

"Yes, my son," answered the monk, "and so it is with gossip and slander. Words are easily dropped; but, no matter how hard you try, you never can get them back again."

—**And reason**—Henry M. Stanley's life was saddened but not embittered by the slanders which were heaped upon him. Instead, he was all the more careful to be truthful and just in his dealings with his fellow men. "I do not belong to that large herd of unthinking souls who say, 'Surely, where there is so much smoke there must be a fire.' Whenever, in the press or in society, a charge is leveled at some person, I put on the brake of reason, to prevent being swept along by the general rage for scandal and abuse, and hold myself unconscious of the charge until it is justified by conviction. No man who addresses himself to me is permitted to launch judgment out in that rash newspaper way, without being made to reflect that he knew less about the matter than he assumed he did."

—**The spread of**—It is difficult to overtake a whisper which quickly swells to a loud and raucous shout. Some years ago, when the character of a prominent man was being assailed, a number of men formed what they called the "Trace-It-Down Club." Their search showed that the evil report was pure calumny. In a multitude of cases this is so. Slander has a swift foot and, once started, is almost impossible to overtake.

In her story of Amos Barton in *Scenes from Clerical Life,* when evil surmises were made as to an innocent friendship, George Eliot thus describes the spread and the growth of the slander: "I can only ask my reader, Did you ever upset your ink bottle and watch in helpless agony the rapid spread of Stygian blackness over your fair manuscript or fairer table cover? With a like inky swiftness did gossip now blacken the reputation of Amos Barton, causing the unfriendly to scorn, and even the friendly to stand aloof at a time when difficulties of another kind were fast thickening around him."

The original whisperer and slanderer could make little headway or do little injury were he not able to enlist the assistance and service of many who repeat his whisper. This is possible only because of that sad trait in human nature which delights in hearing evil of others. There are, alas, many who rejoice in iniquity. So the wicked whisper is repeated, sometimes with an injunction that it is to go no farther and sometimes with an expression of mock sorrow or concern. This sorrow and concern are hypocritical, because if there were such genuine sorrow and concern it would prove itself by a refusal to repeat the whisper.

—**Of those in high place**—Daniel rose so high that he attracted to himself the arrows of slander and defamation. This is one of the prices which distinction and ability must ever pay.

He who ascends to mountain-tops,
* shall find*
The loftiest peaks most wrapt in
* clouds and snow;*
He who surpasses or subdues man-
* kind,*
Must look down on the hate of
* those below.*
—BYRON, *Childe Harold's Pilgrimage*

Slander shows its hideous speech, first of all, in the defamation of men in public life. In his life of Julius Caesar, James Froude writes: "The disposition to speak evil of men who have risen a few degrees above their contemporaries is a feature of human nature as common as it is base; and when to envy there is added fear or hatred, malicious anecdotes spring like mushrooms in a forcing pit."

SLAVERY

When the flag was raised over Fort Sumter in the spring of 1865, a distinguished company of men from the North went to Charleston to take part in the ceremonies. Among them was William Lloyd Garrison, editor of the Abolitionist *Liberator*. When they visited St. Philip's churchyard, where John C. Calhoun lies buried, and stood by his grave, the others drew back and waited to see what the great Abolitionist would have to say by the grave of the great defender of slavery. Garrison stood for a moment looking silently down upon the grave. Then he broke the silence with this sentence: "Down into a grave deeper than this has slavery gone; and for it there will be no resurrection."

SLEEPING—*see also* CHRISTIANS (SLEEP-
ING), TEMPTATION AND SLEEP

—**In church**—Just after John Bunyan's Pilgrim had lost his burden at the foot of the cross, a little farther on, at a bot-

tom and very near the cross, he saw three men fast asleep with fetters on their heels. The name of one was Simple, another Sloth, the third Presumption. When he awoke them, "Simple said, I see no danger; Sloth said, Yet a little more sleep; and Presumption said, Every tub must stand up on its own bottom."

SOLITUDE

At the end of a long debate with the Jews the crowd had dispersed, every man to his home, but Jesus had gone to the Mount of Olives, where he spent the night in meditation and in prayer. If even the Son of God required those turnings aside for periods of contemplation and prayer in order that he might fulfill his great mission, how much more do you and I! As De Quincey puts it in *The Confessions of an English Opium Eater,* "No man will ever develop the possibilities that are in him who does not at least checker his soul with solitude."

By all means use sometimes to be
* alone.*
Salute thyself; see what thy soul
* doth wear.*
—GEORGE HERBERT

One of the most impressive things in the eighty-eight years of John Wesley's long life was when he was taken with his last illness. He returned from the house of a friend, where he had preached his last sermon on the text, "Seek ye the Lord while he may be found" (Isa. 55:6). His friends and housekeeper carried him up to his chambers adjoining the City Road Chapel. Realizing that his end was not far off, the aged saint desired all his friends and his servants to leave him for one half hour by himself. Obedient to his desire, they all went out and left him; and there John Wesley met his God alone, reviewed the incidents of his long life, and prepared for death.

SOLOMON

An Italian artist painted a picture of Solomon in the day of resurrection. Solomon is looking doubtfully upon two processions of souls, some on the way to life eternal, some to darkness and condemnation. He is not sure to which group he belongs. Thus the artist has put into painting the doubt in men's minds as to the final state and fate of Solomon, whether they are to number him among the redeemed souls or think of him as finally apostate and rejected of God. Nothing could have been brighter than Solomon's morning; nothing more glorious than his noonday; nothing darker and gloomier than his evening.

The event which made Solomon famous was his judgment between the two mothers. There have been stories similar to it—for example, the story of Ariphanes of Thrace and the three young men who claimed to be sons of the deceased king of the Cimmerians. Ariphanes ordered that each one hurl a javelin at the father's corpse. Two of the young men at once obeyed. The third refused to do so, and him Ariphanes declared to be the true son and the successor to his father.

SORROW—*see also* ADVERSITY, AFFLICTION, DISAPPOINTMENT, SUFFERING, SYMPATHY

In his enthusiastic support of the long wars with France, Edmund Burke seemed never to think of the sorrows those wars brought home to multitudes of hearts. But when his own son was killed in battle it was as if all world politics and personal pursuits had lost their meaning. "The storms," he wrote, "have gone over me, and I lie like one of those old oaks which the late hurricane has scattered about me. I am stripped of all my honors; I am torn up by the roots and lie prostrate on the earth. I am alone. I have none to meet my enemies in the gate. I live in an inverted order. They who ought to have succeeded me have gone before me. They who should have been to me as posterity are in the place of ancestors."

Margaret Ogilvy, by James M. Barrie, is one of the fairest tributes ever paid to a mother. The first chapter in that moving story is entitled "How My Mother Got Her Soft Face." Margaret Ogilvy had the Scottish mother's ambitions for her sons' advancement in the intellectual world. Her oldest boy had gone far away to school. His younger brother remembered him only as a merry-faced lad who ran like a squirrel up a tree and shook the cherries into his lap. When he was thirteen the terrible news came that he was very ill. The whole family trooped down the brae to the wooden station to see the mother off on her journey to get between death and her boy. Just after the train had gone, the father came out of the telegraph office and said huskily, "He's gone!"

"From that day," writes the son, "I knew my mother forever. When she got home the first thing she expressed a wish to see was the christening robe, and she looked long at it and then turned her face to the wall. That is how she got her soft face and her pathetic ways and her large charity, and why other mothers ran to her when they had lost a child. 'Dinna greet, poor Janet,' she would say to them; and they would answer, 'Ah, Margaret, but you're greeting yourself.'"

That is how all mothers get their soft faces, and all men their soft voices and women their soft touch. They have "greeted" themselves.

—————

—Blessing of—Sometimes men wrestle with sorrow as with a dangerous adversary, only to find out in the end that the sorrow through which they have passed was their friend. One of the most notable preachers of the last century relates how he left his home in Liverpool one day to fill an engagement in the city of Glasgow. As he left the house to go to the station, the last sight on which his eye rested was that of his little daughter held up at the window in her grandmother's arms. As the carriage drove off, the child waved her father a fond and laughing farewell. Many a time, he said, during the railroad trip to Glasgow, that vision of his little daughter rose up before his memory and filled his heart with joy. But he was never to see her again. The next morning he was stunned by a telegram which told of her sudden death. At first it seemed to him a blow that staggered his faith and crushed his hopes, and put out the lamp of his joy. But as the years went by and the vision of that child waving him farewell came back to him, it seemed as if God had set her in the window of heaven to beckon him upward to his eternal home. "I would not give that memory," he said, "for all the gold of earth. I would not part with the inspiration which it stirs within me for all the world could bestow."

—————

—Conquered—In 1862 Eleanor Siddal, the wife of Dante Gabriel Rossetti, who immortalized her beauty in his paintings, died from an overdose of laudanum. In the first paroxysm of his sorrow Rossetti resolved to sacrifice to her memory the poems which he had written and which were still in manuscript. These manuscripts were accordingly buried in her coffin. But seven years afterward they were exhumed and the world greeted them with gladness. The enrichment of English literature was a far higher tribute to his wife than the obliteration of the sepulcher.

—————

—Loneliness in—There are sorrows that come to men, and are noted of others, which may evoke sympathy, but which in their fullness are incommunicable. What a perfect picture of humanity in this respect is our Saviour! When entering into his sorest grief and yearning for human sympathy he took with him into the recesses of the garden Peter and James and John, and then withdrew himself from them a stone's cast, and there entered into his agony. Always there is that distance, the stone's cast, between the heart in the bitterness of its grief and the nearest and the dearest friend.

—————

—And preaching—A great preacher, Joseph Parker, used to say that there is one preacher who is always up to date— the preacher who preaches to aching hearts.

—————

—Unrestrained—When his son William died in 1862 Lincoln resumed his duties —but mechanically, and with a heavy heart. Every Thursday, the anniversary of the lad's death, he observed as a day of mourning. One day the rector of Trinity Church, New York, at the solicitation of Lincoln's friends, called on him and told him that the continued indulgence of such feelings, though natural, was sinful, and unworthy of one who believed in the Christian religion, and that he was unfitting himself for his duties as the leader of his people. From that day Lincoln ceased his mourning, at least that outward mourning at stated seasons which interfered with his own happiness and usefulness.

SOUL—*see also* CHANGES IN THE SOUL, ETERNITY, MAN, PROGRESS AND THE SOUL, SALVATION, SELF, WORLD AND THE SOUL

An unbeliever once went to a minister and said to him, "I know that you are a man of common sense and frankness. I have read your sermons and I know that you will give a man a straightforward answer. Do you believe that I have a soul?"

The minister replied, "Yes, I do."

"Well," answered the man, "that is an extraordinary thing for a man of your ability to think. If you go to the museum, you can see exactly what the component parts of man are—so much lime, so much sugar, so much phosphorus, so much carbon, so much starch." He went on to enumerate sixteen ingredients which make up a man. "You can see them all," he said, "in bottles in a museum. Where, then, does the soul come in?"

The minister looked at him and replied, "Excuse me, but I must decline to continue the argument any further."

The man said, "That was just what I expected. When you cannot meet an argument, you throw up the sponge and will have nothing more to do with it."

"But," said the minister, "I am a reasonable man, and as such I must decline to hold any argument with so many quarts of water, so much phosphorus, so much lime, and so much carbon." Thus the minister answered a fool according to his folly.

———•◦•———

In John Masefield's "The Widow in the Bye Street," the mother comes to say farewell to the prodigal son who is to be executed in prison. When they are parting she says to him:

"*God dropped a spark down into
  everyone,
And if we find and fan it to a
  blaze,
It'll spring up and glow, like—like
  the sun,
And light the wandering out of
  stony ways.*"

Yes, down into every heart God has dropped a divine spark, and when we find it and fan it to a blaze, there is the Kingdom of God.

———•◦•———

In one of Maxim Gorky's tales there is a conversation between two boatmen at the oars on the river Volga. Sergie is full of animalism and sensuality and passion; the other, the frail and pallid Mitia, is awake to the beauty and power of the spiritual world. Mitia says to Sergie: "Law is in the soul. Don't do things that are against your soul, and you will do no evil on the earth. The soul is always as clear as dew. Its voice lies deep down within us, and is difficult to hear. But if we listen, we can never be mistaken. God is in the soul."

———•◦•———

There is said to be a tribe of Indians on the Amazon River who at certain seasons of the year squat on the ground and refuse to move, saying that they are waiting for their souls to catch up with their bodies. That is indeed the great need of the world today. It should sit down for a little and let the soul catch up with the body.

———•◦•———

Over the great doorway of the cathedral at Milan are three inscriptions spanning the arches. Upon one arch is carved a wreath of roses, and underneath is the sentence: "All that which pleases is but for a moment." Over the second is carved a cross with the words: "All that which troubles is but for a moment."

But on the great central arch is the legend: "That only is important which is eternal."

The soul, therefore, is the one important thing with which we have to do in life and in eternity.

———•—•—•———

Some years ago in Charleston, South Carolina, I came across the sermon of a seer-minded and prophetic Negro. The burden of the sermon was this: When the man and the woman were driven out of Eden, and lay down under a tree to sleep, while they slept the spirits of the air, the earth, the waters, and the fire, came and stole away man's soul. Then they fell into a dispute as to what they would do with it. As each one claimed it and no one was able to secure it, all agreed that they would hide man's soul.

But where could they hide it so that man could never find it again? The spirit of the earth said, "Hide the soul of man deep within me, so deep down in the earth that he will never find it."

But the spirit of the water said, "No, man will invent some secret and mysterious power by which he can tell what is under the earth, and he will find his soul again. Do not hide the soul of man in the earth, but hide it in me." Thus spoke the spirit of waters. "Hide it ten thousand fathoms down in the deepest and darkest waters of the sea. There man will never find his soul."

But the spirit of the air said, "No, do not hide the soul of man in the sea. Man will invent a ship which will sail under the sea, and he will search for his soul and find it even in the deepest and coldest and darkest waters of the ocean. Do not hide the soul of man in the sea. Hide it in me. Hide it high up in the highest heavens, clear beyond the remotest star; there man will never find his soul."

But the spirit of fire said, "No, do not hide the soul of man in the heavens, do not hide it among the remotest stars, for with his wonderful mind man will invent some way, some ship of the air, by which he will ascend to the highest heavens and there he will search for his soul until he finds it. No, do not hide the soul of man in the heavens, but hide the soul of man in me." Thus said the Spirit of Fire. "In my white and consuming flame man will never find his soul."

So they hid the soul of man in the spirit of fire, within the flame; but lo, when they put the soul of man in the fire, it came out with a new and more wonderful beauty and clearness than ever before.

Perplexed and in despair as to what to do, and where to put man's soul so that he would never find it, the four spirits returned to their master the devil and asked him what they should do. When he heard of what they had planned, Satan laughed and said, "Fools, I will tell you what to do. I will tell you where to hide man's soul so that he will never find it. Hide it in man."

So the four spirits hurried back to where the man and the woman lay sleeping beneath the tree, and there they hid the soul of man.

Alas, what profound truth there is in that! The priceless and deathless soul hidden right here within the breast of man—and some never find it.

———•—•—•———

—Body, and Holy Ghost—At Carlisle, Pennsylvania, was held the funeral of the son of Dr. Mason, the president of Dickinson College. The crowd was obstructing the funeral procession, and the youth's father exclaimed, "Tread lightly, young men, tread lightly. You bear the temple of the Holy Ghost." A revival was occasioned by those words of the father.

—Caring for the—A man in the penitentiary once wrote me a letter containing the following:

"1st. As to whether anything *can* be done for a man like *me*. I have sinned 'against light,' and in the face of scores of opportunities to be straight. 'All hope gone' is the phrase that most accurately sets forth *my* feelings.

"2nd. I *do not* believe that professedly Christian people feel any deep concern for my soul. Many men and women who never go near a church are moved with the ordinary feelings of charity and humanity—even pagans feel that!—but I *do not* believe that anybody has any real 'burden' for my soul. If I did—well, the evidence of *just one* such case would be enough to make me completely change my life at any cost!

"Do you personally know any 'Christian' man or woman who has the real thing? If so, I wish you would have that man or woman write me."

—Cemetery of the—A cemetery where the dead are buried is a dark and cold place—yet not altogether so. The hand of Christian faith swings the lantern of hope in the darkness of the grave, and love whispers of a tomorrow where love shall find its own, when the trumpet shall sound and the sea shall give up its dead and the grave hers; but in the moral cemetery, where men's characters and souls are buried, there is no light and no hope, for there are the graves of dead—and forever dead—hopes, ideals, joys, innocence.

—Of a child—As the drop of dew on the cheek of a flower at sunrise reflects in that little area all the beauty and mystery of the sun and the glory of the universe, so in the soul of a single infant are all those grand possibilities that God had in mind at the creation when he said, "Let us make man in our image" (Gen. 1:26). I hear the voice of God saying that same sentence every time a child is born into the world.

—Communing with the—"Commune with your own heart . . . and be still." (Ps. 4:4.) This communion is necessary if we are to know our souls ourselves. Your soul is the greatest thing under the stars. Augustine truly said that "man wonders o'er the restless earth, the flowing waters, the sight of stars, and forgets that of all wonders, man himself is the most wonderful." But you cannot know the wonders of yourself unless you commune with your own soul.

—And death—On a late summer day in 1658 the Quaker, George Fox, met Oliver Cromwell riding through Hampton Park. "And before I came to him, as he rode at the head of his lifeguards, I saw and felt a waft of death go forth against him." A few days later the great protector lay dying at Whitehall Palace. His interest in the world receded and his soul fell back on itself as it advanced toward the mysteries of eternity. Nothing now to him was the fact that his voice had been the mightiest in Europe, making kings to tremble; nothing now to him was the memory of his protectorate or the glory of his military conquests at Dunbar and Marston Moor. The only thing which engaged his mind was the welfare of his immortal soul. On the second of September he said to his chaplain, "Is it possible to fall from grace?"

"It is not possible," replied the chaplain.

"Then," said Cromwell, "I am safe, for I know that I was once in grace."

The chief interest and anxiety of Cromwell, about to enter the other world, was how he stood with God. Today it is often taken as a sign of weakness or selfishness to show any interest in the salvation of one's soul. But the soul's Creator and Redeemer has declared that that is the chief business and interest of man, and the source and occasion of his highest joy.

—**And eternity**—Upon how many of the things which you follow and pursue is stamped that word "forever"? Yet "forever" is the only word suitable and appropriate for the immortal soul, which is to endure forever and forever. I hear people now and then speak lightly of it, but I confess I never see it and never read it without being, to a degree, silenced and solemnized and filled with awe and reverence—that question which you sometimes see painted on a great rock by the roadside, or upon a barn or some other building: "Where will you spend eternity?" I could never smile or laugh at that question. And with that question I close this sermon, and these meditations upon the Lord's Prayer. "Thine is the kingdom, and the power, and the glory, for ever." (Matt. 6:13.) Will you share in that "forever"? Where will *you* spend eternity?

—**Greatness of the**—You may talk learnedly about germs and protoplasms, you may display in jars on the shelf specimens of embryonic life in beast and in man, you may stand up against the wall of your museums the skeleton of a man and trace what you call the ascent of man, or the descent of man, but still you have given me no explanation of man, of myself, of you, yourself. You have given me no clue to the mystery of a courageous act, of a smile under the rod of pain, of hopes that rise out of disaster, of a John Huss burning at the stake because, as is written on his great monument, "He lived and spoke and fought, and died for truth." You have given me

no explanation of a landscape of Turner, or the sculpture of Michelangelo, or a canvas of Raphael, or an apostrophe of Isaiah, or a psalm of David, or a sonnet of Shakespeare. Call man a reed if you will, but remember, as Pascal said, "He is a reed that thinks." One single soul is more significant than the whole astronomical universe, because if you give one soul time it can overtake in itself all the emotions and experiences of mankind, from the creation of the world down to the present age.

—**Hidden glory of the**—A man out hunting in the Valley of Virginia, following the game into a depression, or cave, in the fields, heard the sound of flowing water. He followed the stream for a little and listened in wonder as the mysterious river ran off into the subterranean darkness. Coming back with a companion and with a torch, he entered the cave again and followed the sound of the water till they came to a vast cavern through which darkly flowed the river. The flame of the uncertain torch revealed splendors and glories which for generations, for aeons of time, had been hidden from the eye and mind of man. Vaulted domes fretted with gold and brown and silver bands; massive pillars where stalactite and stalagmite met in an eternal embrace, constituting a column such as Karnak could not boast; spiral stairways of transparent limestone; thrones, high and lifted up, which looked as if they had been the judgment seat of departed gods; vast chambers, swept and garnished, whose solitude had never before been disturbed by the fall of man's foot or the sound of his voice. How rich is nature, who can afford to hoard and hide away so much beauty and grandeur! Outside, on the surface, an unattractive, rolling, and barren land. But just beneath the surface a majesty and a loveliness which enthrall the eye and mind of man.

So beneath the dull exterior of man's life, never far away, lies this hidden chamber, this buried life of the soul, with all its wonders and glories.

— — —

—**Loneliness of the**—In his biography of Thomas Gray, Edmund Gosse wrote: "Gray never spoke out. He lived even more than most of us in an involuntary solitude, a pathetic type of the isolation of the soul."

Each man's life is a shrine where none but himself may enter. Stop for a moment to recall the multitude of thoughts, impulses, desires, both good and bad, which have flashed through your mind; and you realize how large a territory there is within you that is absolutely unknown and unexplored, save by yourself. We speak of those whose hearts are as one, and yet in another and deeper sense what seems a very close nearness may be an unmeasurable distance.

— — —

—**A lost**—He said it sadly, yet calmly and deliberately. A man of education, refinement, and Christian faith, who came frequently to our services, he had called to tell me of the death of his only brother. For years this brother had been a prodigal. The appeals of his friends, the entreaties of relatives, his failing in business and worldly prospects—all had been of no avail to win him back from a fatal infatuation. Memories, hopes, family—all had been sacrificed to self-indulgence and the delight of illicit relationships. Now the end had come, as it usually comes. He had died in a brothel, forsaken and dishonored. The patient brother did all that a brother could do, yet with the sorrowful realization that that little was nothing at all. No final decencies and no Christian obsequies could lift the dark shadow that had fallen across his brother's life. Trained to believe and receive the gospel, he could entertain no hope for his brother's soul. He would eagerly grasp at any fact or memory or dying expression which would serve as a raft for his hope. But such there was not. Judged by the light of conduct and by the light of revelation, his brother's soul was lost. "I am afraid my brother's soul is lost."

As he uttered those words, I sat in dumb silence; and the room where we were was still, save for the distant rumble of the traffic on the street. Lost! His brother's soul lost! Could it be possible that he could contemplate such an ending? Lost! Forever banished from the presence of God, and from the life of joy and hope! The mind staggered as it tried to contemplate it. Every ordinary thing, every ordinary sight and object in the room, the usual interest of the day, seemed to melt and shrivel away to nothingness before that dread idea—a soul lost! It was one thing to discuss it as a possibility for an unnamed or imaginary soul, to state the scriptural teachings on the subject, to pronounce in the service or in the sacraments words which assumed such a contingency; but now to hear a man actually say that he thought his brother's soul was lost—that seemed too heavy for the mind to bear.

Yet this man was only taking seriously what he had heard me and other ministers say. He had taken seriously what the great sacraments of the Church, Baptism and the Lord's Supper, assume and signify—that is, the way in which a soul is saved, and therefore the possibility of a soul's being lost. Yes, he had taken seriously the words of Jesus—that it was no mere rhetoric—when he said, "What shall it profit a man if he shall gain the whole world, and lose his own soul?" (Mark 8:36).

— — —

In a well-known picture the devil is represented as gambling with a man, and the stake is the man's soul. It is clear that the devil is winning and the man is losing. Several of the faculties of the soul, several of the man's pawns, such as innocence, purity, and faith, have already been taken. Now hope is going, too, and when it goes, the man has lost and the devil has won. But no poet, no painter, no orator, no thinker, will ever be able to tell us, so that we can take it all in, what that means—the loss of a human soul!

In fancy, we might think of a man who has been so foolish or unfortunate as to trade away his soul, now in the realms of the lost, and in the land of the living also, trying to find something which shall get him back his soul. He comes to the keeper and possessor of his soul and offers him his tears: "I have shed the tears of sorrow and regret over the loss of my soul. These tears surely speak its value. Take my tears and give me back my soul." But the grim custodian tells him his tears will not avail. Again he comes with the sighs and groans of remorse and says, "I have suffered and agonized over the loss of my soul, as Judas did over his. These sighs and groans are the symbols of my remorse. Take them and give me back my soul." But the grim custodian tells him his remorse will not suffice. Again he returns to the keeper of his soul, and this time brings with him his prayers: "Since I traded away my soul I have prayed daily for its restoration. These prayers represent what is holy and eternal. Take them and give me back my soul." But still the grim custodian bids him depart. Again he returns, and this time he brings with him his repentance and good works. "Since I lost my soul, I have repented of my folly, and these good works which I

have done are the proof and the fruit of my repentance. Take my repentance and give me back my soul." But all these proposals are in vain. And if the man who made them had ever heard of Christ, perhaps he could recall his words, "What shall a man give in exchange for his soul?" (Matt. 8:37).

One of Hawthorne's most impressive tales is that of the Intelligence Office. Presiding over this lost-and-found office in the midst of a great city sat a grave figure poring over his volume and looking like the spirit of record. One by one the people came in searching for what they had lost—a faded beauty who sought a lost bloom, another who had lost his shadow of his influence for good, another who searched for a vanished reputation.

At length there came a man looking for a precious, priceless jewel, a prince's treasure, which had fallen from his bosom, where he had worn it in his careless wanderings about the city. The man at the desk opened a cabinet in which was a strange collection of lost articles—wedding rings which had been riveted upon the finger with holy vows and all the mystic potency which the most solemn rites could attain, and yet had proved too slippery for the wearers' vigilance; and others the gold of which was worn thin after the attrition of years of wedlock; and others glittering from the jeweler's shop as if they had been lost during the honeymoon. Here were ivory tablets, too, on the leaves of which were written sentiments and truths of the writer's early years, but to which now he was a complete stranger. White roses, too, withered now, but once emblems of a virgin purity, lost and flung away and trampled in the mire of the streets, and locks of hair faded and lost by faithless lovers.

In the corner of the cabinet, after much search, was found a great pearl, looking like the soul of celestial purity congealed and polished. When the man saw it he exclaimed with joy, "There is my jewel! Give it to me this moment or I perish!" But the intelligence officer reminded the former owner that the pearl was held upon a peculiar tenure, and since he had once let it escape from his keeping he had no greater claim upon it than any other person. No entreaties or pleas could soften the heart of the intelligence man, who was devoid of human sympathy, and the man who had lost his jewel went out disconsolate and empty handed.

How true a picture of life! The best and sacred things are lost, and man of himself has no power to get them back. That was what Christ said about the greatest jewel of all, a man's own soul. "What shall a man give in exchange for his soul?" (Mark 8:37.) That is, when he has lost it, how is he going to get it back? The solemn declaration of Christ is that the Son of Man is come to seek and to save that which was lost.

———◦◦◦———

Thomas Moore somewhere has a line about dissolving the pearl of the soul in the wine of desire. It is a powerful and true figure. It would take a long time to dissolve a pearl in any liquid. It takes a long time to dissolve the soul; indeed, utterly to dissolve it and destroy it is impossible. But it is possible to dissolve the element of righteousness and of happiness in it.

———◦◦◦———

—Neglect of the—About one hundred years ago a man in some way fell overboard from his vessel and was swept down Niagara River toward the falls. Just above the falls, on the American side, there juts out of the water a black rock. The man managed to secure a foot-hold on that rock. Soon his terrible plight was observed by people on the shore. Hundreds gathered together, watching in horror the man on the rock and planning to do what they could to deliver him. They did manage to float food down the river to him. But as the hours and the days went by his strength began to ebb; and at length, in sight of the horror-stricken multitude, he was swept over the thunderous cataract to his death in the cruel waters.

A man's body was in danger of being swept over the falls, and thousands were concerned over him and gathered together to do what they could to deliver him. But if it had been announced that at Niagara Falls a man's soul was in peril, very few of that same crowd would have gathered together. And yet the soul is the immortal part of man, and the disaster which befalls man's body is as nothing compared with that which can overtake his soul.

———◦◦◦———

The psalmist said, "No man cared for my soul." (Ps. 142:4.) If a man's body is in imminent danger and peril, there are plenty who will be interested in his welfare. Suppose a man is working on top of one of the great towers of this church. He loses his footing and, falling, manages to get hold of one of those fierce-looking gargoyles which project from the lower part of the tower. There he clings for dear life. People passing up the avenue hear his cries and see the peril he is in. Soon the street is blocked with anxious, horror-stricken people who shout words of encouragement to him. Soon there is the siren of the fire department, and the firemen get out one of their extension ladders and begin to raise it toward the tower. Then the police come and with a long rope in their hands dash into the church and inquire the way up to the tower. A man's body is in dire peril, and everyone who sees it is concerned over it and ready to do what he can to help the man, to save him from death. But the soul, of infinite value, can be in peril and men will not be moved in the least.

— — —

—Prosperity of the—John wished for his friend a prosperity and bodily health in proportion to the prosperity of his soul —"That thou mayest prosper and be in health, even as thy soul prospereth." (III John v. 2.) In the case of Gaius it was a safe wish. I wonder if you and I would dare to have John, or anyone else, make that wish for *us*—a prosperity of the world, and health of the body, on a level with the prosperity of our soul? Strange transformations would be witnessed if such a wish were literally carried out.

Here is a fine and noble mansion. But look! A change is coming over it: the roof is coming down; the walls of stone or brick or marble are turning to shabby boards; the noble entrance has become a narrow door, entered only by stooping; the spacious yard has been contracted to mean dimensions; inside, the bright lights have been extinguished; the costly oriental rugs have turned to wretched rags. What a moment ago was a mansion and a palace is now a hut or a hovel, because the earthly prosperity of the man who dwelt there has been reduced to a level with his prosperity of soul.

But here is another change. Here is a low, humble dwelling where lives a godly soul. Look! The roof is lifted, until it assumes noble and lofty position and proportions; the unpainted timbers are changing into brick or stone or marble; the mean doorway has become a noble archway; the path that served for a yard has expanded into a beautiful lawn or driveway; inside, the once bare floors are covered with rugs, the once bare walls reflect the light of genius; the

flickering lamps have given way to costly candelabra, hung with silver cords, for the temporal prosperity of this man has been brought up to the level of the prosperity of his soul.

"Even as thy soul prospereth!"

— — —

—Reserves of the—It is a familiar and yet always stirring thing to recount how men have overcome great handicaps in the way of bodily affliction. How Milton, although blind, did not bate one jot, but steered right onward. How Paul, with a thorn in his flesh that would have put most men in a home for incurables, crossed and recrossed the seas, scaled the mountains, and traversed the plains in his great campaign as a soldier of the Lord Jesus Christ. How Parkman could read for just five minutes at a time, how Prescott used a writing case for the blind, and how Walter Scott dipped his pen in the ink of disaster and adversity to write some of his great romances.

All that is familiar to us. But what I think is more remarkable is the repeated exhibitions which we have of frail men and women, who, under adversity of one kind or another, have been transformed into heroes and heroines, and who amaze us and thrill us with their power to do and to achieve. Tribulations shocked them into heroism of life. They called upon the soul's reserves and won their battle, and came off conqueror and more than conqueror. They illustrated and proved the saying of the psalmist, "Thou hast enlarged me when I was in distress" (Ps. 4:1).

— — —

Sometimes affliction itself is a great discoverer of strength and power in one's life. When all was fair and every wind was soft, we hardly knew ourselves. It took the eclipse of the sun and the buffeting of the wind and the contrary waves to show us what was in us.

Love has an expanding and exalting power. Elizabeth Barrett, when she first met Robert Browning, was a chronic invalid confined to her room. They had had some correspondence, but had never met. By some subterfuge Browning contrived to gain access and talk with her in her sick chamber. The first time he came she lifted her head from the pillow. The second time she sat up in bed, and the third time she got up and eloped with him.

———

—Salvation of the—An unsaved man who had been neglecting his soul, and sinning against it, went one night to a theater in England to enjoy himself. At the end of the play one of the characters, a British sailor about to mount the gallows to pay the penalty of his crime, lifted a glass and exclaimed, "Here's to the prosperity of the British nation and the salvation of my immortal soul!" When the curtain fell and the crowd in the theater dispersed, that phrase, "my immortal soul," remained with the man to impress him and to trouble him, until he had made his peace with God and found Christ as the Saviour of his soul. Your immortal soul! What about that soul? Is it well with thy soul?

———

In his account of the German patriot and statesman Stein, who was outlawed by Napoleon with the celebrated description "One named Stein," Andrew White tells of the statesman's death. He says there was no mention of the salvation of the soul, for he took it for granted that his soul would be saved if it were worth saving.

That comment is characteristic of the wisdom of the world, which knows more than the Lord Jesus Christ. Every soul, indeed, is worth saving. The blood which stained the cross on Calvary is the eternal sign of the value of a soul. But only Christ is the Saviour of the soul. Every soul is worth saving, but no soul is good enough, or can do enough, to save itself.

———

John Bunyan in his immortal allegory gave us the story of the pilgrim who set out from the City of Destruction for the City of Life. Now men have suddenly discovered that the famous pilgrim was a selfish and unworthy man, because he made the salvation of his own soul his chief end in life and set out all by himself, leaving his own family in the City of Destruction. But John Bunyan is eternally right. A man who has not himself started for the City of Life will never start others in that direction.

———

The only redeemed soul which we know is in heaven is the soul of the penitent thief. We may feel sure that Peter is there, and John, and Paul, and others nearer to us, some of those we have "loved long since and lost awhile"; but the only one we *know* is in heaven is that penitent thief, and for that knowledge we have the authority and word of Jesus himself.

———

In my vision I saw the King seated upon his throne, and on either side of the throne stood the great angels: Uriel, the angel of light; Raphael, the angel of reason; Michael, the angel of the sword; and Gabriel, the angel of holy song. Before the throne stood another angel, the angel of the book, and by his side stood one of the mortals. The King on the throne said to the angel of the book, "Who is this that you have brought, and what are his claims?"

The angel looked in the book and said, "O King, this man was a great inventor who shed light on the pathway of man through the world."

"Then," said the King on his throne, "send him up, and let him stand here by

360

the side of Uriel, the angel of light." So he went up and stood by the side of Uriel.

Then the angel of the book brought another before the throne. The King looked on him and said, "Who is this, and what are his claims?"

The angel looked in the book and said, "This man was a great philosopher, a thinker, who thought thy thoughts after thee."

Whereupon the King said, "Send him up and let him stand here by the side of Raphael, the angel of reason." So he went up and stood by the side of Raphael.

Then the angel brought a third mortal before the throne. Looking upon him the King said, "Who is this and what are his claims?"

The angel looked in the book and said, "This was a great patriot. With his sword he delivered his people out of the hand of the despots and tyrants."

Then the King said, "Send him up and let him stand here by the side of Michael, the angel of the sword." So he went up and stood by the side of Michael.

Then the angel of the book brought before the throne a fourth mortal. The King looked upon him and said, "Who is this, and what are his claims?"

The angel looked in the book and answered, "This man sang holy songs in praise of God, songs which still echo through the Church of the Living God."

The King said, "Send him up, and let him stand and sing here by the side of Gabriel, the angel of holy song." So the man went up and stood and sung by the side of Gabriel, the singer of holy and prophetic song.

Then the angel brought before the throne a fifth mortal, and when I saw him I wondered who he was, and why he had been brought before the throne, for in his person I saw no note of distinction and in his eye no flash of genius.

Yet in his countenance there was a light that distinguished him from all the rest. Looking upon him the King said, "Who is this, and what are his claims?"

Then the angel looked in the book, and lifting his head said to the King on his throne, "This man brought a soul back to God." And this time I never heard what the King on his throne said, for all heaven rang with a great shout—angels, and archangels, cherubim and seraphim, and all the host of the redeemed, rejoicing together over one soul that had been redeemed!

———————

—A saved—An old and beautiful legend relates how after Zacchaeus had been converted and found Christ, his wife used to note that early every morning he arose from the bed at her side and left the house. Curious to know where he went and what he did, she arose one morning and followed him. At the town well he lowered his bucket, filled it with water, and passed out of the gate of the city until he came to a sycamore tree. There, setting down the bucket of water, he began to gather and cast away the stones and branches and rubbish of any kind that lay about the foot of the tree. Having done this, he poured the water upon the roots of the tree and, gently caressing the trunk of the tree with his hand, stood silent, as if in affectionate reminiscence and contemplation. His amazed wife came out from her hiding place and asked him what he was doing. Whereupon Zacchaeus said: "This is the tree where I found Christ!"

In the great day when God "writeth up the people," may he be able to say of not a few who have passed within the walls of this church during the generations that have gone, or who shall enter its gates in the generations that are to come, "That man was born there." Perhaps even at this historic commemoration, it shall please God's Holy Spirit, tonight, to bring into the Kingdom of our Saviour one of those souls for whom Christ died. And if so, then not only we the living, but angels in Heaven, shall rejoice over a sinner that repenteth.

—And self—Robert Louis Stevenson has a powerful tale of a man, Markheim, who murders a curio dealer so that he may rob the safe. As he is engaged in that task he hears a step mounting the stairs and is confronted by a figure who nods to him in friendly recognition. Then ensues a remarkable conversation between this mysterious intruder and Markheim, the murderer. Markheim is astonished and horrified to find that this visitor knows him to the very soul.

Markheim feels impelled to lay open his heart to this strange man; and he tells him how, although he has done great sins and crimes, there was another and a better self that did not consent. In answer to this the visitor rehearses the gradual progress of Markheim in evil, how three years ago he would have blanched at the name of murder, and how five years hence he will detect him in the very act from which he might now recoil. His way lies downward, and only death can avail to stop his progress.

Suddenly their interview is arrested by the ringing of the bell by the returning housemaid. The visitor suggests to Markheim that he admit her, make some plausible explanation as to his presence in the house, and then dispose of her as he had her master. But Markheim refuses the proposal, telling him that even if his love of good is damned, his hatred of evil still persists. With that the features of the visitor undergo a lovely change, brightening and softening with a tender triumph, and "even as they brightened, faded and dislimned." When he has vanished, Markheim opens the door and asks the maid to go for the police, telling her that he has killed her master.

What is the meaning of this strange tale? Who is the mysterious visitor who seems to know Markheim so well and at times resembles him, one moment the personification of evil and the next the spirit of beauty and virtue? Who but the soul of Markheim? In this tale Stevenson makes a man—a man engaged in an evil enterprise—confront his own soul. You and I may not be criminals, yet what could be more dramatic and awesome than to be confronted by our own soul? The great moment in the drama of the tale is when the ghost of the dead and wronged returns to confront the living. But more appalling than that would be the soul's appearing to itself.

—Selling the—Hawthorne tells how the modern pilgrims came to Vanity Fair, where, in contrast with Christian and his companion, they were quite popular. In the fair almost anything could be purchased for a bit of scrip called Conscience. The dreamer thought he saw some foolish bargains: a young man giving his fortune for disease, a pretty girl who bartered a heart as clear as crystal for an utterly worthless jewel. Still, Vanity Fair sees some strange bargains. How many has it seen today? How many more will it see tonight? What are you doing with your soul? In what way are you wronging it, wounding, defiling it—by open and common practice, or by some secret sin known only to yourself and to God?

Standing amid the ruins of Ephesus, where one hears today only the sigh of the wind in the reeds and sees only the calf, the turtle, and the lizard, one thinks of the great business which once was carried on in that famous metropolis. In his description of the fall of Babylon, John described the business of Ephesus, how men sold there gold, silver, precious stones, pearls, fine linen, ivory, brass, iron, marble, wheat, sheep, horses, chariots, slaves, and souls of men! A magnificent and terrible climax—and souls of men! Alas, in every great city the business of selling the souls of men is still going on.

—**And sin**—There is a great passage in *Pilgrim's Progress,* always grand when it is reproduced in human life. In the fierce battle between Christian and Apollyon, Apollyon had Christian down with his sword fallen out of his hand, and was pressing upon him to destroy him. But just as Apollyon was about to strike the last blow, "Christian nimbly reached out his hand for his sword, and caught it, saying, Rejoice not against me, O mine enemy: when I fall, I shall arise, Mic. 7:8; and with that he gave him a deadly thrust, which made him give back, as one that had received his mortal wound. Christian perceiving that, made at him again, saying, Nay, in all these things we are more than conquerors, through Him that loved us. Rom. 8:37. And with that Apollyon spread forth his dragon wings, and sped him away, that Christian saw him no more. James 4:7." That is the greatest moment in human life—when it turns defeat into victory.

—**Unrest of the**—Sometimes the fountain of unrest within the soul shows itself in the future. Tomorrow it will be different with me. A change of time will set me free from the fever and fret. The burden will slip from my shoulders. The light will come back into my eyes, the bouyancy will come back into my step, the rains will cease, the clouds will drift away, and the sun will shine once more. The saying that distance lends enchantment is true of the moral, as well as of the physical, landscape. Sailing eastward on the Atlantic, one sights first of all the southern coast of Ireland. After the weary and monotonous leagues of gray, heaving ocean, it makes the heart beat with joy to see in the distance the faint blur along the horizon which tells where the land lies. After a little the general contour of the coast becomes clear, then the white towers of the lighthouse, the naked rocks, the white fringe of foam where the waves are breaking, the green grass on the hills, the peasants' cottages, the hamlets and towns. It looks like paradise to a man who for a week has seen nothing but heavy countenance of the ocean. But that is because you look at it from a distance. When you land and examine it at close hand you discover that what three miles out at sea looked so fine is just ordinary; there is much that is mean, ugly, depressing.

—**And the world**—In his tale *Mare Nostrum* the Spanish novelist Blasco-Ibáñez makes the action center about an unworthy, immoral woman, whose better nature has been aroused by the affection of her lover. She shows the awakening of that better nature by an endeavor to avoid him and to persuade him to set his affections upon one more worthy of him. So the mistress of this world has, as it were, moments of compunction and conscience when she repels men from her embrace and tells them to set their affections on higher things and to seek the Kingdom of God.

—**Wreck of the**—There is nothing sadder than a wreck. The wreck of a house where the sacraments of birth and marriage and death have been celebrated.

The wreck of a great ship lying on reef or in the sand with the waves breaking over it, the very symbol of frustration. The wreck of a great building, such as an ancient temple where the gods were once worshiped, or a palace where kings and queens ruled and rioted, but now nothing but a heap of rubbish where the lizards dart and the wild beast makes his lair. The wreck of a great city. To those who knew and loved London, nothing could be more distressing than to see great sections of the ancient city and buildings, which seemed to be the incarnation of the long story of English history, now blasted and gutted with fire and reduced to heaps of stones. But saddest of all is the ruin of a human soul. All the ships on the seven seas might be sunk, all the beautiful buildings of the world reduced to rubbish, all the great cities of the world bombed and blasted, but that could not compare with the ruin of a single soul made in the image of God.

One of the saddest, most melancholy sights that I have ever seen was the great ship *Normandie,* queen of the seven seas, lying on her side in the North River, a charred wreck and ruin, man's mightiest marine achievement upon the sea reduced to a prostrate hulk. A wreck is always a sad sight. There the ship lies on the rocks, or half sunken in the sands, masts gone, sails gone, superstructure gone, the gulls flying above it and the waves sounding a mournful refrain as they break over it.

There are wrecks among men as well as among ships. The greatest wreck of all is the wreck of a human soul. A shipwreck is a symbol of broken and wasted powers. It is the perfect parable of what might have been; so also is the wreck of the soul.

"Saul took a sword, and fell upon it."

(II Sam. 31:4.) But that was only the final act in a long, sad process of self-destruction. It was a fitting end for Saul, for only Saul could destroy himself. The only one who can really hurt or destroy you is yourself. "Thou art the man!" (II Sam. 12:7.)

There is nothing more stirring than to see a great airliner in flight through the heavens, its engines roaring and its silver body silhouetted against the blue empyrean. It strikes the observer as a symbol of man's mastery of the forces of nature. Seen thus in its triumphant flight across the continent, the airship looks as if it would never come down. But they do, sometimes, come down; and they fall and crash, like the daystar falling out of the heavens. What a fall it is! What a scene is a wreck! Trees snapped off, fields plowed up, fragments of the fusilage and the cabin, and the great wings, and the wheels and the rudder, and the engine, strewn over an acre of ground.

The fall of the airplane is a symbol of the conquest of man by nature; transferred to the spiritual and moral world, it is a symbol of the wreck and ruin of a soul. There is no fall like that. Remember it was not a house that Christ was talking about, but the soul of a man, when, at the conclusion of the world's greatest sermon, the Sermon on the Mount, he said, "And it fell: and great was the fall of it" (Matt. 7:27).

—Wronging the—Almost a century ago a man, Caspar Hawser, appeared in the streets of Nuremburg, Germany. He was then a man in middle life, but for the first time he had seen the blue sky and the face of man and heard the sound of the human voice. Since earliest childhood he had been shut in the dark dungeon, never permitted to speak with a fellow being or to look into another face or to behold the sun in the heavens. Now in middle life, with a tongue untrained to speak and a mind untrained to think, he was thrust out into a world for whose life and duties he was altogether unfitted. A distinguished lawyer in Germany wrote a history of this tragic case, which he appropriately entitled, "A Crime Against the Life of the Soul," for such, indeed, it was. Yet there is a crime against the soul of which multitudes are guilty in this world. The soul has an eye that would see God; it has an ear which would hear His voice; it has the possibility and power of reverence, faith, and love. Yet multitudes of men shut their souls down in the dungeon of sensuality and sin.

SOUL WINNING

Some time ago I dined in a restaurant looking out on Boston Common. As I was going through the doors I saw a tablet on the wall which said that on that spot Dwight L. Moody was converted to God, and I thought of that day when Edward Kimball walked up and down in front of the shoe store that stood where the restaurant now stands, mustering up his courage to go into the store and speak to a boy who was wrapping up shoes in the back of the store.

There was a boy there, and that boy was none other than Dwight L. Moody. There was a boy there, and Charles H. Spurgeon brought thousands to Christ. There was a boy there, and William Carey carried the gospel to India. There was a boy there, and Dwight L. Moody brought thousands to Christ and set in motion currents which shall influence the world until time shall be no more.

The church of St. Peter's at Rome is for many reasons the world's most notable place of worship. It is notable, first of all, for its site, for it stands on the very place where the Emperor Nero drove his chariot by night through his gardens, illuminated by the blazing, pitch-covered bodies of the Christian martyrs. It is notable for its chief architect and builder, Michelangelo; for the triumphs of sculpture and painting which adorn it; for its gloomy crypt where sleep the long succession of the bishops of Rome, and, according to the ancient tradition, Peter himself. It is notable for the vastness of its area and the years of its construction; for the famous statue of Peter, worn smooth by the kisses of devout pilgrims from every quarter of the globe; for the prayers for grace and forgiveness that are daily offered there by sinners in every language spoken by man since the confusion of tongue at the Tower of Babel. It is notable for its great golden dome, surmounted by the cross, and which seen afar off by the traveler coming from the north or the south, the east or the west, lets him know that he is approaching the Eternal City. Within and around that great dome are the words of Christ to Peter, "Thou art Peter, and upon this rock I will build my church; and the gates of hell shall not prevail against it" (Matt. 16:18). Standing under that great dome, and reading those words from Matthew's Gospel, one feels that another inscription should be added—this sentence from John's Gospel (1:41-42): "He first findeth his own brother Simon. . . . And he brought him to Jesus." Without Andrew there would have been no Peter.

"No trouble is too great to take for a human soul." So said to me a man whom I had commended for the interest he was taking in the salvation of a brother for whom Christ died. No, no trouble is too great to take for a human soul. I remember what a former distinguished president of one of our American universities once said about the preacher through whom he had come to believe in Christ as his Saviour. He expressed his everlasting gratitude that that humble preacher on this dark winter night had thought it worth his while to travel a long distance through the mud and the rain to preach the gospel of salvation to a few people gathered together in the country church.

The greatest opportunity that comes to us in life is to do something good for an immortal soul. He that winneth souls is wise. He that winneth fame, the honors of this world, gathers that which at length will fade into nothingness. He that winneth wealth heaps up riches and knoweth not who shall gather them. But he that winneth souls, that man is wise.

––––– • • • –––––

Samuel Rutherford's first church was at Anwoth on the Solway. There he wrestled, like Jacob with the angel, with God for his few sheep in the wilderness. His letters express his yearnings for the souls that he ministered to there and his love for that first church. These are not his own words, but they are built about words that he frequently employed; and they express the joy of the true minister of Christ and the privilege of every disciple of Jesus, yes, the high duty of every follower of his:

> O Anwoth by the Solway,
> To me thou still art dear,
> E'en from the gate of Heaven
> I'll drop for thee a tear.
> Oh, if one soul from Anwoth
> Meet me at God's right hand,
> My heaven will be two heavens
> In Immanuel's Land.
> —ANNE R. COUSIN

SOVEREIGNTY—*see* AUTHORITY

SOWING

—In the morning—"In the morning sow thy seed." (Eccles. 11:6.) Sow it in the morning hours of life. Youth is a time not only for preparation for the work of life but also a time to sow. Do not count on high noon, or afternoon, or evening; but now, in the morning, sow thy seed.

Near the gate of the old cemetery at Princeton I used frequently to pause and read the name and date upon a small stone. It was that of a student in the theological seminary who had taken sick and died in his senior year. He was looking forward to ten, twenty, perhaps fifty years, in the ministry of Christ, an under sower for the Great Sower himself. But how brief was his day. Therefore, to everyone in the morning of life I say, "In the morning sow thy seed."

––––– • • • –––––

—And reaping—When it comes to sowing and reaping, we never reap anything different from that which we have sown. "Whatsoever a man soweth, that shall he also reap" (Gal. 6:7), one of the most familiar sayings of the Bible, is yet forever impressive and timely. Many a man has wished, when the time for the harvest came round, that he could alter in some way the law of the sowing and reaping, that now he could reap something different from that which he has sown. But that is always impossible.

Here is a farmer who makes up his mind to sow oats. He plows his field, harrows it, sows it, cultivates it. In due season appears, first the blade, then the ear, then the full corn in the ear. But now the farmer has changed his mind. It is not oats that I want, but rye, or wheat, or timothy, he says; and he reproaches the earth for what it has brought forth. But the patient earth answers him and says, I show no favors.

I deal in complete impartiality with those who sow. What they sow I gladly and generously and faithfully give back to them; but I can never give back to them anything different from what they have sown. This is the grain that you sowed during the springtime. Now this is the harvest that I bring you. "Whatsoever a man soweth, that shall he also reap."

> *The tissue of the life to be,*
> *We weave with colors all our*
> *own;*
> *And on the fields of destiny*
> *We reap as we have sown.*

SPIRITS, EVIL — *see* DEMONS

SPIRITUALISM

One of the books that came out of the revival of spiritualism in the last war was Sir Oliver Lodge's *Raymond,* named after his promising son who was killed in battle. But what was the nature of the information that Sir Oliver Lodge got through the medium concerning his son? It amounted to this: that he lived in a house that seemed to be brick but was not; that he saw the sun but did not feel it; and that in the world where he found himself there were cats, dogs, horses, birds, but no lions, tigers, or children; that some traveled in Fords and some in airplanes. What possible comfort could one derive from such communications as that? Moreover, even if they did seem to be of a more satisfying nature, there is always the haunting question of delusion and illusion—as in the case of the distracted mother quoted by Sir Oliver Lodge, whose difficulty neither he nor anyone else could solve, who thought she had a communication from her son: "I say from him; but the whole torturing question is, Is it from him, or am I self-deceived?"

SPRINGTIME

I drove recently into the country. Around the farmers' houses the forsythia had donned its yellow robe and in the orchards there was just the faintest intimation of the pink blossoms of the peach trees and the white blossoms of the apple trees. In the woods the anemone and hepatica were pushing up their graceful faces about the dead leaves of winter. The sugar maples were flushing with the delicate red that was a forerunner of the new leaf. Far up on the shoulders of the mountains the service trees and the dogwood trees were waving their white banners. Under the blue canopy of heaven floated soft, fleecy clouds. On the hillsides you could see the silver flash of the plowshare as it pierced the breast of yearning mother earth. The plowed fields lay like brown strips of carpet next to the strips of green velvet where the winter wheat had come up. In the meadows the cattle were grazing and the lambs were skipping. The brooks and streams were flowing through the meadows with full-throated music, bound for the Ohio, the Mississippi, the Gulf of Mexico, and "thence to the wide ocean they." Sweetest of all was the music of the song sparrow, the sweetest voice in all the feathered choir.

It was the sublime, the beautiful, the tender, the hope-inspiring, the perennial, miracle of spring. To blind eyes of nature, to blackened and bent and corrupt branches, to barren and stripped limbs, the voice of the Creator was speaking once again, commanding the blind to see, the deaf to hear, the lame to walk, the lepers to be cleansed, and the dead to rise out of their tomb.

Everyone has his recollections associated with the coming of spring. I think of springtime at Beaver Falls. I remember the river. All winter it was covered with ice. Then rains began to lift the ice, and water could be seen between the banks and the ice cakes as the river rose. Soft south winds and warmer suns began to melt the ice. At night—most of the marvels of nature take place at night —the ice would go out, and when we woke in the morning there was the river filled with the swirling, rushing cakes of ice. Higher and higher rose the water, until it overflowed all its banks. Then came a procession of boats that had broken loose, planks, boards, dislodged trees. At last the free river, released from its captivity of the winter, sang its way to the Ohio. After that the wild ducks on the river, then the swallow in the barn, the robins in the orchard, the catbird in the bushes, the orioles in the oak tree, and the wild dove down in the old beech tree—all the old friends back at the old places. Then the anemone and the bloodroot and the trailing arbutus on the hillsides under the leaves; the garter snake in the weeds; out of the soil the moist, pungent odor; the dogwood; the white blossoms; and on the lawn the grass, the forgiveness of heaven. Spring had come!

Whenever the ice went out of the river we knew that spring could not be far off.

All this comes back to me when I read the verse about Israel's captivity being turned "as the streams in the south" (Ps. 126:4).

STAR OF THE MORNING—*see also* HOPE

At the end of John's letter to the church of Ephesus, with its terrific pronouncements of judgment and punishment, comes this beautiful promise, "I will give him the morning star" (Rev. 2:28). One thinks much of the stars in the Bible lands. They seem less astronomical and more companionable than in other climes. Oft have I watched the evening star as our ship sailed past the Aegean Isles, and ere the day dawned I have marveled at the beauty of the morning star. If ever—on a ship tossed with the waves of the sea, or on the mountain, or on the plains, or by the side of the sick bed—you have waited for the coming of the morning, you know what the morning star means. When the morning star appeared on the horizon, you knew that the night was almost over, that the day and the dawn were at hand. How beautiful, then, is this promise which Christ gives to his faithful Church. He himself is the Morning Star. He gives himself to us even now in his Holy Spirit, in the record of his life and death; and one day he will give himself to us in a new and glorious appearance. The Dayspring from on high will visit us; the day will dawn and the Daystar will arise in our hearts.

STARS

—And God—In 1798 Napoleon set out on his expedition to Egypt. Much to the disgust of his soldiers and officers, he took with him a considerable company of scientists and philosophers. On a warm summer night these men were gathered together on the deck of the flagship. The heavens were brilliant, and these scientists were discussing whether or not the planets were inhabited. Some thought they were, and others that they were not. Then they began to discuss the origin of the universe, most of them taking the position that natural law and phenomena were sufficient to account for the origin of the world without a divine Creator. Then Napoleon, who had been standing near them and silently listening to their conversation, introduced himself into the debate and, pointing with his hand to the brilliant host of the stars in the heavens, said, "Gentlemen, who made these?" A simple question, and one which went to the very heart of the matter. Who made the world? The world is a great effect, and common sense tells us it must have a sufficiently great cause. The world is not only a great effect but it is also an intelligent effect, and it must have had a sufficiently intelligent cause. Back of all nebular hypotheses, primordial germs, and stardust, there lies some great secret; and the only key to it is the opening word of the Bible, "In the beginning God."

———— • • • ————

—And the universe—While we have spent this brief period in the house of God the earth which is our home has been plunging forward on its 580,-000-mile journey around the sun at the rate of 1,000 miles a minute, and yet held true to its orbit by the gravitational pull of the sun. Of the eight planets, the earth, which is the third nearest to the sun, and therefore a near neighbor compared with Neptune, is nevertheless 96,-000,000 miles from the sun. The greatest solar distance is from one side of Neptune's orbit to another, and it would take a shell fired out of the heaviest cannon 500 years to traverse that space.

When we go outside our own solar system, then the distance is infinitely increased. The nearest star, Alpha Centauri, is 25,000,000 million miles distant from the earth. It is estimated now that there are between two and three thousand millions of stars. To us, as we look at them on a winter night, they seem close together; but in reality they are so far apart that human arithmetic can hardly count the distance. The most distant stars of the Milky Way are calculated to be one hundred thousand trillions of miles distant from the earth. The successful measurement of the great star, Betelgeuse, makes our vast sun look like a mere dot. Our sun is 860,400 miles in diameter; but it would take 27,000,000

of our suns to make one star like Betelgeuse, whose diameter is 350,000,000 miles.

We boast of our airplanes, although almost every day we read of one crashing, with the immediate annihilation of all who sailed in it; but what shall we say of these great engines of the Creator? An airplane traveling at the rate of 100 miles per hour would require 1,000 years to circumnavigate a star like Betelgeuse, and that without stopping a second for the birth and death of successive generations of pilots.

When we have facts and figures like these pronounced to us, and then remember that we are dealing only with that universe which is visible to man's eye, or within the range of man's vision augmented by the most powerful lens, our mind begins to reel, and we request the astronomer to roll up his chart and put a cap over his telescope and let our amazed and staggering intellects rest.

STEPMOTHER—*see under* MOTHER

STORM, STILLING THE—*see* DEMONS AND CHRIST

SUFFERING—*see also* ADVERSITY, AFFLICTION, PROVIDENCE, SORROW, SYMPATHY, TRIBULATION

—Blessing of—What was the darkest hour that ever struck for this sinful earth? When was it that God seemed most to be absent, and the powers of darkness to have their way and their will? It was when the Son of God hung on the cross, and when even from his lips there broke the mysterious cry, Lord, if thou hadst been here—"My God, my God, why hast thou forsaken me?" (Matt. 27:46.) Yet out of that darkest hour comes the world's brightest light and the soul's fondest hope. Now we know that God was not absent, but present, when Christ died on the cross, for God was in Christ, reconciling the world unto himself.

———•◦•———

A minister and a chorus girl are far apart, and represent different worlds. But from these extremes of life's callings I take this sermon from life.

We commence with the minister. "Let him that thinketh he standeth take heed lest he fall" (I Cor. 10:12), especially those who stand in holy offices, for Satan desires to see them, above all others, step aside from the path of rectitude. This man, either by slow decline and descent or by a sudden fall, had gone far from God. When he gave up his holy calling, he engaged in a business venture, his heart still hardened and his conscience unaroused. In this enterprise he failed. The failure brought in its train humiliation, poverty, absolute want. Then he awoke to his spiritual condition and to a sense of his sin. He was glad that he had not succeeded in his business venture; and though he had suffered much, he counted what he had gained—his spiritual awakening and his return to God—worth the price he had paid in outward struggle and internal distress.

That's what he meant as he sat one day in my study and said to me, "If I had, I would not be here." He meant that had he been successful he might have felt that he could get along without God, and that his material prosperity might have blinded him to his moral nakedness and his spiritual poverty.

The vaudeville dancer, in some ways more sinned against than sinning, had suffered greatly. She had given all that a woman has to give, only to be betrayed and abandoned. Her one compensation, if such it could be called, or rather consolation, was the child. But, as in the case of David, the Lord smote the child,

and it died, leaving the mother dazed, amazed, full of revolt against life, and burning with fierce hatred of the one with whom she had sinned. Yet it was this crushing sorrow, which at first had seemed to put out all the light and hope of her life, that in reality opened for her the door to a new life and kindled the light of hope. It was the beginning of the process of divine visitation and discipline whereby she was brought to the place of confession, of penitence, and faith. Her heart now softened, all hatred and bitterness washed from it by the tears of penitence, she said, "At first I felt it was God's punishment of me; now I think it was his way to win me."

Although in a different language, both the minister and the chorus girl were saying what the psalmist said so many ages ago, "It is good for me that I have been afflicted" (Ps. 119:71).

———•◦•———

She had been taken from one hospital to another, and back to her home, and then from the home back to the hospital. This time she was in her own home, with the foot of the bed lifted higher than the head. On her face were plainly traced the lines of suffering and emaciation. After a visit and a prayer, she took my hand as I rose to go and said, "My sufferings have brought me closer to God." The words were spoken slowly, deliberately, with an air of finality. It was the sure verdict of her heart and mind. Hard and weary as had been the days through which she had passed, they had brought her nearer God.

———•◦•———

—And God—No doubt a part of our probation in this life is the limitation of our knowledge of the ways of God. How different it would be if we could see things as God sees them, could understand the divinity that is shaping our end! In the *Gesta Romanorum,* that fourteenth-century collection of legends and miracles and fables, there is the story "The Hermit and the Angel."

A hermit and an angel once set out on a journey together. The angel was in human form and garb, but he had told the hermit about his exalted rank. The first night they stopped at a humble home by the wayside, where, for the love of God, they were granted food and shelter. In the middle of the night the angel arose and strangled the infant child of their host as he was sleeping in his cradle. The hermit was amazed and horrified at this deed of his companion, but since he knew he was an angel he kept silent. At the end of the next day's journey they were entertained at a mansion in a city, and when they departed the angel stole the beautiful golden cup out of which his host had drunk the wine at dinner.

On the next day's journey they were crossing a bridge over a deep and dangerous stream when they met a pilgrim. The angel said to the pilgrim, "Canst thou show us, good father, the way to the next town?" When the pilgrim turned to point out the road, the angel picked him up and flung him over the parapet of the bridge into the river. Seeing that, the hermit said to himself, "Surely this is a devil with whom I travel, for all his works are evil!" But he said nothing to the angel.

That night, as darkness came on, snow was falling; and they heard the howling of the wolves in the forest. In the distance they saw a light in the window of a cottage, and making their way thither, they asked for refuge. The surly master of the house with oaths and curses turned them away from his door. "Yonder," he said, "is the pig sty. That is the place for dirty beggars like you!" So they passed the night in the pig sty among the swine. In the morning the angel went to the man's house and thanked him for his hospitality, and for a keepsake gave him the stolen goblet.

At this the hermit's anger and horror would no longer be contained. "Get thee gone, wretched spirit!" he cried. "Thou pretendest to be a messenger from heaven; yet thou requitest good with evil and evil with good." Then looking upon him with compassion in his eyes, the angel said: "Listen, short-sighted mortal. For love of that infant son the father had been made covetous, breaking God's commandments to heap up wealth for his boy, which the boy, if he had lived, would have wasted in riotous living and debauchery. My act which seemed to you so cruel saved both parent and child. The owner of the golden goblet which I took had once been abstemious, but he was becoming a drunken sot. The loss of his cup has set him to thinking, and he will mend his ways. The poor pilgrim whom I threw into the river was about to commit a mortal sin, when I interfered and sent his soul unsullied into heaven. As for this wretch who drove God's children from his door, he is, indeed, pleased for the moment with the bauble I have given him; but hereafter he will burn in hell." When the hermit heard these words, he bowed his head and murmured, "Forgive me, Lord, that in my ignorance I misjudged thee."

Although the ways of providence to us are ofttimes inscrutable, one day we shall be able to see, what we can now behold by faith, that

> *There's a wideness in God's mercy,*
> *Like the wideness of the sea;*

and the heart of the Eternal is most wonderfully kind.

When Robert Louis Stevenson first saw the terrible devastations of leprosy he was almost turned into an infidel. But when he saw the miracles of Christian pity and compassion in the leper hospital at Malokai, his faith emerged triumphant, and he wrote in the guest book there:

> To see the infinite pity of this place,
> The mangled limb, the devastated face,
> The innocent sufferer smiling at the rod—
> A fool were tempted to deny his God.
> He sees, he shrinks. But if he gaze again,
> Lo, beauty springing from the breast of pain!
> He marks the sisters on the mournful shores;
> And even a fool is silent and adores.

—And life—One of the famous bells of China is the bell in the Great Tower. Five hundred years ago the ruler of China, the Son of Heaven, commanded the official of this province that he should have a bell made of such size that the sound of it could be heard for a hundred li. The mandarin assembled artisans and bellsmiths from all parts of the empire. But when the metal had been cast it was found that the result was void. The brass, which had been used to strengthen the voice of the bell, and the gold, to deepen it, and the silver, to sweeten it, had rebelled one against the other. A second time the bell was cast, and again the same result. This time the emperor, the Son of Heaven, sent a grim message to the mandarin, saying, "Twice thou hast betrayed thy trust; if thou fail a third time, thy head shall be severed from thy neck. Tremble and obey."

The mandarin's lovely daughter, who had refused a hundred suitors rather than leave her father's home desolate, learned the contents of the message from the emperor, and was in deadly fear for her father. When she consulted an astrologer he said, "Gold and brass will never meet in wedlock. Silver and iron shall never embrace until the flesh of a maiden be melted in the crucible, until the blood of a virgin be mixed with the metals in their fusion."

The day for the third trial of the bell came. The mandarin and his daughter and her servants stood on a platform overlooking the great caldron of liquefied metal. The mandarin was about to give the signal to cast. Then he heard a cry, "For thy sake, O my father!" and, turning his head, he saw his daughter leap into the roaring furnace.

That is the reason, the people say today, that the sound of this bell in the Great Tower is deeper and mellower and mightier than the tones of any other bell, sometimes pealing like the roll of thunder and sometimes as soft as a woman's voice.

This ancient Chinese legend embodies the truth that sacrifice and suffering make their contribution to the strength and richness and beauty of life.

A number of years ago a friend brought me from Austria a beautiful carving of the Lord's Supper, cut out of mother-of-pearl. When I took it to a jeweler to have it mounted, I told him that I thought it would appear to best advantage suspended against a light, so all its colors and beautiful figures would be revealed. But his practiced eye looked at it, and he said, "No, this must be mounted against something dark." So the sorrow and grief and pain in the world are ofttimes a foil against which shine out the virtues of life and the graces of the spirit.

SUICIDE

It is a great tribute to the power of true religion that in the whole history of the Bible, which covers countless centuries and includes all kinds of people in all kinds of circumstances, we have the record of just five suicides: Ahithophel, Absalom's counselor, who, when that rebel put aside his wise counsel and accepted instead the foolish counsel of Hushai, who was really the counselor of David, went to his house and hanged himself; Saul, who, sorely wounded in the battle on Gilboa, took a sword and fell on it—a half-suicide, you might call him; Saul's armor-bearer, who fell likewise upon his sword and died with him; Zimri, the assassin king, who, when retribution was gathering about him, burned his own house over his head; and wretched Judas, who went out and hanged himself. Faith in God is the great anchor. It holds us fast to life. David Hume, the Scottish agnostic, defending suicide, once said, "If we do not hesitate to divert the waters of a great river like the Nile from its course, why should we hesitate to divert from the body of few streams of blood?" But men are held to life not by argument but by conscience and by faith. There is, on the one side, that mysterious, although undefinable, sense of the sacredness of life, and on the other hand, the reasonable and ineradicable dread of fleeing from the ills of this life "to others we know not of."

SUNDAY SCHOOL

One day in the city of Gloucester in England an aged man, his white hair falling over his shoulders, paused on one of the streets of the city and said to the man upon whose arm he was leaning: "This is the place where I first saw and felt the destitution of the children of the city. I said to myself, Can anything be done? A voice seemed to answer me, 'Try it and see.' I tried it, and behold what God hath wrought." It was Robert Raikes, the founder of the Sabbath schools.

SWEARING—*see* PROFANITY

SWORD OF DAVID

Once on a windy November day I climbed the Abbey Craig, near the city of Stirling in Scotland. It was from that eminence that William Wallace, the Scottish patriot, watched the English army on the eleventh of September, 1207, when it attempted to follow Wallace across the Firth of Forth and was cut to pieces by the Scottish army. In the memorial tower which now marks the scene of the battle there is preserved the sword of Wallace. As I looked upon the huge two-edged weapon and wondered at the strength of the arm that could wield it, I felt that I had come closer to William Wallace than *The Scottish Chieftains,* or any legend, or any painting had ever brought me. All his proud defiance of King Edward, his victories, his defeats, his wanderings, his escapes, his wild adventures, and his final death on the scaffold came back to me as I gazed upon that sword. There was his own sword! It had been wet with the blood of his foes. His followers and his enemies had seen it flashing in the sunlight, as with his tremendous strength he brought it down upon the heads of the English soldiers. That sword is a symbol of all the struggles and all the heroism of the Scottish people.

The habit of preserving weapons of famous warriors is a very ancient one. It goes clear back to the days of David and King Saul. The Tabernacle was at the town of Nob, and where the Tabernacle was, there was the nation's shrine. The sword of Goliath, with which David had cut off the Philistine giant's head after he had felled him with the stone out of his sling, was deposited at the Tabernacle. Behind the ephod, the sacred breastplate with its mystic gleaming stones, and the Urim and the Thummin, carefully wrapped in a cloth, rested this historic sword.

SYMPATHY

It is always a good thing to think of the sorrow of others. In Longfellow's famous poem "The Bridge," a man whose heart was hot and restless and who thought to end his life, went out on the parapet of the bridge to do so. Hearing the clock in the steeple strike the hour, he began to think of the great number of burdened and sorrowing souls who had passed over that bridge before him, and as he thought of the sorrows of others the burden of his own sorrow fell from him.

But now it has fallen from me,
It is buried in the sea;
And only the sorrow of others
Throws its shadow over me.

Ian Maclaren (Dr. John Watson) author of *Beside the Bonnie Brier Bush,* in his first church in the Highlands, attempting to preach without notes, would sometimes have to stop in the midst of his sermon and say to the congregation, "Friends, that is not very clear. It was clear in my study on Saturday, but now I will begin again."

After a service when his memory had failed him a gaunt old elder came forward and, taking him by the hand, said: "When you are not remembering your sermon, just give out a psalm, and we will be singing that while you are taking a rest; for we all are loving you and praying for you."

With such elders and such parishion-ers, who would not have become a great preacher and a great master of the deep things of the heart? That first Highland church made Ian Maclaren. Years afterward he said: "I am in the ministry today because of the tenderness and charity of those country folk, those perfect gentlemen and Christians."

Once on a midnight visit to a police station in Edinburgh a young Scottish preacher, afterward famous, Thomas Guthrie, saw the homeless waifs who had come there to seek shelter. On an open space before the stove, where the light shone full on his face, lay a little lad who attracted his special attention. The boy was about eight years old, with a sweet and innocent face: "his pillow a brick, and as he lay calm in sleep, forgetful of his sorrows, he might have served for a picture of injured innocence. He knew neither father nor mother, brothers nor friend. In the wide world his only friends were the police. How he lived they did not know. But there he was at night."

Guthrie said that for days and nights he could not get that boy out of his mind or heart. It was scenes like this which moved him to inaugurate his great work for the guarding and reformation of the outcast children of Edinburgh. Today on beautiful Princes Street you can see the monument of the great preacher, with the "street Arabs" taking refuge under his arm. "I have the satisfaction," said Guthrie, "when I lay my head upon my pillow of always finding one part of it soft, and that is that God has made me an instrument in his hands by saving many a poor creature from a life of misery and crime."

There is an old tradition that once when Moses, keeping the flocks of Jethro in the wilderness, saw a lamb caught in the thicket he left his path and at great peril to himself extricated the lamb and bore it to a place of safety. Then God said, "Moses, thou hast sympathy; I will make thee the minister of my people."

———

—Of Christ—Recently I received a letter from a woman who had suffered greatly through the death of a much-beloved father. With his dying breath he had enjoined her to be sure to care for her sister, a helpless blind girl. This she had done with great fidelity. Yet she was conscious of a great loneliness. What she asked was, "Does God really care? Can we count upon the sympathy of Christ?"

It just happened that I had been reading from Mark's Gospel the story of the storm on the Sea of Galilee. So my answer was right at hand. She wanted to know if she could count on the sympathy of God. I told her to read the story of this miracle, and especially this verse: "The ship was in the midst of the sea, and he alone on the land. And he saw them toiling in rowing; for the wind was contrary unto them" (Mark 6: 47-48). Yes, we can always count on the knowledge and sympathy of Christ. "There is no place where earth's sorrows are more felt than up in heaven."

T

TALENT

I enroll myself as a student in the Academy of Fine Arts. I listen to the instruction of skilled teachers, and I view the works of accomplished artists. After much toil and thought I may be able to draw what will be at least a fair likeness of this church beneath whose roof we now sit. If I happen to have unusual talent, I may in time produce something that will be worthy of your attention, perhaps of your admiration.

You will say that my teachers taught me. Yes, but the talent has to be there before they can draw it out. And if they do teach me, who taught them? It makes no difference whether you stand in rapt wonder before a master-piece of Turner or Reynolds or Watts, or look at the daubing of the latest apprentice, you are confronted by that mystery of a gift that is in man, which man himself can stir

up, can develop, can hand down from generation to generation, but never can originate.

———

Shortly before Theodore Parker's death in 1860, at Florence, where his ashes now repose, an old friend said to Parker, "You have done much, you have given your life to God, to his truth, and to his work, as truly as any old martyr of them all."

"I don't know," was the reply, "I had great powers committed to me; I have but half used them."

No one who reads the sermons of Theodore Parker, no matter how he may disagree with the sentiments expressed therein, can question the fact that great powers had been committed to him.

———

—Undeveloped—To our view, accidents seem to bring great men to the front.

But when you read how a feud in the Republican Party in Pennsylvania and a dispute between Greeley and Seward and Weed in New York resulted in the nomination of Lincoln at Chicago; or how a great man of letters has been introduced to the world through someone's happening to unroll his manuscript, as Johnson did with Goldsmith's *Vicar of Wakefield;* and how, but for apparently small incidents, Newton would have been a farmer, Faraday a bookbinder, and Pasteur a tanner, we conclude that if these great talents were in this way brought out and given the arena of opportunity, there must be thousands of men whom chance has not discovered, whose talents have not been brought to the surface. You can wander into any rural cemetery and say what Thomas Gray said of those venerable graves at Stokes Poges:

Perhaps in this neglected spot is laid
    Some heart once pregnant with
      celestial fire;
Hands, that the rod of empire might
    have swayed,
    Or waked to ecstasy the living
      lyre.

It is this reflection, the unevoked and undiscovered greatness in man, which makes us wonder about immortality, and the use God will make hereafter of those whom in this Life no man hath hired, when the trumpet of the Resurrection shall call them out of their graves and say to them, "Awake, awake, put on thy strength."

———————

—Using what we have—It was only an oxgoad, but there was a man's arm behind the oxgoad and a great spirit behind the arm. The oxgoad had been baptized with the spirit of courage and determination and faith. Thus it suffered a metamorphosis and became an irresistible weapon. There was no sword —no, not even Goliath's mighty weapon —nor spear nor lance among the host of Philistines that could match itself with the oxgoad in the hands of the Spirit-filled judge.

Shamgar is the kind of man who accomplishes much with little. He reminds us that it is not so much what we have as how we use what we have. It is not so much the tool as the man who holds the tool. It is not so much the sword, the weapon, that counts, as the spirit of the man who holds the sword.

TEACHER

I have thought, as any college man here today has also thought, of the instructors under whom I sat. Who are the ones who now stand out, whose faces are easily recalled and whose ways and manners are easily remembered? The men who were noted for having written this or that book? By no means. The man that I remember as the most noted author was the least of them all. Are they the men who were spoken of as making original research in the laboratory or in the obscure field of history of economics? By no means. The least impressive of any of my instructors was a man who was one of the few authorities in the Ethiopic dialects. No; the men who impressed themselves upon you, and therefore educated you, were men who had intellectual ability but who had big hearts as well. They had personality because they had beating hearts, sympathy, and interest; and for that reason they remain still your teachers, your companions and friends, when the walking dictionary, or the man who wrote so-and-so, has passed completely out of the range of your life. These men were useful teachers and professors because the issues of education proceed from the heart.

Two temples once were built. The one was built with hands. Marble and stone, gold and silver, iron and brass were brought from afar. When at length all had been completed and the grand structure stood there in all the glory of vast roof, mighty foundations, groined walls, flying buttresses, soaring arches, and colossal pillars, men marveled at the plan and the achievement of the builder, and exclaimed, "This temple shall never know decay."

Meanwhile another temple was being built, but not with hands. None saw the toil of the builder. None saw the stone, the marble, the gold and silver and precious woods that were gathered for this temple. But at length it was completed, although none wondered at the finished work. None praised the builder or predicted immortality for the builder.

The first temple has long ago disappeared. Roof, pillars, arches, and aisles all have sunk into dust. But the temple built by the teacher still abides and shall abide forever, for it was the temple of a child's immortal soul. What manner of child shall this be!

TEMPER—*see also* ANGER

A bad temper, an unpleasant disposition, can destroy the joy and happiness of marriage—and dissolve marriage itself. A man quite aged went once to his physican for a physical examination. The physician expressed astonishment at his robust vigor in spite of his advanced years. The man explained that he had been compelled to live an "out-of-doors life." He then went on to say that when he and his wife were married they made a compact that when he lost his temper she was to keep silent, and when she lost her temper he was to go out of doors! A sudden flash and flame of anger can wither the flowers in the fairest paradise of any earthly home.

Lafontaine, chaplain of the Prussian army, once preached an earnest sermon on the sin and folly of yielding to a hasty temper. The next day a major of the regiment accosted him in no very good humor, saying: "Well, sir! I think you made use of the prerogative of your office to annoy me with some very sharp hits yesterday."

"I certainly thought of you while I was preparing the sermon," the chaplain answered, "but I had no intention of being personal or sharp."

"Well, it is of no use," said the major, "I have a hasty temper and I cannot help it. I cannot control it; the thing is impossible."

The following Sabbath, Lafontaine preached on self-deception, and the vain excuses which men are accustomed to make. "Why," said he, "a man will declare it is impossible to control his temper, when he very well knows that were the same provocation to happen in the presence of his sovereign, he not only could, but he would, control himself entirely. And yet he dares to say that the continual presence of the King of kings imposes upon him neither restraint nor fear."

The next day the preacher again met the officer, who said humbly: "You were right yesterday, chaplain. Hereafter, whenever you see me in danger of falling remind me of the King."

There is a tradition that Jonathan Edwards, third president of Princeton and America's greatest thinker, had a daughter with an ungovernable temper. But, as is often the case, this infirmity was not known to the outside world. A worthy young man fell in love with this daughter and sought her hand in marriage.

"You can't have her," was the abrupt answer of Jonathan Edwards.

"But I love her," the young man replied.

"You can't have her," said Edwards.

"But she loves me," replied the young man.

Again Edwards said, "You can't have her."

"Why?" asked the young man.

"Because she is not worthy of you."

"But," he asked, "she is a Christian, is she not?"

"Yes, she is a Christian, but the grace of God can live with some people with whom no one else could ever live."

TEMPERANCE—*see* DRINK, TOTAL ABSTINENCE

TEMPEST—*see* DEMONS AND CHRIST

TEMPTATION—*see also* AMBITION (PERILS OF), CHOICE, INFLUENCE (RESISTING EVIL), PRAYER AND TEMPTATION

A man is just as strong as his weakest moment. You could hardly say that Esau was a man of mere sensuality, who had no appreciation at all of the birthright or the blessing. That could not have been so, for we read of the bitter remorse that afterward seized him because he had once despised his birthright, and how, carefully and with tears, he besought Isaac to give it back to him. He was not a man of pronounced and uninterrupted materialism and animalism but a man who, in the temptation of a moment, threw away his birthright. He was just as strong as that weak moment when he came, hungry and thirsty from the fields, and smelled the pottage of his brother. A man's character is just as strong as the weakest link in

it. It is arresting and solemnizing to remember that in the last analysis we are to be judged and tested not by our excellencies, not by our so-called strong points, but by our weakness. The real trial will be the trial and test of your weak place and your weak moment. A battle line is just as strong as the weakest point or place in the whole length of the line.

———•———

Once when a soldier was going off to the wars his sweetheart gave him a talisman which he was to take with him as a protection against temptation. The talisman consisted of a moth suspended between a star and a flame. When the soldier's heart inclined toward evil the moth sank toward the flame; but when his heart inclined toward good and resisted evil, the moth rose toward the star.

———•———

Perhaps the most beautiful paraphrase of the Lord's Prayer ever written is that to be found in the eleventh canto of Dante's *Purgatory*, where the souls that are being purged of their sins repeat the Lord's Prayer, not so much for themselves as for those who come after them on the dangerous path of life. Dante's rendering of the sixth petition is as follows:

Our virtue, which so soon doth harm receive,
Put not to peril with our ancient Foe;
But from his evil sting deliverance give.

———•———

—Avoiding—There is a legend that Augustine, accosted on the street by a former mistress shortly after his conversion, turned and walked in the opposite direction. Surprised, the woman cried out, "Augustine, it is I."

But Augustine, proceeding on his way, cried back to her, "Yes, but it is not I."

What he meant was that there was a new Augustine, and that this new Augustine would avoid the very territory and appearance of evil.

—·•◆•·—

There is an old legend of a monk who, when assailed by the devil in a low and immoral theater, asked the devil how he could be so bold as to tempt a servant of the Lord. The devil answered, "What business has a servant of the Lord in my territory?"

The command given to the man and the woman was not merely that they should not *eat* of the tree of the knowledge of good and evil, but that they should not even *touch* it.

—·•◆•·—

William Jennings Bryan used to tell of a man in his home town in Illinois who had been the victim of drink. He reformed, signed the pledge, and apparently was delivered out of his evil habit. But when he rode into town he continued to hitch his horse to the rail in front of the tavern. He pitched his tent toward Sodom, and soon was again a drunkard. The way to avoid evil is to avoid the appearance of it.

—·•◆•·—

A man would not jump into the Niagara River above the falls, and then expect that by some miracle God would keep him from being swept over the falls. A man would not put a match to a keg of powder and then expect that God would keep him from being blown to atoms. And yet there are rational men and women, who have—outwardly at least—turned away from evil and given their allegiance to God, who walk in the way of temptation and seem to expect that they will be delivered.

—·•◆•·—

To say "Lead us not into temptation" (Matt. 6:13) is to ask that God will keep us from reading those books, going to those entertainments, meeting those associates, that stir up the evil which is in every man's nature, for every soul has its own ladder down to hell.

We can lead ourselves, or permit others to lead us, into circumstances where temptation is certain to strike and where sin is almost equally certain to wound us. The thing is to avoid those circumstances.

There is not much use in a man's trying to row when his boat is only a hundred yards above Niagara Falls. When evil passions are once on the wing they are not easily recalled. When the desire for evil is roused within a man's breast, through his own willfulness and carelessness, he may not be able to restrain his evil desires any more than a man can persuade an enraged, blood-excited tiger not to leap, or induce a hooded cobra not to strike.

—·•◆•·—

Trochilus, one of the disciples of Plato, miraculously escaped from a storm at sea in which the ship was sunk and he himself almost perished. When he reached home, the first thing he did was to order his servants to wall up two windows in one of his chambers which looked out upon the sea. His fear was that on some fine, bright day, looking out upon the sea when it was calm and tranquil and flashing in the sunlight, he should again be tempted to venture upon its treacherous waters. There are not a few windows looking out upon the sea of temptation which the soul would do well to wall up.

—·•◆•·—

One of the noted publishers of Great Britian tells the story of how he came as a youth from Scotland to take a job in London. One of the first companions that he fell in with took him one night to a house of shame; but as soon as he realized the nature of the place, without a moment's hesitation, he fled from it. To that quick and immediate decision he attributed his subsequent life of success and of honor.

—Beginning of—The trees once rebelled against the ax and formed a league binding themselves that none of them would allow the ax to have wood for his helve, or handle. But the ax attended the convention of the trees and persuaded them to give him wood for his handle, so that he could cut down just the small bushes and trees which hid from view the stately splendor of the ash and the oak and the cedar. Thus beguiled, they gave him wood for that purpose. But the moment he was thus furnished he fell to and chopped down the trees, sparing none of them. Watch the beginnings of evil. If you avoid the very appearance of evil, as the Bible puts it, you will escape the reality of evil.

—Christ's help in—If the thought of a godly father, or a praying mother, or a faithful wife, or an innocent child, will sometimes hold a man back from sin, how much more will the thought of the presence of Christ deliver the soul in the time of temptation.

Every night at sunset four bugles are sounded from the castle rock at Edinburgh as night comes down over the great rock and the picturesque city. There is a tradition that after the fourth bugle has sounded over the darkening city those on the streets below can hear the sound of a fifth bugler—a bugler who long ago was slain. That is mere legend. But when a tried, troubled, tempted, or sin-wounded soul sounds the trumpet of resistance and repentance

and recovery, out of the unseen comes the clear and unmistakable note of another trumpet. It is the answer of Christ to the soul which turns to him and seeks in the battle of life his presence and his help.

—Defense against—In the engrossing story of his life the Russian novelist Maxim Gorky tells of his experiences as a cabin boy on a steamer on the Volga River. Depraved, degraded, corrupted and corrupting men and women were all around him. Particularly evil in speech and action was the stewardess of the boat.

But Gorky relates that he suffered no harm, because his world was different from their world. "I did not grasp," he says, "the meaning of her speech, although I dimly guessed at it. But I was not disturbed by it. I lived far away from the stewardess, and from all that went on in that world. I lived behind a great rugged rock that hid me from all that world." You can have your own world if you are determined to have it. What kind of world do you want?

When he passed the haunt of the sirens Ulysses had his sailors bind him to the mast of the ship, so that even if he was tempted by their music to desert the path of honor and of duty his bonds would hold him fast. But the Argonauts, who went sailing into the Black Sea, seeking for the Golden Fleece in that very peninsula where not long ago a Russian army resisted the German hordes, took Orpheus with them on their ship; and when any danger beset them they had Orpheus play on his magic harp. So Christ in our hearts is the chief defense against temptation.

In an article dealing with the habits of tigers in a country of the Far East, the author tells of a man who, overcome with the heat, left the shelter of his cabin and lay down to sleep in the open with only a small frail mosquito netting stretched over him. Awakened by a mysterious warning such as men sometimes get, he saw approaching his place of bivouac a tiger, his eyes glaring in the night. Closer and closer the tiger came, and then he was joined by another. Repeatedly they came up to that mosquito netting, until their very breath made it quiver, but each time they drew back, mystified and alarmed, until with a wild roar of fear the man frightened them off.

The veil of innocence which God has wrapped around the soul will save it from destruction—until a man rends it himself by his own deliberate will and invites the foe to come in.

—◆—

A man in a dream once saw himself in a glass cage surrounded by furious foes who sought with all manner of weapons to destroy him. But their weapons could not penetrate the wall of glass, and he looked down serenely upon their rage. Something like that Christ meant when he said, "These things I have spoken unto you, that in me ye might have peace. In the world ye shall have tribulation: but be of good cheer; I have overcome the world" (John 16:33).

—◆—

When Theseus set out on his dangerous journey through the Cretan labyrinth to slay the Minotaur, Ariadne put into his hand a silken thread. That thread would remind him of her and would guide him through the perils of the labyrinth and to the upper world again. But the Christian disciple in the dangerous passages of human life has something better than that—he has the promise of the presence of the Living Christ.

—◆—

—**By flattery**—"She brought him butter in a lordly dish." (Judges 5:25.) This lordly dish was used only when the most honored and distinguished guests were in the home. The use of this dish by Jael made Sisera feel that Jael thought it a high honor to entertain him, and thus any suspicions he might have had were set at rest. Under the spell of flattery men are often fools immeasurable, and in its intoxication are led to do things that in the clear light of reason they would never have done. "She brought him butter in a lordly dish." That has spelled the downfall of many a man. In the memorable chapter in the book of Proverbs where a woman leads a man down to the chambers of death, it is the weapon of flattery which she employs. "With her much fair speech she caused him to yield, with the flattering of her lips she forced him. He goeth after her straightway, as an ox goeth to the slaughter, or as a fool to the correction of the stocks; till a dart strike through his liver; as a bird hasteth to the snare, and knoweth not that it is for his life." (Prov. 7:21-23.)

—◆—

—**By a friend**—Marco Polo, the famous medieval traveler, tells of a great desert near the town of Lop where evil spirits lured travelers to destruction by means of an extraordinary delusion. If a traveler had fallen behind the caravan and was by himself, he would hear his name called in a familiar tone of voice. Thinking it was the voice of a companion and friend, he would leave the road and follow the voice, and so perish.

Probably no such place as Marco Polo describes ever existed. Nevertheless, what he relates is a parable which describes the temptation of a friend. The temptations which come to us through friendship are ofttimes the most dangerous.

———•◦•———

—**Ministers'**—A minister who had done great service in the church, and for God and man, had this to say: "I have had some degree of experimental acquaintance with Jesus Christ for almost forty years. I have borne the ministerial character for upwards of twenty-five years. I have been perhaps of some little use in the Church of God, and I have had a greater share of esteem among religious people than I had any reason to expect. Yet after all, it is possible for me in one single hour of temptation to blast my character, to ruin my public usefulness, and to render my warmest Christian friends ashamed of owning me."

———•◦•———

—**And a moment of time**—On a soft summer evening King David, walking on the roof of his palace, saw a woman bathing. In that moment of time David plunged into a deep abyss of sin and murder and crime. In the courtyard of the high priest, while Jesus was being examined within, Peter and John stood by the fire warming themselves. Peter had shown great bravery so far that night. It looked as if his boast that he would be faithful to Christ even unto prison and unto death would be made good. But a maidservant pointed her finger at him, and said, "Thou art one of them" (Mark 14:70), and in that moment Peter began to curse and to swear, and to say, "I know not this man."

———•◦•———

One look, and Lot's wife was a pillar of salt. Just a look! There is "life for a look"; there is also death for a look. Augustine in his *Confessions* relates the story of a young man at Rome who had been won from a life of sin and licentiousness to Christ. He forsook his old ways. One day some of his friends persuaded him to go with them to the Colosseum. He took a seat with his companions far up on the topmost bench of that colossal ellipse. As soon as the trumpet rang for the spectacle to commence, he firmly closed his eyes, resolved not to look upon the unholy sights. So the spectacles passed. But at one act, or conflict, the excited and blood-intoxicated thousands put up a mighty roar of acclaim. At the sound, Alypius opened his eyes, just for a moment. But by the one look he was lost. He forsook Christ and went back to the world.

Do not imagine that it is safe to take even one look at sin, just for a moment to caress it with the touch of furtive imagination. One look turned Lot's wife to a pillar of salt.

———•◦•———

—**A moral testing**—There is no fatalism in Christianity. We are not tempted beyond our powers to resist. King Edward III, looking down on the hills around Abbeyville, where the Black Prince was fighting and seemed to be engulfed by the enemy, refused to send any succor to his aid which might withdraw from him the honor of a well-contested victory. He saw in the danger of the Black Prince an opportunity for glory. So in our temptations our Great Commander wants us to win spiritual and moral strength and renown.

———•◦•———

—**Power of**—Only the rock which throws itself up against the current of a rapidly flowing river gives any idea of how strong the current is. It is when sin is resisted that we discover its power. Sin unresisted is as noiseless as the gliding stream and as viewless as the wind which sweeps over land and ocean.

—**And prayer**—In one of my churches there was a fine old elder who used to lead in prayer at the Wednesday night meetings. There were certain verses of familiar hymns which he never failed to quote. One of them was this verse by Cowper:

And Satan trembles when he sees
The weakest saint upon his knees.

Not bad poetry that; but there is more truth than poetry in it.

— • • • —

In a story so popular a number of years ago, *The Garden of Allah,* the strongest and the most dramatic passage is that where the author describes the recreant and apostate monk thrown into the greatest distress and alarm when he beheld a man at prayer. The sight of a man so engaged cooled the ardor of his passion and reminded him of the vows he had broken and the sin he had committed. There would be less sinning in the world if there were more praying.

— • • • —

Homer tells us that when Ulysses came to the Aeaean isle where the daughter of the sun, Circe, lived, he climbed a hill and saw in the center of the island a palace embowered with trees. He sent forward one half of his crew under the command of Eurylochus to see if he could find hospitality. When the men approached the palace, which was surrounded by wild animals that had once been men now changed into beasts by Circe's art, they heard the sounds of soft music from within. When they entered—all but their leader, Eurylochus, who suspected danger—Circe served them with wine and other delicacies. When they had eaten and drunk heartily she touched them one by one

with her wand, and they then were immediately changed into swine. When Eurylochus brought the story of this disaster to Ulysses, he went forth to rescue his men. As he was going, he was met on the way by Mercury, who warned him of the dangerous arts of Circe. But as Ulysses would not be dissuaded from his efforts, Mercury put in his hand a flower, the fragrance of which he was to inhale, which had the power to resist all sorceries. Armed with this flower, Ulysses entered the palace of Circe, who entertained him as she had his companions; and when he had eaten and drunk, she touched him with her wand, saying, "Hence, seek the sty and wallow with thy friends!" But, protected from her spell by the flower which he carried, Ulysses drew his sword and compelled her to release his companions and restore them to their human form.

The Christian has a flower with which he can disarm temptation, and that flower is prayer.

— • • • —

—**Preparing for**—In his famous *Two Years Before the Mast* Richard Henry Dana relates how at San Diego, on the California coast, the sailors got out their needles and scissors and prepared for themselves heavy garments—coats lined with wool and painted on the outside with tar; also heavy mittens, jerseys, and scarves. Why did they do this? Their ship was lying in the lovely bay at San Diego, where a tropical sun was smiling down upon them. Where was the ship going that these men were getting ready heavy winter garments? The ship was going around the Horn, where for days and weeks they would be sailing through icy seas, driven with arctic gales, and the ship's rigging would be coated with ice. Long before they reached the dangerous passage they were getting ready for it.

It is wise to take a survey of our life, and to be ready for every eventuality.

* * *

—**Resisting**—Ahab was a weak and wicked king, yet he had a certain respect for himself and for his people. He told Ben-hadad that although he had consented to the first conditions laid down, this other he would not do: "This thing I may not do" (I Kings 20:9)! Every man ought to have a *thus far and no farther in his character,* a "This thing I may not do," in answer to the tempter.

* * *

A man once came to his physician complaining of physical weakness and low spirits, and how he was tempted to rely upon stimulants. The physician told him that to resort to stimulants in his condition would be injurious. When the patient declared that unless he drank he would be unequal to his work and would sink, the doctor said, "Then sink like a man."

* * *

Archimedes, the man who said, "Give me a place on which to rest my lever and I can move the world," is said to have destroyed the Roman fleet which was besieging Syracuse—where the Allied armies of the second World War landed for the Italian campaign—by setting them on fire by the reflection of mirrors. An unarmed and weak mathematician destroyed the armada of a great kingdom because he put himself in touch with the forces of the physical universe. One unarmed and humble mortal can overthrow Satan and all his hosts if he will only put himself, and keep himself, in touch with that source of all spiritual power, the Lord Jesus Christ.

* * *

In Bunyan's great dream of Mansoul, that fortress and capital, although besieged by strong, cruel, subtle, and malignant foes, could not fall, and did not fall, until its gates were opened from within. Not until you and I enter into conspiracy with the foe at the gate of our soul can that enemy win the victory. We are able to bear it if we will.

* * *

In the days of the Civil War it was illegal to trade in cotton; but many unscrupulous speculators tried to buy cotton in the South, run it through the Union lines, and sell it at great profit in the North. One of these speculators approached a Mississippi steamboat captain and offered him $100 if he would run his cotton up the river for him. The captain declined, reminding him that it was illegal.

"I will give you $500," said the man.

"No," answered the captain.

"I will give you $1000."

"No," the captain said again.

"I will give you $3000."

At that the captain drew his pistol, and pointing it at the man said, "Get off this boat. You are coming too near my price."

That is the way to deal with temptation. That is the way Christ dealt with it. There was no parley, no delay; he said, "Get thee behind me, Satan" (Matt. 16:23).

* * *

—**In school**—The great teacher Arnold of Rugby once wrote: "Of all the painful things connected with my employment nothing is equivalent to the grief of seeing a boy come to the school innocent and promising, and tracing the corruption of his character from the influence of the temptations around him, in the very place which ought to have strengthened it and improved it." He hints there at two principles of conduct—the importance and tragic fatality of companionship, and also the importance of the spiritual or unseen environment of every man's life. The influence of bad environment cannot be fatal to the soul unless the soul itself is friendly and receptive to that evil influence.

———•••———

—**And sleep**—Burglars when they rob a house sometimes chloroform those who dwell there so they may rob and loot at their pleasure. It would seem that Satan acts in much the same way when he despoils men of their souls. He casts them into a deep sleep, gives them a false sense of safety, the conviction that while temptation and evil might destroy others, it could never destroy them. It is while men sleep that the devil does his work. It was when Sisera, exhausted after the great Battle of Kishon, lay asleep in the house of Jael, where he had taken refuge, that that patriotic Hebrew took a hammer and drove a tent pin through the temple of the unconscious captain of Canaan. It was when Samson lay asleep on the lap of Delilah that the Philistines sheared him of his locks and stripped him of his great strength, and then put his eyes out and cast him into the dungeon to do the work of a slave.

———•••———

The dramatic events that took place in Russia during the second World War recalled the disastrous retreat of Napoleon from Moscow in 1801. The best account we have of that retreat is by Caulaincourt, the Duke of Vicenza, Napoleon's master of horse, who was with him in intimate contact all through the Russian campaign. Caulaincourt describes how the soldiers of the Guard, overcome by the cold, fell out of the ranks and lay prostrate in the snow, too weak or too numb to stand. Once they fell asleep they were dead. To sleep was to die.

He relates how on a number of occasions he tried to arouse men who had thus fallen to the ground, warning them that they would perish; but the drowsiness engendered by the cold was irresist-

ibly strong. To all his entreaties the drowsy soldiers were deaf. The only words they uttered were to beg him for the love of God to go away and let them sleep.

So is it with the sleep of the soul, with the fatal allurement of temptation and of sin.

———•••———

—**A treacherous enemy**—Temptation is a sleepless, unwearying enemy. The Scotch-Irish forefathers who settled and conquered the wilderness of Western Pennsylvania, as they went about their daily toil, clearing the forests, cultivating the fields, looking after the stock, did so ever mindful of the fact that there was a cruel, crafty, merciless, and blood-thirsty foe always lurking about, waiting for an opportunity to find the settler off his guard and fire the fatal shot or hurl his tomahawk and rush forward with the encircling knife.

So, although we are often supinely oblivious of it, you and I have an enemy who is waiting and watching to find us off our guard; and his patience is never worn out and his enmity is unsleeping. How powerful a figure did the Lord use when he spoke to Cain, warning him against the temptation of hatred and jealousy that at length moved him to his dreadful crime: "Sin coucheth at the door" (Gen. 4:7). The figure is that of a wild animal, flattened against the ground or a rock, or against the limb of the tree, watching and waiting to make his fatal spring.

———•••———

A man once watched an Indian preparing a snare with which to catch a wild animal. He was surprised to learn that the Indian never sprang the trap or pulled the noose the first time the animal appeared. Instead of that, he would let it come repeatedly and feed where the trap was, and then, when it had become bold and thoroughly familiar with the surroundings, he would set the trap so that the next time it came the animal would be caught in the snare.

That is the way temptation works. It does not drive its shaft into the heart of its victim at first, but deceives it and lures it on; and then the fatal blow is delivered.

———•◦•———

I once spent a number of weeks in a village on the banks of the Wisconsin River. It is a broad river flowing between grassy banks, with noble hills on either side. In front of the town the river ran under an old-fashioned wooden bridge, and the cool shadowed waters as they ran under the bridge seemed to invite one to come into them and bathe. But I had not been long there before I discovered that none boated on the river and none ever went down to swim in it. When I asked why this was so, the villagers pointed out to me this or that spot in the river where someone had been drowned. Even during the time I was there the river claimed another victim. Several times I went to the river to swim by myself but found it a lonely and unpleasant spot, for the specters of the river tragedies could not be banished; and at length I, like all the others, gave it up altogether. It was hard to realize that this beautiful stream deserved such a reputation; and yet it was well deserved, for where the river seemed so placid and calm it was in reality rushing toward the Mississippi with a force of current that the strongest swimmers could not overcome, and from those inviting sand bars that seemed to tell of a gradually declining beach one stepped off into bottomless pits or engulfing sands.

The river of temptation is very much like that river. One who has not had experience with it would never imagine that it is so dangerous and treacherous. In the river there is the peril of the deep pool. One steps suddenly and unexpectedly into water that is over the head. Life has much of what seems to be regularity and conformity; and, looking on it from the outside, one would hardly believe that it is filled with mortal tragedy and that on every side men and women are going down, some with a loud cry, others without a sound. The pleasure of what is not positively wicked, but which tends in that direction, deceives and allures many an unsuspecting soul. As long as they can feel the bottom beneath their feet they think they are safe. Then suddenly, another step, and with a cry they are gone!

———•◦•———

The ship which carried Paul was lured to its destruction by the south wind. Paul admonished the men to remain safe in the harbor at Fair Havens, but when the south wind blew softly, supposing that they had gained their purpose, they put out to sea on the last voyage, which ended on the rocks of Malta. All temptations come along the line of least resistance—the easy, the pleasant, the desirable. The thief is told that there is an easier and a more pleasant way to make money than by the sweat of the brow and the labor of the mind.

Gehazi saw the flashing colors of the Syrian raiment, not the leprous scars on the face. Achan saw the Babylonian garments, not the execrations of the people and the lamentations of his wife and children. Judas saw the glitter of the gold, not the darkness of remorse. The man who fools with whisky sees only the immediate stimulus and the good fellowship, and hears only the roaring chorus of his companions. He does not see the poisonous stuff eating out the vitality of his body and dulling the windows of his mind and defiling the temple of his spirit.

The young man who goes down into the swamp of impure and unclean living sees only the gratification of his curiosity, the strange excitement of his mysterious adventure. He does not see the awful retribution which nature exacts of those who break her laws; he does not see himself, his body devoured with ulcers, his will broken, his spirit degraded to a level far below that of the brute. He knows only that stolen waters are sweet and that bread eaten in secret is pleasant; he does not know that Death is there, and that her guests are in the depths of hell.

—The unexpected—Mere disinclination is no guarantee against any evil that men have done. The great doers of evil were the men who thought they could never do it. As a youth Napoleon wrote an essay for the Lyons Academy on the dangers of ambition. "Would that this hand had never learned to write!" exclaimed Nero when asked to sign his first death warrant. The same Robespierre who during the Reign of Terror sent thousands to the guillotine resigned his office as a provincial judge because he could not bring himself to pronounce sentence of death upon a man convicted of a capital crime.

The young king David, told that he would live to darken the closing days of his reign with murder and adultery, would have said, "Is thy servant a dog?" (II Kings 8:13). If Solomon had been told, as he knelt that holy night on Gideon's sacred slope to ask God for wisdom to discern between good and evil and to judge his people, that he would forsake his father's God and bend his aged knees to heathen deities and follow after strange women, he would have said it— "Is thy servant a dog?" Peter, told on

that last night, as he boasted of his fidelity to Jesus, that before the sacramental wine was dry upon his lips he would have denied his Lord with an oath— surely Peter would have said it.

Clothe yourself with power to discern the secrets of men's hearts and foresee their actions, and tell this man or this woman of the offenses which they will one day commit, and they, too, will rise up to denounce you as an impostor and to exclaim against such a possibility. But in many a life your prophecy may be fulfilled, yea, more than fulfilled. How often the tears of Elisha would be our tears, did we have his power to search men's hearts! "Who can understand his errors?" (Ps. 19:12.)

Thousands of men are wrecked on the hill of what they considered improbable, if not impossible, temptations. When the thing has happened, men say, "Who would have thought it?" "The last person in the world I would have supposed . . . ," and so on. In his autobiography Senator George F. Hoar speaks of the atrocious murder committed by one of the faculty at Harvard when he was a student there, and says, "John W. Webster gave lectures on chemistry and geology. There was no person among the faculty at Cambridge less likely to commit such a bloody and cruel crime as that for which he was executed." On the whole territory of temptation, whether we are going down a hill which we think is safe for us, although dangerous for others, or descending a hill which is admittedly full of peril, the wise thing is to take precaution—to watch and to pray.

—The universality of—Standing in one of the great limestone caves of Bermuda, you can hear the flow of an underground stream. Those waters, ceaselessly flowing, have eroded the cavernous depths with their vast resounding chambers and fantastic decorations. The mind reels as it tries to estimate how long that stream has been running.

While empires have risen and fallen, while new continents have been discovered and added to the map of the world, while generation after generation of men have come forth like the leaves of the forest, and like the leaves have fallen and perished, strewing the world with their dust, that stream which swiftly murmurs at your feet has been flowing on and on, never interrupted, never ceasing, never getting through with its work, a symbol of the tireless energy of those forces in the natural world which make and unmake the seas and the continents, extending the first verse of Genesis—"In the beginning God created the heaven and the earth"—over all the ages that have been and all that are yet to come. So temptation flows like a river through the life of man. Old races die out, and new races take their place. New powers are thought out and new devices invented, but through each generation of men there flows this river of temptation. How long temptation has been here! How old it is! How unchanging it is! It is as new as birth and as old as death. It touches the life of the philosopher and the fool, the prince and the pauper, the sage and the savage, Christ and Judas. Wherever man has gone temptation has gone. It is man's shadow, haunting him wherever he goes and wherever he appears. It is the warfare from which there is no discharge.

A number of years ago I spent a Sabbath on the lovely isle of Bute. In the evening we walked along the shores of the eastern side of the Island until we came to an ancient stone church standing on a grassy eminence which projected out into the sea. We were late for the service and, unwilling to disturb either the preacher or the congregation, sat down on the stone steps of the church. The door being open, we could hear distinctly the words of the minister. The long Scottish summer day was beginning to fade, and the light was commencing to flash from many a white tower lighthouse in the distance. The subject of the minister's sermon was "Temptation." There is nothing worse than a poor sermon, nothing better than a good one. This was a good one. He was no ordinary preacher; and he said many things worth hearing, things which, having been heard once, are remembered. One sentence particularly stands out in my memory. It was this: "Every man has his own ladder down to hell."

As I sat gazing on the beautiful twilight panorama of sea, mountains, islands, and sky, this sentence sounded like a voice from another world. "Every man has his own ladder down to hell." The sentence tells the truth about human nature: it reminds us of those capacities for evil which reside in every breast. There are ladders by which we can rise to heaven; there are also ladders which lead down into the abyss.

I was attempting one day to fix an electric lamp in the cellar of my home. Whenever I touched the lamp I was severely shocked by the electric current. Finally I sent for the electrician. He tried it with the same result. Then he took a heavy piece of timber and laid it on the floor and, standing on it, adjusted the light without injury. The damp earth on which we had been standing was congenial to the play of that electric current. When the electrician got off the ground he was safe. Man would be safe, absolutely safe, if he could break his contact with the evil that is inherent in human nature. But that he cannot do. He must stand upon the mother earth of humanity through which evil expresses itself.

———

—**The unlikely**—Men often fall on their strongest side. "Wherefore let him that thinketh he standeth take heed lest he fall" (I Cor. 10:12). Moses was the meekest of men, yet he fell in a moment of angry presumption, when he smote the rock thrice and denounced the people as rebels. Elijah was the prophet of magnificent courage, and yet when Jezebel sought to kill him, Elijah, under the juniper tree, asked God to take away his life. Peter was the apostle of natural and impulsive courage. In the garden of Gethsemane, he drew his sword against the whole mob, and yet the same night he went down before the pointed finger of a serving maid.

The ancient city of Sardis fronted the broad valley of the Hermos River with the Tmolus Mountain at its back. The citadel toward the mountain was regarded as so naturally strong and impregnable that no defense was made on that side, and there it was that the soldiers of Cyrus made their ascent and took Sardis. Abraham, the man of great faith, at two times in his life resorted to miserable and cowardly falsehood.

———

Walking one summer day along the historic Cumberland Road, high upon the summit of the Alleghenies, I saw in the midst of a field and in the shadow of venerable pine trees a mountain grave. I left the road and crossed the field to see whose lonely grave this might be. As I drew near I read upon the wooden marker the name Brigadier General Edward Braddock.

At once my mind ran back a century and a half, and I saw the long procession of red-coated regulars, blue-coated colo-nials, and lumbering wagons pass down that mountain highway until they were lost in the recesses of the primeval forest. After the disastrous defeat at the fords of the Monongahela, Braddock, mortally wounded, had been borne along in the retreat as far as this spot where now he lies buried.

After his grave had been filled, the artillery carriages and the wagon trains were driven over it to hide the body from the profaning hands of the savages. Just before he died, Braddock, reclining in the arms of Washington and looking up into the faces of his officers, and past them to the calm heavens, exclaimed, *"Who would have thought it!"* Who would have thought that the British general who had won renown on the fields of Europe would have been defeated by a handful of French and Indian allies in the midst of the American bush!

"Who would have thought it!" It is an expression which comes to mind when we think not only of military disasters but of those crushing moral disasters and ambushes which suddenly overwhelm the souls of men.

———

—**Victory over**—Mr. Valiant-for-Truth, when summoned to go over the river, said, "I am going to my Father's; and though with great difficulty I have got hither, yet now I do not repent me of all the trouble I have been at to arrive where I am. My sword I give to him that shall succeed me in my pilgrimage, and my courage and skill to him that can get it. My marks and scars I carry with me, to be a witness for me that I have fought His battles who will now be my rewarder."

———

When Paul shook the viper off his arm he shook it off into the fire. He did not shake it off into the bundle of fagots, or upon the ground, where it might strike him again, or bury its fangs in some other survivor of the shipwreck. He shook it off into the flame. That particular viper would never again menace the life of Paul, or the life of any other man.

To resist a temptation half-heartedly, to say No with a certain tone of reservation in our minds, as if we might give it consideration tomorrow, is to make sure that temptation will return, and return stronger than it was before, because we ourselves are weaker. Although Saul tried to kill himself on the bloody field of Gilboa, the finishing blow was given to him by an Amalekite, one of those people whom, contrary to the commandment of God, Saul had spared. You spare your temptation today, shake it off into the bushes, or to the ground, instead of into the fire, into the flames, where it will be reduced to ashes, and it will come back to hiss and to strike and to curse tomorrow.

————•—•—————

"Angels came and ministered unto him." (Matt. 4:11.) What unconscious beauty and grandeur in that sentence! Still these angels come to crown and acclaim the soul that has resisted temptation and has said to the tempter, "Get thee behind me, Satan" (Matt. 16:23).

After his desperate battle with Apollyon, Christian was ministered to by a hand which had in it the leaves of healing. Wounds received in resisting evil can always be healed. There is no poison in them. A hand invisible is reached reached down with leaves in it from the tree of life, which is for the healing of the soul. The only wounds which cannot be healed are those which you inflict upon yourself.

THANKS

In the midst of the storm, when the storm-battered vessel was plunging at its four anchors off the coast of Malta, Paul "gave thanks to God in presence of them all" (Acts 27:35). He could do that because he had faith in the word and promise God had given him.

————•—•—————

Paul's reasons for gratitude to God cover the whole territory of human life and experience. He gives thanks for:

1) His daily bread (Acts 27:35)
2) Men who have faith in Christ (Rom. 1:8)
3) Deliverance from anxiety (II Cor. 2:14)
4) Deliverance from temptation (Rom. 7:25)
5) The memory of his friends (Phil. 1:3)
6) Kindness in the day of trouble (Acts 28:15)
7) The "unspeakable" gift (II Cor. 9:15)

THIEF, THE PENITENT

The thief and brigand on the cross has stolen horses, jewels, money, children; he has spoiled and plundered caravans. But now he steals heaven. He picks the lock of the gate of heaven with the key of repentance.

————•—•—————

An old legend gives the names of the two thieves as Titus and Dumacus, and tells us that when they were crucified they were both well advanced in years. Long years before, when Joseph and Mary were in flight to Egypt with the infant Jesus, their caravan was waylaid by these brigands. Dumacus was for destroying Joseph and Mary and the child; but Titus, caught with the beauty of the child in Mary's arms, persuaded his companion to spare their lives and, addressing the child, said: "O blessed child, if the day should ever come when I shall need mercy, then on that day remember this deed."

THIRST

On September 22, 1586, Sir Philip Sidney, whose name is like ointment poured forth, was desperately wounded in a cavalry charge before the walls of Zutphen. As he was being carried to a dressing station, there occurred that beautiful incident forever associated with his name. "Being thirsty with excess of bleeding, he called for drink, which was presently brought him. But as he was putting the bottle to his mouth, he saw a poor soldier carried along who had eaten his last at the same feast, ghastly casting up his eyes at the bottle. Which Sir Philip perceiving, took it from his head before he drank and delivered it to the poor man with these words: 'Thy necessity is greater than mine,' and when he had pledged this poor soldier he was presently carried to Arnheim."

———◆———

Probably few persons in this country know what the torment of extreme hunger is, and fewer still the torment of intense thirst. But they who have tasted this cup of bitterness testify to the fact that the torment of thirst is the worst suffering that can come upon the human frame. Soldiers lying desperately wounded upon the field of battle between the hostile lines, where none dared venture to their rescue, have harrowed the hearts of friend and foe alike with their piteous cries for water. Patients in the hospital recovering from a desperate operation call for water and eagerly swallow the few drops permitted them. Travelers lost in the desert or on the plains have dug like animals in the sand for a sign of water, or with glaring, distended eyeballs have rushed frantically toward the mirage that they thought was water. Shipwrecked persons tossing for days in the sea in an open boat, crazed by thirst, in spite of all threats and warnings and entreaties, will bail up the salt water and drink it. Crucifixion was a form of punishment and execution designed by a cruel people to put criminals to death, and to do it with the greatest degree of humiliation and torture. But the most unmitigated of the sources of anguish combined in that worst form of death was the terrible thirst.

THOUGHT

On a church board, whereon was displayed one of those brief sayings calculated to arrest and impress the casual reader as he passes by, I recently read this: "You are not what you think you are, but you *are* what you *think*." "As [a man] thinketh in his heart, so is he." (Prov. 23:7.) In this hidden realm all disguise and pretense are thrown off, and we worship what we really desire and admire.

TIME—*see also* TOMORROW

From the nave of the Strasbourg Cathedral I walked over to the south transept. There is the great and justly renowned clock. It, too, like the cathedral, has had many builders. This clock not only preaches from hour to hour a great and solemn sermon but is a monument to the greatness of the human mind. Among its many intricate devices is one which marks the eclipses. So ingenious is the combination that it will last forever. As long as the earth wheels round the sun, that device, if it be preserved, will mark the eclipses. At the hour of noon statues of the Twelve Apostles emerge and pass in reverent procession before the figure of Christ, who lifts his hand to bless them, while a cock flaps his wings and crows three times. In the center are four figures representing the four ages of life, and in the midst of them stands Death. At the first quarter glad Childhood emerges and strikes the bell; at the second quarter rosy Youth comes forth; at the third, sober Manhood, and lifts his robust arm; and at the last quarter, feeble and decrepit Old Age lifts wearily his hammer to strike. When he has finished, Death lifts his arm and strikes the hour. Childhood, Youth, Manhood, Old Age, Death!

Some of those who stood watching belonged to the first quarter, some to youth's golden morn, some to manhood's sober day, and some to the last quarter and the feebleness of old age; and one could see too plainly that ere long death would lift his hammer and strike the passing of their life.

To stand and watch the figures strike the quarter hour, one after the other, was subduing, impressive, solemnizing. It made one think of applying his heart unto wisdom. As he put himself in one of the four groups, one wondered how much time was left—the third age, the fourth, or soon the stroke of Death? It made one ask himself, "What have I done with my life? What am I doing with it now?"

Even while the curious onlookers stand and silently watch the hands of that clock proceed around the face of the dial, and one after the other the five figures come forth to strike their blows, my life, your life, is marching inexorably onward to the end. No prayer, no entreaty, no skill of physician, can hold it back.

There are two ways of dealing with time. Perhaps I can express it by such a metaphor as this. In the squares and gardens of our cities, the streams of water from the fountains shoot out of the mouths of marble boys, or play through the outstretched hands of water nymphs. To them water is nothing save something to play with. But men adrift in a boat on the high sea, or crossing

the desert, measure out the water drop by drop, for they know that that water is their life.

Too often we are like those artistic fountains and play with time as if it were the least valuable thing in the world. But experience, whether we think of those who are gone or think of our own unfulfilled purposes and resolutions and our unfinished characters, has taught us that time is the most valuable thing we have and that whatsoever heart or hand findeth to do, we ought to do it *now,* and with our might.

—New Year—At the threshold of the new year, we stand today at one of those divisions of time which man has established for his own convenience. The division is altogether imaginary and arbitrary. This day is no more the beginning of a new year than yesterday or the day before. Yet even this imaginary division gives pause for thought.

The man who pauses to rest on the bridge may think of the course of the river, how in a short time the water into which he is gazing will flow under the bridge at Sewickley, and then under the bridge at Rochester, and then past Wheeling, and then under the bridges at Cincinnati, and then past Cairo, and thus into the Mississippi, and past St. Louis, Memphis, Vicksburg, New Orleans, into the Gulf of Mexico and so to the Atlantic Ocean. He pauses to think of the course of the river, but the river never stops for a moment in its eager course toward the ocean.

So, between the two eternities, the river of time flows ever on, ever seeking the sea; and even while we pause on a New Year's morning to contemplate the stream, its rapidity, its slowness, its destination, or its source, the river of our life flows ever onward. Days of pain and sorrow will make the stream seem to flow very slowly; days of happiness and bliss will give it a rapid velocity; but always its rate of flow is the same, and never for a single moment does it stop.

Time, like an ever-rolling stream,
Bears all its sons away.
                              —ISAAC WATTS

TOLERANCE—*see also* INTOLERANCE

Forbear to judge, for we are sinners
all.
Close up his eyes and draw the cur-
tain close;
And let us all to meditation.

—SHAKESPEARE (*King Henry VI*)

Whitefield, the great preacher, belonged to the Calvinistic wing of the Methodists, and the early and ardent friendship between him and Wesley cooled perceptibly toward the end of their ministry. But when Whitefield died in New England and the news came back to England, at the close of a memorial sermon on the life of his eloquent colleague, a little bigoted woman who thought none but Calvinists could enter the Kingdom of Heaven, and imagined that Wesley thought none but Arminians could enter, came forward and asked him if he expected to see "dear Dr. Whitefield in heaven."

Wesley answered, "No!"

"Ah!" said the woman, "I was afraid you would say that."

Then Wesley rejoined, "Do not misunderstand me. George Whitefield will be so near the throne that men like me will never get a glimpse of him." Would that all Christians could at least wish that for their brethren with whom they differ in points of doctrine and practice!

TOLERATION

When we speak of the necessity of the great beliefs, we do not mean a flat uniformity as to matters in Christian doctrine about which men may differ. When Charles V was trying to bring the world to a uniformity of belief, and employing the thumbscrew and the rack to that end, he was one day experimenting with three clocks in his retreat at Yuste. Unable to make the three clocks keep exactly the same time, he gave it up in disgust, exclaiming, "Here I was trying to make a whole world believe exactly alike, and I can't even make three clocks keep the same time."

Carlyle wrote of John Knox: "Tolerance has to tolerate the unessential and see well what that is. Tolerance has to be noble, measured, just in its very wrath, when it can tolerate no longer. But on the whole, we are not here altogether to tolerate! We are here to resist, to control and vanquish withal. We do not tolerate Falsehoods, Thieveries, Iniquities, when they fasten upon us; we say to them, Thou art false, thou art not tolerable!"

One Saturday evening a visitor appeared at Pastor Rutherford's door. Being welcomed as a guest, he took his place with the rest of the family at family worship that evening and was catechized in his turn. Rutherford asked him, "How many Commandments are there?" His reply was, "Eleven." Rutherford corrected him, but his guest maintained his position, quoting for authority the words of Christ, "A new commandment I give unto you, That ye love one another" (John 13:34).

Early Sabbath morning Rutherford arose, as was his custom, and went out for meditation to a near-by thicket. Arrived there, he was surprised to hear the voice of prayer in behalf of the souls that day to assemble for worship. Rutherford was now beginning to suspect that he was entertaining angels unawares, and soon his guest made known his identity. He was none other than the celebrated Archbishop Usher. They had sweet converse together, and at the morning service the Archbishop entered the Covenanter pastor's pulpit and preached on "The New Commandment."

Wesley once said: "I have no more right to object to a man holding a different opinion from mine, than I have to differ from a man because he wears a wig and I wear my own hair. But if he takes his wig off, and shakes the powder in my eyes, I shall consider it my duty to get rid of him as soon as possible."

TOMORROW—*see also* OPPORTUNITY, PROCRASTINATION, TIME

They were having a great banquet one night at Thebes in Greece. The chief ruler, Archias, and the other magnates of the city had taken their seats at the banqueting table; and the dancers and singers had commenced their entertainment. There were enemies plotting against the life of Archias and his companions. In the midst of the banquet a friend brought to him a sealed letter, warning him that he was in peril of assassination. Archias glanced at it and then, laying it aside, said, "Pleasure tonight. Business tomorrow." In a short time the assassins, who were diguised as female entertainers, drew their daggers and slew Archias and his companions.

For the great business of eternal life there is only one time, and that it today.

The only convenient season is God's season. Clement L. Vallandigham—the eloquent, powerful, and somewhat notorious "Copperhead" and opponent of Lincoln's administration—came of godly parents, his father being the pastor of the Presbyterian church at Lisbon, Ohio. Although he was the subject of many prayers and had before him daily the example of true Christian living, Vallandigham deferred till well along in life a profession of faith in Christ as his Saviour.

In a beautiful letter written in 1855 to his brother he pays an eloquent tribute to his godly home and his saintly father and mother, and then says: "Yet in all this have I not seen God visibly, palpably, seen and felt him as my God and Redeemer. Religion has ever been to me a thing belonging to the future, a something some day to be sought after, certainly to be sought after, but tomorrow. That tomorrow never came: there was no such thing in all God's creation to come; and I knew and realized it not these many years. Fool that I was! Tomorrow was ever one day in advance. Yesterday, this day, was the morrow. It came, but it was no longer tomorrow, but Today with all its terribleness, and it was all that belonged to me."

Listen! I hear the strains of music—glad, joyous, triumphant music. It is the song of those who overcame, who reached their goal, who won the prize, who escaped from the bondage of sin and habit, who stood on the stage of influence and usefulness, who drank the golden cup of happiness, who came off conquerors and more than conquerors. They are the men who said "Today."

Listen! I hear another music—not the music of triumph and gladness, but the music of a dirge, a lamentation, rising and falling in mournful measures. It is the song of those who lost the way and now wander in darkness, who threw away their talents and wasted their gifts, who are hopelessly enwound with the chains of evil habit, who cry in vain for loved ones hid in death's dateless night, whose lights went out while they slept and who now cry in vain at the golden gates of eternal life, "Open to us!" But the only answer that comes back is that word "Too late!"

When we say, "Boast not thyself of tomorrow" (Prov. 27:1), we do not mean that a man is not to take wise forethought for tomorrow. Any worthy life must plan nobly for tomorrow. Most of the blessings of civilization and liberty which we enjoy are fruit sown by men who thought about tomorrow. We should all plan for greater things, statelier mansions, a nobler life, tomorrow— and a life tomorrow that is better than today's. But no one can boast of tomorrow. No one can count on tomorrow. How many good things were going to be done tomorrow but were never done; for tomorrow was always one day ahead, or always one day behind—Yesterday.

*He was going to be all that a mortal
　should be
　　To-morrow.
No one should be kinder or braver
　than he
　　To-morrow.
A friend who was troubled and
　weary he knew,
Who'd be glad of a lift and who
　needed it, too;
On him he would call and see what
　he could do
　　To-morrow.*

*Each morning he stacked up the letters he'd write
　　To-morrow.
And thought of the folks he would
　fill with delight
　　To-morrow.
It was too bad, indeed, he was busy
　to-day,*

*And hadn't a minute to stop on his
　way;
More time he would have to give
　others, he'd say,
　　To-morrow.*

*The greatest of workers this man
　would have been
　　To-morrow.
The world would have known him,
　had he ever seen
　　To-morrow.
But the fact is he died and faded
　from view,
And all that he left here when living was through
Was a mountain of things he intended to do
　　To-morrow.*[1]

A man once had a vision in which he seemed to be standing in the midst of an assembly of evil spirits. On the throne sat their dark ruler, Satan, grasping the scepter of wickedness in his hand. Summoning his subjects about him, Satan said in a loud voice, "Who will go to earth and persuade men to accomplish the ruin of their souls?"

One of the attendant spirits said, "I will go."

"And how will you persuade them?" asked the grim monarch.

"I will persuade them," was the answer, "that there is no heaven."

But Satan replied: "No, that will not do. You will never be able to force such a belief on the generality of mankind."

Then a second spoke up and said, "I will go."

"And how will you persuade them?" asked Satan.

"I will persuade them that there is no hell."

[1] Edgar A. Guest, from the book *A Heap o' Livin'*, copyright 1916. Used by permission of The Reilly & Lee Company, Chicago.

But again Satan answered: "That will not do. You will never persuade the generality of men that that is so, for conscience will witness against you. We must have something else, something which will appeal to all classes and ages and dispositions and which will be acceptable to the human race as a whole."

Thereupon a dark spirit glided forward and said, "Satan, I will go."

"And what wilt thou tell them?" asked Satan.

"I will tell them," answered the spirit, "that there is no hurry."

He was the spirit chosen to go—and still he is abroad in the earth.

Tomorrow is the chain that binds men to loathsome habit. Tomorrow is the barred and bolted door that shuts man out from the house of his dreams. "Tomorrow" is the epitaph upon the graves of those who failed and came short of life's true goal. Tomorrow is the downward path that leads men into the land of regret. Tomorrow is the siren's song that seduces men from the path of duty. Tomorrow is the slumber that paralyzes the energies of man. Tomorrow is the snare that traps men's feet. Tomorrow is the sword of self-destruction upon which men fall. "Tomorrow" is the word cut over the realms of the lost. "Tomorrow" is the word which, in that kingdom of the lost, blends with that other word "Never, nevermore." "Today" is the Holy Ghost's word. "Tomorrow" is the word of the tempter and deceiver of mankind.

TONGUE, SINS OF THE—*see also* GOSSIP, SLANDER

A woman once came to one of the old Puritan divines of London and told him that the bands which he wore with his pulpit gown were altogether too long, and that they annoyed her greatly. She would like his permission to shorten them. Confident of his acquiescence, she had come armed with a pair of scissors. The minister mildly acquiesced and handed over the offending bands to the woman, who shortened them according to her taste with her scissors and then handed the fragments back to the minister.

When he received them, he thanked her and said: "Now, my good woman, there is something about you that is altogether too long, and which has annoyed me greatly, and since one good turn deserves another, I would like permission to shorten it."

"Certainly," said the woman, "you have permission to do so, and here are the shears."

Whereupon the worthy divine said, "Very well, madam, put out your tongue."

TOTAL ABSTINENCE—*see also* DRINK, FRIENDS (VALUE OF), INFLUENCE (RESISTING EVIL, 2nd entry; UNCONSCIOUS), LOVE FOR WOMAN

One of the dashing soldiers of the Confederacy was the great cavalry leader "Jeb" Stuart, who was killed at Yellow Tavern in 1864 in battle with the troopers of Sheridan, and who, when he was dying, had members of his staff sing "Rock of Ages" to help him over the river. Someone proffered Stuart a flask of whisky to relieve him in his great suffering, but he would not drink of it, saying that he had promised his mother that he would abstain from strong drink.

One of the most outspoken Christians of the Union army was General O. O. Howard. When Howard came from the Army of the Potomac to join Sherman in the campaign from Chattanooga at Atlanta, many of the officers joked about his Christian ways and his total abstinence. On one occasion when one of the high generals was urging Howard to go with them and have a drink, and was twitting him with his peculiarity, Sherman, who was present and who himself was not noted for his piety, spoke up in his abrupt, severe manner: "Let Howard alone! I want one general in this army who doesn't drink."

TRAINING—*see* CHILDREN, HOME, HOME TRAINING

TRIALS

The particular thorn which troubles you, whether it be the positive distress of something present or the lack of something desired and sought after, is undoubtedly for your good. You may not see it, but it may be keeping you humble, keeping you safe, and teaching you to lean upon God.

Samuel Rutherford, writing once a letter of consolation to a sorely tried friend, reminded him that Christ, in selecting a cross for him, had ten thousand upon which he might have drawn and that, of this great number, this was the particular cross which he had chosen for him. This is worth thinking about when your thorn seems sharper than you can endure. This is the cross and this the thorn which Christ has chosen for you.

TRIBULATION—*see also* ADVERSITY, SUFFERING

It takes tribulation to make a Corinthian column. The mighty monarch of the forest in Wisconsin or Georgia felt the fierce blows of the ax, until at length it fell with a vast sigh to the earth, leaving a lonely place against the sky. Tribulation cast it into the river and floated it to the sawmills; tribulation sawed it and cut it and shaped it and hammered it.

But there it stands now, recalling the temple of Olympian Zeus and holding the dome over our heads as we worship the invisible God.

—**And God**—Trouble may be sent to us by God, but it is not necessary for us to know why. That old saint of Scotland, Samuel Rutherford, once in deep distress was tempted to murmur and almost gave up hope. But ere long he was given comfort and strength in his distress, and began to see the purpose of it. It was then he wrote that we must never try to read God's messages through the envelope in which they come. He meant that it takes time for God's purpose to be made clear to us. "Fool that I was," wrote Rutherford, "not to know that the messages of God are not to be read through the envelope in which they are enclosed."

Two men were once discussing why it is that you cannot see the stars by day. The stars are still there; the distance is not greater by day than by night; why, then, cannot these mighty lamps be seen by day? One man maintained that they could be seen if one went far enough down in a well. The other denied the proposition but permitted himself to be lowered into the well. After he had been lowered a certain distance, he was asked if he could see the stars, and said, "No." Still farther down the same question was asked, with the same answer. But when he had been lowered to a great depth, then, looking up toward the heavens, he said he was able to see the stars.

Go down deep enough into a well, and you can see the stars by day. So to those who are willing to co-operate with God, and to will for themselves the things which he hath willed for them, the deep well of adversity and trouble is a place whence they can see the stars of the spiritual heavens and know that in all and above all and through all is God, and that God is love.

—Shall pass away—Even the heaviest troubles will pass away. Lincoln used to say to himself so often in the midst of his many distresses, "This, too, shall pass away." That was the word engraved upon an emerald given to an Eastern king by his daughter. Unable to control his anxious moments, he asked his wise men for a motto suitable alike in prosperity and adversity. After many suggestions had been rejected, his daughter gave him an emerald with this inscription upon it, "This, too, shall pass away."

—And strength—The tried man is the strong man, not the untried one. Thomas Guthrie, after he left Edinburgh, pursued scientific studies at the Sorbonne, in France. In the chemistry lecture one day the professor, lecturing on iron, produced a Damascus blade. "To put it to the trial, he placed the sword in the hands of a very powerful man, his assistant, desiring him to strike it with all his might against a bar of iron. With the arm of a giant the assistant sent the blade flashing around his head, and then down on the iron block, into which, instead of being shivered like glass, it imbedded itself, quivering, but uninjured." The lecturer stated that he believed these swords owed their remarkable temper to the fact that the iron of which they were made was smelted by the charcoal of a thorn bush that grew in the desert. The life that has had thorns in it, that has had its blade tempered with the ashes of the thorns—with trial, adversity, temptation—is the strong, the flashing, the penetrating, the conquering life.

There is an old Greek story of a soldier under Antigonus who had a disease that was extremely painful and likely at any time to destroy his life. In every campaign he was in the forefront of the hottest battle. His pain prompted him to fight in order to forget it, and his expectation of death at any time made him court death on the martial field. His general, Antigonus, so admired the bravery of the man that he had him cured of his malady by a renowned physician. From that moment the valiant soldier was no longer seen at the front. He avoided danger instead of seeking it, and sought to protect his life instead of risking it on the field. His tribulation made him fight well; his health and comfort destroyed his usefulness as a soldier.

Were you relieved of some burden, or healed of some disease, or set free from some worry, you might lose in moral and spiritual power and influence.

In my university days I used to walk in the early spring mornings by the shore of a beautiful lake. Its waters were as clear as crystal, and its banks were thick with forests. The beach was strewn with stones. But they were ugly and irregular. It is not the gentle lapping of the waves of the inland lake which grinds and polishes stones into white, smooth, rounded pebbles. It takes the grinding and tossing and crushing of the ocean breakers to do that; and there it is, by the side of the ocean, and not upon the shore of the lake, that you find the fair and shapely stones.

—And sympathy—In a magazine article a prominent newspaper editor of the South tells what tribulation did for him. He was often bitterly attacked, and answered railing with railing and reviling with reviling. He was successful from a business standpoint, but he lived in an atmosphere of bitterness and scorn and belligerency.

One day he was taken sick, and for weary weeks lay at the point of death. In the great silence and quiet of the antechamber of death he had time to look into the heart of things. When he was convalescent, he saw about him the flowers that friends had sent, heard his wife real telegrams and letters and repeat messages that had come, and saw how the churches, which he had long attacked because he thought they had attacked him, had prayed for him.

He emerged from the shadow country a new man. "I still walk," he says, "down the streets of Elizabeth City, and to all appearances I may seem the same to all my neighbors. But I am not the same. My little excursion into the Valley of the Great Shadow, and the revelation of the beauty of human nature that it brought me, has softened me and made me a more humble, a more grateful, and a more reverent individual. There has come back to me a line which I read years and years ago, and which had little meaning for me at the time: 'In a world where death is, I have no time for hate.'"

—Uses of—Henry Ward Beecher, who himself came up out of the severest kind of tribulation which can befall mortal man, has a noble paragraph on the subject: "No man can enter into the Kingdom of God without strife. No virtue can be wrought out without strife. Our virtues are like crystals hidden in rocks. No man shall find them by any soft ways, but by the hammer and by fire. If there is anything which is to endure the fear of death, and the strifes of the eternal world, it is that to which we come by suffering. And we are to account nothing too heavy, nothing too sharp, nothing too long, in this life that shall bring us at last, crowned and robed and sceptred, into the presence of our own God to be participators of His immortality."

The English poet Southey, whose "The Inchcape Rock" and "The Battle of Blenheim" many learned in their childhood, illustrated in his life the purifying and uplifting power of tribulation. His life was bound up in his son Herbert, who died at the age of nine. When the tidings were first brought to him, and when he was first able to speak, Southey uttered the words of Job: "The Lord gave, and the Lord hath taken away; blessed be the name of the Lord" (1:21). The blow was a terrible one. "The head and flower of my earthly happiness is cut off," he wrote, "but I am not unhappy." In the *Fragmentary Thoughts* occasioned by his son's death, broken fragments without connection, we catch echoes of his grief, but also of his Christian submission and faith. Here are some of those fragments:

"Thy life was a day, and, sum it well, life is but a week of such days, with how much storm and cold and darkness!"

> *Come, then,*
> *Pain and infirmity—appointed guests,*
> *My heart is ready.*

But the key to his victory is summed up in this fragment:

> *My soul*
> *Needed perhaps a longer discipline,*
> *Or sorer penance, here.*

In the great grief that had overtaken him, Southey strove to find the meaning in the discipline and refinement of his own spirit.

"It takes tribulation to make a man!" The remark was made to me by a friend at whose side I was sitting in a crowded car. We had been discussing a popular writer: how a serious note had been coming into his books; how in one book, where he traced a moral awakening and a moral development, it was generally supposed that he was describing his own life; how sorrow and adversity had awakened into life the spiritual nature that was in him. "Yes," declared my friend, bringing his fist down upon his knee, "it takes tribulation to make a man!"

One of the cousins of John Brown speaks in a letter of a remark made by his famous relative one day when the theory of human perfection was being discussed. Meaning that you could never judge a man's true character until you saw him in the midst of trial, he said: "We never know ourselves till we are thoroughly tried. As the heating of an old smooth coin will make the effaced stamp visible again, so the fire of temptation reveals what is latent even to ourselves."

TRINITY

Norman Macleod used to sum up his Christian faith in these words: "There is a Father in heaven who loves us, a Brother-Saviour who died for us, a Spirit who helps us to be good, and a home where we shall all meet at last."

On one of the Canadian rivers, which flows through a fearful chasm, which stand confronting one another two mighty crags, whose pinnacles tower hundreds of feet into the heavens, and whose roots lay hold upon the foundations of the earth. They have been named "Trinity" and "Eternity." So in the Christian revelation, con-

fronting one another and inseparable from any true thought of God, there stand these two doctrines of the Christian God—his eternity, the successionless and timeless existence of the everlasting I Am, and his trinity, his threefold expression of himself as God the Father, God the Son, and God the Holy Ghost. Both of these ideas baffle human comprehension. When we try to grasp either one of them, the words of Job come to our lips: "Canst thou by searching find out God? canst thou find out the Almighty unto perfection?" (11:7). The question answers itself. When we try to behold the triune God, we feel like a man who gazes upon the midday sun.

TRIUMPH OF CHRIST—*see also* CHRIST (TRIUMPH OF), CHURCH (TRIUMPH OF THE)

All hail to the Conqueror! Standing one fourteenth of July by the *Arc de Triomphe,* I saw a great French military parade. First of all came the cavalry on their beautiful chestnut horses, and then the infantry, and then the artillery, and then all the equipment and paraphernalia of war. And loud cheers went up as this great host, led by mounted musicians who played on their French horns the stirring air of the march from *Aida,* marched around the great arch inscribed with the victories of Napoleon and down the sunlit avenue. But what was that compared with that day when Christ shall see of the travail of his soul and be satisfied, when he shall take captivity captive and divide the spoils with the great?

TROUBLE—*see* ADVERSITY, SUFFERING, TRIBULATION

TRUST—*see also* FAITH

Strength comes to us equal to our need. "As thy days, so shall thy strength be." (Deut. 33:25.) How many promises of God's Word there are which are of a nature to deliver us from fear! They are like moles, or sea walls, thrust out into the deep, and within their shelter all is peace and quiet.

Dwight L. Moody's favorite verse was Isaiah 12:2: "I will trust, and not be afraid." He used to say: "You can travel first class or second class to heaven. Second class is, 'What time I am afraid, I will trust.' First class is, 'I will trust, and not be afraid.'" That is the better way. Why not buy a first-class ticket?

———

A man was once being conducted by a guide over a dangerous Alpine trail. At length they came to a place where a great rock jutted out over the precipice, leaving only the fragment of a pathway. The guide laid hold on the rock with one hand and put his other hand down on what was left of the trail, the hand extending out over the abyss. He told the other man to step on his hand and forearm and thus pass around the rock in safety. The man hesitated and was afraid; but the guide said, "Do not fear to stand on my hand. That hand has never yet lost a man!"

The pierced hand of Christ has never yet lost a man who took that hand and put his trust in him.

TRUTH

On the great rocks and crags of the California coast near Monterey, one can see cedars of Lebanon growing in the very midst of the rock. In some way the seed found a place in the rock and, with nature's mighty and mysterious power of germination and growth, drove its way straight up and through the heart of the rock until it found the sun and the light and waved its branches over the surges of the Pacific. So is the power of one single seed of divine truth.

———

In the Apocryphal book of First Esdras (chaps. 3-4) it is related that after a great feast which Darius, the king of Persia, had given to the governors of 127 provinces, from India to Ethiopia, four young men of the king's guard agreed that each of them should speak a sentence, and that he whose sentence should seem wiser than the others should be clothed in purple, drink in gold, sleep on gold, have a chariot with bridles of gold, a chain about his neck, sit next to Darius, and be called his cousin. Each one wrote his sentence, sealed it, and laid it under the pillow of the king. In the morning the king found the writings under his pillow and called the young men before him to defend their statements.

The first had written: "Wine is strongest." In defense of his proposition he cited the well-known effects of strong drink, how it leveled all distinctions of rank, making the fatherless child and the king on the throne as one; how it could cause a man to forget pain and remember neither sorrow nor debt; how it made the poor imagine themselves rich; but also how it made men forget both friends and brethren, and fight one with another, arousing a hidden personality of evil within them so that afterward they could not remember what they had done or said. For these reasons wine was strongest.

The second had written: "The king is strongest." In defense of his proposition he pointed to the unlimited sway over land and sea of such a monarch as Darius. In remotest parts his word was law. If he commanded one people to make war upon another, it was done. Men slew and were slain at his bidding. The farmers brought forth their increase and bore it unto the king as tribute. Only one man, yet none dared to depart without his permission; and what he desired, that they fulfilled. What could be stronger than such a power?

The third had written: "Women are strongest." In defense of his proposition he reminded his judges how kings might be great upon the earth, but that it was women who bore them, and that without women men could not be. Gold and silver and all goodly things men forsake in behalf of a woman. Even a man's own father and mother he would forsake for love of a woman. His country, too, he would forego if love called upon him to do it. All the fruit of his labor man will give to a woman. For woman's sake man sails the seas and crosses the rivers and fights with wild beasts and walks in darkness. For a woman men make fools of themselves and become slaves of passion, "For her sake" being the epitaph of many a man. By thousands men sinned and perished because they were drawn on by the awful and mysterious power of love for woman.

The fourth had written: "Truth is strongest." In defense of his proposition he told his judges how all the earth called upon the truth, how heaven had blessed it, and how evil works trembled in the presence of the truth. Wine and kings and women are strong, and they are wicked—but all of them perish. Truth endureth forever. She is the source of justice and order. She is the strength, kingdom, power, and majesty of all ages. When he had finished, all the people shouted and said, "Great is Truth!"

------◆◆◆------

Fox wrote of John Wycliff: "For though they digged up Wiclif's body, burned his bones, and drowned his ashes, yet the word of God, and truth of His doctrine, with the truth and success thereof, they could not burn; which yet

to this day for the most part of his articles do remain."

"The brook," wrote Thomas Fuller, "did convey his ashes into Avon; Avon into the Severn; Severn into the narrow seas, they into the main ocean. And thus the ashes of Wiclif are the emblem of his doctrine, which now is dispersed all the world over."

And Wordsworth, following the lead of Fox and Fuller, has preserved the same simile for us in the well-known sonnet:

> *As thou these ashes, little Brook!*
> *wilt bear*
> *Into the Avon, Avon to the tide*
> *Of Severn, Severn to the narrow*
> *seas,*
> *Into main ocean they, this deed ac-*
> *curst*
> *An emblem yields to friends and*
> *enemies,*
> *How the bold Teacher's Doctrine,*
> *sanctified*
> *By truth, shall spread, throughout*
> *the world dispersed.*

TURNING POINT—*see also* CONVERSION, DESTINY

The purpose of the sermon was to show how there are turning points in a man's life, and how what we do, or say, or will, or accept, or refuse, influences our life ever after. At the conclusion of the sermon I said: "This may be a tenth hour for some life. Let that bring a solemn earnestness into our preaching and praying, the thought that we speak now to some soul whose tenth hour is now beginning to strike." I was drawing the bow at a venture, but the arrow found its mark, for I was indeed speaking to at least one soul whose tenth hour was beginning to strike.

The next week I received a letter

which told of a dark struggle, a great fear, and the joy of deliverance. Of the soul which passed through this tenth hour, suffice it to say that it had been called upon to drink as bitter a cup as is ever pressed to human lips. It was a trial which involved bitter disappointment, the surrender of what was most precious, and the incomparable pain of heartlessness and faithlessness. This soul knew that it was suffering; but the actual peril that it was in, the crisis through which it was passing, was, by the Spirit of God, brought home by the refrain of the text, "It was about the tenth hour" (John 1:39). The soul saw its peril and rallied all its powers. The letter to me was one of gratitude, the best salary of any minister, but also a letter of self-revelation. The unforgettable thing in that letter was this: "For some time I have been on the verge of a pit, the pit of self-destruction. In other words, the tenth hour struck for me this evening. I feel that I am past the crisis, and I am praying for strength to brace me up and keep my wandering footsteps from that pit."

U

UNBELIEF—*see also* BELIEF

P. T. Barnum was not only a great showman but something of a homely philosopher. He once observed that more people were humbugged into believing too little than were humbugged into believing too much. The danger today is that people will be humbugged into believing nothing.

＊＊＊

Years ago a great Christian scholar, Dr. Franz Delitzsch of Leipzig University, made this prediction. Speaking to his students, he said: "Young men, the battle is now raging around the Old Testament. Soon it will pass into the New Testament field—it is already beginning there. Finally it will press forward to the citadel of your faith, the Person of Jesus Christ. There the last struggle will occur. I shall not be here then, but some of you will. Be true to Christ, stand up for him, preach Christ and him crucified."

UNIVERSE

In his *History of the Conquest of Peru* Prescott describes the first impressions made by the Spanish invaders upon the Peruvians. When they saw the Spanish ships like floating castles riding in their bays, and looked with dread upon the knights astride their war horses, or fled in terror before the discharge of their artillery, and beheld with awe the white faces of the strangers, as if they were children of that luminary which the Peruvians worshiped, and heard in silence the haughty invader's account of the might of his emperor and the vastness of his dominions, they interpreted it all as the handwriting in the heavens by which the god of the Incas proclaimed the approaching downfall of their empire.

Now they knew for a certainty that their empire was not the only deity, and they suspected that this handful of strangers was the advance army of a great host which would someday sweep the Incas from their seats of power.

Suppose that some of the interesting fancies about the other worlds of our universe should prove to be true, and that one day there should suddenly arrive in our midst a company of beings from another world, armed with superior powers and bearing the unmistakable evidences of a superior civilization, in comparison with which ours would be as the barbarism of Peru was to the glory of Spain, what effect would such a visit and such a demonstration have upon mankind? Would it sadden him or depress him, or fill him with dread lest one day he should see the heavens filled with squadrons of airy warriors and our proudest and oldest civilizations falling before a ruthless invader?

V

VICTORY—*see* ADVERSITY (PHYSICAL HANDICAPS), CHRIST (VICTORY IN)

VIRGIN BIRTH

Where does Mark's Gospel begin? With the baptism of Jesus—that is, with his public life and ministry. The fact that Mark does not write about the birth and childhood of Jesus in no way invalidates the facts related by Matthew and Luke. It discredits them no more than McMaster, in his history of the United States which commences with the year 1784, invalidates the facts about the Colonial history of the United States which are related by Bancroft.

You might as well argue that there was no Declaration of Independence and no Bunker Hill because there is no mention of these events in a history of the United States which commenced with the Civil War as to argue that there was no virgin birth because Mark, who records the public life of Jesus, makes no reference to it. The birth and childhood of Jesus lay outside the scope and plan of his treatise.

VISIONS—*see also* INSPIRATION, IMPULSES

In his book *The Wilson Era,* Josephus Daniels, secretary of the navy under Wilson, relates how he once asked Andrew Carnegie what was the secret of his remarkable success. Carnegie replied, "I owe it all to my flashes."

Mystified, Daniels said, "What do you mean by 'flashes'?"

"All my life," replied Carnegie, "I woke up early in the morning, and always there came into my mind with the waking a flash telling me what to do that day, and if I followed those matin flashes, I always succeeded."

"You mean," said Daniels, "that you have heavenly visions, and like the man in the Scriptures you were not disobedient to your visions?"

"Call it that if you like," answered Carnegie, "or call it flashes; but it was the following of those silent admonitions and directions which brought me the success you say I have achieved."

Whatever may be said about the flashes in the business world, there is no doubt about flashes of divine impulse in the moral and spiritual world. When they come, happy is the man who, like Paul, is not disobedient to the heavenly vision.

VOICE OF GOD—*see* BURNING BUSH

W

WAR—*see also* COURAGE IN WAR

In the midst of the darkness and misery and sin and horror of world conflict, nevertheless something there is stirring and uplifting about the fact that so many splendid young men rise up to say, "Here am I; send me" (Isa. 6:8). That, indeed, is their splendor and glory. Over the gate of the Soldier's Field at Harvard University—the athletic stadium dedicated by Henry Lee Higginson to Charles Russell Lowell, James Lowell, and Robert Gould Shaw, "friends, comrades, kinsmen who died for their country"—are cut these lines by Emerson:

> *Though love repine, and reason*
> *chafe,*
> *There came a voice without*
> *reply,*
> *" 'Tis man's perdition to be safe,*
> *When for the truth he ought to*
> *die."*

—And Christianity—The two most famous legions in the Roman army were the Tenth Legion and the Thundering Legion. The Tenth Legion was composed of Caesar's veteran shock troops. In every great emergency it was upon that legion that he called, and it never failed him. The Thundering Legion was the name given to the Militine Legion in the days of the philosopher emperor —and yet one of the worst persecutors of the Church—Marcus Aurelius.

Tertullian tells us how the legion won that name, the "Thundering Legion." In A.D. 176 the army of the emperor was engaged in a campaign against the Germans. In their march the Romans found themselves encircled by precipitous mountains which were occupied by their savage enemies. In addition to this danger the army was tormented by thirst because of the drought. It was then that the commander of the Praetorian Guard informed the emperor that the Militine Legion was made up of Christians, and that they believed in the power of prayer.

"Let them pray, then," said the emperor. The soldiers of the Legion then bowed on the ground and earnestly besought God in the name of Christ to deliver the Roman army. They had scarcely risen from their knees when a great thunderstorm arose, accompanied by hail. The storm drove the barbarians out of their strongholds; and, descending from the mountains, they entreated the Romans for mercy. His army delivered from death at the hands of the barbarians, and delivered from death by the drought, the emperor decreed that this legion should be thereafter called the "Thundering Legion." He also abated somewhat his persecution of the Christians.

—Horrors of—At Compiègne I left the train and, driving past one of Napoleon's old castles, was soon in the midst of the beautiful forest of Compiègne. Suddenly we came to a clearing in the forest, a deep glade one hundred yards or more in length. In the center of this clearing were two sections of train rails—on one side the rails where the train of the German plenipotentiaries had stood, and on the other side the rails on which the car of Marshal Foch had stood. Between them was a great granite slab, on which I read the words: "Here on the 11th of November, 1918, succumbed the criminal plot of the German Empire, vanquished by the Free Peoples which it hoped to enslave."

On the edge of the wood, and not far from the Armistice Monument, I saw a little stand where souvenirs were sold. I stepped toward the counter to see what I could purchase—and then suddenly stopped, as if an arrow had transfixed me. My God, what a face! The noble image of God in man marred and broken, and this voice which came from nowhere in that face, more like the shrill whistle of a frightened beast than the voice which spake amid the solitudes of Eden. Better, one thought, that the surgeons who patched up this face had let the man die rather than wear forever that awful, terrible mask. Never will mother or sister or lover kiss that face. The French government honored the wounds and the scars of this man by appointing him to that post in the Armistice Wood, where the great conflict came to an end. There, then, are two monuments—the granite stone commemorating the collapse of the plot against the freedom of the world, and that poor, wrecked human countenance, a monument to the horrors and shame of war.

On the fourteenth of July, the day of the fall of the Bastille, I stood in the midst of the great crowd near the *Arc de Triomphe* and watched the military parade. It was a bright warm day, and Paris was at her best. The grand arch with Napoleon's victories engraved upon it dominated the scene like the very incarnation of military glory.

It was a beautiful picture—the sky-blue uniforms, the prancing steeds, the bedecked generals, the July sun flashing from the naked steel of thousands of bayonets, and high above, the droning of the airplanes. The mighty names graven on the Arch of Triumph seemed to come to life at the stirring beat of the drum—Grouchy, Soult, Lannes, Macdonald, Bernandotte, Murat, Ney, and over them all the Man of Destiny himself, with cockade hat and hand thrust into the breast of his coat.

But as I looked, I thought I discerned another face looking down upon the scene; it was that marred, that sinister, hideous face from which I had recoiled in the Wood of Compiègne. As I looked at it the sound of the music and the marching died away and all the rich splendor of the scene faded from view. The marred face was the only reality; all others had faded. There I saw war stripped of its romance and glory, revealed in all its naked shame and horror.

———•◆•———

At the Battle of Shiloh, where Johnston tried to push Grant into the Tennessee River, there was nothing but victory and enthusiasm for the Confederates on the first day. Yet this was Henry M. Stanley's arraignment of war:

"It was the first Field of Glory I had seen in my May of life, and the first time that Glory sicked me with its repulsive aspect and made me suspect it was all a glittering lie. My thoughts reverted to the time when these festering bodies were idolized objects of their mothers' passionate love, their fathers standing by, half-fearing to touch the fragile little things, and the wings of civil law outspread to protect parents and children in their family loves, their coming and going followed with pride and praise, and the blessing of the Almighty overshadowing all.

"Then, as they were nearing manhood, through some strange warp of Society, men in authority summoned them from school and shop, field and farms, to meet in the weeds in a Sunday morning for mutual butchery with the deadliest instruments ever invented, Civil Law, Religion, Morality complaisantly standing aside while 90,000 young men who had been preached and moralized to for years were let loose to engage in the carnival of slaughter."

—**And peace**—A man was once asked, "Is it true that all the peoples of the earth could get into Texas?" "Yes," he said, "it is true—provided they went in as friends."

On the cottage at Rijnsburg where the philosopher Spinoza lodged from 1660 to 1670 is this inscription:

Alas, if all men were but wise,
And would be good as well,
The earth would be a Paradise,
Where now 'tis mostly Hell.

WARNING—*see also* TEMPTATION

From the steeple of St. Mary's Church in Cracow, Poland, a bugle has been sounded every day for the last seven hundred years. The last note on the bugle is always muted and broken, as if some disaster had befallen the bugler. This seven-hundred-year commemoration is in memory of a heroic trumpeter who one night sounded a blast on his trumpet and summoned the people to defend their city against the hordes of the invading Tartars. As he was sounding the last blast on his trumpet, an arrow from one of the Tartars struck him and killed him. Hence the muffled note at the end.

WASHINGTON, GEORGE

The Washington Monument at the national capital makes one think of Washington's pure and lofty character. Speaking at the laying of the cornerstone, July 4, 1848, Robert C. Winthrop, Speaker of the House, said: "Lay the cornerstone of a monument which shall adequately bespeak the gratitude of the whole American people. Build it to the skies, you cannot outreach the loftiness of his principles; found it on the massive and eternal rock, you cannot make it more enduring than his fame. Construct it of peerless Parian marble, you cannot make it purer than his life. Exhaust upon it the rules and principles of ancient and modern art, you cannot make it more proportionate than his character."

Pure and lofty like that noble shaft, splendidly upright and heroic, George Washington today rebukes every sordid motive, all party spirit, every fear and misgiving, and bids us love and serve this America for what it has been, for what it is today, and for what, under God, it is yet to be in the ages to come.

WATER OF LIFE—*see also* CHRIST THE WATER OF LIFE

Water is man's great necessity. Without it no child can thrive, no nation can exist. What is the word that you hear from the lips of the traveler lost on the face of the scorched desert? "Water!" What is the word that you hear on the lips of the sick and feverish man as he tosses on his bed? "Water!" What is the piteous appeal and murmur that you hear on the lips of the wounded in battle as they lie on the field of carnage? "Water." How beautiful, then, is this metaphor, "the water of life"! As the body must have water, so the soul must have the water of life. The Bible closes with an invitation to drink of that water. The invitation takes in everyone: "Whosoever will, let him take the water of life freely" (Rev. 22:17).

WELLS, REDIGGED

Once on a hot summer day, floating down the Ohio River, our boat grounded on the sands of a large and densely wooded island some distance below Parkersburg. Disembarking, we roamed over the island and soon came upon the evidences of a former habitation. Fragments of well-cut stones that had once marked the lines of a noble driveway, and here and there the vestiges of a once splendid mansion.

It had been the home of the expatriated Englishman Harman Blennerhasset, who there in that island wilderness had built for himself and his beautiful lady the first mansion west of the Alleghenies. But ambition and unfortunate association with Aaron Burr in the conspiracy to invade Mexico wrecked the fortune, scattered the family, and ruined the happiness of the master of that home.

Now the island is a river solitude, with only here and there a few stones or broken pillars to remind one of the time when the hospitality of kings was dealt out with a lavish hand and the parks and lawns resounded with European music and cultivated conversation.

Wandering over the place, we came upon an old well that had been digged more than a century before. In recent years someone had rigged a windlass over it. We lowered the bucket to a great depth, raised it again, and drank eagerly of the pure and refreshing water, just as cool and just as refreshing as when Burr and Blennerhasset drank of it a century before.

If one today were to purchase that island and rear another great mansion, his first necessity would still be water; and he could do no better than to dig again the well which was digged so long ago. The water is still there, and the well that found it over a century ago will still find it today.

That was what Isaac did. He digged again the wells which his father, Abraham, had digged before him.

WHISKY — *see* DRINK, TOTAL ABSTINENCE

WIFE — *see* ENCOURAGEMENT (3rd entry), LOVE FOR WIFE

John Roebling, Pittsburgh's famous bridge builder, builder of Brooklyn Bridge, settled first at Saxonburg, Pennsylvania, where he manufactured the first wire rope. Here he married Johanna Herting, one of the settlers who had come with the colony from Germany. In 1864, when Roebling was building the Cincinnati-Covington bridge, his wife died. He wrote in the family Bible this beautiful tribute to her:

"Of those angels in human form who are blessing this earth by their unselfish love and devotion, this dear departed wife was one. She never thought of herself, she only thought of others. No trace of ill-will toward any person ever entered her unselfish bosom. And, oh, what a treasure of love she was toward her own children! No faults were ever discovered, she knew only forbearance, patience, and kindness. My only regret is that such pure unselfishness was not sufficiently appreciated by myself. In a higher sphere of life I hope to meet you again, dear Johanna. And I also hope that my own love and devotion will then be more deserving of yours."

———————

Too often an angelic wife, an angel on earth, goes to heaven before we realize that she is an angel. In Browning's "Paracelsus" the philosopher who made fame and ambition his god, at the expense and sacrifice of human affection and love, confesses his error to Festus in the hospital at St. Sebastian:

And she is gone; sweet human love
is gone!
'Tis only when they spring to
heaven that angels
Reveal themselves to you; they sit
all day
Beside you, and lie down at night
by you
Who care not for their presence,
muse or sleep,
And all at once they leave you, and
you know them!

WILL OF GOD

Worshiping once in a church in Edinburgh, Scotland, I saw a venerable, white-headed old man sitting in a chair on the pulpit platform directly under the pulpit. He joined heartily in the singing and listened reverently and eagerly to the reading and the preaching. I asked who the old man was and learned that it was Sir Alexander Simpson, a great figure in the world of medicine and the son of a yet more famous father, the discoverer of chloroform. He had concluded his distinguished career in the faculty of Edinburgh University. When the students were for this last time presented to him for their degrees, he took farewell of them and of the university and active life in these words:

"It may chance that some July day, far down the century, when I have long been in the ether, one or other of you will talk with child or grandchild of the years when the century was young. Among its forgotten scenes there will arise before your mind the memory of the days when you at last burst the chrysalis shell of pupilage to lift free wings into the azure. You will recall the unusual occurrence of the simultaneous leave-taking of the university of the graduates and their promoter. 'We came away,' you will say to the child, 'a goodly company, all together through

the gateway that leads to the rosy dawn. He passed out all alone through the door that looks to the sunset and the evening star. He was an old man like me,' I forehear you say, 'not in himself a great man.

" 'He had been a friend of great men, and came out of a great time in the nineteenth century, when there was the midsea and the mighty things, and it looked to the men of his generation as if old things had passed away and a new world had begun. And he told us that the great lesson he had learned in his way through life was the same that that disciple who leaned on Jesus' breast at supper taught to the fathers, the young men, and the little children of his time, when he said, The world passeth away, and the lust thereof: but he that doeth the will of God abideth for ever' " (I John 2:17).

———·◆·———

The last words of Richard Baxter, the famous English Puritan divine, author of the celebrated work *The Saints' Everlasting Rest* and the man "who preached as a dying man to dying men, and never sure to preach again," were these: "Lord, what thou wilt, where thou wilt, and when thou wilt."

WILL, LAST

One August day, touring through the Shenandoah Valley, I stopped at Charleston and visited the old courthouse where John Brown was tried, convicted, and sentenced, following his ill-timed attempt upon the United States arsenal at Harper's Ferry. Out of one of the vaults the clerk drew an enormous ledger of the year 1859 and opened it to the page on which was written the last will and testament of John Brown.

As I read it through I was amazed at the poverty of the man. In his will he directs what shall be done with his silver watch, his Bible, and a few Sharps rifles. That was all he had to leave. But when I went out again into the bright sunlight and looked off toward the mountains with their drapery of infinite blue, and with the Potomac and the Shenandoah washing their base, I could not help thinking of the contrast between the material bequest of the man and the spiritual.

All that the courts could take cognizance of was a watch and a Bible and a few old guns. But to humanity he had left a firmer faith in virtue and in liberty; and in less than three years those same mountain-walled valleys were resounding with the song of marching men at arms:

John Brown's body lies a-mouldering in the grave,
But his soul goes marching on.

WITNESSING—*see also* COURAGE (MORAL)

In Bulwer-Lytton's *The Last Days of Pompeii* there is a beautiful example of how the gospel spread as one man told it to another. Glaucus, falsely charged with the crime of murder, was condemned to fight with a lion in the arena. He was led to the revolving door under the temple of Jupiter, and through the narrow opening thrust into the dungeon. A pitcher of water and a loaf of bread were placed before him; the door closed, and he was left in darkness.

As the handsome young Athenian, suddenly thrust down to the lowest abyss of ignominy and horror, realized his plight, the bitterness of his soul gave vent to a groan of anguish. With that, a voice from the recess of the darkness answered his groan: "Who is my companion in this awful hour? Athenian Glaucus, is it thou?"

The speaker was Olynthus, only yesterday converted to Christianity and now condemned as an atheist to fight with a tiger.

Now near to death, the Christian exgladiator and prizefighter crept in the darkness to the side of the cultivated Greek pagan and hurried to tell him of his Christian faith: how his God was with him in the dungeon, how God's smile penetrated the darkness, and how on the eve of death his heart whispered of immortality and earth receded from him but to bring his weary soul nearer to heaven. "And there, as oft in the early ages of the Christian creed, it was in the darkness of the dungeon, and over the approach of death, that the dawning Gospel shed its soft and consecrating rays."

I heard of an infidel who said that if he believed as Christians say they believe, that a man's life in the world to come depends upon his life here in this world, then he would give men no rest, he would be at them day and night, urging them and entreating them to lead godly lives and to become men of faith that they might inherit eternal life. If this means much to us, then we must testify unto the world, and both by our lives and by our words persuade men to live godly lives, that they not only may get the most out of this life but also may inherit life eternal.

WOMAN—*see also* ENCOURAGEMENT (3rd entry), LOVE (FOR WIFE; FOR WOMAN)

—And Christ—The disciples, John tells us—and he was one of them—marveled to find their Master talking with a woman. Alone, too! And yet none of them asked him why he did it, or what it was he hoped to get out of a conversation with her. That brief comment of John, that the disciples "marveled that he talked with the woman" (John 4:27), shows how Christ has changed the world.

Woman, who made it fit and decent and moral for a prophet to talk with thee? Who threw a zone of mercy and protection about thy little child? Who lifted thee up and changed thee from man's plaything to man's companion? Who changed thee from man's chattel and property to man's friend and equal and inspirer? Who obliterated the brand of the slave from thy face and put on thy brow the halo of chivalry and tenderness and romance? Who so changed thy lot that, instead of marveling today that a prophet should talk with a woman, what men marvel at is that there was ever a day when men should have marveled that Christ talked with a woman? Come, then, Woman; bring thine alabaster box, filled with the ointment precious and very costly. Come, break thy box and pour thine ointment of love and gratitude upon his head and feet. Come, wash his feet with thy tears of love and wipe them with thy hair for a towel!

—Her influence for evil—A brilliant and eccentric professor in a theological seminary used to tell the men in his classes never to marry a woman unless they were willing to go to hell for her sake. In the sense in which he meant it—that they should have a love which many waters could not quench and a devotion which laughed at death and hell—the advice was not unwholesome. But in another sense it is true that many a man has gone to hell for the sake of a woman, and also that many a woman has gone to hell for the sake of some man.

WORDS

—Of encouragement—Sir Walter Scott relates how, when he was a lad of fifteen, he was at a house to which came Scot-land's famous poet Robert Burns. Some question was asked about a painting on the wall. Scott was the only one who knew the facts, and with a timid voice he told the great poet what he wanted to know. Long after, Scott treasured the light in the eye of Burns and the kindly greeting and recognition that he gave him. According to another account, Burns not only gave Scott a kind look but on another occasion said to him: "You will be a great man in Scotland, my lad. You have it in you to be a writer." Scott went home and cried all night for joy at this word of recognition and encouragement from the great poet.

When Martin Luther was entering Worms to make his great stand before the emperor and the Diet, that stand that means so much to mankind today, an old knight clapped him on the shoulder, and said: "My dear monk, my poor monk, thou art going to make such a stand as neither I nor any of my companions in arms have ever made in our hottest battles. If thou art sure of the justice of thy cause, then forward in God's name, and be of good courage, God will not forsake thee."

—Fitly spoken—The Bible has wonderful examples of the power of speech and the blessedness of the "word fitly spoken" (Prov. 25:11). There was the incident of Naaman and Elisha. Naaman had come all the way from Syria to be cured of his leprosy; but when Elisha sent out his servant to meet him and told him to go wash seven times in the Jordan, Naaman was in a rage and, turning his chariot about, started homeward. But one of his officers spoke the word in season and said to him, "My father, if the prophet had bid thee do some great thing, wouldest thou not have done it? how much rather then, when he saith

411

to thee, Wash, and be clean?" (II Kings 5:13).

Naaman saw the sense in this, put down his pride and anger, went and washed in the Jordan, and his flesh became as the flesh of a little child.

—Of gratitude—When Grant received the news, after his great victories in the West, that the Senate had confirmed his nomination to the grade of lieutenant general and commander in chief of all the armies of the Union, almost the first thing he did was to write a letter to Sherman. In that letter he says: "While I have been eminently successful in this war, in at least gaining the confidence of the public, no one feels more than I how much of this success is due to the energy and skill, and the harmonious putting forth of that energy and skill, of those whom it has been my good fortune to have occupying subordinate positions under me. There are many officers to whom these remarks are applicable to a greater or lesser degree proportionate to their ability as soldiers; but I want to express my thanks to you and McPherson as the men to whom, above all others, I feel indebted for whatever I had of success. How far your advice and suggestions have been of assistance, you know. How far your execution of whatever has been given you to do entitled you to the reward I am receiving, you cannot know as well as I do."

There, indeed, was a beautiful word of gratitude and thanks, and "fitly spoken . . . like apples of gold in pictures of silver" (Prov. 25:11).

—Influence of—Addison has a passage in *The Spectator* about the Roman Catholic doctrine of purgatory, how some authors must stay there until the influence of their evil writings has disappeared. But who can tell when that influence will come to an end?

—Judgment on—We stand by the side of him from whose loved eyes the light of this life is fading, and eagerly do we strive to catch the word which the lips of the dying man are struggling to pronounce. Often, even to the most attent ears, that word is lost. The man would like to speak but cannot. How strange is that moment when the great stillness comes down and it is clear to the watchers that these lips have spoken in this life their last word. Now not a single word can be added; now not a single word can be retracted. What we have spoken, we have spoken.

O friends, let our words be words which shall have a sweet echo yonder in the Great Day, words which have blessed and not cursed, helped and not hindered, encouraged and not discouraged, heartened and not disheartened, increased and not diminished men's faith in man and in God, brightened and not dimmed the hopes of man for life here and glory hereafter. "Set a watch, O Lord, before my mouth; keep the door of my lips!" (Ps. 141:3.)

—Power of—The rule of silence enforced by the Trappist monks is a searching comment on the power of ill-advised speech to do injury. Words are the ambassadors of the soul. Imagine a spring landscape without the light of the sun! So would history be without the life and the color given it by words. It was said of Luther that his words were like battles.

*Religion, freedom, vengeance, what
 you will—
A word's enough to raise mankind
 to kill.*

Likewise, a word is enough to hold mankind back from killing and to inspire him to noble thinking and glorious living.

———•◦•———

—Of warning—No one ever used words with such beauty and charm as John Bunyan. Take *Pilgrim's Progress* out of English literature and how much it has been impoverished! In *Grace Abounding* John Bunyan tells how one day he was sitting on a bench outside a neighbor's shop window, "cursing, and swearing, and playing the madman, after my wonted manner." Within the window sat a woman, herself loose and ungodly but who, shocked at Bunyan's profanity, expostulated with him and told him that his words made her tremble.

This reproof silenced and sobered him, and from that time forward he was able to leave off swearing. Bunyan relates this incident as one of the steps in his conversion. Who knows what part that courageous and spontaneous rebuke and warning played in the history of Bunyan's glorious life?

WORKS—*see* FAITH AND WORKS

WORLD
—End of the—The world—that is, our physical world, this planet on which we live and our solar universe—will one day come to an end. It had a beginning, when God created the heavens and the earth. "Through faith we understand that the worlds were framed by the word of God, so that things which are seen were not made of things which do appear" (Heb. 11:3). This is the conclusion, not only of faith, but of reason. When men begin to speculate as to possible ways in which the earth might come to an end, there is much difference of opinion. Some tell us that the earth in its rotation, held back by the tides, will gradually slow down until it lies dead and inert, only the corpse of a world. It is said, too, that the sun will withdraw its energies, that its fires will go out and that our planet will become an empire of cold and night. In his *The Foundations of Belief* Lord Balfour wrote: "After a period long compared to the dimensions of time open to our investigation, the energies of our system will decay. The glory of the sun will be dimmed, and the earth, tideless and inert, will not longer tolerate the race which has for a moment disturbed its solitude."

———•◦•———

—Its deceit—The world is like the statue of a virgin made of wood and iron which used to stand in the museum at Strassburg. When a victim approached, the virgin opened her arms to receive him; but, when once she had enfolded her victim, she closed on him with a hundred knives and lances, and then dropped him into a gulf. So the world mocks her lovers. But Daniel was never mocked by the world, because he loved not this present world but loved God.

———•◦•———

Wherever men prove traitors to their best selves, wherever Christian disciples forsake Jesus, the reason is the same—the love of this present world.

O world, O world, what a deceiver thou art! How quickly thou canst shrink and fade for us into mere nothingness! In how brief a moment, by one single blow on the head, or a fever in the blood, or a tumult in the heart, we are through with thee forever, and thy vain show is over! Yet how thou dost seduce us with thy flattery and charm us with thy painted face, so that, in our blind infatuation and flaming love for thee, for one little moment more of thine unreal corruptive joys, we gladly sell our souls, forget our God, crucify our Lord afresh, and forego our hopes of eternal happiness!

—**And the soul**—All the pleasures, all the achievements, leave the soul with a something not yet tasted, a something beyond. There is something that the world cannot bestow. I remember a man who made a wise comment upon people of wealth and fashion who were pursuing the things of this world and forgetting the things of God. "They are trying," he said, "to get more out of this world than there is in it." How true that is. There is nothing in this world for the soul, and those who try to get out of the world lasting satisfactions for the soul are trying to get out of the world more than there is in it.

—**Vanity of the**—She was a woman who even in the decline of old age showed vestiges of a remarkable beauty. Daughter of a governor of one of the Eastern states, she had been a great belle in her youth, and her beauty had even led one distracted suitor to shoot another. Well do I remember what she said to me one day when some reference was made to the world of society which she had abandoned completely for the Church, its services, its friendships, and its sacred causes: "I've been all through that. There's nothing in it."

WORRY—*see also* CARE, FEAR

A large percentage of the things which we dread never happen. Probably, if a man could keep a register of his fears through twenty-five or fifty years of life, it would show that a very small percentage of the things which he dreaded came to pass.

In his house in Chelsea in London they show you the sound-proof chamber, a sort of vaulted apartment, which Carlyle had built in his house so that all the noise of the street would be shut out and he could do his work in unbroken silence. One of his neighbors, however, kept a cock that several times in the night and in the early morning gave way to vigorous self-expression. When Carlyle protested to the owner of the cock, the man pointed out to him that the cock crowed only three times in the night, and that after all that could not be such a terrible annoyance. "But," Carlyle said to him, "if you only knew what I suffer waiting for that cock to crow!" There are a lot of people like that in life—harassed and suffering because they are waiting for something disastrous and unpleasant to happen.

Some time ago the United States public health service issued a statement in connection with the prevalence of nervous diseases and the tendency of worry to weaken and shorten life. In this statement was the following observation, no doubt suggested by the words of Jesus: "So far as is known, no bird ever tried to build more nests than its neighbor. No fox ever fretted because he had only one hole in which to hide. No squirrel ever died of anxiety lest he should not lay by enough for two winters instead of one, and no dog ever lost any sleep over the fact that he had not enough bones laid aside for his declining years."

There is a world of sense in that observation. Even in the hardest times it is a remote, a very remote, chance that anyone in the population will starve to death or freeze to death, and in the case of those who fear God it becomes so remote as to be practically an impossibility. A long time ago the psalmist said, "I have been young, and now am old; yet have I not seen the righteous forsaken, nor his seed begging bread" (Ps. 37:25).

There is no doubt about the fact of worry in life, and no doubt either about the effect of worry. There is a great passage in *Faust* on this subject. In one of the last scenes in Act V, four gray sisters appear at midnight at the palace door. These are Want, Guilt, Necessity, and Care. The first three are unable to enter the palace, but the keyhole is free to the entrance of Care. When Faust addressed Care after she had entered the palace, Care answered:

*Though no ear should choose to
    hear me,
Yet the shrinking heart must fear
    me;
Though transformed to mortal eyes,
Grimmest power I exercise.
On the land or ocean, yonder,
I, a dread companion, wander,
Always found, yet never sought.*

*Whom I once possess shall never
Find the world worth his endeavour
Endless gloom around him folding,
Rise nor set of sun beholding,
And he knows not how to measure
True possession of his treasure.
Be it happiness or sorrow,
He postpones it till the morrow:
To the future only cleaveth.
Nothing, therefore, he achieveth.*

This Care breathed in the face of Faust and blinded him. This is a true description of the effects of care. It weakens men and saddens them, frightens them and blinds them to the satisfactions of life. Too often, no matter what men profess as to their faith, worry and anxiety make them practical atheists, for worry fears the future more than it fears God.

———•◦•———

When Lincoln was on his way to Washington to be inaugurated, he spent some time in New York with Horace Greeley and told him an anecdote which was meant to be an answer to the question which everybody was asking him: Are we really to have Civil War? In his circuit-riding days Lincoln and his companions, riding to the next session of court, had crossed many swollen rivers. But the Fox River was still ahead of them; and they said one to another, "If these streams give us so much trouble, how shall we get over Fox River?"

When darkness fell, they stopped for the night at a log tavern, where they fell in with the Methodist presiding elder of the district who rode through the country in all kinds of weather and knew all about the Fox River. They gathered about him and asked him about the present state of the river. "Oh, yes," replied the circuit rider, "I know all about the Fox River. I have crossed it often and understand it well. But I have one fixed rule with regard to Fox River —I never cross it till I reach it."

WORSHIP

Tintagel is a little village on the rugged cliffs of Cornwall in England. On one of the wave-beaten rocks are the ruins of a castle said to have been the castle of King Arthur and the knights of the Round Table. It was at Tintagel, too, that the great sword of King Arthur, Excalibur, was hurled back into the sea by one of his knights. On a Sabbath morning I walked out from the little village to a little stone church that stood in a field near the sea, so near indeed that during the service we heard the breaking of the waves and the wind blew the spray against the church door. The sermon was a very brief one, and a very poorly delivered one; but it had one thing in it that I have always remembered, although a quarter of a century has passed since I worshiped in that church. The preacher said that we do not really love or worship God until we love and admire the things which God requires and which God loves. In other words, worship is that to which we give our interest, our enthusiasm, and our devotion.

———————

—Architecture in—The glory of Cordova is its mosque, now a Christian cathedral. Pushing the door open, we entered the mosque. At first we were confronted with what, after the brilliant sunlight outside, seemed to be only gloom. But slowly the gloom began to take form and outline. We were looking down a seemingly endless lane, or avenue. On either side were graceful pillars twelve feet high—pillars of jasper, porphyry, and marble of every color. Africa, Europe, and Asia, and the temples of pagan and Christian had been levied upon for these pillars. Above all the pillars ran beautiful arches, also twelve feet high. Turning to the right, we saw more aisles and lanes. To the left it was the same. Whichever way we looked or moved, it was the same dim, vanishing, fading, majestic, uplifting perspective. The entire vast area of the mosque is a forest of marble pillars. Nineteen aisles run in one direction, and twenty-nine in another. Glorious even today in its decline and alteration, what must this mosque have been like when the worshipers of the False Prophet thronged through its nineteen gateways and bowed toward Mecca by the twelve hundred pillars in the light of ten thousand lamps, the perfumed oil of which not only shed light for the eyes but diffused sweet odors to the senses. The feeling you have in the mosque is akin to that sense of awe and mystery which comes over you when you walk through the silent aisles of a vast primeval forest.

In the center stood a Christian altar.

Yet it was not this altar, nor the sonorous and monotonous chanting of the priests at the altar, which made me think of God; rather, it was that labyrinth of aisles and arches and that forest of twelve hundred marble pillars, all seeming to say, "Holy, holy, holy! Lord God Almighty!"

———————

—Atmosphere of—One of the world's greatest cathedrals is that at Toledo. He who has seen it can never forget it. It is worthy of the description of Bescauer. In this description he speaks not only of the beauty of architecture but of the beauty of worship also when he says: "Imagine a world of stone, immense as the spirit of our religion, somber as its traditions, enigmatic as its parables, and yet you will not have even a remote idea of this eternal monument of the enthusiasm and faith of our ancestors—a monument upon which the centuries have emulously lavished their treasures of knowledge, inspiration, and the arts. In the cathedral heart dwells silence, majesty, the poetry of mysticism, and a holy dread which guards those thresholds against worldly thoughts, and the paltry passions of earth. Consumption of the body is stayed by breathing pure mountain air; atheism should be cured by breathing the atmosphere of faith."

———————

—Church going—On the Gothic towers of this church, looking down upon you as you come into the church and leave it, are the gargoyles, not less hideous than those which are to be found on the towers of the medieval churches. There is something mysterious about putting a gargoyle with his devilish countenance on the house of God. The gargoyle seems to have been a symbol of how worship and faith in Christ cast out the evil spirit from the heart of man.

However that may be as a true explanation of an architectural monstrosity, there is no doubt that worship and prayer in the church subdue passion and cast out evil spirits. There are those who have entered the doors of this church who had evil purposes in their hearts, or who were about to yield to what would have been fatal temptation; but they left the church changed, emancipated, and delivered.

————————

The noble Cathedral of Milan, with its thousands of statues floating like a dream in the air, has a great central door on which are wrought characters and scenes from the Old Testament.

Standing before this door, I saw two figures in particular that struck me. One on the left wing of the door was that of the young David holding the head of Goliath in his hand; the other, on the right wing of the door, was Moses smiting the rock at Rephidim, and the water was gushing out of the rock for a thirsty multitude.

These two figures confronting the worshiper as he enters the great cathedral seem to be symbols of the opportunity, the blessing, and the power of worship, and of a relationship to the house of God. David slaying the giant in the name of the Lord stands for our victory over temptation, and the water gushing out of the rock stands for the satisfaction of the highest instincts and aspirations of our souls.

————————

—Family—Of all the psalms the 121st is nearest and dearest to me because of family associations and traditions of childhood. "The Travelers Psalm," it was called—and still is by the Scottish people. Whenever a guest, a friend, or a member of the family was leaving the home, this psalm was sung at family worship. Father and mother starting on long journeys across the seas were bid-

den farewell with this song, and the dangers of them that go down to the sea in ships seemed less menacing because they had been saluted with the psalm. Sons or daughters starting off for school or college were thus commended to Him that keepeth Israel and slumbers not nor sleeps.

In gray days of gloom or dark days of domestic sorrow trembling voices picked up the tune and made its noble invocation their heartfelt prayer. Many things fade and fail, and drop altogether away, as the years slip by and new interests crowd out the old; but the psalm, the old meter to which it was sung, the group which used to sing it, the room in which it was sung, the glimpse of river and hills through the windows as they sang, the occasional deep-toned accompaniment of the morning bell in the college tower—all this remains fixed and forever.

"Thy going out and in, God keep forever will," ended the noble psalm. How many goings out and comings in at that home! Some now are through with their journeyings out and in; more are to go out, never again to come in, safe in that other home where they shall go no more out and come no more in, and singing some "new" song.

That "new song," whatever it may be, will no doubt be the right song for that new world. But for this world I ask no better song than this old song of the Hebrew singer. Continually, like a deep undertone, it vibrates within the soul. And when my own goings out and comings in are over and this poor world fades and fails, let this be the song which shall continue to make its sound heard after all earthly voices, pleasant and unpleasant, have been forever hushed. Let this be the prayer with which I go down the hill and into the mists:

I to the hills will lift mine eyes,
*   From whence doth come mine*
*   aid;*
My safety cometh from the Lord,
*   Who heaven and earth hath*
*   made.*

Thy foot He'll not let slide, nor will
He slumber that thee keeps:
Behold, He that keeps Israel,
*   He slumbers not, nor sleeps.*

The Lord thee keeps, the Lord thy
*   shade*
*   On thy right hand doth stay:*
The moon by night thee shall not
*   smite,*
*   Nor yet the sun by day.*

The Lord shall keep thy soul; He
*   shall*
*   Preserve thee from all ill:*
Henceforth Thy going out and in
God keep for ever will.

* * *

—And God—The Jews have a legend that when Abraham started on his journeys he saw the stars in the heavens and said, "I will worship the stars." But ere long the stars set. Then Abraham saw the constellations—the Pleiades and the rest of them—and he said, "I will worship the constellations." But the constellations also set. Then Abraham saw the moon sailing high in the heavens and he said, "I will worship the moon." But the moon also vanished when her season was over. Then Abraham saw the sun in all his majesty, coming out of his chamber like a bridegroom and rejoicing as a strong man to run a race. But when the day was spent, he saw the sun sink on the western horizon. Stars, constellations, moon, and sun—all were unworthy of his worship, for all had set and all had disappeared. Then Abraham

said, "I will worship God, for he abides forever."

God alone is worthy of your worship. Whatever else you worship—ambition, money, appetite, beauty, affections, friends—all of them, one by one, like the heavenly bodies, set and disappear. But God remains. Jesus Christ remains. He is the same yesterday, today, and forever. Give him first place in your life. Give him your devotion, your strength, and your love.

* * *

—Singing in—I have heard the grand music of St. Isaac's Cathedral, where, in the gorgeous liturgy of the Greek Orthodox Church, choir answers choir as the golden doors of the iconostasis swing open 'mid rising clouds of incense. I have heard the pilgrim monks sing vesper hymns about the supposed tomb of the great apostle in St. Paul's without the walls of Rome. But there is no music to me like that of a Protestant congregation singing together the psalms or hymns of their fathers. I have heard the Protestant Waldensians sing their songs on a Sabbath in one of their valleys, with the great mountains looking down upon them—the mountains which had been wet with the blood of their fathers who had died for the faith of the gospel.

When a congregation sing together, speaking to themselves, to one another, and to God in psalms and hymns and spiritual songs, and making melody in their hearts to the Lord—then come to the surface all the great traditions of the past, all the great convictions of the present, and all the glorious hopes for the future.

* * *

—In Utopia—In More's *Utopia* the people have beautiful churches and a rich ritual, with lights and incense and sweet odors, not because these have any particular power with the Deity, but because this "unhurtful and harmless kind of worship pleaseth them." All the people at church wear white apparel. The holy days are two each month, the first and the last. On these days, before repairing to the churches, the wives fall down before the husbands and the children before the parents, confessing their faults or omissions. "Thus if an cloud of privy displeasure was risen at home, by this satisfaction it is overblown, that they may be present at the sacrifices with pure

and charitable minds. For they be afraid to come there [to church] with troubled conscience. Therefore, if they know themselves to bear any hatred or grudge towards any man, they presume not to come to the sacrifices before they have reconciled themselves and purged their consciences, for fear of great vengeance and punishment for their offence."

WOUNDED, THE—*see* RESURRECTION OF THE BODY

Y

YOUTH—*see also* CHILDHOOD, DREAMS (LOST; OF YOUTH), SOWING IN THE MORNING

—**And character making**—In his vision Jeremiah saw the potter working on the wheels, and the vessel he was forming was marred; but, because it was still soft, the potter was able to make another vessel out of it, not the one originally designed, but still one of use and honor. Later on the prophet was commanded to take a potter's bottle, completely formed and hardened, not capable of being worked over, and break it in the valley of Hinnom. The clay had been made into the bottle, and the bottle had been hardened in the fire. Its quality was fixed, and, since it did not suit the owner's purpose, it was good for nothing and was shivered into fragments.

Youth is a picture of the first vision; its clay is soft and ductile, and the mistakes made may be remedied. But middle life and age—that is a picture of the second vision. The vessel has been completely formed, and hardened in the fire of experience; no improvement can be

made, and all the mistakes and marrings must remain.

—————

—**Ideals of**—Take the man who has failed in the race of life or who, if successful, wears honors that are tainted and does, as a matter of habit, things that once he would have scorned to do— take that man back to the morning of his consecration, to the day when he left the doors of the college with the fires of high resolution and lofty ambition burning in his heart; and let him contrast his present disenchanted, disillusioned, easy-principled self with that youth of long ago, when the fleece was filled with dew and God spake on every wind that blew.

Oh, these abandoned, forgotten, sinned-against Ophrahs of the past! Now the fleece is dry; no flame goes up from the altar; no voice of God makes the heart beat quick and the eye look up.

"Even in Ophrah!" You would think that if Gideon was going to forget God and worship idols, he would have set up his idol anywhere save in Ophrah, with the great and holy memories of his

419

youth. Yet is not this what we often see in life, idols built in Ophrah? Take the man who has long ceased to name the name of God back to the church of his youth, back to the old family pew, and let him sit there and call up the days and the faces that are gone; let him think of the youth, the child, that once sat there with a heart that was free from the stain of sin; and let him compare that child, as pure as the morning dew, with the sated sinner worshiping the idols of this world.

* * *

—Opportunities of—Winston Churchill, whose marvelous gift of words rallied his nation and all free peoples when invasion threatened England, in an autobiography written in 1930, *My Early Life, A Roving Commission,* expresses his regret that he did not have a university training. But that regret was tempered by his observation of how college men wasted their time, and he wrote: "But I now pity undergraduates, when I see what frivolous lives many of them lead in the midst of precious, fleeting opportunity. After all, a man's life must be nailed to a cross, either of thought or of action. Without work, there is no play."

* * *

Youth is like one of those fountains in the park at Versailles, or in the gardens of Peterhof in Russia. What wonderful reflections, combinations, sparklings, scintillations, and radiant iridescence are to be seen in the play of a fountain when the sunlight builds a rainbow through the jet of water and a million drops are transfigured into jewels like those which flashed and flamed upon the walls of the Holy City —jasper, sapphire, calcedony, emerald, sardonyx, sardius, chrysolite, beryl, topaz, chrysoprase, jacinth, and amethyst—and

fall, mingled with fire, upon the watery pavement.

But yonder an unseen hand turns an invisible valve, and the column of water begins to sink lower and lower. The glorious color fades from the drops, the ripples disappear, and the face of the pool becomes smooth and still. All its splendor is gone, all its music is hushed. The spirit is gone out of the pool. So flashes and flames for a little in all its beauty and glory the fountain of youth. And then it sinks. Make the most of it!

* * *

Youth faces an open door. It whispers its great messages, points to its great goals, calls for hard labor and application, for clean living and the avoidance of that which will hurt or defile the soul, and measures the ground for laying the foundations of future strength and character. In the bracing air and golden light of youth things can be planned and things can be done which afterward cannot be planned, cannot be achieved. The metals of life are molten and can be worked into almost any form that is desired. But when this metal has cooled with the years it cannot be worked. One day, whether youth has been used or misused, slowly but inexorably its golden door begins to close, and soon the door is shut. No self-deception, no assumed but unreal energies, no art of the beauty shop or the dressmaker or the hairdresser, can hide the fact that the door is shut and youth is gone.

That voice which rings out of the Old Testament, "Remember now thy Creator in the days of thy youth" (Eccles. 12:1), applies not only to that greatest interest of life, the soul's relationship to God, but to all that is good and desirable in life.

* * *

One day an Oxford undergraduate, after a night of dissipation, was lying on

420

his bed in his chambers when one of his own set of idlers came into his room and said to him, "You are a fool. You are wasting your time and your chance. Your way of going on is silly and senseless. Why not rouse yourself and do something worthy?"

That very moment the young man, who had been letting youth's precious moments pass by unused, like the water of an ornamental fountain through the hands of a nymph or a child, came to himself and resolved to change his way. He ordered his servant to lay the fire the next morning at five o'clock. Thus he began to pursue that course of study and application which in time made him one of the noted men of his day, and, through his celebrated book—Paley's *Evidences*—a great defender of the Christain faith.

———◦•◦•◦•◦———

—Possibilities of—In one of our great missions I spoke recently to almost a thousand failures and mistakes. It was a sad array. How many hearts would have broken to see them there! How many leaves of promise did I see blasted before me! How many vessels of bright hopes shattered! It was hard to know what to say.

But in the same room on another day I addressed a far different company— not men ragged and unkempt, marred with all the sad and dismal tragedy of dissipation and hardship, but little children with life before them, the innocence not faded from their cheeks nor the luster from their bright and sparkling eyes. It was not hard to speak to them. For there were collected before me, not a group of failures and mistakes, but a group of angelic possibilities. The angels had not yet gone.

I speak to you in the interset of the angel of youth. While he tarries, up and be doing! Think of the mind; store it with what is good. Think of the memory; act now so that its harvest will be pleasant. Think of the body; honor it as the temple of the Holy Ghost lest God destroy the defiled temple. Think of God! "Remember now thy Creator in the days of thy youth!" (Eccles. 12:1.)